DAVID LIVINGSTONE:

A CATALOGUE OF DOCUMENTS

Compiled by

G.W. CLENDENNEN

assisted by

I.C. CUNNINGHAM

EDINBURGH

NATIONAL LIBRARY OF SCOTLAND

for the

DAVID LIVINGSTONE DOCUMENTATION PROJECT

1979

ISBN 0 902220 22 5

Knowledge is of two kinds.   We know a subject ourselves,

or we know where we can find information upon it.

SAMUEL JOHNSON

CONTENTS

ILLUSTRATIONS

PREFACE

The need for a comprehensive listing of the manuscript writings of David Livingstone has been widely felt: by members of his family, by librarians, and by scholars working in the many fields which come into contact with the work of this missionary, traveller, scientist, and humanitarian. In particular the complexity of his character, shown in the various styles of his formal writing and his letters to different correspondents, and the wide range of his scientific and other interests cannot be fully appreciated from the limited primary material so far available. These feelings came to a head at a seminar 'David Livingstone and Africa' held in 1973 by the Centre of African Studies in the University of Edinburgh to celebrate the centenary of Livingstone's death, and were given tangible form in a paper by Mr. D.H. Simpson (Royal Commonwealth Society). The formation of the David Livingstone Documentation Project followed and the present catalogue is the first step in making the documents accessible.

Its appearance is due first and foremost to those persons and bodies who provided the funds for research and printing. These are:

Mrs. D.L. Harryhausen, Livingstone's great-grand-daughter;
The Social Science Research Council;
The Centenary Pilgrimage Trust;
The Dulverton Trust;
The Overseas Council of the Church of Scotland;
The Congregational Union of Scotland;
The Bank of Scotland;
The Clydesdale Bank Ltd.

Our sincere thanks are due to all of these; also to the National Library of Scotland, which has given services in kind (office space, typing, publication), and to the Scottish National Memorial to David Livingstone, whose treasurer Mr. D.J. Macleod has safeguarded the funds.

In the second place acknowledgement must be made to the members of the Committee which has under the chairmanship of Professor G.A. Shepperson (University of Edinburgh) directed the policy of the Project from its inception and laid down the general shape of the Catalogue: Dr. R.C. Bridges (University of Aberdeen and Royal Geographical Society), Mr. I.C. Cunningham (National Library of Scotland) who has acted as secretary, Mr. W. Cunningham (Scottish National Memorial to David Livingstone), Dr. K.J. McCracken (University of Stirling), Dr. A.D. Roberts (University of London), Professor E.F.D. Roberts (National Library of Scotland), Professor I. Schapera, Mr. D.H. Simpson (Royal Commonwealth Society), Mr. A.F. Walls (Scottish Institute of Missionary Studies), and Rev. Dr. G.D. White (University of Glasgow).

Thirdly we are all much indebted to the compiler of the Catalogue, Dr. G.W. Clendennen. In circumstances not always easy he has brought the hopes of many to fruition; in three years he has collected material in three continents, corresponded even more widely, devised the detailed layout of the Catalogue, and edited the material which he had collected. Subsidiary pieces of collecting have been done by Messr. I.C. Cunningham, W. Cunningham, and D.H. Simpson of the Committee. At the editing stage Mr. I.C. Cunningham was responsible for some of Sections 2 and 3 and Appendix 4, for the Addenda, and for the final preparation of the copy for printing.

Fourthly the Project is grateful to the following for a variety of services rendered: Dr. and Mrs. V.L. Bosazza, Johannesburg; Mr Frank Bradlow, Cape Town; Mr. D.R. Burton, Salisbury; Mrs. A.M. Cunningham, Johannesburg; Mrs. Alberto (Jill) Dias, Lisbon; Mr. Richard A.G. Dupuis, London; Mr. Robin Fryde, Johannesburg; Mrs. Edna Healey, London; Mr. David Livingstone, Scarboro, Ontario; Mr. P. Livingstone-Armstrong, Féchy (Vaud); Mrs.

Sheila Loseby, Johannesburg; Dr. P.M. Nottingham, Hamilton, New Zealand; Dr. and Mrs. Q.N. Parsons, Swaziland; Dr. and Mrs. O.N. Ransford, Bulawayo; Miss Rozina Visram, London; Mr. John Whitney, London; the late Dr. H.F. Wilson, St. Fillans; Mrs. H.F. Wilson, St. Fillans; and the editors of those newspapers (too numerous to list) who published appeals for information.

Last but not least the Project could not have succeeded without the cooperation of the owners of the actual documents, who are listed below. To all we are grateful for allowing their property to be inspected and included in this Catalogue, particularly to the private persons and organisations: Argyll Muniments, Brenthurst Library, Charles J. Sawyer Ltd., Mrs. D. Foskett, Mrs. D.L. Harryhausen, John Murray, Livingstone Memorial Church, Library of St. Boniface College Council, Parish Church of Canon's Garth, St. Michael's Church in Harare, the executors of Dr. H.F. Wilson, and others who wish to remain anonymous; even more so to those who have gone beyond the call of duty in searching for documents, copying them freely, and offering hospitality. For permission to reproduce the documents illustrated we are indebted to the Trustees of the National Library of Scotland and the Scottish National Memorial to David Livingstone.

A work such as this can never be final. New material will certainly appear, omissions will be noted, errors uncovered. The Committee would much appreciate if such were notified to the Secretary, at the National Library of Scotland, Edinburgh, for inclusion or correction in any future edition. It is hoped that such an edition may also include some desirable features which have been unavoidably omitted from this, such as a list of Livingstone's autograph maps, and notes on letters which he is known to have written but which have not been located in any form. One omission which is deliberate is that of a general index: Section 2 is basically an index to Section 1, and it was felt that an index to Sections 2 — 4 would have been more misleading (because some letters are not summarised and because of the different scales inevitably employed in describing letters, journals, notebooks, etc.) than useful.

In conjunction with the Project the National Library of Scotland has acquired photocopies of a large proportion of the material located, and this is indicated in the Catalogue. These copies may be consulted freely by any accredited reader in the Library; but all questions relating to publication of, quotation from, or photographic reproduction of such documents should be addressed to the owner of the original; where the owner is a private individual not named in the Catalogue the Secretary of the Project will forward letters.

Compiler's note.

Mr. Clendennen would further like to record his sincere gratitude to

Sra Rosalina Cunha, Librarian, Calouste Gulbenkian Museum, for opening many doors in Lisbon is a most generous and gracious manner;

Mrs. Sheila Suttner, Dean, Jubilee Hall, the University of the Witwatersrand, for forwarding both Project and personal communications throughout the period of research in southern Africa;

Professor Derek Wagg, Department of Hispanic Studies, the University of Edinburgh, for a great deal of instruction in the Portuguese language, and for improving the translation of letter 1419;

Dr. James A. Casada, Department of History, Winthrop College, Rock Hill, South Carolina, for bringing several letters to the Project's attention, reading the typescript and kindly offering several valuable corrections and additions, and being generally helpful over the entire period of research and publication;

Mr. and Mrs. William Cunningham, Scottish National Memorial to David Livingstone, Blantyre, Scotland, for a great deal of cooperation beyond the norm when working in the Memorial, and for a very generous portion of that endearing hospitality for which the west of Scotland is justifiably renowned;

Professor George Shepperson, Project Chairman, for serving as a fountainhead of sage advice, and for continuing optimism and encouragement at times when positive results seemed impossible to achieve, which made an inestimable contribution to the existence of the catalogue in its present form;

and last but furthest from least

Mr. Ian Cunningham, Project Secretary, for cheerfully and competently taking on innumerable tasks which were completely unanticipated, including a mass of research, checking and rechecking elusive details, revising and improving often messy typescripts, and seeing the entire collection of sections and essays through publication, to name only a few. His contributions to this work are nothing short of monumental.

LIST OF ARCHIVES AND LIBRARIES

The following is a list of the archives, libraries, and others which hold material referred to in this catalogue.

AGSNY	Library, American Geographical Society, Broadway at 156th Street, New York, New York 10032, the United States.
AHUL	Arquivo Histórico Ultramarino, Ministério da Cooperação (Palácio da Ega), Calçada da Boa Hora 30 (à Junqueira), Lisboa 3, Portugal.
ALUSG	Andersonian Library, University of Strathclyde, McCance Building, 16 Richmond Street, Glasgow G1 1XQ, Scotland.
AMI	Argyll Muniments, Inverary Castle, Inverary, Argyllshire, Scotland.
APLANZ	Auckland Public Library, Lorne Street (Box 4138), Auckland 1, New Zealand.
BLJ	Brenthurst Library, 44 Main Street, Johannesburg 2000, South Africa.
BLL	Department of Manuscripts, British Library, Great Russell Street, London WC1B 3DG, England.
BLO	Bodleian Library, Oxford OX1 3BG, England.
BMNHL	General Library, British Museum (Natural History), Cromwell Road, London SW7 5BD, England.
BSGL	Biblioteca da Sociedade de Geográfia de Lisboa, Rua das Portas de Santo Antão 100, Lisboa, Portugal.
CLRUGSA	Cory Library for Historical Research, Rhodes University Library, P.O. Box 184, Grahamstown 6140, South Africa.
CMSL	Church Missionary Society, 157 Waterloo Road, London SE1 8UU, England.
CNSMUN	Centre for Newfoundland Studies, Memorial University of Newfoundland, St. John's, Newfoundland, Canada A1C 5S7.
CSBL	Messrs. Charles J. Sawyer Ltd., Booksellers, 1 Grafton Street, London W1X 3LB, England.
DMAGLHMDSA	Durban Museum and Art Gallery, Local History Museum, Old Court House, Aliwal Street, Durban 4000, South Africa.
DMLDSA	Durban Municipal Library, City Hall, P.O. Box 917, Durban 4000, South Africa.
DPLDS	Dundee Public Library, Albert Square, Dundee DD1 1DB, Scotland.
ERSHH	Educational Resource Service Headquarters [formerly Lanark County Library], 4 Auchingramont Road, Hamilton, Scotland.
FMC	Fitzwilliam Museum, Cambridge CB2 1RB, England.

Foskett Collection	Mrs. D. Foskett, Ambleside.
GACT	Government Archives, Private Bag 9025, Queen Victoria Street, Cape Town 8000, South Africa.
GLUCBGRS	General Reference Service, the General Library, University of California, Berkeley, California 94720, the United States.
GMAG	Glasgow Museums and Art Gallery, Kelvingrove, Glasgow G3 8AG, Scotland.
GRMSA	Graaff-Reinet Museum, P.O. Box 104, Graaff-Reinet 6280, South Africa.
Harryhausen Collection	Mrs. D.L. Harryhausen, London. (At present deposited in NLS.)
ICSTLL	Archives, Imperial College of Science and Technology Library, Prince Consort Road, London SW7 2SZ, England.
IOLL	India Office Library, 197 Blackfriars Road, London SE1 8NG, England.
JLUCT	J.W. Jagger Library, University of Cape Town, Rondebosch 7700, South Africa.
JMPL	John Murray, Publishers, 50 Albemarle Street, London W1X 4BD, England.
JPLAM	Johannesburg Public Library, Africana Museum, Market Square, Johannesburg 2001, South Africa.
KCLUND	Killie Campbell Africana Library, University of Natal, Muckleneuk, 220 Marriott Road, Durban 4001, South Africa.
KPLSA	Kimberley Public Library, 65 Du Toitspan Road, P.O. Box 627, Kimberley 8300, South Africa.
LCUSWDC	Manuscript Division, Library of the Congress of the United States, Washington, D.C. 20540, the United States.
LMCBS	Livingstone Memorial Church, 286 Glasgow Road, Blantyre, Glasgow G72 9DB, Scotland.
LPCT	Library of Parliament, Parliament House, Cape Town 8000, South Africa.
MALCITPC	Munger Africana Library, California Institute of Technology, Pasadena, California 91125, the United States.
MDNHLL	Ministry of Defence Naval Historical Library, Empress State Building, Lillie Road, London SW6 1TR, England.
MLG	The Mitchell Library, North Street, Glasgow G3 7DN, Scotland.
NARS	National Archives of Rhodesia, Causeway, Salisbury, Rhodesia.

NCLE	New College Library, Mound Place, Edinburgh EH1 2LU, Scotland.
NMLZ	National Museum, Livingstone, Zambia.
NLS	Department of Manuscripts, National Library of Scotland, George IV Bridge, Edinburgh EH1 1EW, Scotland.
NLWA	Department of Manuscripts and Records, National Library of Wales, Aberystwyth SY23 3BU, Wales.
NYPL	New York Public Library, Fifth Avenue, New York, New York 10018, the United States.
OCLOO	Oberlin College Library, Seeley G. Mudd Learning Center, Oberlin College, Oberlin, Ohio 44074, the United States.
PACO	Public Archives of Canada, 395 Wellington Street, Ottawa, Ontario K1A 0N3, Canada.
PCCGHYE	Parish Church, Canon's Garth, Helmsley, Yorkshire YO6 5SQ, England.
PMSM	Library, Peabody Museum, Salem, Massachusetts 01970, the United States.
PROL	Public Record Office, Chancery Lane, London WC2A 1LR, England.
RBGK	Library, Royal Botanical Gardens, Kew, Richmond, Surrey TW9 3AB, England.
RCPSG	Royal College of Physicians and Surgeons, 242 St. Vincent Street, Glasgow G2 5RJ, Scotland.
RCSL	Library, Royal Commonwealth Society, Northumberland Avenue, London WC2N 5BJ, England.
RGSL	Royal Geographical Society, Kensington Gore, London SW7 2AR, England.
RHLO	Rhodes House Library, Oxford OX1 3RG, England.
RSALL	Library, Royal Society of Arts, John Adam Street, Adelphi, London WC2N 6EZ, England.
SALCT	South African Library, Queen Victoria Street, Cape Town 8001, South Africa.
SMCHR	St. Michael's Church, Harare, Rhodesia.
SNMDL	Scottish National Memorial to David Livingstone, Station Road, Blantyre, Glasgow G72 9BT, Scotland.
SPMRIP	Service Protestant de Mission et de Relations Internationales, 102 Boulevard Arago, 75014 Paris, France.
UFHLFHSA	Library, University of Fort Hart, P.O. Fort Hare, Cape Province, South Africa.

ULSOASL Library, University of London School of Oriental and African Studies, Malet Street, London WC1E 7HP, England.

UNLNNE Manuscript Department, University of Nottingham Library, University Park, Nottingham, Nottinghamshire NG7 2RD, England.

USPGL Archives, United Society for the Propogation of the Gospel, 15 Tufton Street, London SW1P 3QQ, England.

UTSNYC Archives, Union Theological Seminary, Broadway and 120th Street, New York, New York 10027, the United States.

WCLUWJ William Cullen Library, University of the Witwatersrand, 1 Jan Smuts Avenue, Johannesburg 2001, South Africa.

WIHMLL Library, Wellcome Institute for the History of Medicine, 183 Euston Road, London NW1 2BP, England.

Wilson Collection Executors of the late Dr. H.F. Wilson, St. Fillans.

LIST OF PUBLICATIONS

A. BOOKS

Almeida de Eça, Gastão Felipe de.　**Inéditos do Dr. David Livingstone?**　Lourenço Marques: Imprensa Nacional de Moçambique, 1953.　(Almeida, **IdDDL.**)

Argyll, the Dowager Duchess of (ed.).　**George Douglas, Eighth Duke of Argyll, KG, KT (1823 – 1900), Autobiography and Memoirs.**　2 vols. London:　John Murray, 1906.　(Argyll, **DAAM.**).

Baines, Thomas.　**The Gold Regions of South Eastern Africa.**　London and Port Elizabeth: Stanford, Mackay, 1877.　(Baines, **GRSEA.**)

Bennett, Norman Robert, and Ylvisaker, Marguerite (eds.).　**The Central African Journal of Lovell J. Procter, 1860 – 1864.**　Boston, Massachusetts:　Boston University, African Studies Center, 1971.　(Bennett & Ylvisaker, **CAJLJP.**)

Blaikie, William Garden.　**The Personal Life of David Livingstone.**　London:　John Murray, 1880.　(Blaikie, **PLDL.**)

Boase, Frederic.　**Modern English Biography** (and Supplement).　6 vols. Truro:　Netherton & Worth, 1892 – 1912.　(Boase, **MEB.**)

Campbell, J. R.　**Livingstone.**　London:　Ernest Benn Ltd., 1929.　(Campbell, **Liv.**)

Chadwick, Owen.　**Mackenzie's Grave.**　London:　Hodder & Stoughton, 1959.　(Chadwick, **MG.**)

Chamberlin, David (ed.).　**Some Letters from Livingstone, 1840 – 1872.**　London:　Oxford University Press, 1940.　(Chamberlin, **SLFL.**)

Coupland, R.　**Kirk on the Zambesi:　a Chapter of African History.**　Oxford:　the Clarendon Press, 1928.　(Coupland, **KotZ.**)

Coupland, Reginald.　**Livingstone's Last Journey.**　London:　Collins, 1945.　(Coupland, **LLJ.**)

Dawson, R.B.　**Livingstone, the Hero of Africa.**　London:　Seeley, Service, & Co. Ltd., 1918.　(Dawson, **LtHA.**)

Debenham, Frank.　**The Way to Ilala:　David Livingstone's Pilgrimage.**　London, New York, and Toronto:　Longmans, Green, & Co., 1955.　(Debenham, **TWtI.**)

Dictionary of American Biogrpahy.　20 vols. London:　Humphrey Milford, 1928 – 36.　(**DAmerB.**)

Dictionary of National Biography.　22 vols. London:　Smith, Elder, & Co., 1885 – 1901.　(**DNB.**)

Dictionary of South African Biography.　2 vols. publ. Cape Town.　Nasionale Boekhandel Bpk., 1968 –.　(**DSAfrB.**)

Ewing, William.　**Annals of the Free Church of Scotland 1843 – 1900.**　2 vols. Edinburgh: T. & T. Clark, 1914.　(Ewing, **Annals.**)

Foskett, R. (ed.).   **The Zambesi Doctors: David Livingstone's Letters to John Kirk, 1858 —
1872.**   Edinburgh: the University Press, 1964.   (Foskett, **ZmDc.**)

Foskett, Reginald   (ed.).   **The Zambesi Journal and Letters of Dr. John Kirk, 1858 — 1863.**
2 vols. Edinburgh and London: Oliver & Boyd, 1965.   (Foskett, **ZJJK.**)

Foster, Joseph.   **Hand-list of Men at the Bar,** part of his **Collectanea Genealogica.**   London:
privately printed, 1881 — 5.   (Foster, **HMB.**)

Fraser, A.Z.   **Livingstone and Newstead.**   London: John Murray, 1913.   (Fraser, **L&N.**)

Gelfand, Michael.   **Livingstone the Doctor;   His Life and Travels: A Study in Medical History.**
Oxford: Basil Blackwell, 1957.   (Gelfand, **LtD.**)

Goodwin, Harvey.   **Memoir of Bishop Mackenzie.**   Cambridge, England: Deighton, Bell, & Co.,
1864.   (Goodwin, **MoBM.**)

Grande Enciclopédia Portuguesa e Brasiliera.   40 vols.   Lisboa & Rio de Janeiro: Editorial
Enciclopédia Limitada, 1936 — 60.   (**GrEncPort.**)

Hall, Richard.   **Stanley: An Adventurer Explored.**   London: Collins, 1974.   (Hall, **Stanley.**)

Hughes, Thomas.   **David Livingstone.**   London & New York: Macmillan and Co., 1889.
(Hughes, **DL.**)

Izett, William.   **Jubilee of John Ness.**   Hamilton, Scotland: Hamilton Herald Printing and
Publishing Co. Ltd., 1906.   (Izett, **JJN.**)

Jeal, Tim.   **Livingstone.**   London: Heinemann, 1973.   (Jeal, **Liv.**)

Johnston, H.H.   **Livingstone and the Exploration of Central Africa.**   London: George Philip &
Son Ltd., [1912?].   (Johnston, **LECA.**)

Kumm, H.K.W.   **African Missionary Heroes and Heroines.**   New York: Macmillan, 1917.
(Kumm, **AMHaH.**)

Lamb, John A.   **The Fasti of the United Free Church of Scotland 1900 — 1929.**   Edinburgh and
London: Oliver & Boyd, 1956.   (Lamb, **FUF.**)

Listowel, Judith.   **The Other Livingstone.**   Lewes, Sussex: Julian Friedmann Publishers Ltd.,
1974.   (Listowel, **TOL.**)

Livingstone, David.   **Analysis of the Language of the Bechuanas.**   London: privately printed,
1858.   (Livingstone, **ALB.**)

Livingstone, David.   **Missionary Travels and Researches in South Africa** (etc.).   London: John
Murray, 1857.   (Livingstone, **MT.**)

Livingstone, David and Livingstone, Charles.   **Narrative of an Expedition to the Zambesi and its
Tributaries** (etc.).   London: John Murray, 1895.   (Livingstone, **NEZT.**)

Lloyd, B.W. (ed.).   **Livingstone, 1873 — 1973.**   Cape Town: C. Struik (Pty) Ltd., 1973.
(Lloyd, **Liv.**)

London Missionary Society.   A Register of Missionaries, Deputations, etc. from 1796 to 1923. 4th ed. London, 1923. (LMSReg.)

Macaulay, Dr. **Livingstone Anecdotes.** London: Religious Tract Society, [1886?]. (Macaulay, **LivA.**)

Mackelvie, William. **Annals of the United Presbyterian Church.** Edinburgh: Oliphant & Co., 1873. (Mackelvie, **AUPC.**)

Macnair, James I. **Livingstone the Liberator: A Study of a Dynamic Personality.** London and Glasgow: Collins, 1940. (Macnair, **LtL.**)

Marsh, Zoë. **East Africa through Contemporary Records.** Cambridge: University Press, 1961. (Marsh, **EAtCR.**)

Martelli, George. **Livingstone's River: A History of the Zambesi Expedition, 1858 – 1864.** London: Chatto & Windus, 1970. (Martelli, **LR.**)

Martineau, John. **The Life and Correspondence of Sir Bartle Frere.** 2 vols. London: John Murray, 1895. (Martineau, **LCBF.**)

McLeod, Lyons. **Travels in Eastern Africa, with the Narrative of a Residence in Mozambique.** 2 vols. London: Hurst and Blackett, 1860. (McLeod, **TiEA.**)

Moffat, Robert U. **John Smith Moffat.** London: John Murray, 1921. (Moffat, **JSM.**)

Moir, Fred. L.M. **After Livingstone: an African Trade Romance.** London: Hodder & Stoughton, 1923. (Moir, **ALATR.**)

Monk, William (ed.).   **Dr. Livingstone's Cambridge Lectures** (etc.).   Cambridge, England: Deighton, Bell, and Co., and London: Bell and Daldy, Second Edition, 1860. (Monk, **DLCL,** 2nd edition, 1860.)

Napier, James. **Life of Robert Napier.** Edinburgh & London: William Blackwood and Sons, 1904. (Napier, **LRN.**)

Neue Deutsche Biographie. 10 vols. publ. Berlin: Duncker & Humblot, 1953–. (**NDB.**)

Northcott, Cecil. **Robert Moffat: Pioneer in Africa.** London: Lutterworth Press, 1961. (Northcott, **RM.**)

Oliver, R.A. et al. **History of East Africa.** 3 vols. Oxford: Clarendon Press, 1963 – 76. (Oliver et al., **HEA.**)

Oswell, W. Edward. **William Cotton Oswell, Hunter and Explorer.** 2 vols. London: William Heinemann, 1900. (Oswell, **WCO.**)

Pachai, Bridglal (ed.). **Livingstone: Man of Africa. Memorial Essays, 1873 – 1973.** London: Longman Group Ltd., 1973. (Pachai, **LMA.**)

Paul, Sir James Balfour (ed.). **The Scots Peerage.** 9 vols. Edinburgh; David Douglas, 1904 – 14. (Paul, **SP.**)

Peel, Albert. **Letters to a Victorian Editor.** London: Independent Press Ltd., 1929. (Peel, **LVE.**)

Ransford, Oliver. **Livingstone's Lake: the Drama of Nyasa.** London: John Murray, 1966. (Ransford, **LLDN.**)

Russell, Mrs. Charles E.B. **General Rigby, Zanzibar and the Slave Trade** (etc.). London: George Allen & Unwin Ltd., 1935. (Russell, **RZST.**)

Schapera, I. (ed.). **David Livingstone: Family Letters, 1841 – 1856.** 2 vols. London: Chatto & Windus, 1959. (Schapera, **DLFL.**)

Schapera, I. (ed.). **David Livingstone: South African Papers, 1849 – 1853.** Cape Town: Van Riebeck Society, 1974. (Schapera, **DLSAP.**)

Schapera, I. (ed.). **Livingstone's African Journal, 1853 – 1856.** 2 vols. London: Chatto & Windus, 1963. (Schapera, **LAJ.**)

Schapera, I. (ed.). **Livingstone's Missionary Correspondence, 1841 – 1856.** London: Chatto & Windus, 1961. (Schapera, **LMC.**)

Schapera, I. (ed.). **Livingstone's Private Journals, 1851 – 1853.** London: Chatto & Windus, 1960. (Schapera, **LPJ.**)

Scott, Hew. **Fasti Ecclesiae Scoticanae.** New edition. 7 vols. Edinburgh and London: Oliver & Boyd, 1915 – 28. (Scott, **FES.**)

Seaver, George. **David Livingstone: His Life and Letters.** London: Lutterworth Press, 1957. (Seaver, **DLLL.**)

Shepperson, George (ed.). **David Livingstone and the Rovuma: a Notebook.** Edinburgh: the University Press, 1965. (Shepperson, **DLatR.**)

Simmons, Jack. **Livingstone and Africa.** London: the English Universities Press Ltd., 1955. (Simmons, **LaA.**)

Simpson, Donald. **Dark Companions: the African Contribution to the European Exploration of East Africa.** London: Paul Elek, 1975. (Simpson, **DC.**)

Smith, Edwin W. **The Mabilles of Basutoland.** London: Hodder & Stoughton, 1939. (Smith, **MoB.**)

Smith, George. **Life of Alexander Duff.** 2 vols. London: Hodder & Stoughton, 1879. (Smith, **LoAD.**)

Stanley, Henry M. **How I Found Livingstone** (etc.). London: Sampson Low, Marston, Low, and Searle, 1872. (Stanley, **HIFL,** 1872.)

Stanley, Henry M. **How I Found Livingstone** (etc.). London: Sampson Low, Marston, Searle & Rivington Ltd., 1890. (Stanley, **HIFL,** 1890.)

Starritt, S. Stuart. **Livingstone the Pioneer.** London: The Religious Tract Society, [1927?]. (Starritt, **LtP.**)

Tabler, Edward C.   **The Zambezi Papers of Richard Thornton, Geologist to Livingstone's Zambezi Expedition.**   2 vols. London: Chatto & Windus, 1963.   (Tabler, **ZPRT.**)

Waller, Horace (ed.).   **The Last Journals of David Livingstone in Central Africa from 1865 to his Death.**   2 vols. London: John Murray, 1874.   (Waller, **LJDL.**)

Wallis, J.P.R.   **Thomas Baines of King's Lynn.**   London: Jonathen Cape Ltd., 1941.   (Wallis, **TBKL.**)

Wallis, J.P.R. (ed.).   **The Matabele Mission: A Selection from the Correspondence of John and Emily Moffat, David Livingstone and others, 1858 – 1878.**   London: Chatto & Windus, 1945.   (Wallis, **TMaM.**)

Wallis J.P.R. (ed.).   **The Zambesi Expedition of   David Livingstone, 1858 – 1863.**   2 vols.   London: Chatto & Windus, 1956.   (Wallis, **ZEDL.**)

Wallis, J.P.R. (ed.).   **The Zambesi Journal of James Stewart, 1862 – 1863, with a Selection from his Correspondence.**   London: Chatto & Windus, 1952.   (Wallis, **ZJJS.**)

Wells, James.   **Stewart of Lovedale: the Life of James Stewart.**   London: Hodder & Stoughton, Second edition, 1909.   (Wells, **SoL.**)

Author not identified.   **The Life and Finding of Dr. Livingstone.**   London: Dean & Son, [1873?].   (**LFDL.**)

Author not identified (H.G. Adams?).   **A Narrative of Dr. Livingstone's Discoveries in South-Central Africa from 1849 – 1856.**   London: Routledge & Co., 1857. (**NDLDSCA.**)

B. PERIODICAL LITERATURE

1. Articles.

Bennett, 'LLWFS' Bennett, Norman R.   'Livingstone's Letters to William F. Stearns.' **African Historical Studies** (Boston, Mass., 1968–), vol. 1, no. 2 (1968), pp. 243 – 254.

Clendennen, **DLJW** Clendennen, Gary W. (ed.) 'David Livingstone on the Zambesi: Letters to John Washington, 1861 – 1863.' **Munger Africana Library Notes** (Pasadena, 1970–), vol. VI, no. 32 (Jan. 1976).

Macnair, **Greatheart** Macnair, James I. **Greatheart** (Children's Missionary Magazine of the [United Free] Church of Scotland, Edinburgh, 1912–), new series, vol. XVI, no. 5 (May 1936), pp. 106 – 108.

Moffat, 'DL' Moffat, Rev. Dr. [Robert]. 'David Livingstone'. **The Sunday at Home** (London, 1854–), no. 1061 (29 Aug. 1874), pp. 549 – 554.

OCDD Mission, **OP** 1862 Oxford, Cambridge, Dublin and Durham Mission to Central Africa. **Occasional Paper** (London, 1862).

RTMBA Livingstone, D[avid]. 'On the Latest Discoveries in South-Central Africa'. **Report of the Thirtieth Meeting of the British Association for the Advancement of Science.** (Held at Oxford, Jun. – Jul. 1860.) Subsection 'Geography and Ethnology' of Section 2, 'Notices and Abstracts of Miscellaneous Communications to the Sections', pp. 164 – 168.

RTSMBA 'A Letter from Dr. Livingstone communicated by Sir Roderick Murchison.' **Report of the Thirty-Second Meeting of the British Association for the Advancement of Science.** (Held at Cambridge, Oct. 1862.) Subsection 'Geography and Ethnology' of Section 2, 'Notices and Abstracts of Miscellaneous Communications to the Sections', pp. 146 – 147.

Wilson, **DLSR** Wilson, Hubert F. 'David Livingstone: Some Reminiscences.' **The Nyasaland Journal** (Blantyre, Malawi, 1948–), vol. 12, no. 2 (Jul. 1959), pp. 12 – 21.

2. Newspapers, periodicals, and yearbooks.

Allen's Indian Mail (London, 1843–).

Army List **The Official Army List** (London, 1880–).

Athenaeum **The Athenaeum** (London, 1828–).

The Atlantic Monthly (Boston, Mass., 1857–).

ACW **Australian Christian World**

BOdGGdPdA **Boletim Official do Governo Geral da Provincia de Angola**

BOdGGdPdM	**Boletim Official de Governo Geral da Provincia de Moçambique**
	The Bombay Gazette (, 1790—).
	British Banner (London, 1848—).
	The British Quarterly Review (London, 1845—).
Bull., Amer Geog. and Stat. Soc.	**Bulletin of the American Geographical and Statistical Society of New York** (New York, 1852—).
Bull., Paris Geog. Soc.	**Bulletin de la Société de Géographie de Paris** (Paris, 1822—).
	Cape Argus
	Cape Monitor
	Cape Monthly Magazine (Cape Town, 1853—).
	Cape of Good Hope Almanac (Cape Town, 1840—).
	Cape Town Mail
	Catholic Presbyterian (London, 1879—).
	Christian News (Glasgow, 1846—).
	Christian World (London, 1857—).
	The College Courant (Glasgow, 1948—).
	Colonial Intelligencer (London, 1847 — 66).
Congr. Yearbook	**The Congregational Yearbook** (London, 1846—).
	The Congregationalist (Cape Town, 1895—).
Crockford	**Crockford's Clerical Directory** (London, 1858—).
	The Daily News (London, 1846—).
DD	**Dew Drop** (Glasgow, 1848—).
	The Dundee Advertiser (Dundee, 1801—).
EIHC	**Essex Institute Historical Collections** (Salem, Mass., 1859).
	Evangelical Christendom (London, 1847—).
F.O. List	**The Foreign Office List** (London, 1852—).
	The Glasgow Herald (Glasgow, 1805—).
GMJ	**Glasgow Medical Journal** (Glasgow, 1853—).

The Globe (Toronto).

Good Words (Edinburgh, 1860–).

Illustrated London News (London, 1842–).

I.O. List   The India Office List (London, 1886–).

Ind. Army List   The Indian Army and Civil Service List (London, 1861 – 76; previously The East-India Register, 1803–, later The India List, 1877–).

Irish Monthly (Dublin, 1873–).

John Bull (London, 1820 –).

JFHS   Journal of the Friends' Historical Society (London and Philadelphia, 1903–).

JRAS   Journal of the Royal African Society (London, 1901–).

JRGSL   Journal of the Royal Geographical Society of London (London, 1832–).

The Lancet (London, 1823–).

Liverpool Mercury (Liverpool, 1811–).

Medical Register (London, 1859–).

MTG   Medical Times and Gazette (London, 1839 – 85).

MH   Missionary Herald (previously Panoplist; Boston, Mass., 1805–).

MJPGA   Mittheilungen aus Justus Perthes' Geographischer Anstalt (Gotha, 1855–).

The Morning Post (London, 1772–).

The Navy List (London, 1815–).

The New York Herald (New York, 1835–).

OB   Outward Bound (London, 1920–).

PP   Parliamentary Papers, Great Britain.

PRGSL   Proceedings of the Royal Geographcial Society of London (London, 1855–).

PRSE   Proceedings of the Royal Society of Edinburgh (Edinburgh, 1855–).

RLJ   Rhodes-Livingstone Journal (Human Problems in British Central Africa) (Oxford, 1944–).

The Scotsman (Edinburgh, 1817–).

SC	The Scottish Congregationalist (Edinburgh, 1881—).
	South African Advertiser and Mail
	South African Commerical Advertiser (Cape Town, 1824—).
	The Times (London, 1788—).
	Wesleyan Times (London, 1849—).
	Who Was Who (London, 1929—).

C. BOOKSELLERS' AND AUCTIONEERS' CATALOGUES

Christie's, 8 King Street, St. James's, London SW1Y 6QT, England.

Edwards, Francis, Ltd., 83 Marylebone High Street, London W1M 4AL, England.

Fletcher, C.A. Kyrle, 2/26 Medway Street, London SW1P 2BD, England.

K Books, Waplington Hall, Allerthorpe, York, England.

Maggs Bros. Ltd., 50 Berkeley Square, London W1X 6EL, England.

Myers, Winifred A. (Autographs) Ltd., Suite 52, 91 St. Martin's Lane, London WC2, England.

Phillips in Scotland, 65 George Street, Edinburgh EH2 2JG, Scotland.

Rendell, Kenneth W., Inc., 154 Wells Avenue, Newton, Massachusetts 02159, the United States.

Sawyer, C.J., 1 Grafton Street, London W1X 3LB, England.

Sotheby's, 34/35 New Bond Street, London W1A 2AA, England.

SECTION 1

CHRONOLOGICAL TABLES OF LIVINGSTONE'S LETTERS

The following tables contain what may be termed a statistical presentation of the letters of David Livingstone, designed to aid users in locating quickly and efficiently all known letters written during the various stages of the great missionary-explorer's life. They are an extension of the less detailed list of the National Library of Scotland's holdings published in the **Bulletin of the Scottish Institute of Missionary Studies**, no. 13, 1973, pp. 3 — 14. On each left-hand page one finds seven columns of information, and on the corresponding right-hand page there are an additional five columns. There follows a detailed explanation of the kind of information presented in each of the twelve columns, treated from left to right across the double page.

No   This is the number of the letter, assigned to each one according to its position in the chronological sequence adopted in this catalogue. Due to corrections made after the letters had been numbered, there are a few numbers to which no letters are assigned. In the Addenda the usual four-digit number is augmented by a decimal point and a fifth digit, which entire number indicates the position the letter would have occupied in the major sequence had the relevant information been known earlier.

Recipient   This is the name of the person(s), institution, or organization to whom/which the letter was sent, when known. When the greeting heading the letter differs from the name of the person to whom the letter is addressed on the envelope or the address panel, the person(s) named in the greeting are deemed the recipients. Livingstone frequently addressed letters to his father, but opened them with "My Dear Parents:" such letters are listed to "Neil & Ag. Livingston(e) 1" in this column.

When more than one person shares the same name (there were three "Agnes Livingstones") the digits 1, 2 & 3 are added after their surname in the order in which they received letters from Livingstone. In all cases save one, this number also indicates seniority; the exception is James Gordon Bennett the younger, to whom Livingstone wrote prior to writing to his father.

In the many cases where Livingstone wrote several persons on the same day, the letters are listed alphabetically by the recipients' surnames, even though in some cases the texts of the letters make it clear that, for example, he wrote Murchison in the morning and Clarendon in the evening. Whenever a recipient's name appears in brackets, it indicates that his or her name does not appear on the manuscript: all such names not explained in the notes are the responsibility of the compiler. A question mark following any entry in this or any other column indicates that there is reason to recognize a small doubt exists, while two question marks indicate that this is merely what may be termed an "educated guess."

Only one recipient is represented in this column by two different names: Mary Moffat (Livingston) becomes Mary Livingston after 9 January 1845. (The final 'e' is added to the names of all Livingstons after November 1852: see "Observations on the Spelling of Livingstone" in the Appendix.) 'Mrs.' is used only when the given name of a married woman is not known, and 'Miss' is used similarly with single women. Titles of persons such as "Captain" are also used when the given name is not known, but in cases where the person is titled, such as the Earl of Clarendon, the person is referred to by his or her title, by which they are universally known. In all such cases, the person's name is listed in Section 2.

Date   Obviously, this is the date the letter was written, and it is usually taken directly from the manuscript (or whatever version of it is referred to in the 'Type' column). The most common type of date is the simple date, consisting of the day, the month and the year, which indicates that the letter was completely written on one day. The invariable first two digits of the year, 18, are omitted for spacing reasons. There are two types of compound dates, the first of which is indicated by two or more dates separated by a comma: this indicates that the letter was begun on one day and finished on another (with perhaps further additions in between that Livingstone failed to date); hence this is the manner in which postscripts are presented. However, it should not be assumed that letters with simple dates have no postscripts: Livingstone's postscripts often appear in the margins of preceding pages and are easily overlooked, and in some cases postscripts were overlooked in published versions. Many of the latter will appear where the contents of the letter are summarized. The second type of compound date shows two dates separated by a hyphen. In this case, the letter is presumed to have been written on or between the two dates, as the letter itself is not dated by Livingstone. Again, any such dates in brackets which are not explained in the notes are the responsibility of the compiler. Compound dates always appear in the chronological sequence according to the earliest date if known and to the last possible date if unknown. Thus a letter of 18 Jan, 20 Mar will be listed under 18 Jan, while one of 27 Mar — 23 Sep will be listed under 23 Sep. The only items presented with no regard for their date are the inclosures with Livingstone's dispatches to the Foreign Office, which in every case immediately follow the dispatch.

Place   This is the place from which the letter was written, and usually appears on the letter itself. Occasional paraphrasing or shortening of place names goes unmarked, but most such changes are recorded in the notes; such will appear in brackets. Also in brackets are places not written on the document. Spelling of place names is taken directly from the document, hence the spelling may differ between autograph manuscripts and manuscript copies. All spellings in brackets are those of the compiler.

Length   This column is designed to give an idea of the length of each letter, although this can be deceiving since Livingstone's script varies in size. The length as presented here consists of three elements, each separated by a /: 1/4/3 indicates that one sheet of paper is so folded as to yield four pages, upon three of which Livingstone has written. Since many manuscripts have been completely torn at the fold, what was originally a 1/4/4 length might well appear as a 2/4/4 length. When such detail was not easily ascertained, the length was recorded simply in pages, and for some fragments of letters, the number of lines is given. Where booksellers' catalogues give a length in fractions, the fraction is rounded off to the next highest whole number: 1½ becomes 2. For printed letters, length is given simply in pages.

Size   The size consists of two numbers giving the height and width of the page, respectively, in millimeters. When this detail is not available, the terms lge fol (= large folio, more than 325 x 200 mm), fol (= folio, ca. 300 x 200 mm), 4to (= quarto, ca. 230 x 185 mm), and 8vo (= octavo, ca. 212 x 135 mm) are used; misc. indicates that the pages in the letter fall into two or more of these categories. It should be remembered that as page sizes are not uniform, any size expressed in anything other than millimeters is at best only an approximation. Size is omitted from many types of copies as irrelevant, but sizes are given for some MS copies, and for Pr copies where the size is indicated in a bookseller's catalogue. For manuscripts that are irregularly torn, maximum dimensions are given. Normally, manuscripts were measured vertically along the left side and horizontally across the top; where letters are not square, other measurements will differ. Letters consisting of more than one page show measurements of the first page only, unless the sizes varied so much (more than a few millimeters) that several measurements were necessary: such fall into the 'misc.' category. Time did not permit the actual measuring of the vast collection in the PROL, but most such items are on uniformly-sized government paper of approximately 325 x 200 mm; for all such, 'fol' is column entry.

Type   When the work of this Project began, it was planned that the catalogue would include only information about manuscripts which were in the hand of Livingstone himself. However, it soon became obvious that many of Livingstone's letters existed only in other forms, and their number made them too important to be overlooked. The following types of letters are referred to in this column;

MS aut	Manuscript autograph: the letter is the original in Livingstone's hand.
MS aut in	Manuscript autograph incomplete, from which a page or pages are missing.
MS aut fr	Manuscript autograph fragment, indicating that part of a page has been torn away (and thus perhaps in some cases further pages are missing). This designation is not used for letters which have had only the signature removed.
MS aut copy	A copy in Livingstone's hand, often taken from one of his journals, and like all other copies noted here, never listed (except in the notes) when the location of the original is known.
MS copy	A copy of a letter in a hand other than Livingstone's. When known, the scribe is named in the notes, and if the copy is dated prior to 1900, this is also mentioned in the notes.
Ph copy	Photocopy of an MS aut. Photocopies of other types of letters are mentioned in the notes.
Mf copy	Microfilm copy of an MS aut.
Facs	Facsimile: a published form of the letter in facsimile.
Pr copy	Printed copy: a published form of the letter.
NS copy	Newspaper copy: when known, the paper is identified in the "Publication" column.
TS copy	Typescript copy, most of which were prepared at times unknown by persons unidentified; the few exceptions are mentioned in the notes.
TG copy	Telegram copy — not, of course, in Livingstone's hand.

With one frequent exception, the kind of copy listed in the "Type" column refers directly to the item listed in the "Location" column. The exceptions are the Pr and NS copies, which always refer to the "Publication" column. Usually, entries in a bookseller's catalogue refer to an MS aut, but in this catalogue all such are Pr copies, unless the location of the MS aut is known. This should not be taken to imply that the bookseller's catalogues print the letter in its entirety: on the contrary, this is almost never the case, but some such extracts are quite long, and some of the short ones are nevertheless very significant. Here is a potential source of vital information which students of Livingstone would often do well not to overlook. No bookseller's catalogue is listed in the "Publication" column unless the editors are unaware of the existence of any other published version.

No N   Crossing the page, the reader is again confronted by the letter number, which is placed here to help the eye make the transition from page to page. In every case, it should agree with the number on the left-hand page. The **N** heads one of the most useful columns in the tables, as a lower-case 'n' beside the letter number indicates the presence of a note concerning that particular letter. This note will be found in Appendix I, identified by the letter number. In addition to the various kinds of information presented in the notes which were listed under **Type** above, the notes also tell of the actual condition of the letter, list additional published versions of the letter, elaborate upon the date or place of the letter — in short, the notes offer a variety of types of information which may be of interest to the reader.

Location   In this column is listed the place where the type of letter indicated in the "Type" column may be found today.   The abbreviation of the archive or library is followed by the house classification number of the manuscript.   The abbreviations of the holding institutions are listed above.   No location is given for Pr copies.

NLS Copy   Here is indicated the MS number of a copy of the letter which may be found in the National Library of Scotland, which now houses the world's largest collection of Livingstone documents.   Space prevented identifying the type of copy which the library holds, but in most cases it is either an Mf copy or a Ph copy.   No mention is made here of Pr copies even though the library houses the overwhelming majority of the Pr copies listed in these tables.   This column will also be blank when NLS appears in the "Location" column.

Publication   The final column indicates where the reader may find a published version of the letter, and in many cases the published form is the only form presently known to the editors. All abbreviations of published works are also elaborated upon above.   In some cases, the symbol "ex" follows the pagination of the publication citation, and it indicates that the published version is merely an extract.   The reader must exercise vigilance on this matter, because almost all of the published versions omit some part, with the exception of those letters edited by Prof. Isaac Schapera.   In some cases the reader will be disappointed to check the source and find that the extract is merely a sentence or two in length: such items are included here because a part of the letter exists in published form, and hence there is no doubt that the letter exists, or at least existed at one time.   When more complete versions of such items surface, it is hoped that the finder will bring them to the attention of this Project, and the same holds true for any versions of Livingstone's letters, complete or fragmentary, which our readers may discover from time to time.   In another way must the reader be wary when dealing with published items: if the Type column lists a letter as being an MS aut, and the corresponding Publication column lists Wallis, **ZEDL** as the published source, there is a possibility that the published form differs from the original, since Wallis did not publish MS aut letters in this work;   he published MS aut copies from Livingstone's journals.   It should also be noted that letters lacking the designation "ex" are not necessarily published in full: if the only surviving example of a letter is an NS or a Pr copy, there is no way of telling whether the printed version is faithful to the original or not.   Furthermore, in many cases it was not possible to compare the published form of a letter with the original even when the location of the original is known.

With the above information at his or her fingertips, the reader should have little difficulty in understanding the kinds of information which this catalogue offers, and using it to the best of his or her advantage.   Sometimes the tables may prove useful in ways which are not always obvious;   for example, the sum of the entries in the Place column constitute the most comprehensive and detailed table of Livingstone's movements yet published, and the Date and Place columns used in conjunction serve as an aid to identifying letters which are only partially dated or completely undated.   Many such uses will only become evident after the catalogue has been used over a period of time.

Yet in spite of all efforts, the catalogue has certain deficiencies which are regrettable but none the less present.   No suitable method of presenting the information found in postmarks was devised, nor was it possible to indicate the colour of the paper on which the letter was written.   Whether or not the envelope survives is not indicated, and no attempt was made to include the address of the recipient at the time that the letter was written.   The number of letters from which Livingstone's signature has been removed is legion, yet this also is omitted from this catalogue. To note all such mutilations would have swelled the appendix of notes to even greater proportions, so this category must be left for future publications of the letters themselves. In many cases these types of information were recorded, and specific cases will be made available to anyone who wishes to write the Project Secretary.

Another major problem concerns the presence in the tables of what may best be termed "phantom" letters. These are letters which appear in two places in the tables (inadvertently, of course) and thus have two letter numbers. In such cases, a copy of some kind was found, usually a short extract, which cannot with certainty be identified with any known MS aut. This often happens when the copyist misdated the copy, or when a photocopy of an original letter was not made available to the editors for comparison, or for similar reasons. Some such phantoms were discovered in the tables after the letters had been numbered; this is why there are no letters under some numbers.

As at this time future revised editions of this catalogue are planned, the Project cordially invites anyone with ideas on how it may be improved to share them with the Project Secretary. All such suggestions will be given most serious consideration.

NO	RECIPIENT	DATE	PLACE	LENGTH	SIZE		TYPE
0001	[John Arundel]	5 Sep 37	Blantyre Works	1/ 4/ 4	228	184	MS aut
0002	John Arundel	[Jan—Jul 38]	Blantyre	11pp	325	215	MS aut
0003	Janet Livingston	3 Oct 38	Ongar, Essex	1/ 4/ 1	230	186	MS aut
0004	Janet Livingston	5 May 39	Ongar	1/ 4/ 4	233	187	MS aut
0005	John Arundel	2 Jul 39	Ongar	1/ 4/ 4	242	197	MS aut
0006	Agnes Livingston 1	[1838–1939]	Ongar, Essex	1/ 4/ 4	229	186	MS aut
0007	Arthur Tidman	[Apr 40]	[London]	1/ 2/ 2	225	183	MS aut
0008	Henry Dickson	8 May 40	London	2/ 8/ 8	245	200	MS aut
0009	[Thomas L. Prentice?]	17 Jun 40	London	1/ 2/ 2	234	183	MS aut
0010	George Drummond	25 Jul 40	London	3/10/10	250	198	MS aut
0011	Margaret Sewell	3 Aug 40	Hamilton	4/ 4/ 4		fol	Ph copy
0012	Margaret Sewell	8 Aug 40	Hamilton	4/ 4/ 4		fol	Ph copy
0013	Margaret Sewell	25 Aug [40]	Hamilton	1/ 4/ 3	184	110	MS aut
0014	John Arundel	16 Nov 40	Glasgow	1/ 2/ 2	249	204	MS aut
0015	James Maclehose	21 Nov 40	London	4/ 4/ 4		fol	Ph copy
0016	Joseph Houlton	28 Nov 40	London	2 pp		8vo	Pr copy
0017	Benjamin T. Pyne	8 Dec 40	"George" off Gravesend	1/ 4/ 4	230	185	MS aut
0018	John Arundel	27 Jan 41	At sea off Rio de Janeiro	1/ 4/ 4	226	185	MS aut
0019	Thomas L. Prentice	27 Jan 41	At sea off Rio de Janeiro	1/ 4/ 4	226	185	MS aut in
0020	Catherine Ridley	26 Feb [41]	"George" Lt 33°S, Ln 12°W	1/ 4/ 4	226	183	MS aut
0021	Thomas L. Prentice	5, 17 Mar 41	"George" at sea — Cape Town	1/ 4/ 4	265	201	MS aut
0022	George Drummond	10,18 Mar 41	"George" at sea — Cape Town	1/ 4/ 4	320	200	MS aut
0023	Richard Owen	29 Mar 41	Cape Town	1/ 4/ 4	253	203	MS aut
0024	Janet & Ag. Livingston 2	30 Mar 41	Cape Town	1/ 4/ 4	268	203	MS aut
0025	Richard Cecil	13 May 41	Port Elizabeth	1/ 4/ 4	250	201	MS aut
0026	Benjamin T. Pyne	13 May 41	Port Elizabeth	1/ 4/ 4	250	200	MS aut
0027	Neil & Ag. Livingston 1	19 May 41	Port Elizabeth	1/ 4/ 4	230	184	MS aut
0028	David G. Watt	7 Jul, 4 Aug 41	[Past Colesberg] — Kuruman	1/ 4/ 4	324	200	MS aut
0029	Thomas L. Prentice	3 Aug 41	Kuruman	1/ 4/ 4	226	185	MS aut
0030	Henry Drummond	4 Aug 41	Kuruman	1/ 4/ 4	228	187	MS aut
0031	Klaso Whitboy	4 Aug 41	Kuruman	1/ 2/ 1	160	183	MS aut
0032	Peter Wright	4 Aug 41	Kuruman	1/ 4/ 4	225	190	MS aut
0033	James Kitchingman	[4 Aug 41?]	Kuruman	1/ 4/ 4	228	185	MS aut
0034	Mrs. John Philip	5 Aug 41	Kuruman	4 pp		4to	Ph copy
0035	Joseph J. Freeman	23 Sep 41	Kuruman	1/ 4/ 4	323	200	MS aut
0036	Parents & Sisters	29 Sep 41	Kuruman	1/ 4/ 4	323	203	MS aut
0037	Catherine McRobert	2 Dec 41	Kuruman	1/ 4/ 4		4to	MS copy
0038	John Naismith, Sr.	2 Dec 41	Kuruman	4 pp		fol	Ph copy
0039	Thomas L. Prentice	2, 15 Dec 41	Kuruman	2/ 8/ 8	320	197	MS aut
0040	Janet & Ag. Livingston 2	8 Dec 41	Kuruman	1/ 4/ 4	323	202	MS aut
0041	James MacLehose	8 Dec 41	Kuruman	2/ 8/ 8	325	200	MS aut
0042	Robert N. Hayward	10 Dec 41	Kuruman	1/ 4/ 4		fol	Pr copy
0043	John Arundel	22 Dec 41	Kuruman	1/ 4/ 4	322	200	MS aut
0044	J. Risdon Bennett	22 Dec 41	Kuruman	1/ 4/ 4	320	200	MS aut in
0045	Joseph J. Freeman	22 Dec 41	Kuruman	1/ 4/ 4	324	202	MS aut
0046	Benjamin T. Pyne	22 Dec 41	Kuruman	1/ 4/ 4	325	201	MS aut
0047	Peter Wright	Jan 42	Kuruman	1/ 4/ 4	324	202	MS aut
0048	Peter Wright	7 Feb 42	Kuruman	1/ 4/ 4	230	182	MS aut
0049	Benjamin T. Pyne	11 Mar, 17 May 42	Tropic Capricorn —[Ln 28°E]	4 pp		fol	Ph copy
0050	Agnes Livingston 2	4 Apr 42	Bakwain Country	1/ 4/ 4	227	184	MS aut

NO N	LOCATION	NLS COPY	PUBLICATION
0001	ULSOASL, Africa, Wooden Box of L's letters.	MS.10778	Listowel, **TOL**, pp. 6—7, ex.
0002 n	ULSOASL, Africa, Wooden Box of L's letters.	MS.10778	
0003 n	NLS, MS.10701, ff. 1—2.		
0004 n	NLS, MS.10701, ff. 5—6.		Blaikie, **PLDL**, p. 30, ex.
0005 n	ULSOASL, Africa, Wooden Box of L's letters.	MS.10778	Gelfand, **LtD**, pp. 20—21.
0006 n	NLS, MS.10701, ff. 3—4.		
0007 n	ULSOASL, Africa, Wooden Box of L's letters.	MS.10778	
0008 n	NLS, MS.10707, ff. 1—4.		Chamberlin, **SLFL**, pp. 5—7.
0009 n	ULSOASL, Africa, Wooden Box of L's letters.	MS.10778	
0010	NLS, MS.10707, ff. 5—9.		Chamberlin, **SLFL**, pp. 7—10.
0011	SALCT, S. A. MSS. Coll., Sect. A.	MS.10780 (1)	
0012	SALCT, S. A. MSS. Coll., Sect. A.	MS.10780 (1)	
0013	SMCHR.	MS.10777 (29)	
0014 n	ULSOASL, Africa, Wooden Box of L's letters.	MS.10778	Gelfand, **LtD**, p. 25.
0015	SALCT, S. A. MSS. Coll., Sect. A.	MS.10780 (1)	
0016			Myers' Cat. No. 379 (Spring, 1954), no. 271.
0017	Privately owned.	MS.10769 (1)	
0018 n	NLS, MS.10768, ff. 1—2.		
0019	NMLZ, on display.	MS.10779 (20)	Chamberlin, **SLFL**, pp. 10—12.
0020 n	NMLZ, on display.	MS.10779 (20)	Chamberlin, **SLFL**, pp. 12—16.
0021	NMLZ, on display.	MS.10779 (20)	Chamberlin, **SLFL**, pp. 16—19.
0022	NLS, MS,10707, ff. 10—11.		Chamberlin, **SLFL**, pp. 19—21.
0023	WIHMLL, MS.64754.	MS.10779 (15)	
0024	NLS, MS.10701, ff. 8—9.		Schapera, **DLFL** I, pp. 28—32.
0025 n	JPLAM.	MS.10779 (8)	**The Congregationalist**, Oct 1925, pp. 15—17.
0026	Privately owned.	MS.10769 (2)	
0027	NLS, MS.10701, ff. 10—11.		Schapera, **DLFL** I, pp. 32—37.
0028 n	ULSOASL, Africa, Wooden Box of L's letters.	MS.10778	Johnston, **LECA**, pp. 63—69.
0029	NMLZ, on display.	MS.10779 (20)	Chamberlin, **SLFL**, pp. 22—24.
0030	ULSOASL, Africa, Wooden Box of L's letters.	MS.10778	Chamberlin, **SLFL**, pp. 24—27.
0031	SNMDL, on display.	MS.10708 (2)	
0032	Privately owned.	MS.10779 (9)	
0033	NARS, LI 2/1/1.		
0034	ULSOASL, Africa, Odds, Box 9.		Chamberlin, **SLFL**, pp. 27—28.
0035	ULSOASL, Africa, Wooden Box of L's letters.	MS.10778	Schapera, **LMC**, pp. 1—4.
0036	NLS, MS.10701, ff. 12—13.		Schapera, **DLFL** I, pp. 37—43.
0037	ULSOASL, Africa, Odds, Box 10, folder 1.		
0038	ULSOASL, Africa, Odds, Box 22.	MS.10779 (21)	
0039	NMLZ, on display.	MS.10779 (20)	Debenham, **TWtI**, p. 22, ex.
0040	NLS, MS.10701, ff. 14—15.		Schapera, **DLFL** I, pp. 43—50.
0041	NLS, MS.656, ff. 76—79.		
0042			Phillips in Scotland Cat. 20 Oct. 1976, lot 222.
0043	ULSOASL, Africa, Wooden Box of L's letters.	MS.10778	Schapera, **LMC**, pp. 8—12.
0044 n	SNMDL, on display.	MS.10708, f. 3	Chamberlin, **SLFL**, pp. 28—31.
0045	ULSOASL, Africa, Wooden Box of L's letters.	MS. 10778	Schapera, **LMC**, pp. 4—8.
0046	RHLO, MSS. Afr. s. 141, ff. 7—8.	MS.10779 (19)	
0047 n	Privately owned.	MS.10779 (9)	
0048	Privately owned.	MS.10777 (3)	
0049 n	Privately owned.	MS.10769 (3)	
0050	NLS, MS.10701, ff. 16—17.		Schapera, **DLFL** I, pp. 51—58.

NO	RECIPIENT	DATE	PLACE	LENGTH	SIZE	TYPE
0051	Margaret Sewell	7 Apr 42	Bakwain Country	2/ 8/ 8	230 184	MS aut
0052	Manning Prentice	8 Apr 42	[Bakwain Country]	1/ 4/ 4	230 205	MS aut
0053	Thomas Prentice	8 Apr, 8 May 42	Bakwain Country	1/ 4/ 4	230 185	MS aut
0054	David G. Watt	14 Apr, 18 Jun 42	Bakwain Country — [Kuruman]	1/ 4/ 4	230 185	MS aut
0055	James MacLehose	28 May, 18 Jun 42	Bakwain Country — Kuruman	4/10/10	misc	MS aut
0056	Joseph J. Freeman	3, 7 Jul 42	Kuruman	3/12/12	327 202	MS aut
0057	Richard Cecil	11 Jul 42	Kuruman	7 pp	fol	Pr copy
0058	Neil & Ag. Livingston 1	13 Jul 42	Kuruman	1/ 4/ 4	258 203	MS aut
0059	Ami Bost	14 Jul 42	Kuruman	1/ 4/ 4	251 204	MS aut
0060	Margaret Sewell	14 Jul 42	Kuruman alias Lattakoo	1/ 4/ 4	250 200	MS aut
0061	Joseph J. Freeman	18 Jul 42	Kuruman	1/ 4/ 4	325 202	MS aut
0062	Peter Wright	11 Aug 42	Kuruman	1/ 4/ 4	325 200	MS aut
0063	Neil Livingston	[1 Sep 42?]	[Kuruman?]	3 pp		MS copy
0064	— McRobert	1 Sep 42	Kuruman	4 pp	4to	MS copy
0065	Neil & Ag. Livingston 1	26 Sep 42	Kuruman	1/ 4/ 4	251 203	MS aut
0066	Hamilton M. Dyke	24 Feb 43	Motito	2/ 6/ 6	325 200	MS aut
0067	Neil & Ag. Livingston 1	21 Mar 43	Bakwain Country	1/ 4/ 4	320 204	MS aut in
0068	Agnes Livingston 1	[21 Mar 43??]	[Bakwain Country??]	1/ 2/ 2	251 202	MS aut
0069	[Margaret Sewell??]	17 Jun 43	Kuruman	1/ 4/ 4	251 200	MS aut
0070	David G. Watt	18 Jun 43	Kuruman	2/ 6/ 6	250 201	MS aut
0071	George Drummond	20 Jun 43	Kuruman	1/ 4/ 4	320 200	MS aut
0072	James MacLehose	20 Jun 43	Kuruman	3/12/12	250 200	MS aut
0073	[Cambuslang Girls School]	21 Jun 43	Kuruman	1/ 4/ 4	4to	Ph copy
0074	[Elizabeth?] Pyne	22 Jun 43	Kuruman	1/ 4/ 4	fol	MS aut
0075	Catherine McRobert	24 Jun 43	Kuruman	1/ 4/ 4	320 200	MS aut
0076	Arthur Tidman	24 Jun 43	Kuruman	4/16/16	320 200	MS aut
0077	Benjamin T. Pyne	25 Jun 43	Kuruman	1/ 4/ 4	fol	MS aut
0078	J. Risdon Bennett	30 Jun 43	Kuruman	2/ 8/ 8	320 200	MS aut
0079	John McRobert	14 Jul 43	Kuruman	6 pp	4to	MS copy
0080	Richard Cecil	15 Jul 43	Kuruman	4 pp	4to	Pr copy
0081	Alexander Brownlee Jr.	17 Jul 43	Lattakoo	2/ 6/ 6	250 200	MS aut
0082	Robert N. Hayward	17 Jul 43	Kuruman	2/ 8/ 8	251 201	MS aut
0083	Fergus Ferguson	28 Jul 43	[Kuruman]	2/ 6/ 6	250 200	MS aut
0084	Henry Drummond	29 Jul 43	Kuruman	2/ 6/ 6	250 200	MS aut
0085		Jul 43	Kuruman	5 pp		MS copy
0086	Neil Livingston	[6 Aug 43?]	[Kuruman]	1/ 2/ 2	263 203	MS aut in
0087	Janet Livingston	2 Aug 43	[Hills of the Bakatla]	2/ 8/ 8	252 204	MS aut
0088	Catherine McRobert	1 Sep 43	Mabotsa	4 pp	4to	MS copy
0089	David G. Watt	27 Sep 43	Kuruman	2/ 8/ 8	250 201	MS aut
0090	Margery Wright	29 Sep 43	Lattakoo	1/ 4/ 3	fol	MS aut
0091	[Elizabeth?] Pyne	5 Oct 43	Kuruman	1/ 4/ 4	250 200	MS aut
0092	[Cambuslang Girls School]	6 Oct 43	Lattakoo	1/ 4/ 4	4to	Ph copy
0093	Thomas L. Prentice	9 Oct 43	Lattakoo	1/ 4/ 4	325 200	MS aut
0094	William Buckland	10 Oct 43	Lattakoo	3/12/12	250 204	MS aut
0095	Arthur Tidman	30 Oct 43	Lattakoo	2/ 8/ 8	325 200	MS aut
0096	Margery Wright	5 Nov [43]	Kuruman	1/ 4/ 3	fol	MS aut
0097	Neil & Ag. Livingston 1	16 Dec 43	Kuruman	1/ 4/ 4	251 202	MS aut
0098	Robert Moffat 1	15 Feb 44	Mabotsa	1/ 4/ 4	4to	MS aut
0099	Neil & Ag. Livingston 1	27 Apr 44	Mabotsa	1/ 4/ 4	324 203	MS aut in
0100	John H. Parker	11 May 44	Mabotsa	1/ 4/ 4	249 198	MS aut

NO N	LOCATION	NLS COPY	PUBLICATION
0051	NLS, MS.656, ff. 93—96.		
0052	ULSOASL, Africa, Wooden Box of L's letters.	MS.10778	Seaver, **DLLL**, p. 55, p. 57, ex.
0053	ULSOASL, Africa, Wooden Box of L's letters.	MS.10778	
0054	NLS, MS.10707, ff. 12—13.		Seaver, **DLLL**, pp. 55—56, 58, ex.
0055	NLS, MS.656, ff. 80—84.		
0056 n	ULSOASL, Africa, Wooden Box of L's letters.	MS.10778	Schapera, **LMC**, pp. 14—25.
0057 n			Hughes, **DL**, pp. 21—22, ex.
0058	NLS, MS.10701, ff. 18—19.		Schapera, **DLFL** I, pp. 59—63.
0059	SPMRIP.	MS.10777 (25)	
0060	NLS, MS.656, ff. 97—98.		
0061 n	ULSOASL, Africa, Wooden Box of L's letters.	MS.10778	Schapera, **LMC**, pp. 26—28.
0062	Privately owned.	MS.10779 (9)	
0063 n	NLS, MS.10773, ff. 157—159.		
0064 n	ULSOASL, Africa, Odds, Box 10, folder 1.	MS.10773.	
0065	NLS, MS.10701, ff. 20—21.		Schapera, **DLFL** I, pp. 63—68.
0066 n	CLRUGSA.	MS.10777 (19)	
0067	NLS, MS.10701, ff. 22—23.		Schapera, **DLFL** I, pp. 69—74.
0068 n	NLS, MS.10701, f. 24.		Schapera, **DLFL** I, pp. 74—76.
0069	NLS, MS.656, ff. 99—100.		
0070	ULSOASL, Africa, Wooden Box of L's letters.	MS.10778.	
0071	NLS, MS.10707, ff. 14—15.		Chamberlin, **SLFL**, pp. 40—41.
0072	NLS, MS.656, ff. 85—90.		
0073 n	NLS, MS.10709, ff. 1—3.		Blaikie, **PLDL**, p. 56, ex.
0074	RHLO, MSS. Afr. s. 141, ff. 9—10.	MS.10779 (19)	
0075	SNMDL, on display.	MS.10708, f. 7	Campbell, **Liv**, p. 92 (n), ex.
0076 n	ULSOASL, Africa, Wooden Box of L's letters.	MS.10778	Schapera, **LMC**, pp. 30—45.
0077	Privately owned.	MS.10769 (4)	
0078 n	NLS, MS.10707, ff. 16—17; SNMDL, on display.	MS.10708, f. 11	Chamberlin, **SLFL**, pp. 49—58.
0079	ULSOASL, Africa, Odds, Box 10, folder 1.	MS.10773	
0080			Sotheby's Cat.,22 Dec 1915, lot 496.
0081	RCPSG.		**GMJ**, vol. 128, (Oct. 1937) pp. 161—164.
0082	BLJ, Book no. 5318, Acc. Reg. 4669		Sotheby's Cat.,29 Jun 1939, lot 1475.
0083	NLS, MS.2521, ff. 122—124.		
0084 n	ULSOASL, Africa, Wooden Box of L's letters.	MS.10778	Chamberlin, **SLFL**, pp. 59—62.
0085	ULSOASL, Africa, Wooden Box of L's letters.	MS.10778	
0086 n	NLS, MS.10701, f. 25.		Schapera, **DLFL** I, pp. 76—78.
0087 n	NLS, MS.10701, ff. 26—29.		Schapera, **DLFL** I, pp. 78—86.
0088	ULSOASL, Africa, Odds, Box 10, folder 1.	MS.10773	Campbell, **Liv**, pp. 92—93 (n), ex.
0089	ULSOASL, Africa, Wooden Box of L's letters.	MS.10778	Blaikie, **PLDL**, p. 65, ex.
0090	Privately owned.	MS.10779 (9)	
0091	RHLO, MSS. Afr. s. 141, ff. 11—12.	MS.10779 (19)	
0092	NLS, MS.10709, f. 5.		
0093	NMLZ, on display.	MS.10779 (20)	Chamberlin, **SLFL**, pp. 62—64.
0094	BLL, Add. MS.42581, ff. 53—58.	MS.10780 (3)	
0095	ULSOASL, Africa, Wooden Box of L's letters.	MS.10778	Schapera, **LMC**, pp. 46—51.
0096	Privately owned.	MS.10779 (9)	
0097	NLS, MS.10701, ff. 30—31.		Schapera, **DLFL** I, pp. 87—89.
0098	ULSOASL, Africa, Odds, Box 18.	MS.10780 (6)	Schapera, **DLFL** I, pp. 90—92.
0099	NLS, MS.10701, ff. 32—33.		Schapera, **DLFL** I, pp. 92—97.
0100	WIHMLL, MS.67518.	MS.10779 (15)	

NO	RECIPIENT	DATE	PLACE	LENGTH	SIZE		TYPE
0101	Janet Livingston	21 May 44	Mabotsa	1/ 4/ 4	293	203	MS aut
0102	Catherine McRobert	5 Jun 44	Mabotsa	6 pp	4to		MS copy
0103	Benjamin T. Pyne	6 Jun 44	Mabotsa	4 pp	4to		MS aut
0104	Arthur Tidman	9 Jun 44	Mabotsa	1/ 4/ 4	325	200	MS aut
0105	John Philip	21 Jul 44	Kuruman	1/ 2/ 1	150	185	MS aut
0106	John Philip	29 Jul 44	Kuruman	1/ 2/ 1	164	208	MS aut
0107	Mary Moffat (Livingston)	1 Aug 44	Motito	1/ 4/ 4	228	187	MS aut
0108	John McRobert	4 Sep 44	Mabotsa	5 pp	4to		MS copy
0109	Mary Moffat (Livingston)	12 Sep 44	Mabotsa	1/ 4/ 4	228	187	MS aut
0110	[Sunday School Children]	17 Sep 44	Mabotsa	1/ 4/ 4	325	200	MS aut
0111	Mary Moffat (Livingston)	[Oct 44]	[Mabotsa?]	2 pp			Pr copy
0112	George Drummond	21 Nov 44	Mabotsa	1/ 4/ 4	320	200	MS aut
0113	Arthur Tidman	2 Dec 44	Mabotsa	1/ 4/ 4	315	198	MS aut
0114	Benjamin T. Pyne	28 Jan 45	[Kuruman]	1/ 4/ 4	fol		MS aut
0115	Robert Moffat 1	10 Mar 45	Motito	2 pp	4to		Pr copy
0116	Arthur Tidman	23 Mar 45	Banks of the Molopo	1/ 4/ 4	405	247	MS aut
0117	Robert Moffat 1	[1 Apr 45]	[Mabotsa]	1/ 2/ 2	150	196	MS aut fr
0118	David G. Watt	2 Apr 45	Mabotsa	1/ 4/ 4	250	200	MS aut
0119	Robert Moffat 2	28 Apr 45	Mabotsa	1/ 4/ 4	320	198	MS aut fr
0120	Samuel Roberts	29 Apr 45	Mabotsa	1/ 4/ 4	fol		MS aut
0121	Robert Moffat 1	12 May 45	Mabotsa	2/ 8/ 8	fol		MS aut
0122	Agnes Livingston 1	14 May 45	Mabotsa				MS aut
0123	David G. Watt	23 May 45	Mabotsa	1/ 4/ 4	323	198	MS aut
0124	Robert N. Hayward	28 May 45	Mabotsa	1/ 4/3	fol		MS aut
0125	Robert Moffat 1	6, 18 Jun 45	Mabotsa	3/10/10	lge fol		MS aut
0126	Robert Moffat 1	[18 Jul 45]	[Mabotsa]	1/ 4/ 4	4to		MS aut in
0127	Robert Moffat 1	13 Aug 45	Mabotsa	2/ 8/ 8	4to		MS aut in
0128	Robert Moffat 1	[13 Aug 45]	[Mabotsa]	6 lines			Pr copy
0129	David G. Watt	15 Aug 45	Mabotsa	1/ 4/ 4	250	203	MS aut in
0130	Robert Moffat 1	5 Sep 45	Mabotsa	2/ 8/ 8	250	202	MS aut in
0131	Robert Moffat 1	5 Sep 45	Mabotsa	1/ 2/ 2	161	118	MS aut fr
0132	Robert Moffat 1	22 Sep 45	Mabotsa	1/ 4/ 4	250	202	MS aut in
0133	Robert Moffat 1	[Jun—Oct 45?]	[Mabotsa?]	1/ 2/ 2	250	187	MS aut in
0134	Robert Moffat 1	[Jun—Oct 45??]	[Mabotsa??]	14 lines			Pr copy
0135	Robert Moffat 1	[Aug 43—Oct 45??]	[Mabotsa??]	12 lines			Pr copy
0136	Neil & Ag. Livingston 1	1 Oct 45	Mabotsa	1/ 4/ 4	256	202	MS aut
0137	Arthur Tidman	17 Oct 45	Mabotsa	4/16/16	400	250	MS aut
0138	Robert Moffat 1	[1 Nov 45?]	[Chonuane?]	1/ 2/ 2	246	202	MS aut fr
0139	Agnes Livingston 2	11 Nov 45	Chonuane	1/ 4/ 4	320	199	MS aut
0140		15 Nov 45	Chonuane	4 pp	4to		MS copy
0141	J. Risdon Bennett	26 Dec 45	Chonuane	1/ 4/ 4	400	250	MS aut
0142	[John Philip?]	[1845??]	Mabotsa	4 pp	fol		Pr copy
0143	Benjamin T. Pyne	1 Jan 46	Chonuane	1/ 4/ 4	fol		MS aut
0144	Neil Livingston	17 Jan 46	Chonuane	1/ 4/ 4	320	198	MS aut in
0145	Catherine McRobert	18 Jan 46	Chonuane	1/ 4/ 4	319	198	MS aut fr
0146	Robert Moffat 1	11 Feb 46	Chonuane	3/12/12	225	184	MS aut in
0147	James MacLehose	26 Feb 46	Chonuane	1/ 4/ 4	225	185	MS aut
0148	Robert Moffat 1	11 Mar 46	Chonuane	2/ 8/ 8	226	184	MS aut in
0149	Arthur Tidman	10, 12 Apr 46	Mabotsa	2/ 8/ 7	223	191	MS aut
0150	Benjamin T. Pyne	28 May 46	Kolobeng	1/ 4/ 4	315	186	MS aut in

NO N	LOCATION	NLS COPY	PUBLICATION
0101	NLS, MS.10701, ff. 34—35.		Schapera, **DLFL** I, pp. 98—102.
0102	NLS, MS.10773, pp. 181—186.		
0103	Privately owned.	MS.10769 (5)	
0104	ULSOASL, Africa, Wooden Box of L's letters.	MS.10778	Schapera, **LMC**, pp. 52—55.
0105	ULSOASL, Africa, Wooden Box of L's letters.	MS.10778	
0106	ULSOASL, Africa, Wooden Box of L's letters.	MS.10778	
0107 n	BLL, Add. MS.50184, ff. 1—2.	MS.10780 (3)	Schapera, **DLFL** I, pp. 102—104.
0108	NLS, MS.10773, pp. 147—151.		
0109 n	BLL, Add. MS.50184, ff. 3—4.	MS.10780 (3)	Schapera, **DLFL** I, pp. 104—106.
0110 n	ULSOASL, Africa, Wooden Box of L's letters.	MS.10778	
0111 n			Schapera, **DLFL** I, pp. 106—108.
0112	NLS, MS.10707, ff. 19—20.		Chamberlin, **SLFL**, pp. 74—75.
0113	ULSOASL, Africa, Wooden Box of L's letters.	MS.10778	Schapera, **LMC**, pp. 58—61.
0114	NLS, MS.3650, ff. 151—152.		
0115			Sotheby's Cat., 21 Jul 1965, lot 761.
0116	ULSOASL, Africa, Wooden Box of L's letters.	MS.10778	Schapera, **LMC**, pp. 61—65.
0117 n	WIHMLL, MS.68213.	MS.10779 (15)	Schapera, **DLFL** I, pp. 110—111.
0118	ULSOASL, Africa, Wooden Box of L's letters.	MS.10778	
0119	BLJ, Book no. 5318, Acc. Reg. 4669.		
0120	NLWA, MS.13198.	MS.10779 (2)	**DD**, vol. 1, no. 7 (Oct 1848), pp. 133—136.
0121	ULSOASL, Africa, Odds, Box 18.	MS.10780 (6)	Schapera, **DLFL** I, pp. 111—119.
0122	Privately owned.		Schapera, **DLFL** I, pp. 120—123.
0123	ULSOASL, Africa, Wooden Box of L's letters.	MS.10778	
0124	SNMDL, on display.	MS.10708, f. 15	Campbell, **Liv**, pp. 96—97.
0125	ULSOASL, Africa, Odds, Box 18.	MS.10780 (6)	Schapera, **DLFL** I, pp. 123—135.
0126 n	ULSOASL, Africa, Odds, Box 18.	MS.10780 (6)	Schapera, **DLFL** I, pp. 136—137.
0127	ULSOASL, Africa, Odds, Box 18.	MS.10780 (6)	Schapera, **DLFL** I, pp. 137—143.
0128 n			Myers' Cat. No. 8 (1972), no. 5, item 1.
0129	ULSOASL, Africa, Wooden Box of L's letters.	MS.10778	
0130	ULSOASL, Africa, Odds, Box 18.	MS.10780 (6)	Schapera, **DLFL** I, pp. 143—147.
0131 n	WCLUWJ, Hist. and Lit. Papers, A348/A1.	MS.10779 (10)	Sotheby's Cat., 3 Dec 1913, lot 299, item 4.
0132	ULSOASL, Africa, Odds, Box 18.	MS.10780 (6)	Schapera, **DLFL** I, pp. 148—150.
0133 n	SNMDL, Misc. MS. Material.	MS.10709, f. 21	
0134 n			Myers' Cat. No. 8 (1972), no. 5, item 3.
0135 n			Myers' Cat. No. 8 (1972), no. 5, item 2.
0136	NLS, MS.10701, ff. 36—37.		Schapera, **DLFL** I, pp. 150—153.
0137	ULSOASL, Africa, Wooden Box of L's letters.	MS.10778	Schapera, **LMC**, pp. 65—85.
0138	ULSOASL, Africa, Odds, Box 18.	MS.10780 (6)	Schapera, **DLFL** I, pp. 154—155.
0139	NLS, MS.10701, ff. 38—39.		Schapera, **DLFL** I, pp. 155—158.
0140	NLS, MS.10773, pp. 177—180.		
0141	NLS, MS.10707, ff. 21—22.		Chamberlin, **SLFL**, pp. 83—86.
0142 n			Sotheby's Cat., 29 Jun 1939, lot 1474.
0143	Privately owned	MS.10769 (6)	
0144	NLS, MS.10701, ff. 40—41.		Schapera, **DLFL** I, pp. 159—163.
0145	WIHMLL, MS.64765.	MS.10779 (15)	
0146 n	ULSOASL, Africa, Odds, Box 18.	MS.10780 (6)	Schapera, **DLFL** I, pp. 163—170.
0147	NLS, MS.656, ff. 91—92.		
0148	ULSOASL, Africa, Odds, Box 18.	MS.10780 (6)	Schapera, **DLFL** I, pp. 170—174.
0149	ULSOASL, Africa, Wooden Box of L's letters.	MS.10778	Schapera, **LMC**, pp. 88—92.
0150	WIHMLL, MS.68188.	MS.10779 (15).	

NO	RECIPIENT	DATE	PLACE	LENGTH	SIZE		TYPE
0151	David G. Watt	8 Jun 46	Chonuane	1/ 4/ 4	250	204	MS aut in
0152	Robert Moffat 1	1, 31 Jul 46	Chonuane	1/ 4/ 4	lge	fol	MS aut in
0153	Robert Moffat 1	8 Sep 46	Chonuane	1/ 4/ 4	250	202	MS aut in
0154	Robert Moffat 1	[Feb—Sep 46??]		1/ 2/ 2	228	184	MS aut fr
0155	Robert Moffat 1	5 Oct 46	Chonuane	1/ 4/ 4	312	186	MS aut
0156	Charles Whish	9 Oct 46	Chonuane	1/ 4/ 4	400	247	MS aut
0157	Robert Moffat 1	27 Oct 46	[Chonuane]	2/ 6/ 6	250	202	MS aut in
0158	Benjamin T. Pyne	Dec 46, 20 Mar 47	Banks of the Botetle	4 pp		fol	MS copy
0159	Catherine McRobert	9 Jan 47	Chonuane	3 pp		4to	MS copy
0160	David G. Watt	17 Jan 47	Chonuane	1/ 4/ 4	250	204	MS aut
0161	Neil & Ag. Livingston 1	15 Mar 47	Kuruman	1/ 4/ 4	251	203	MS aut
0162	Charles Livingston	16 Mar 47	Kuruman	1/ 4/ 4	400	248	MS aut
0163	Arthur Tidman	17 Mar 47	Kuruman	4/12/11	378	240	MS aut
0164	Young Friends	22 Mar 47	Kuruman	1/ 2/ 2		4to	MS aut in
0165	William C. Oswell	22 Mar 47	Kuruman	1/ 4/ 4	250	202	MS aut fr
0166	Agnes Livingston 1	4 May 47	Kuruman	1/ 4/ 4	251	203	MS aut
0167	Hamilton M. Dyke	20 May 47	Kuruman	1/ 4/ 4	270	218	MS aut
0168	Benjamin T. Pyne	31 May 47	Kuruman	1/ 4/ 4	lge	fol	MS aut
0169	Andrew Murray	10 Jun 47	Kuruman	2/ 8/ 8	266	216	MS aut
0170	Catherine McRobert	9 Jul 47	Chonuane	5 pp		4to	MS copy
0171	Robert Moffat 1	Jul 47	Banks of the Notoane	1/ 4/ 4	227	185	MS aut in
0172	Robert Moffat 1	[Jul 47?]	[Banks of the Notoane?]	1/ 2/ 2	226	185	MS aut in
0173	Joseph Moore	9 Aug 47	Kolobeng, Bakwain Country	2/ 4/ 4	228	185	MS aut
0174	Robert Moffat 2	13 Aug, Sep, 30 Sep 47	Kolobeng, Bakwain Country	1/ 4/ 4	375	238	MS aut
0175	Robert Moffat 1	[Jul—Aug 47?]	[Kolobeng]	1/ 2/ 2	227	184	MS aut fr
0176	Margaret Sewell	20 Sep 47	Kolobeng, Bakwain Country	5 pp			TS copy
0177	Robert Moffat 1	29 Sep 47	Kolobeng	5/20/20		misc	MS aut
0178	Janet Livingston	7 Nov 47, 3 Jan 48	Kolobeng	1/ 4/ 4	251	203	MS aut
0179	Robert Moffat 1	[Nov 47?]	[Kolobeng]	1/ 2/ 2	323	203	MS aut in
0180	Arthur Tidman	[30 Dec 47]	[Kolobeng]	2/ 8/ 8	325	200	MS aut
0181	David G. Watt	13 Feb [48]	Kolobeng, Bakwain Country	1/ 4/ 4	321	200	MS aut
0182	Robert Moffat 1	[Mar 48?], 23 Mar [48]	[Kolobeng]	3/ 8/ 7		misc	MS aut fr
0183	Hamilton M. Dyke	7 Apr 48	Kolobeng	1/ 4/ 4	228	186	MS aut
0184	William C. Oswell	10 Apr 48	Kolobeng	1/ 4/ 4	400	250	MS aut
0185	Henry Drummond	19 Jun 48	Kolobeng, Bakwain Country	1/ 4/ 4	378	240	MS aut
0186	Neil & Ag. Livingston 1	5 Jul 48	Kolobeng	1/ 4/ 4	377	240	MS aut
0187	Robert Moffat 1	[11 Aug 48]	[Kolobeng]	1/ 4/ 4	227	183	MS aut in
0188	Robert Moffat 1	2 Sep 48	Kolobeng	3/12/12	226	184	MS aut
0189	Arthur Tidman	1 Nov 48	Kolobeng	2/ 8/ 8	325	203	MS aut in
0190	Henry Drummond	Nov, 20 Dec 48	Kolobeng	1/ 4/ 4	323	200	MS aut
0191	Robert Moffat 1	Nov 48	Kolobeng	3/12/12	230	185	MS aut
0192	John McRobert	24 Dec 48, 26 Jan 49	Kolobeng	1/ 4/ 4	325	206	Ph copy
0193	J. Risdon Bennett	1848 [?]		1 p			NS copy
0194	Robert Moffat 1	[1848?]		1/ 4/ 4	181	113	MS aut in
0195	Robert Moffat 1	[1848]		1/ 2/ 2	78	184	MS aut fr
0196	Robert Moffat 1	18 Jan 49	Kolobeng	1/ 4/ 4	lge	fol	MS aut in
0197	Janet Livingston	31 Jan 49	Kolobeng	1/ 4/ 4	248	202	MS aut
0198	Robert Moffat 1	31 Jan 49	Kolobeng	1/ 4/ 4	lge	fol	MS aut
0199	Robert Moffat 1	23 Mar 49	Kolobeng	3/12/12	250	200	MS aut in
0200	William Ashton	1 Apr 49	Kolobeng	4 pp		4to	MS copy

NO N	LOCATION	NLS COPY	PUBLICATION
0151	ULSOASL, Africa, Wooden Box of L's letters.	MS.10778	
0152	ULSOASL, Africa, Odds, Box 18.	MS.10780 (6)	Schapera, **DLFL** I, pp. 174—178.
0153	ULSOASL, Africa, Odds, Box 18.	MS.10780 (6)	Schapera, **DLFL** I, pp. 178—181.
0154 n	NLS, MS.10768, f. 83.		Maggs' Cat. No. 920, (Nov 1969), no. 9.
0155	ULSOASL, Africa, Odds, Box 18.	MS.10780 (6)	Schapera, **DLFL** I, pp. 181—183.
0156	SNMDL, on display.	MS.10708, f. 19	Chamberlin, **SLFL**, pp. 90—94.
0157	ULSOASL, Africa, Odds, Box 18.	MS.10780 (6)	Schapera, **DLFL** I, pp. 183—185.
0158	ULSOASL, Africa, Odds, Box 10, folder 2.		
0159	NLS, MS.10773, pp. 152—154.		
0160	ULSOASL, Africa, Wooden Box of L's letters.	MS.10778	
0161	NLS, MS.10701, ff. 42—43.		Schapera, **DLFL** I, pp. 186—189.
0162	SNMDL, on display.	MS.10708, f. 23	Schapera, **DLFL** I, pp. 189—195.
0163	ULSOASL, Africa, Wooden Box of L's letters.	MS.10778	Schapera, **LMC**, pp. 94—109.
0164	SNMDL, on display.	MS.10708, f. 27	
0165	NMLZ, G5.		Oswell, **WCO** I, pp. 147—149.
0166	NLS, MS.10701, ff. 44—45.		Schapera, **DLFL** I, pp. 195—200.
0167	NLS, MS.10707, ff. 23—24.	MS.10709, f. 9	
0168	Privately owned.	MS.10769 (7)	
0169	GRMSA.	MS.10777 (18)	Schapera, **DLSAP**, p. 4, ex.
0170	ULSOASL, Africa, Odds, Box 10, folder 2.		
0171	ULSOASL, Africa, Odds, Box 18.	MS.10780 (6)	Schapera, **DLFL** I, pp. 200—202.
0172	RHLO, MSS. Afr. s. 16, vol. I, f. 279.	MS.10780 (8)	Sotheby's Cat., 20 Dec 1939, lot 690.
0173	NARS, LI 2/1/1.	MS.10773	Sotheby's Cat., 17 Dec 1951, lot 213.
0174	BLJ, Book no. 4730.		Schapera, **DLFL** I, pp. 202—211.
0175 n	NLS, MS.10768, f. 3.		
0176	RGSL, Library, Y 224.11.		
0177	ULSOASL, Africa, Odds, Box 18.	MS.10780 (6)	Schapera, **DLFL** I, pp. 211—226.
0178	NLS, MS.10701, ff. 46—47.		Schapera, **DLFL** I, pp. 226—230.
0179	ULSOASL, Africa, Odds, Box 18.	MS.10780 (6)	Schapera, **DLFL** I, pp. 231—233.
0180 n	ULSOASL, Africa, Wooden Box of L's letters.	MS.10778	Schapera, **LMC**, pp. 111—117.
0181	NMLZ, on display.	MS.10779 (20)	Chamberlin, **SLFL**, pp. 115—118.
0182	ULSOASL, Africa, Odds, Box 18.	MS.10780 (6)	Schapera, **DLFL** I, pp. 234—243.
0183	NLS, MS.10707, ff. 25—26.	MS.10709, f. 13	
0184	APLANZ, MS.116.	MS.10777 (10a)	Sotheby's Cat., 2 Jun 1932, lot 448.
0185	NLS, MS.10707, ff. 27—28.		Chamberlin, **SLFL**, pp. 118—123.
0186	NLS, MS.10701, ff. 48—49.		Schapera, **DLFL** I, pp. 243—249.
0187 n	ULSOASL, Africa, Odds, Box 18.	MS.10780 (6)	Schapera, **DLFL** I, pp. 249—251.
0188 n	ULSOASL, Africa, Odds, Box 18.	MS.10780 (6)	Schapera, **DLFL** I, pp. 251—258.
0189	ULSOASL, Africa, Wooden Box of L's letters.	MS.10778	Schapera, **LMC**, pp. 118—124.
0190	ULSOASL, Africa, Wooden Box of L's letters.	MS.10778	
0191	ULSOASL, Africa, Odds, Box 18.	MS.10780 (6)	Schapera, **DLFL** I, pp. 259—266.
0192	NLS, MS.10709, f. 15.		**SC**, n.s. vol. 39 (Feb 1943), p. 13.
0193 n	ULSOASL, Africa, Odds, Box 11, folder 5.		**ACW**, 7 Oct 1932.
0194	JPLAM.	MS.10779 (8)	
0195	NLS, MS.10768, f. 84.		
0196	ULSOASL, Africa, Odds, Box 18.	MS.10780 (6)	Schapera, **DLFL** II, pp. 7—13.
0197	NLS, MS.10701, ff. 50—51.		Schapera, **DLFL** II, pp. 17—20.
0198	ULSOASL, Africa, Odds, Box 18.	MS.10780 (6)	Schapera, **DLFL** II, pp. 13—17.
0199	ULSOASL, Africa, Odds, Box 18.	MS.10780 (6)	Schapera, **DLFL** II, pp. 20—28.
0200 n	ULSOASL, Africa, Odds, Box 10, folder 2.		

NO	RECIPIENT	DATE	PLACE	LENGTH	SIZE	TYPE
0201	Robert Moffat 1	11 Apr 49	Kolobeng	1/ 4/ 4	lge fol	MS aut
0202	Janet Livingston	20 Apr 49	Kolobeng	1/ 4/ 4	400 250	MS aut
0203	Robert Moffat 1	[4 May?] 49	[Kolobeng]	3/12/12	250 202	MS aut in
0204	Charles Livingston	16 May 49	Kolobeng	1/ 4/ 4	400 250	MS aut
0205	Robert Moffat 1	26 May 49	Kolobeng	1/ 4/ 4	250 200	MS aut
0206	Arthur Tidman	26 May 49	Kolobeng	1/ 4/ 4	400 250	MS aut
0207	Charles Livingston	19 Aug, 10, 18 Oct 49	Banks of the River Zouga	6 pp		Pr copy
0208	Arthur Tidman	3 Sep, 14 Oct 49	Banks of the River Zouga	2/ 8/ 8	255 200	Ph copy
0209	Robert Moffat 1	[17 Sep?] 49		3/ 8/ 8	misc	MS aut fr
0210	Margaret Sewell	21 Sep 49	Desert north of Kolobeng	5 pp		TS copy
0211	Neil & Ag. Livingston 1	25 Sep 49	Kolobeng			MS aut
0212	Robert Moffat 1	[1?] Oct, 12 Oct 49	Kolobeng	1/ 4/ 4	226 183	MS aut in
0213	William C. Oswell	11 Oct 49	Kolobeng	2/ 6/ 6	227 186	MS aut
0214	Benjamin T. Pyne	15 Oct 49	Kolobeng	1/ 4/ 4	229 186	MS aut
0215	Thomas Steele	Sep—Oct 49		3 pp		Pr copy
0216	Joseph J. Freeman	14 Nov 49	Kolobeng	1/ 4/ 4	226 186	MS aut
0217	Robert Moffat 1	[Nov?] 49	[Kolobeng]	1/ 2/ 2	227 186	MS aut in
0218	Henry Denny	7 Dec 49	Kolobeng, Bakwain Country	1/ 4/ 4	228 185	MS aut
0219	Joseph J. Freeman	9 Jan 50	Kolobeng	2/ 8/ 8	250 200	MS aut
0220	David G. Watt	13 Jan 50	Kolobeng	1/ 4/ 4	400 250	MS aut
0221	Robert Moffat 1	[Jan,] 4 Feb 50	[Kolobeng]	1/ 4/ 4	250 200	MS aut in
0222	Agnes Livingston 2	5 Feb 50	Kolobeng	1/ 4/ 4	250 201	MS aut
0223	Margaret Sewell	20 Feb, 2 Mar 50	Kolobeng	5 pp		TS copy
0224	Henry H. Methuen	[1 Nov 49—28 Feb 50??]	[Kolobeng??]	1/ 2/ 2	251 200	MS aut in
0225	Benjamin T. Pyne	4 Mar, 2 Aug 50	Kolobeng	6 pp	4to	MS aut
0226	Robert Moffat 1	4 Mar 50	Kolobeng	1/ 4/ 4	250 202	MS aut
0227	Robert Moffat 1	8, 18, 31 Jul; 1 Aug 50	[Logagneñ – Kolobeng]	2/ 8/ 8	lge fol	MS aut
0228	Parents & Sisters	28 Jul 50	Kolobeng	1/ 4/ 4	400 250	MS aut
0229	David G. Watt	18 Aug 50	Kolobeng	1/ 4/ 4	400 250	MS aut
0230	Joseph J. Freeman	24 Aug 50	Kolobeng	1/ 4/ 4	400 248	MS aut
0231	Robert Moffat 1	24 Aug 50	Kolobeng	1/ 4/ 4	250 201	MS aut
0232	Arthur Tidman	24 Aug 50	Kolobeng	2/ 8/ 8	400 250	MS aut
0233	Benjamin T. Pyne	27 Aug 50	[Kolobeng]	7 pp		MS copy
0234	William Thompson	27 Aug 50	Kolobeng	1/ 4/ 4	225 190	MS aut
0235	Margaret Sewell	9 Sep 50	Kolobeng	5 pp		TS copy
0236	Robert Moffat 1	18, 27 Sep 50	Kolobeng	1/ 4/ 4	250 200	MS aut
0237	Robert Moffat 1	2, [7] Oct 50	Kolobeng	2/ 8/ 6	226 185	MS aut
0238	Robert Moffat 1	17 Oct 50	Kolobeng	2/ 8/ 8	250 201	MS aut
0239	Robert Moffat 1	27 Oct 50	Kolobeng	1/ 4/ 4	251 201	MS aut
0240	Parents & Sisters	4 Dec 50	Kuruman	1/ 4/ 4	251 201	MS aut
0241	Benjamin T. Pyne	4 Dec 50	Kuruman	1/ 4/ 4	260 200	Ph copy
0242	David G. Watt	10 Jan 51	Kuruman	1/ 4/ 4	420 252	MS aut
0243	William Fairbrother	14 Jan 51	Kuruman	1/ 4/ 4	228 184	MS aut
0244	H. Norton Shaw	[Aug 50—Jan 51]		1 p.		Pr copy
0245	Parents & Sisters	9 Feb 51	Kuruman	2/ 8/ 8	252 198	MS aut
0246	Charles Livingston	25 Mar, 26 Apr 51	Kolobeng	3 pp		Pr copy
0247	Robert Moffat 1	14 Apr 51	Kolobeng	1/ 4/ 4	252 200	MS aut in
0248	Margaret Sewell	19, 26 Apr 51	Kolobeng	8 pp		TS copy
0249	Robert Moffat 1	26 Apr 51	Logageñ	1/ 4/ 4	252 201	MS aut
0250	Janet & Ag. Livingston 2	28 Apr 51	Kolobeng	1/ 4/ 4	252 201	MS aut

NO	N	LOCATION	NLS COPY	PUBLICATION
0201		ULSOASL, Africa, Odds, Box 18.	MS.10780 (6)	Schapera, **DLFL** II, pp. 28—32.
0202		NLS, MS.10701, ff. 52—53.		Schapera, **DLFL** II, pp. 32—38.
0203		ULSOASL, Africa, Odds, Box 18.	MS.10780 (6)	Schapera, **DLFL** II, pp. 39—48.
0204		NLS, MS.10707, ff. 29—30.		Schapera, **DLFL** II, pp. 48—57.
0205		ULSOASL, Africa, Odds, Box 18.	MS.10780 (6)	Schapera, **DLFL** II, pp. 57—60.
0206		ULSOASL, Africa, Wooden Box of L's letters.	MS.10778	Schapera, **LMC**, pp. 126—130.
0207	n			**MH**, May 1922, pp. 173—178.
0208	n	SNMDL, on display.	MS.10708, f. 29	Schapera, **LMC**, pp. 131—138.
0209		ULSOASL, Africa, Odds, Box 18.	MS.10780 (6)	Schapera, **DLFL** II, pp. 60—64.
0210		RGSL, Library, Y 224.11.		
0211		Privately owned.		Schapera, **DLFL** II, pp. 64—68.
0212		NLS, MS.10768, ff. 4—5.		Sawyer's Cat. No. 281 (1970), no. 392.
0213		NLS, MS.10701, ff. 54—56.		
0214		BLJ, Book no. 5318, Acc. Reg. 4669.		Sotheby's Cat., 29 Jun 1939, lot 1476.
0215				**JRGSL**, vol. 20 (1850), pp. 138—142, ex.
0216		ULSOASL, Africa, Wooden Box of L's letters.	MS.10778	Schapera, **LMC**, pp. 138—140.
0217		ULSOASL, Africa, Odds, Box 18.	MS.10780 (6)	Schapera, **DLFL** II, pp. 68—70.
0218		BLJ, Book no. 5318, Acc. Reg. 4669.		Sotheby's Cat., 29 Jun 1939, lot 1477.
0219		ULSOASL, Africa, Wooden Box of L's letters.	MS 10778	Schapera, **LMC**, pp. 140—144.
0220		ULSOASL, Africa, Wooden Box of L's letters.	MS.10778	
0221		ULSOASL, Africa, Odds, Box 18.	MS.10780 (6)	Schapera, **DLFL** II, pp. 71—73.
0222		NLS, MS. 10701, ff. 57—58.		Schapera, **DLFL** II, pp. 73—77.
0223		RGSL, Library, Y 224.11.		
0224		WIHMLL, MS.67464.	MS.10779 (15)	
0225		Privately owned.	MS.10769 (8)	
0226		ULSOASL, Africa, Odds, Box 18.	MS.10780 (6)	Schapera, **DLFL** II, pp. 77—79.
0227	n	ULSOASL, Africa, Odds, Box 18.	MS.10780 (6)	Schapera, **DLFL** II, pp. 79—92.
0228		NLS, MS.10701, ff. 59—60.		Schapera, **DLFL** II, pp. 92—100.
0229		SNMDL, on display.	MS.10708, f. 37	
0230		ULSOASL, Africa, Wooden Box of L's letters.	MS.10778	Schapera, **LMC**, pp. 146—154.
0231		ULSOASL, Africa, Odds, Box 18.	MS.10780 (6)	Schapera, **DLFL** II, pp. 100—102.
0232	n	ULSOASL, Africa, Wooden Box of L's letters.	MS.10778	Schapera, **LMC**, pp. 154—164.
0233	n	KCLUND.		**The Times**, 22 Aug 1938, p. 7, c. 1, ex.
0234		ULSOASL, Africa, Wooden Box of L's letters.	MS.10778	Schapera, **LMC**, pp. 164—166.
0235		RGSL, Library, Y 224.11.		
0236		ULSOASL, Africa, Odds, Box 18.	MS.10780 (6)	Schapera, **DLFL** II, pp. 103—105.
0237		ULSOASL, Africa, Odds, Box 18.	MS.10780 (6)	Schapera, **DLFL** II, pp. 105—107.
0238		ULSOASL, Africa, Odds, Box 18.	MS.10780 (6)	Schapera, **DLFL** II, pp. 107—111.
0239		ULSOASL, Africa, Odds, Box 18.	MS.10780 (6)	Schapera, **DLFL** II, pp. 112—114.
0240		NLS, MS.10701, ff. 61—62.		Schapera, **DLFL** II, pp. 114—117.
0241	n	SNMDL.	MS.10708, f. 42	Chamberlin, **SLFL**, pp. 141—144.
0242		ULSOASL, Africa, Wooden Box of L's letters.	MS.10778	Campbell, **Liv**, p. 69, n, ex.
0243		NMLZ, on dispaly.	MS.10779 (20)	Sotheby's Cat., 9 Jun 1936, lot 470.
0244	n			**JRGSL**, vol. 21 (1851), p. 24, n.
0245		NLS, MS.10701, ff. 63—66.		Schapera, **DLFL** II, pp. 118—124.
0246	n			**MH**, Jun 1922, pp. 219—221.
0247		ULSOASL, Africa, Odds, Box 18.	MS.10780 (6)	Schapera, **DLFL** II, pp. 125—128.
0248		RGSL, Library, Y 224.11.		
0249		ULSOASL, Africa, Odds, Box 18.	MS.10780 (6)	Schapera, **DLFL** II, pp. 128—130.
0250		NLS, MS.10701, ff. 67—68.		Schapera, **DLFL** II, pp. 132—136.

NO	RECIPIENT	DATE	PLACE	LENGTH	SIZE	TYPE
0251	Robert Moffat 2	28 Apr 51	Kolobeng	2/ 4/ 4	4to	MS aut
0252	Benjamin T. Pyne	30 Apr 51	Boatlanama	1/ 4/ 4	4to	MS aut
0253	Arthur Tidman	30 Apr 51	Boatlanama	2/ 6/ 6	252 200	MS aut in
0254	Robert Moffat 1	29 Sep 51	Banks of the Zouga	1/ 4/ 4	252 200	MS aut in
0255	David G. Watt	29 Sep 51	Banks of the Zouga	2/ 6/ 5	252 200	MS aut
0256	Arthur Tidman	1 Oct 51	Banks of the Zouga	2/ 8/ 8	252 200	MS aut
0257	Charles Livingston	8 Oct 51	Banks of the Zouga	5 pp		Pr copy
0258	Arthur Tidman	17 Oct 51	Banks of the Zouga	4/16/16	252 200	MS aut fr
0259	Parents & Sisters	Oct, 14 Nov 51	Banks of the Zouga	3/12/12	misc	MS aut
0260	William C. Oswell	[15 Nov 51]	[North of Shokotsa]	1/ 4/ 4	250 197	Ph copy
0261	Robert Moffat 1	29 Nov 51	Kolobeng	1/ 4/ 4	228 186	MS aut
0262	Hamilton M. Dyke	1 Dec 51	Kolobeng	1/ 4/ 4	380 235	MS aut
0263	Agnes Livingston 2	29 Dec 51	Kuruman	1/ 4/ 4	397 250	MS aut
0264	Robert Moffat 1	22 Jan 52	Past Scheit Fontein	1/ 2/ 2	400 250	MS aut fr
0265	Robert Moffat 1	Jan 52		1/ 2/ 2	282 258	MS aut fr
0266	Arthur Tidman	17 Mar 52	Cape Town	1/ 4/ 4	396 248	MS aut
0267	David G. Watt	Mar 52	Cape Town	1/ 4/ 4	250 200	MS aut
0268	Robert Moffat 1	2 Apr 52	Cape Town	1/ 4/ 4	400 250	MS aut
0269	[Benjamin T. Pyne]	2 Apr 52	Cape Town	1/ 4/ 4	179 112	MS aut
0270	Charles Livingston	12, [24?] Apr 52	Cape Town	3 pp		Pr copy
0271	Robert Moffat 1	26 Apr 52	Cape Town	1/ 4/ 4	273 218	MS aut
0272	Arthur Tidman	26 Apr 52	Cape Town	1/ 4/ 4	250 198	MS aut
0273	Arthur Tidman	26 Apr 52	Cape Town	1/ 4/ 4	274 218	MS aut
0274	William C. Oswell	27 Apr 52	Cape Town	1/ 4/ 4	275 219	Ph copy fr
0275	Mary Livingston	5 May 52	Cape Town	1 p		Pr copy
0276	Thomas Maclear	7 May 52	Cape Town	1/ 4/ 2	172 113	MS aut
0277	Agnes Livingston 3	18 May 52	Cape Town	1/ 4/ 4	8vo	MS aut
0278	Robert M. Livingston	18 May 52	Cape Town	1/ 4/ 4	182 223	MS aut
0279	Thomas Maclear	24 May 52	Cape Town	1/ 4/ 4	199 126	MS aut
0280	Mary Livingston	28 May 52	Cape Town	4 pp	4to	Pr copy
0281	Charles Livingston	29 May 52	Cape Town	2pp		Pr copy
0282	William Thompson	9 Jun 52	Paarl	1/ 4/ 3	245 200	MS aut
0283	William Thompson	[20?] Jul 52	Scheit Fontein	2/ 8/ 8	284 208	MS aut
0284	William Thompson	6, 20 Sep 52	Kuruman	1/ 4/ 4	400 250	MS aut
0285	H.E. Rutherfoord	8 Sep [52]	Kuruman	4 pp	lge 4to	Pr copy
0286	Charles Livingston	10 Sep 52	Kuruman	2 pp		Pr copy
0287	Mary Livingston	20 Sep 52	Kuruman	1/ 4/ 4	255 200	MS aut
0288	William C. Oswell	20 Sep 52	Kuruman	1/ 4/ 4	fol	MS aut
0289	Neil & Ag. Livingston 1	26 Sep 52	Kuruman	1/ 4/ 4	396 248	MS aut
0290	Charles H. Darling	29 Sep 52	Kuruman	1/ 4/ 4		MS copy
0291	William Thompson	30 Sep 52	Kuruman	1/ 4/ 4	400 248	MS aut
0292	Livingston Children	[Sep 52?]	[Kuruman]	1/ 4/ 4	113 92	MS aut
0293	William Thompson	12 Oct 52	Kuruman	4/14/13	275 220	MS aut
0294	Benjamin T. Pyne	15 Oct 52	Kuruman	1/ 4/ 4	191 118	MS aut
0295	David G. Watt	Oct 52	Kuruman	1/ 4/ 4	274 218	MS aut
0296	Arthur Tidman	2, 12 Nov 52	Kuruman	2/ 8/ 8	275 220	MS aut
0297	Margaret Sewell	22 Nov 52	Kuruman	2/ 4/ 4	275 215	MS aut
0298	Thomas Spencer	22 Nov 52	Kuruman	2 pp		MS aut copy
0299	Joseph Moore	23 Nov 52	Kuruman	1/ 4/ 4	275 220	MS aut
0300	William Thompson	24 Nov 52	Kuruman	2/ 6/ 6	220 138	MS aut

NO	N	LOCATION	NLS COPY	PUBLICATION
0251		DMAGLHMDSA, on display.	MS.10777 (14)	Schapera, **DLFL** II, pp. 130—132.
0252		NLS, MS.2521, ff. 125—126.		
0253		ULSOASL, Africa, Wooden Box of L's letters.	MS.10778	Schapera, **LMC**, pp. 169—173.
0254		ULSOASL, Africa, Odds, Box 18.	MS.10780 (6)	Schapera, **DLFL** II, pp. 136—140.
0255		ULSOASL, Africa, Wooden Box of L's letters.	MS.10778	
0256		ULSOASL, Africa, Wooden Box of L's letters.	MS.10778	Schapera, **LMC**, pp. 173—178.
0257	n			**The Atlantic Monthly**, Jul 1922, pp. 1—5, ex.
0258		ULSOASL, Africa, Wooden Box of L's letters.	MS.10778	Schapera, **LMC**, pp. 178—192.
0259		NLS, MS.10701, ff. 69—74.		Schapera, **DLFL** II, pp. 140—154.
0260	n	NMLZ.	MS.10777 (20)	
0261		ULSOASL, Africa, Odds, Box 18.	MS.10780 (6)	Schapera, **DLFL** II, pp. 154—155.
0262		NLS, MS.10707, ff. 31—32.	MS.10709, f. 23	
0263		NLS, MS.10701, ff. 75—76.		Schapera, **DLFL** II, pp. 156—162.
0264		ULSOASL, Africa, Odds, Box 18.	MS.10780 (6)	Schapera, **DLFL** II, pp. 163—166.
0265	n	NMLZ, on display.	MS.10779 (20)	Schapera, **DLFL** II, pp. 166—167.
0266		ULSOASL, Africa, Wooden Box of L's letters.	MS.10778	Schapera, **LMC**, pp. 193—197.
0267		ULSOASL, Africa, Wooden Box of L's letters.	MS.10778	
0268		ULSOASL, Africa, Odds, Box 18.	MS.10780 (6)	Schapera, **DLFL** II, pp. 167—176.
0269		WIHMLL, MS.52325.	MS.10779 (15)	
0270				**The Atlantic Monthly**, Jul 1922, pp. 6—8, ex.
0271		ULSOASL, Africa, Odds, Box 18.	MS.10780 (6)	Schapera, **DLFL** II, pp. 177—181.
0272		ULSOASL, Africa, Wooden Box of L's letters.	MS.10778	Schapera, **LMC**, pp. 200—202.
0273		ULSOASL, Africa, Wooden Box of L's letters.	MS.10778	Schapera, **LMC**, pp. 202—204.
0274	n	WCLUWJ.	MS.10779 (10)	Oswell, **WCO** II, pp. 2—3, ex.
0275	n			Schapera, **DLFL** II, p. 182.
0276		NARS, LI 1/1/1, ff. 4—5.		
0277	n	NLS, MS.10704, ff. 1—2.		Schapera, **DLFL** II, p. 183.
0278	n	MLG, James Cowie Collection, MS.301.	MS.10777 (16)	
0279		GACT, Maclear Papers, Acc. 515.	MS.10779 (4)	
0280				Sotheby's Cat., 20 Feb 1967, lot 178.
0281				**The Atlantic Monthly**, Jul 1922, pp. 8—9, ex.
0282		ULSOASL, Africa, Wooden Box of L's letters.	MS.10778	Schapera, **LMC**, pp. 204—206.
0283	n	ULSOASL, Africa, Wooden Box of L's letters.	MS.10778	Schapera, **LMC**, pp. 208—213.
0284		ULSOASL, Africa, Wooden Box of L's letters.	MS.10778	Schapera, **LMC**, pp. 214—218.
0285				Sotheby's Cat., 25 Feb 1946, lot 201.
0286				**The Atlantic Monthly**, Jul 1922, pp. 9—10, ex.
0287	n	BLL, Add. MS. 50184, ff. 5—6.	MS.10780 (3)	Schapera, **DLFL** II, pp. 184—186.
0288		RGSL, Archives, DL 1/1/3.	MS.10780 (5)	
0289		NLS, MS.10701, ff. 78—79.		Schapera, **DLFL** II, pp. 187—191.
0290	n	ULSOASL, Africa, Wooden Box of L's letters.	MS.10778	Schapera, **DLSAP**, pp. 55—59.
0291		ULSOASL, Africa, Wooden Box of L's letters.	MS.10778	Schapera, **LMC**, pp. 219—222.
0292	n	NLS, MS.10701, ff. 77—78.		Schapera, **DLFL** II, p. 187.
0293	n	ULSOASL, Africa, Wooden Box of L's letters.	MS.10778	Schapera, **LMC**, pp. 222—228.
0294		WCLUWJ, Hist. and Lit. Papers, A348/A2.	MS.10779 (10)	Sotheby's Cat., 3 Dec 1913, lot 299, item 5.
0295		ULSOASL, Africa, Wooden Box of L's letters.	MS.10778	
0296		ULSOASL, Africa, Wooden Box of L's letters.	MS.10778	Schapera, **LMC**, pp. 228—233.
0297		RGSL, Archives, DL 1/4.		
0298	n	NARS, LI 1/4/1, Journal no. 2.		Schapera, **LPJ**, pp. 92—93.
0299		NARS, LI 2/1/1.	MS.10773	Sotheby's Cat., 17 Dec 1951, lot 214.
0300		ULSOASL, Africa, Wooden Box of L's letters.	MS.10778	Schapera, **LMC**, pp. 234—236.

NO	RECIPIENT	DATE	PLACE	LENGTH	SIZE	TYPE
0301	Agnes Livingstone 3	26 Nov 52	Kuruman	1/ 4/ 4	½ 8vo	MS aut
0302	Thomas S. Livingstone	26 Nov 52	Kuruman	1/ 4/ 4	126 101	MS aut
0303	Livingstone Children	Nov 52	Kuruman	1/ 4/ 4	169 114	MS aut
0304	John S. Pakington	12 Dec 52	Kuruman	4 pp		MS copy
0305	Arthur Tidman	12 Dec 52	Kuruman	1/ 4/ 4	275 220	MS aut
0306	Thomas Maclear	13 Dec 52	Kuruman	1/ 4/ 4	275 219	MS aut
0307	Agnes Livingstone 1	19 Dec 52	Kuruman	1/ 4/ 4	247 200	MS aut
0308	Robert Moffat 1	28 Dec 52	Kuruñkue	1/ 4/ 4	251 203	MS aut
0309	John Snow	12 Jan 53	Litubaruba	4 pp	4to	Ph copy
0310	Mary Livingstone	14,16 Jan 53	Litubaruba	1/ 4/ 4	400 255	MS aut
0311	Charles Livingstone	6 Feb, 18 Mar, 7 Jun 53	[Motlatsa-Dinyanti]	1/ 4/ 4	400 250	MS aut
0312	Livingstone Children	[10–14 Feb 53]	Lotlakané	1/ 4/ 4	218 136	MS aut
0313	Mary Livingstone	6 Jun 53	Sekeletu's Town	1/ 4/ 3	400 251	MS aut
0314	Robert Moffat 1	16 Sep 53	Sekeletu's Town, Linyanti	1/ 4/ 4	400 250	MS aut
0315	William Thompson	17 Sep 53	Sekeletu's Town	1/ 4/ 4	400 250	MS aut
0316	[John Livingstone]	20 Sep 53	Sekeletu's Town, Linyanti	1 p		NS copy
0317	William C. Oswell	20 Sep, 2 Oct 53	Sekeletu's Town, Linyanti	2/ 8/ 8	400 250	MS aut
0318	Thomas Steele	20 Sep 53	Town of Sekeletu, Linyanti	2/ 8/ 8	fol	MS aut
0319	Charles Livingstone	21 Sep 53	Sekeletu's Town, Linyanti	4 pp		Pr copy
0320	Arthur Tidman	24 Sep 53	Town of Sekeletu, Linyanti	2/ 6/ 6	396 250	MS aut
0321	Jean Frédoux	28 Sep 53	Town of Sekeletu, Linyanti	1/ 4/ 4	335 245	MS aut
0322	Paris Geographical Soc.	28 Sep 53	Town of Sekeletu, Linyanti	9 pp		Pr copy
0323	Thomas Maclear	29 Sep 53	Town of Sekeletu, Linyanti	1/ 4/ 4	400 250	MS aut
0324	Parents & Sisters	30 Sep 53	Sekeletu's Town, Linyanti	1/ 4/ 4	275 200	MS aut
0325	Livingstone Children	2 Oct [53]	Sekeletu's Town, Linyanti	4 pp	8vo	Pr copy
0326	J.H. Wilson	2 Oct 53	Sekeletu's Town, Linyanti	1/ 4/ 4	400 251	MS aut copy
0327	David G. Watt	3 Oct 53	Linyanti	1 p		Pr copy
0328	William Thompson	11, 17 Oct 53	Linyanti	1/ 4/ 4	275 220	MS aut
0329	Robert Moffat 1	1, 9, 10 Nov 53	Linyanti	4/12/12	400 251	MS aut
0330	Arthur Tidman	8 Nov 53	Linyanti	1/ 4/ 4	275 200	MS aut
0331	Thomas Maclear	7 Apr, 8 Jun, 15 Aug 54	[Banks of the Quango-Loanda]	1/ 4/ 4	400 250	MS aut
0332	Charles Livingstone	8 Apr, 17 Jun 54	Cassange-Loanda	3 pp		Pr copy
0333	Alfredo Duprat	9 Apr 54	Cassange	2 pp		Pr copy
0334	William Thompson	14 May, 14 Aug 54	Calimba-Loanda	2/ 8/ 8	249 197	MS aut
0335	Robert Moffat 1	19 May, 9 Aug 54	Golungo Alto-Loanda	1/ 4/ 4	248 190	MS aut
0336	Thomas Maclear	8 Jun, 15 Aug 54	Loanda	2/ 8/ 8	276 225	MS aut in
0337	Roderick I. Murchison	20 Aug 54	Loanda	1/ 4/ 4	4to	MS aut
0338	Edmund Gabriel	1 Oct 54	Golungo Alto	3/12/12	248 187	MS aut
0339	Edmund Gabriel	13, 17, 21 Oct 54	Massangano-Golungo Alto	4/16/16	4to	MS aut
0340	Edmund Gabriel	21 Oct 54	Golungo Alto	4/12/12	4to	MS aut
0341	Edmund Gabriel	24 Oct 54	Golungo Alto	1/ 4/ 4	4to	MS aut
0342	Edmund Gabriel	25 Oct [54]	Golungo Alto	1/ 2/ 2	4to	MS aut
0343	Mary Livingstone	25 Oct 54	Golungo Alto	3 pp		Pr copy
0344	Edmund Gabriel	28 Oct 54	Golungo Alto	4/16/16	4to	MS aut in
0345	Edmund Gabriel	1 Nov 54	Golungo Alto	1/ 4/ 4	4to	MS aut
0346	Edmund Gabriel	5 Nov 54	Golungo Alto	2/ 8/ 8	4to	MS aut in
0347	Charles Livingstone	8 Nov 54	Golungo Alto	3/12/12	4to	MS aut
0348	Edmund Gabriel	9 Nov 54	Golungo Alto	1/ 4/ 4	4to	MS aut
0349	Edmund Gabriel	12 Nov 54	Golungo Alto	1/ 4/ 4	4to	MS aut
0350	Edmund Gabriel	15 Nov 54	Golungo Alto	1/ 4/ 4	4to	MS aut

NO	N	LOCATION	NLS COPY	PUBLICATION
0301		Privately owned.	MS.10779 (1)	
0302		NLS, MS.10701, ff. 82—83.		Schapera, **DLFL** II, pp. 192—193.
0303		NLS, MS.10701, ff. 80—81.		Schapera, **DLFL** II, pp. 191—192.
0304	n	NLS, MS.10777 (26).		Schapera, **DLSAP**, pp. 59—62.
0305		ULSOASL, Africa, Wooden Box of L's letters.	MS.10778	Schapera, **LMC**, pp. 236—238.
0306		NARS, LI 1/1/1, pp. 51—54.		
0307		NLS, MS.10701, ff. 84—85.		Schapera, **DLFL** II, pp. 193—194.
0308		ULSOASL, Africa, Odds, Box 18.	MS.10780 (6)	Schapera, **DLFL** II, pp. 195—197.
0309	n	ULSOASL, Africa, Odds, Box 21.		Seaver, **DLLL**, p. 167, ex.
0310		BLL, Add.MS.50184, ff. 7—8.	MS.10780 (3)	Schapera, **DLFL** II, pp. 199—203.
0311	n	NLS, MS.10707, ff. 33—34.		Schapera, **DLFL** II, pp. 206—214.
0312	n	NLS, MS.10704, ff. 3—4.		Schapera, **DLFL** II, pp. 204—206.
0313	n	NARS, ST 1/1/1, pp. 174—176.		**School**, vol. II, No. 2 (1945), pp. 35—39.
0314		ULSOASL, Africa, Odds, Box 18.	MS. 10780 (6)	Schapera, **DLFL** II, pp. 214—222.
0315		ULSOASL, Africa, Wooden Box of L's letters.	MS.10778	Schapera, **LMC**, pp. 239—246.
0316	n	RGSL, Archives, DL 2/2.		
0317		NLS, MS.10768, ff. 6—9.		
0318		RGSL, Archives, DL 2/1.	MS.10780 (5)	**JRGSL**, vol. 24 (1854), pp. 291—306.
0319				**The Atlantic Monthly**, Aug 1922, pp. 213—216.
0320		ULSOASL, Africa, Wooden Box of L's letters.	MS.10778	Schapera, **LMC**, pp. 246—253.
0321		SNMDL, on display.	MS.10708, f.46	Schapera, **DLFL** II, pp. 222—225.
0322	n		MS.10777 (10)	**Bull., Paris Geog Soc**, May 1854, pp. 364—372.
0323		NLS, MS.10768, ff. 10—11.		
0324		NLS, MS.10701, ff. 86—87.		Schapera, **DLFL** II, pp. 226—229.
0325	n			Schapera, **DLFL** II, pp. 229—231.
0326	n	NARS, LI 1/1/1, pp. 78—81.	MS.10777 (10)	Schapera, **DLSAP**, pp. 119—123.
0327				Blaikie, **PLDL**, p. 128, ex.
0328	n	ULSOASL, Africa, Wooden Box of L's letters.	MS.10778	Schapera, **LMC**, pp. 253—256.
0329		ULSOASL, Africa, Odds, Box 18.	MS.10780 (6)	Schapera, **DLFL** II, pp. 231—242.
0330		ULSOASL, Africa, Wooden Box of L's letters.	MS.10778	Schapera, **LMC**, pp. 256—259.
0331		NARS, LI 1/1/1, pp. 86—89.		**PP** Sess. 1856, v.LXII, [174] Class A pp. 86—87.
0332				**MH**, Jul 1922, pp. 262—264.
0333				**PP** Sess. 1856, v. LXII, [174] Class A pp. 84—85.
0334		ULSOASL, Africa, Wooden Box of L's letters.	MS.10778	Schapera, **LMC**, pp. 260—266.
0335		ULSOASL, Africa, Odds, Box 18.	MS.10780 (6)	Schapera, **DLFL** II, pp. 243-248.
0336		NARS, LI 1/1/1, pp. 94—101.		
0337		RGSL, Archives, DL 2/5/10.	MS.10780 (5)	
0338		BLL, Add. MS.37410, ff. 1—6.	MS.10780 (3)	
0339	n	BLL, Add. MS.37410, ff. 7—14.	MS.10780 (3)	
0340		BLL, Add. MS.37410, ff. 15—20.	MS.10780 (3)	
0341		BLL, Add. MS.37410, ff. 21—22.	MS.10780 (3)	
0342		BLL, Add. MS.37410, f. 23.	MS.10780 (3)	
0343	n			Schapera, **DLFL** II, pp. 248—250.
0344		BLL, Add. MS.37410, ff. 24—31.	MS.10780 (3)	
0345		BLL, Add. MS.37410, ff. 32—33.	MS.10780 (3)	
0346	n	BLL, Add. MS.37410, ff. 34—37.	MS.10780 (3)	
0347		SNMDL.	MS.10708, f. 50	Schapera, **DLFL** II, pp. 250—257.
0348		BLL, Add. MS.37410, ff. 38—39.	MS.10780 (3)	
0349		BLL, Add. MS.37410, ff. 40—41.	MS.10780 (3)	
0350		BLL, Add. MS.37410, ff. 42—43.	MS.10780 (3)	

NO	RECIPIENT	DATE	PLACE	LENGTH	SIZE	TYPE
0351	Edmund Gabriel	17 Nov 54	Golungo Alto	1/ 4/ 4	4to	MS aut
0352	Edmund Gabriel	21 Nov 54	Golungo Alto	6/16/16	4to	MS aut
0353	Edmund Gabriel	7 Dec 54	Ambaca	4/14/14	4to	MS aut
0354	Edmund Gabriel	20 Dec 54	Pungo Adongo	1/ 4/ 3	288 235	MS aut
0355	Roderick I. Murchison	24 Dec 54	Pungo Adongo, Angola	5/20/20	fol	MS aut
0356	Edmund Gabriel	26 Dec 54	Pungo Adongo	4/16/15	225 187	MS aut
0357	Edmund Gabriel	31 Dec 54	Pungo Adongo	3/12/12	8vo	MS aut
0358	Roderick I. Murchison	31 Dec 54	Pungo Adongo	2/ 8/ 8	misc	MS aut
0359	Edmund Gabriel	5, 18, 20, 23 Jan 55	Malange-Cassange	10/40/40	225 188	MS aut
0360	Arthur Tidman	14 Jan 55	Cassange, Angola	5/20/20	225 188	MS aut
0361	Thomas Maclear	29 Jan 55	Cassange, Angola	1/ 4/ 4	290 233	MS aut
0362	Edmund Gabriel	30 Jan 55	Cassange	2/ 8/ 8	225 187	MS aut
0363	Edmund Gabriel	4 Feb 55	Cassange	2/ 8/ 8	4to	MS aut
0364	Arthur Tidman	10 Feb 55	Cassange	1/ 4/ 4	178 112	MS aut fr
0365	Edmund Gabriel	12, 13 Feb 55	Cassange	2/ 8/ 8	4to	MS aut
0366	Roderick I. Murchison	13 Feb 55	Cassange	2/ 8/ 8	fol	MS aut
0367	Parents & Sisters	14 Feb 55	Cassange	1/ 4/ 4	8vo	MS aut
0368	Edmund Gabriel	14, 15 Feb 55	Cassange	2/ 8/ 8	250 198	MS aut
0369	Edmund Gabriel	2, 18 Mar, 19 Apr, 18 May	Banks of the Quango-Cobango	6/24/24	4to	MS aut
0370	Thomas Maclear	2 Mar 55	Banks of the River Quango	2/ 8/ 8	249 198	MS aut
0371	Mary Livingstone	[20 Mar 55]	[Bashinge]	2 pp		Pr copy
0372	Roderick I. Murchison	17 May 55	Cabango, Lunda Country	2 pp		Pr copy
0373	[Thomas Maclear]	18 May 55	Cabango	4 pp		MS copy
0374	Rawson W. Rawson	18 May 55	Cabango	4 pp	8vo	Pr copy
0375		[Jul 55]	Banks of the Leeba	1 p		Pr copy
0376	Edmund Gabriel	12 Aug 55	Naliele, Barotse Country	2/ 8/ 8	4to	MS aut
0377	Roderick I. Murchison	[Aug 55]		4/16/16	fol	MS aut in
0378	Alfredo Duprat	12 Sep 55	Banks of the River Chobe	1/ 4/ 4	178 115	MS aut
0379	The Bishop of Angola	12 Sep 55	[Linyanti]	3 pp		TS copy
0380	Edmund Gabriel	12 Sep 55	Town of Sekeletu	3/12/12	250 197	MS aut
0381	Thomas Maclear	12 Sep 55	Town of Sekeletu	1/ 4/ 4	249 193	MS aut fr
0382	Robert Moffat 1	12 Sep 55	Linyanti, R. Chobe	3/12/12	249 197	MS aut
0383	Alberto Schut	12 Sep 55	Capital of Sekeletu, Linyanti	2 pp		TS copy
0384	Thomas Maclear	13 Sep 55	Linyanti	5/18/17	248 199	MS aut
0385	William Thompson	13 Sep 55	Linyanti	3/10/10	250 198	MS aut
0386	Mary Livingstone	14 Sep 55	Linyanti, R. Chobe	1/ 4/ 4	250 197	MS aut
0387	Mary Moffat	26 Sep 55	Linyanti	4/14/14	248 189	MS aut in
0388	William Thompson	27 Sep 55	Linyanti	2/ 8/ 8	250 197	MS aut
0389	Arthur Tidman	12 Oct 55	Linyanti, River Chobe	3/12/12	400 250	MS aut
0390	Roderick I. Murchison	16 Oct 55, 3 Mar 56	Linyanti, River Chobe	12 pp	fol	MS aut
0391	Charles Livingstone	20 Dec 55	[Kafue/Zambezi: Confluence]	5 pp		Pr copy
0392	Roderick I. Murchison	25 Jan 56	Hill Chanyuné	27 pp	fol	MS aut
0393	Edmund Gabriel	7 Feb, 3 Mar 56	R. Zambesi, above Tete-Tete	11 pp		Pr copy
0394	Thomas Maclear	15 Feb, 2 Mar 56	Near Tete or Nyunkwe-Tete	3/12/12	400 252	MS aut
0395	King Pedro V of Portugal	24 Feb 56	Above Tete or Nyunkwe	1/ 4/ 4	400 250	MS aut copy
0396	[Thomas Maclear]	[22 Feb—1 Mar 56]	[Southwest of Tete]	1/ 4/ 4	308 215	MS aut
0397	[Thomas Maclear]	2 Mar 56	Tete or Nyunkwe	1/ 4/ 4	270 210	MS aut
0398	Robert Moffat 1	[2 Mar 56??]	[Tete??]	1/ 4/ 4	226 180	MS aut in
0399	William Thompson	2 Mar 56	Tete or Nyungwe	1/ 4/ 4	270 211	MS aut
0400	Arthur Tidman	2 Mar 56	Tete or Nyungwe	1/ 4/ 4	270 210	MS aut

NO N	LOCATION	NLS COPY	PUBLICATION
0351	BLL, Add. MS.37410, ff. 44—45.	MS.10780 (3)	
0352	BLL, Add. MS.37410, ff. 46—53.	MS.10780 (3)	
0353	BLL, Add. MS.37410, ff. 54—60.	MS.10780 (3)	
0354	BLL, Add. MS.37410, ff. 61-62.	MS.10780 (3)	
0355	RGSL, Archives, DL 2/6/3.	MS.10780 (5)	JRGSL, vol. 25 (1855), pp. 219—229.
0356	BLL, Add. MS.37410, ff. 63—70.	MS.10780 (3)	
0357	BLL, Add. MS.37410, ff. 71—76.	MS.10780 (3)	
0358	RGSL, Archives, DL 2/6/1.	MS.10780 (5)	JRGSL, vol. 25 (1855), pp. 218—219.
0359 n	BLJ, Book no. 6754.	MS.10769	OB (details in note).
0360	ULSOASL, Africa, Wooden Box of L's letters.	MS.10778	Schapera, LMC, pp. 268—273.
0361 n	NARS, LI 1/1/1, pp. 102—105.		
0362	BLL, Add. MS.37410, ff. 77—80.	MS.10780 (3)	
0363	BLL, Add. MS.37410, ff. 81—84.	MS.10780 (3)	
0364	ULSOASL, Africa, Wooden Box of L's letters.	MS.10778	Schapera, LMC, p. 274.
0365	BLL, Add. MS.37410, ff. 85—88.	MS.10780 (3)	
0366	RGSL, Archives, DL 2/6/4.	MS.10780 (5)	JRGSL, vol. 25 (1855), pp. 229—235.
0367	NLS, MS.3650, ff. 153—4.		
0368	BLL, Add. MS.37410, ff. 89—92.	MS.10780 (3)	
0369	BLL, Add. MS.37410, ff. 93—104.	MS.10780 (3)	
0370	NARS, LI 1/1/1, pp. 106—113.		
0371 n			Schapera, DLFL II, pp. 258—259.
0372			JRGSL, vol. 26 (1856), pp. 80—81.
0373 n	NARS, LI 1/1/1, pp. 142—145.		
0374			Maggs' Cat., no. 894, 1964, no. 620.
0375 n			NDLDSCA, p. 43.
0376	BLL, Add. MS.37410, ff. 105—108.	MS.10780 (3)	
0377	RGSL, Archives, DL 2/6/5.	MS.10780 (5)	
0378	SALCT, Grey Collection,13b.	MS.10780 (1)	
0379	NLS, MS.10777 (10)		BOdGGdPdA, No. 575 (4 Oct 1856).
0380 n	BLJ, Book no. 6754.		OB, vol. III, No. 28 (Jan 1923), pp. 292—293.
0381	NARS, LI 1/1/1, pp. 152—155.		Gelfand, LtD (facs. of a page) opposite p. 96.
0382	ULSOASL, Africa, Odds, Box 18.	MS.10780 (6)	Schapera, DLFL II, pp. 260—267.
0383	NLS, MS.10777 (10)		BOdGGdPdA, No. 580 (8 Nov 1856).
0384 n	NARS, LI 1/1/1, pp. 156—173.		
0385	ULSOASL, Africa, Wooden Box of L's letters.	MS.10778	Schapera, LMC, pp. 278—283.
0386	BLL, Add. MS.50184, ff. 9—10.	MS.10780 (3)	Schapera, DLFL II, pp. 267—269.
0387	ULSOASL, Africa, Odds, Box 18.	MS.10780 (6)	Schapera, DLFL II, pp. 269—275.
0388	ULSOASL, Africa, Wooden Box of L's letters.	MS.10778	Schapera, LMC, pp. 284—287.
0389 n	ULSOASL, Africa, Wooden Box of L's letters.	MS.10778	Schapera, LMC, pp. 287—302.
0390 n	RGSL, Archives, DL 2/8/1.	MS.10780 (5)	JRGSL, vol.27 (1857), pp. 349—357.
0391 n			The Atlantic Monthly, Aug 1922, pp. 216—220, ex.
0392 n	RGSL, Archives, DL 2/8/2.	MS.10780 (5)	
0393 n			EIHC, vol. 12 (1874), pp. 285—295.
0394 n	SALCT, Grey Collection, 13b.	MS.10780 (1)	PP Sess. 2 1857, v.XLIV, [212] Class A pp. 32—35.
0395 n	NARS, LI 1/1/1, pp. 376—379.		Wallis, ZEDL I, xv, ex.
0396 n	NARS, LI 1/1/1, pp. 379—382.		
0397 n	NARS, LI 1/1/1, pp. 383—386.		
0398	ULSOASL, Africa, Odds, Box 18.	MS.10780 (6)	Schapera, DLFL II, pp. 276—278.
0399	ULSOASL, Africa, Wooden Box of L's letters.	MS.10778	Schapera, LMC, pp. 303—305.
0400	ULSOASL, Africa, Wooden Box of L's letters.	MS.10778	Schapera, LMC, pp. 302—303.

NO	RECIPIENT	DATE	PLACE	LENGTH	SIZE		TYPE
0401	Alfredo Duprat	4 Mar 56	Tette	4 pp		fol	Pr copy
0402	Roderick I. Murchison	4 Mar 56	Tette or Nyungwe	16 pp		fol	MS aut
0403	Joseph Moore	16 Mar 56	Tette or Nyungwe	1/ 4/ 4		fol	MS aut
0404	Parents & Sisters	18 Mar, 28 Aug 56	Tette-Mauritius	1/ 4/ 4	333	213	MS aut
0405	The Earl of Clarendon	19 Mar 56	Tete or Nyungwe.	5 pp			Pr copy
0406	José R. Coelho do Amaral	25 Mar, [25 Jun 56?]	Tete-Quilimane	3 pp			Pr copy
0407	Alfredo Duprat	26 Mar 56	Tete or Nyungwe	1/ 4/ 4	335	210	MS aut
0408	Jean and Ann Frédoux	26 Mar, 12 Jul, 12 Aug 56	Tete or Nyungwe	1/ 4/ 4	334	212	MS aut
0409	Edmund Gabriel	[2 Mar–3 Apr 56]	[Tette]	1/ 4/ 4	250	197	MS aut in
0410	Thomas Maclear	3, 23 Apr 56	Tete	2/ 6/ 6	308	213	MS aut
0411	Edmund Gabriel	4 Apr 56	Tete	1/ 4/ 4	341	222	MS aut
0412	William C. Oswell	4 Apr 56	Tete or Nyungwe	1/ 4/ 4	332	213	MS aut
0413	Robert Moffat 1	5 Apr, 12 Aug 56	Tete or Nyungwe-Mauritius	1/ 4/ 4		fol	MS aut
0414	Roderick I. Murchison	23 May, 26 Aug 56	Quilimane-Mauritius	12/46/46		fol	MS aut
0415	Arthur Tidman	23 May 56	Quilimane, East Africa	3/12/12	308	203	MS aut
0416	Arthur Tidman	23 May 56	Quilimane	3/12/12	247	197	MS aut
0417	[Thomas Maclear]	27 May 56	Quilimane	1/ 4/ 4	272	214	MS aut in
0418	Joaquim de Azevedo Alpoim	30 May 56	Quilimane	1/ 4/ 4	310	202	MS aut
0419	Parents & Sisters	1 Jun 56	Quilimane, Eastern Africa	2/ 8/ 8	273	214	MS aut
0420	V. Guedes Carvalho e M.	20 Jun 56	Quilimane	1/ 4/ 4	272	214	MS aut
0421	Edmund Gabriel	27 Jun 56	Quilimane	2/ 8/ 8	247	197	MS aut
0422	William Thompson	[Nov 55–Jun 56], 2 Jul [56]		1/ 2/ 2	233	167	MS aut
0423	Roderick I. Murchison	5 Aug 56	H.M.B. "Frolic" at sea	3/12/12	320	202	MS aut
0424	William Thompson	8, 12 Aug 56	At sea — Port Luis	3/12/12	251	200	MS aut
0425	Thomas Maclear	14 Aug 56	Port Luis, Isd Mauritius	3/12/12	251	200	MS aut
0426	Thomas Maclear	17 Aug 56	H.M.B. "Frolic", Mauritius	1/ 4/ 4	201	125	MS aut
0427	Robert Moffat 1	17 Aug 56	H.M.B. "Frolic", Mauritius	1/ 4/ 4	251	200	MS aut
0428	José M. Nuñes	20 Aug 56	Mauritius	4 pp			MS copy
0429	The Earl of Clarendon	26 Aug 56	Claremont, Mauritius	3 pp			MS copy
0430	Arthur Tidman	26 Aug 56	Claremont, Mauritius	1 p			Pr copy
0431	William Thompson	17, 28 Sep 56	Claremont, Mauritius	2/ 8/ 8	229	186	MS aut
0432	Lumley W. Peyton	26 Sep 56	Mauritius	3 pp		4to	Pr copy
0433	Gunroom Officers, HMBF	26 Sep 56	Claremont, Mauritius	1 p			MS copy
0434	Henry D. Trotter	9 Oct 56	Mauritius	7 pp			MS copy
0435	Mrs. Robinson	18 Oct 56	Port Luis	1/ 4/ 4	180	105	MS aut
0436	William Thompson	31 Oct, 3 Nov 56	On board S.S. "England"	1/ 4/ 4	227	185	MS aut
0437	José M. Nuñes	1 Nov [56]	S.S. "England"	4 pp			MS copy
0438	Mary Livingstone	27 Nov, 6 Dec 56	P. +O. Co. S.S. "Candia"	1/ 4/ 4	227	185	MS aut
0439	Agnes Livingstone 1	11 Dec 56	Southampton	1/ 4/ 4	185	115	MS aut
0440	Roderick I. Murchison	12 Dec 56	Southampton	2/ 8/ 8	185	115	MS aut
0441	George Back	13 Dec 56	Blomfield St., London	1/ 4/ 2	185	115	MS aut
0442		13 Dec [56]	Blomfield St., [London]	1/ 4/ 2	182	114	MS aut
0443	Benjamin T. Pyne	15 Dec 56	Mission House	1/ 4/ 4	185	115	MS aut
0444	Editor of the "Times"	18 Dec 56	Mission House	2 pp		8vo	Pr copy
0445	Robert Kerr	19 Dec 56	Ship Hotel, Charing Cross	1/ 4/ 3	181	113	MS aut
0446	Roderick I. Murchison	22 Dec 56	Ship Hotel, Charing Cross	2/ 8/ 8	225	188	MS aut
0447	Robert Kerr	27 Dec 56	Hamilton	1 p			Pr copy
0448	James Loudon	[30 Dec 56??]	[Hamilton]	1/ 4/ 3	185	115	MS aut
0449	Anthony H. Hoskins	5 Jan 57	Mission House	1/ 4/ 4	180	113	MS aut
0450	Roderick I. Murchison	6 Jan 57	15 Finsbury Square	1/ 4/ 4	137	88	MS aut

NO	N	LOCATION	NLS COPY	PUBLICATION
0401	n			Almeida, **IdDDL**, pp. 7—8.
0402	n	RGSL, Archives, DL 2/8/3.	MS.10780 (5)	**JRGSL**, vol 27 (1857), pp. 367—374.
0403		BLL, Add. MS.36525, ff. 9—10.	MS.10780 (3)	
0404		NLS, MS.10701, ff. 88—89.		Schapera, **DLFL** II, pp. 278—281.
0405	n			**PP** Sess. 2 1857, v. XLIV, [212] Class A pp. 62—66.
0406			MS.10779 (11a)	**BOdGGdPdA**, No. 618 (1 Aug 1857), pp. 6—8.
0407		SALCT, Grey Collection, 13b.	MS.10780 (1)	
0408		BLJ, Book no. 6092.		Sotheby's Cat., 19 Jul 1949, lot 348.
0409	n	BLJ, Book no. 6754.	MS.10769	**OB**, vol. III no. 29 (23 Feb 1923), pp. 369—370.
0410		NARS, LI 1/1/1, pp. 407—412.		
0411	n	BLJ, Book no. 6754.	MS.10769	**OB**, vol. III, No. 29 (23 Feb 1923), pp. 371—372.
0412		NLS, MS.10768, ff. 12—13.		
0413		ULSOASL, Africa, Odds, Box 18.	MS.10780 (6)	Schapera, **DLFL** II, pp. 281—284.
0414	n	RGSL, Archives, DL 2/8/4.	MS.10780 (5)	**JRGSL**, vol. 27 (1857), pp. 374—387.
0415	n	NARS, LI 1/1/1, pp. 457—468.	MS.10773	Schapera, **LMC**, pp. 306—312.
0416	n	NARS, LI 1/1/1, pp. 445—456.	MS.10773	Schapera, **LMC**, pp. 313—317.
0417		NARS, LI 1/1/1, pp. 469—472.		
0418		NARS, LI 1/1/1, pp. 475—478.		
0419		NLS, MS.10701, ff. 90—93.		Schapera, **DLFL** II, pp. 284—290.
0420		NARS, LI 1/1/1, pp. 495—498.		
0421	n	BLJ, Book no. 6754.	MS.10769	**OB**, vol. III, No. 29 (23 Feb 1923). pp. 373—375.
0422		ULSOASL, Africa, Wooden Box of L's letters.	MS.10778	Schapera, **LMC**, p. 305.
0423	n	NARS, LI 1/1/1, pp. 499—509.		Wallis, **ZEDL** I, xviii—xxi.
0424		ULSOASL, Africa, Wooden Box of L's letters.	MS.10778	Schapera, **LMC**, pp. 317—321.
0425		NARS, LI 1/1/1, pp. 510—521.		
0426		NARS, LI 1/1/1, pp. 522—525.		
0427		ULSOASL, Africa, Odds, Box 18.	MS.10780 (6)	Schapera, **DLFL** II, pp. 290—292.
0428	n	NARS, LI 1/1/1, pp. 525a—525d.	MS.10779 (21)	
0429	n	AHUL, Moçambique Papeis, Caixo 1, Diversos.	MS.10779 (11a)	**BOdGGdPdA**, No. 603 (18 April 1856).
0430				Schapera, **LMC**, p. 321.
0431		ULSOASL, Africa, Wooden Box of L's letters.	MS.10778	Schapera, **LMC**, pp. 322—324.
0432				Sawyer's Cat., no. 266 (1964), no. 481.
0433	n	NLS, MS.10773, p. 176.		Maggs' Cat., No. 254 (Summer 1973), no. 91.
0434		NARS, LI 1/1/1, pp. 536—543.		Christie's Cat., 29 Jul 1971, lot 466.
0435		NLS, MS.10768, ff. 14—15.		
0436		ULSOASL, Africa, Wooden Box of L's letters.	MS.10778	Schapera, **LMC**, pp. 324—326.
0437		NARS, LI 1/1/1, pp. 544—547.	MS.10779 (21)	
0438		NLS, MS.10701, ff. 94—95.		Schapera, **DLFL** II, pp. 292—294.
0439		NLS, MS.10701, ff. 96—97.		Schapera, **DLFL** II, pp. 294—295.
0440		NARS, LI 1/1/1, pp. 572—579.		
0441	n	RGSL, Back Collection.		
0442		BLJ, Book no. 5318, Acc. Reg.4669.		
0443		Privately owned.	MS.10769 (9)	
0444	n			Myers' Cat., No. 366 (Spring, 1951), no. 2.
0445	n	SNMDL.	MS.10779 (3)	Izett, **JJN**, p. 19.
0446		NARS, LI 1/1/1, pp. 584—591.		
0447	n			Izett, **JJN**, p. 20.
0448	n	SNMDL.	MS.10708, f. 130	
0449		WIHMLL, MS.68571.	MS.10779 (15)	
0450		NARS, LI 1/1/1, pp. 593—596.		

NO	RECIPIENT	DATE	PLACE	LENGTH	SIZE	TYPE
0451		6 Jan [57]	Mission House	1/ 4/ 4	182 113	MS aut
0452	John N Goulty	9 Jan 57	London	1/ 4/ 1	183 115	MS aut
0453	William O. Livingstone	9 Jan 57	London	1/ 4/ 4	155 113	MS aut
0454	[James?] MacLehose	20 Jan [57]	Mission House	2 pp	8vo	Pr copy
0455	H. Norton Shaw	20 Jan 57	57 Sloane Street	2/ 8/ 8	8vo	MS aut
0456	Thomas Maclear	21 Jan 57	Mission House, Blomfield St.	1/ 4/ 4	226 185	MS aut
0457	Mrs. Lumley Peyton	22 Jan 57	Mission House	4 pp	8vo	Pr copy
0458	Roderick I. Murchison	23 Jan 57	57 Sloane Street	1/ 4/ 4	183 115	MS aut
0459	Ragged School, Stockport	23 Jan 57	Mission House	1/ 4/ 4	228 188	MS aut
0460	Roderick I. Murchison	26 Jan 57	57 Sloane Street	3/ 4/12	fol	MS aut
0461	Arthur Tidman	26 Jan 57	57 Sloane Street	2/ 6/ 6	184 116	MS aut
0462	Frederick Fitch	27 Jan 57	57 Sloane Street	4 pp	4to	Ph copy
0463		27 Jan [57]	57 Sloane Street, London	1/ 4/ 4	184 115	MS aut
0464	H. Norton Shaw	[2 Feb 57]	57 Sloane Street	1/ 4/ 4	8vo	MS aut
0465	John Murray	4 Feb 57	57 Sloane Street	1/ 4/ 4	181 112	MS aut
0466	William Hooker	5 Feb 57	57 Sloane Street	1/ 4/ 4	180 111	MS aut
0467	William Hooker	8 Feb [57]	57 Sloane Street	4 pp	sm 8vo	Pr copy
0468	George Back	9 Feb [57]	57 Sloane Street	1/ 4/ 3	137 87	MS aut
0469	José M. Nuñes	14 Feb 57	London	12 pp		MS copy
0470	Thomas Maclear	16 Feb 57	London	1/ 4/ 4	226 184	MS aut
0471	H. Norton Shaw	20 Feb [57]	57 Sloane Street	1/ 4/ 4	4to	MS aut
0472	Neil Livingstone 2	27 Feb 57	57 Sloane Street, London	1 p		MS copy
0473	H. Norton Shaw	3 Mar 57	57 Sloane Street	1/ 4/ 4	8vo	MS aut
0474	John Murray	5 Mar [57]	57 Sloane Street	1/ 4/ 4	183 115	MS aut
0475	[Arthur Tidman?]	13 Mar 57	57 Sloane Street	4 pp	8vo	Pr copy
0476	The Earl of Clarendon	19 Mar 57	57 Sloane Street	2/ 8/ 7	fol	MS aut
0477	Editor of the "Athenaeum"	19 Mar [57]	[57] Sloane Street	1 p		Pr copy
0478	George Clowes	22 Mar 57	57 Sloane Street	3 pp	8vo	Pr copy
0479	John Murray	22 Mar [57]	57 Sloane Street	1/ 4/ 4	182 116	MS aut
0480	Alexander Hare	23 Mar 57	57 Sloane Street	1 p		MS copy
0481	[H. Norton Shaw?]	[23 Mar 57?]	[57 Sloane Street ?]	1/ 2/ 1	8vo	MS aut
0482	John Murray	24 Mar [57]	57 Sloane Street	1/ 4/ 4	178 110	MS aut
0483	Roderick I. Murchison	25 Mar [57]	57 Sloane Street	1/ 4/ 4	183 116	MS aut
0484	John Murray	25 Mar [57??]		2 pp	8vo	Pr copy
0485	H. Norton Shaw	25 Mar [57]	[57] Sloane Street	2/ 4/ 4	8vo	MS aut
0486	Jorge C. de Figanière	25 Mar 57	57 Sloane Street	2 pp		MS copy
0487	[H. Norton Shaw]	26 Mar [57]	[London]	1 p	8vo	MS aut
0488	John Murray	27 Mar [57]	57 Sloane Street	1/ 4/ 3	183 116	MS aut
0489	John Murray	30 Mar 57	57 Sloane Street	1/ 4/ 4	182 113	MS aut
0490	Roderick I. Murchison	[Feb—Mar 57]	[London]	1/ 4/ 4	135 87	MS aut
0491	Roderick I. Murchison	[Feb—Mar 57]	57 Sloane Street	1/ 4/ 4	135 88	MS aut
0492	Edward Grimstone	2 Apr [57]	[London]	1/ 2/ 1	203 143	MS aut
0493	Henry Labouchere	2 Apr 57	57 Sloane Street	13 pp		MS copy
0494	J. Bevan Braithwaite	4 Apr 57	57 Sloane Street	1 p		MS aut
0495	John Murray	6 Apr [57]	57 Sloane Street	2/ 8/ 8	181 110	MS aut
0496	John Murray	7 Apr 57	57 Sloane Street	1/ 4/ 3	182 111	MS aut
0497	Arthur Tidman	7 Apr 57	57 Sloane Street	3 pp		MS copy
0498	John Murray	10 Apr [57]	[London]	1/ 4/ 4	182 111	MS aut
0499	Thomas Maclear	11 Apr 57	R.G.S. [15 Whitehall Place]	1/ 4/ 4	323 204	MS aut
0500	[Charles Manby]	14 Apr 57	57 Sloane Street	1/ 4/ 4	184 111	MS aut

NO	N	LOCATION	NLS COPY	PUBLICATION
0451	n	UTSNYC, Archives.	MS.10779 (16a)	
0452	n	SALCT, S.A. MSS. Coll., Sect. A.	MS.10780 (1)	
0453	n	SNMDL.	MS.10708, f. 62	Macnair, **Greatheart,** (May 1936), pp. 106—108.
0454				Sotheby's Cat., 12 Nov 1968, lot 560.
0455	n	RGSL, Archives, DL 2/15/14.	MS.10780 (5)	
0456		NARS, LI 1/1/1, pp. 613—616.		Blaikie, **PLDL,** p. 210, ex.
0457				Sawyer's Cat., No. 266 (1964), no. 481.
0458		NARS, LI 1/1/1, pp. 625—628.		
0459	n	ULSOASL, Africa, Wooden Box of L's letters.	MS.10778	Macaulay, **LivA,** pp. 63—65.
0460	n	BLO, Clarendon dep. C. 80, ff. 224—229.	MS.10709, f. 31	Seaver, **DLLL,** pp. 298—299, ex.
0461		ULSOASL, Africa, Wooden Box of L's letters.	MS.10778	
0462		NARS, LI 2/1/1.	MS.10779 (21)	
0463	n	WIHMLL, MS.68011A.	MS.10779 (15)	
0464		RGSL, Archives, DL 2/15/1.	MS.10780 (5)	
0465		JMPL.		
0466		RBGK, African Letters, 1844—1858, LIX f. 189.	MS.10779 (10a)	
0467				Myers' Cat., No. 1 (Spring, 1958), no. 176.
0468		RGSL, Back Collection.		
0469		NARS, LI 1/1/1, pp. 629—640.	MS.10779 (21)	
0470		NARS, LI 1/1/1, pp. 641—644.		
0471		RGSL, Archives, DL 2/15/2.	MS.10780 (5)	
0472	n	NLS, MS.10710, f. 49.		
0473	n	RGSL, Archives, DL 2/15/3.	MS.10780 (5)	
0474		JMPL.		
0475	n			Maggs' Cat., No. 907 (Summer 1967), no. 83.
0476		BLO, Clarendon dep. C. 80, ff. 203—206.	MS.10709, f. 43	Seaver, **DLLL,** p. 299, ex.
0477				**Athenaeum** 21 Mar 1857, No. 1534, p. 375.
0478				Myers' Cat., No. 902 (1966), no. 92.
0479		JMPL.		
0480		NLS, MS.10773, f. 170.		
0481		RGSL, Archives, DL 2/15/18.	MS.10780 (5)	
0482		ULSOASL, Africa, Wooden Box of L's letters.	MS.10778	
0483		NARS, LI 1/1/1, pp. 645-648.		
0484	n			Sotheby's Cat., 24 Jun 1975, lot 278.
0485		RGSL, Archives, DL 2/15/4.	MS.10780 (5)	
0486	n	AHUL, Moçambique Papeis, Caixo 1, Diversos.	MS.10779 (11a)	
0487		RGSL, Archives, DL 2/15/15.	MS.10780 (5)	
0488		JMPL.		
0489		JMPL.		
0490		NARS, LI 1/1/1, pp. 617-620.		
0491	n	NARS, LI 1/1/1, pp. 609-612.		
0492		WCLUWJ, Hist. and Lit. Papers, A348/A4.	MS.10779 (10)	
0493	n	Wilson Collection, Journal no. 6.	MS.10775	
0494	n	E.M. privately owned.	MS.10769	
0495		JMPL.		
0496		JMPL.		
0497		Wilson Collection, Journal no. 6.	MS.10775	
0498		JMPL.		
0499		NARS, LI 1/1/1, pp. 654-657.		
0500		Privately owned.	MS.10777 (7)	

NO	RECIPIENT	DATE	PLACE	LENGTH	SIZE	TYPE
0501	Roderick I. Murchison	15 Apr 57	57 Sloane Street	2/ 8/ 7	183 112	MS aut
0502	George Rough	15 Apr 57	57 Sloane Street	6 pp	184 111	MS aut
0503	The Conde do Lavradio	17 Apr 57	[57] Sloane Street	3 pp		MS copy
0504	[James Young?]	17 Apr 57	57 Sloane Street	1/ 4/ 4	228 186	MS aut
0505	H. Norton Shaw	21 Apr 57	57 Sloane Street	1/ 4/ 4	8vo	MS aut
0506	[J. Bevan Braithwaite]	23 Apr 57	57 Sloane Street	1/ 4/ 4	229 185	MS aut
0507	James MacLehose	24 Apr 57	57 Sloane Street	1/ 4/ 4	8vo	Ph copy
0508	James Macqueen	24 Apr [57]	57 Sloane Street	3 pp	8vo	Pr copy
0509	J. Bevan Braithwaite	27 Apr 57	57 Sloane Street	1 p		MS aut
0510	John Murray	28 Apr 57	57 Sloane Street	1/ 4/ 3	181 111	MS aut
0511	J. Bevan Braithwaite	29 Apr 57	57 Sloane Street	2 pp		MS copy
0512	John Murray	29 Apr 57	57 Sloane Street	2/ 6/ 6	182 111	MS aut
0513	[Arthur Tidman]	[20 Jan—30 Apr 57]	[London?]	1 p		TS copy
0514	The Earl of Clarendon	2 May 57	57 Sloane Street	1/ 4/ 3	fol	MS aut
0515	John Murray	8 May 57	57 Sloane Street	1/ 4/ 4	182 110	MS aut
0516		8 May 57	57 Sloane Street	1/ 4/ 3	182 110	MS aut
0517	Thomas Maclear	13 May 57	[London]	3/12/11	182 112	MS aut
0518	Mrs. Thomas Binney	16 May 57	57 Sloane Street	1/ 4/ 4	182 111	MS aut
0519	William Hooker	16 May 57	57 Sloane Street	1/ 4/ 4	181 111	MS aut
0520	Lady Eastlake	18 May 57	[London]	2 pp	8vo	Pr copy
0521	Mr. MacSkimming	18 May 57	57 Sloane Street	1/ 4/ 4	182 110	MS aut
0522	John Murray	[4, 11 or 18 May 57]	57 Sloane Street	1/ 4/ 4	182 110	MS aut
0523	Heinrich Barth	20 May 57	57 Sloane Street	1 p		TS copy
0524	John Murray	22 May [57]	57 Sloane Street	2/ 8/ 8	182 110	MS aut
0525	George Back	23 May 57	57 Sloane Street	1/ 4/ 4	181 111	MS aut
0526	Alexander Hare	23 May 57	57 Sloane Street	1 p		MS copy
0527		[20 Jan—23 May 57]	57 Sloane Street	1/ 4/ 3	183 115	MS aut
0528		[20 Jan—23 May 57]	57 Sloane Street	1/ 2/ 2	106 67	MS aut
0529	John Murray	26 May 57	Hadley Hurst, Barnet	2/ 8/ 8	182 111	MS aut
0530	Lady Eastlake	30 May 57	Hadley Green	1/ 4/ 4	182 111	MS aut
0531	John Murray	30 May [57]	Hadley Green, Barnet	2/ 8/ 8	182 111	MS aut
0532	John Murray	30 May 57	[Hadley Green?]	3/12/11	182 111	MS aut
0533	John Murray	31 May 57	Hadley Green	2/ 8/ 8	183 113	MS aut
0534						
0535	John Murray	3 Jun 57	Hadley Green	1/ 4/ 4	183 111	MS aut
0536	H. Norton Shaw	5 Jun 57	Hadley Green	3/12/12	8vo	MS aut
0537	Thomas Milne	13 Jun 57	Hadley Green	1/ 4/ 4	228 186	MS aut
0538	Charles Daubeny	17 Jun 57	Hadley Green, Barnet	1/ 4/ 4	183 112	MS aut
0539	Mrs. Haldane	17 Jun 57	Hadley Green	1/ 4/ 4	182 112	MS aut
0540	John Murray	17 Jun [57]	Hadley Green	2/ 8/ 8	182 112	MS aut
0541	Mrs. Way	19 Jun 57	[London?]	3 pp	8vo	Pr copy
0542	John Murray	20 Jun 57	Hadley Green, Barnet	1/ 4/ 4	182 110	MS aut
0543	Miss Moysey	27 Jun 57	Hadley Green	1/ 4/ 4	183 111	MS aut
0544	John Murray	27 Jun 57	Hadley Green	1/ 4/ 4	183 112	MS aut
0545	H. Norton Shaw	27 Jun 57	Hadley Green	1/ 4/ 4	8vo	MS aut
0546	Miss Moysey	Jun 57	Hadley Green	4 pp	8vo	Pr copy
0547	H. Norton Shaw	1 Jul 57	Hadley Green	2/ 8/ 8	8vo	MS aut
0548	G. Watkins	2 Jul 57	[Hadley Green?]	2 pp	8vo	Pr copy
0549	Edward Buxton	4 Jul 57	Hadley Green	4 pp	8vo	Pr copy
0550	[John S. Moffat]	[4 Jul 57]	[Hadley Green]	1/ 4/ 4	182 112	MS aut

NO N	LOCATION	NLS COPY	PUBLICATION
0501	NARS, LI 1/1/1, pp. 658-664.		
0502	NLS, MS. Acc. 6682.		Sotheby's Cat., 11 May 1970, lot 158a.
0503	Wilson Collection, Journal no. 6.	MS10775	Wallis, **ZEDL** I, xxiv—xxv.
0504	WIHMLL, MS. 63006.	MS.10779 (15)	
0505 n	RGSL, Archives, DL 2/15/5.	MS.10780 (5)	
0506	NLS, MS. Dep. 237.		
0507	SALCT, S.A. MSS. Coll., Sect. A.	MS.10780 (1)	
0508			Sawyer's List No. 8 (1955), no. 45.
0509 n	E.M. privately owned.	MS.10769	
0510	JMPL.		
0511 n	NLS, MS. Dep. 237.		
0512	JMPL.		
0513 n	ULSOASL, Africa, Odds, Box 10, folder 3.		
0514 n	BLO, Clarendon dep. C.80, ff. 201—202	MS.10709, f. 50	
0515	JMPL.		
0516 n	WIHMLL, MS. 68011B.	MS.10779 (15)	
0517	NARS, LI 1/1/1, pp. 665—673.		
0518	NARS, LI 2/1/1.		
0519	RBGK, African Letters, 1844—1858, LIX f, 191.	MS.10779 (10a)	
0520			Rendell Cat. No. 26, no. 151.
0521 n	SNMDL.	MS.10708, f. 64	
0522 n	JMPL.		
0523	RGSL, Barth Correspondence.		
0524	JMPL.		
0525	RGSL, Back Collection.		
0526	NLS, MS. 10773, f. 170.		
0527	WIHMLL, MS. 58622.	MS.10779 (15)	
0528	WCLUWJ, Hist. and Lit. Papers, A348/A3.	MS.10779 (10)	Sotheby's Cat., 3 Dec 1913, lot 299, item 11.
0529	JMPL.		
0530	WIHMLL, MS. 68010A.	MS.10779 (15)	
0531	JMPL.		
0532	JMPL.		
0533	JMPL.		
0534 n			
0535	JMPL.		
0536	RGSL, Archives, DL 2/15/6.	MS.10780 (5)	
0537	NLS, MS. 10768, ff. 17—18.		
0538	WIHMLL, MS. 63003.	MS.10779 (15)	
0539	WIHMLL, MS. 68011C.	MS.10779 (15)	
0540	JMPL.		
0541			Rendell Cat. No. 78 (1972), no. 85.
0542	JMPL.		
0543	NARS, LI 2/1/1.		
0544	JMPL.		
0545	RGSL, Archives, DL 2/15/7.	MS.10780 (5)	
0546			Sotheby's Cat., 19 Dec 1933, lot 430.
0547	RGSL, Archives, DL 2/15/8.	MS.10780 (5)	
0548			Rendell Cat. No. 23, no. 100.
0549			Maggs' Cat. No. 927 (Autumn 1970), no. 129.
0550 n	NARS, MO 1/1/6, pp. 258—261.		

NO	RECIPIENT	DATE	PLACE	LENGTH	SIZE	TYPE
0551	John Murray	6 Jul 57	Hadley Green	1/ 4/ 4	182 110	MS aut
0552	H. Norton Shaw	8 Jul 57	Hadley Green	1/ 4/ 4	8vo	MS aut
0553	J.E. Grey	9 Jul [57]	London	4 pp	8vo	Pr copy
0554	Frederick Fitch	10 Jul 57	Hadley Green	1/ 4/ 3	8vo	Ph copy
0555	H. Norton Shaw	10 Jul [57]	Hadley Green	1/ 4/ 4	8vo	MS aut
0556	Joseph D. Hooker	11 Jul 57	Hadley Green, Barnet	2/ 8/ 8	183 111	MS aut
0557	John Murray	11 Jul 57	Hadley Green	1/ 4/ 4	183 112	MS aut
0558	John Murray	14 Jul 57	Hadley Green	1/ 4/ 4	182 111	MS aut
0559	[Henry Toynbee?]	25 Jul 57	Hadley Green, Barnet	1/ 4/ 4	182 111	MS aut
0560	Joseph D. Hooker	28 Jul 57	Hadley Green	2/ 8/ 8	182 111	MS aut
0561	John Murray	[1 Mar–30 Jul 57]	London	1/ 4/ 4	180 112	MS aut
0562	John Murray	[1 Mar–30 Jul 57]	[London]	1/ 4/ 4	183 115	MS aut
0563	J.E. Grey	31 Jul [57]	[50 A Albemarle St., London]	1/ 4/ 4	178 114	MS aut
0564	John Murray	4 Aug 57	Hadley Green	1/ 4/ 4	182 111	MS aut
0565		6 Aug 57	Hadley Green	1/ 4/ 4	180 110	MS aut
0566	Robert Cooke	10 Aug [57]	Hadley Green	1/ 4/ 4	180 115	MS aut
0567		13 Aug 57	Hadley Green	1/ 4/ 4	230 187	MS aut
0568		16 Aug 57	Hadley Green	2/ 8/ 8	230 189	MS aut
0569	J. Aspinall Turner	19 Aug 57	Hadley Green	1/ 4/ 3	182 112	MS aut
0570	Henry Toynbee	20 Aug 57	Hadley Green	2/ 8/ 8	184 111	MS aut
0571	Henry Toynbee	22 Aug 57	Hadley Green	1/ 4/ 4	230 188	MS aut
0572	John Murray	24 Aug 57	Hadley Green	2/ 8/ 7	183 112	MS aut
0573	Henry Toynbee	[22–27 Aug 57]	[Hadley Green?]	1/ 4/ 4	181 113	MS aut
0574	John Murray	[24 May–27 Aug] 57	Hadley Green	1/ 4/ 4	183 112	MS aut
0575	[Charles Livingstone?]	28 Aug 57	Drumcondra Castle [Dublin]	1/ 4/ 4	8vo	MS aut
9576	Mary Livingstone	[28 Aug 57]	Drumcondra Castle	1/ 4/ 4	8vo	MS aut
0577	Mary Livingstone	[29 Aug 57]	[Drumcondra Castle]	1/ 4/ 2	8vo	MS aut in
0578	Mary Livingstone	29 Aug 57	Dublin	2 pp		Pr copy
0579		29 Aug 57	Dublin	4 pp	8vo	Pr copy
0580	H. Norton Shaw	4 Sep 57	London	1/ 4/ 4	8vo	MS aut
0581	Henry Toynbee	4 Sep 57	London	1/ 4/ 4	179 112	MS aut in
0582	H. Norton Shaw	9 Sep 57	Manchester	1/ 4/ 4	8vo	MS aut
0583	H. Norton Shaw	12 Sep 57	Kendal	1/ 4/ 4	8vo	MS aut
0584	Mrs. Cowan	14 Sep 57	Hamilton	1/ 4/ 4	189 115	MS aut
0585	Agnes Livingstone 3	14 Sep 57	Burnbank, Hamilton	1/ 4/ 4	203 128	MS aut
0586	[Arthur Tidman]	14 Sep 57	Hamilton	4 pp	8vo	Pr copy
0587	Lady Murchison	14 Sep 57	Hamilton	2/ 8/ 8	189 116	MS aut
0588	William Wilson	14 Sep 57	Burnbank, Hamilton	1/ 4/ 4	190 115	MS aut
0589		21 [Sep 57]	Burnbank, Hamilton	1/ 4/ 4	204 128	MS aut
0590		[14–21 Sep 57?]	4 Athol Place, Glasgow	1/ 4/ 4	185 114	MS aut
0591	Edward Baines	27 Sep 57	Dundee	1/ 4/ 4	183 112	MS aut
0592	Agnes Livingstone 3	27 Sep 57	Rossie Priory	1/ 4/ 4	8vo	MS aut
0593	Miss MacGregor	27 Sep 57	Dundee	1/ 2/ 2	202 129	MS aut
0594	Roderick I. Murchison	27 Sep 57	Rossie Priory near Dundee	1/ 4/ 4	183 112	MS aut
0595	John Murray	27 Sep 57	near Dundee	1/ 2/ 1	255 151	MS aut
0596	T.B. Johnston	3 Oct 57	Carlisle	1/ 4/ 4	178 115	MS aut
0597	Miss Mackenzie	3 Oct 57	Carlisle	2/ 8/ 8	177 114	MS aut
0598	Henry White	3 Oct 57	Carlisle	1/ 4/ 4	8vo	MS aut
0599		3 Oct 57	Carlisle	3 pp	8vo	Pr copy
0600	Roderick I. Murchison	6 Oct 57	Kendal	1/ 4/ 4		MS aut

NO	N	LOCATION	NLS COPY	PUBLICATION
0551		JMPL.		
0552		RGSL, Archives, DL 2/15/9.	MS.10780 (5)	
0553				Sotheby's Cat., 19 Feb 1945, lot 194.
0554		NARS, LI 2/1/1.	MS.10779 (21)	
0555		RGSL, Archives, DL 2/15/10.	MS.10780 (5)	
0556		RBGK, English Letters, 1865—1900, 92, f. 126.	MS.10779 (10a)	
0557		JMPL.		
0558		JMPL.		
0559		ULSOASL, Africa, Wooden Box of L's letters.	MS.10778	
0560		RBGK, English Letters, 1865—1900, 92, f. 128.	MS.10779 (10a)	
0561	n	JMPL.		
0562		JMPL.		
0563	n	BLJ, Book no. 5352.		
0564		JMPL.		
0565		Privately owned.		
0566		Privately owned.		
0567	n	NARS, LI 1/1/1, pp. 674—677.		
0568		NARS, LI 1/1/1, pp. 678—685.		
0569		NLS, MS. 3219, ff. 119—120.		
0570		WIHMLL, MS. 91798.	MS.10779 (15)	
0571		WIHMLL, MS 91798.	MS.10779 (15)	
0572		JMPL.		
0573		WIHMLL, MS. 91798.	MS.10779 (15)	
0574		JMPL.		
0575		ULSOASL, Africa, Odds, Box 18.	MS.10780 (6)	
0576		BLL, Add. MS. 50184, ff. 11—12.	MS.10780 (3)	
0577	n	BLL, Add. MS. 50184, ff. 13—14.	MS.10780 (3)	
0578				Blaikie, PLDL, pp. 217—218.
0579				Maggs' Cat. No. 801 (1951), no. 714.
0580		RGSL, Archives, DL 2/15/16.	MS.10780 (5)	
0581		WIHMLL, MS. 91798.	MS.10779 (15)	
0582		RGSL, Archives, DL 2/15/17.	MS.10780 (5)	
0583		RGSL, Archives, DL 2/15/11.	MS.10780 (5)	
0584		WIHMLL, MS. 67464.	MS.10779 (15)	
0585		BLL, Add. MS. 50184, f. 15.	MS.10780 (3)	
0586				Sotheby's Cat., 11 Apr 1967, p. 418.
0587		NARS, LI 1/1/1, pp. 686—693.		
0588		ULSOASL, Africa, Wooden Box of L's letters.	MS.10778	
0589		NLS, MS.10774 (194).		
0590	n	Privately owned.	MS.10769 (12)	
0591		CSBL.		
0592		BLL, Add. MS. 50184, ff. 16—17.	MS.10780 (3)	
0593		CSBL.		Christie's Cat., 1 Jul 1970, lot 24.
0594		NARS, LI 1/1/1, pp. 694—697.		
0595		JMPL.		
0596		WIHMLL, MS. 56360.	MS.10779 (15)	
0597		NARS, LI 1/1/1, pp. 704—711.		
0598		NLS, MS. 10707, ff. 35—36.	MS.10709, f. 64	
0599				Rendell Cat. No. 35 (1968), no. 75.
0600		NARS, LI 1/1/1, pp. 700—703.		

NO	RECIPIENT	DATE	PLACE	LENGTH	SIZE	TYPE
0601	[Edward Baines?]	12 Oct 57	Halifax	1/ 4/ 4	184 112	MS aut
0602	John Murray	13 Oct 57	Liverpool	1/ 4/ 4	177 113	MS aut
0603	J. Collingwood Bruce	21 Oct 57	50 Albemarle St. London	1/ 4/ 4	180 114	MS aut
0604	T.B. Johnston	21 Oct 57	50 Albemarle St.	1/ 4/ 4	8vo	MS aut
0605	Arthur Tidman	21 Oct 57	50 Albemarle St.	1/ 4/ 4	8vo	MS aut
0606	Thomas Milne	24 Oct 57	London	1/ 4/ 3	223 179	MS aut
0607		24 Oct 57	50 Albemarle Street	2/ 8/ 8	8vo	Ph copy
0608	Joseph D. Hooker	26 Oct 57	50 Albemarle Street	2/ 6/ 6	189 115	MS aut
0609		26 Oct 57	50 Albemarle Street	1/ 4/ 2	180 115	MS aut
0610	J. Bevan Braithwaite	27 Oct 57	10 Soho Square	2/ 8/ 8	8vo	MS aut
0611	Frederick Fitch	28 Oct 57	50 Albemarle Street	2 pp	8vo	Ph copy
0612	Edward Sabine	30 Oct 57	Soho Square	1/ 4/ 3	180 115	MS aut
0613		30 Oct 57	50 Albemarle Street	1/ 2/ 2	180 114	MS aut
0614	H. Norton Shaw	2 Nov [57]	10 Soho Square	4 pp	8vo	MS aut
0615	Charles Daubeny	3 Nov 57	50 Albemarle Street	4 pp	8vo	Pr copy
0616	Heinrich Barth	10 Nov 57	50 Albemarle Street	1 p		TS copy
0617	Thomas Maclear	10 Nov 57	50 Albemarle Street	2/ 8/ 8	227 190	MS aut
0618	Titus Salt	10 Nov 57		4 pp	8vo	Pr copy
0619	[John Washington]	11 Nov 57	10 Soho Square	1/ 4/ 4	191 116	MS aut
0620	John Murray	12 Nov 57	Highbury New Park	1/ 4/ 4	178 110	MS aut
0621	John Murray	18 Nov 57	Oxford	1/ 4/ 4	185 114	MS aut
0622	Edward Baines	21 Nov 57	50 Albemarle Street	8 pp	8vo	Pr copy
0623	John Darlington	21 Nov 57	London	4 pp	8vo	Pr copy
0624	Miss Moysey	21 Nov 57	Highbury New Park	1/ 4/ 4	8vo	MS aut
0625	George Rough	21 Nov 57	50 Albemarle Street	1/ 4/ 4	8vo	MS aut
0626	Thomas S. Livingstone	22 Nov 57	St. Anne's Hall, Chertsey	4 pp	8vo	Pr copy
0627	Samuel Wilberforce	23 Nov 57	50 Albemarle Street	1/ 4/ 4	8vo	MS aut
0628	J. Bevan Braithwaite	27 Nov 57	50 Albemarle Street	1/ 4/ 4	8vo	MS aut
0629	[Wilbraham?] Taylor	28 Nov 57	50 Albemarle Street	1/ 4/ 4	177 110	MS aut
0630	Charles Grey	30 Nov 57	50 Albemarle Street	1/ 4/ 4	178 110	MS aut copy
0631	James Young	Nov 57		1 p		Pr copy
0632	[The Earl of Clarendon?]	1 Dec 57	London	2/ 8/ 8	4to	MS aut
0633		1 Dec 57	Highbury New Park	1/ 4/ 4	185 115	MS aut
0634	James Vavasseur	7 Dec 57	50 Albemarle Street	2 pp	8vo	Pr copy
0635		7 Dec 57	50 Albemarle Street	1/ 4/ 4	183 112	MS aut
0636	John Washington	9 Dec 57	Admiralty	2/ 8/ 8	185 115	MS aut
0637	[Thomas Archer?]	11 Dec 57		1 p		Pr copy
0638	Jonson Gedge	11 Dec 57		3 pp	8vo	Pr copy
0639	Henry Stephens	11 Dec 57	50 Albemarle Street	1/ 4/ 4	176 110	MS aut
0640	Robert Napier & Sons	15 Dec 57	20 Bedford Square	2/ 8/ 7	179 110	MS aut
0641	Joseph D. Hooker	16 Dec 57	20 Bedford Square	1/ 4/ 4	183 112	MS aut
0642	Henry Howard	16 Dec 57		4 pp	8vo	Pr copy
0643	John Murray	17 Dec 57		2 pp	8vo	Pr copy
0644		17 Dec 57	20 Bedford Square	1/ 4/ 4	177 110	MS copy
0645	John Washington	18 Dec 57		1/ 4/ 1	254 202	MS aut
0646	J. Bennett	19 Dec 57	London [20 Bedford Square]	2 pp	8vo	Pr copy
0647	The Earl of Shelburne	21 Dec 57	20 Bedford Square	1/ 2/ 1	4to	MS aut
0648	John Washington	22 Dec 57	20 Bedford Square	1/ 4/ 2	252 202	MS aut
0649	George Wilson	22 Dec 57	20 Bedford Square	2/ 8/ 8	178 118	Ph copy
0650		22 Dec 57	20 Bedford Square	3 pp	4to	Pr copy

NO	N	LOCATION	NLS COPY	PUBLICATION
0601		CSBL.		
0602		JMPL.		
0603		SALCT, S.A. MSS. Coll. Sect A.	MS.10780 (1)	
0604		NLS, MS. 10707, ff. 37—38.	MS.10709, f. 66	
0605		NMLZ, on display.		
0606		NLS, MS. 10768, ff. 20—21.		Sotheby's Cat., 11 Apr 1969, lot 417.
0607		ULSOASL, Africa, Odds, Box 10, folder 3.		
0608		RBGK, English Letters, 1865—1900, 92, f. 130.	MS.10779 (10a)	
0609		WIHMLL, MS. 64758.	MS.10779 (15)	
0610	n	E.M. privately owned.	MS.10769	
0611		NARS, LI 2/1/1.	MS.10779 (21)	
0612		NLS, MS. 10768, ff. 22—23.		
0613		WIHMLL, MS. 63380.	MS.10779 (15)	
0614		RGSL, Archives, DL 2/15/12.	MS.10780 (5)	
0615	n			Sotheby's Cat., 13 Jul 1976, lot 502.
0616		RGSL, Barth Correspondence.		
0617		NARS, LI 1/1/1, pp. 714—721.		Blaikie, **PLDL**, pp. 213—214, 225, ex.
0618				Sotheby's Cat., 10 Jul 1950, lot 267.
0619		MDNHLL, MSS. 120.	MS.10777 (23)	
0620	n	JMPL.		
0621		JMPL.		
0622				Sotheby's Cat., 31 Oct 1961, lot 262.
0623				Maggs' Cat. No. 785 (1949), no. 743.
0624		WIHMLL, MS. 67478.	MS.10779 (15)	
0625		DPLDS.	MS.10777 (13)	
0626				Sotheby's Cat., 23 Jun 1958, lot 258.
0627		BLO, MSS. Wilberforce, C.12, ff. 83—84.	MS.10780 (7)	
0628	n	E.M. privately owned.	MS.10769	
0629		WIHMLL, MS. 67464.	MS.10779 (15)	
0630	n	NARS, LI 1/1/1, pp. 725—728.		
0631				Blaikie, **PLDL**, p. 218, n.1,ex.
0632		PROL, FO 63/842, ff. 1—8.	MS.10780 (4)	
0633		NARS, LI 2/1/1.		
0634				Sotheby's Cat., 17 Dec 1975, lot 841
0635		WIHMLL, MS. 63010.	MS.10779 (15)	
0636		MDNHLL , MSS. 120.	MS.10777 (23)	
0637				Sotheby's Cat., 12 Jun 1973, lot 590.
0638				Rendell Cat. No. 116 (May 1976), no. 117.
0639		NMLZ, on display.	MS.10779 (20)	
0640		Privately owned.	MS.10709, f. 69	
0641		RBGK, English Letters, 1865—1900, 92, f. 132.	MS.10779 (10a)	
0642				Christie's Cat., 29 Jul 1971, lot 560.
0643				Sotheby's Cat., 19 May 1926, lot 632.
0644		KCLUND.	MS.10779 (6)	
0645	n	MDNHLL, MSS. 120.	MS.10777 (23)	
0646				Sotheby's Cat., 15 Dec 1931, lot 339.
0647		PROL, FO 63/842, ff. 29—30.	MS.10780 (4)	
0648		MDNHLL, MSS. 120.	MS.10777 (23)	
0649		SNMDL, Misc. MS. Material.	MS.10779 (3)	
0650	n			Sawyer's Cat. SA/56, addenda, 1967, no. 115.

NO	RECIPIENT	DATE	PLACE	LENGTH	SIZE	TYPE
0651	John Murray	25 Dec 57	Burnbank, Hamilton	1/ 4/ 3	185 114	MS aut
0652	Joseph D. Hooker	28 Dec 57	Burnbank, Hamilton NB	2/ 8/ 8	178 112	MS aut
0653	Lord Shaftesbury	[Nov-Dec 57?]		4 pp		MS aut
0654	William Monk	1 Jan 58	12 Kensington Palace Gdns	4 pp		Pr copy
0655	[John Kirk]	4 Jan 58	Hamilton	2/ 8/ 8	182 114	MS aut
0656	The Earl of Clarendon	7 Jan 58	50 Albemarle Street	4/16/16	fol	MS aut
0657	Henry Fleetwood	7 Jan 58	20 Bedford Square	1/ 4/ 3	227 188	MS aut
0658	Alexander Macmillan	8 Jan 58	50 Albemarle Street	1/ 4/ 4	8vo	Ph copy
0659	John Washington	9 Jan 58	20 Bedford Square	2/ 8/ 8	227 186	MS aut
0660	Thomas Ballantyne	11 Jan 58	50 Albemarle Street	1/ 4/ 3	202 125	MS aut
0661	Lord Ebury	14 Jan 58	12 Kensington Palace Gdns	2/ 8/ 8	203 126	MS aut
0662	[John Kirk]	14 Jan 58	12 Kensington Palace Gdns	1/ 4/ 4	231 185	MS aut
0663	John S. Moffat	14 Jan 58	12 Kensington Palace Gdns	2/ 6/ 6	232 185	MS aut
0664	John S. Moffat	14 Jan 58	12 Kensington Palace Gdns	1/ 4/ 4	202 125	MS aut
0665	William H. Smyth	18 Jan 58	12 Kensington Palace Gdns	1/ 4/ 4	202 125	MS aut
0666	James Young	18 Jan 58	12 Kensington Palace Gdns	1/ 4/ 4	203 125	MS aut
0667		19 Jan 58	12 Kensington Palace Gdns	1/ 4/ 4	4to	MS aut
0668	[John Kirk]	21 Jan 58	12 Kensington Palace Gdns	1/ 4/ 4	257 200	MS aut
0669	William Hope	21 Jan 58	12 Kensington Palace Gdns	1/ 4/ 3	252 200	MS aut
0670		21 Jan 58	London	2 pp	8vo	Pr copy
0671		21 Jan 58		2 pp	8vo	Pr copy
0672	[John Kirk]	22 Jan 58	15 Whitehall Place	1/ 4/ 4	181 110	MS aut
0673	[John Kirk]	26 Jan 58	50 Albemarle Street, London	1/ 4/ 3	252 199	MS aut
0674	Henry Labouchere	26 Jan 58		4 pp	fol	Pr copy
0675	Joseph Moore	26 Jan 58	50 Albemarle Street	3 pp	8vo	Pr copy
0676	Annarella Smyth	26 Jan 58	50 Albemarle Street	1/ 4/ 3	202 125	MS aut
0677	Thomas Baines	28 Jan 58	Manchester	2/ 8/ 8	181 114	MS aut
0678	Angela Burdett-Coutts	28 Jan, 1 Feb 58	Manchester	1/ 4/ 4	177 114	MS aut
0679	[John Kirk]	28 Jan 58	Manchester	1/ 4/ 4	181 114	MS aut
0680	Agnes Livingstone 3	28 Jan 58	Manchester	1/ 4/ 4	180 112	MS aut
0681	David L. Ratcliffe	28 Jan 58	50 Albemarle St., London	1/ 4/ 4	176 113	MS aut
0682	[Reginald C.E. Abbot??]	28 Jan 58	50 Albemarle St., London	1/ 4/ 4	177 114	MS aut
0683	Mrs. Ratcliffe	1 Feb 58	50 Albemarle Street	1/ 4/ 3	227 186	MS aut
0684	Thomas S. Livingstone	2 Feb 58	London	1 p		Pr copy
0685	Angela Burdett-Coutts	3 Feb 58	18 Hart St., Bloomsbury Sq.	1/ 4/ 4	252 200	MS aut
0686	Thomas Maclear	3 Feb 58	50 Albemarle Street	1/ 4/ 4	320 200	MS aut
0687	Frederick Fitch	5 Feb [58]	18 Hart Street	3 pp	8vo	Ph copy
0688	Henry Allon	6 Feb 58	18 Hart St., Bloomsbury Sq.	1/ 4/ 4	183 112	MS aut
0689	John S. Moffat	6 Feb 58	18 Hart St., Bloomsbury	2/ 8/ 8	183 112	MS aut
0690	Adam Sedgwick	6 Feb 58	50 Albemarle Street	1/ 4/ 4	228 185	MS aut
0691	Whitwell Elwin	8 Feb 58	50 Albemarle Street	2/ 4/ 4	172 118	MS aut
0692	John Murray	8 Feb 58	18 Hart St., Bloomsbury Sq.	1/ 4/ 4	183 112	MS aut
0693	Frederick Fitch	9 Feb 58	18 Hart Street	4 pp	8vo	Ph copy
0694	Edmund Hammond	9 Feb 58	18 Hart Street	2/ 8/ 7	4to	MS aut
0695	J. Board	10 Feb 58	London	3 pp	4to	Pr copy
0696		10 Feb 58	18 Hart St., Bloomsbury Sq.	1/ 2/ 2	8vo	MS aut
0697	Joseph Denman	11 Feb 58		2 pp	8vo	Pr copy
0698	Frederick Fitch	11 Feb 58	18 Hart Street	1/ 4/ 3	8vo	Ph copy
0699	Edmund Hammond	11 Feb 58	18 Hart St., Bloomsbury Sq.	4 pp	fol	MS aut
0700	H. Norton Shaw	11 Feb 58	18 Hart Street	1/ 4/ 4	8vo	MS aut

NO	N	LOCATION	NLS COPY	PUBLICATION
0651		JMPL.		
0652	n	RBGK, English Letters, 1865—1900, 92, f. 133.	MS.10779 (10a)	
0653	n	E.M. privately owned.		
0654	n			Monk, **DLCL**, 2nd edition (1860), pp. 303—305.
0655	n	Foskett Collection.		Foskett, **ZmDc**, pp. 29—30.
0656		PROL, FO 63/842, ff. 60—68.	MS.10780 (4)	Coupland, **KotZ**, pp. 77—78.
0657		Privately owned.	MS.10777 (2)	
0658		SNMDL.	MS.10708, f. 67	
0659		MDNHLL, MSS. 120.	MS.10777 (23)	
0660		FMC, MS. 134—1947.	MS.10777 (12)	
0661		NLS, MS. 10768, ff. 24—28.		Sotheby's Cat., 27 Feb 1962, lot 520.
0662		Foskett Collection.		Foskett, **ZmDc**, p. 31.
0663		NARS, MO 1/1/6, pp. 278—283.		Wallis, **TMaM**, pp. 2—3.
0664		NARS, MO 1/1/6, pp. 284—287.		Wallis, **TMaM**, pp. 3—4.
0665	n	WIHMLL, MS. 91798.	MS.10779 (15)	
0666		NMLZ, G5.		
0667		NLS, MS. 3813, ff. 203—204.		
0668		Foskett Collection.		Foskett, **ZmDc**, pp. 32—33.
0669		WIHMLL, MS. 67550.	MS.10779 (15)	
0670				Maggs' Cat. No. 870 (1960), no. 153.
0671				Sotheby's Cat., 30 Jul 1926, lot 228.
0672		Foskett Collection.		Foskett, **ZmDc**, p. 34.
0673	n	NLS, MS. 10707, ff. 42—43.		Foskett, **ZmDc**, p. 35.
0674				Sotheby's Cat., 6 Jun 1950, lot 317.
0675				Sotheby's Cat., 22 Jun 1955, lot 681.
0676		WIHMLL, MS. 64760.	MS.10779 (15)	
0677		BLJ, Book no. 5445.		
0678		Privately owned.		
0679	n	Foskett Collection.		Foskett, **ZmDc**, p. 36.
0680		NLS, MS. 10704, ff. 5—6.		
0681	n	USPGL, B4 ii, (30).	MS.10779 (14)	
0682	n	NLS, MS. 10768, ff. 29—30.		
0683	n	USPGL, B4 ii, (31).	MS.10779 (14)	
0684				Blaikie, **PLDL**, p. 240, ex.
0685		Privately owned.		
0686		NLS, MS. 10768, ff. 31—32.		Sotheby's Cat., 15 Apr 1975, lot 538.
0687		NARS, LI 2/1/1.	MS.10779 (21)	
0688		WIHMLL, MS. 68566.	MS.10779 (15)	
0689		NARS, MO 1/1/6, pp. 289—296.		Wallis, **TMaM**, pp. 4—5.
0690	n	NMLZ, on display.	MS.10779 (20)	Seaver, **DLLL**, p. 308. ex.
0691		WCLUWJ, Hist. and Lit. Papers, A348/A5.	MS.10779 (10)	Sotheby's Cat., 3 Dec 1913, lot 299, item 6.
0692		JMPL.		
0693		NARS, LI 2/1/1.	MS.10779 (21)	
0694		PROL, FO 63/842, ff. 139—142.	MS.10780 (4)	
0695				Maggs' Cat. No. 857 (1958), no. 366.
0696	n	PMSM, H.M. Stanley Papers.	MS.10777 (28)	
0697				Sotheby's Cat., 30 Nov 1938, lot 825.
0698		NARS, LI 2/1/1.	MS.10779 (21)	
0699		PROL, FO 63/842, ff. 145—147.	MS.10780 (4)	
0700		RGSL, Archives, DL 2/15/19.	MS.10780 (5)	

NO	RECIPIENT	DATE	PLACE	LENGTH	SIZE	TYPE
0701	John T. Quekett	11 Feb 58		4 pp	8vo	Pr copy
0702	J.H. Wilton	11 Feb 58	18 Hart Street	3 pp	8vo	Pr copy
0703	William B. Woodman	11 Feb 58	18 Hart Street	2/ 4/ 4	180 111	MS aut
0704		11 Feb 58	Hart Street	2 pp	8vo	Pr copy
0705	James Paget	11 Feb 58	18 Hart Street	3 pp	8vo	Pr copy
0706		11 Feb 58	18 Hart Street	4 pp	8vo	Ph copy
0707	J. Bevan Braithwaite	12 Feb 58	18 Hart Street	1/ 4/ 4	8vo	Ph copy
0708	John Murray	12 Feb 58	18 Hart Street	1/ 4/ 4	184 112	MS aut
0709	John Washington	12 Feb 58	18 Hart St., Bloomsbury	3/12/12	180 110	MS aut
0710	John S. Moffat	13 Feb 58	18 Hart Street	4 pp		Ph copy
0711	John Washington	13 Feb 58	18 Hart Street	1/ 4/ 4	180 110	MS aut
0712	Angela Burdett-Coutts	14 Feb 58	18 Hart St., Bloomsbury	2/ 6/ 6	229 187	MS aut
0713	Thomas Baines	15 Feb 58	[18] Hart Street	4 pp	8vo	Pr copy
0714	Frederick Fitch	15 Feb58	18 Hart Street	1 p	8vo	Ph copy
0715	Roderick I. Murchison	15 Feb 58	18 Hart Street	1/ 4/ 4	180 110	MS aut
0716	[C.S. Hanbury??]	[19 Jan—15 Feb 58]		1/ 2/ 2	201 126	MS aut
0717	Edmund Hammond	16 Feb 58	18 Hart Street	1/ 4/ 3	4to	MS aut
0718	Edmund Hammond	16 Feb 58	18 Hart Street	1/ 4/ 4	8vo	MS aut
0719	John Murray	16 Feb 58	[50 Albemarle Street]	1/ 4/ 4	180 114	MS aut
0720	George Back	17 Feb 58	18 Hart St., Bloomsbury	1/ 4/ 4	8vo	MS aut
0721	T. Sam Fletcher	17 Feb 58	18 Hart St., Bloomsbury	1/ 4/ 3	179 112	MS aut
0722	[John Kirk]	17 Feb 58	18 Hart Street	1/ 4/ 4	181 111	MS aut
0723	John Washington	17 Feb 58	18 Hart Street	2/ 8/ 8	180 110	MS aut
0724		17 Feb 58	18 Hart Street	1/ 4/ 3	180 112	MS aut
0725	Frederick Fitch	18 Feb 58	18 Hart Street	4 pp	8vo	Ph copy
0726	John Livingstone	18 Feb 58	50 Albemarle St., London	1/ 4/ 4	228 185	MS aut
0727	J.E. Goodman	19 Feb 58	18 Hart Street	1/ 4/ 4	233 183	MS aut
0728	Edward Marjoribanks	19 Feb 58	18 Hart St., Bloomsbury Sq.	2/ 8/ 8	230 183	MS aut
0729	Edmund Hammond	20 Feb 58	18 Hart Street	1/ 2/ 2	fol	MS aut
0730	John S. Moffat	20 Feb 58	Foreign Office	1/ 4/ 4	321 200	MS aut
0731	[John Kirk]	22 Feb 58	London	1/ 4/ 4	187 118	MS aut
0732	Roderick I. Murchison	22 Feb 58	18 Hart Street	1/ 4/ 4	182 115	MS aut
0733	Arthur Tidman	22 Feb 58	18 Hart Street	1/ 4/ 3	230 183	MS aut
0734	Henry Labouchere	[27 Jan—22 Feb 58]	London	4 pp	8vo	Pr copy
0735	Lady Belhaven	24 Feb 58	Burnbank [Hamilton]	1/ 4/ 4	184 114	MS aut
0736	[Samuel?] Macnab	24 Feb 58	11 Sardinia Ter., Glasgow	1/ 4/ 4	210 124	MS aut
0737						
0738	[John Kirk]	28 Feb 58	Glasgow	1/ 4/ 3	185 113	MS aut
0739	John Washington	28 Feb 58	4 Athol Place, Glasgow	1/ 4/ 4	180 110	MS aut
0740	William B. Woodman	28 Feb 58	Glasgow	1/ 4/ 4	8vo	MS aut
0741	Mburuma & Sekeletu	[Feb 58]	London	2/ 6/ 6	fol	MS aut
0742	John Douglas	2 Mar 58	4 Athol Place	1/ 4/ 3	187 101	MS aut
0743	Edmund Hammond	2 Mar 58	4 Athol Place	1/ 2/ 2	fol	MS aut
0744	John S. Moffat	2 Mar 58	4 Athol Place	1/ 4/ 4	187 116	MS aut in
0745	William C. Oswell	2 Mar 58		3 pp	8vo	Pr copy
0746	[Wilbraham?] Taylor	2 Mar 58	Kendal	1/ 4/ 4	178 113	MS aut
0747	Angela Burdett-Coutts	4 Mar 58	Birkenhead	1/ 4/ 4	254 203	MS aut
0748	J. Bevan Braithwaite	6 Mar 58	Birkenhead	1/ 4/ 4	255 203	MS aut
0749	Leigh Clare	6 Mar 58	Birkenhead	1/ 2/ 1	8vo	MS aut
0750	Edmund Hammond	6 Mar 58	Birkenhead	1/ 4/ 3	fol	MS aut

NO	N	LOCATION	NLS COPY	PUBLICATION
0701				Rendell Cat. No. 26, no. 149.
0702				Myers' Cat. No. 390 (1957), no. 175.
0703		ULSOASL, Africa, Wooden Box of L's letters.	MS.10778	
0704				Fletcher's Cat. No. 201 (Spring, 1962), no. 143.
0705				Sotheby's Cat., 23 Jun 1958, lot 259.
0706		NARS, LI 2/1/1.	MS.10779 (21)	
0707		NLS, MS. Acc. 6509.		Edwards' Bulletin No. 38 (1975), no. 129.
0708		JMPL.		
0709		MDNHLL, MSS. 120.	MS.10777 (23)	
0710	n	NLS, MS. Acc. 6509.		Wallis, **TMaM**, p. 5.
0711		MDNHLL, MSS. 120.	MS.10777 (23)	
0712		Privately owned.		
0713				Maggs' Cat. Christmas 1918, no. 2401.
0714		NARS, LI 2/1/1.	MS.10779 (21)	
0715		NARS, LI 1/1/1, pp. 739–742.		
0716		WIHMLL, MS. 68325.	MS.10779 (15)	
0717		PROL, FO 63/842, ff. 188–189.	MS.10780 (4)	
0718		PROL, FO 63/842, ff. 185–186.	MS.10780 (4)	
0719	n	JMPL.		
0720		RGSL, Back Collection.		
0721		WIHMLL, MS. A 365.	MS.10779 (15)	
0722	n	Foskett Collection.		Foskett, **ZmDc**, p. 37.
0723		MDNHLL, MSS. 120.	MS.10777 (23)	
0724		CSBL.		Sotheby's Cat., 30 Apr 1968, p. 105.
0725		NARS, LI 2/1/1.		
0726		ULSOASL, Africa, Wooden Box of L's letters.	MS.10778	Seaver, **DLLL**, pp. 315–316.
0727		SALCT, S.A. MSS. Sect. A.	MS.10780 (1)	Sawyer's Cat. SA/56, addenda (1967), no. 117.
0728		NLS, MS. 2618, ff. 239–242.		
0729		PROL, FO 63/842, ff. 221–222.	MS.10780 (4)	
0730		NARS, MO 1/1/6, pp. 300–302.		Wallis, **TMaM**, pp. 7–9.
0731	n	Foskett Collection.		Foskett, **ZmDc**, p. 38.
0732		NARS, LI 1/1/1, pp. 766–769.		
0733		ULSOASL, Africa, Wooden Box of L's letters.	MS.10778	Sotheby's Cat., 30 Oct 1973, lot 386.
0734	n			Maggs' Cat. No. 823 (1954), no. 168.
0735		WIHMLL, MS. 64764	MS.10779 (15)	
0736	n	JPLAM.	MS.10779 (8)	
0737	n			
0738	n	Foskett Collection.		Foskett, **ZmDc**, p. 39.
0739		MDNHLL, MSS. 120.	MS.10777 (23)	
0740		ULSOASL, Africa, Odds, Box 11, "odd items".		
0741	n	PROL, FO 63/842, ff. 199–201.	MS.10780 (4)	
0742		SNMDL.	MS.10708, f. 68	
0743		PROL, FO 63/842, f. 239.	MS.10780 (4)	
0744		NARS, MO 1/1/6, pp. 304–307.		Wallis, **TMaM**, pp. 9–10.
0745				Rendell Cat. No. 26, no. 150.
0746		WIHMLL, MS. 63518.	MS.10779 (15)	
0747		Privately owned.		
0748		NLS, MS. Dep. 237.		
0749		WCLUWJ, Hist. and Lit. Papers, A348/A10.	MS.10779 (10)	Sotheby's Cat., 3 Dec 1913, lot 229, item 3.
0750		PROL, FO 63/842, ff. 253–254.	MS.10780 (4)	

NO	RECIPIENT	DATE	PLACE	LENGTH	SIZE		TYPE
0751	Agnes Livingstone 3	6 Mar 58	Birkenhead	1/ 4/ 4	181	113	MS aut
0752	Mrs. Lowe	6 Mar 58	Birkenhead	1/ 4/ 4	180	113	MS aut
0753	John Murray	6 Mar 58	Birkenhead	1/ 4/ 4	182	112	MS aut
0754	Arthur Tidman	6 Mar 58	Birkenhead	1/ 4/ 4	255	204	MS aut
0755	[Mrs. J.A.?] Turner	6 Mar 58	Birkenhead	1/ 4/ 4	8vo		MS aut
0756		6 Mar 58	Birkenhead	1/ 4/ 4	182	113	MS aut
0757	John Washington	8, 9 Mar 58	Birkenhead	1/ 4/ 4	223	183	MS aut
0758	[Adam Sedgwick??]	8 Mar 58	Birkenhead	1 p	8vo		Pr copy
0759	John Washington	9 Mar 58	Birkenhead	1/ 4/ 4	223	183	MS aut
0760	John Washington	9 Mar 58	Birkenhead	1/ 4/ 4	223	183	MS aut
0761	George Back	10 Mar 58	"Pearl" — Mersey	1/ 4/ 4	202	125	MS aut
0762	Agnes Livingstone 3	10 Mar 58	"Pearl"	1/ 4/ 3	8vo		MS aut
0763	Thomas S. Livingstone	10 Mar 58	"Pearl" in the Mersey	1 p			Pr copy
0764	John Washington	10 Mar 58	"Pearl" 1½ PM	1/ 4/ 2	223	183	MS aut
0765	John Kirk	18 Mar 58	"Pearl" at Sea off Madiera	7 pp			Pr copy
0766	Angela Burdett-Coutts	22 Mar 58	"Pearl" off Senegal	1/ 4/ 4	222	185	MS aut
0767	Whitwell Elwin	22 Mar 58	Screw Steamer "Pearl"	1/ 4/ 4	322	203	MS aut
0768	Agnes Livingstone 3	22 Mar 58	"Pearl" off Senegal	1/ 4/ 4	228	186	MS aut
0769	The Earl of Malmesbury	22 Mar 58	Steamer "Pearl"	2/ 8/ 8	fol		MS aut
0770	The Earl of Malmesbury	23 Mar 58	Steamer "Pearl"	2/ 8/ 7	fol		MS aut
0771	[George L. Conyngham??]	25 Mar 58	Steamer "Pearl"	1/ 4/ 4	321	204	MS aut
0772	Edmund Hammond	25 Mar 58	"Pearl" off Sierra Leone	1/ 4/ 2	fol		MS aut
0773	Robert M. Livingstone	25 Mar 58	"Pearl" near Sierra Leone	1/ 4/ 4	228	185	MS aut
0774	Roderick I. Murchison	30 Mar 58	Sierra Leone	2/ 6/ 5	misc		MS aut
0775	[Richard Owen]	30 Mar 58	Sierra Leone	1/ 4/4	322	202	MS aut
0776	Francis Skead	3 Apr 58	Steamer "Pearl"	1/ 2/ 2	4to		MS aut
0777	Norman Bedingfeld	10 Apr 58	S.S. "Pearl"	8 pp			MS copy
0778	John Kirk	15 Apr 58	"Pearl"	1 p			Pr copy
0779	George Rae	15 Apr 58	Screw Steamer "Pearl"	2 pp			Pr copy
0780	[John S. Moffat]	16 Apr, 1 May 58	"Pearl" Steamer	1/ 4/ 4	317	204	MS aut
0781	Richard Thornton	16 Apr 58	Steamer "Pearl" at Sea	3/12/12	322	202	MS aut
0782	Thomas Baines	18 Apr 58	Screw Steamer "Pearl" at Sea	2 pp			Pr copy
0783	John Washington	19,28 Apr 58	"Pearl" at Sea — [Cape Town]	1/ 4/ 4	322	203	MS aut
0784	Custodio José da Silva	26 Apr 58	Cape Town	1 p			MS copy
0785	William Porter	30 Apr 58	[Cape Town]				MS copy
0786	William Thompson	30 Apr 58	Cape Town	1/ 4/ 3	202	124	MS aut
0787	The Earl of Malmesbury	1 May 58	Cape of Good Hope	2/ 8/ 7	fol		MS aut
0788	Angela Burdett-Coutts	6 May, 21 Jun 58	Screw Steamer "Pearl"	1/ 4/ 4	327	203	MS aut
0789	Agnes Livingstone 3	7 May 58	Steamer "Pearl" [off Natal]	1/ 4/ 4	206	165	MS aut
0790	Robert M. Livingstone	7 May 58	Screw Steamer "Pearl"	1/ 4/ 4	205	165	MS aut
0791	Thomas S. Livingstone	7 May 58	Steamer "Pearl"	1/ 4/ 4	205	165	MS aut
0792	[J. Bevan Braithwaite]	10 May 58	Screw Steamer "Pearl"	1/ 4/ 4	330	204	MS aut
0793	Charles Livingstone	10 May 58	S.S. "Pearl"	2/ 8/ 7	322	201	MS aut
0794	Robert Moffat 1	10 May, 25 Jun 58	"Pearl" [off Delagoa Bay]	1/ 4/ 4	328	205	MS aut
0795	James Young	10 May 58	"Pearl" off Cape Corrientes	2 pp			Pr copy
0796	Henry Allon	26 May, 8 Jun 58	Steamer "Pearl"	1/ 4/ 4	fol		Ph copy
0797	William E.A. Gordon	9 Jun 58	S.S. "Pearl"	2 pp			MS copy
0798	Norman Bedingfeld	12 Jun 58	S.S. "Pearl"	2 pp			Pr copy
0799	John Laird	21 Jun 58	"Ma-Robert", Zambesi	3 pp			MS copy
0800	Morton Peto	21 Jun 58	Zambesi River	4 pp	fol		TS copy

NO N	LOCATION	NLS COPY	PUBLICATION
0751	NLS, MS. 10704, ff. 7—8.		
0752	USPGL.	MS.10779 (14)	
0753	JMPL.		
0754	ULSOASL, Africa, Wooden Box of L's letters.	MS.10778.	
0755	Privately owned.	MS.10777 (6)	
0756	NARS, LI 2/1/1.		
0757	MDNHLL, MSS. 120.	MS.10777 (23)	
0758 n			Myers' Cat. No. 360 (Winter, 1949), no. 6.
0759	MDNHLL, MSS. 120.	MS.10777 (23)	
0760	MDNHLL, MSS. 120.	MS.10777 (23)	
0761	RGSL, Back Collection.		
0762	NLS, MS. 10704, ff. 9—10.		
0763			Blaikie, **PLDL**, p. 240, ex.
0764	MDNHLL, MSS. 120.	MS.10777 (23)	
0765 n			Foskett, **ZmDc**, pp. 40—47.
0766	Privately owned.		
0767	WIHMLL, MS. 63154.	MS.10779 (15)	
0768	BLL, Add. MS. 50184, ff. 18—19.	MS.10780 (3)	
0769 n	PROL, FO 63/842, ff. 273—277.	MS.10780 (4)	Wallis, **ZEDL** II, pp. 263—264.
0770 n	PROL, FO 63/842, ff. 278—281.	MS.10780 (4)	Wallis, **ZEDL** II, pp. 264—265.
0771	BLJ, Book no. 5700.		
0772	PROL, FO 63/842, ff. 271—272.	MS.10780 (4)	
0773	NLS, MS. 10701, ff. 98—99.		Blaikie, **PLDL**, pp. 244—245, ex.
0774	NARS, LI 1/1/1, pp. 781—785.		**The Times**, 24 Apr 1858, p. 12, c. 4.
0775	NLS, MS. Acc. 7077.		Maggs' Cat. No. 801 (1951), no. 712.
0776	DPLDS.	MS.10777 (13)	
0777	PROL, FO 63/843 II, ff. 48—55.	MS.10780 (4)	Wallis, **ZEDL** II, pp. 413—417.
0778 n			Foskett, **ZmDc**, p. 53.
0779			Wallis, **ZEDL** II, pp. 418—419.
0780 n	NARS, MO 1/1/6, pp. 331—334.		Wallis, **TMaM**, pp. 10—11.
0781	NMLZ, on display.	MS.10779 (20)	Wallis, **ZEDL** II, pp. 432—433.
0782			Wallis, **ZEDL** II, pp. 434—435.
0783	MDNHLL, MSS. 120.	MS.10777 (23)	
0784 n	AHUL, Moçambique Papeis, Pasta 15 (1858).		
0785 n	GACT, Maclear Papers, Acc. 515.		
0786	ULSOASL, Africa, Wooden Box of L's letters.	MS.10778	
0787 n	PROL, FO 63/843 I, ff. 1—4.	MS.10780 (4)	
0788	Privately owned.		
0789	BLL, Add. MS. 50184, ff. 20—21.	MS.10780 (3)	
0790	Wilson Collection.	MS.10775 (14)	
0791	NLS, MS. 10701, ff. 100—101.		
0792	NLS, MS. Dep. 237.		
0793	OCLOO, Autographs.	MS.10779 (17a)	Wallis, **ZEDL** II, pp. 431—432.
0794 n	BLL, Add. MS. 50184, ff. 22—23.	MS.10780 (3)	Blaikie, **PLDL**, p. 248, ex.
0795			Blaikie, **PLDL**, pp. 247—248, ex.
0796	ULSOASL, Africa, Odds, Box 9.		Peel, **LVE**, pp. 324—326.
0797	PROL, FO 63/843 I, ff. 81—83.	MS.10780 (4)	Wallis, **ZEDL** I, p. 10.
0798			Wallis, **ZEDL** I, pp. 14—15.
0799 n	MDNHLL, MSS. 120.		Monk, **DLCL**, 2nd edition (1860), pp. 345—346.
0800 n	NMLZ.		Sotheby's Cat., 6 Jun 1950, lot 308.

NO	RECIPIENT	DATE	PLACE	LENGTH	SIZE		TYPE
0801	Frederick Fitch	22 Jun 58	"Ma-Robert," Zambesi River	1/ 4/ 4		fol	Ph copy
0802	The Earl of Malmesbury	22 Jun 58	Steamer "Pearl," Zambesi	6/22/22		fol	MS aut
0803	Samuel Wilberforce	22 Jun 58	Steamer "Pearl," Zambesi	2/ 8/ 8		fol	MS aut
0804	[James Young?]	23 Jun 58	"Ma-Robert," Zambesi	1 p			NS copy
0805	George L.Conyngham	26 Jun 58	Zambesi	1/ 4/ 4	229	184	MS aut
0806		26 Jun 58	River Zambesi				NS copy
0807	Thomas Maclear	26 Jun 58	Steamer "Pearl," Zambesi	1/ 4/ 4	330	203	MS aut
0808	Norman Bedingfeld	28 Jun 58	Nyika Island	2 pp			MS copy
0809	José M. Nuñes	10 Jul 58	Zambesi, near Sena	3 pp			MS copy
0810	Norman Bedingfeld	13 Jul 58	Senna	1/ 4/ 3	218	172	MS aut
0811	John Kirk	21 Jul 58	Off Shupunga	2 pp			Pr copy
0812	Norman Bedingfeld	31 Jul 58	Expedition Island	10 pp		fol	MS aut copy
0813	Thomas Maclear	31 Jul 58	Nyika or Expedition Island	2/ 4/ 4	330	203	MS aut
0814	The Earl of Malmesbury	31 Jul 58	Expedition Island, Zambesi	20 pp		fol	MS aut
0815	Norman Bedingfeld	12 Aug 58	Expedition Island	3 pp			MS copy
0816	[Commander, H.M. Ship]	13 Aug 58	Expedition Island	1/ 4/ 4	322	203	MS aut
0817	The Earl of Malmesbury	16 Aug 58	Shupanga	12 pp		fol	MS aut
0818	José M. Nuñes	17 Aug 58	Shupanga	4 pp			MS copy
0819	John Kirk	25 Aug 58	Is. of Pita, above Senna	1/ 4/ 4	333	204	MS aut
0820	Richard Thornton	25 Aug 58	Island of Pita	1/ 4/ 4	325	204	MS aut
0821	Angela Burdett-Coutts	28 Aug 58	Steamer "Ma-Robert"	1/ 4/ 4	327	205	MS aut
0822	[Wilbraham Taylor]	[Aug 58] , 28 Sep [58]		1/ 4/ 4	325	205	MS aut in
0823	The Earl of Malmesbury	9 Sep 58	Tette	2/ 8/ 8	330	202	MS aut
0824	Thomas Maclear	10 Sep 58	Tette	1/ 4/ 4	325	202	MS aut
0825	The Earl of Malmesbury	10 Sep, 2 Oct 58	Tette-Kongone	26 pp		fol	MS aut
0826	John Washington	13 Sep 58	Tette	2/ 8/ 8	323	202	MS aut
0827	[James Young?]	14 Sep 58	Tete				NS copy
0828	Morton Peto	17 Sep 58	"Ma-Robert," Zambesi River	4 pp		4to	TS copy
0829	Thomas Baines	19 Sep 58	Senna	4 pp			Facsimile
0830	Frederick Grey	21 Sep 58	Shupanga	2/ 6/ 6	338	202	MS aut
0831	William Robertson	23 Sep 58	Shupanga	1/ 4/ 4	330	202	MS aut copy
0832	The Earl of Malmesbury	25 Sep 58	Zambesi	1/ 4/ 4		fol	MS aut
0833	Andrew Drew	27 Sep 58	Kongone Harbour	1/ 4/ 4	328	204	MS aut
0834	[J. Bevan Braithwaite]	28 Sep 58	Kongone Harbour	3/ 8/ 8		misc	MS aut
0835	George Grey	28 Sep 58	Kongone River				NS copy
0836	Agnes Livingstone 3	28 Sep 58	Steamer "Ma-Robert"	1/ 4/ 4	250	200	MS aut
0837							
0838	John Washington	28 Sep 58	Kongone Harbour	2/ 8/ 8	203	165	MS aut
0839	John S. & Emily Moffat	2 Oct 58	"Ma-Robert," River Kongone	1/ 4/ 4	325	202	MS aut
0840	William Thompson	4 Oct 58	River Kongone	1/ 4/ 4	325	204	MS aut
0841	George L. Conyngham	5 Oct 58	Zambesi River	1/ 4/ 4	252	200	MS aut
0842	The Earl of Malmesbury	5 Oct 58	Kongone Harbour	4 pp		fol	MS aut
0843	John Murray	5 Oct 58	Kongone Harbour	1/ 4/ 4	237	204	MS aut
0844	Agnes Livingstone 1	6 Oct 58	[Kongone Harbour]	1/ 4/ 4	228	184	MS aut fr
0845	Thomas Maclear	6 Oct 58	Kongone River	6/24/24	330	202	MS aut
0846	John Washington	6 Oct 58	Kongone River	1/ 4/ 4	329	203	MS aut
0847	Edmund Gabriel	7 Oct 58	Kongone, Steamer "Ma-Robert"	2/ 8/ 8	332	202	MS aut
0848	Frederick Grey	13 Oct 58	Shupanga	1/ 4/ 4	338	202	MS aut
0849	José M. Nuñes	13 Oct 58	Shupanga	4 pp			MS copy
0850	Richard Thornton	[29 Nov 58]	[Caborra Basa Rapids]	1/ 2/ 2	120	63	MS aut

NO	N	LOCATION	NLS COPY	PUBLICATION
0801		NARS, LI 2/1/1.	MS.10779 (21)	
0802	n	PROL, FO 63/843 I, ff. 93—103.	MS.10780 (4)	Wallis, **ZEDL** II, pp. 266—271.
0803		BLO, MSS. Wilberforce, C. 12, ff. 114—117.	MS.10780 (7)	
0804				**The Times**, 5 Jan 1859, p.12, c.1.
0805		BLJ, Book no. 5700.		
0806	n	AHUL, Moçambique Papeis, Pasta 15 (1858).		**BOdGGdPdA**, No. 690 (18 Dec 1858), pp. 8—9.
0807		NARS, LI 1/1/1, pp. 805—808.		
0808		PROL, FO 63/843 II, ff. 61—62.	MS.10780 (4)	Wallis, **ZEDL** I, p. 18.
0809		NARS, LI 1/1/1, pp. 809—811.	MS.10779 (21)	
0810		NLS, MS. 10768, ff. 33—34.		Maggs' Cat. No. 971 (Spring, 1976), no. 93.
0811	n			Foskett, **ZmDc**, pp. 54—55.
0812	n	PROL, FO 63/843 II, ff. 68—73.	MS.10780 (4)	Wallis, **ZEDL** I, pp. 24—25.
0813		NARS, LI 1/1/1, pp. 814—821.		
0814	n	PROL, FO 63/843 II, ff. 30—39.	MS.10780 (4)	Wallis, **ZEDL** II, pp. 272—278.
0815	n	NARS, LI 1/1/1, p.813.		Wallis, **ZEDL** I, pp. 27—29.
0816	n	SNMDL, on display.		
0817	n	PROL, FO 63/843 II, ff. 41—46.	MS.10780 (4)	Wallis, **ZEDL** II, pp. 280—283.
0818		NARS, LI 1/1/1, pp. 870—873.	MS.10779 (21)	
0819	n	BLJ, Book no. 6401.		Foskett, **ZmDc**, pp. 55—57.
0820		NMLZ, on display.	MS.10779 (20)	Tabler, **ZPRT** I, pp. 63—65.
0821		Privately owned.		
0822	n	NARS, LI 2/1/1.	MS.10779 (21)	Edwards' Cat. 691 (1948), no. 355.
0823	n	NARS, LI 1/1/1, pp. 881—888.		
0824		NARS, LI 1/1/1, pp. 889—892.		
0825		PROL, FO 63/843 II, ff. 96—107.	MS.10780 (4)	Wallis, **ZEDL** II, pp. 283—290.
0826		MDNHLL, MSS. 120	MS.10777 (23)	
0827				**The Times**, 5 Jan 1859, p. 12, c. 1.
0828	n	NMLZ.		Sotheby's Cat., 6 Jun 1950, lot 308.
0829		JPLAM.	MS.10708, f. 70	Baines, **GRSEA**, between pp. xii and xiii.
0830		RCSL, MSS. Sc. 99.	MS.10779 (13)	
0831	n	BLL, Add. MS. 50184, ff. 24—25.	MS.10780 (3)	
0832		PROL, FO 63/843 I, ff. 137—138.	MS.10780 (4)	
0833		WIHMLL, MS. 56318.	MS.10779 (15)	
0834		NLS, MS. Dep. 237.		
0835	n	ULSOASL, Africa, Wooden Box of L's letters.	MS.10778	Monk, **DLCL**, 2nd edition (1860), pp. 346—348.
0836		BLL, Add. MS. 50184, ff. 26—27.	MS.10780 (3)	
0837	n			
0838		MDNHLL, MSS. 120.	MS.10777 (23)	
0839	n	NARS, MO 1/1/6, pp. 504—507.		Wallis, **TMaM**, pp. 42—44.
0840	n	ULSOASL, Africa, Wooden Box of L's letters.	MS.10778	Chamberlin, **SLFL**, pp. 266—268.
0841		BLJ, Book no. 5318, Acc. Reg. 4669.		Sotheby's Cat., 29 Jun 1939, lot 478.
0842	n	PROL, FO 63/843 II, ff. 111—112.	MS.10780 (4)	
0843		JMPL.		
0844		NLS, MS. 10701, ff. 102—103.		
0845	n	NARS, LI 1/1/1, pp. 904—927.		
0846		MDNHLL, MSS. 120.	MS.10777 (23)	
0847	n	BLJ, Book no. 6754.	MS.10769	**OB**, vol III, No. 29 (Feb 1923), pp. 375—376, ex.
0848		RCSL, MSS. Sc. 99.	MS.10779 (13)	
0849		NARS, LI 1/1/1, ff. 928—931.	MS.10779 (21)	
0850		KPLSA.	MS.10779 (11)	

NO	RECIPIENT	DATE	PLACE	LENGTH	SIZE	TYPE
0851	James Young	8 Dec 58	Tette	1 p		MS copy
0852	Joseph Sturge	11 Dec 58	Tette	1/ 4/ 4	fol	MS aut
0853	The Earl of Malmesbury	17 Dec 58	Tette	31 pp	fol	MS aut
0854	George Grey	18 Dec 58	Tette	1/ 4/ 4	325 200	MS aut
0855	John Washington	18 Dec 58	Tette	2/ 8/ 8	325 201	MS aut
0856	Mrs. [Andrew?] Buchanan	19 Dec 58		2 pp		Pr copy
0857	Thomas Maclear	19 Dec 58	Tette	2/ 6/ 6	326 200	MS aut
0858	Angela Burdett-Coutts	20 Dec 58	Tette	1/ 4/ 4	328 203	MS aut
0859	Frederick Grey	25 Dec 58	Senna	1/ 4/ 4	323 200	MS aut
0860	José M. Nuñes	27 Dec 58	Senna	4 pp		MS copy
0861	Thomas Maclear	13 Jan [59]	Morambala	2/ 8/ 8	330 202	MS aut
0862	José M. Nuñes	15 Jan 59	Shupanga	4 pp		MS copy
0863	John Blanche	20 Jan 59	Zambesi River, Africa	1/ 4/ 4	325 203	MS aut
0864	William Thompson	5 Feb 59	Tette	1/ 4/ 4	325 204	MS aut
0865	The Earl of Malmesbury	14 Feb 59	Tette, Zambesi River	12 pp	fol	MS aut
0866	Frederick Grey	15 Feb 59	Tette	2/ 8/ 8	323 200	MS aut
0867	Roderick I. Murchison	15 Feb 59	Tette	2/ 4/ 4	325 202	MS aut
0868	James Young	15 Feb 59	Tette	1 p		MS copy
0869		15 Feb 59	Tette	3 pp		Pr copy
0870	John Washington	16 Feb 59	Tette	2/ 8/ 8	325 201	MS aut
0871	José M. Nuñes	18 Feb 59	Tette	4 pp		MS copy
0872	Joseph Denman	19 Feb 59	Tette	4 pp	fol	Pr copy
0873	George Grey	19 Feb 59	Tette	2/ 8/ 8	325 205	MS aut
0874	W.K.R. von Haidinger	[21 Feb 59]	[Tette]	12 pp	179 118	MS aut
0875	Amer. Geog. & Stat. Soc.	22 Feb 59	Tette, Zambesi	4/16/16	280 215	MS aut
0876	Richard Thornton	24 Feb 59	Tette			TS copy?
0877	Lord Kinnaird	2 Mar 59	Tette, River Zambesi	8 pp	misc	Ph copy
0878	William Monk	3 Mar 59	Tette			MS copy
0879	The Earl of Malmesbury	4 Mar 59	Tette	2/ 8/ 8	fol	MS aut
0880	The Duke of Argyll	5 Mar 59	Tette	1 p		Pr copy
0881	José M. Nuñes	9 Mar 59	Tette	3 pp		MS copy
0882	J. Aspinall Turner	9 Mar 59	Tette	3 pp		Pr copy
0883	William C. Oswell	2 Apr, 14 May 59	Chibisa's-Shupanga	2/ 6/ 6	325 202	MS aut
0884	Angela Burdett-Coutts	8 May 59	Senna	1/ 4/ 4	327 202	MS aut
0885	James Young	8 May 59	Senna	1 p		MS copy
0886	Roderick I. Murchison	9 May 59	Senna	1/ 4/ 4	322 202	MS aut
0887	[Thomas Maclear]	12 May 59	Senna	4 pp	fol	MS aut in
0888	The Earl of Malmesbury	12 May 59	Senna	24 pp	fol	MS aut
0889	Lord Palmerston	13 May 59	Senna	1/ 4/ 4	322 204	MS aut
0890	Henry Venn	15 May 59	Senna	1/ 4/ 4	323 200	MS aut
0891	Charles L. Braithwaite	24 May 59	Kongone Harbour	10 pp	8vo	MS copy
0892	John Washington	25 May 59	Kongone Harbour	3/10/10	323 202	MS aut
0893	Commander, H.M. Ship	25 May 59	Kongone Harbour	1/ 4/ 4	325 202	Ph copy
0894						
0895	Adam Sedgwick	27 May 59	River Zambesi, East Africa	1/ 4/ 4	337 208	MS aut
0896	José M. Nuñes	28, 30 May 59	Maruru-Shupanga	3 pp		MS copy
0897	J. Bevan Braithwaite	[30 May 59]	[River Zambesi]	1/ 2/ 2	247 202	MS aut fr
0898	Richard Owen	[May], 30 May 59	Zambesi [-Shupanga]	1/ 4/ 4	fol	MS aut in
0899	J. Aspinall Turner	30 May 59	River Zambesi	2 pp		Pr copy
0900	Robert M. Livingstone	31 May 59	River Zambesi	4 pp	fol	TS copy

NO	N	LOCATION	NLS COPY	PUBLICATION
0851	n	MDNHLL, MSS. 120.		
0852		BLL, Add. MS. 43845, ff. 63—64.	MS.10780 (3)	Chamberlin, **SLFL**, pp. 268—270.
0853	n	PROL, FO 63/843II, ff. 114—130.	MS.10780 (4)	Wallis, **ZEDL** II, pp. 292—300.
0854	n	APLANZ, GL: L30.	MS.10777 (10a)	Monk, **DLCL**, 2nd edition (1860), pp. 348—349.
0855		MDNHLL, MSS. 120.	MS.10777 (23)	
0856				Monk, **DLCL**, 2nd edition (1860), pp. 349—350.
0857		NARS, LI 1/1/1, pp. 943—948.		**JRGSL**, vol. 31 (1861), pp. 279—280.
0858		Privately owned.		Monk, **DLCL**, 2nd edition (1860), pp. 350—351.
0859		RCSL, MSS. Sc 99.	MS.10779 (13)	
0860		NARS, LI 1/1/1, pp. 949—952.	MS.10779 (21)	
0861	n	NARS, LI 1/1/1, pp. 964—971.		**JRGSL**, vol. 31 (1861), pp. 280—283.
0862		NARS, LI 1/1/1, pp. 978—981.	MS.10779 (21)	
0863		ULSOASL, Africa, Wooden Box of L's letters.	MS.10778	
0864	n	ULSOASL, Africa, Wooden Box of L's letters.	MS.10778	
0865	n	PROL, FO 63/871, ff. 38—44.	MS.10780 (4)	Wallis, **ZEDL** II, pp. 300—302, ex.
0866		RCSL, MSS. Sc 99.	MS.10779 (13)	
0867	n	NARS, LI 1/1/1, pp. 985—992.		Seaver, **DLLL**, pp. 341—342, 346, ex.
0868		MDNHLL, MSS. 120.		
0869				Monk, **DLCL**, 2nd edition (1860), pp. 351—353.
0870		MDNHLL, MSS. 120.	MS.10777 (23)	
0871		NARS, LI 1/1/1, pp. 1001—1004.	MS.10779 (21)	
0872				Sotheby's Cat., 6 Jun 1950, lot 309.
0873	n	APLANZ, GL: L30.	MS.10777 (10a)	Monk, **DLCL**, 2nd edition (1860), pp. 354—356.
0874		WCLUWJ, Hist. and Lit. Papers, A348/A6.	MS.10779 (10)	Sotheby's Cat., 3 Dec 1913, lot 299, item 7.
0875	n	AGSNY.	MS.10779 (16)	**New York Herald**, 7 Jan 1860.
0876	n			Sotheby's Cat., 10 Nov 1936, lot 509.
0877		SNMDL.	MS.10708, f. 74	
0878	n	KPLSA.		Monk, **DLCL**, 2nd edition (1860), pp. 356—357.
0879	n	PROL, FO 84/1082, ff. 214—217.		Wallis, **ZEDL** II, pp. 306—308.
0880				Argyll, **DAAM** II, p. 512, ex.
0881		NARS, LI 1/1/1, pp. 1005—1007.	MS.10779 (21)	
0882				Monk, **DLCL**, 2nd edition (1860), pp. 358—360.
0883		NMLZ, on display.	MS.10779 (20)	Oswell, **WCO** II, pp. 56—59.
0884		Privately owned.		Monk, **DLCL**, 2nd edition (1860), pp. 360—361.
0885		MDNHLL, MSS. 120.		
0886		NARS, LI 1/1/1, pp. 1014—1017.		
0887	n	SALCT, S.A.MSS. Sect. A.		**JRGSL**, vol. 31 (1861), pp. 283—284.
0888	n	PROL, FO 63/871, ff. 84—95.	MS.10780 (4)	Wallis, **ZEDL** II, pp. 315—321.
0889		NLS, MS.10768, ff. 35—36.		Maggs' Cat. No. 828 (1955), no. 744.
0890		CMSL.	MS.10779 (12)	Monk, **DLCL**, 2nd edition (1860), pp. 361—362.
0891		Privately owned.	MS.10777 (4)	**OB**, vol. III, No. 32 (May 1923), pp. 597—598, **ex.**
0892		MDNHLL, MSS. 120.	MS.10777 (23)	
0893		Privately owned.	MS.10709, f. 77	Lloyd, **Liv.** end papers (facsimile).
0894	n			
0895	n	BLJ, Book no. 5521.		Monk, **DLCL**, 2nd edition (1860), pp. 362—364.
0896		NARS, LI 1/1/1, pp. 1021—1024.	MS.10779 (21)	
0897		NLS, MS. Dep. 237.		
0898		BLL, Add. MS. 39954, ff. 378—380.	MS.10780 (3)	
0899				Monk, **DLCL**, 2nd edition (1860), pp. 364—365.
0900	n	ULSOASL, Africa, Odds, Box 10, folder 4.	MS.10769	Seaver, **DLLL**, pp. 344—345, ex.

NO	RECIPIENT	DATE	PLACE	LENGTH	SIZE	TYPE
0901	The Earl of Malmesbury	31 May 59	River Zambesi	4 pp	fol	MS aut
0902	Andrew Smith	31 May 59	River Zambesi	1/ 4/ 4	fol	MS aut
0903	Commander, H.M. Ship	31 May 59	Shupanga	1/ 4/ 4	fol	Ph copy
0904	George Grey	1 Jun 59	River Shire	1/ 4/ 4	325 200	MS aut
0905	Agnes Livingstone 3	1 Jun 59	River Shire	1/ 4/ 4	330 200	MS aut
0906	Edmund Gabriel	4 Jun 59	River Shire	18 pp	misc	MS aut fr
0907	José M. Nuñes	11 Jun 59	Senna	2 pp		MS copy
0908	Tito Augosto d'A. Sicard	23 Jun 59	Tette	2 pp		Pr copy
0909	Tito Augosto d'A. Sicard	23 Jun 59	Tette	1 p		Pr copy
0910	Richard Thornton	25 Jun 59	Tette	1/ 4/ 4	322 203	MS aut
0911	Tito Augosto d'A. Sicard	26 Jun 59	Tette	1 p		MS copy
0912	Angela Burdett-Coutts	5, 22 Jul 59	Tette-Senna	2/ 6/ 6	322 203	MS aut
0913	Thomas Baines	11 Jul 59	Tette	1 p		MS copy
0914	Thomas Baines	21 Jul 59	Senna	1 p		Pr copy
0915	Roderick I. Murchison	22, 30 Jul 59	Senna	2/ 8/ 8	227 185	MS aut
0916	James Young	22 Jul 59	Senna	1 p		MS copy
0917	The Earl of Malmesbury	26 Jul 59	River Zambesi	12 pp	fol	MS aut
0918	Inclosure No. 2	[21−25 Jul 59]	[River Zambesi]	19 pp	fol	MS aut
0919	José M. Nuñes	27 Jul 59	Mazaro	4 pp		MS copy
0920	George Grey	30 Jul 59	Kongone Harbour	1/ 4/ 4	325 200	MS aut
0921	Philip Saumarez	30 Jul 59	Kongone Harbour			TS copy
0922	Thomas Maclear	31 Jul 59	Kongone Harbour	1/ 4/ 4	227 186	MS aut
0923	Messrs. Pye Brothers	31 Jul 59	Kongone Harbour	1/ 4/ 4	227 185	MS aut
0924	[Frederick Grey??]	31 Jul 59	Kongone Harbour	1/ 4/ 4	226 185	MS aut
0925	Stephen J. Hill	1 Aug 59	Kongone Harbour	4 pp	4to	Pr copy
0926	Edward Marjoribanks	6 Aug 59	River Zambesi	4 pp	fol	Pr copy
0927	James Young	6 Aug 59	River Zambesi	1 p		MS copy
0928	José M. Nuñes	8 Aug 59	Near Mazaro	3 pp		MS copy
0929	Roderick I. Murchison	8 Aug 59	River Zambesi	1/ 4/ 4	225 186	MS aut
0930	The Earl of Shelburne	9 Aug 59	River Zambesi	1/ 4/ 4	fol	MS aut
0931	Angela Burdett-Coutts	10 Oct 59	Chibisa's, River Shire	1/ 4/ 4	217 185	MS aut
0932	Roderick I. Murchison	10 Oct 59	Murchison's Cat., R. Shire	1/ 4/ 4	326 200	MS aut
0933	John Washington	10 Oct 59	Murchison's Cataract, Shire	1/ 4/ 4	325 201	MS aut
0934		10 Oct 59	River Shire	1 p		Pr copy
0935	James Young	12 Oct 59	Murchison's Cataracts	1/ 4/ 2	8vo	MS copy
0936	Thomas Maclear	14 Oct 59	Dakanamoio Is., Shire	1/ 4/ 4	325 202	MS aut
0937	John S. Moffat	15 Oct 59	River Shire	1/ 4/ 4	325 202	MS aut
0938	Lord John Russell	15 Oct 59	Murchison's Cat., R. Shire	19 pp	fol	MS aut
0939	Inclosure No. 1	7 Dec 59	Kongone	7 pp	fol	MS aut
0940	Inclosure No. 2	7 Dec 59	Kongone Harbour	4 pp	fol	MS aut
0941	Inclosure No. 3	7 Dec 59	Kongone Harbour	3 pp	fol	MS aut
0942	Henry Venn	15 Oct 59	[River Shire]	1/ 4/ 4	323 200	MS aut
0943	José M. Nuñes	17 Oct 59	River Shire	2 pp		Facsimile
0944	John Kirk	17 Oct 59	Dakana Moio Island	2 pp		Pr copy
0945	[Robert Gray]	20 Oct 59	River Shire	1/ 4/ 4	324 204	MS aut
0946	Agnes Livingstone 3	20 Oct 59	River Shire	1/ 4/ 4	215 185	MS aut
0947	Lord Palmerston	20 Oct 59	River Shire	1/ 4/ 4	322 204	MS aut
0948	[Wilbraham Taylor]	20 Oct 59	River Shire	2/ 8/ 8	215 185	MS aut
0949	John Washington	20 Oct, 30 Nov [59]	[River Shire]	2/ 8/ 8	misc	MS aut
0950	William Whewell	20 Oct 59	River Shire	3 pp		Pr copy

NO	N	LOCATION	NLS COPY	PUBLICATION
0901		PROL, FO 63/871, ff. 98—100	MS.10780 (4)	Wallis, **ZEDL** II, pp. 322—323.
0902		SNMDL.	MS.10708, f. 82	
0903	n	SNMDL.	MS.10707, f. 47	
0904	n	APLANZ, GL: L30.	MS.10777 (10a)	Monk, **DLCL**, pp. 367—368.
0905		BLL, Add. MS. 50184, ff. 28—29.	MS.10780 (3)	Blaikie, **PLDL**, pp. 255—257.
0906	n	BLJ, Book no. 6754.	MS.10769	**OB**, vol. III, No.30 (March 1923), pp.447—450.
0907		NARS, LI 1/1/1, pp, 1025—1026.	MS.10779 (21)	
0908	n			Wallis, **ZEDL** I, pp. 109—110.
0909				Wallis, **ZEDL** I, pp. 110.
0910	n	NLS, MS. 10707, ff. 49—50.		Tabler, **ZPRT** I, pp. 103—104.
0911	n	AHUL, Moçambique Papeis, Pasta 16 (1859).		Wallis, **ZEDL** I, p. 112.
0912		Privately owned.		Monk, **DLCL**, 2nd edition (1860), pp. 368—370.
0913	n	PROL, FO 63/871, f. 222.	MS.10780 (4)	Wallis, **ZEDL** I, pp. 115—116.
0914	n			Wallis, **ZEDL** I, p. 118.
0915		NARS, LI 1/1/1, pp. 1029—1036.		
0916		MDNHLL, MSS. 120.		
0917	n	PROL, FO 63/871, ff. 116—122.	MS.10780 (4)	Wallis, **ZEDL** II, pp. 323—326.
0918	n	RGSL, Archives, DL 3/4/2.	MS.10780 (5)	Wallis, **ZEDL** II, pp. 326—331.
0919		NARS, LI 1/1/1, pp. 1037—1040.	MS.10779 (21)	
0920	n	APLANZ, GL: L30.	MS.10777 (10a)	Monk, **DLCL**, 2nd edition (1860), pp. 366—367.
0921		ULSOASL, Africa, Odds, Box 10, folder 4.		
0922		NARS, LI 1/1/1, pp. 1041—1044.		Blaikie, **PLDL**, p. 262, ex. (?).
0923		WIHMLL, MS. 67480.	MS. 10779 (15)	
0924		NARS, LI 2/1/1.		Sotheby's Cat., 29 Jun 1948, lot 492. (?)
0925	n		MS.10769	Christie's Cat., 23 Jun 1976, lot 212.
0926				Sotheby's Cat., 1 Aug 1939, lot 815.
0927	n	MDNHLL, MSS. 120.		
0928		NARS, LI 1/1/1, pp. 1050—1052.	MS.10779 (21)	
0929		NARS, LI 1/1/1, pp. 1046—1049.		
0930		PROL, FO 84/1082, ff. 218—219.		
0931		Privately owned.		
0932		NARS, LI 1/1/1, pp. 1059—1062.		**The Times**, 2 Mar 1860, p. 10 c. 6.
0933		MDNHLL, MSS. 120.	MS.10777 (23)	
0934	n			Monk, **DLCL**, 2nd edition (1860), p. 376.
0935	n	NLS, MS. Dep. 237.		
0936		NARS, LI 1/1/1, pp. 1063—1066.		
0937	n	NARS, MO 1/1/6, pp. 648—651.		Wallis, **TMaM**, pp. 82—85.
0938	n	PROL, FO 63/871, ff. 232—241.	MS.10780 (4)	Wallis, **ZEDL** II, pp. 332—335.
0939		PROL, FO 63/871, ff. 261—264.	MS.10780 (4)	Wallis, **ZEDL** II, pp. 336—337.
0940		PROL, FO 63/871, ff. 265—266.	MS.10780 (4)	Wallis, **ZEDL** II, pp. 337—338.
0941		PROL, FO 63/871, ff. 267—268.	MS.10780 (4)	Wallis, **ZEDL** II, pp. 338—339.
0942	n	CMSL.	MS.10779 (12)	
0943	n			Moir, **ALATR**, between pp. 8 and 9.
0944	n			Foskett, **ZmDc**, pp. 58—59.
0945		NARS, LI 1/1/1, pp. 1067—1070.		
0946		BLL, Add. MS. 50184, ff. 30—31.	MS.10780 (3)	
0947		NLS, MS. 10768, ff. 37—38.	MS.10780 (4)	Maggs' Cat. No. 828 (1955), no. 744.
0948	n	NARS, LI 2/1/1.	MS.10708, f. 86	Ransford, **LLDN**, facs. opp. p. 102, ex.
0949		MDNHLL, MSS.120.	MS.10777 (23)	
0950				Monk, **DLCL**, 2nd edition (1860), pp. 376—378.

NO	RECIPIENT	DATE	PLACE	LENGTH	SIZE		TYPE
0951		20 Oct 59	River Shire				NS copy
0952	[J. Bevan Braithwaite]	24 Oct 59	River Shire	1/ 4/ 4	322	203	MS aut
0953	Thomas & Mary Archer	26 Oct 59	River Shire, Eastern Africa	1/ 4/ 4	fol		MS aut
0954	Frederick Fitch	28 Oct 59	River Shire, East Africa	2/ 8/ 8	4to		Ph copy
0955	Frederick Grey	28 Oct 59	River Shire	1/ 4/ 4	323	200	MS aut
0956	Thomas Milne	28 Oct 59	River Shire, Eastern Africa	1/ 4/ 4	322	203	MS aut
0957	Lyon Playfair	28 Oct 59	River Shire	3 pp			Pr copy
0958	John Kirk	29 Oct 59	Shamoara	1/ 4/ 4	227	185	MS aut
0959	Agnes Livingstone 1	31 Oct 59	River Zambesi	1/ 4/ 4	215	185	MS aut
0960	John Murray	1 Nov 59	River Shire	1/ 4/ 4	210	185	MS aut
0961		1 Nov 59	River Shire				NS copy
0962	William E.A. Gordon	3 Nov 59	[River Shire]	2 pp			Pr copy
0963	John Kirk	3 Nov 59		1/ 2/ 2	86	184	MS aut
0964	Thomas Maclear	3 Nov 59	Mouth of the Shire	1/ 4/ 4	325	203	MS aut
0965	British Association	4 Nov 59	River Shire	5 pp			Pr copy
0966	Andrew Drew	4 Nov 59	Mouth of Shire, Zambesi	4 pp	fol		MS aut
0967	John Washington	5 Nov 59	River Zambesi, Shupanga	2/ 8/ 8	323	203	MS aut
0968	John Kirk	6 Nov 59	Shupanga	1/ 4/ 4	144	92	MS aut
0969	Roderick I. Murchison	6 Nov 59	Shupanga	1/ 4/ 4	325	203	MS aut
0970	William C. Oswell	7 Nov 59	River Shire	1/ 4/ 4	325	204	MS aut
0971	John Washington	10 Nov 59	Kongone Harbour	1/ 4/ 4	325	201	MS aut
0972	Inclosure No. 1	13 Nov 59	[Kongone Harbour]	1/ 4/ 4	327	202	MS aut
0973	Lord John Russell	20 Nov 59	Kongone Harbour	14 pp	fol		MS aut
0974	Inclosure No. 1	6 Dec 59	[Kongone Harbour]	8 pp	fol		MS aut
0975	Lord John Russell	9 Dec 59	Kongone Harbour	2 pp	fol		MS aut
0976	Inclosure No. 1	9 Dec 59	Kongone Harbour	3 pp	fol		MS aut
0977	Inclosure No. 2	12 Dec 59	Kongone	1 p	fol		MS aut
0978	Frederick Grey	10 Dec 59	Kongone Harbour	2/ 6/ 6	323	200	MS aut
0979	Roderick I. Murchison	10 Dec 59	Kongone	1/ 4/ 4	202	114	MS aut
0980	José M. Nuñes	24 Dec 59	Mazaro	3 pp			MS copy
0981		[1 Sep—31 Dec 59?]		1/ 2/ 2	136	200	MS aut
0982	James Young	[1859]		1/ 4/ 4	226	186	MS aut in
0983	José M. Nuñes	9 Jan 60	Shupanga	6 pp			MS copy
0984	Peter Le Neve Foster	12 Jan 60	River Zambesi, East Africa	4 pp			MS copy
0985	J. Bevan Braithwaite	26 Jan, 7 Feb 60	River Zambesi	3/12/12	323	202	MS aut
0986		26 Jan 60	River Zambesi				MS copy
0987	James Young	28 Jan 60	Zambesi	1/ 4/ 4	321	201	MS aut
0988	John Washington	4 Feb 60	Tette	3/12/12	322	202	MS aut
0989	Heinrich Barth	6 Feb 60	Tette				TS copy
0990	Richard Thornton	6 Feb 60	Tette	1/ 4/ 4			MS aut
0991	Roderick I. Murchison	7 Feb 60	Tette	1/ 4/ 4	215	185	MS aut
0992	Lord John Russell	7 Feb 60	Tette	7 pp	fol		MS aut
0993	Inclosure No. 2	20 Feb 60	Kongone	6 pp	fol		MS aut
0994	James Young	[7 Feb 60??]	[Tette]	2/ 8/ 4	267	215	MS aut in
0995	Richard Thornton	8 Feb 60	Tette	1/ 4/ 4	182	111	MS aut
0996	José M. Nuñes	16 Feb 60	Senna	4 pp			MS copy
0997	Mr. Randall	20 Feb 60	Zambesi	3 pp			MS copy
0998	John Washington	20 Feb 60	Shupanga	2/ 8/ 8	216	185	MS aut
0999	Thomas Maclear	22 Feb, 12 Mar 60	Kongone	3/12/12	215	186	MS aut
1000	Agnes Livingstone 3	28 Feb 60	Kongone	1/ 4/ 2	265	215	MS aut

NO	N	LOCATION	NLS COPY	PUBLICATION
0951				**Glasgow Herald**, 8 May 1860, p. 2, c. 3.
0952		NLS, MS. Dep. 237.		
0953		NLS, MS. 10707, ff. 52—53.		
0954		NARS, LI 2/1/1.	MS.10779 (21)	
0955		RCSL, MSS. Sc 99.	MS.10779 (13)	
0956		NLS, MS. 10768, ff. 39—40.		
0957				**PRSE**, vol. IV (Nov 1857—Apr 1862), pp. 311—313.
0958		Foskett Collection.		Foskett, **ZmDc**, p. 60.
0959		NLS, MS. 10701, ff. 104—105.		
0960		JMPL.		
0961	n			**Athenaeum**, No. 1688 (3 Mar 1860), p. 304.
0962	n			Wallis, **ZEDL** I, pp. 129—130.
0963		Foskett Collection.		Foskett, **ZmDc**, p. 61.
0964		NARS, LI 1/1/1, pp. 1074—1077.		
0965				**RTMBA**, pp. 164—168.
0966	n	E.M. privately owned.		Sotheby's Cat., 7 Dec 1956, lot 408.
0967		MDNHLL, MSS. 120.	MS.10777 (23)	
0968		Foskett Collection.		Foskett, **ZmDc**, p. 62.
0969		NARS, LI 1/1/1, pp. 1078—1081.		
0970		NMLZ, on display.	MS.10779 (20)	Oswell, **WCO** II, pp. 62—65.
0971		MDNHLL, MSS. 120.	MS.10777 (23)	
0972	n	MDNHLL, MSS. 120.	MS.10777 (23)	
0973	n	PROL, FO 63/871, ff. 250—256.	MS.10780 (4)	Wallis, **ZEDL** II , pp. 340—343.
0974	n	PROL, FO 63/871, ff. 257—260.	MS.10780 (4)	Wallis, **ZEDL** II, pp. 343—345.
0975	n	PROL, FO 63/871, f. 269.	MS.10780 (4)	Wallis, **ZEDL** II, p. 339.
0976		PROL, FO 63/871, ff. 271—272.	MS.10780 (4)	
0977		PROL, FO 36/871, f. 273.	MS.10780 (4)	Wallis, **ZEDL** II, pp. 339—340.
0978		RCSL, MSS. Sc 99.	MS.10779 (13)	
0979		NARS, LI 1/1/1, pp. 1082—1085.		
0980		NARS, LI 1/1/1, pp. 1086—1088.	MS.10779 (21)	
0981		NLS, MS. 10768, f. 41.		Maggs' Cat. No. 894 (1964), no. 621.
0982		NMLZ, G5.		
0983		NARS, LI 1/1/1, pp. 1089—1094.	MS.10779 (21)	
0984		KCLUND.		
0985		NLS, MS. Dep. 237.		Blaikie, **PLDL**, p. 267, ex.
0986	n	NARS, ST 1/1/1.		Wallis, **ZJJS**, pp. 205—208.
0987		NMLZ, G5.		
0988		MDNHLL, MSS. 120.	MS.10777 (23)	
0989		RGSL, Barth Correspondence.		
0990		NLS, MS. 10707, ff. 54—56.		Wallis, **ZEDL** I, p. 149.
0991		NARS, LI 1/1/1, pp. 1099—1102.		Blaikie, **PLDL**, p. 268, ex.
0992	n	PROL, FO 63/871, ff. 384—387.	MS.10780 (4)	Wallis, **ZEDL** II, pp. 345—346.
0993	n	PROL, FO 63/871, ff. 390—393.	MS.10780 (4)	Wallis, **ZEDL** II, pp. 346—348.
0994		NMLZ, G5.		
0995		KPLSA.	MS.10779 (11)	
0996		NARS, LI 1/1/1, pp. 1103—1106.	MS.10779 (21)	
0997		NLS, MS. 10773, pp. 173—175.		
0998		MDNHLL, MSS. 120	MS.10777 (23)	
0999		NARS, LI 1/1/1, pp. 1107—1118.		
1000		NLS, MS. 10704, ff. 11—12.		

NO	RECIPIENT	DATE	PLACE	LENGTH	SIZE	TYPE
1001	Thomas S. Livingstone	28 Feb 60	Kongone	1/ 4/ 4	210 185	MS aut
1002	James Young	29 Feb 60	Kongone	1 p		MS copy
1003	Roderick I. Murchison	10 Mar 60	Kongone	1/ 4/ 4	201 161	MS aut
1004	Edward Baines	12 Mar 60	[Zambesi]	3 pp	4to	Pr copy
1005	Frederick Grey	21 Mar 60	River Zambesi	2 pp		Pr copy
1006	[Robert Gray]	21 Mar 60	River Zambesi	1/ 4/ 4	320 201	MS aut
1007	Edmund Gabriel	25 Mar 60	Mazaro, Zambesi River	1/ 4/ 4	326 200	MS aut
1008	George Grey	25 Mar 60	Mazaro, Zambesi River	3/12/11	265 215	MS aut
1009	José M. Nuñes	25 Mar 60	Mazaro	2 pp		MS copy
1010	John Washington	25 Mar 60	Mazaro, Zambesi	1/ 4/ 3	267 215	MS aut
1011	Robert Gray	26 Mar 60	Mazaro, River Zambesi	4 pp		MS copy
1012	The Duke of Wellington	[Mar 60?]				TS copy
1013	George Grey	6 Apr 60	Senna	1/ 4/ 4	325 200	MS aut
1014	[Edgar L.] Layard	7 Apr 60	Senna	1/ 4/ 3	267 214	MS aut
1015	[Samuel Wilberforce]	7 Apr 60	Senna	1/ 4/ 4	323 203	MS aut
1016	Robert Gray	8 Apr 60	Senna	1/ 4/ 4	322 202	MS aut
1017	George Grey	[10 Apr 60]	[Senna]	1 p		Pr copy
1018	José M. Nuñes	10 Apr 60	Senna	3 pp		MS copy
1019	Lord John Russell	10 Apr 60	Senna, River Zambesi	10 pp	fol	MS aut
1020	Inclosure No. 1	10 Apr 60	Senna	1 p		Pr copy
1021	John S. Moffat	20 Apr, 7 May 60	Lupata-Tette	1/ 4/ 4	325 202	MS aut
1022	Thomas Maclear	7 May 60	Kaimbe Is. opposite Tette	1/ 4/ 4	327 201	MS aut
1023	José M. Nuñes	14 May 60	Tette	4 pp		MS copy
1024	[Candido Cardoso]	16 May 60	Tette	1 p		Pr copy
1025	[Candido Cardoso]	25 May 60	[10 days N.W. of Tette]	2 pp		Pr copy
1026	James Young	22 Jul, 10 Aug [60]	Near Kalosi Is., Zambesi	7 pp		MS copy
1027	Robert Moffat 1	10 Aug 60	Zambesi Falls	1 p		Pr copy
1028	Thomas Maclear	17 Aug, 25 Dec 60	Sesheke-Is. 1 day above Senna	8 pp	fol	MS aut
1029	John S. Moffat	21 Aug 60	Sesheke	1/ 4/ 4	265 214	MS aut
1030	Angela Burdett-Coutts	4 Sep 60	[Town of Sesheke]	1/ 4/ 4	320 201	MS aut
1031	Lord John Russell	6 Sep 60	Town of Sesheke	20 pp	fol	MS aut
1032	Inclosure No. 1	6 Sep 60	Sesheke	4 pp	fol	MS aut
1033	Inclosure No. 2	9 Sep 60	Sesheke	6 pp	fol	MS aut
1034	Inclosure No. 3	[9 Sep 60?]	[Sesheke?]	1 p		Pr copy
1035		8 Sep, 28 Nov 60	Sesheke-Tete	1 p		NS copy
1036	Roderick I. Murchison	10 Sep 60	Sesheke	4 pp	fol	MS aut
1037	John Washington	12 Sep 60	Sesheke	2/ 8/ 8	226 186	MS aut
1038	Arthur Tidman	10 Nov 60	Chicova, Zambesi	3/12/ 5	268 213	MS aut
1039	Inclosure No. 1	26 Nov 60	Tette	1/ 2/ 1	318 202	MS aut
1040	Lord John Russell	24 Nov 60	Tette	11 pp	fol	MS aut
1041	Inclosure No. 1	[24 Nov 60]	[Tette]	3 pp	fol	MS aut
1042	Inclosure No. 2	29 Dec 60	Senna	1 p	fol	MS aut
1043	Inclosure No. 3	29 Dec 60	Senna	1 p	fol	MS aut
1044	[Inclosure No. 4?]	28 Dec 60	Senna	1 p	fol	MS aut
1045	Angela Burdett-Coutts	24 Nov 60	Tette	1/ 4/ 4	215 186	MS aut
1046	Charles M. Hay	26 Nov 60	Tette	1/ 4/ 4		MS copy
1047	Roderick I. Murchison	26 Nov 60	Tette	4 pp	fol	MS aut in
1048	John Washington	26 Nov, 20 Dec 60	Tette	2/ 8/ 8	200 163	MS aut in
1049	[Robert Gray?]	28 Nov 60	Tette	1/ 4/ 4	222 187	MS aut
1050	Agnes Livingstone 3	28 Nov 60	Tette	1/ 4/ 2	267 215	MS aut

NO	N	LOCATION	NLS COPY	PUBLICATION
1001		NLS, MS.10701, ff. 106—107.		
1002	n	NLS, MS. Dep. 237.		
1003		NARS, LI 1/1/1, pp. 1122—1125.		Blaikie, **PLDL**, p. 269, ex.
1004				Sotheby's Cat., 31 Oct 1961, lot 264.
1005				Wallis, **ZEDL** I, pp. 157—158.
1006		WIHMLL, MS. 63005.	MS.10779 (15)	
1007	n	BLJ, Book no. 6754.	MS.10769	Sotheby's Cat., 3 May 1971, lot 279.
1008	n	APLANZ, GL: L30.	MS.10777 (10a)	
1009		NARS, LI 1/1/1, pp. 1130—1131.	MS.10779 (21)	
1010		MDNHLL, MSS. 120.	MS.10777 (23)	
1011		USPGL, B4 ii, (54—55)	MS.10779 (14)	
1012		RGSL, Library, Y 224.11.		
1013	n	APLANZ, GL: L30.	MS.10777 (10a)	
1014		NLS, MS. 10768, ff. 43—44.		Sawyer's Cat. SA/44 (1965), no. 73.
1015	n	NARS, LI 1/1/1, pp. 1132—1135.		**The Times**, 4 Dec 1860, p. 9, c.5.
1016	n	BLJ, Book no. 5318, Acc. Reg. 4669.		Sotheby's Cat., 29 Jun 1939, lot 479.
1017				Wallis, **ZEDL** II, p. 351.
1018		NARS, LI 1/1/1, pp. 1136—1138.	MS.10779 (21)	
1019	n	PROL, FO 63/871, ff. 441—446.	MS.10780 (4)	Wallis, **ZEDL** II, pp. 348—350.
1020				Wallis, **ZEDL** II, p. 351.
1021		NARS, MO 1/1/6, pp. 667—670.		Wallis, **TMaM**, pp. 89—92.
1022		NARS, LI 1/1/1, pp. 1164—1167.		
1023		NARS, LI 1/1/1, pp. 1168—1171.	MS.10779 (21)	
1024	n			Wallis, **ZEDL** I, p. 165.
1025	n			Wallis, **ZEDL** I, pp. 167—168.
1026	n	ALUSG, Jas. Young Papers, Copy Book 1860—63.		**Glasgow Herald**, 20 Apr 1861, p. 2, c. 3.
1027				Blaikie, **PLDL**, p. 275, ex.
1028	n	SNMDL, Journal no. 9.	MS.10715	
1029		NARS, MO 1/1/6, pp. 752—755.		Wallis, **TMaM**, pp. 103—105.
1030	n	Privately owned.		
1031	n	PROL, FO 63/894 I, ff. 47—57.	MS.10780 (4)	Wallis, **ZEDL** II, pp. 387—392.
1032		PROL, FO 63/894 I, ff. 58—59.	MS.10780 (4)	Wallis, **ZEDL** II, P. 393.
1033		PROL, FO 63/894 I, ff. 60—63.	MS.10780 (4)	Wallis, **ZEDL** II, pp. 395—396.
1034	n			Wallis, **ZEDL** II, p. 394.
1035	n			**Glasgow Herald**, 11 Jun 1861, p. 2.
1036		RGSL, Archives, DL 3/6/1.	MS.10780 (5)	**The Times**, 23 Apr 1861, p. 5, c. 5.
1037		MDNHLL, MSS. 120.	MS.10777 (23)	
1038		ULSOASL, Africa, Wooden Box of L's letters.	MS.10778	Chamberlin, **SLFL**, pp. 270—272.
1039		ULSOASL, Africa, Wooden Box of L's letters.	MS.10778	
1040	n	PROL, FO 63/894 I, ff. 36—41.	MS.10780 (4)	Wallis, **ZEDL** II, pp. 396—399.
1041		PROL, FO 63/894 I, ff. 42—43.	MS.10780 (4)	Wallis, **ZEDL** II, pp. 399—400.
1042		PROL, FO 63/894 I, f. 44.	MS.10780 (4)	Wallis, **ZEDL** II, pp. 400—401.
1043	n	PROL, FO 63/894 I, f. 64.	MS.10780 (4)	
1044		PROL, FO 63/894 I, f. 45.	MS.10780 (4)	
1045		Privately owned.		
1046		NARS, LI 1/1/1, pp. 1176—1179.	MS.10779 (21)	
1047		RGSL, Archives, DL 3/6/2.	MS.10780 (5)	**The Times**, 23 Apr 1861, p. 5, c.5.
1048		MDNHLL, MSS. 120.	MS.10777 (23)	
1049	n	WIHMLL, MS. 67259.	MS.10779 (15)	
1050		BLL, Add. MS. 50184, ff. 33—34.	MS.10780 (3)	

NO	RECIPIENT	DATE	PLACE	LENGTH	SIZE	TYPE
1051	Thomas S. Livingstone	28 Nov 60	Tette	1/ 2/ 2	265 215	MS aut
1052	Joseph Moore	28 Nov 60	Tette	1/ 4/ 4	210 185	MS aut
1053	John Washington	28 Nov 60	Tette	2/ 8/ 8	322 203	MS aut
1054	James McWilliam	28 Nov 60	[Tette]	3 pp		Pr copy
1055		28 Nov 60	[Tette]	3 pp		Pr copy
1056	John S. Moffat	29 Nov 60	Tette	1/ 4/ 4	320 202	MS aut
1057	Hon. Secs. Ox & C Mission	29 Nov 60,14, 22 Jan 61	Tette-Kongone	6/22/22	322 200	MS aut
1058	Agnes Livingstone 2	30 Nov 60	Tette	1/ 2/ 2	218 185	MS aut
1059	George Back	30 Nov 60	Tette	1/ 4/ 4	320 200	MS aut
1060	[William C. Oswell?]	[Aug—Nov 60]		1/ 2/ 2	177 114	MS aut in
1061	James Young	4, 20 Dec 60	Lupata—[Sena]	6 pp		MS copy
1062	Richard Owen	29 Dec 60	Senna	6 pp	4to	MS aut
1063	José M. Nuñes	1 Jan 61	Shupanga	4 pp		MS copy
1064	Richard Thornton	1 Jan 61	Shupanga	1/ 4/ 3	226 186	MS aut
1065	John S. & Emily Moffat	14 Jan 61	Kongone	2/ 4/ 4	222 185	MS aut
1066	Lord Palmerston	15 Jan 61	Kongone mouth of Zambesi	1/ 4/ 4	322 200	MS aut
1067	Frederick Fitch	19 Jan 61	Kongone	1/ 4/ 4	4to	Ph copy
1068	J. Bevan Braithwaite	24 Jan 61	Kongone	1/ 4/ 4	323 202	MS aut
1069	[Robert Moffat 1??]	28 Jan 61	Kongone	1/ 4/ 4	213 186	MS aut
1070	James Young	[Jan 61]		2 pp		Pr copy
1071	Thomas Maclear	1 Feb 61	Kongone	1/ 4/ 4	175 114	MS aut
1072	Roderick I. Murchison	1 Feb 61	Kongone	1/ 4/ 4	215 185	MS aut
1073	John Washington	1 Feb 61	Kongone	1/ 4/ 4	217 186	MS aut
1074	José M. Nuñes	7 Feb 61	Kongone	4 pp	8vo	Pr copy
1075	Richard B. Crawford	9 Feb 61	Kongone	1/ 4/ 2	325 201	MS aut copy
1076	Lord John Russell	9 Feb 61	Kongone Harbour	7 pp	fol	MS aut
1077	James Hannan	15 Feb 61	"Pioneer" at Sea	1/ 4/ 4	182 111	MS aut
1078	William King	15 Feb 61	On Board "Pioneer"	1/ 4/ 4	185 113	MS aut
1079	Agnes Livingstone 3	20 Feb 61	"Pioneer" off Madagascar	1/ 4/ 4	204 132	MS aut
1080	Roderick I. Murchison	20 Feb 61	"Pioneer" at Sea	1/ 4/ 4	215 186	MS aut
1081	Christopher P. Rigby	25 Feb 61	"Pioneer" off Rovuma	7 pp		Pr copy
1082	H. Norton Shaw	1 Mar 61	"Pioneer" off Rovuma	6 pp		MS aut
1083	Lord John Russell	4, 10 Mar 61	HMS "Pioneer" in Rovuma Bay	1/ 4/ 4	325 200	MS aut copy
1084	John Washington	5 Mar 61	Rovuma Bay	2/ 8/ 8	182 112	MS aut
1085	[James McWilliam?]	[5 Mar 61?]	[Rovuma Bay?]	1/ 2/ 2	181 110	MS aut
1086	Robert Moffat 1	6 Mar 61	HMS "Pioneer"	1/ 4/ 4	182 110	MS aut
1087	Francis Skead	6 [Mar] 61	Rovuma Bay	2/ 8/ 8	185 114	MS aut
1088	Editor of the "Times"	[5 Feb?—] 6 Mar 61		5/20/20	182 111	MS aut
1089	J. Bevan Braithwaite	7 Mar 61	HMS "Pioneer" at Rovuma Bay	1/ 4/ 4	182 111	MS aut
1090	Henry [Keppel?]	7 Mar 61	HMS "Pioneer" in Rovuma Bay	2/ 8/ 8	182 111	MS aut
1091	[Edmund Gabriel]	8 Mar 61	Rovuma Bay	4 pp		MS copy
1092	Andrew Drew	11 Mar 61	"Pioneer"[Rovuma Bay]	2 pp	4to	MS aut
1093	Lord John Russell	11, 13 Mar 61	HMS "Pioneer" in Rovuma Bay	7 pp	fol	MS aut
1094	John Washington	11 Mar 61	"Pioneer," Rovuma Bay	1/ 4/ 2	251 202	MS aut
1095	Thomas Maclear	12 Mar 61	HMS "Pioneer"	1/ 4/ 4	251 203	MS aut
1096	Angela Burdett-Coutts	13 Mar 61	HMS "Pioneer"	1/ 4/ 3	251 202	MS aut
1097	Mary Livingstone	14 Mar 61	Rovuma River	1/ 4/ 4	202 160	MS aut
1098	Editor of the "Times"	[15 Mar 61?]	[Rovuma River?]	1/ 4/ 4	251 203	MS aut
1099	Daniel J. May	25 Mar [61]	River Rovuma	2 pp		Pr copy
1100	George Grey	4, [8 or 9] Apr 61	Mohilla Is., near Comoro	2/ 8/ 8	325 200	MS aut

NO	N	LOCATION	NLS COPY	PUBLICATION
1051		NLS, MS. 10701, ff. 108–109.		
1052		NLS, MS. 10768, ff. 45–46.		Blaikie, **PLDL**, pp. 278–279.
1053		MDNHLL, MSS. 120.	MS.10777 (23)	
1054				**The Lancet**, 24 August 1861, pp. 184–186.
1055				**JFHS**, vol. 14, no. 1 (1917), p. 28.
1056		JPLAM.	MS.10779 (8)	Wallis, **TMaM**, pp. 120–122.
1057	n	USPGL, B4 ii, ff. 63–71.	MS.10779 (14)	Wallis, **ZEDL** II, pp. 351–362.
1058		NLS, MS. 10701, ff. 110–111.		
1059		RGSL, Back Collection.		
1060		NMLZ, G5.		
1061	n	ALUSG, Jas. Young Papers, Copy Book 1860–63.		Blaikie, **PLDL**, pp. 277–278.
1062		BMNHL, OC 62.	MS.10777 (21)	
1063		NARS, LI 1/1/1, pp. 1202–1205.	MS.10779 (21)	
1064	n	NLS, MS. 10707, ff. 60–61.		Tabler, **ZPRT** II, pp. 220–221.
1065		NARS, MO 1/1/6, pp. 849–852.		Wallis, **TMaM**, pp. 129–131.
1066		NLS, MS. 10768, ff. 47–48.		Maggs' Cat. No. 828 (1955), no. 744.
1067		NARS, LI 2/1/1.	MS.10779 (21)	
1068		NLS, MS. Dep. 237.		
1069	n	WIHMLL, MS. 67259.	MS.10779 (15)	
1070				Blaikie, **PLDL**, pp. 279–280.
1071		SALCT, S.A. MSS. Sect. A.	MS.10780 (1)	
1072		NARS, LI 1/1/1, pp. 1222–1225.		
1073		MDNHLL, MSS.120.	MS.10777 (23)	Clendennen, **DLJW**, pp. 11–13.
1074				Sawyer's Cat. No. 266 (1964), no. 483.
1075	n	NARS, LI 1/1/1, pp. 1230–1231.		
1076	n	PROL, FO 63/894 I, ff. 65–68.	MS.10780 (4)	
1077		WIHMLL, MS. 91833.	MS.10779 (15)	**Wesleyan Times**, 26 Aug 1861, p. 533.
1078		PACO, King Papers, vol I, pp. 566–569.	MS.10777 (24)	
1079		BLL, Add. MS. 50184, ff. 35–36.	MS.10780 (3)	
1080		NARS, LI 1/1/1, pp. 1240–1243.		
1081				Russell, **RZST**, pp. 226–227.
1082		RGSL, Archives, DL 3/9/1.	MS.10780 (5)	
1083	n	NARS, LI 1/1/1, pp. 1244–1247.		
1084		MDNHLL, MSS. 120.	MS.10777 (23)	Clendennen, **DLJW**, pp. 13–14.
1085	n	WCLUWJ, Hist. and Lit. Papers.	MS.10779 (10)	
1086		BLL, Add. MS. 50184, ff. 37–37*.	MS.10780 (3)	
1087	n	MALCITPC.	MS.10777 (8)	Sotheby's Cat., 13 May 1963, lot 253.
1088		NLS, MS. Dep. 237.		
1089		NLS, MS. Dep. 237.		
1090		NLS, MS.10768, ff. 49–52.		
1091		RGSL, Archives, DL 3/9/2.		
1092		E.M. privately owned.		Sawyer's Cat. No. 266 (1964), no. 484.
1093	n	PROL, FO 63/894 I, ff. 87–90.	MS.10780 (4)	
1094		MDNHLL, MSS. 120.	MS.10777 (23)	Clendennen, **DLJW**, p. 14.
1095		NARS, LI 1/1/1, pp. 1251–1254.		
1096		Privately owned.		
1097		NARS, LI 1/1/1, pp. 1256–1259.		
1098		NLS, MS. Dep. 237.		
1099	n			Wallis, **ZEDL** II, pp. 308–309.
1100	n	APLANZ, GL: L30.	MS.10777 (10a)	**Glasgow Herald**, 7 Nov 1861, p. 4, c. 3.

NO	RECIPIENT	DATE	PLACE	LENGTH	SIZE		TYPE
1101	[Roderick I. Murchison?]	9 Apr 61	Pomony Bay, Johanna	2 pp			Pr copy
1102	William Sunley	[10 Apr 61??]	Johanna	1/ 2/ 1	231	172	MS aut
1103	Editor of the "Times"	[11 Apr 61]	Johanna	7 pp	228	187	MS aut
1104	Lord John Russell	16 Apr 61	Johanna	11 pp		fol	MS aut
1105	Inclosure No. 1	[20 Apr 61]	[Johanna]	3 pp		fol	MS aut
1106	Inclosure No. 2	[20 Apr 61]	[Johanna]	1 p		fol	MS aut
1107	Inclosure No. 3	[20 Apr 61]	[Johanna]	1 p		fol	MS aut
1108	William Sunley	17 Apr 61	Johanna	1/ 4/ 3	228	184	MS aut
1109	John Washington	18 Apr 61	Johanna	2/ 8/ 7	325	200	MS aut
1110	Henry Keppel	20 Apr 61	Johanna				MS copy
1111	Thomas Maclear	20 Apr 61	Johanna	1/ 4/ 4	325	202	MS aut
1112	Daniel J. May	20 Apr 61	Johanna	2 pp		fol	MS aut copy
1113	Roderick I. Murchison	20 Apr 61	Johanna	1/ 4/ 4	228	187	MS aut
1114	Henry Keppel	1 May 61	Kongone				MS copy
1115	José M. Nuñes	1 May 61	Kongone	4 pp			MS copy
1116	Custódio José da Silva	1 May 61	Kongone Harbour	2 pp			MS copy
1117	John Washington	1 May 61	Kongone Harbour	1/ 4/ 4	227	187	MS aut
1118	James Young	14 May 61	HMS "Pioneer"	1/ 4/ 4	325	200	MS aut
1119	Thomas Maclear	17 May 61	Shamo, River Shire	1/ 4/ 4	229	185	MS aut
1120	Agnes Livingstone 3	20 May 61	HMS "Pioneer," R. Shire	1/ 4/ 4	228	187	MS aut
1121	José M. Nuñes	20 May 61	River Shire	5 pp			MS aut
1122	Lord John Russell	20 May 61	HMS "Pioneer," R. Shire	3 pp		fol	MS aut
1123	Inclosure No. 1	20 May 61	River Shire	2 pp		fol	MS aut
1124	John Washington	20 May 61	R. Shire	1/ 2/ 1	326	202	MS aut
1125	Henry Keppel	21 May 61	River Shire				MS copy
1126	Robert Moffat 1	26 Aug 61	Murchison's Cataract, Shire	1/ 2/ 1	140	182	MS aut fr
1127	Robert Moffat 1	23 Sep [61]	Lake Nyassa	1/ 2/ 1	227	189	MS aut in
1128	Roderick I. Murchison	23 Sep, 26 Oct, 11, 25 Nov	Lake Nyassa – River Shire	4/16/16	227	185	MS aut
1129	[George Denman??]	[26 Sep 61?]	[120 miles up Lake Nyassa]	2/ 8/ 8	207	128	MS aut in
1130	Robert M. Livingstone	26 Sep 61	Lake Nyassa	1/ 4/ 4	208	129	MS aut
1131	Agnes Livingstone 3	12 Oct 61	Lake Nyassa	1/ 4/ 4	182	114	MS aut
1132	Thomas S. Livingstone	12 Oct 61	Lake Nyassa	1/ 4/ 4	182	113	MS aut
1133	William O. Livingstone	14 Oct 61	Lake Nyassa	1/ 4/ 4	171	106	MS aut
1134	William K. Tweedie	2, 18 Nov 61,1 Mar 62	River Shire – [Zambesi River]	2/ 8/ 8		fol	MS aut
1135	James Young	7 Nov 61	[River Shire]	1/ 4/ 4	208	129	MS aut
1136	Charles Mackenzie	9 Nov 61	[River Shire]	1 p			MS copy
1137	Lord John Russell	10 Nov 61 – [17 Dec 61]	HMS "Pioneer," R. Shire	16 pp		fol	MS aut
1138	Inclosure No. 1	15 Nov 61	Shire	4 pp		fol	MS aut
1139	Inclosure No. 2	[Nov 61]	[Shire]	2 pp		fol	MS aut
1140	Inclosure No. 3	[Nov 61]	[Shire]	3 pp		fol	MS aut
1141	J. Bevan Braithwaite	12 Nov 61	HMS "Pioneer"	1/ 4/ 4	228	185	MS aut
1142	[Thomas Maclear?]	12 Nov 61	HMS "Pioneer"				MS copy
1143	Lord Palmerston	12 Nov 61	River Shire	12 pp		4to	Pr copy
1144	George Frere	13 Nov 61	"Pioneer," Murchison's Cats.	1/ 4/ 4	228	187	MS aut
1145	George Grey	15 Nov 61	HMS "Pioneer"	1/ 4/ 4	230	185	MS aut
1146	William Sunley	18 Nov 61	River Shire	1/ 4/ 4	228	187	MS aut
1147	Arthur Tidman	24 Nov 61	River Shire, East Africa	2 pp		fol	MS aut copy
1148	Frederick Fitch	25 Nov 61	"Pioneer" or Moroñwi, Shire	2/ 8/ 8		misc	Ph copy
1149	Lord Kinnaird	25 Nov 61	HMS "Pioneer," R. Shire	3/12/12	225	180	Ph copy
1150	[Robert Moffat 1?]	25 Nov 61	HMS "Meroñue" or "Pioneer"	1/ 4/ 4	227	187	MS aut fr

NO	N	LOCATION	NLS COPY	PUBLICATION
1101				**PRGSL**, vol. VI (1861—2), pp. 20—21.
1102		SNMDL, Misc. MS. Material.	MS.10779 (3)	
1103	n	RGSL, Archives, DL 3/14.	MS.10780 (5)	
1104	n	PROL, FO 63/894 I, ff. 110—115.	MS.10780 (4)	
1105		PROL, FO 63/894 I, ff. 116—117.	MS.10780 (4)	
1106		PROL, FO 63/894 I, f.120.	MS.10780 (4)	
1107		PROL, FO 63/894 I, f. 121.	MS.10780 (4)	
1108		Privately owned.	MS.10777 (9)	
1109		MDNHLL, MSS. 120.	MS.10777 (23)	Clendennen, **DLJW**, pp. 14—17.
1110		MDNHLL, MSS. 120.		
1111		NARS, LI 1/1/1, pp. 1280—1283.		
1112	n	PROL, FO 63/894 I, ff. 118—118½.	MS.10780 (4)	
1113		NARS, LI 1/1/1, pp. 1276—1279.		
1114		MDNHLL, MSS. 120.		
1115		NARS, LI 1/1/1, pp. 1285—1288.	MS.10779 (21)	
1116	n	AHUL, Moçambique Papeis, Pasta 19 (1862).		
1117		MDNHLL, MSS. 120.	MS.10777 (23)	Clendennen, **DLJW**, pp. 17—18.
1118		NMLZ, G5.		
1119		NARS, LI 1/1/1, pp. 1298—1301.		
1120		BLL, Add. MS. 50184, ff. 38—39.	MS.10780 (3)	
1121		NARS, LI 1/1/1, pp. 1303—1307.	MS.10779 (21)	
1122	n	PROL, FO 63/894 I, ff. 139—140.	MS.10780 (4)	
1123		PROL, FO 63/894 I, ff. 141—144.	MS.10780 (4)	
1124		MDNHLL, MSS. 120.	MS.10777 (23)	Clendennen, **DLJW**, pp. 19—20.
1125		MDNHLL, MSS. 120.	MS.10777 (23)	
1126		BLL, Add. MS. 50184, f. 40.	MS.10780 (3)	
1127	n	BLL, Add. MS. 50184, f. 43.	MS.10780 (3)	
1128	n	NARS, LI 1/1/1, pp. 1317—1332.		For details see note.
1129		FMC, 1926 Box "General Series".	MS.10777 (12)	
1130	n	NLS, MS. 10701, ff. 112—113.		Blaikie, **PLDL**, p. 286.
1131		BLL, Add. MS. 50184, ff. 44—45.	MS.10780 (3)	
1132		NLS, MS. 10701, ff. 114—115.		Wilson, **DLSR**, pp. 19—21.
1133		LMCBS.	MS.10769 (11)	
1134		NLS, MS. 7792, ff. 1—4.		Smith, **LoAD**, pp. 451—457.
1135		NMLZ, G5.		
1136	n	USPGL, A1(I)A, Book 1, f. 24.		
1137	n	PROL, FO 63/894 I, ff. 163—170.	MS.10780 (4)	**PP** Sess. 1863, v. LXXI, [58] Class B pp. 191—194.
1138	n	PROL, FO 63/894 I, ff. 171—172.	MS.10780 (4)	**PP** Sess. 1863, v. LXXI, [58] Class B pp. 194—195.
1139	n	PROL, FO 63/894 I, f. 173.	MS.10780 (4)	**PP** Sess. 1863, v. LXXI, [58] Class B p. 195.
1140	n	PROL, FO 63/894 I, ff. 175—177.	MS.10780 (4)	**PP** Sess. 1863, v. LXXI, [58] Class B pp. 195—196.
1141		NLS, MS. Dep. 237.		
1142	n	GACT, Maclear Papers, Acc. 515.		**South African Advertiser and Mail**, 21 May 1862.
1143				Maggs' Cat. No. 823 (1954), no. 169.
1144		NMLZ, on display.	MS. 10779 (20)	OCDD Mission, **OP**, 1862, pp. 5—6.
1145	n	APLANZ, GL: L30.	MS.10777 (10a)	Foskett, **ZmDc**, pp. 160—162.
1146		BLJ, Book no. 5318, Acc. Reg. 4669.		Sotheby's Cat., 29 Jun 1939, lot 1480.
1147		SNMDL, Journal no. 9, pp. 235—236.	MS.10715	
1148		NARS, LI 2/1/1.	MS.10779 (21)	
1149		SNMDL.	MS.10708, f. 94.	
1150		BLL, Add. MS. 50184, ff. 41—42.	MS.10780 (3)	

NO	RECIPIENT	DATE	PLACE	LENGTH	SIZE	TYPE
1151	Agnes Livingstone 1	29 Nov 61	HMS "Pioneer'	1/ 4/ 4	228 188	MS aut
1152	John Washington	6, 20 Dec 61	HMS "Pioneer'	3/12/12	325 202	MS aut
1153		7 Dec 61	River Shire	1/ 4/ 4	220 186	MS aut
1154	Joseph D. Hooker	9 Dec 61	River Shire	2/ 6/ 6	228 185	MS aut
1155	Lyon Playfair	10 Dec 61	River Shire	1/ 4/ 4	230 187	MS aut
1156	John Washington	20 Dec 61	HMS "Pioneer"	1/ 4/ 3	325 201	MS aut
1157	[William Sunley]	[18 Nov–22 Dec 61]	["Pioneer," River Shire]	1/ 4/ 4	210 172	MS aut
1158		24 Dec 61	River Shire	1/ 4/ 4	320 193	MS aut
1159	John S. Moffat	24 Dec 61	River Shire	1/ 4/ 4	320 188	MS aut
1160	Lord John Russell	25 Dec 61	River Shire	1 p	fol	MS aut
1161						
1162	[The Earl of Clarendon?]	[Nov–Dec 61?]		20 pp	8vo	Pr copy
1163	Janet Livingstone	1 Jan 62	River Shire	1/ 4/ 4	322 192	MS aut
1164	William Monk	2 Jan 62	HMS "Pioneer," R. Shire	1 p		NS copy
1165	John Washington	6 Jan 62	River Shire	1/ 4/ 4	325 202	MS aut
1166	Amer. Geog. & Stat. Soc.	6 Jan 62	River Shire	1/ 4/ 4	320 205	MS aut
1167	Thomas S. Livingstone	7 Jan 62	River Shire	1/ 4/ 4	228 184	MS aut
1168	José M. Nuñes	22 Jan 62	Shupanga	3 pp		MS copy
1169	Christopher P. Rigby	23 Jan 62	River Shire	2 pp		Pr copy
1170	[Frederick Fitch]	31 Jan 62	Luabo Mouth of Zambesi	4 pp	fol	Ph copy
1171	John Washington	31 Jan 62	HMS "Pioneer," R. Zambesi	1/ 4/ 4	322 194	MS aut
1172	H. Norton Shaw	[13 Nov 61–31 Jan 62]		1/ 4/ 4	4to	MS aut
1173	John C. Wilson	1 Feb 62	Luabo Mouth of Zambesi			MS copy
1174	José M. Nuñes	5 Feb 62	Kongone	8 pp		MS copy
1175	[James Young]	[2–7 Feb 62]		1/ 4/ 4	322 195	MS aut fr
1176	[James Young]	[7 Feb 62?]		1/ 2/ 2	213 140	MS aut fr
1177	Robert Moffat 1	8 Feb 62	HM Exploring Ship "Pioneer"	1/ 4/ 4	228 187	MS aut in
1178	[Robert Moffat 1]	[8 Feb 62?]		1/ 2/ 1	228 185	MS aut in
1179	John Kirk	17 Feb 62	Maruru, 1′ above Paulo's	1/ 2/ 1	166 220	MS aut
1180	Baldwin W. Walker	17 Feb 62	River Zambesi	4/16/16	232 184	MS aut
1181	Heinrich Barth	18 Feb 62	HM Exploring Ship "Pioneer"			TS copy
1182	James Young	19 Feb 62	"Pioneer" in Zambesi	1/ 2/ 2	201 138	MS aut fr
1183	José M. Nuñes	21 Feb 62	HMS "Pioneer"	4 pp		MS copy
1184	John Washington	21 Feb 62	R. Zambesi	1/ 4/ 4	325 202	MS aut
1185	Lord John Russell	22 Feb 62	River Zambesi	6 pp	fol	MS aut
1186	Inclosure No. 1	[22 Feb 62]	[River Zambesi]	2 pp	fol	MS aut
1187	Inclosure No. 2	22 Feb 62	River Zambesi	3 pp	fol	MS aut
1188	John S. Moffat	23 Feb 62	Zambesi	2/ 8/ 8	228 186	MS aut
1189	Arthur Tidman	25 Feb 62	HMS Exploring Ship "Pioneer"	2/ 6/ 6	misc	MS aut
1190	Thomas Binney	27 Feb 62	HM Exploring Ship "Pioneer"	1/ 4/ 4	4to	MS aut
1191	[Frederick Fitch]	1 Mar 62	Zambesi	2 pp	4to	Ph copy
1192	Thomas Maclear	1 Mar 62	Zambesi	1/ 4/ 4	233 180	MS aut
1193	José M. Nuñes	6 Mar 62	Zambesi	4 pp		MS copy
1194	John Washington	7 Mar 62	near Shupanga, Zambesi	2/ 8/ 8	228 186	MS aut
1195	Robert S. Candlish	12, 15 Mar 62	Shupanga	1/ 4/ 4	228 184	MS aut
1196	[Robert Gray]	15 Mar 62	Shupanga	1/ 4/ 4	258 185	MS aut
1197	Roderick I. Murchison	15 Mar 62	Shupanga	1/ 4/ 4	211 135	MS aut
1198	Lovell J. Procter	15 Mar 62	Shupanga	2/ 6/ 5		MS aut
1199	Henry Rowley	15 Mar 62	Shupanga	1/ 4/ 4	211 135	MS aut
1200	Lord John Russell	15 Mar 62	Shupanga, River Zambesi	4 pp	fol	MS aut

NO	N	LOCATION	NLS COPY	PUBLICATION
1151		NLS, MS. 10701, ff. 116—117.		
1152		MDNHLL, MSS. 120.	MS.10777 (23)	Clendennen, **DLJW**, pp. 20—26.
1153		NLS, MS. 10768, ff. 53—54.		**JRGSL**, vol. 33 (1863), p. 251, ex.
1154		RBGK, African Letters, 1859—1865, LX, f. 179.	MS.10779 (10a)	
1155		ICSTLL, Playfair Correspondence, no. 927.	MS.10777 (22)	
1156		MDNHLL, MSS. 120.	MS.10777 (23)	Clendennen, **DLJW**, pp. 26—27.
1157	n	Privately owned.	MS.10777 (9)	
1158	n	NARS, LI 1/1/1, pp. 1333—1336.		
1159		NARS, MO 1/1/6, pp. 1018—1021.		Wallis, **TMaM**, pp. 157—160.
1160	n	PROL, FO 63/894 II, f. 1.	MS.10780 (4)	
1161	n			
1162				Sotheby's Cat., 8 Nov 1960, lot 202.
1163		NLS, MS. 10701, ff. 118—119.		Seaver, **DLLL**, p. 420, ex.
1164	n		MS.10779 (10)	**John Bull**, 26 July 1862, pp. 474—475.
1165		MDNHLL, MSS. 120.	MS.10777 (23)	Clendennen, **DLJW**, pp. 27—29.
1166		AGSNY.	MS.10779 (16)	
1167		NLS, MS. 10701, ff. 120—121.		
1168		NARS, LI 1/1/1, pp. 1340—1342.	MS.10779 (21)	
1169				Russell, **RZST**, pp. 277—278.
1170		NARS, LI 2/1/1.		
1171		MDNHLL, MSS. 120.	MS.10777 (23)	Clendennen, **DLJW**, pp. 29—30.
1172		RGSL, Archives, DL 3/12.	MS.10780 (5)	
1173		JLUCT, Baldwin Walker Papers, Incl. to AE 316.		
1174		NARS, LI 1/1/1, ff. 362—364.	MS.10779 (21)	Wallis, **ZEDL** II, pp. 362—364.
1175	n	NMLZ, G5.		
1176	n	NMLZ, G5.		
1177		BLL, Add. MS. 50184, ff. 46—47.	MS.10780 (3)	
1178	n	BLL, Add. MS. 50184, f.32.	MS.10780 (3)	
1179		SNMDL.	MS.10708, f. 116	
1180	n	JLUCT, Baldwin Walker Papers, AE 314.	MS.10779 (5)	
1181		RGSL, Barth Correspondence.		
1182		NMLZ, G5.		
1183		NARS, LI 1/1/1, pp. 1351—1354.	MS.10779 (21)	
1184		MDNHLL, MSS. 120.	MS.10777 (23)	Clendennen, **DLJW**, pp. 30—31.
1185	n	PROL, FO 63/894 II, ff. 2—5.	MS.10780 (4)	**PP** Sess. 1863, v. LXXI, [58] Class B pp. 196—197.
1186	n	PROL, FO 63/894 II, ff. 6—7.	MS.10780 (4)	**PP** Sess. 1863, v. LXXI, [58] Class B p. 197.
1187	n	PROL, FO 63/894 II, ff. 8—9.	MS.10780 (4)	
1188		NARS, MO 1/1/6, pp. 1042—1049.		Wallis, **TMaM**, pp. 164—168.
1189	n	ULSOASL, Africa, Wooden Box of L's letters.	MS.10778	
1190		NLS, MS. 1809, ff. 132—133.		
1191		NARS, LI 2/1/1.	MS.10779 (21)	
1192		NARS, LI 1/1/1, pp. 1373—1376a.		
1193		NARS, LI 1/1/1, pp. 1377—1380.	MS.10779 (21)	
1194		MDNHLL, MSS. 120.	MS.10777 (23)	Clendennen, **DLJW**, pp. 31—33.
1195	n	NLS, MS. 7792, ff. 5—6.		Smith, **LoAD** II, pp. 457—458.
1196	n	NARS, LI 1/1/1, pp. 1385—1388.	MS.10779 (21)	
1197		NARS, LI 1/1/1, pp. 1389—1392.		
1198		NLS, MS. 10707, ff. 62—64.		
1199	n	NLS, MS. 10768, ff. 55—56.		**Christian World**, 2 Feb 1933, p. 5, c. 3.
1200	n	PROL, FO 63/894 I, ff. 161—162.	MS.10780 (4)	

NO	RECIPIENT	DATE	PLACE	LENGTH	SIZE	TYPE
1201	Editor of the "Times"	[17 Mar 62]	[Zambesi Mouth]	2/ 8/ 8	212 135	MS aut
1202	J. Bevan Braithwaite	17 Mar 62	Zambesi	1/ 2/ 1	211 135	MS aut
1203	John Washington	17 Mar 62	Kongone	3/12/12	211 135	MS aut
1204	Robert Gray	18 Mar 62	Kongone	3 pp		Pr copy
1205	Baldwin W. Walker	19 Mar 62	Kongone Harbour	1/ 4/ 4	325 205	MS aut
1206	John Washington	24 Mar 62	Kongone	2/ 8/ 8		MS aut
1207	José M. Nuñes	25 Mar 62	Kongone	4 pp		MS copy
1208	Sidney Strong	25 Mar 62	Kongone Mouth of Zambesi	2/ 8/ 8	324 204	MS aut
1209	Thomas Maclear	28 Mar 62	Kongone	4/16/16	216 137	MS aut
1210	James Stewart	1 Apr 62	Kongone	1/ 4/ 4	212 135	MS aut
1211	John Washington	1 Apr 62	Kongone	1/ 2/ 2	216 136	MS aut
1212	John S. Moffat	[3 Apr 62]	[off Kongone]	1/ 4/ 4	212 135	MS aut in
1213	John Washington	3 Apr 62	HMS "Pioneer" off Kongone	1/ 4/ 4	212 135	MS aut
1214	Charles Hardesty	10 Apr 62		1 p		MS aut copy
1215	Lord Kinnaird	25 Apr, 8 May 62	Shupanga	4 pp	8vo	Ph copy
1216	Agnes Livingstone 3	28 Apr 62	Shupanga	1/ 4/ 4	4to	MS aut
1217	Thomas S. Livingstone	28 Apr 62	Shupanga	1/ 4/ 4	228 185	MS aut
1218	William O. Livingstone	28 Apr 62	Shupanga	1/ 4/ 4	228 184	MS aut
1219	Robert Moffat 1	28, 29 Apr 62	Shupanga	2/ 8/ 8	228 188	MS aut
1220	Mrs. Frederick Fitch	29 Apr 62	Shupanga	4 pp	235 132	Ph copy
1221	Agnes Livingstone 1	29 Apr 62	Shupanga	2/ 8/ 8	4to	MS aut
1222	Lady Murchison	29 Apr 62	Shupanga	1/ 4/ 4	228 182	MS aut
1223	Roderick I. Murchison	29 Apr 62	Shupanga, R. Zambesi	1/ 4/ 4	228 182	MS aut
1224	Frederick Fitch	1 May 62	Shupanga	4 pp	240 135	Ph copy
1225	Janet Livingstone	5 May 62	Shupanga	2/ 4/ 4	210 180	MS aut
1226	Thomas Maclear	5 May 62	Shupanga	1/ 4/ 4	228 182	MS aut
1227	John Washington	5 May 62	Shupanga	3/10/10	misc	MS aut
1228	James Young	5 May 62	Shupanga	3/12/ 7		MS aut
1229	John Washington	15 May 62	Shupanga	2/ 8/ 8	325 200	MS aut
1230	John Washington	21 May 62	Shupanga	1/ 4/ 4	228 185	MS aut
1231	James Young	28 May 62	Kongone Harbour	1/ 4/ 4	230 185	MS aut
1232	John S. Moffat	29 May 62	Kongone	2/ 8/ 8	215 137	MS aut
1233	Austin H. Layard	2 Jun 62	Kongone harbour	4 pp	fol	MS aut
1234	P. Vigors	2 Jun 62	Kongone			NS copy
1235	[Lord John Russell]	5 Jun 62	Kongone harbour, R. Zambesi	1/ 2/ 1	162 200	MS aut
1236	John Washington	6 Jun 62	Kongone	2/ 6/ 6	209 130	MS aut
1237	Robert Moffat 1	17 Jun 62	Shupanga	1/ 4/ 4	208 128	MS aut in
1238	Robert Gray	20 Jun 62	Shupanga	2/ 8/ 8	216 137	MS aut
1239	Thomas Maclear	21 Jun, 25 Jul 62	Shupanga-Kongone	8/18/18	216 137	MS aut
1240	Lord John Russell	27 Jun 62	Shupanga, Zambesi River	4/ 8/ 7	fol	MS aut
1241	Lord John Russell	1 Jul 62	Shupanga, Zambesi	3 pp	fol	MS aut
1242	Joseph Moore	2 Jul 62	Shupanga, R. Zambesi	9 pp	fol	MS copy
1243	Roderick I. Murchison	7 Jul 62	Kongone	1/ 4/ 4	209 130	MS aut
1244	Horace Waller	7 Jul 62	Shupanga	4/12/12	215 135	MS aut
1245	António Tavares de Almeida	10 Jul 62	HMS "Pioneer," Shupanga	2 pp	fol	MS aut copy
1246	[João Tavares de Almeida]	12 Jul 62	HMS "Pioneer," Shupanga	5 pp	fol	MS aut copy
1247	Agnes Livingstone 3	12 Jul 62	Shupanga	2/ 8/ 8	217 130	MS aut
1248	Custódio José da Silva	14 Jul 62	HMS "Pioneer," Shupanga	4 pp	fol	MS copy
1249	William M. Coghlan	18 Jul 62	HMS "Pioneer," R. Zambesi	2 pp		MS copy
1250	John Washington	22 Jul 62	East Luabo	2/ 8/ 8	322 202	MS aut

NO N	LOCATION	NLS COPY	PUBLICATION
1201 n	NLS, MS. Dep. 237.		
1202	NLS, MS. Dep. 237.		
1203	MDNHLL, MSS. 120.	MS.10777 (23)	Clendennen, DLJW, pp. 33—35.
1204			OCDD Mission, OP, 1862, pp. 34—36.
1205 n	JLUCT, Baldwin Walker Papers, AE 315.	MS.10779 (5)	
1206	MDNHLL, MSS. 120.	MS.10777 (23)	Clendennen, DLJW, pp. 35—37.
1207	NARS, LI 1/1/1, pp. 1393—1396.	MS.10779 (21)	
1208	USPGL, B4 ii, ff. 81—84.	MS.10779 (14)	OCDD Mission, OP, 1862, pp. 36—38.
1209	NARS, LI 1/1/1, pp. 1396—1411.	MS.10779 (10)	Wallis, ZEDL II, pp. 365—368.
1210	NARS, ST 1/1/1.		Wallis, ZJJS, pp. 208—209.
1211	MDNHLL, MSS. 120.	MS.10777 (23)	Clendennen, DLJW, pp. 37—38.
1212 n	NARS, MO 1/1/6, pp. 1054—1057.		Wallis, TMaM, pp. 169—170.
1213	MDNHLL, MSS. 120.	MS.10777 (23)	Clendennen, DLJW, p. 38.
1214	SNMDL, Journal no. 9, p. 34.	MS.10715	
1215	SNMDL.	MS.10708, f. 110	
1216	NLS, MS.10704, ff. 15—16.		Blaikie, PLDL, p. 303, ex.
1217	NLS, MS.10701, ff. 122—123.		
1218	NLS,MS.Acc. 6903.		Christie's Cat., 6 Apr 1977, lot 22(1).
1219	NLS, MS.10701, ff. 124—127.		
1220	NARS, LI 2/1/1.	MS.10779 (21)	
1221	NLS, MS. 10704, ff. 17—20.		Blaikie, PLDL, pp. 302—303.
1222	NARS, LI 1/1/1, pp. 1418—1421.		Blaikie, PLDL, p. 304, ex.
1223	NARS, LI 1/1/1, pp. 1414—1417.		RTSMBA, pp. 146—147.
1224	NARS, LI 2/1/1.	MS.10779 (21)	
1225	NLS, MS. 10701, ff. 128—131.		Seaver, DLLL, p. 421, ex.
1226	NARS, LI 1/1/1, pp. 1422—1425.		
1227	MDNHLL, MSS. 120.	MS.10777 (23)	Clendennen, DLJW, pp. 38—41.
1228	NMLZ, G5.		
1229	MDNHLL, MSS. 120.	MS.10777 (23)	Clendennen, DLJW, pp. 41—44.
1230	MDNHLL, MSS. 120.	MS.10777 (23)	Clendennen, DLJW, pp. 44—45.
1231	Wilson Collection.	MS.10775 (14)	
1232	NARS, MO 1/1/6, pp. 1086—1093.		Wallis, TMaM, pp. 177—178.
1233	PROL, FO 63/894 II, ff. 80—81.	MS.10780 (4)	
1234	RGSL, Archives, DL 3/13/8.		JRGSL, vol. 33 (1863), p. 273, ex.
1235	PROL, FO 63/891 (unnumbered folio).		
1236	MDNHLL, MSS. 120.		Clendennen, DLJW, pp. 45—46.
1237	BLL, Add. MS. 50184, ff. 48—49.	MS.10780 (3)	
1238 n	WCLUWJ, Hist. and Lit. Papers, AB 867/ID IV.	MS.10779 (10)	JRGSL, vol. 33 (1863), p. 274, ex.
1239 n	NARS, LI 1/1/1, pp. 1436—1454.		Wallis, ZEDL II, pp. 368—371.
1240 n	PROL, FO 84/1177, ff. 366—369.	MS.10715	PP Sess. 1863, v. LXXI, [58] Class B, pp. 196—197.
1241 n	PROL, FO 63/894 II, ff. 83—84.	MS.10780 (4)	
1242	NLS, MS. 10773, pp. 37—45.		Sotheby's Cat., 17 Dec 1951, lot 211
1243	NARS, LI 1/1/1, pp. 1471—1474.		
1244	RHLO, Waller MSS. Afr. s. 16, I, ff, 1—6.	MS.10780 (8)	
1245 n	SNMDL, Journal no. 9, pp. 63—64.	MS.10715	
1246	SNMDL, Journal no. 9, pp. 69—73.	MS.10715	
1247	BLL, Add. MS. 50184, ff. 50—53.	MS.10780 (3)	
1248 n	AHUL, Moçambique Papeis, Pasta 19 (1862).		
1249	NLS, MS. 10773, pp. 171—172.		
1250	MDNHLL, MSS. 120.	MS.10777 (23)	Clendennen, DLJW, pp. 46—50.

NO	RECIPIENT	DATE	PLACE	LENGTH	SIZE	TYPE
1251	[Roderick I. Murchison]	25 Jul 62	Kongone	1/ 4/ 4	215 137	MS aut
1252	Radulphus B. Oldfield	26 Jul 62	Kongone	1 p	fol	MS aut copy
1253	Lovell J. Procter	30 Jul 62	Kongone	2 pp		Pr copy
1254	James Stewart	30 Jul 62	Kongone	1/ 4/ 4	203 161	MS aut
1255	Richard Thornton	30 Jul 62	Kongone	1/ 4/ 4	203 161	MS aut
1256	Horace Waller	30 Jul 62	Kongone	2/ 8/ 8	215 135	MS aut
1257	J.J. Wesley Bennett	5 Aug 62	Kongone	1/ 4/ 3	216 137	MS aut
1258	Austin H. Layard	5 Aug 62	Kongone	14 pp	fol	MS aut
1259	Austin H. Layard	5 Aug 62	Kongone	4 pp	fol	MS aut
1260	Edward D. Young	8 Aug 62	HM Exploring Ship "Pioneer"	1 p	fol	MS aut copy
1261	John Washington	15 Aug 62	HM Exploring Ship "Pioneer"	1/ 4/ 4	323 203	MS aut
1262	William O. Livingstone	21 Aug 62	HM Exploring Ship "Pioneer"	2/ 8/ 8	203 164	MS aut
1263	Agnes Livingstone 1	30 Aug, 21 Oct 62	Johanna-Johanna	1/ 4/ 4	216 137	MS aut
1264						
1265	Agnes Livingstone 3	1 Sep 62	Johanna	1/ 4/ 4	205 162	MS aut
1266	Roderick I. Murchison	2 Sep 62	Johanna	2/ 8/ 8	216 136	MS aut
1267	Lord John Russell	2 Sep 62	Johanna	2 pp	fol	MS aut
1268	John Washington	2 Sep 62	Johanna	1/ 2/ 2	325 204	MS aut
1269	Alan H. Gardner	3 Sep 62	HMS Exploring Ship "Pioneer"	1/ 4/ 4	326 206	MS aut
1270	Agnes Livingstone 3	[26 Aug–4 Sep 62]	[Pomony Bay?]	1/ 2/ 1	217 136	MS aut
1271	John Washington	4 Sep 62	Johanna	1/ 4/ 4	325 205	MS aut
1272	William O. Livingstone	10 Oct 62	R. Rovuma	4 pp	8vo	Pr copy
1273	Anges Livingstone 3	10, 21 Oct 62	Rovuma-Johanna	2/ 8/ 8	180 110	MS aut
1274	Thomas S. Livingstone	10 Oct 62	Rovuma Bay	1/ 4/ 4	326 205	MS aut
1275	Roderick I. Murchison	10 Oct 62	River Rovuma	2/ 4/ 4	326 205	MS aut
1276	Alan H. Gardner	15 Oct 62	Rovuma			MS copy
1277	Thomas Maclear	15, 27 Oct 62	Rovuma-Johanna	6/24/23	181 111	MS aut
1278	John Washington	15 Oct 62	Rovuma	2/ 8/ 8	181 111	MS aut
1279	Lord Palmerston	16 Oct 62	Rovuma Bay	1/ 4/ 4	325 206	MS aut
1280	Lord John Russell	16, 21 Oct 62	Rovuma Bay-Johanna	14 pp	fol	MS aut
1281	[Lord John Russell]	21 Oct 62	Johanna	1/ 2/ 1	163 200	MS aut
1282	[Livingstone]	21 Oct 62	Johanna	1/ 4/ 4	181 112	MS aut
1283	Mrs. Robinson	24 Oct 62	Johanna	7 pp		TS copy
1284	Robert and Mary Moffat	25 Oct 62	Johanna	1/ 4/ 4	330 205	MS aut in
1285	John Washington	1 Nov 62	Johanna	3/10/ 9	misc	MS aut
1286	[Galdino Nuñes?]	12 Nov 62	Bara de Quillimane	1/ 4/ 2	216 136	MS aut
1287	Thomas Maclear	17 Nov 62	Quillimane	1/ 4/ 4	247 190	MS aut
1288		17 [Nov] 62	Quillimane	1/ 4/ 4	247 190	MS aut
1289	George Frere	19 Nov 62	Quillimane	1/ 4/ 4	245 190	MS aut
1290	William Sunley	19 Nov 62	Quillimane	1/ 4/ 4	247 192	MS aut
1291	Thomas Maclear	20 Nov 62	Quillimane River	2/ 4/ 4	326 203	MS aut
1292	J. Bevan Braithwaite	21 Nov 62	Quillimane River	1/ 4/ 4	325 207	MS aut
1293	John S. Moffat	25 Nov 62	Kongone	1/ 4/ 4	325 206	MS aut
1294	George Frere	2 Dec 62, 6 Jan 63	Zambesi	2/ 8/ 8	misc	MS aut
1295	Roderick I. Murchison	14 Dec 62	R. Zambesi	1/ 4/ 4	326 205	MS aut
1296	Livingstone's Trustees	15 Dec 62	River Zambesi	1/ 4/ 4	205 163	MS aut copy
1297	Lord John Russell	15 Dec 62	River Zambesi	1 p	fol	MS aut
1298	John Washington	15 Dec 62	River Zambesi	1/ 4/ 4	325 204	MS aut
1299	James Young	15 Dec 62	River Zambesi	2/ 8/ 8	207 128	MS aut
1300	Agnes Livingstone 3	18 Dec 62	Shupanga	2/ 8/ 8	268 208	MS aut

NO	N	LOCATION	NLS COPY	PUBLICATION
1251		NARS, LI 1/1/1, pp. 1475—1478.		
1252		SNMDL, Journal no. 9, p. 92.	MS.10715	
1253				Bennett & Ylvisaker, **CAJLJP**, pp. 340—341.
1254		NARS, ST 1/1/1.		Wallis, **ZJJS**, p. 209.
1255		KPLSA.	MS.10779 (11)	Sotheby's Cat., 9 Jun 1936, lot 495.
1256		RHLO, Waller MSS. Afr. s.16, I, ff. 7—10.	MS.10780 (8)	
1257		WIHMLL, MS. 64762.	MS.10779 (15)	
1258	n	PROL, FO 63/894 II, ff. 85—91.	MS.10780 (4)	
1259	n	PROL, FO 63/894 II, ff. 97—98.	MS.10780 (4)	
1260		SNMDL, Journal no. 9, p. 95.	MS.10715	
1261		MDNHLL, MSS. 120.	MS.10777 (23)	Clendennen, **DLJW**, pp. 50—51.
1262	n	NLS, MS. 10701, ff. 132—133 + MS. Acc. 6903.		Wallis, **ZEDL** II, pp. 214—215.
1263		NLS, MS. 10701, ff. 134—135.		Wallis, **ZEDL** II, pp. 215—216.
1264	n			
1265		BLL, Add. MS. 50184, ff. 54—55.	MS.10780 (3)	Wallis, **ZEDL** II, pp. 216—217.
1266		NARS, LI 1/1/1, pp. 1490—1497.		
1267	n	PROL, FO 63/894 II, f. 100.	MS.10780 (4)	Shepperson, **DLatR**, p. 158.
1268		MDNHLL, MSS. 120.	MS.10777 (23)	Clendennen, **DLJW**, pp. 51—52.
1269	n	NARS, LI 1/1/1, pp. 1498—1501.	MS.10715	
1270	n	BLL, Add. MS. 50184, f. 148.	MS.10780 (3)	
1271		MDNHLL, MSS. 120.	MS.10777 (23)	Clendennen, **DLJW**, pp. 52—53.
1272				Myers' Cat. No. 8 (1972), no. 4.
1273		BLL, Add. MS. 50184, ff. 56—59.	MS.10780 (3)	Wallis, **ZEDL** II, pp. 220—221.
1274		NLS, MS. 10701, ff. 138—139.		Wallis, **ZEDL** II, pp. 217—220.
1275	n	NARS, LI 1/1/1, ff. 1510—1513.		Wallis, **ZEDL** II, pp. 371—374.
1276	n	GACT, Maclear Papers, Acc. 515.		Shepperson, **DLatR**, pp. 176—177.
1277	n	NARS, LI 1/1/1, pp. 1514—1536.		Wallis, **ZEDL** II, pp. 374—377.
1278		MDNHLL, MSS, 120.	MS.10777 (23)	Clendennen, **DLJW**, pp. 53—54.
1279		NLS, MS. 10768, ff. 57—58.		Maggs' Cat. No. 828 (1955), no. 744.
1280	n	PROL, FO 63/894 II, ff. 102—108.	MS.10780 (4)	Shepperson, **DLatR**, pp. 159—164.
1281		PROL, FO 63/891 (unnumbered folio).		
1282	n	NLS, MS. 10701, ff. 136—137.		Seaver, **DLLL**, pp. 419—420, ex.
1283		ULSOASL, Africa, Odds, Box 10, folder 4.		Sotheby's Cat., 18 Jun 1934, lot 217.
1284		BLL, Add. MS. 50184, ff. 60—61.	MS.10780 (3)	Wallis, **ZEDL** II, pp. 221—224.
1285		MDNHLL, MSS. 120.	MS.10777 (23)	Clendennen, **DLJW**, pp. 54—55.
1286	n	NARS, LI 1/1/1, pp. 1538—1539.		
1287		NARS, LI 1/1/1, pp. 1540—1543.		
1288	n	BLJ, Book no. 6098.		
1289		NMLZ, on display.	MS.10779 (20)	
1290		BLJ, Book no. 5318, Acc. Reg. 4669.		Sotheby's Cat., 29 Jun 1939, lot 1481.
1291		NARS, LI 1/1/1, pp. 1545—1549.		
1292		NLS, MS. Dep. 237.		
1293		NARS, MO 1/1/6, ff. 1147—1150.		Wallis, **TMaM**, pp. 185—188.
1294		NMLZ, on display.	MS.10779 (20)	
1295		NARS, LI 1/1/1, pp. 1550—1553.		Wallis, **ZEDL** II, pp. 377—379.
1296	n	NARS, LI 1/1/1, pp. 1554—1556.		
1297	n	PROL, FO 97/322, f. 87.	MS.10780 (4)	
1298		MDNHLL, MSS. 120.	MS.10777 (23)	Clendennen, **DLJW**, pp. 56—58.
1299	n	NMLZ, G5.		
1300		BLL, Add. MS. 50184, ff. 62—65.	MS.10780 (3)	Wallis, **ZEDL** II, pp. 224—228.

NO	RECIPIENT	DATE	PLACE	LENGTH	SIZE		TYPE
1301	António Tavares de Almeida	22 Dec 62	Shupanga	1/ 4/ 1			MS copy
1302	Robert Gray	23 Dec 62	Shupanga	4/16/16	181	111	MS aut
1303	Thomas Maclear	23 Dec 62	Shupanga	4/16/16	181	111	MS aut
1304	James Stewart	24 Dec 62	Shupanga	1/ 4/ 4	325	202	MS aut
1305	Lord John Russell	29 Dec 62	River Zambesi	1 p		fol	MS aut
1306	Lord John Russell	29 Dec 62	River Zambesi	8/16/15		fol	MS aut
1307	Inclosure No. 4	[29 Dec 62]	River Zambesi	2/ 8/ 8		fol	MS aut
1308	[Custódio José da Silva]	5 Jan 63	Shupanga	1/ 4/ 4		fol	MS copy
1309	James Stewart	7 Jan 63	River Zambesi	1/ 4/ 4	325	205	MS aut
1310		8 Jan 63	River Zambesi	4 pp		4to	Pr copy
1311	George Rae	10 Jan 63	Shupanga	1 p		fol	MS aut copy
1312	Lord Palmerston	14 Jan 63	River Shire	8 pp		fol	Pr copy
1313	Culling E. Eardley	23 Jan 63	River Shire				Pr copy
1314	José M. Nuñes	27 Jan 63	River Shire	6 pp			MS copy
1315	Lovell J. Procter	27 Jan 63	Elephant Swamp	2/ 6/ 6	182	112	MS aut
1316	Lord John Russell	28 Jan 63	River Shire	1/ 4/ 4		fol	MS aut
1317	Samuel Wilberforce	12 Feb 63	River Shire	1/ 4/ 4	360	231	MS aut
1318	[George Frere?]	14 Feb 63	River Shire	1/ 4/ 4	360	230	MS aut
1319	Adam Sedgwick	16 Feb 63	River Shire	2/ 6/ 6	361	232	MS aut
1320	James Stewart	19 Feb 63	River Shire	1 p			Pr copy
1321	Richard Thornton	19 Feb 63	R. Shire	1/ 4/ 3	232	180	MS aut
1322	Robert M. Livingstone	20 Feb 63	River Shire	1/ 4/ 4		fol	MS aut
1323	[William Logan]	20 Feb 63	River Shire	1/ 4/ 4	362	232	MS aut
1324	[Galdino Nuñes]	21 Feb 63	River Shire	1 p			MS copy
1325	Jose M. Nuñes	21 Feb 63	River Shire	4 pp			MS copy
1326	John Washington	23, 24 Feb 63	River Shire	2/ 8/ 8	362	231	MS aut
1327	The Earl of Clarendon	24 Feb 63	River Shire	1/ 4/ 4	360	233	MS aut
1328	Agnes Livingstone 3	24 Feb 63	River Shire	1/ 4/ 4	360	230	MS aut
1329	Captain, Man of War	25 Feb 63	River Shire				MS copy
1330	Lovell J. Procter	26 Mar 63	HMS "Pioneer"	2 pp			Pr copy
1331	Horace Waller	26 Mar 63	1' above Mankokwe's	1/ 4/ 4	230	180	MS aut
1332	Horace Waller	20 Apr 63		1/ 4/ 4	180	110	MS aut
1333	Horace Waller	21 Apr 63		1/ 4/ 4	230	180	MS aut
1334	George Thornton	22 Apr 63	Murchison's Cataracts	1/ 4/ 4	325	205	MS aut
1335	John Washington	23, 27, 28 Apr, 12 May 63	Murchison's Cataracts	14 pp		fol	MS copy
1336	Horace Waller	24 Apr 63	Cataracts	2/ 8/ 7	230	180	MS aut
1337	Roderick I. Murchison	25 Apr 63	Murchison's Cataracts	2/ 8/ 7	207	128	MS aut
1338	Captain, HM Ship	28 Apr 63	Murchison's Cataracts	1/ 2/ 2	253	215	MS copy
1339	Lord John Russell	28 Apr 63	Murchison's Cataracts	4 pp		fol	MS aut
1340	Inclosure No. 1	28 Apr 63	Murchison's Cataracts	3 pp		fol	MS aut
1341	Inclosure No. 2	28 Apr 63	Murchison's Cataracts	3 pp		fol	MS aut
1342	Horace Waller	28 Apr 63	[Murchison's Cataracts]	3/12/12	205	130	MS aut
1343	[John Kirk]	[28 Apr 63]	[Murchison's Cataracts]	2/ 6/ 5	231	176	MS aut in
1344	[John Washington]	29 Apr 63	Murchison's Cataracts	1/ 2/ 1	325	204	MS aut
1345	Horace Waller	30 Apr 63	Cataracts	1/ 4/ 3	205	130	MS aut
1346	James Young	30 Apr 63	Murchison's Cataracts	1/ 4/ 4	329	202	MS aut
1347	Lord John Russell	1 May 63	Murchison's Cataracts	4 pp		fol	MS aut
1348	[George Thornton]	1 May 63	[Murchison's Cataracts]	1/ 4/ 4	207	129	MS aut
1349	Horace Waller	1 May 63	Cataracts	1/ 2/ 1		fol	MS aut
1350	Agnes Livingstone 3	18 May 63	Murchison's Cataracts	1/ 4/ 3	208	128	MS aut

NO	N	LOCATION	NLS COPY	PUBLICATION
1301	n	AHUL, Moçambique Papeis, Pasta 21 (1863).	MS.10715	
1302		NARS, LI 1/1/1, pp. 1557—1572.		
1303		NARS, LI 1/1/1, pp. 1573—1588.		
1304	n	NARS, ST 1/1/1.		Wallis, **ZJJS**, pp. 214—215.
1305	n	PROL, FO 97/322, f. 88.	MS.10780 (4)	
1306	n	PROL, FO 84/1177, ff. 370—377.	MS.10715	**PP** Sess. 1864, v. LXVI, [60] Class B, pp. 118—120.
1307	n	PROL, FO 84/1200, ff. 397—400.	MS.10715	**PP** Sess. 1864, v. LXVI, [60] Class B, pp. 121—122.
1308	n	AHUL, Moçambique Papeis, Pasta 21 (1863).	MS.10715	
1309		NARS, ST 1/1/1.		Wallis, **ZJJS**, p. 244.
1310	n			Bonner Cat., 1952, p. 7.
1311		SNMDL, Journal no. 9, p. 142.	MS.10715	
1312				Maggs' Cat. No. 823 (1954), no. 170.
1313	n			**Evangel. Christendom**, v. XVII (1 Sep 63), pp. 438—439.
1314		NARS, LI 1/1/1, ff. 1592a—f.	MS.10779 (21)	
1315		WIHMLL, MS. 64755.	MS.10779 (15)	Bennett & Ylvisaker, **CAJLJP**, p. 397.
1316	n	PROL, FO 84/1200, ff. 395—396.	MS.10715	**PP** Sess. 1864, v. LXVI, [60] Class B, pp. 123—124.
1317		BLO, MSS. Wilberforce c. 14, ff. 16—17.	MS.10780 (7)	
1318		USPGL, B4 ii, ff. 6—7.	MS.10779 (14)	
1319		NARS, LI 2/1/1.		Sotheby's Cat., 12 Nov 1935, lot 437.
1320				Wells, **SoL**, p. 87.
1321		NMLZ, G5.		Sotheby's Cat., 9 Jun 1936, lot 497.
1322		NLS, MS. 10704, ff. 21—22.		
1323		NLS, MS. 10768, ff. 59—60.	MS.10710, f. 50	**The Scotsman**, 22 March 1913.
1324	n	USPGL, Tozer letters, A1(I) A.		
1325		NARS, LI 1/1/1, pp. 1644—1647.	MS.10779 (21)	
1326		MDNHLL, MSS. 120.	MS.10777 (23)	Clendennen, **DLJW**, pp. 58—61.
1327		BLJ, Book no. 5318, Acc. Reg. 4669.		Sotheby's Cat., 29 Jun 1939, lot 1482.
1328		BLL, Add. MS. 50184, ff. 70—71.	MS.10780 (3)	
1329	n	JLUCT, Baldwin Walker Papers, S745.		
1330				Bennett & Ylvisaker, **CAJLJP**, pp. 417—418.
1331		RHLO, Waller MSS. Afr. s. 16, I, ff. 11—12.	MS.10780 (8)	
1332		RHLO, Waller MSS. Afr. s. 16, I, ff. 19—20.	MS.10780 (8)	
1333		RHLO, Waller MSS. Afr. s. 16, I, ff. 13—14.	MS.10780 (8)	
1334	n	NMLZ, on display.	MS.10779 (20)	Tabler, **ZPRT** II, pp. 303—304.
1335		PROL, FO 97/322, ff. 114—121.	MS.10780 (4)	
1336		RHLO, Waller MSS. Afr. s. 16, I, ff. 15—18.	MS.10780 (8)	
1337	n	NARS, LI 1/1/1, pp. 1693—1699.	MS.2618, f. 286	**The Times**, 14 Oct 1863, p. 5, c. 5.
1338	n	RHLO, Waller MSS. Afr. s. 16, I, f. 215.	MS.10780 (8)	
1339	n	PROL, FO 97/322, ff. 59—61.	MS.10780 (4)	
1340	n	PROL, FO 97/322, ff. 63—64.	MS.10780 (4)	
1341	n	PROL, FO 97/322, ff. 65—66.	MS.10780 (4)	
1342	n	RHLO, Waller MSS. Afr. s. 16, I, ff. 21—26.	MS.10780 (8)	
1343	n	Foskett Collection.		Foskett, **ZmDc**, pp. 67—68.
1344		MDNHLL, MSS. 120.	MS.10777 (23)	Clendennen, **DLJW**, pp. 61—62.
1345		RHLO, Waller MSS. Afr. s. 16, I, ff. 27—28.	MS.10780 (8)	
1346		NMLZ, G5.		
1347	n	PROL, FO 97/322, ff. 67—68.	MS.10780 (4)	
1348	n	NARS, LI 2/1/1.		
1349		RHLO, Waller MSS. Afr. s. 16, I, f. 29.	MS.10780 (8)	
1350		BLL, Add. MS. 50184, ff. 74—75.	MS.10780 (3)	

NO	RECIPIENT	DATE	PLACE	LENGTH	SIZE		TYPE
1351	Robert Moffat 1	18 May 63	Murchison's Cataracts	1/ 4/ 3	208	128	MS aut
1352	Horace Waller	23 May 63	Cataracts	1/ 4/ 4	207	128	MS aut
1353	Horace Waller	30 May 63		1/ 4/ 4	205	130	MS aut
1354	John Kirk	2 Jun 63	Cataracts	2 pp			Pr copy
1355	Horace Waller	2 Jun 63	Cataracts	1/ 4/ 4	205	130	MS aut
1356	Lovell J. Procter	5 Jun 63	Cataracts	1/ 4/ 4		8vo	MS aut
1357	Horace Waller	10 Jun 63	Cataracts	1/ 2/ 2		fol	MS aut
1358	Horace Waller	14 Jun 63	Moembedzi	1/ 4/ 4	204	132	MS aut
1359	[George C. Cato]	3 Jul 63	Cataracts of the Shire	2/ 8/ 6		8vo	MS aut
1360	Horace Waller	3 Jul 63	Cataracts of Shire	2/ 8/ 8	205	130	MS aut
1361	Philip Wodehouse	3 Jul 63	Murchison Cataracts	4 pp		fol	MS aut copy
1362	James Young	3 Jul 63	Murchison Cataracts	1 p			Pr copy
1363	Charles T. Jago	4 Jul 63	Murchison's Cataracts	4 pp			MS copy
1364	Thomas Maclear	4 Jul 63	Murchison's Cataracts	2/ 4/ 4	330	203	MS aut
1365	John Kirk	5 Jul 63	Cataracts of Shire	2/ 8/ 8	208	128	MS aut
1366	Horace Waller	5 Jul 63	Cataracts	1/ 4/ 4	205	130	MS aut
1367	Robert Gray	8 Jul 63	Murchison's Cataracts	2/ 8/ 8	207	129	MS aut
1368	Agnes Livingstone 3	8 Jul 63	Murchison's Cataracts	2/ 8/ 8	208	128	MS aut
1369	Thomas Maclear	8 Jul 63	Cataracts	3/12/12	207	128	MS aut
1370	John S. Moffat	8 Jul 63	Murchison's Cataracts	2 pp			TS copy
1371	Horace Waller	[10 Jul 63?]		1/ 2/ 2		fol	MS aut
1372	[Robert Moffat 1??]	[5–11 Jul 63?]	[River Shire]	1/ 4/ 4	200	132	MS aut in
1373	Mrs Robert Gray	14 Jul 63	Shire Cataracts				MS aut
1374	[George Tozer]	[14 Jul 63?]	[Cataracts]	1/ 2/ 2	204	163	MS aut in
1375	Horace Waller	14 Jul 63	Cataracts	1/ 4/ 3	195	125	MS aut
1376	John Washington	14 Jul 63	Murchison's Cataracts	1 p		fol	MS copy
1377	Baldwin W. Walker	15 Jul 63	Cataracts of Shire	4 pp			MS copy
1378	[Lord John Russell?]	17 Jul 63	Murchison's Cataracts	1/ 4/ 4	325	202	MS aut
1379	[Horace Waller]	17 Jul 63	In medias Res	3/12/11	205	130	MS aut
1380	[Edward D.]Young	17 [Jul 63]	[Cataracts of the Shire]	1/ 4/ 4	206	133	MS aut
1381	Charles Meller	20 Jul 63	Cataracts	1/ 4/ 4	205	129	MS aut
1382	Lord John Russell	20 Jul 63	Murchison's Cataracts	7 pp		fol	MS aut
1383	Inclosure No. 1	20 Jul 63	[Murchison's Cataracts]	5 pp		fol	MS aut
1384	[– Livingstone]	25 Jul 63	Cataracts of the Shire	1/ 4/ 4	205	133	MS aut
1385	[J. Bevan Braithwaite]	28 Jul 63	Shire Cataracts	1/ 4/ 4	325	202	MS aut
1386	Horace Waller	6 Aug 63	Above Tedzane	1/ 4/ 4	205	130	MS aut
1387	John Kirk	8 Aug 63	Malango	3/12/12	204	132	MS aut
1388	Horace Waller	8 Aug 63	Malango	1/ 4/ 4	205	130	MS aut
1389	William Hooker	10 Aug 63	Cataracts of Shire	1/ 4/ 4	205	133	MS aut
1390	Agnes Livingstone 3	10 Aug 63	Cataracts of Shire	1/ 4/ 4	204	132	MS aut
1391	Thomas S. Livingstone	10 Aug 63	Cataracts of Shire	1/ 4/ 4		8vo	MS aut
1392	Robert Moffat 1	10 Aug 63	Shire Cataracts	1/ 4/ 4	204	132	MS aut in
1393	Horace Waller	15 Aug 63	Cataracts	3/12/12	205	130	MS aut
1394	Baldwin W. Walker	18 Aug 63	Upper Shire	1 p			Pr copy
1395	[James Young]	[Jul–Aug 63?]	[River Shire]	3/12/12	204	133	MS aut
1396	Thomas Maclear	5 Nov 63	Murchison's Cataracts	2/ 8/ 8	328	208	MS aut
1397	Adam Sedgwick	5 Nov, 24 Dec 63	Murchison's Cataracts	4/16/16	205	133	MS aut
1398	Horace Waller	28 Nov 63	Murchison's Cataracts	1/ 4/ 4	205	130	MS aut
1399	Roderick I. Murchison	4 Dec 63, 10 Feb[64]	Murchison's Cat.—Shupanga	4 pp		fol	MS aut
1400	John Washington	4, 22 Dec 63	Murchison's Cataracts	8 pp		fol	MS aut

NO	N	LOCATION	NLS COPY	PUBLICATION
1351		BLL, Add. MS.50184, ff. 72—73.	MS.10780 (3)	
1352		WIHMLL, MS. 64757.	MS.10779 (15)	
1353		RHLO, Waller MSS. Afr. s. 16, I, ff. 30—31.	MS.10780 (8)	
1354	n			Foskett, **ZmDc**, pp. 63—64.
1355		RHLO, Waller MSS. Afr. s. 16, I, ff. 32—33.	MS.10780 (8)	
1356		NLS, MS. 10707, ff. 74—75.		
1357		RHLO, Waller MSS. Afr. s. 16, I, f. 34.	MS.10780 (8)	
1358		RHLO, Waller MSS. Afr. s. 16, I, ff. 35—36.	MS.10780 (8)	
1359		CLRUGSA.	MS.10777 (19)	
1360		RHLO, Waller MSS. Afr. s. 16, I, ff. 37—40.	MS. 10780 (8)	
1361		SNMDL, Journal no. 9, pp. 201—204.	MS.10715	
1362				Blaikie, **PLDL**, p. 313, ex.
1363		PROL, FO 97/322, ff. 186—187.	MS.10780 (4)	
1364		NARS, LI 1/1/1, pp. 1737—1740.		**The Times**, 27 Jan 1864, p. 7, c. 4.
1365	n	BLJ, Book no. 6523.		Foskett, **ZmDc**, pp. 65—66.
1366		RHLO, Waller MSS. Afr. s. 16, I, ff. 41—42.	MS.10780 (8)	
1367		WCLUWJ, Records, Archbishop CT, AB 867/ID IV.	MS.10779 (10)	
1368		BLL, Add. MS. 50184, ff. 76—79.	MS.10780 (3)	
1369		NARS, LI 1/1/1, pp. 1745—1756.		
1370		ULSOASL, Africa, Odds, Box 10, folder 4.		Wallis, **ZEDL** II, pp. 218—219.
1371		RHLO, Waller MSS. Afr. s. 16, I, f. 182.	MS.10780 (8)	
1372		BLL, Add. MS. 50184, ff. 68—69.	MS.10780 (3)	
1373		PCCGHYE.		
1374		NARS, LI 1/1/1, pp. 2349—2350.		
1375		UFHLFHSA.	MS.10777 (15)	
1376		PROL, FO 97/322, f. 208.		
1377		PROL, FO 97/322, ff. 188—191.	MS.10780 (4)	
1378	n	NARS, LI 1/1/1, pp. 1758—1761.		
1379		RHLO, Waller MSS. Afr. s. 16, I, ff. 43—48.	MS.10780 (8)	
1380	n	KPLSA.	MS.10779 (11)	
1381			MS.10769	Sotheby's Cat., 18 Nov 1969, lot 384.
1382	n	PROL, FO 97/322, ff. 237—240.	MS.10780 (4)	
1383	n	PROL, FO 97/322, ff. 241—243.	MS.10780 (4)	
1384	n	KPLSA.	MS.10779 (11)	
1385		NLS, MS. Dep. 237.		
1386		RHLO, Waller MSS. Afr. s. 16, I, ff. 49—50.	MS.10780 (8)	
1387		Foskett Collection.		Foskett, **ZmDc**, pp. 69—72.
1388		RHLO, Waller MSS. Afr. s. 16, I, ff. 51—52.	MS.10780 (8)	
1389		RBGK, African Letters, 1859—1865, LX, f. 180.	MS.10779 (10a)	
1390		BLL, Add. MS. 50184, ff. 80—81.	MS.10780 (3)	
1391		NLS, MS. 10704, ff. 23—24.		
1392		BLL, Add. MS. 50184, ff. 82—83.	MS.10780 (3)	
1393		RHLO, Waller MSS. Afr. s. 16, I, ff. 53—58.	MS.10780 (8)	
1394	n	NLS, MS. 7905, f. 71v.		
1395		NMLZ, G5.		
1396		NARS, LI 1/1/1, pp. 1777—1784.		
1397		BLJ, Book no. 5521.		Sotheby's Cat., 9 Jun 1936, lot 502.
1398		RHLO, Waller MSS. Afr. s. 16, I, ff. 59—60.	MS.10780 (8)	
1399		RGSL, Archives, DL 3/16/1.	MS.10780 (5)	**JRGSL**, vol. 34 (1864), pp. 245—249.
1400	n	RGSL, Archives, DL 3/16/2.	MS.10780 (5)	**PRGSL**, vol. VIII (1863—64), pp. 256—258.

NO	RECIPIENT	DATE	PLACE	LENGTH	SIZE		TYPE
1401	Agnes Livingstone 3	7 Dec 63	Murchison's Cataracts	3/12/12	205	134	MS aut
1402	John Kirk	9 Dec 63	Murchison's Cataracts	5 pp			Pr copy
1403	Robert Moffat 1	10, 17 Dec 63	Murchison's Cataracts	3/12/12	205	135	MS aut in
1404	J.N. Whitaker	10 Dec 63	Murchison's Cataracts	3 pp		8vo	Pr copy
1405	Frederick Fitch	12, 17 Dec 63	Murchison Cataracts	2/ 8/ 8		8vo	Ph copy
1406	John S. Moffat	12, 17 Dec 63	Murchison's Cataracts	2/ 8/ 8	204	133	MS aut
1407	Lord John Russell	12 Dec 63, 24 Feb 64	Cataracts — Mosambique	15 pp	fol		MS aut
1408	Inclosure No. 1	12 Dec 63, 24 Feb 64	[Cataracts] — Mosambique	3 pp	fol		MS aut
1409	Christian Kirk	17 Dec 63	Murchison's Cataracts	2 pp			Pr copy
1410	George Tozer	18 Dec 63	Murchison's Cataracts	1/ 4/ 4	321	207	MS aut copy
1411	Horace Waller	18 Dec 63	Murchison's Cataracts	4/12/12	205	130	MS aut
1412	[Thomas Maclear]	19, 30 Dec 63, 18 Feb 64	[Cataracts—Kongone]	5/18/17	204	133	MS aut
1413	Lord John Russell	19 Dec 63	River Shire	1 p	fol		MS aut
1414	George Frere	22 Dec 63	Murchison's Cataracts	2/ 8/ 8	204	132	MS aut
1415	[Agnes Livingstone 3]	24 Dec 63	Murchison's Cataracts	1/ 4/ 4		8vo	MS aut
1416	[Anna Mary Livingstone]	26 Dec 63	River Shire			8vo	facsimile
1417	Thomas S. Livingstone	26 Dec 63	River Shire	1/ 4/ 4	204	133	MS aut
1418	William O. Livingstone	26 Dec 63	River Shire	1/ 4/ 4	202	130	MS aut
1419	José Torresão	31 Dec 63	Os Cataractos do Shire	3/12/12			facsimile
1420	Samuel Wilberforce	31 Dec 63	River Shire	2/ 8/ 8	204	132	MS aut
1421	Joseph Moore	14 Jan 64	River Shire	2/ 8/ 8	205	132	MS aut
1422	George H. Richards	10 Feb 64	Shupanga	1/ 4/ 4	228	187	MS aut
1423	[James Young?]	[10 Feb 64?]	[Shupanga?]	1/ 2/ 2	206	165	MS aut
1424	José M. Nuñes	12 Feb 64	Kongone	7 pp			MS copy
1425	Agnes Livingstone 3	25 Feb 64	Mosambique	2/ 8/ 8		8vo	MS aut
1426	Thomas Maclear	26 Feb 64	Mosambique	4/16/16	205	131	MS aut
1427	Edward Marjoribanks	27 Feb 64	Mosambique	1/ 4/ 4	204	132	Ph copy
1428	Robert Gray	27 Feb 64	Mosambique	3/10/10	182	110	MS aut
1429	George Thornton	27 Feb 64	Mosambique	2/ 8/ 8	205	132	MS aut
1430	Baldwin W. Walker	27 Feb 64	Mosambique	5 pp			MS copy
1431	[Roderick I. Murchison?]	[Feb 64]		4 pp			MS aut
1432	William Sunley	4 Mar 64	Mosambique	2/ 8/ 8	182	111	MS aut
1433	Alan H. Gardner	7 Mar 64	Mosambique	2 pp	fol		MS copy
1434	[John Pennell]	7 Mar 64	Mosambique	1/ 2/ 1	fol		MS aut
1435	Thomas Ward	7 Mar 64	Mosambique	1 p	4to		Pr copy
1436	Edward D. Young	7 Mar 64	Mosambique	1 p			Pr copy
1437	Thomas Maclear	22 Mar 64	Mosambique	2/ 8/ 8	229	184	MS aut
1438	Robert Gray	30 Mar 64	Mosambique	2/ 8/ 8	204	132	MS aut fr
1439	[E.D. Young & H. Waller]	2 Apr 64	Mosambique	1/ 4/ 1		8vo	MS aut
1440	George H. Richards	11 Apr 64	Mosambique	10 pp	190	118	MS aut copy
1441	José M. Nuñes	12 Apr 64	Mosambique	4 pp			MS copy
1442	William Sunley	25 Apr 64	Zanzibar	2/ 4/ 4	182	110	MS aut
1443	Agnes Livingstone 3	29, 30 Apr 64	Zanzibar	1/ 4/ 4	204	132	MS aut
1444	H. Bartle E. Frere	14 Jun 64	"Lady Nyassa," Bombay	1/ 2/ 2	204	132	MS aut
1445	Depty Comm. of Customs	[14 Jun 64]	[Bombay]	5 pp	190	118	MS aut copy
1446	Roderick I. Murchison	18 Jun, 17 Jul 64	Poonah—Malta	4 pp	fol		MS aut
1447	H. Bartle E. Frere	23 Jun 64	Bombay	2/ 8/ 8		8vo	MS aut
1448	[Agnes Livingstone 3]	[30 Apr—23 Jun 64?]	[Zanzibar or India?]	1/ 2/ 1	268	210	MS aut in
1449	Thomas Maclear	5 Jul 64	Near Aden	1/ 4/ 4	345	210	MS aut
1450	E. Mary Burrup	28 Jul 64	Tavistock Hotel	1/ 2/ 2	202	135	MS aut

NO	N	LOCATION	NLS COPY	PUBLICATION
1401		BLL, Add. MS.50184, ff. 84—89.	MS.10780 (3)	
1402	n			Foskett, **ZmDc**, pp. 73—77.
1403		BLL, Add. MS. 50184, ff. 90—94.	MS.10780 (3)	
1404				Sawyer's Cat. SA/56 addenda (1967), no. 114.
1405		NARS, LI 2/1/1.	MS.10779 (21)	
1406		NARS, MO 1/1/6, pp. 1217—1224.		Wallis, **TMaM**, pp. 225—227.
1407	n	PROL, FO 97/322, ff. 244—251.	MS.10780 (4)	
1408	n	PROL, FO 97/322, ff. 252—253.	MS.10780 (4)	
1409				Foskett, **ZmDc**, pp. 162—163.
1410	n	NARS, LI 1/1/1, pp. 1792—1794.	MS.10715	
1411		RHLO, Waller MSS. Afr. s. 16, I, ff. 61—66.	MS.10780 (8)	
1412		NARS, LI 1/1/1, pp. 1825—1840.		
1413		PROL, FO 97/322, f. 254.	MS.10780 (4)	
1414		NMLZ, on display.	MS.10779 (20)	
1415	n	NLS, MS. 10704, ff. 25—26.		
1416			MS.10777 (26)	Dawson, **LtHA**, p. 96.
1417		NLS, MS. 10701, ff. 142—143.		
1418		NLS, MS. Acc. 6769.		
1419	n			Almeida, **IdDDL**, between pp. 18 and 19.
1420		BLO, MSS. Wilberforce c. 19, ff. 16—19.	MS.10780 (7)	
1421		NARS, LI 2/1/1.	MS.10773	Sotheby's Cat., 17 Dec 1951, lot 210.
1422		RGSL, Archives, DL 3/16/3.	MS.10780 (5)	
1423	n	NMLZ, G5.		
1424		NARS, LI 1/1/1, pp. 1802—1808.	MS.10779 (21)	
1425	n	BLL, Add. MS.50184, ff. 95—97.	MS.10780 (3)	Wallis, **ZEDL** II, pp. 382—385.
1426		NARS, LI 1/1/1, pp. 1809—1824.		
1427		NLS, MS. 10709, f. 84.		
1428		USPGL, B4 ii, ff. 8—11.	MS.10779 (14)	
1429		NARS, LI 2/1/1.		
1430		PROL, FO 97/322, ff. 267—269.	MS.10780 (4)	
1431		RGSL, Archives, DL 3/16/4.	MS.10780 (5)	
1432		BLJ, Book no. 5318, Acc. Reg. 4669.		Sotheby's Cat., 29 Jun 1939, lot 1483.
1433	n	Wilson Coll., Journal no. 10.	MS.10775 (4)	
1434		SNMDL, on display.	MS.10708, f. 113	
1435				Myers' Cat. No. 6 (Spring, 1967) no. 13.
1436	n	NLS, MS. 7905, f. 72.		
1437		NARS, LI 1/1/1, pp. 1842—1849.		
1438		USPGL, B4 ii, ff. 12—15.	MS.10779 (14)	
1439		RHLO, Waller MSS. Afr. s. 16, I, ff. 67—68.	MS.10780 (8)	
1440		Wilson Coll., Journal no. 10.	MS.10775 (4)	
1441		NARS, LI 1/1/1, pp. 1856—1859.	MS.10779 (21)	
1442		BLJ, Book no. 5318, Acc. Reg. 4669.		Sotheby's Cat., 29 Jun 1939, lot 1484.
1443		BLL, Add. MS. 50184, ff. 98—99.	MS.10780 (3)	
1444	n	WIHMLL, MS. 64759.	MS.10779 (15)	
1445	n	Wilson Coll., Jounral no. 10.	MS.10775 (4)	
1446		RGSL, Archives, DL 3/16/5.	MS.10780 (5)	**JRGSL**, vol. 34 (1864), pp. 249—250, ex.
1447		NLS, MS. 3278, ff. 192—195.		
1448	n	BLL, Add. MS. 50184, f. 100.	MS.10780 (3)	
1449		NARS, LI 1/1/1, pp. 1862—1865.		Wallis, **ZEDL** II, pp. 385—387.
1450	n	USPGL, on display.	MS.10779 (14)	

NO	RECIPIENT	DATE	PLACE	LENGTH	SIZE		TYPE
1451	John Kirk	28 Jul 64	Tavistock Hotel, Covent Gar.	2/ 8/ 8	200	128	MS aut
1452	Agnes Livingstone 3	29 Jul 64	Tavistock Hotel	1/ 4/ 4	205	127	MS aut
1453	[George Thornton]	29 Jul 64	Tavistock Hotel	1/ 4/ 4		8vo	Ph copy
1454	Frederick & Mrs Fitch	30 Jul 64	Tavistock Hotel	3 pp		8vo	Ph copy
1455	Roderick I. Murchison	2 Aug 64	Hamilton	2/ 8/ 8	180	115	MS aut
1456	John Murray	2 Aug 64	Burnbank Road, Hamilton	1/ 4/ 4	182	114	MS aut
1457	Samuel Wilberforce	2 Aug 64	Hamilton	1/ 4/ 3		8vo	MS aut
1458	James Young	2 Aug 64	Hamilton	1/ 4/ 2	181	115	MS aut
1459	Horace Waller	4 Aug 64	Hamilton	1/ 4/ 2		8vo	MS aut
1460	Joseph Moore	5 Aug 64	Hamilton	1/ 2/ 2	181	115	MS copy
1461	Samuel Wilberforce	5 Aug [64]	Hamilton	3/12/12		8vo	MS aut
1462	Horace Waller	6 Aug 64	Hamilton	1/ 4/ 4		8vo	MS aut
1463	Edward Baines	8 Aug 64	Hamilton	1/ 4/ 4	180	112	MS aut
1464	Roderick I. Murchison	8 Aug 64	Hamilton	1/ 4/ 4	180	115	MS aut
1465	Mrs. Noel	8 Aug [64]	Hamilton	1/ 4/ 4	180	114	MS aut
1466	Joseph D. Hooker	9 Aug 64	Hamilton	1/ 4/ 4	181	113	MS aut
1467		15 Aug 64	Hamilton	1/ 4/ 1	180	114	MS aut
1468	Roderick I. Murchison	16 Aug 64	Hamilton	1/ 4/ 4	202	126	MS aut
1469	James Stewart	17 Aug 64	Hamilton	1/ 2/ 2	181	113	MS aut
1470		17 Aug 64	Hamilton	7 pp		8vo	Pr copy
1471	Agnes Livingstone 3	27 Aug 64	4 Atholl Place, Glasgow	1/ 4/ 4	159	200	MS aut
1472	Roderick I. Murchison	27 Aug 64	Hamilton	1/ 4/ 4	181	114	MS aut
1473	T.M.B. Paterson	27 Aug 64	Hamilton	2 pp	188	163	Ph copy
1474	[Edward D. Young??]	29 Aug 64	Hamilton	1/ 2/ 2	202	127	MS aut in
1475	J.H. Morris	30 Aug 64	Hamilton	2 pp		8vo	Pr copy
1476	[John A. Blair]	1 Sep 64	Hamilton	1 p			Pr copy
1477	Cumming	1 Sep 64	Hamilton	4 pp		8vo	Pr copy
1478	John Kirk	1 Sep 64	Hamilton	1/ 4/ 4	181	113	MS aut
1479	Horace Waller	1 Sep 64	Hamilton	1/ 4/ 3	204	127	MS aut
1480	J.R. Stebbing	1 Sep 64	Hamilton	1/ 2/ 2		8vo	MS aut
1481		1 Sept 64	Hamilton	1/ 4/ 3	181	114	MS aut
1482	Roderick I. Murchison	5 Sep 64	Hamilton	1/ 4/ 4	204	130	MS aut
1483	Matilda Coneys	6 Sep 64	Hamilton	2 pp		8vo	Pr copy
1484	Horace Waller	6 Sep 64	Hamilton	1/ 4/ 3	205	127	MS aut
1485	John Burns	10 Sep 64	Hamilton	1/ 4/ 3	201	129	MS aut
1486	William Sunley	13 Sep 64	Hamilton	1/ 4/ 4	210	130	MS aut
1487	Mrs. Williamson	18, 19 Sep 64	Bath	1/ 4/ 4	178	112	MS aut fr
1488	Horace Waller	[19 Sep 64]	[Bath]	1/ 4/ 2		8vo	MS aut
1489		[18–23 Sep 64]	British Association, Bath	1/ 2/ 1	178	113	MS aut
1490	John S. Moffat	24 Sep 64	Newstead Abbey	1/ 4/ 4	182	120	MS aut in
1491	John S. Moffat	[24 Sep 64]	Newstead Abbey	1/ 2/ 2	60	120	MS aut fr
1492	John Murray	24 Sep 64	Clifton	1/ 4/ 4	182	120	MS aut
1493	Horace Waller	24 Sep 64	Clifton	1/ 4/ 3		8vo	MS aut fr
1494	F. Williams	24 Sep 64	Clifton	2 pp		8vo	Pr copy
1495	James Young	26 Sep 64	Newstead Abbey	1/ 4/ 4	177	113	MS aut
1496	George L. Conyngham	30 Sep 64	Newstead Abbey	1/ 4/ 4	177	114	MS aut
1497	John Murray	30 Sep 64	Newstead Abbey	1/ 4/ 4	177	114	MS aut
1498	William Hooker	1 Oct 64	Newstead Abbey	1/ 4/ 3	177	114	MS aut
1499	Arthur Tidman	1 Oct 64	[Newstead Abbey]	1/ 4/ 3	178	115	MS aut
1500	Horace Waller	1 Oct 64	Newstead Abbey	1/ 4/ 4		8vo	MS aut

NO	N	LOCATION	NLS COPY	PUBLICATION
1451		Foskett Collection.		Foskett, **ZmDc**, pp. 78—79.
1452		BLL, Add. MS. 50184, ff. 103—104.	MS.10780 (3)	
1453		NLS, MS. 10709, ff. 86—87.		Sotheby's Cat., 10 Nov 1936, lot 505.
1454		NARS, LI 2/1/1.	MS.10779 (21)	
1455		NARS, LI 1/1/1, pp. 1879—1886.		
1456		JMPL.		
1457		BLO, MSS. Wilberforce c. 19, ff. 22—23.	MS.10780 (7)	
1458		NMLZ, G5.		
1459		RHLO, Waller MSS. Afr. s. 16, I, ff. 69—70.	MS.10780 (8)	
1460		NLS, MS. 10773, p. 55.		Sawyer's Cat. SA/70 (1971), no. 29.
1461		BLO, MSS. Wilberforce c. 19, ff. 24—29.	MS.10780 (7)	
1462		RHLO, Waller MSS. Afr. s. 16, I, ff. 71—72.	MS.10780 (8)	
1463		CSBL.		
1464		NARS, LI 1/1/1, pp. 1887—1890.		
1465		NLS, MS. 10768, ff. 62—63.		
1466		RBGK, English Letters, 1865—1900, 92, f. 134.	MS.10779 (10a)	
1467		WIHMLL, MS. 91831.	MS.10779 (15)	
1468		NARS, LI 1/1/1, pp. 1891—1894.		
1469		NARS, ST 1/1/1.		Wallis, **ZJJS**, p. 231.
1470	n			Maggs' Cat. No. 804 (1951), no. 997.
1471		NLS, MS. 10704, ff. 27—28.		
1472		NARS, LI 1/1/1, pp. 1895—1898.		
1473	n	Privately owned.	MS.10779 (3)	
1474		RHLO, Waller MSS. Afr. s. 16, I, f. 73.	MS.10780 (8)	
1475	n			Maggs' Cat. No. 889 (1963), no. 372.
1476		USPGL, AI (XXVIII), f. 77.		
1477				Sawyer's Cat. No. 266 (1964), no. 485.
1478		Foskett Collection.		Foskett, **ZmDc**, p. 80.
1479		RHLO, Waller MSS. Afr. s. 16, I, ff. 74—75.	MS.10780 (8)	
1480		WCLUWJ, Hist. and Lit. Papers, A348/A7.	MS.10779 (10)	Sotheby's Cat., 3 Dec 1913, lot 299, item 8.
1481		BLJ, Book no. 5318, Acc. Reg. 4669.		Sotheby's Cat., 29 Jun 1939, lot 1485.
1482		NARS, LI 1/1/1, pp. 1903—1906.		
1483				Fletcher Cat. No. 163 (Autumn, 1953), no. 201.
1484		RHLO, Waller MSS. Afr. s. 16, I, ff. 76—77.	MS.10780 (8)	
1485		NLS, MS. 10707, ff. 76—77.	MS.10709, f. 88	
1486		WIHMLL, MS. 68010D.	MS.10779 (15)	
1487		WIHMLL, MS. 63381.	MS.10779 (15)	Sotheby's Cat., 28 Jul 1930, lot 111.
1488		RHLO, Waller MSS. Afr. s. 16, I, ff. 78—79.	MS.10780 (8)	
1489		SNMDL.		
1490		NARS, MO 1/1/6, pp. 1253—1256.		Wallis, **TMaM**, p. 234.
1491		ULSOASL, Africa, Wooden Box of L's letters.	MS.10778	
1492		JMPL.		
1493		RHLO, Waller MSS. Afr. s. 16, I, ff. 80—81.	MS.10780 (8)	
1494				Myers' Cat. No. 10 (1977), no. 6.
1495	n	NMLZ, G5.		
1496		WIHMLL, MS. 63008.	MS.10779 (15)	
1497		JMPL.		
1498		RGBK, English Letters, 1862—1865, XLII, f. 17.	MS.10779 (10a)	
1499		ULSOASL, Africa, Wooden Box of L's letters.	MS.10778	
1500		RHLO, Waller MSS. Afr. s. 16, I, ff. 82—83.	MS.10780 (8)	

NO	RECIPIENT	DATE	PLACE	LENGTH	SIZE	TYPE
1501	James Stewart	7 Oct 64	Newstead Abbey	1/ 4/ 4	177 114	MS aut
1502		7 Oct 64	Newstead Abbey	1/ 4/ 3	177 113	MS aut
1503	William C. Oswell	8 Oct 64	Newstead Abbey	2/ 8/ 8	177 114	MS aut
1504		8 Oct 64	Mansfield	2 pp	8vo	Pr copy
1505	Roderick I. Murchison	9 Oct 64	Newstead Abbey	1/ 4/ 4	177 113	MS aut
1506	Joseph D. Hooker	12 Oct 64	Newstead Abbey	1/ 4/ 4	177 113	MS aut
1507	Charles Meller	12 Oct 64	Newstead Abbey	1/ 4/ 4	178 115	MS aut
1508	John Murray	12 Oct 64	Newstead Abbey	1/ 4/ 4	179 113	MS aut
1509	Horace Waller	13 Oct 64	Newstead Abbey	1/ 4/ 4	8vo	MS aut
1510	The Duchess of Argyll	14 Oct 64	Newstead Abbey	1/ 4/ 4	178 114	MS aut
1511	John Kirk	17 Oct 64	Newstead Abbey			Pr copy
1512	Joseph D. Hooker	19 Oct 64	Newstead Abbey	1/ 4/ 2	179 112	MS aut
1513	John Kirk	21 Oct 64	Newstead Abbey	1/ 4/ 4	182 114	MS aut
1514	John Murray	21 Oct 64	Newstead Abbey	1/ 4/ 4	179 113	MS aut
1515	William C. Oswell	21 Oct 64	Newstead Abbey	1/ 4/ 4	180 112	MS aut
1516	Roderick I. Murchison	23 Oct 64	Newstead Abbey	1/ 4/ 4		MS aut
1517	Richard Glynn	25 Oct 64	Newstead Abbey	1/ 4/ 3	170 115	MS aut
1518	Austin H. Layard	25 Oct 64	Newstead Abbey	2 pp	fol	MS aut
1519	[Thomas Binney??]	27 Oct 64	Newstead Abbey	1/ 4/ 4	8vo	MS aut
1520	John Murray	30 Oct 64	Newstead Abbey	1/ 4/ 4	177 113	MS aut
1521	R.M. Smith	31 Oct [64]	Newstead Abbey	4 pp	8vo	Pr copy
1522	Horace Waller	31 Oct 64	Newstead Abbey	1/ 4/ 4	8vo	MS aut
1523	Austin H. Layard	2 Nov 64	Newstead Abbey	2 pp	fol	MS aut
1524	Thomas Maclear	3 Nov 64	Newstead Abbey	2/ 8/ 8		MS aut
1525	John Murray	5 Nov 64	Newstead Abbey	1/ 4/ 4	177 114	MS aut
1526	Samuel Wilberforce	5 Nov 64	[Newstead Abbey]	2/ 8/ 8	8vo	MS aut
1527	John Kirk	7 Nov 64	Newstead Abbey			Pr copy
1528	John Murray	7 Nov 64	Newstead Abbey	1/ 4/ 4	179 113	MS aut
1529	Horace Waller	8 Nov 64	Newstead Abbey	1/ 4/ 4	8vo	MS aut
1530	Roderick I. Murchison	12 Nov 64	Newstead Abbey	1/ 4/ 4	177 114	MS aut
1531	John Kirk	[14 Nov 64?]	Newstead Abbey	1/ 2/ 1	178 112	MS aut
1532	Roderick I. Murchison	15 Nov 64	51, Upper Brook St., W.	1/ 4/ 4	185 111	MS aut
1533	Roderick I. Murchison	17 Nov 64	Newstead Abbey	1/ 4/ 4		MS aut
1534	Roderick I. Murchison	18 Nov 64	Newstead Abbey	1/ 4/ 4	173 114	MS aut
1535	Richard Owen	18 Nov 64	Newstead Abbey	1/ 4/ 4	177 115	MS aut
1536	Horace Waller	18 Nov 64	Newstead Abbey	1/ 4/ 4	8vo	MS aut
1537	Mrs. Williamson	18 Nov 64	Newstead Abbey	4 pp	8vo	Pr copy
1538	Richard Owen	22 Nov 64	Newstead Abbey	1/ 4/ 4	176 113	MS aut
1539	John Murray	23 Nov 64	Newstead Abbey	1/ 4/ 3	177 114	MS aut
1540	Horace Waller	23 Nov 64	Newstead Abbey	1/ 4/ 4	8vo	MS aut
1541	John Kirk	24 Nov 64	Newstead Abbey	1/ 4/ 4	177 113	MS aut
1542	R.M. Smith	24 Nov 64	Newstead Abbey	1/ 4/ 4	175 115	MS aut
1543	John Kirk	25 Nov 64	Newstead Abbey	1/ 4/ 4	178 113	MS aut
1544	John Kirk	27 Nov 64	Newstead Abbey	1/ 4/ 4	180 114	MS aut
1545	John Murray	27 Nov 64	Newstead Abbey	3/ 8/ 8	177 113	MS aut
1546	Rodrick I. Murchison	28 Nov 64	Newstead Abbey	1/ 4/ 4	8vo	MS aut
1547	John Kirk	30 Nov 64	Newstead Abbey	1/ 4/ 4	177 113	MS aut
1548	John Murray	30 Nov 64	Newstead Abbey	1/ 4/ 3	177 113	MS aut
1549	James Young	30 Nov 64	Newstead Abbey	2/ 6/ 6	182 114	MS aut
1550	John Kirk	1 Dec 64	Newstead Abbey			Pr copy

NO	N	LOCATION	NLS COPY	PUBLICATION
1501		NARS, ST 1/1/1.		Wallis, **ZJJS**, pp. 232—233.
1502		WIHMLL, MS. 56319.	MS.10779 (15)	
1503		NMLZ, on display.	MS.10779 (20)	Oswell, **WCO** II, p. 78, ex.
1504				Fletcher Cat. No. 233 (1971), no. 179.
1505		NARS, LI 1/1/1, pp. 1909—1912.		
1506		RBGK, English Letters, 1865—1900, 92, f. 135.	MS.10779 (10a)	
1507			MS.10769	Sotheby's Cat., 18 Nov 1969, lot 384.
1508		JMPL.		
1509		RHLO, Waller MSS. Afr. s. 16, I, ff. 84—85.	MS.10780 (8)	
1510		AMI.	MS.10777 (1)	
1511				Foskett, **ZmDc**, p. 83.
1512		RBGK, Letters to J.D. Hooker, 14, f. 109.	MS.10779 (10a)	
1513		Foskett Collection.		Foskett, **ZmDc**, pp. 84—85.
1514		JMPL.		
1515		NMLZ, on display.	MS. 10779 (20)	Oswell, **WCO** II, p. 79, ex.
1516		NARS, LI 1/1/1, pp. 1921—1924.		Seaver, **DLLL**, pp. 454—455, ex.
1517		Privately owned.		
1518		PROL, FO 97/322, ff. 286—287.	MS.10780 (4)	
1519		NLS, MS. 1809, ff. 134—135.		
1520		JMPL.		
1521	n			Rendell Cat. No. 60, no. 101
1522		RHLO, Waller MSS. Afr. s. 16, I, ff. 86—87.	MS.10780 (8)	
1523		PROL, FO 97/322, f. 290.	MS.10780 (4)	
1524		NARS, LI 1/1/1, pp. 1925—1932.		
1525		JMPL.		
1526		BLO, MSS. Wilberforce c. 19, ff. 30—33.		
1527				Foskett, **ZmDc**, pp. 86—87.
1528		JMPL.		
1529		RHLO, Waller MSS. Afr. s. 16, I, ff. 88—89.	MS.10780 (8)	
1530		NARS, LI 1/1/1, pp. 1942—1945.		
1531	n	WIHMLL, MS. 67463.	MS.10779 (15)	
1532	n	NARS, LI 1/1/1, pp. 1948—1951.		
1533		NARS, LI 1/1/1, pp. 1952—1955.		
1534		WIHMLL, MS. 63318.	MS.10779 (15)	
1535		NARS, LI 2/1/1.		
1536		RHLO, Waller MSS. Afr. s. 16, I, ff. 90—91.	MS.10780 (8)	
1537				Sotheby's Cat., 28 Mar 1972, lot 290.
1538		USPGL, B4 ii, ff. 16—17.	MS.10779 (14)	
1539		JMPL.		
1540		RHLO, Waller MSS. Afr. s. 16, I, ff. 92—93.	MS.10780 (8)	
1541	n	Foskett Collection.		Foskett, **ZmDc**, pp. 88—89.
1542		Privately owned.		
1543		Foskett Collection.		Foskett, **ZmDc**, p. 90.
1544		Foskett Collection.		Foskett, **ZmDc**, pp. 91—92.
1545		JMPL.		
1546		NARS, LI 1/1/1, pp. 1957—1960.		
1547	n	Foskett Collection.		Foskett, **ZmDc**, pp. 85—86.
1548		JMPL.		
1549		NMLZ, G5.		
1550				Foskett, **ZmDc**, pp. 92—93.

NO	RECIPIENT	DATE	PLACE	LENGTH	SIZE		TYPE
1551	James Atlay	6 Dec 64	Newstead Abbey	1/ 4/ 4	172	113	MS aut
1552	Peter Le Neve Foster	8 Dec 64	Newstead Abbey	1/ 4/ 3	177	113	MS aut
1553	John Kirk	8 Dec 64	Newstead Abbey	1/ 4/ 4	177	113	MS aut
1554	Christopher P.Rigby	8 Dec 64	Newstead Abbey				Pr copy
1555	Horace Waller	8 Dec 64	Newstead Abbey	1/ 4/ 4		8vo	MS aut
1556	John Kirk	12 Dec 64	Newstead Abbey	1/ 4/ 4	176	113	MS aut
1557	Horace Waller	14 Dec 64	Newstead Abbey	1/ 4/ 4		8vo	MS aut
1558	John Murray	15 Dec 64	Newstead Abbey	1/ 4/ 4	177	113	MS aut
1559	Horace Waller	18 Dec 64	Newstead Abbey	1/ 4/ 4		8vo	MS aut
1560	John Kirk	19 Dec 64	Newstead Abbey	1/ 4/ 4	176	113	MS aut
1561	James Stewart	22 Dec 64	Newstead Abbey	1/ 4/ 3	177	114	MS aut
1562	John Kirk	[24, 25 Dec 64]	[Newstead Abbey]	1/ 2/ 2		8vo	MS aut
1563	Horace Waller	28 Dec 64	Newstead Abbey	1/ 4/ 4		8vo	MS aut
1564	Horace Waller	[Dec 64]	Newstead Abbey	1/ 4/ 3		8vo	MS aut
1565	Horace Waller	[26 Sep -31 Dec 64]	Newstead Abbey	1/ 2/ 2		8vo	MS aut
1566	Horace Waller	[26 Sep—31 Dec 64]	Newstead Abbey	1/ 4/ 4		8vo	MS aut in
1567	John Murray	3 Jan 65	Newstead Abbey	1/ 4/ 4	177	113	MS aut
1568	Horace Waller	4 Jan 65	Newstead Abbey	1/ 4/ 3		8vo	MS aut
1569	[James Young]	4 Jan 65	Newstead Abbey	1/ 4/ 4	179	113	MS aut in
1570	Roderick I. Murchison	6 Jan 65	Newstead Abbey	3/12/12		misc	MS aut
1571	James Young	7 Jan 65	Newstead Abbey	1/ 4/ 4	176	114	MS aut
1572	William C. Oswell	8 Jan 65	Newstead Abbey	1/ 4/ 4	180	114	MS aut
1573	Horace Waller	8 Jan 65	Newstead Abbey	1/ 4/ 4		8vo	MS aut
1574	William C. Oswell	11 Jan 65	Newstead Abbey	1/ 4/ 4	179	113	MS aut
1575	Horace Waller	12 Jan 65	Newstead Abbey	1/ 4/ 4		8vo	MS aut
1576	William C. Oswell	12 Jan 65	Newstead Abbey	1/ 4/ 4	179	113	MS aut
1577	Roderick I. Murchison	16 Jan 65	Newstead Abbey	1/ 4/ 4		8vo	MS aut
1578	John Murray	17 Jan 65	Newstead Abbey	1/ 4/ 2	177	113	MS aut
1579	George Thornton	19 Jan 65	Newstead Abbey	1/ 4/ 3	179	114	MS aut
1580	John Murray	20 Jan 65	Newstead Abbey	1/ 4/ 4	179	113	MS aut
1581	James Young	20 Jan 65	[Newstead Abbey?]	1 p			Pr copy
1582	William C. Oswell	21 Jan 65	Newstead Abbey	1/ 4/ 4	179	114	MS aut
1583	John Murray	24 Jan 65	[Newstead Abbey?]	4 pp		8vo	Pr copy
1584	Horace Waller	24 Jan 65	[Newstead Abbey?]	1/ 4/ 4		8vo	MS aut
1585	William C. Chapman	25 Jan 65	Newstead Abbey	1/ 4/ 4	177	114	MS aut
1586	William C. Oswell	25 Jan 65	Newstead Abbey	2/ 6/ 6	179	113	MS aut
1587	Horace Waller	25 Jan 65	Newstead Abbey	1/ 4/ 4		8vo	MS aut
1588	John Murray	26 Jan 65	[Newstead Abbey?]	1/ 4/ 4		8vo	Pr copy
1589	J. Aspinall Turner	26 Jan 65	Newstead Abbey	1/ 4/ 4	177	112	MS aut
1590	William C.Oswell	[Jan 65?]	Newstead Abbey	1/ 4/ 4	180	113	MS aut
1591	Charles A. Alington	3 Feb 65	Newstead Abbey	1/ 4/ 4		8vo	MS aut
1592	William C. Oswell	3 Feb 65	Newstead Abbey	1/ 4/ 4	181	119	MS aut
1593	Horace Waller	3 Feb 65	Newstead Abbey	1/ 4/ 4		8vo	MS aut
1594	William C. Chapman	6 Feb 65	Newstead Abbey	2 pp		8vo	Pr copy
1595	George H. Richards	6 Feb 65	Newstead Abbey	8 pp		fol	MS aut
1596	Horace Waller	7 Feb 65	Newstead Abbey	1/ 4/ 4		8vo	MS aut
1597	William C. Oswell	8 Feb 65	Newstead Abbey	1/ 4/ 4	179	114	MS aut
1598	William C. Oswell	[8 Feb 65?]	Newstead Abbey	2/ 6/ 6	177	111	MS aut in
1599	[Richard?] Owen	8 Feb 65	Newstead Abbey	1/ 4/ 3	179	114	MS aut
1600	Henry Rowley	8 Feb [65]	[Newstead Abbey?]	1/ 4/ 3		8vo	MS aut

NO	N	LOCATION	NLS COPY	PUBLICATION
1551		WIHMLL, MS. 64763.	MS. 10779 (15)	
1552		RSALL.		The Times, 24 Aug 1938, p. 11, c. 5.
1553		Foskett Collection.		Foskett, **ZmDc**, p. 94.
1554				Russell, **RZST**, p. 229.
1555		RHLO, Waller MSS. Afr. s. 16, I, ff. 94—95.	MS. 10780 (8)	
1556		Foskett Collection.		Foskett, **ZmDc**, p. 95.
1557		RHLO, Waller MSS. Afr. s. 16, I, ff. 96—97.		
1558		JMPL.		
1559		RHLO, Waller MSS. Afr. s. 16, I, ff. 98—99.	MS.10780 (8)	
1560		Foskett Collection.		Foskett, **ZmDc**, p. 96.
1561		NARS, ST 1/1/1.		Wallis, **ZJJS**, p. 234.
1562		RHLO, Waller MSS. Afr. s. 16, I, f. 100.	MS.10780 (8)	
1563		RHLO, Waller MSS. Afr. s. 16, I, ff. 101—102.	MS.10780 (8)	
1564		RHLO, Waller MSS. Afr. s. 16, I, ff. 195—196.	MS.10780 (8)	
1565		RHLO, Waller MSS. Afr. s. 16, I, f. 205.	MS.10780 (8)	
1566	n	RHLO, Waller MSS. Afr. s. 16, I, ff. 190—191.	MS.10780 (8)	
1567		JMPL.		
1568		RHLO, Waller MSS. Afr. s. 16, I, ff. 103—104.	MS.10780 (8)	
1569		NMLZ, G5.		
1570		NARS, LI 1/1/1, pp. 2010—2021.		Blaikie, **PLDL**, pp. 349—350, ex.
1571		NMLZ, G5.		
1572		NMLZ, G5.	MS.10779 (20)	
1573		RHLO, Waller MSS. Afr. s. 16, I, ff. 105—106.	MS.10780 (8)	
1574		NMLZ, G5.	MS.10779 (20)	
1575		RHLO, Waller MSS. Afr. s. 16, I, ff. 107—108.	MS.10780 (8)	
1576		NMLZ, G5.		Oswell, **WCO** II, p. 81, ex.
1577		NARS, LI 1/1/1, pp. 2026—2029.		
1578		JMPL.		
1579	n	NARS, LI 2/1/1.		
1580		JMPL.		
1581				Blaikie, **PLDL**, p. 351.
1582		NMLZ, G5.		Oswell, **WCO** II, p. 81, ex.
1583				Sotheby's Cat., 30 Nov 1938, lot 825.
1584		RHLO, Waller MSS. Afr. s. 16, I, ff. 109—110.	MS.10780 (8)	
1585		WIHMLL, MS. 68010E.	MS.10779 (15)	
1586		NMLZ, G5.		
1587		RHLO, Waller MSS. Afr. s. 16, I, ff. 111—112.	MS.10780 (8)	
1588				Sotheby's Cat., 22 Jun 1955, lot 652.
1589		NLS, MS. Acc. 6682.		Sawyer's Cat. SA/84 (May, 1975), no. 67.
1590		NMLZ, G5.		
1591		NLS, MS. 3651, ff. 81—82.		
1592		NMLZ, G5.		
1593		RHLO, Waller MSS. Afr. s. 16, I, ff. 113—114.	MS.10780 (8)	
1594				Maggs' Cat. 916 (Spring 1969), no. 101.
1595		PROL, FO 97/322, ff. 306—309½.	MS.10780 (4)	
1596		RHLO, Waller MSS. Afr. s. 16, I, ff. 115—116.	MS.10780 (8)	
1597		NMLZ, G5.	MS.10779 (20)	
1598		NARS, LI 2/1/1.		Maggs' Cat. 794 (1950), no. 180.
1599		WIHMLL, MS. 68010F.	MS.10779 (15)	
1600		WCLUWJ, Hist. and Lit. Papers, A348/A8.	MS.10779 (10)	Sotheby's Cat., 3 Dec 1913, lot 299, item 9.

NO	RECIPIENT	DATE	PLACE	LENGTH	SIZE		TYPE
1601	Horace Waller	8 Feb [65]	Newstead Abbey	1/ 4/ 3	177	111	MS aut
1602	William C. Oswell	9 Feb 65	Newstead Abbey	1/ 4/ 3	179	113	MS aut
1603	Horace Waller	9 Feb 65	Newstead Abbey	1/ 4/ 4		8vo	MS aut in
1604	Charles A. Alington	11 Feb 65	Newstead Abbey	1/ 4/ 4		8vo	MS aut
1605	John Kirk	11 Feb 65	Newstead Abbey	1 p			Pr copy
1606	Roderick I. Murchison	11 Feb 65	Newstead Abbey	1/ 4/ 4	179	113	MS aut
1607	John Kirk	13 Feb 65	Newstead Abbey	1/ 4/ 4	180	113	MS aut
1608	John Murray	13 Feb 65	Newstead Abbey	1/ 2/ 2	182	119	MS aut
1609	John Kirk	14 Feb 65	Newstead Abbey	2/ 6/ 6	182	118	MS aut
1610	Horace Waller	14 [Feb 65?]	[Newstead Abbey?]	1/ 2/ 2	155	119	MS aut
1611	William C. Oswell	15, 18 Feb 65	Newstead Abbey	2/ 8/ 8	180	112	MS aut
1612	[Austin H. Layard?]	17 Feb 65	Newstead Abbey	1/ 4/ 3	177	114	MS aut
1613	Horace Waller	17 [Feb 65?]	Newstead Abbey	1/ 4/ 4		8vo	MS aut
1614	Charles A. Alington	18 Feb 65	Newstead Abbey	2/ 8/ 7		8vo	MS aut
1615	John Murray	18 Feb 65	Newstead Abbey	1/ 4/ 2	177	113	MS aut
1616	John Murray	20 Feb 65	Newstead Abbey	1/ 4/ 4	179	114	MS aut
1617	Peter Le Neve Foster	23 Feb 65	Newstead Abbey	1/ 4/ 4	177	113	MS aut
1618	John Kirk	24 Feb 65	Newstead Abbey	1/ 2/ 1	182	114	MS aut
1619	John Murray	24 Feb 65	Newstead Abbey	1/ 4/ 4	177	112	MS aut
1620	William C. Oswell	24 [Feb65?]	[Newstead Abbey?]	1/ 2/ 2	204	163	MS aut in
1621	Horace Waller	24 Feb 65	Newstead Abbey	1/ 4/ 4		8vo	MS aut
1622	[J. Bevan Braithwaite??]	24 Feb 65	Newstead Abbey	1/ 4/ 4	177	114	MS aut
1623	John Kirk	28 Feb 65	Newstead Abbey	1/ 4/ 4	182	119	MS aut
1624	[Horace Waller]	[Feb 65??]	Newstead Abbey	1/ 4/ 4		8vo	MS aut
1625	John Murray	[Oct 64—Feb 65]	[Newstead Abbey]	4/12/ 6	225	150	MS aut in
1626		[25 Jan —28 Feb 65?]	[Newstead Abbey?]	1/ 2/ 2	179	112	MS aut in
1627	[William C. Oswell]	1 Mar [65]	[Newstead Abbey?]	1/ 2/ 2	181	120	MS aut in
1628	John Richardson	2 Mar 65	Newstead Abbey	1/ 4/ 4	178	114	MS aut
1629	Thomas Maclear	3 Mar 65	Newstead Abbey	1/ 4/ 4	176	113	MS aut
1630	John Murray	3 Mar 65	[Newstead Abbey?]	2/ 6/ 6	177	112	MS aut
1631	John Murray	4 Mar 65	Newstead Abbey	1/ 4/ 4	182	119	MS aut
1632	John Kirk	5 Mar 6[5]	Newstead Abbey	1/ 4/ 4	177	112	MS aut
1633	Roderick I. Murchison	5 Mar 65	Newstead Abbey	1/ 4/ 4			MS aut
1634	Horace Waller	8 Mar 65	Newstead Abbey	1/ 4/ 3		8vo	MS aut
1635	William C. Oswell	9 Mar 65	Newstead Abbey	1/ 4/ 4	177	112	MS aut
1636	Agnes Livingstone 3	11 Mar 65	19 Bucklersbury, London	1/ 4/ 4	200	124	MS aut
1637	John S. Moffat	[20 Feb—11 Mar 65?]	[Newstead Abbey?]	7 pp			MS aut copy
1638	Agnes Livingstone 3	[13 Mar 65?]	[London?]	1/ 4/ 3	182	120	MS aut
1639	J. Bevan Braithwaite	15 Mar 65	Newstead Abbey	2/ 8/ 6	178	113	MS aut
1640	John Murray	18 Mar 65	Newstead Abbey	3/ 8/ 6	177	113	MS aut
1641	Samuel Wilberforce	18 Mar 65	Newstead Abbey	1/ 4/ 4		8vo	MS aut
1642	Robert Cooke	20 Mar 65	Newstead Abbey	2/ 8/ 8	180	114	MS aut
1643	William C. Oswell	20 Mar 65	Newstead Abbey	1/ 4/ 3		8vo	MS aut
1644	John Kirk	21 Mar 65	Newstead Abbey	1 p			Pr copy
1645	John Murray	21 Mar 65	Newstead Abbey	1/ 4/ 4	178	111	MS aut
1646	William C. Oswell	21 Mar 65	Newstead Abbey	1/ 4/ 4	177	112	MS aut
1647	John Murray	23 Mar 65	[Newstead Abbey?]	2/ 8/ 6	180	112	MS aut in
1648	[James Napier]	23 Mar 65	Newstead Abbey	1/ 4/ 3	220	180	MS aut
1649	William C. Oswell	23 Mar 65	Newstead Abbey	3/12/12	177	112	MS aut
1650	John Kirk	24 Mar 65	Newstead Abbey	2/ 6/ 6	180	112	MS aut

NO	N	LOCATION	NLS COPY	PUBLICATION
1601		WCLUWJ, Hist. and Lit. Papers, A348/A9.	MS.10779 (10)	Sotheby's Cat., 3 Dec 1913, lot 299, item 10.
1602		NMLZ, G5.		Oswell, **WCO** II, p. 82, ex.
1603		RHLO, Waller MSS. Afr. s. 16, I, ff. 117—118.	MS.10780 (8)	
1604		NLS, MS. 3651, ff. 83—84.		
1605				Foskett, **ZmDc**, p. 97.
1606		NARS, LI 1/1/1, pp. 2038—2041.		
1607		Foskett Collection.		Foskett, **ZmDc**, p. 98.
1608		JMPL.		
1609		Foskett Collection.		Foskett, **ZmDc**, pp. 99—100.
1610		RHLO, Waller MSS. Afr. s. 16, I, f. 194.	MS.10780 (8)	
1611		NMLZ, on display.	MS.10779 (20)	Oswell, **WCO** II, pp. 83—84, ex.
1612		NLS, MS. Acc. 6847.		Sotheby's Cat., 23 Jul 1974, lot 541.
1613		RHLO, Waller MSS. Afr. s. 16, I, ff. 184—185.	MS.10780 (8)	
1614		NLS, MS. 3651, ff. 85—88.		
1615		JMPL.		
1616		JMPL.		
1617		RSALL.		
1618		Foskett Collection.		Foskett, **ZmDc**, p. 101.
1619		JMPL.		
1620		NMLZ, G5.		
1621		RHLO, Waller MSS. Afr. s. 16, I, ff. 119—120.	MS.10780 (8)	
1622		WIHMLL, MS.67707.	MS.10779 (15)	
1623		Foskett Collection.		Foskett, **ZmDc**, pp. 102—103.
1624		RHLO, Waller MSS. Afr. s. 16, I, ff. 192—193.	MS.10780 (8)	
1625	n	JMPL.		
1626		ULSOASL, Africa, Wooden Box of L's letters.	MS.10778	
1627		NMLZ, G5.		
1628		WIHMLL, MS. 64761.	MS.10779 (15)	
1629		NARS, LI 1/1/1, pp. 2046—2049.		
1630		JMPL.		
1631		JMPL.		
1632		Foskett Collection.		Foskett, **ZmDc**, pp. 103—104.
1633		NARS, LI 1/1/1, pp. 2051—2054.		
1634		RHLO, Waller MSS. Afr. s. 16, I, ff. 121—122.	MS.10780 (8)	
1635		BLJ, Book no. 5225.		
1636	n	BLL, Add. MS. 50184, f. 105.	MS.10780 (3)	
1637		Wilson Coll., Journal no. 10.	MS.10775	
1638	n	BLL, Add. MS. 50184, ff. 101—102.	MS.10780 (3)	
1639		NLS, MS. Dep. 237.		
1640		JMPL.		
1641		BLO, MSS. Wilberforce c. 19, ff. 34—35.		
1642		JMPL.		
1643		NMLZ, on display.		
1644				Foskett, **ZmDc**, p. 105.
1645		JMPL.		
1646		NMLZ, G5.	MS.10779 (20)	
1647		JMPL.		
1648		ALUSG.	MS.10779 (7)	
1649		NMLZ, G5.	MS.10779 (20)	
1650		Foskett Collection.		Foskett, **ZmDc**, pp. 106—107.

NO	RECIPIENT	DATE	PLACE	LENGTH	SIZE		TYPE
1651	James Stewart	24,25 Mar 65	Newstead Abbey	2/ 8/ 5	180	112	MS aut
1652	Roderick I. Murchison	25 Mar 65	Newstead Abbey	1/ 4/ 4			MS aut
1653	John Murray	25 Mar 65	Newstead Abbey	1/ 4/ 4	180	112	MS aut
1654	Adam Sedgwick	26 Mar 65	Newstead Abbey	3/12/12	180	112	MS aut
1655	John Kirk	27, 28 Mar 65	Newstead Abbey	1/ 4/ 4	180	112	MS aut
1656	[John Kirk]	28 Mar 65	Newstead Abbey	1/ 2/ 2	180	112	MS aut
1657	John Murray	31 Mar 65	Newstead Abbey	1/ 4/ 4	180	112	MS aut
1658	James Stewart	31 Mar 65	Newstead Abbey	1/ 4/ 4	177	112	MS aut
1659	Charles Meller	[1 Nov 64—31 Mar 65]	[Newstead Abbey?]	1/ 2/ 1	183	112	MS aut
1660	[James Young]	[Mar 65?]	[Newstead Abbey?]	1/ 2/ 2	177	112	MS aut in
1661	[John Murray]	1 Apr 65	Newstead Abbey	1/ 4/ 4	177	112	MS aut
1662	William C. Oswell	1 Apr 65	Newstead Abbey	1/ 4/ 4	177	112	MS aut
1663	John Kirk	3 Apr 65	[Newstead Abbey?]	2/ 6/ 6	182	118	MS aut
1664	William C. Oswell	3, 6 Apr [65]	Newstead Abbey	2/ 6/ 6	177	112	MS aut
1665		3 Apr 65	Newstead Abbey	3 pp	8vo		Pr copy
1666	Roderick I. Murchison	4 Apr 65	Newstead Abbey	1/ 4/ 4			MS aut
1667	William C. Oswell	4 Apr 65	Newstead Abbey	1/ 4/ 4	177	112	MS aut
1668	John Kirk	5 Apr 65	Newstead Abbey	2 pp			Pr copy
1669	Horace Waller	6 Apr 65	Newstead Abbey	1/ 4/ 4	8vo		MS aut
1670	William F. Webb	6 Apr 65	Newstead Abbey	2/ 6/ 6	177	111	MS aut
1671	[Robert Arthington?]	7 Apr 65	Newstead Abbey	1/ 4/ 4	184	118	MS aut
1672	William C. Oswell	7 Apr 65	[Newstead Abbey?]	1/ 4/ 4	184	118	MS aut fr
1673	[William C. Oswell]	8 Apr 65	[Newstead Abbey?]	1/ 4/ 4	184	119	MS aut
1674	William C. Oswell	10 Apr 65	Newstead Abbey	2/ 4/ 4	8vo		MS aut fr
1675	James Stewart	13 Apr 65	[Newstead Abbey?]	2/ 4/ 3			MS aut
1676	John Kirk	14 Apr 65	Newstead Abbey	1/ 4/ 4	176	112	MS aut
1677	William C. Oswell	14 Apr 65	Newstead Abbey	1/ 4/ 4	177	112	MS aut
1678	William C. Oswell	15 Apr 65	[Newstead Abbey ?]	1 p			Pr copy
1679	William C. Oswell	16 Apr 65	Newstead Abbey	3/ 8/ 8	misc		MS aut fr
1680	[William C. Oswell]	17 [Apr 65?]	[Newstead Abbey?]	1/ 2/ 2	176	113	MS aut
1681	William C. Oswell	21 Apr 65	Newstead Abbey	3/ 8/ 8	180	113	MS aut
1682	Robert Cooke	22 Apr 65	Newstead Abbey	1/ 4/ 4	179	114	MS aut
1683	William C. Oswell	22 Apr 65	Newstead Abbey	2/ 6/ 6	179	113	MS aut
1684	Horace Waller	23 Apr 65	Newstead Abbey	1/ 4/ 4	8vo		MS aut
1685	William C. Oswell	24 Apr 65	Newstead Abbey	1/ 2/ 2	180	113	MS aut in
1686	Mr. Frost	25 Apr 65	Newstead Abbey	1/ 2/ 2	8vo		MS aut
1687	Roderick I. Murchison	25 Apr 65	Storey's Hotel, 8 Dover St.	1/ 4/ 4	182	119	MS aut
1688	William C. Oswell	25 Apr 65	Newstead Abbey	1/ 4/ 4	179	113	MS aut
1689	Frederick and Mrs Fitch	26 Apr 65	8 Dover St., Piccadilly	3 pp	8vo		Ph copy
1690	William C. Oswell	28 Apr 65	Storey's Hotel	1/ 4/ 4	180	111	MS aut fr
1691	William C. Oswell	[Apr 65]		1/ 4/ 2	181	111	MS aut
1692	Roderick I. Murchison	1 May 65	8 Dover Street	1/ 4/ 4	180	111	MS aut
1693	William C. Oswell	1 May 65	8 Dover Street	1/ 4/ 4	180	111	MS aut
1694	[William C. Oswell]	[1 May 65]		1/ 4/ 4	201	125	MS aut
1695	Horace Waller	2 May 65	8 Dover Street	1/ 4/ 3	8vo		MS aut in
1696	[Robert Arthington?]	4 May 65	8 Dover Street	1/ 4/ 4	181	115	MS aut
1697	James Hamilton	4 May 65	8 Dover Street, Piccadilly	1/ 4/ 4	180	114	MS aut
1698	William C. Oswell	4 May 65		1/ 4/ 4	180	115	MS aut in
1699	Austin H. Layard	5 May 65	8 Dover Street, Piccadilly	1/ 2/ 1	fol		MS aut
1700	William C. Oswell	5 May 65	8 Dover Street	1/ 4/ 4	176	112	MS aut

NO	N	LOCATION	NLS COPY	PUBLICATION
1651		NARS, ST 1/1/1.		Wallis, **ZJJS**, pp. 236—237.
1652		NARS, LI 1/1/1, pp. 2063—2066.		
1653		JMPL.		
1654		NMLZ, on display.	MS.10779 (20)	Sotheby's Cat., 9 Jun 1936, lot 503.
1655		Foskett Collection.		Foskett, **ZmDc**, p. 108.
1656		Foskett Collection.		Foskett, **ZmDc**, pp. 109—110.
1657		JMPL.		
1658		NARS, ST 1/1/1.		Wallis, **ZJJS**, pp. 237—238.
1659			MS.10769	Sotheby's Cat., 18 Nov 1969, lot 384.
1660	n	ALUSG.	MS.10779 (7)	
1661		JMPL.		
1662		NMLZ, G5.		
1663	n	Foskett Collection.		Foskett, **ZmDc**, pp. 113—114.
1664		NMLZ, G5.		
1665				Sotheby's Cat., 20 Feb 1967, p. 52.
1666		NARS, LI 1/1/1, pp. 2070—2073.		
1667		NMLZ, G5.		
1668				Foskett, **ZmDc**, pp. 110—111.
1669		RHLO, Waller MSS. Afr. s. 16, I, ff.123—124.	MS.10780 (8)	
1670		NLS, MS. 10707, ff. 78—81.		
1671	n	WIHMLL, MS. 56118.	MS.10779 (15)	
1672		NMLZ, G5.		
1673		NMLZ, G5.		
1674		NMLZ, G5.		
1675		NARS, ST 1/1/1.		Wallis, **ZJJS**, pp. 238—239.
1676		Foskett Collection.		Foskett, **ZmDc**, p. 112.
1677		NMLZ, G5.		
1678				Oswell, **WCO** II, p. 84, ex.
1679		NMLZ, G5.		Oswell, **WCO** II, p. 85, ex.
1680		NMLZ, G5.		
1681		NMLZ, G5.		
1682		WIHMLL, MS. 63007.	MS.10779 (15)	
1683		NMLZ, G5.		
1684		RHLO, Waller MSS. Afr. s. 16, I, ff. 125—126.	MS.10780 (8)	
1685		NMLZ, G5.		
1686		NLS, MS. 2522, f. 69.		
1687		NARS, LI 1/1/1, pp. 2078—2081.		
1688		NMLZ, G5.		Oswell, **WCO** II, p. 85, ex.
1689		NARS, LI 2/1/1.	MS.10779 (21)	
1690		NMLZ, G5.		
1691	n	WIHMLL, MS. 63318.	MS.10779 (15)	
1692		NARS, LI 1/1/1, pp. 2082—2085.		
1693		NMLZ, G5.		
1694	n	NMLZ, G5.		Oswell, **WCO** II, p. 84, ex.
1695		RHLO, Waller MSS. Afr. s. 16, I, ff. 127—128.	MS.10780 (8)	
1696	n	WIHMLL, MS. 56119.	MS.10779 (15)	
1697		SNMDL.	MS.10708, f. 115	
1698		NMLZ, G5.		
1699		PROL, FO 84/1249, f. 101.		
1700		USPGL, SPG Autographs XIV.	MS.10779 (14)	Oswell, **WCO** II, p. 86, ex.

NO	RECIPIENT	DATE	PLACE	LENGTH	SIZE		TYPE
1701	Austin H. Layard	8 May 65	8 Dover Street, London	2 pp	fol		MS aut
1702	Robert Moffat 1	8 May 65	50 Albemarle St., London	1/ 4/ 4	180	115	MS aut
1703	William C. Oswell	8 May 65	8 Dover Street	1/ 4/ 4	187	121	MS aut
1704	William C. Oswell	10 May 65		1/ 4/ 4	180	114	MS aut
1705	[James Young?]	10 May 65	19 Bucklersbury, London	1/ 4/ 3	199	128	MS aut in
1706	John Kirk	11 May 65		1/ 4/ 3	209	128	MS aut
1707	William C. Oswell	11 May 65		1/ 2/ 2	208	125	MS aut in
1708	Horace Waller	11 May 65	8 Dover Street	1/ 4/ 4	210	130	MS aut
1709	Charles A. Alington	[12 May 65?]	[Dover Street?]	1/ 2/ 1	208	128	MS aut
1710	Arthur Mills	12 May 65	8 Dover St., Piccadilly	4 pp	8vo		Pr copy
1711	John Kirk	13 May 65	8 Dover Street, London	2/ 8/ 8	180	115	MS aut
1712	William C. Oswell	[15 May 65]		1/ 2/ 2	180	115	MS aut
1713	[James Young]	[8 or 15 May 65]		1/ 2/ 2	181	114	MS aut in
1714	William C. Oswell	18 May 65		1/ 2/ 1	210	130	MS aut
1715	Charles B. Adderley	19 May 65	8 Dover Street	1/ 4/ 4	8vo		Ph copy
1716	[Lord John Russell]	19 May 65		1/ 2/ 1	fol		MS aut
1717		[25 Apr—19 May 65?]	8 Dover Street, Piccadilly	4 pp	8vo		Pr copy
1718	William C. Oswell	22 May 65		2 / 6/ 6	180	114	MS aut
1719	Angela Burdett-Coutts	23 May 65	London	6 pp	8vo		Pr copy
1720	Arthur Mills	23 May 65		2 pp	8vo		Pr copy
1721	Lord John Russell	23 May 65	50 Albemarle Street	1 p	fol		MS aut
1722	William C. Oswell	25 May 65	Burnbank Road, Hamilton	1/ 4/ 4	180	114	MS aut
1723	Arthur Tidman	25 May 65	Burnbank Road, Hamilton	1/ 4/ 4	180	115	MS aut
1724	Charles A. Alington	26 May 65	Burnbank Road, Hamilton	1/ 4/ 4	8vo		MS aut
1725	Thomas Maclear	27 May 65	Burnbank Road, Hamilton	3/12/12	185	115	MS aut
1726	William F. Webb	27 May 65		1 p			Pr copy
1727	John Murray	31 May 65	Burnbank Road, Hamilton	1/ 4/ 4	185	114	MS aut
1728	John Phillips	[Sep 64—May 65??]		2 pp	8vo		Pr copy
1729	William C. Oswell	[Feb—May 65]		2 pp			Pr copy
1730	John Murray	1 Jun 65		1/ 2/ 2	184	115	MS aut
1731	Horace Waller	1 Jun 65	Burnbank Road, Hamilton	1/ 4/ 4	8vo		MS aut
1732	William Sunley	2 Jun 65	Burnbank Road, Hamilton	1/ 4/ 4	176	110	MS aut
1733	Arthur Tidman	2 Jun 65	Burnbank Road, Hamilton	1/ 4/ 4	175	111	MS aut
1734		2 Jun 65	Burnbank Road, Hamilton	1/ 2/ 1	172	112	MS aut
1735	John Murray	3 Jun 65	Burnbank Road, Hamilton	1/ 4/ 3	174	112	MS aut
1736	Horace Waller	5 Jun 65	Hamilton	1/ 4/ 4	8vo		MS aut
1737	Harriette I. Livingstone	6 Jun 65	Burnbank Road, Hamilton	6 pp			Mf copy
1738	William C. Oswell	6 Jun 65	Hamilton	1/ 4/ 4	180	114	MS aut
1739	John W. Festing	8 Jun 65	Burnbank Road, Hamilton	1/ 4/ 4	181	113	MS aut
1740	John Kirk	8 Jun 65	Burnbank Road, Hamilton	2/ 8/ 8	182	114	MS aut
1741	John Murray	9 Jun 65	Burnbank Road, Hamilton	1/ 4/ 4	181	114	MS aut
1742	William C. Oswell	9 Jun 65	Burnbank Road, Hamilton	1/ 4/ 4	181	114	MS aut in
1743	Horace Waller	9 Jun 65	Burnbank Road, Hamilton	1/ 4/ 4	8vo		MS aut
1744	Roderick I. Murchison	15 Jun 65	Botanic Garden, Oxford	1/ 4/ 3	180	114	MS aut
1745	[Adam Sedgwick?]	15 Jun 65	Botanic Garden, Oxford	1/ 4/ 3	180	114	MS aut
1746	John Murray	17 Jun 65	Botanic Garden, Oxford	1/ 4/ 3	181	114	MS aut
1747	Roderick I. Murchison	19 Jun 65	Botanic Garden, Oxford	1/ 4/ 2	180	114	MS aut
1748	John Murray	19 Jun 65	Botanic Garden, Oxford	1/ 4/ 2	182	113	MS aut
1749	Charles A. Alington	20 Jun 65	Burnbank Road, Hamilton	1/ 4/ 4	184	115	MS aut
1750	John Livingstone	20 Jun 65	Burnbank Road, Hamilton	1/ 4/ 4	185	115	MS aut

NO	N	LOCATION	NLS COPY	PUBLICATION
1701		PROL, FO 84/1249, ff. 104—105.		
1702		BLL, Add. MS. 50184, f. 106.	MS.10780 (3)	
1703		NMLZ, G5.		
1704		NMLZ, G5.		
1705	n	NMLZ, G5.		
1706		USPGL.	MS.10779 (14)	
1707		NMLZ, G5.		
1708		RHLO, Waller MSS. Afr. s. 16, I, ff. 129—130.	MS.10780 (8)	
1709		NLS, MS. 3651, f. 96.		
1710				Sotheby's Cat., 14 Dec 1976, lot 142.
1711		Foskett Collection.		Foskett, ZmDc, pp. 115—116.
1712	n	NMLZ, G5.		
1713	n	NMLZ, G5.		
1714	n	NMLZ, G5.		
1715		SNMDL.	MS.10708, f. 117	
1716	n	PROL, FO 84/1249, f. 106.		
1717				Sotheby's Cat., 14 Feb 1929, lot 842.
1718		NMLZ, on display.	MS.10779 (20)	Oswell, WCO II, pp. 86—87, ex.
1719	n			Maggs' Cat. No. 804 (1951), no. 998.
1720				Rendell Cat. No. 85, no. 125.
1721		PROL, FO 84/1249, f. 108		
1722		NMLZ, on display.	MS.10779 (20)	
1723		ULSOASL, Africa, Wooden Box of L's letters.	MS.10778	
1724		NLS, MS. 3651, ff. 91—92.		
1725		Privately owned.		
1726	n			Oswell, WCO II, p. 88, ex.
1727		JMPL.		
1728				Sotheby's Cat., 28 Mar 1960, lot 140.
1729				Oswell, WCO II, pp. 87—88, ex.
1730		JMPL.		
1731		RHLO, Waller MSS. Afr. s. 16, I, ff. 131—132.	MS.10780 (8)	
1732	n	WIHMLL, MS. 67519.	MS.10779 (15)	Seaver, DLLL, p. 478, ex.
1733		ULSOASL, Africa, Wooden Box of L's letters.	MS.10778	
1734		WCLUWJ, HA16f.	MS.10779 (10)	
1735		JMPL.		
1736		RHLO, Waller MSS.Afr. s. 16, I, ff. 133—134.	MS.10780 (8)	
1737		LCUSWDC, Mss. Div., AC 6907, L. Family Mf.	MS.10779 (22)	
1738		NMLZ, on display.	MS.10779 (20)	
1739		USPGL, B4 ii, ff. 18—19.	MS.10779 (14)	
1740		Foskett Collection.		Foskett, ZmDc, pp. 117—119.
1741		JMPL.		
1742		NMLZ, G5.		
1743		RHLO, Waller MSS. Afr. s. 16, I, ff. 135—136.	MS.10780 (8)	
1744	n	NARS, LI 1/1/1, pp. 2086—2088.		
1745		NARS, LI 2/1/1.		
1746		JMPL.		
1747		NARS, LI 1/1/1, pp. 2089—2090.		
1748		JMPL.		
1749	n	NLS, MS. 3651, ff. 94—95.		
1750		NLS, MS. 2522, ff. 70—71.		Sotheby's Cat., 29 Mar 1922, lot 616.

NO	RECIPIENT	DATE	PLACE	LENGTH	SIZE		TYPE
1751	James Young	20 Jun 65	Burnbank Road, Hamilton	1/ 4/ 4	185	115	MS aut
1752	Roderick I. Murchison	21 Jun 65	Burnbank Road, Hamilton	3/10/ 9	190	114	MS aut fr
1753	Horace Waller	21 Jun 65	Burnbank Road, Hamilton	1/ 4/ 4		8vo	MS aut
1754	Horace Waller	22 Jun 65	Burnbank Road, Hamilton	1/ 4/ 4		8vo	MS aut
1755	John Kirk	24 Jun 65	Burnbank Road, Hamilton	1 p			Pr copy
1756	Robert Napier	24 Jun 65	Burnbank Road, Hamilton	1/ 4/ 4	189	118	MS aut
1757	James Young	24 Jun 65	Burnbank Road, Hamilton	1/ 4/ 4	185	115	MS aut
1758	William C. Oswell	27 Jun 65	Burnbank Road, Hamilton	1/ 4/ 4	180	113	MS aut
1759	Horace Waller	27 Jun 65	Burnbank Road, Hamilton	1/ 4/ 4		8vo	MS aut
1760	Roderick I. Murchison	30 Jun 65	Limefield, by West Calder	1/ 4/ 4	175	111	MS aut
1761	John Murray	30 Jun 65	Limefield, by West Calder	1/ 4/ 4	175	110	MS aut
1762	[Horace Waller]	[Jun 65?]	[Burnbank Road, Hamilton?]	1/ 2/ 2		8vo	MS aut
1763	James Loudon	[30 May–4 Jul 65?]	[Hamilton]	1/ 2/ 2		8vo	MS aut
1764	John Burns	6 Jul 65	Burnbank Road, Hamilton	1/ 4/ 4		8vo	MS aut
1765	William Logan	6 Jul 65	[Hamilton]	4 pp		8vo	Pr copy
1766	[James Young]	[1 Aug 64–6 Jul 65?]		1/ 2/ 2	181	114	MS aut in
1767	Thomas Guthrie	13 Jul 65	48 Euston Square, London	2/ 6/ 6	181	113	MS aut
1768	Horace Waller	13 Jul 65	48 Euston Square, London	1/ 4/ 1		8vo	MS aut
1769	Alan H. Gardner	15 Jul 65	48 Euston Square, London	2/ 6/ 6	179	115	MS aut
1770	Roderick I. Murchison	21 Jul 65	Newstead Abbey	2/ 8/ 8	180	113	MS aut
1771	Horace Waller	21 Jul 65	Newstead Abbey	1/ 4/ 4		8vo	MS aut
1772	Horace Waller	21 Jul 65	Newstead Abbey	1/ 4/ 2		8vo	MS aut
1773	William C. Oswell	24 Jul 65	Newstead Abbey	1/ 4/ 4	179	113	MS aut
1774	Frederick Fitch	25 Jul 65	48 Euston Square	4 pp		8vo	Ph copy
1775	William C. Oswell	25 Jul 65	48 Euston Square	1/ 4/ 1		8vo	MS aut
1776	James Young	[25 Jul 65]		1/ 2/ 1	181	114	MS aut in
1777	Adam Sedgwick	27 Jul 65	48 Euston Square	4 pp		8vo	Pr copy
1778	Horace Waller	27 Jul 65	48 Euston Square	1/ 4/ 4		8vo	MS aut
1779	Arthur Mills	28 Jul 65		4 pp		8vo	Pr copy
1780	Adam Sedgwick	28 Jul 65	48 Euston Square	2 pp		8vo	Pr copy
1781		28 Jul 65	48 Euston Square	1/ 4/ 3	177	115	MS aut
1782		28 Jul 65	[48 Euston Square?]	3 pp			MS aut copy
1783	John Kirk	30 Jul 65	Newstead Abbey	2/ 8/ 8	180	113	MS aut
1784	James Hamilton	30 Jul 65	Newstead Abbey	1/ 4/ 4	178	114	MS aut
1785	Horace Waller	[26 Sep 64–30 Jul 65]	Newstead Abbey	1/ 4/ 4		8vo	MS aut
1786	[Horace Waller]	[26 Sep 64–30 Jul 65]	Newstead Abbey	2/ 6/ 6		8vo	MS aut in
1787	[Horace Waller]	[26 Sep 64–30 Jul 65]	Newstead Abbey	1/ 4/ 4		8vo	MS aut in
1788	[James Young]	[26 Sep 64–30 Jul 65]	Newstead Abbey	1/ 4/ 4	179	113	MS aut in
1789	[Lady Franklin]	7 Aug 65	50 Albemarle Street	1/ 4/ 3	182	113	MS aut
1790	William C. Oswell	7 Aug 65	50 Albemarle Street	1/ 4/ 4	184	114	MS aut
1791	Roderick I. Murchison	7 Aug 65	London	8 pp			MS aut copy
1792	Roderick I. Murchison	[7 Aug 65]		2/ 8/ 8	176	113	MS aut in
1793	Horace Waller	8 Aug 65	48 Euston Square	1/ 4/ 3		8vo	MS aut
1794	James Young	8 Aug 65	48 Euston Square	1/ 4/ 4	177	114	MS aut
1795	William C. Oswell	10 Aug 65	48 Euston Square	1/ 4/ 4	177	114	MS aut
1796	Horace Waller	10 Aug 65	Euston Square	3 pp		8vo	Pr copy
1797	[John Loader?]	11 Aug 65	50 Albemarle Street	1/ 4/ 2	181	115	MS aut
1798	Wilbraham Taylor	[12 Aug 65?]	48 Euston Square	1/ 2/ 2	181	114	MS aut
1799	William F. Webb	12 Aug 65	[48 Euston Square?]	1 p			Pr copy
1800	James Young	12 Aug 65	48 Euston Square	1/ 4/ 3	176	114	MS aut

NO	N	LOCATION	NLS COPY	PUBLICATION
1751		NMLZ, G5.		
1752		NARS, LI 1/1/1, pp. 2091—2099.		
1753		RHLO, Waller MSS. Afr. s. 16, I, ff. 137—138.	MS.10780 (8)	
1754		RHLO, Waller MSS. Afr. s. 16, I, ff. 139—140.	MS.10780 (8)	
1755				Foskett, **ZmDc**, p. 119.
1756		KCLUND.	MS.10779 (6)	Napier, **LRN**, pp. 216—217.
1757		NMLZ, G5.		
1758		NMLZ, on display.	MS.10779 (20)	Oswell, **WCO** II, pp. 88—89, ex.
1759		RHLO, Waller MSS.Afr. s. 16, I, ff. 141—142.	MS.10780 (8)	
1760	n	NARS, LI 1/1/1, pp. 2100—2103.		
1761		JMPL.		
1762		RHLO, Waller MSS. Afr. s. 16, I, f. 199.	MS.10780 (8)	
1763		SNMDL.	MS.10708, f. 132	
1764		CLRUGSA.	MS.10777 (19)	**SC**, May 1923, p. 11.
1765				Sotheby's Cat., 28 Feb 1949, lot 163.
1766		NMLZ, G5.		
1767	n	NLS, MS. 10768, ff. 64—66.		Christies' Cat. 22 Jul 1970, lot 70.
1768		RHLO, Waller MSS. Afr. s. 16, I, ff. 143—144.	MS.10780 (8)	
1769		NLS, MS.10768, ff. 67—69.		Sotheby's Cat., 14 Jul 1970, lot 563.
1770		NARS, LI 1/1/1, pp. 2104—2111.		
1771		RHLO, Waller MSS. Afr. s. 16, I, ff. 147—148.	MS.10780 (8)	
1772	n	RHLO, Waller MSS. Afr. s. 16, I, ff. 145—146.	MS.10780 (8)	
1773		NMLZ, G5.	MS.10779 (20)	
1774		NARS, LI 2/1/1.	MS.10779 (21)	
1775		NMLZ, G5.		
1776		NMLZ, G5.		
1777	n			Sotheby's Cat., 9 Jun 1950, lot 310.
1778		RHLO, Waller MSS. Afr. s. 16, I, ff. 149—150.	MS.10780 (8)	
1779				Rendell Cat. No. 88, no. 97.
1780				Sotheby's Cat., 9 Jun 1936, lot 506.
1781		NLS, MS. 10768, ff. 70—71.		
1782	n	Wilson Coll., Journal no. 10.	MS.10775	
1783		Foskett Collection.		Foskett, **ZmDc**, pp. 120—121.
1784		NLS, MS. 10768, ff. 72—73.		Sotheby's Cat., 30 Oct 1973, lot 383.
1785		RHLO, Waller MSS. Afr. s. 16, I, ff. 186—187.	MS.10780 (8)	
1786	n	RHLO, Waller MSS. Afr. s. 16, I, ff. 188—189, 206.	MS.10780 (8)	
1787		RHLO, Waller MSS. Afr. s. 16, I, ff. 197—198.	MS.10780 (8)	
1788		NMLZ, G5.		
1789	n	JMPL.		Maggs' Cat. 927 (Autumn, 1970), no. 130
1790		WIHMLL, MS. 63002.	MS.10779 (15)	
1791	n	Wilson Coll., Journal no. 10.	MS.10775	Seaver, **DLLL**, pp. 355—356.
1792	n	NARS, LI 1/1/1, pp. 2112—2119.		
1793		LSBCCWSWW.		
1794		NMLZ, G5.		
1795		NMLZ, G5.		
1796				Myers' Cat. No. 2 (1959), no. 218.
1797	n	WIHMLL, MS. A167.	MS.10779 (15)	
1798	n	WIHMLL, MS. 63318.	MS.10779 (15)	
1799				Oswell, **WCO** II, p. 89, ex.
1800		NMLZ, G5.		

NO	RECIPIENT	DATE	PLACE	LENGTH	SIZE		TYPE
1801	John Murray	13 Aug 65	48 Euston Square	1/ 4/ 4	177	113	MS aut
1802							
1803	[Horace Waller]	[26 Sep 64—13 Aug 65]		1/ 2/ 2		8vo	MS aut in
1804	[Horace Waller]	[26 Sep 64—13 Aug 65]		1/ 2/ 2		8vo	MS aut
1805	[Horace Waller]	[26 Sep 64—13 Aug 65]		1/ 2/ 2		8vo	MS aut in
1806							
1807	[Horace Waller]	[1 Jan —13 Aug 65]		1/ 2/ 1	182	113	MS aut in
1808	Agnes Livingstone 3	19 Aug 65	Marseilles	1/ 4/ 4	205	134	MS aut
1809	Roderick I. Murchison	19 Aug 65	Marseilles	2/ 8/ 7	205	133	MS aut
1810	William C. Oswell	19 Aug 65	Marseilles	1/ 4/ 4	205	133	MS aut
1811	Agnes Livingstone 3	22 Aug 65	At sea on board "Massilia"	1/ 4/ 4	205	130	MS aut
1812	James Young	22 Aug 65	On board S.S. "Massilia"	1/ 4/ 4	205	133	MS aut
1813	Agnes Livingstone 3	26 Aug 65	Near Alexandria	2/ 8/ 4		8vo	MS aut
1814	Horace Waller	26 Aug 65	Near Alexandria	2/ 8/ 6	205	130	MS aut
1815	Agnes Livingstone 3	3 Sep 65	Gulph of Aden	2/ 8/ 8	205	130	MS aut
1816	[Agnes Livingstone 3]	[22 Aug—10 Sep 65]	[At sea, en route to Bombay]	1/ 2/ 1		8vo	MS aut in
1817		[27 Aug—10 Sep 65]		2 pp		8vo	Pr copy
1818	Agnes Livingstone 3	11, 20, 28 Sep 65	Kambala Hill, Bombay	3/12/12	205	133	MS aut
1819	Capt. White	11 Sep 65	Kambala Hill, Bombay	4 pp		8vo	Pr copy
1820	John Kirk	20 Sep 65	Poonah	1/ 4/ 4	205	133	MS aut
1821	W.S. Price	27 Sep 65	Bombay	3/10/ 9		8vo	MS aut
1822	Horace Waller	27 Sep 65	Bombay	1/ 4/ 4	205	130	MS aut
1823	Austin H. Layard	28 Sep 65	Bombay	1/ 4/ 4		8vo	MS aut
1824	Roderick I. Murchison	28 Sep 65	Bombay	1/ 4/ 4	177	113	MS aut
1825	John Murray	28 Sep 65	Bombay	1/ 4/ 4	177	113	MS aut
1826	William C. Oswell	29 Sep 65	Bombay	1/ 4/ 4	177	113	MS aut in
1827	[C.S.de N. Lucas?]	6 Oct 65	Poonah	1/ 4/ 4		8vo	Ph copy
1828	Agnes Livingstone 3	12 Oct 65	Bombay	1/ 4/ 4	215	132	MS aut
1829	Agnes Livingstone 3	26, 28 Oct 65	Bombay	2/ 8/ 8	200	125	MS aut
1830	Roderick I. Murchison	26 Oct 65	Bombay	1/ 4/ 4	180	113	MS aut
1831	Horace Waller	26 Oct 65	Remington & Co., Bombay	2/ 8/ 8		8vo	MS aut
1832	Thomas Maclear	28 Oct 65	Remington & Co., Bombay	3/12/12	200	122	MS aut
1833	C.S. de N. Lucas	30 Oct 65	Cambala Hill	1/ 4/ 4	178	115	MS aut
1834	W.S. Price	7 Nov 65	Bombay	4 pp		8vo	Pr copy
1835	Agnes Livingstone 3	9 Nov 65	Surat	1/ 4/ 4	179	113	MS aut
1836	Agnes Livingstone 3	14 [Oct or Nov 65]		1/ 2/		8vo	MS aut
1837	John Kirk	15 Nov 65	Bombay	2 pp			Pr copy
1838	Horace Waller	15 Nov 65	Bombay	1/ 4/ 4	202	125	MS aut
1839	J.S. Willans	16 Nov 65		3 pp		8vo	Pr copy
1840	Agnes Livingstone 3	17 Nov 65	Bombay	1/ 4/ 4	180	114	MS aut in
1841	Agnes Livingstone 3	24, 27 Nov 65	Bombay	1/ 4/ 4	179	114	MS aut in
1842	Roderick I. Murchison	27 Nov 65	Bombay	2/ 8/ 8	208	126	MS aut
1843	James Hamilton	28 Nov 65	Bombay	1/ 4/ 4	180	114	MS aut
1844	Lord John Russell	28 Nov 65	Bombay	6 pp		fol	MS aut
1845	W.S. Price	[Nov 65]	Malabar Hill	2 pp		8vo	Pr copy
1846	John Kirk	2 Dec 65	Bombay	1/ 4/ 4	201	125	MS aut
1847	Agnes Livingstone 3	2 Dec 65	Bombay	1/ 4/ 4	200	125	MS aut
1848	Thomas S. Livingstone	2 Dec 65	Bombay	2/ 8/ 8	202	127	MS aut
1849	Horace Waller	2 Dec 65	Bombay	1/ 4/ 4	202	126	MS aut
1850	Horace Waller	4 Dec 65	Bombay	1/ 4/ 3	196	162	MS aut

NO	N	LOCATION	NLS COPY	PUBLICATION
1801		JMPL.		
1802	n			
1803		RHLO, Waller MSS. Afr. s. 16, I, f. 201.	MS.10780 (8)	
1804		RHLO, Waller MSS. Afr. s. 16, I, f. 202.	MS.10780 (8)	
1805		RHLO, Waller MSS. Afr. s. 16, I, f. 204.	MS.10780 (8)	
1806	n			
1807		RHLO, Waller MSS. Afr. s. 16, I, f. 183.	MS.10780 (8)	
1808		BLL, Add. MS. 50184, ff. 107—108.	MS.10780 (3)	
1809		NARS, LI 1/1/1, pp. 2120—2126.		
1810	n	NMLZ, G5.		Oswell, **WCO** II, p. 90, ex.
1811		BLL, Add. MS. 50184, ff. 109—110.	MS.10780 (3)	
1812		NMLZ, G5.		
1813	n	BLL, Add. MS. 50184, ff. 111—114.	MS.10780 (3)	
1814	n	RHLO, Waller MSS. Afr. s. 16, I, ff. 151—154.	MS.10780 (8)	
1815		BLL, Add. MS. 50184, ff. 117—119.	MS.10780 (3)	
1816	n	BLL, Add. MS. 50184, f. 115.	MS.10780 (3)	
1817				Sotheby's Cat., 3 Dec 1974, lot 70.
1818		BLL, Add. MS. 50184, ff. 120—125.	MS.10780 (3)	Blaikie, **PLDL**, pp. 361—362, ex.
1819	n			Edwards' Cat. No. 971 (1973), no. 242.
1820		Foskett Collection.		Foskett, **ZmDc**, pp. 125—126.
1821		BLJ, Book no. 5318, Acc. Reg. 4669.		Sotheby's Cat., 29 Jun 1939, lot 1486.
1822		RHLO, Waller MSS. Afr. s. 16, I, ff. 155—156.	MS.10780 (8)	
1823		BLL, Add. MS. 39117, ff. 190—191.	MS.10780 (3)	
1824		NARS, LI 1/1/1, pp. 2127—2130.		
1825		JMPL.		
1826		NMLZ, on display.	MS.10779 (20)	Oswell, **WCO** II, pp. 91—92, ex.
1827		SNMDL.	MS.10708, f. 122	
1828		BLL, Add. MS. 50184, ff. 126—127.	MS.10780 (3)	
1829		BLL, Add. MS. 50184, ff. 128—131.	MS.10780 (3)	
1830		NARS, LI 1/1/1, pp. 2131—2134.		
1831		RHLO, Waller MSS. Afr. s. 16, I, ff. 157—160.	MS.10780 (8)	
1832		NARS, LI 1/1/1, pp. 2135—2147.		
1833		WIHMLL, MS. 57496.	MS.10779 (15)	
1834				Maggs' Cat. 1919, no. 480.
1835		BLL, Add. MS. 50184, ff. 132—133.	MS.10780 (3)	
1836	n	BLL, Add. MS. 50184, f. 116.	MS.10780 (3)	
1837				Foskett, **ZmDc**, pp. 127—128.
1838		RHLO, Waller MSS. Afr. s. 16, I, ff. 161—162.	MS.10780 (8)	
1839				Sotheby's Cat., 30 Nov 1938, lot 825.
1840		NLS, MS. 10704, ff. 29—30.		
1841		NLS, MS. 10704, ff. 31—32.		
1842		NARS, LI 1/1/1, pp. 2148—2155.		
1843		NLS, MS. 10768, ff. 74—75.		Sotheby's Cat., 30 Oct 1973, lot 384.
1844	n	PROL, FO 84/1249, ff. 110—113.		
1845				Sotheby's Cat., 16 Mar 1971, lot 593.
1846		BLJ, Book no. 6401.		Foskett, **ZmDc**, pp. 128—130.
1847		BLL, Add. MS. 50184, f. 134.	MS.10780 (3)	
1848		NLS, MS. 10701, ff. 144—147.		
1849		RHLO, Waller MSS. Afr. s. 16, I, ff. 165—166.	MS.10780 (8)	
1850	n	RHLO, Waller MSS. Afr. s. 16, I, ff. 163—164.	MS.10780 (8)	

NO	RECIPIENT	DATE	PLACE	LENGTH	SIZE		TYPE
1851	Miss Cole	7 Dec 65	Malabar Hill	4 pp	8vo		Pr copy
1852	Agnes Livingstone 3	7, 13 Dec 65	Bombay	3/10/10	204	127	MS aut
1853	John Kirk	13 Dec 65	Bombay	1/ 4/ 4	202	124	MS aut
1854	Agnes Livingstone 3	20 Dec 65	Bombay	1/ 4/ 4	198	123	MS aut
1855	Anna Mary Livingstone	24 Dec 65	Bombay	2/ 6/ 6	180	113	MS aut
1856	Agnes Livingstone 3	26 Dec 65	Bombay	2/ 8/ 8	204	125	MS aut
1857	W.S. Price	27 Dec 65	Kambala Hill	3 pp	8vo		Pr copy
1858	Roderick I. Murchison	28 Dec 65	Bombay	1/ 4/ 4	202	126	MS aut
1859		31 Dec 65	Bombay	4 pp	8vo		Pr copy
1860	[Agnes Livingstone 3]	[Dec 65]	[Bombay]	1/ 4/ 4	204	127	MS aut in
1861	[Agnes Livingstone 3]	[11 Sep–31 Dec 65]	[Bombay]	1/ 4/ 4	202	127	MS aut in
1862		[11 Sep–31 Dec] 65	Bombay	4 pp	8vo		Pr copy
1863		[Nov–Dec 65?]	Malabar Hill	1 p	8vo		Pr copy
1864	[John Kirk]	[1 Jan 66?]	[Bombay?]	1/ 2/ 2	8vo		MS aut in
1865	John Kirk	1, 7 Jan 66	Bombay	2/ 6/ 6	180	112	MS aut
1866	William C. Oswell	1 Jan 66	Bombay	2/ 8/ 8	202	125	MS aut
1867	[Horace Waller]	[1 Jan 66?]	[Bombay?]	1/ 2/ 2	8vo		MS aut in
1868	Horace Waller	1 Jan 66	Bombay	1/ 4/ 4	8vo		MS aut
1869	[James Young]	[2 Jan 66?]	[Bombay?]	1/ 4/ 4	209	131	MS aut
1870	[Anna Mary Livingstone]	22 Jan 66	Crossing the Line, 49º Lon.	1/ 4/ 4	176	114	MS aut
1871	Agnes Livingstone 3	22, 29 Jan, 6 Feb 66	[At Sea]–Zanzibar	4/16/16	8vo		MS aut
1872	James Young	26 Jan 66	At sea, 300 miles from Zan.	2 pp			Pr copy
1873	Roderick I. Murchison	29 Jan 66	Zanzibar	3/12/12	177	113	MS aut
1874	[Thomas Maclear]	30 Jan 66	[Zanzibar]	1/ 4/ 4	177	114	MS aut
1875	William F. Stearns	2 Feb 66	Zanzibar	2 pp			Pr copy
1876	C. Gonne	6, 7 Feb 66	Zanzibar	3 pp			MS copy
1877	[Thomas S. Livingstone?]	6 Feb [66]	Zanzibar	1/ 4/ 4	178	114	MS aut
1878	Agnes Livingstone 3	8 Feb 66	Zanzibar	2/ 8/ 8	8vo		MS aut
1879	William F. Stearns	15 Feb 66	Zanzibar	1 p			Pr copy
1880	Horace Waller	[16 Feb] 66	Zanzibar	1/ 2/ 2	170	133	MS aut in
1881	Agnes Livingstone 3	17 Feb 66	Zanzibar	1/ 4/ 4	177	114	MS aut
1882	William F. Stearns	19 Feb 66	[Zanzibar]	2 pp			Pr copy
1883	Thomas Maclear	2 Mar 66	Zanzibar	2/ 8/ 8	180	113	MS aut
1884	George Frere	7 Mar 66	Zanzibar	2/ 8/ 8	180	112	MS aut
1885	Agnes Livingstone 3	7 Mar 66	Zanzibar	1/ 4/ 4	180	113	MS aut
1886	William Sunley	14 Mar 66	Zanzibar	1/ 4/ 4	202	158	MS aut
1887	Edmund St. John Garforth	16 Mar 66	Zanzibar	4 pp	fol		MS copy
1888	The Earl of Clarendon	22, 24 Mar 66	Rovuma Bay, HMS "Penguin"	4 pp	fol		MS aut
1889	Edmund St. John Garforth	22 Mar 66	Rovuma Bay, HMS "Penguin"	3 pp	fol		MS aut copy
1890	Agnes Livingstone 3	22, 24 Mar 66	Rovuma Bay	1/ 4/ 4	210	172	MS aut
1891	G.E. Seward	5 Apr 66	Kindany harbour	1/ 4/ 4	210	134	MS aut
1892	The Earl of Clarendon	18 May 66	Ngomano	8 pp	fol		MS aut
1893	Agnes Livingstone 3	18 May 66	Ingomano	1/ 4/ 4	179	114	MS aut
1894	Roderick I. Murchison	18 [May] 66	Ingomano	1/ 4/ 4	181	110	MS aut
1895		4 Jun 66	Ngomano	1/ 2/ 2	315	190	MS aut
1896	The Earl of Clarendon	11 Jun, 20 Aug 66	[East Africa]–Lake Nyassa	16 pp	fol		MS aut
1897	Inclosure No. 1	11 Jun, 20 Aug 66	Interior of Africa–L. Nyassa	2 pp	fol		MS aut
1898		18 Jun 66	Ngozo	1/ 2/ 2	314	200	MS aut
1899	Friends in Scotland	20 Aug 66	Lake Nyassa				NS copy
1900	Lords Comm. Admiralty	20 Aug 66	Lake Nyassa				TS copy

NO	N	LOCATION	NLS COPY	PUBLICATION
1851				Rendell Cat. No. 32 (1968), no. 134.
1852		BLL, Add. MS. 50184, ff. 135—139.	MS.10780 (3)	
1853		BLJ, Book no. 6401.		Foskett, **ZmDc**, pp. 131—132.
1854		BLL, Add. MS. 50184, ff. 142—143.	MS.10780 (3)	
1855		Wilson Collection.	MS.10775 (14)	Blaikie, **PLDL**, p. 365, ex.
1856		BLL, Add. MS.50184, ff. 144—147.	MS.10780 (3)	
1857	n			Sawyer's List No. 11 (1958), no. 78.
1858		NARS, LI 1/1/1, pp. 2156—2159.		
1859				Sotheby's Cat., 6 Jun 1950, lot 312.
1860	n	BLL, Add. MS. 50184, ff. 140—141.	MS.10780 (3)	
1861		BLL, Add. MS. 50184, ff. 66—67.	MS. 10780 (3)	
1862				Rendell Cat. No. 33 (1968), no. 312.
1863				Sotheby's Cat., 17 Dec 1935, lot 526.
1864		RHLO, Waller MSS. Afr. s. 16, I, f. 207.	MS.10780 (8)	
1865		Foskett Collection.		Foskett, **ZmDc**, pp. 132—133.
1866		NMLZ, G5.	MS.10779 (20)	Oswell, **WCO** II, pp. 92—93, ex.
1867		RHLO, Waller MSS. Afr. s. 16, I, f. 203.	MS.10780 (8)	
1868		RHLO, Waller MSS. Afr. s. 16, I, ff. 167—168.	MS.10780 (8)	
1869		NMLZ, G5.		
1870		Wilson Collection.	MS.10775 (14)	
1871	n	NLS, MS. 10704, ff. 33—40.		Blaikie, **PLDL**, pp. 367—368.
1872				Blaikie, **PLDL**, pp. 366—367.
1873		NARS, LI 1/1/1, pp. 2172—2183.		
1874		GACT, Maclear Papers, Acc. 515.	MS.10779 (4)	
1875	n			Bennett, "LLWFS" pp. 247—248.
1876		IOLL, L/P 8 S/6/569.	MS.10777 (22a)	
1877		NLS, MS. 10701, ff. 148—149.		
1878		NLS, MS. 10704, ff. 41—44.		
1879	n			Bennett, "LLWFS" p. 248.
1880		RHLO, Waller MSS. Afr. s. 16, I, f. 169.	MS.10780 (8)	
1881		BLL, Add. MS. 50184, ff. 149—150.	MS.10780 (3)	
1882	n			Bennett, "LLWFS" pp. 248—249.
1883		NARS, LI 1/1/1, pp. 2184—2191.		
1884		NMLZ, on display.	MS.10779 (20)	
1885		BLL, Add. MS. 50184, ff. 151—152.	MS.10780 (3)	
1886		BLJ, Book no. 5318, Acc. Reg. 4669.		Sotheby's Cat., 29 Jun 1939, lot 1487.
1887	n	NLS, MS. 10707, ff. 83—84.		**PP** Sess. 1867, v.LXXIII, [65] Class A, p. 97.
1888	n	PROL, FO 84/1265, ff. 450—451.		
1889		PROL, FO 84/1265, ff. 452—453.		**PP** Sess. 1867, v. LXXIII, [65] Class A, p. 97.
1890		BLL, Add. MS. 50184, ff. 153—154.	MS.10780 (3)	
1891		BLL, Add. MS. 50184, ff. 155—156.	MS.10780 (3)	
1892	n	PROL, FO 84/1265, ff. 454—457.		**PP** Sess. 1867, v. LXXIII, [66] Class B pp. 39—40.
1893		BLL, Add. MS. 50184, ff. 157—158.	MS.10780 (3)	
1894	n	NARS, LI 1/1/1, pp. 2192—2195.		
1895		NARS, LI 1/1/1, pp. 2196—2197.		
1896	n	PROL, FO 84/1265, ff. 458—465.		**PP** Sess. 1868—69, v. LVI, [145] Class B pp. 13—17.
1897		PROL, FO 84/1265, f. 467.		
1898		NARS, LI 1/1/1, pp. 2198—2199.		
1899		RGSL, Archives, DL 4/4/1.		**Morning Post**, 24 Apr 1868.
1900	n	RCSL, Copy Book I.		

82

NO	RECIPIENT	DATE	PLACE	LENGTH	SIZE	TYPE
1901	Adam Sedgwick	24 Aug 66, 1 Feb 67	Lake Nyassa—Bemba	1/ 4/ 4	325 200	MS aut
1902	Thomas S. Livingstone	28 Aug 66, 1 Feb 67	Lake Nyassa—Bemba	1/ 4/ 4	316 203	MS aut
1903	Norman McLeod	28 Aug 66	Lake Nyassa	6 pp	misc	TS copy
1904	Horace Waller	3 Nov 66, 1 Feb 67	Country of the Chipeta	1/ 4/ 4	fol	MS aut
1905	Robert Moffat 1	[3—10 Nov 66] , 1 Feb 67	Chipeta Country—[Bemba]	3 pp		Pr copy
1906	James Young	10 Nov 66, Jan, 1 Feb 67	Country of the Chipeta—Bemba	1/ 4/ 4	317 203	MS aut
1907		10 Nov 66	Country of the Chipeta	1 p		Pr copy
1908	The Earl of Clarendon	1 Feb 67	Bemba	4/ 8/ 8	fol	MS aut
1909	H. Bartle E. Frere	1 Feb 67	Bemba	5 pp		MS copy
1910	Friends in Scotland	1 Feb 67	Bemba			NS copy
1911						
1912	G.E. Seward	1 Feb 67	Bemba	4 pp	fol	MS aut
1913	Friends in Scotland	2 Feb 67	Chitapangwa's vill., Bemba			NS copy
1914	Agnes Livingstone 3	2 Feb 67	Chitapangwa's vill., Bemba	2/ 8/ 8	8vo	MS aut
1915	T. Maclear & W. Mann	2 Feb 67	Chitapangwa's vill., Bemba	4/16/15	8vo	MS aut
1916	Roderick I. Murchison	2 Feb 67	Bemba	4 pp	fol	MS aut
1917	T. Maclear & W. Mann	4 Feb 67	[Lobemba, village Molemba]	1/ 4/ 4	325 210	MS aut
1918	[John Kirk??]	[28 Jul 66—23 Feb 67]	[East Africa]	2/ 8/ 7	178 114	MS aut in
1919	[John Kirk]	12 Sep 67	Msama's country	1 p		Pr copy
1920	G.E. Seward	25 Sep 67	Lopone	4 pp		MS copy
1921	John Kirk	Oct 67	Lopone	2 pp		MS copy
1922	H. Bartle E. Frere	3 Dec 67	Town of Cazembe	1/ 4/ 4	325 200	MS aut
1923	The Earl of Clarendon	10 Dec 67	Town of Cazembe	17 pp	fol	MS aut copy
1924	Roderick I. Murchison	10 Dec 67	Town of Cazembe	2/ 6/ 6	325 200	MS aut
1925	G.E. Seward	14 Dec 67	Town of Cazembe			TS copy
1926	Robert Moffat 1	7 Mar 68	Near Lake Moero	2/ 4/ 4	186 116	MS aut in
1927	Agnes Livingstone 3	4 Jul 68	Near Lake Bangweolo	1/ 4/ 4	162 204	MS aut
1928	John Kirk	8 Jul 68	Near Lake Bangweolo	1 p		Pr copy
1929	Thomas Maclear	8 Jul 68	Near Lake Bangweolo	10 pp	fol	MS aut
1930	Roderick I. Murchison	8 Jul 68	Near Lake Bangweolo	3/ 6/ 6	180 111	MS aut
1931	William C. Oswell	8 Jul 68	Near Lake Bangweolo	1/ 2/ 2	180 112	MS aut
1932	The Earl of Clarendon	Jul 68	Near Lake Bangweolo	1/ 4/ 4	325 200	MS aut copy
1933	H. Bartle E. Frere	Jul 68	Near Lake Bangweolo, S.C.A.	7 pp		Pr copy
1934	[James Young]	[Jul 68?]	[Near Lake Bangweolo?]	2/ 4/ 4	180 111	MS aut in
1935	Lord Stanley	26 Mar 69	Ujiji	9 pp	fol	MS aut copy
1936	Abdallah	19 Apr 69	Ujiji	2 pp	fol	MS aut copy
1937	Majid ibn Sa'id	20 Apr 69	Ujiji	3 pp	fol	MS aut copy
1938	J. Kirk or R. Playfair	30 May 69	Ujiji	1/ 4/ 4	183 119	MS aut
1939	Thomas S. Livingstone	24 Sep 69	Moenekuss, Manyuema Country	1/ 4/ 4	fol	MS aut
1940	Agnes Livingstone 3	Sep 69	Manyuema Country	2/ 6/ 6	182 119	MS aut
1941	John Livingstone	[Sep 69?]	Manyuema or Cannibal Country	1 p		Pr copy
1942	T. Maclear & W. Mann	Sep 69, May 70	Town of Moenekuss, Manyuema	1/ 4/ 4	315 202	MS aut
1943	H. Bartle E. Frere	Oct 69, May 70	Manyuema Country	18 pp		MS copy
1944	William C. Oswell	Oct 69	[Manyuema, West of Ujiji]	1/ 2/ 2	320 200	MS aut
1945	James Hamilton	8 Apr 70	[Manyuema country]	1/ 2/ 2	315 202	MS aut
1946	Roderick I. Murchison	Apr—Jul 70	[Manyuema country]	5 pp		Pr copy
1947						
1948						
1949						
1950	Lord Stanley	15 Nov 70	[Bambarre, Manyuema Country]	16 pp	fol	MS aut

NO N	LOCATION	NLS COPY	PUBLICATION
1901 n	NMLZ, on display.	MS.10779 (20)	Seaver, **DLLL**, p. 476, ex.
1902 n	NLS, MS.10701, ff. 150—151.		Blaikie, **PLDL**, pp. 373, 381—382, ex.
1903 n	RCSL, Copy Book I.		**Good Words,** Jun 1868, pp. 354—356.
1904 n	RHLO, Waller MSS. Afr. s. 16, I, ff. 170—171.	MS.10780 (8)	Waller, **LJDL** I, p. 109.
1905 n			Moffat, "DL" pp. 551—552, 554.
1906	NMLZ, G5.		
1907 n			**The Times,** 22 Apr 1868, p. 12, c. 2.
1908 n	PROL, FO 84/1277, ff. 217—220.		**PRGSL,** vol. XII (1867—68), pp. 177—178.
1909	RGSL, Archives, DL 4/4/3.		**PRGSL,** vol. XII (1867—68), pp. 182—183.
1910	RGSL, Archives, DL 4/4/1.		**Morning Post,** 24 Apr 1868.
1911 n			
1912 n	E.M. privately owned.		Sotheby's Cat., 6 Jul 1977, lot 238.
1913	RGSL, Archives, DL 4/4/1.		
1914	NLS, MS. 10704, ff. 45—48.		
1915	NARS, LI 1/1/1, pp. 2209—2223.		
1916	RGSL, Archives, DL 4/4/6.	MS.10780 (5)	**PRGSL,** vol. XII (1867—68), pp. 175—176.
1917 n	NARS, LI 1/1/1, pp. 2224—2227.		
1918 n	BLL, Add. MS. 50184, ff. 159—162.	MS.10780 (3)	
1919			Foskett, **ZmDc**, p. 137.
1920	RGSL, Archives, DL 4/6/2.		PP Sess. 1868—69, v. LVI,[145] Class B, pp. 80—81.
1921	RGSL, Archives, DL 4/6/3.		
1922	NARS, LI 1/1/1, pp. 2229—2232.		
1923 n	SNMDL, Journal no. 11, pp. 333—349.	MS.10734	Waller, **LJDL** I, pp. 254—268.
1924	NARS, LI 1/1/1, pp. 2233—2238.		
1925 n	RCSL, Copy Book I.		PP Sess. 1868—69, v. LVI,[145] Class B, p. 81.
1926	BLL, Add. MS. 50184, ff. 163—164.	MS.10780 (3)	
1927	BLL, Add. MS. 50184, f. 165.	MS.10780 (3)	
1928 n			**PRGSL,** vol. XIV (1869—70), p. 8, ex.
1929	RGSL, Archives, DL 4/5/3.	MS.10780 (5)	
1930 n	NARS, LI 1/1/1, pp. 2239—2244.		**PRGSL,** vol. XIV (1869—70), pp. 12—13, ex.
1931	NMLZ, on display.	MS.10779 (20)	Oswell, **WCO** II, pp. 101—102, ex.
1932 n	GACT, Maclear Papers, Acc. 515.		**PRGSL,** vol. XIV (1869—70), pp. 8—12.
1933 n	GLUCBGRS.	MS.10777 (11)	**PRGSL,** vol. XIV (1869—70), pp. 13—16, ex.
1934	NMLZ, G5.		
1935	SNMDL, Journal no. 11, pp. 493—501.	MS.10734	
1936	SNMDL, Journal no. 11, pp. 504—505.	MS.10734	
1937	SNMDL, Journal no. 11, pp. 502—504.	MS.10734	Blaikie, **PLDL**, pp. 388—389.
1938 n	Foskett Collection.		Foskett, **ZmDc**, pp. 138—139.
1939 n	NLS, MS. 10701, ff. 152—153.		Blaikie, **PLDL**, pp. 394—397.
1940 n	BLL, Add. MS. 50184, ff. 166—168.	MS.10780 (3)	Blaikie, **PLDL**, p. 399.
1941 n			Starritt, **LtP**, p. 132, ex.
1942 n	NARS, LI 1/1/1, pp. 2260—2263.		Blaikie, **PLDL**, pp. 397—399.
1943 n	RGSL, Archives, DL 4/9/1.		**PRGSL,** vol.XVIII (1873—74), pp. 255—261.
1944 n	NMLZ, on display.	MS.10779 (20)	Oswell, **WCO** II, pp. 108—113.
1945 n	NLS, MS. 10768, f. 76.		Sotheby's Cat., 30 Oct 1973, lot 385.
1946 n			**PRGSL,** vol.XVIII (1873—74), pp. 274—278.
1947 n			
1948 n			
1949 n			
1950 n	PROL, FO 2/49B, ff. 58—65½.	MS.10780 (4)	PP Sess. 1872, v. LXX, C—598, pp. 1—5.

84

NO	RECIPIENT	DATE	PLACE	LENGTH	SIZE	TYPE
1951	Lord Stanley	15 Nov 70	[Manyuema Country]	1/ 4/ 4	fol	MS aut
1952	[William C. Oswell]	24 Nov 70	[Manyuema Country]	1/ 2/ 2	295 136	MS aut
1953	H. Bartle E. Frere	27 Nov 70	[Manyuema Country]	5 pp		MS copy
1954	J. Bevan Braithwaite	Nov 70	[Manyuema Country]	2/ 4/ 4	305 134	MS aut
1955	Lord Kinnaird	Nov 70	Manyema Country, Cent. Afr.			NS copy
1956	J. Kirk or R. Playfair	Nov 70	Bambarre, Manyema Country	1/ 4/ 4	123 119	MS aut
1957	Thomas Maclear	Nov 70	Manyema	2 pp		Pr copy
1958	William F. Stearns	Nov 70	Manyema Country, Cent. Afr.	4 pp		Pr copy
1959	[Agnes Livingstone 3??]	Nov 70	[Manyuema Country]	1/ 2/ 2	297 140	MS aut
1960	J. Bevan Braithwaite	Dec 70	Manyema Country	1/ 2/ 2	127 120	MS aut
1961	John Kirk	5 Feb 71	Bambarre, Manyuema	2/ 4/ 4	345 205	MS aut
1962	Agnes Livingstone 3	5 Feb 71	Bambarre, Manyema Country	1/ 4/ 4	205 164	MS aut fr
1963	Horace Waller	5 Feb 71	Manyema	4 pp	fol	Pr copy
1964		7 Feb 71	Manyema	6 pp	fol	MS copy
1965	[John Kirk??]	[11 Feb 71]	[Manyuema Country]	1/ 2/ 2	395 105	MS aut
1966		12 Feb 71	Bambarre, Manyema	6 pp	fol	MS copy
1967	John Kirk	13 Feb 71	Manyema Country	1/ 2/ 2	fol	MS aut
1968	John Kirk	25 Mar 71	[Webb's Lualaba]	1/ 2/ 2	341 118	MS aut
1969	Agnes Livingstone 3	Mar 71	[Webb's Lualaba]	1/ 2/ 2	fol	MS aut
1970	John Kirk	14 May 71		1/ 2/ 1	202 208	MS aut
1971	John Kirk	26 Jun 71		1/ 2/ 1	202 208	MS aut
1972	Barghash ibn Sa'īd	29 Oct 71, Feb 72	Ujiji—Unyanyembe	1 p		Pr copy
1973	John Kirk	30 Oct, 16 Nov 71	Ujiji	7 pp	fol	MS aut copy
1974	The Earl of Clarendon	1 Nov 71	Ujiji	15 pp	fol	MS aut
1975	The Earl of Clarendon	1, 15 Nov 71	Ujiji	4 pp	fol	MS aut
1976	John Kirk	1 Nov 71	Ujiji	1/ 4/ 4	343 214	MS aut
1977	Lord Granville	14 Nov 71	Ujiji	18 pp	fol	MS aut
1978	Captain White	15 Nov 71	Ujiji	2 pp	fol	MS aut
1979	John Livingstone	16 Nov 71	Ujiji			NS copy
1980	John Kirk	17 Nov 71	Ujiji	2 pp	fol	MS aut copy
1981	T. Maclear and W. Mann	17 Nov 71	Ujiji	5 pp		Pr copy
1982	Agnes Livingstone 3	18 Nov 71	Tanganyika	1/ 4/ 4	340 215	MS aut
1983	James Gordon Bennett 1	Nov 71	Ujiji on Tanganyika, E. Afr.	4 pp		Pr copy
1984	Horace Waller	Nov 71	Ujiji	1/ 4/ 4	lge fol	MS aut
1985	Agnes Livingstone 3	16 Dec 71	Ujiji	3/12/12	179 114	MS aut
1986	[James Young]	16 Dec 71	Ujiji	1/ 4/ 1	183 113	MS aut copy
1987	Lord Granville	18 Dec 71	Ujiji	8 pp	fol	MS aut copy
1988	[William C. Oswell]	6 Jan 72	Tanganyika	2/ 8/ 8	180 112	MS aut
1989	J. Bevan Braithwaite	8 Jan 72	[Tanganyika]	1/ 2/ 2	340 215	MS aut
1990	Lord Kinnaird	17 Jan, 13 Mar 72	[Tanganyika]—Unyanyembe			NS copy
1991	John Wilson	24 Jan, 13 Mar 72	[Tanganyika]—Unyanyembe	1/ 4/ 4	fol	MS aut
1992	George H. Richards	8 Feb 72	[Ngombe Nullah]	2/ 8/ 8	180 110	MS aut
1993	Francis Skead	8 Feb 72	Ngombe Nullah	1/ 4/ 4	8vo	Ph copy
1994	[Horace Waller]	19 Feb 72	Unyanyembe	1/ 2/ 2	lge fol	MS aut
1995	Henry W. Bates	20 Feb 72	[Unyanyembe]	4 pp	330 190	MS aut
1996	Lord Granville	20 Feb 72	[Unyanyembe]	20 pp	fol	MS aut
1997						
1998	John Kirk	20 Feb 72	Unyanyembe	2 pp		Ph copy
1999	James Gordon Bennett 2	Feb 72	South Eastern Central Africa	22 pp	344 212	MS aut
2000						

NO N	LOCATION	NLS COPY	PUBLICATION
1951 n	PROL, FO 2/49A, ff. 1—4.	MS.10780 (4)	
1952 n	NMLZ, on display.	MS.10779 (20)	Oswell, **WCO** II, pp. 113—115.
1953	RGSL, Archives, DL 4/9/1, 11—15.		**PRGSL**, vol. XVIII (1873—74), pp. 265—267.
1954 n	NLS, MS. 10768, ff. 77—78.		**PRGSL**, vol. XVIII (1873—74), pp. 278—279, ex.
1955	SNMDL, Misc. MS. Mat.	MS.10779 (3)	**Dundee Advertiser**, 9 Aug 1872.
1956 n	Foskett Collection.		Foskett, **ZmDc**, pp. 140—144.
1957 n			**PRGSL**, vol. XVII (1872—73), pp. 68—69.
1958 n			Bennett, "LLWFS" pp. 249—252.
1959 n	BLL, Add. MS. 50184, f. 170.	MS.10780 (3)	
1960 n	NLS, MS. 10768, f. 79.		**PRGSL**, vol. XVIII (1873—74), pp. 278—279, ex.
1961 n	NARS, LI 1/1/1, pp. 2281—2284.	MS.10734	
1962 n	BLL, Add. MS.50184, ff. 172—173.	MS.10780 (3)	Seaver, **PLDL**, pp. 555—556, ex.?
1963			Sotheby's Cat., 28 Nov 1966, lot 170.
1964 n	RGSL, Archives, DL 4/10/1.		
1965 n	BLL, Add. MS. 50184, f. 171.	MS.10780 (3)	
1966 n	RGSL, Archives, DL 4/10/2.		
1967 n	NLS, MS. 10701, f. 154.		
1968 n	NLS, MS. 10768, f. 80.		Foskett, **ZmDc**, pp. 145—150.
1969 n	NLS, MS. 10707, f. 85.		
1970 n	NLS, MS. 10768, f. 81.		Foskett, **ZmDc**, pp. 151—152.
1971 n	NLS, MS. 10768, f. 81v.		Foskett, **ZmDc**, pp. 153—154.
1972 n	RGSL, Archives, DL 4/11.		
1973 n	PROL, FO 2/49B, ff. 84—87.	MS.10780 (4)	Stanley, **HIFL** (1872), pp. 704—707.
1974 n	PROL, FO 2/49B, ff. 66—73.	MS.10780 (4)	**LFDL**, pp. 262—273.
1975 n	PROL, FO 2/49B, ff. 74—75½.	MS.10780 (4)	**LFDL**, pp. 258—261.
1976	NARS, LI 1/1/1, pp. 2286—2289.		
1977 n	PROL, FO 2/49B, ff. 76—83.	MS.10780 (4)	**LFDL**, pp. 274—290.
1978 n	E.M. privately owned.	MS.10769	Christies' Cat. 12 Jul 1972, lot 238.
1979	RGSL, Archives, DL 4/20.		**Globe**, 18 Aug 72.
1980 n	SNMDL, Journal no. 11, pp. 590—591.	MS.10734	
1981 n			**PRGSL**, vol. XVII (1872—73), pp. 69—73.
1982	BLL, Add. MS. 50184, ff. 174—175.	MS.10780 (3)	Blaikie, **PLDL**, p. 425.
1983 n			Stanley, **HIFL** (1872), pp. 616—619.
1984	RHLO, Waller MSS. Afr. s. 16, I, ff. 173—174.	MS.10780 (8)	**The Times**, 2 Aug 1872, p. 5, c. 5.
1985 n	BLL, Add. MS. 50184, ff. 176—179.	MS.10780 (3)	
1986	NMLZ, G17/13.		
1987 n	SNMDL, Journal no. 11, pp. 592—599.	MS.10734	**LFDL**, pp. 297—303.
1988	NMLZ, on display.	MS.10779 (20)	Oswell, **WCO** II, pp. 116—118.
1989 n	NLS, MS. 10768, f. 82.		**PRGSL**, vol. XVIII (1873—74), pp. 279—280.
1990 n	SNMDL, Misc. MS. Mat.	MS.10779 (3)	**Dundee Advertiser**, 9 Aug 1872.
1991 n	NLS, MS. 7792, ff. 7—8.		
1992 n	Privately owned.		Sotheby's Cat., 21 Jun 1960, lot 439.
1993	PMSM.	MS.10777 (28)	
1994 n	RHLO, Waller MSS. Afr. s. 16, I, f. 175.	MS.10780 (8)	**The Times**, 2 Aug 1872, p. 5., c. 5.
1995 n	E.M. privately owned.	MS.10710, f. 58	
1996 n	PROL, FO 2/49B, ff. 89—98.	MS.10780 (4)	**LFDL**, pp. 303—317.
1997 n			
1998 n	SNMDL.	MS.10708, f. 124	Foskett, **ZmDc**, pp. 155—157.
1999 n	BLJ, Book no. 5318, Acc. Reg. 4669.		**LFDL**, pp. 225—245.
2000 n			

NO	RECIPIENT	DATE	PLACE	LENGTH	SIZE	TYPE
2001	Agnes Livingstone 3	Feb 72	[Unyanyembe]	1/ 4/ 4	340 213	MS aut
2002	[Horace Waller]	8 Mar 72	[Unyanyembe]	1/ 4/ 4	108 114	MS aut
2003	Wm. R.S.V. Fitzgerald	13 Mar 72	Unyanyembe, East Africa	12 pp	fol	MS copy
2004	[Agnes Livingstone 3]	13 Mar 72	[Unyanyembe]	1/ 4/ 4	170 108	MS aut
2005	Roderick I. Murchison	13 Mar 72	Unyanyembe District			Pr copy
2006	William F. Stearns	13 Mar 72	[Unyanyembe]	2 pp		Pr copy
2007	[Henry M. Stanley]	14 Mar 72	Unyanyembe	1/ 2/ 1	8vo	MS aut
2008	Henry M. Stanley	15, 16 Mar 72	Kwihara	2 pp		Pr copy
2009	Thomas Maclear	[Mar 72?]	[Unyanyembe?]	1 p		Pr copy
2010	Agnes Livingstone 3	2 Jun, 1 Jul 72	[Unyanyembe–Kwihara]	1/ 4/ 4	342 210	MS aut
2011	John Kirk	Jun 72	[Unyanyembe?]			TS copy
2012	H. Bartle E. Frere	1 Jul 72	Unyanyembe			NS copy
2013	Lord Granville	1 Jul 72	Unyanyembe	8 pp	fol	MS aut
2014	John F. Webb	2 Jul 72	Unyanyembe	2 pp		Pr copy
2015	[James Young]	[15 Mar–Jul 72?]	[Unyanyembe?]	1/ 4/ 2	333 206	MS aut
2016	Agnes Livingstone 3	15 Aug 72	[Unyanyembe?]	1 p		Pr copy
2017						
2018	Agnes Livingstone 3	23 Aug 72	Unyanyembe	1/ 2/ 1	167 210	MS aut fr
2019	Horace Waller	2 Sep 72	East of Tanganyika	2/ 8/ 8	325 205	MS aut
2020	Robert Moffat 1	Sep 72	Near Tanganyika	2 pp		Pr copy
2021	William Thompson	Nov 72	South Central Africa	1/ 4/ 4	205 169	MS aut
2022	John Livingstone	Dec 72	Lake Bangweolo, S.C.A.	2/ 4/ 4	340 210	MS aut
2023						
2024	T. Maclear & W. Mann	[1872?]		2/ 8/ 4	343 215	MS aut fr
2025	Janet Livingstone	[Dec72–Jan 73]	Lake Bangweolo	1 p		Pr copy
2026	H. Bartle E. Frere	[Jan 73?]	Lake Bangweolo, S.C.A.	5 pp		Pr copy
2027	T. Maclear & W. Mann	[Jan 73?]	Lake Bangweolo, S.C.A.			TS copy
2028	Henry Rawlinson	[Jan?] 73	South Central Africa	4 pp	fol	MS aut
2029	Henry Rawlinson	[Jan 73?]	South Central Africa	4 pp	fol	MS aut
2030	Henry M. Stanley	[Jan 73?]	Lake Bangweolo, S.C.A.			NS copy
2031	James Young	[Jan 73?]	[Lake Bangweolo?]	1 p		Pr copy
2032		[1873?]		2 pp	fol	MS aut

NO	N	LOCATION	NLS COPY	PUBLICATION
2001	n	BLL, Add. MS. 50184, ff. 182—183.	MS.10780 (3)	
2002	n	RHLO, Waller MSS. Afr. s. 16, I, ff. 176—177.	MS.10780 (8)	
2003	n	RGSL, Archives, DL 4/10/3.		**Allen's Indian Mail**, 30 Sep 1872, p. 946.
2004	n	BLL, Add. MS. 50184, ff. 184—185.	MS.10780 (3)	
2005	n			**PRGSL**, vol. XVI (1871—72), pp. 433—436.
2006	n			Bennett, "LLWFS" pp. 252—253.
2007	n	SNMDL, on display.	MS.10708, f. 129	Stanley, **HIFL** (1872), p. 663.
2008	n			Stanley, **HIFL** (1872), pp. 628—629.
2009				**PRGSL**, vol. XVII (1872—73). p. 68, ex.
2010	n	BLL, Add. MS. 50184, ff. 186—187.	MS.10780 (3)	
2011	n	RCSL, Copy Book II.		
2012	n	RGSL, Archives, DL 4/20. p.10, c.2.		**The Times**, 22 Oct 1872, p. 10, c. b.
2013	n	PROL, FO 2/49B, ff. 148—152.	MS.10780 (4)	Stanley, **HIFL** (1872), pp. 713—717.
2014				Stanley, **HIFL** (1890), pp. 499—500.
2015	n	NMLZ, G5.		
2016				Blaikie, **PLDL**, p. 444, ex.
2017	n			
2018		BLL, Add. MS.50184, f. 188.	MS.10780 (3)	
2019		RHLO, Waller MSS. Afr. s. 16, I, ff. 178—181.	MS.10780 (8)	
2020				Macaulay, **LivA**, pp. 121—122.
2021		ULSOASL, Africa, Wooden Box of L's letters.	MS.10778	Chamberlin, **SLFL**, pp. 272—274.
2022	n	Privately owned.		Blaikie, **PLDL**, p. 444, ex.
2023	n			
2024		NARS, LI 1/1/1, pp. 2334—2337.		
2025	n			Seaver, **DLLL**, p. 601, ex.
2026	n			**PRGSL**, vol. XVIII (1873—74), pp. 261—265.
2027	n	RCSL, Copy Book II.		Blaikie, **PLDL**, pp. 441—443, ex.
2028		RGSL, Archives, DL 4/18/1.	MS.10780 (5)	**PRGSL**, vol. XVIII (1873—74), pp. 267, 270—274.
2029	n	E.M. Privately owned.		**PRGSL**, vol. XVIII (1873—74), pp. 267—270.
2030				**The Times**, 7 Apr 1874, p. 5, c. 3 (ex).
2031				Blaikie, **PLDL**, p. 443, ex.
2032	n	PROL, FO 2/49A, ff. 5—6.	MS.10780 (4)	

SECTION 2

SUMMARIES OF LETTERS

In this section Livingstone's correspondents are arranged alphabetically. For each is given basic biographical information (where this is available) with references to standard sources. Then comes a chronological list of all Livingstone's letters to the person concerned, with the briefest summary of its contents. However letters which have been published in full in works which can be assumed to be available to any serious student are not summarised. These works are:

Blaikie, **PLDL**;
Chamberlin, **SLFL**;
Clendennen, **DLJW**;
Foskett, **ZmDc**;
Moir, **ALATR**;
Schapera, **DLFL**; id., **DLSAP**; id., **LMC**;
Shepperson, **DLatR**;
Tabler, **ZPRT**;
Waller, **LJDL**;
Wallis, **TMaM**; id., **ZEDL**; id., **ZJJS**.
(For fuller details see the List of Publications.)

Letters about the identity of whose recipient there is some doubt are prefixed by a †. An * indicates that the summary is based on incomplete information, generally an extract in a printed source or a bookseller's catalogue. It has been possible to include in this section those letters which were discovered too late for inclusion in the main chronological list and which appear in the Addenda.

These summaries have been compiled at different times by different persons and from different types of source. No attempt has been made to iron out the resultant variations in style and format. But it has been the aim throughout to present Livingstone himself with the minimum of distortion. The object is merely to indicate the subjects discussed; a four-line summary of a letter of four folio pages (to name a common case) can do no more.

ABBOT, Hon. Reginald Charles Edward (1842—1919).
Educated at Eton and Christ Church, Oxford.   Became a barrister.
Succeeded as 3rd Baron Colchester in 1867.   (Who Was Who 1916—1928.)

0682   † 28 Jan. 1858.   Need for commitment to the Lord.

ADDERLEY, Charles Bowyer, 1st Baron Norton (1814—1905).
Tory Member of Parliament 1841—78.   He was interested in colonial development and
chaired the House of Commons Committee which took evidence from Livingstone in
1865.   He was Under-Secretary for the Colonies 1866—8 and President of the Board of
Trade 1874—8.   Knighted 1869 and created baron 1878.   (DNB.)

1715   9 May 1865.   Cannot come to dinner as he has to go to Lord Mayor's feast, where in
terror his health will be proposed he will eat nothing.   Grateful for kind way in which
examination was conducted.

ADMIRALTY, Lords Commissioners of.

1900   20 Aug. 1866.   *Recommendations to curtail the slave trade.

ALINGTON, Charles Argentine (?—1899).
A Church of England clergyman who was for a time chaplain to Bishop Tozer.   He was
later Rector of Swinhope 1884—99.   (Crockford.)

1591   3 Feb. 1865.   Welcome home.   Will enquire and send word about box.   Mrs Moffat of
Natal is his sister-in-law.   Does Alington speak Zulu?   Is going to the Rovuma and will
probably meet Zulus.   Tenacity necessary to fight slavery.   Portuguese anger at his
speech, the book will be worse.   Terrão lost his money in Bombay.

1604   11 Feb. 1865.   Box probably one of Kirk's sent back by Burrup;   send to Royal Botanic
Gardens.   Going out as soon as book is published.   Did he hear of any other boxes?
Young brought all Thornton's.

1614   18 Feb. 1865.   Box Thornton's;   send to his brother.   Information from John Moffat
about Mosilikatze.   Means to get opening north of the Portuguese.   Offers of help.   No
word of Terrão's son.   Tito is dead.   Zulus crossed Zambesi 30 years ago;   can Alington
speak Zulu?   Names of Nyassa peoples.   Portuguese claim to have discovered Nyassa.
Female warriors.   Spider common in Bechuana country.

1709   [12 May 1865?]   Shall be in at 4 p.m. and delighted to see him.

1724   26 May 1865.   Regrets Alington cannot go with him.   Other offers unsatisfactory.
Should like the cot, if very strong.

1749   20 Jun. 1865.   His mother's death.   Thanks for present.   Met his friend Reid.

ALLON, Henry (1818—1892).
Congregational minister at Union Chapel, Islington after 1844; editor of the **British Quarterly Review**, 1866—86. In addition to serving Cheshunt College in several capacities, Allon was a prolific writer, producing many sermons and pamphlets, and editing several hymns and collections of hymns. **(DNB.)**

0688   6 Feb. 1858.   I have only Tuesday of next week open, and was too busy earlier to visit you.   The mission authorities refused my brother-in-law permission to go to Africa, and instead want him to study medicine for two months!

0796   26 May 1858.   Sorry I was too busy at Liverpool to write to thank you and your friends for the encyclopedia.   Good weather thus far;   have parted with Mrs L. at the Cape. Rev. Moffat says my men still at Tette.   We cannot relax Saturdays or Sundays until we get through the delta.   8 Jun.   Local people now at war with the Portuguese and supposedly have swept them from every station.   Slave traders use the delta for their own purposes.

AMERICAN GEOGRAPHICAL AND STATISTICAL SOCIETY.
Founded in New York in 1851 for the purpose of advancing mankind's knowledge and understanding of the world and its peoples, this society invited Livingstone to become a corresponding member early in January, 1857, several months before his name was added to the rolls of its London counterpart.

0875   22 Feb. 1859.   A review of the expedition to date: exploration of the delta region; problems between Portuguese and rebels on the lower Zambezi;   course and depth of the river below Tette;   first visit up the Shire;   evidence of cotton;   description and drawing of the pelele;   the Kebrabasa rapids;   and efforts to prevent fever when in the mangrove swamps of the delta.

1166   6 Jan. 1862.   On the recent exploration of Lake Nyassa: description of the upper Shire below the lake;   depth, shape, size and storms of the lake;   inhabitants of the shores; region well-suited for cotton cultivation;   and the hope for success by the Universities' Mission.

ARCHER, Mary, née Gray.
Wife of Thomas.

0953   26 Oct. 1859.   Thank you for your kindness;   apologies for not having written. Recently reached Lake Nyassa, and hope to go to Makololo country next year.   Wishes for the success of the Makololo mission.   No word from home since we left.   My wife was at Kuruman some time ago.   We counted 10 herds of elephants here before dark.

ARCHER, Thomas (1805—1864).
Minister of Oxendon Street Presbyterian Church, London 1832—64.   (Mackelvie, **AUPC**, p. 495.)

0637   11 Dec. 1857.   *Asking for admission for Dr. Archer and his friends.

ARGYLL, Duchess of (1824–1878).
Elizabeth Georgiana Campbell, née Leveson-Gower, 1st wife of the 8th Duke of Argyll.

1510   14 Oct. 1864.   Encloses letter for his little friend.   Glad that she is pleased with his speech at Bath;   what was said and what was in the papers were verbally different but to the same effect.   Now writing book.   Staying with Webbs, friends made in Africa. Spirit of Newstead very different from Byron's day.   P.S. Thank Dr. Cumming for book.

ARGYLL, 8th Duke of (1823–1900).
George Douglas Campbell, succeeded to the title in 1847.   A Liberal, he held several Government posts, including Secretary for India 1868–74.   He was much interested in ecclesiastical affairs.   **(DNB.)**

0880   5 Mar. 1859.   *The slave trade, under the pretense of the French emigration scheme, convinces me more strongly that an English colony ought to be attempted in the interior. You threw out this idea once when I called upon you, and since then the scheme has grown daily in importance.

ARTHINGTON, Robert.
A philanthropist from Leeds.

1671   † 7 Apr. 1865.   Cannot find Silva's address, but it is not necessary.   No obstacle would be put in way of a settler, but he could hardly get testaments past the customs on his first arrival.   Plan feasible;   let me know how it succeeds.   Consult Foreign Office about English commissioner at Loanda.

1696   † 4 May 1865.   Silva is a Protestant at least in name.   Meet him through Walter Brodie, an elder in Hamilton's church, and he will give all required information.

ARUNDEL, John (1778–1848).
Home Secretary of the London Missionary Society 1819–46, hence Livingstone's first contact with the Society.   **(Congr. Yearbook** 1848, pp. 211–13.)

0001   5 Sep. 1837.   Statement of his Christian experience: doubt and unhappiness from age 12 to 19, relieved by reading 'The Philosophy of a Future State'.   Doctrinal position.

0002   [Jan. – Jul.] 1838.   Replies to 17 questions as to religious belief and experience, education, health, vocation, etc.

0005   2 Jul. 1839.   Wishes to go to South Africa rather than the West Indies, where he would be in conflict with medical men in pursuit of gain, and which would not be a sufficiently missionary sphere.

0014   16 Nov. 1840.   Has been elected a member of the Faculty of Physicians and Surgeons of Glasgow.   After visiting parents will return to London.   Books to be presented to J. R. Bennett.   Taylor and Inglis well and pursuing studies.

0018   27 Jan. 1841.   Compelled by accident to foremast to make for Rio, where they propose to distribute tracts.   Voyage pleasant.   Divine service held without visible effect on sailors.

0043   22 Dec. 1841.   Published in Schapera, **LMC** no. 3.

ASHTON, William (1817—1897).
Missionary in South Africa 1843—97, mainly at Kuruman where he was in charge of printing.   (**LMS Reg.** No. 455.)

0200   1 Apr. 1849.   Frequent threats by the Boers to attack him and Sechele.   On Potgieter and Kruger.

ATHENAEUM, Editor of.

0477   19 Mar. [1857].   As I am preparing my own narrative, I am surprised to find pirates extracting from my letters without my knowledge or permission.   I know neither the author nor the publisher.

ATLAY, James (1817—1894).
Vicar of Madingley 1847—52 and of Leeds 1859—68;   Bishop of Hereford 1868—94. (**Crockford.**)

1551   6 Dec. 1864.   Cannot attend missionary meeting at Leeds.   His love for Bishop Mackenzie and regret at the suspension of his mission.

AZEVEDO ALPOIM, Joaquim de.
Colonel, Governor of Quilimane 1854—7.   (Schapera, **LAJ** II, p. 469 n.1.)

0418   30 May 1856.   Recommends moving Senna to a location more healthy and more suitable for foreign trade.

BACK, Sir George (1796—1878).
With Franklin on his voyage into Arctic waters in 1819, he also commanded an expedition to the north to find Capt. John Ross in 1833.   Promoted to rank of Admiral in 1857.   (**DNB.**)

0441   13 Dec. 1856.   Thank you for your note of welcome and congratulations, which is gratifying from one of your exploratory experience.

0468   9 Feb. [1857].   Mrs L. and I will be pleased to meet your worthy rector, and accept your kind invitation for Monday 16th.

0525   23 May 1857.   Have been busy with the narrative, and now proceed to the country to finish the work in quiet and order.   This morning I received a copy of Luke in Esquimo; hope people don't think I need cooling.   The thought of your icebergs makes me shiver.

0720   17 Feb. 1858.   Am ashamed that I never called nor thanked you for your kind gifts: first part of furlough spent in writing, second in speechifying, third in preparation for leaving.   I feel deeply the sympathy you showed for my work, and thank you and your lady for your kindness.

0761   10 Mar. 1858.   Sorry always that I failed to respond to your polite attentions in person. Have been in an unnatural state and anxiously return to the quiet.   Anchor to be lifted at 1 p.m. today;   a photo of the launch will be sent you.

1059   30 Nov. 1860.   Saw about 100 miles of river which tsetse prevented me from seeing in 1855.   The Batoka country is suited for cotton raising, and contains much coal.   I send more details on the Falls, in which you expressed an interest, and also a small map. Your knife is always with me.

BAINES, Sir Edward (1800—1890).
Journalist and economist, Baines was editor of the **Leeds Mercury** for several years, and represented Leeds in Parliament 1859—74.   (DNB.)

0591   27 Sep. 1857.   Cannot "speechify" the date I will see you.   I will contact you when I reach Kendal.

0601   12 Oct. 1857.   When leaving you I left my boots behind;   please send them to Liverpool. I enclose a piece of Angola cotton for Mr. Fairbairn.

0622   21 Nov. 1857.   *Concerning his attitude to alcoholic drink and his abstinence when in Africa.   Enquiring about the Arabic Testaments printed in Leeds for Mungo Park, which he would like to give to literate Arabs in Africa.

1004   12 Mar. 1860.   *Have opened a cotton field, which permits a direct influence on the East coast slave trade.   Lawful commerce and the Gospel will diminish the traffic.   We try to get freedom of navigation and hope to place a small steamer on Lake Nyassa.

1463   8 Aug. 1864.   Cannot lecture before the Leeds Philosophical and Literary Society.

BAINES, Thomas (1820—1875).
Having shown himself both energetic and competent as an artist with the 74th Highlanders in South Africa during the War of the Axe (2nd phase;   1850—3) and as artist-storekeeper to J.C. Gregory's expedition in north-west Australia (1855—7), Baines was appointed artist-storekeeper to the Zambezi Expedition.   After being dismissed by Livingstone for the misuse of Government property, Baines journeyed to the Victoria Falls with James Chapman, and published the first paintings of the Falls by a competent artist (1865).   For the remainder of his life he travelled widely in southern Africa.
(DNB.)

Letters to him of 18 Apr. 1858 (0782), 11 Jul. 1859 (0913), and 21 Jul. 1859 (0914) are published in Wallis, **ZEDL**.

0677   28 Jan. 1858.   Have ordered 1600 lbs of beads from Mr. Kendal and 5 bales of calico; take a note of them.   Contact Bedingfeld.   Your paintings still at Peto's;   Duke of Argyll would like to see them.   Pay begins on 1 Feb., so be ready on 15th.   I'll be in London on Saturday.

0713   15 Feb. 1858.   *You are right to decline £200 p.a., you deserve £300.   Salary of artist was put at £200 without any reference to you.   I shall do all I can for you.

0829   19 Sep. 1858.   Advising him of the visit of Medlycott and Cooke.   Sicard intends to aid Baines in reaching Tete.   Thornton's foot keeps him from working.   Bedingfeld in an official letter refers to a certificate signed by Baines, of which the Secretary of State should have a copy.

BALLANTYNE, Thomas (1806—1871).

A journalist who was editor of among others the **Manchester Guardian, Liverpool Journal, Leader,** and **Statesman.**   A student of the works of Thomas Carlyle, he was also associated with Cobden and Bright in their stand against the Corn Laws.   **(DNB.)**

0660   11 Jan. 1858.   I could not write although your letter has been before me since 25th ult. I agree in all you advance but am busy preparing to leave the country.   I wish you success in your noble undertaking.

BARGHASH IBN SAID (ca.1837—1888).

Son of Said ibn Sultan, the first Omani ruler of Zanzibar, and himself Sultan in succession to his brother Majid ibn Said 1870—88.   He agreed to abolish slave trading and came more and more under British domination.   (Oliver **et al.,** I, pp. 237—51.)

1972   29 Oct. 1871.   *Asks assistance due to bad conduct by Sherif Basha in pilfering goods. Feb. 1872.   Send headman of good character.

BARTH, Heinrich (1821—1865).

After being granted the Ph.D. degree by the University of Berlin in 1844, Barth embarked on a trip through the Mediterranean coast of Africa (1845—47).   From 1850 to 1855 he made his greatest journey, and established himself as one of the great explorers of Africa in the 19th century.   Crossing the Sahara twice, he visited Tripoli, Fezzan, Air, Sokoto, Bornu, Timbuktu, Kanem and all points between.   Barth resided in London from 1855—8, and he struck up a friendship of sorts with Livingstone during the latter's first return to Britain from Africa.   (**NDB.**)

0523   20 May 1857.   Thank you for sending a copy of your book.   I was not aware that the questions to which you refer had been raised.   We have overcome them and nothing more need be said of them.

0616   10 Nov. 1857.   Meant to acknowledge your kindness at R.G.S. meeting but lost you in the crowd.   I'm saving the remaining volumes for when I get back to Africa.   My mother is ill due to excitement of sending three sons off to different parts of the world on one day.   I hope to reach my "adopted land" in January, but first will visit Portugal.   My work is a poor little thing compared to yours: you are at least five times more persevering with the pen than I.

0989   6 Feb. 1860.   Thank you for sending the remaining volumes of your work.   The wretched vessel prevented our going to the Makololo country, but we went up the Shire and discovered two magnificent lakes.   Congratulations on the honour conferred upon you by Her Majesty the Queen.

1181   18 Feb. 1862.   Shall be engaged 12 months carrying parts of a steamer past the cataracts. Explored the lake last year, but failed to ascertain whether or not the Rovuma issues therefrom.   Slaving the only trade known in that region.   Establishment of the Universities' mission and the encounter with the Ajawa.   Me write another book?   One in a man's life is quite enough.

BATES, Henry Walter (1825—1892).
Naturalist who made important discoveries in the Amazon basin.   Assistant Secretary of the Royal Geographical Society 1864—92.   (DNB.)

1995   20 Feb. 1872.   Has received his letter of 1869 which took 16 months to come from Zanzibar.   Kirk's sending supplies by slaves has been useless: long delays and plundering. Now supplied by Stanley, who will brief Bates on the geography of Tanganyika.   Kirk's naivety has lost 2 years, 1800 miles, and much money.   Maps and observations to May 1869 destroyed by Governor.   Pained and dejected by Murchison's illness.   Webb's success in sending packages to Stanley contrasts with Kirk's failure.

BEDINGFELD, Norman Bernard (1824—1894).
Commander, R.N. and Second-in-Command of the Zambezi Expedition, Bedingfeld had seen service off West Africa prior to joining Livingstone.   Although dismissed by Livingstone for insubordination, he was promoted to Captain in 1862, retired in 1877, and was promoted to Rear-Admiral and Vice-Admiral in 1878 and 1884 respectively.
(Navy List.)

Letters to him of 10 Apr. 1858 (0777), 12 Jun. 1858 (0798), 28 Jun. 1858 (0808), 31 Jul. 1858 (0812), and 12 Aug. 1858 (0815) are published in Wallis, ZEDL.

0810   13 Jul. 1858.   Portuguese say Nyaruka is nearer this than any other point;   steam down to it in the morning and I shall meet you there at 10 o'clock.   Portuguese have no canoes or launches here at present: all are down to meet the Governor.   Sr. Ferrao has put two rooms at our service.   Please wind my watch.   Other side of the river said to be deepest and best.

BELHAVEN, Lady (?—1873).
Hamilton Hamilton, née Campbell, wife of 8th Lord Belhaven.   (Paul, SP II, p. 54.)

0735   24 Feb. 1858.   Sorry I have been unable to call you and thank you for remembering my African friends.   I had hoped to spend a few days here, but arrived yesterday and leave for Glasgow tonight.

BENNETT, J.J. Wesley.
A resident of Shepton Mallet, Somerset.

1257   5 Aug. 1862.   I normally don't mind replying to a request for an autograph from a lady, but feel silly in doing so to a man.   Instead of wasting money on postage and plaguing people, why not support a child in a ragged school?

BENNETT, James (1774—1862).
Congregational minister, at Silver Street and later Falcon Square, London. Livingstone attended Falcon Square when in London in 1838—9; Bennett left this pastorate in 1860. He authored many works on religion, and was the father of Livingstone's friend, J. Risdon Bennett. He was also a Secretary to the London Missionary Society.   (DNB.)

0646   19 Dec. 1857.   *I don't expect to try any new schemes. With the big sleep before our eyes, we must be wary of experiments when surrounded by other difficulties.

BENNETT, James Gordon (1) (1841—1918).
Son and successor of the following.   In 1869, as manager of the **New York Herald**, he instructed Stanley to find Livingstone.   (DAmer B.)

1983   Nov. 1871.   His depressed state when he met Stanley, whose presence revived him.   The watershed now largely known, but has yet to see the most interesting part, where he has heard there are four fountains.   Asks for assistance in ending slave trade.

BENNETT, James Gordon (2) (1800—1872).
A native of Keith, he emigrated to the United States in 1819, became a journalist in Boston, and founded the **New York Herald** in 1835.   (DAmer B.)

1999   Feb. 1872.   Dreadful nature of East African slave trade.   Slaves are ugly, but are not typical Africans, who are like other men;   the women's beauty is spoiled only by adornment.   Slaughter caused by kidnapping of families.   Men captured may escape or die of broken hearts.   Slavers callous.   Belief in haunting.   Watershed: fountains converge into trough with three rivers and five lakes.   To find exit from Lake Moero had to venture into Manyuema country.   May be mistaken but thinks it is the Nile, with the fountains as told by Herodotus.   Troubles caused by Banians.   Nature of the Manyuema, who are cannibals despite much food and game.   Their markets.   Bloodshed caused by Banians.

2009.2 9 Apr. 1872.   Truly scientific people abhor slavery.   Foolish beliefs of a visitor to Mabotsa about inferiority of natives.   Arab belief in badness of women;   visit to a harem. Kindness of native chiefs.   Life at Chitambwa's.   Missions in Madagascar.   Need for mission in East Africa.   Roscher's death.   Plateau could support missionaries, who are needed everywhere.

BENNETT, Sir James Risdon (1809—1891).
A son of a secretary of the London Missionary Society, he graduated in medicine at Edinburgh in 1833.   He practised at Aldersgate Street Dispensary and Charing Cross Hospital in London, where he befriended Livingstone.   He was later at St Thomas's, became President of the Royal College of Physicians in 1876, and was knighted in 1881.
(DNB.)

0044   22 Dec. 1841.   Published in Chamberlin, **SLFL** no. 10 (omitting a long passage on the Bechuanas in general, differences of language and superstition, and the manufacture of iron;   and a few sentences on native agents and bird specimens).

0078   30 Jun. 1843.   Published in Chamberlin, **SLFL** no. 15 (omitting passages on Bakhatla and their iron, Mosilikatze, Sebegwe's loss of people by fever near Lake Mokhoro, request for Bennett's explanation of hydrocephalus, and a postscript on scrofula;   pp. 50—2 **passim** Sebegwe, p. 58 1.27 Sichuana).

0141   26 Dec. 1845.   Published in Chamberlin, **SLFL** no. 23 (omitting passages on Bennett's connection with the Sydenham society, sketch of his fractured humerus, description of Bakwain country, prevention of war, and character of Sechele).

0193   1848[?].   *On his repair to his arm broken by the lion, and on iron-making in the interior.

BINNEY, Mrs.
Wife of Thomas.

0518   16 May 1857.   Expresses hope that her husband is recovering.

BINNEY, Thomas (1798—1874).
A Congregational minister, he served at Weigh House, London (1829—1869) and was also a Director of the London Missionary Society.   He was noted for his nonconformist and hence controversial views.   (DNB.)

1190   27 Feb. 1862.   Thank you for the book and for the kind words spoken to Mrs L. on her departure from England.   We plan to carry a boat past the cataracts and float it on Lake Nyassa.   Explored 200 miles along west shore of the lake and found it deep and stormy. Saw an Arab dhow taking slaves across the lake.   19,000 slaves pass through Zanzibar annually.   Free Church may begin a mission in this region.   After we freed slaves in Shire highlands, we were attacked and forced to defend ourselves: since then the Bishop has taken an aggressive role.

1519   † 27 Oct. 1864.   Have not heard of you in a long time, please write.   I met Allon at Bath and he did not give a favourable report of your health.   I am writing another book at Webb's, where Byron lived.   Colenso proposed my health at Bath and a Scotch paper became exercised about it;   I knew nothing until the moment and had to respond.   I do not intend to be in London until well through my work.

BLAIR, John Andrew.
Printer and handyman attached to the Universities' Mission, frequently in charge of stores. He arrived in the Zambezi region on the "Hetty Ellen" in Jan. 1862 and left early in 1864.

1476   1 Sep. 1864.   Does not intend to go up Shire again.   Little propect of the mission being resumed by Tozer.

BLANCHE, John.
Gunmaker, Gracechurch Street, London.

0863   20 Jan. 1859.   Thank you for your gift of a revolver, which I value very highly.   I have not tried it on game yet.   Had to send our naval officer away, and continue to be plagued by a badly-constructed engine.   Saw enormous herds of elephant on the Shire 10 days ago, and chased some of them with the steamer.   Wanted one for fuel for our engine.   People never saw whites and were suspicious.   Large vessel could now go up to Tette with ease.   No fever except among Kroomen.   Regards to your son.

BLEEK, Wilhelm Heinrich Immanuel (1827–1875).
A German philologist who specialised in South African languages, he settled in Cape Town in 1856, and was appointed by Sir George Grey as interpreter in 1857 and librarian of his collection in 1860.   (**DSAfrB** I, p. 82.)

0875.2 22 Feb. 1859.   Enclosed are Lord's Prayer and the Creed in local language, as nearly as possible to what the Jesuits taught 100 years ago.   Linguistic notes: Batsuana; the diminutive.

0875.3 Incl. 1, 5 Jun. 1859.   The Pater Noster and Credo in dialect, with notes thereon.

BOARD, J.

0695   10 Feb. 1858.   Thank you for the beautiful stereoscope which you left to aid me in the elevation of the African races.   Wishing that you in attempting to aid others **may be** abundantly blessed yourself.

BOMBAY, Deputy Commissioner of Customs.

1445   [14 Jun. 1864].   Describing the service to which the "Lady Nyassa" has been put since launching, in accordance with customs regulations.   No merchandise on board except cloth used to introduce legitimate commerce into the Zambesi, which amounts to approximately 4 bales of calico;   also a box of beads not intended for sale unless vessel is disposed of;   our stores are nearly expended and the crew has only its clothing.   Please consider this an exceptional case and forgive my not filling out the usual form;   I am consigned to nobody and do not know a soul in the place.

BOST, Ami.
A metal broker in Glasgow from about 1842 to 1861.

0059   14 Jul. 1842.   Gratified by news of recipient's brother John.   His pleasure in meeting French missionaries at Motito.   Population very scattered.   Has been received with friendliness by all tribes, who have scarcely any idea of God.   Some natives at Motito and Kuruman have risen a little from the general degradation.   Exhortation.

BRAITHWAITE, Charles Lloyd (?1813–1893).
Brother of Joseph Bevan.

0891   24 May 1859.   On the first two visits up the Shire, and of the discovery of Lake Shirwa on the second.   Kirk and Livingstone enjoyed good health on the latter, and the new region seems like a good place for a mission.

BRAITHWAITE, Joseph Bevan (1818–1905).
A barrister and member of the Society of Friends whom Livingstone met in 1857 and corresponded with for the rest of his life.   Braithwaite was a friend of the Moffats, and Mary Livingstone and her children often stayed in Braithwaite's home in Kendal.
(Foster, HMB, p. 51.)

0494   4 Apr. 1857.   Thanks for the Greek Testament.   My full report on the Kaffir Wars denounced the party which became rich by the state of warfare;   the revised edition was toned down.

0506   23 Apr. 1857.   Livingstone explains why he is at odds with the Directors of the L.M.S.

0509   27 Apr. 1857.   On the financial situation of his sisters and mother following his father's death, and further details about his relations with the L.M.S.

0511   29 Apr. 1857.   L.M.S. paid all of my travel expenses, and my wife's: these with allowances for last 4½ years come to £1570.   My brother arrives from Hamilton tomorrow to put me in my intended work.

0610   27 Oct. 1857.   You long ago offered to draw up a deed for my children;   I should like Buchanan, Hannan, and Young to act as my Trustees.   Interview with Clarendon pending. Soon I go to Portugal to request free navigation of the Zambesi for all nations.

0628   27 Nov. 1857.   As I did not read Anderson's work, I cannot withdraw any of my conclusions.   Mr Wolf showed me his plates just after I reached England, and they were used in Anderson's book.

0707   12 Feb. 1858.   I gave my brother-in-law an advance of £500, £150 per year, and £300 in the event of my death, to form a mission near the Zambesi.   He wants a legal document: may I have your assistance?   Mr Moffat will explain his wishes;   I am too busy now to come myself.

0748   6 Mar. 1858.   Further details on the dispute between Livingstone and the L.M.S. Livingstone encloses a letter from Tidman, his own reply, and a relevant letter from J.S. Moffat.

0792   10 May 1858.   Met R. Moffat Sr. in Cape Town and learned my men are still in Tette. The Makololo will not be pleased with the absence of Ma-Robert.   On the lack of difference between the British and the African intellect: the one has merely had more training than the other.   Sierra Leone colony not perfect, but a good example nevertheless of the English philanthropic spirit.

0834   28 Sep. 1858.   On the behavior and double resignation of Bedingfeld.   I consider this expedition experimental in many respects, one of which concerns the health of the men. Zambesi a sand river, unlike the muddy rivers of the west.   Disagreement with two Dutch clergymen of the Transvaal.

0897   [30 May 1859.]   *Please forward to the editor of the "Times" the enclosed letter describing the discovery of Lake Shirwa.

0952   24 Oct. 1859.   One sowing of cotton here serves for three years.   A 33 mile road may be erected around cataracts.   Cotton grown on all three terraces east of the Shire.   Lake Shirwa 90 miles long;   Mt. Zomba 20 miles in diameter at base.   Purchased malachite from slavers at foot of Lake Nyassa.

0985   26 Jan. 1860.   Derogatory comments on the engine of the "Ma-Robert", and his wish to have another boat.   Baines fell before the moral atmosphere of this place.   Further criticism of Bedingfeld, Thornton, and missionaries at Kuruman.
7 Feb.   You may think me uncharitable about Bedingfeld, but he lied to me about his health.   He could not lie to Dr. Kirk.   A Portuguese sergeant aided me in the rescue of da Silva.

1068   24 Jan. 1861.   Awaiting new steamer.   Fever caused death among missionaries at Linyanti;   I advised J.S. Moffat to go north to the Makololo if he is not allowed to teach the Matibele.   Good opinion of **Evangelical Christendom,** bad opinion of **Evangelical Alliance.**   I intend to appeal to the Society of Friends for aid in establishing lawful trade.   What do you think of that?

1089   7 Mar. 1861.   Sister Janet allowed someone to petition Lords of the Treasury for an annual fee, in my name.   This will bring public censure.   I enclose a letter for the "Times".

1141   12 Nov. 1861.   I refused Bishop's request to go drive away another party of Ajawa: he has since gone himself.   Rowley and Procter write and do little else.   Mr. Clegg sent us a bale of remnants for which he received full price;   also one of damaged pieces.

1202   17 Mar. 1862.   Tells of the death of Mackenzie;   imagine men going east who meant to go south.   The chief who attacked Scudamore and Procter was in habit of attacking the Portuguese.

1292   21 Nov. 1862.   Cutting wood in order to reach the Zambesi.   When going 156 miles up Rovuma we twice touched slave route.   A suspected slaver in Quilimane now.   A London missionary and 6 Scotchmen plan to join me: do you know Jehan?

1385   28 Jul. 1863.   I suspected the recall before we ascended this river, but had I known it in reality I would have stayed closer to the sea.   We could go to India now and sell "Lady Nyassa" there.   The squadron on the West coast has made missionary progress possible. Portuguese taxed new Bishop highly at Quilimane.

1639   15 Mar. 1865.   His commission to the chiefs between the Portuguese and Abyssinia; will be useful among Arabs.   Russell refuses salary.   Possibility of getting 'Daily Telegraph' to take back unjust criticism.

1954   Nov. 1870.   Want of paper.   Following central drainage system.   The fountains; native reports.   Difficulties of travel.   Will not give up.   Errors of Macqueen and Speke. Ancient knowledge.   Hopes to confirm scriptures.   Anxious about Thomas.   Doubt on salary;   insulting letter from Foreign Office clerk.   Palmerston's offer;   he thought only of Africa.   Prince Albert's opposition.   Support for this expedition;   blockheads in the Royal Geographical Society.   Would Bright help to get salary?

1960   Dec. 1870.   Criticism of Hannan's actions as trustee concerning Robert and money. Break trust if possible.

1989   8 Jan. 1872.   Gives up idea of Bright's help.   Plan to move settlement from west to east coast to halt slave trade.   Loss of money through Kirk.   Do not let literary thieves get letters.   Regards.

BRITISH ASSOCIATION

0965   4 Nov. 1859.   Description of the Shire River;   the highlands east of the river;   the inhabitants of the region and some of their customs;   abundance of cotton;   drunkenness proliferates.

BROWNLEE, Alexander Jr.
Lived at 22 Orr Street, Mile-end, Glasgow, and was apparently of about the same age as Livingstone.

0081   17 Jul. 1843.   Could not reply sooner because, having found the language easier than expected, has been on several journeys to acquire local knowledge.   On slow wagons or oxen has been farther into the interior than any European.   Degradation of Bechuanas; cowardly murderers, dependent on female labour, superstitious.   Deceit of a native doctor. Need for prayer.   New station to be established near primitive iron foundries.   Regards. Treatment for prurigo.

BRUCE, John Collingwood (1805 – 1892).
Presbyterian minister, proprietor of Percy St. Academy, Newcastle 1834 – 1863 (LL.D. 1853).   A noted antiquary, he was especially interested in Hadrian's Wall.   (DNB.)

0603   21 Oct. 1857.   My trip went through Carlisle, Kendal and Leeds, and not Newcastle, though it would have given me great pleasure to have walked in the hills with you.   Soon I hope to be on my way to Portugal.

BUCHANAN, Mrs.
Wife of Andrew (see under Livingstone's Trustees)?

0856   19 Dec. 1858.   Thornton found three seams of coal. With coal and iron ore, Africa was not destined to be a slave market.   Cotton is growing everywhere.   I was wrong saying the natives do not make sugar.

BUCKLAND, William (1784 — 1856).
A clergyman (Dean of Westminster 1845–56) and a distinguished geologist and paleontologist (Professor of Mineralogy at Oxford 1813–56, and of Geology there 1818–56), who always attempted to reconcile his scientific findings with Biblical statements.
(DNB.)

0094   10 Oct. 1843.   Buckland had asked before he left England for information about the decrease in water supply in the Kuruman area. Describes old water channels and springs. Contrast between vegetation of hills and plains.   Geology of hills.   Trees flourish if irrigation provided.   Water supply in last four years exceeds that of preceding four: probably fluctuation in the process of desiccation.   Cause probably rise in level of an oblong tract of land.   Hopes soon to have accurate information of a lake. Expeditions generally carry too much weight.   Animals of the area.

BURDETT-COUTTS, Angela Georgina (1814 — 1906).
Business administrator (Coutts' Bank), socialite and philanthropist of universal interest. She used her vast fortune to benefit hundreds of causes, including the conditions of the poor, treatment of animals, and churches and missionary efforts throughout the world. She married in 1881.   **(DNB.)**

0678   28 Jan. 1858.   Wrote to the boy of the lady who sat on my left at dinner, but forgot her name. 1 Feb. We sail from Liverpool on the 15th.   Lord Grey wrote me and a lady and put the letters in the wrong envelopes.

0685   3 Feb. 1858.   Have removed from Peto's and am packing in the Paraffin Light Co. Kindly send presents to this point.   Pleased to meet the Bishop of Oxford.   Lord Grey thinks Wood's reasons for refusing to count Bedingfeld's time are conclusive and good: I wonder what they are?   Thank you for sending Lady Colchester's note.   Caesar called women impedimenta, but my wife does her best.

0712   14 Feb. 1858.   I accept your gifts in the name of Him whom we serve.   I did not pursue the notoriety I received: it followed me.   The microscope and souvenirs will be heirlooms in my family.   If the Launch is so weak as to force me to lose it in the Zambèsi, woe betide Macgregor Laird.   Queen said in parting "best wishes would follow me."

0747   4 Mar. 1858.   Yesterday at Kendal an amateur photographer made a good likeness of me, which I will send to friends.   Last night performed bitter parting ceremonies with my children.   "Pearl" came from the Clyde last night.   The Launch is a nice little thing: I think I'll name her the "Ma-Robert."

0766   22 Mar. 1858.   Good trip so far; the Captain a good Christian and the men mostly Scotchmen.   There is no cross-grained specimen among my men, and all come to prayers regularly.

0788   6 May 1858.   Mrs. L. sick since Sierra Leone.   My men still at Tette.   Boers supply Sechele with brandy, gratis.   3 Hanoverian missionaries have settled at his place.   Grey wants an institution for chiefs' sons at the Cape, and he also wishes to establish overland communication with us near the Kafue.   Mentions some persons he met in Cape Town. 21 June: a brief review of work thus far and plans for the near future.

0821   28 Aug. 1858.   You may remember I had apprehensions about this boat: she requires a hundredweight and a half each hour to produce 4½ knots, and ought to be called the "Asthmatic."   I made friends with Bonga, the brother of the rebel chief.   Governor of Quilimane was a Raspailite who would take no medicine: in every glass of water I gave him 10 grams of quinine and he was over it in three days.   Had prayers and litany on Sunday, but no psalms and lessons, as I had to get my men out of the delta.   The bishop of Oxford will support me in this.

0858   20 Dec. 1858.   Rapids not what we expected.   We steamed 4 miles beyond their beginning and walked 12 miles on foot, returned to steamer then walked 30 miles through the region.   10-12 knots of power will stem the flood.   We take no quinine.   I have long got over the feeling of belonging to one section of the church.   I lost the drinking cup you gave me in wading the Lui River.

0884   8 May 1859.   Have recently discovered Lake Shirwa, and this is the first letter I write of it.   It is separated from Nyinyesi by a small bit of land.   Did Burton reach it?   It is said to reach the Equator.

0912   5 Jul. 1859.   Pleased to hear that you send the gospel to accompany the forming of a new English colony: I think the same should happen here.   Further thoughts on Laird and the "Ma-Robert."   Priest of Tette keeps Chibisa's daughter as a slave, and will not be persuaded to part with her.   Send a paper on fever to Sir James Clark.   22 Jul.   We must part with the Kroomen: they cannot travel on land, and the boat cannot carry their provisions.

0931   10 Oct. 1859.   Ascended Mt. Zomba at its southern edge.   Not knowing if the Government send out another steamer, we plan to build one of our own for the Lake.   We have no doubt of it paying as a commerical speculation.   We cannot carry our Makololo, but tow them astern.

1030   4 Sep. 1860.   Followed the north bank, then turned west into the highlands.   Visited the Victoria Falls, and hope to visit the Muamba Falls on the way back.   Tells of the sad fate of the Linyanti mission, and of Sekeletu's illness.   Proposed mission of the Universities.   Warburg's drops worked well in India, but not here.   The rugs are very highly valued.   This goes south with an elephant hunter.

1045   24 Nov. 1860.   J.S. Moffat reports that Schroeder, a Hanoverian, has had success with Sechele at Kolobeng.   We are to have a real steamer soon, and expect to explore the Rovuma.   While the Makololo are the best people for a mission, the Manganja have the best country.   A canoe of ours was upset, but it was no adventure worth telling.

1096   13 Mar. 1861.   Could not in good conscience let the missionaries go up the river in the unhealthy season, so we went to the Rovuma.   Mary writes that you agree that I am wrong to leave her for so long.   Although the Rovuma was difficult, the natives know of no cataracts.   All believe that the Rovuma comes out of the "Nyassa of the Maravi."

1719   23 May 1865.   *Recommending Horace Waller as the man to carry out her plans for sending a mission to Borneo.   He is an active honourable upright man and true Christian missionary, is kindly disposed toward the natives and gets on well with them, and behaved nobly towards the orphans of Bishop Mackenzie.

1789   †7 Aug. 1865.   We did not forget your invitation, but as we were departing we were met by letters announcing the illness of a friend, and hurried off to render medical aid. Hearing that you are having an evening for Queen Emma, may I come and bring daughter?

BURNS, John (1829 – 1901).
Son of Sir George Burns, shipowner and one of the founders of the Cunard Company; succeeded his father as manager of the company in Glasgow in 1860 and became chairman in 1880.   Created Baron Inverclyde in 1897.   (DNB. Suppl. s.v. Sir George Burns.)

1485   10 Sep. 1864.   Going south, so cannot attend meeting of the Gaiter Club, whose motto suggests rollicking in the country, to which he has a strong propensity.

1764   6 Jul. 1865.   Called two days ago to say farewell and thank him for service in respect of his son, for whom it will never be needed.   Time in Scotland totally spend in attending his mother.

BURRUP, E. Mary.
Widow of Henry de Wint Burrup, a member of the UMCA who died shortly after Bishop Mackenzie in 1862.   She travelled with Mary Livingstone on the **Gorgon**.

1450   28 Jul. 1864.   Thanks for condolence and welcome.   Cowardly abandonment of mission is a sore disappointment and makes one mourn the more the loss of Bishop Mackenzie.

BUXTON, Sir Edward North (1812 – 1858).
Member of Parliament for South Essex 1847-52 and Norfolk 1857-8.   (DNB.)

0549   4 Jul. 1857.   Declining an invitation as he has retired to this quiet place to complete his book.   Intends to call soon after the book is finished.

CAMBUSLANG GIRLS' SCHOOL.
Pupils of the Rev. John and Mrs. McRobert.

0073   21 Jun. 1843.   Fond of travel stories in his youth (when he did not know Christian happiness), and supposes they will be likewise.   Therefore tells of a dangerous incident in the Bakalahari country, when failure to do his duty and consequent lack of water almost killed him.   [End missing.]

0092   6 Oct. 1843.   Lesson to be learned from death of three of his friends.   Death of Sehanne from fever, not poison.

CANDLISH, Robert Smith (1806 — 1873).
Preacher and theologian, Minister of St. George's, Edinburgh 1833—43, and St. George's Free Church, Edinburgh, 1843—73. Very active in the formation of the Free Church of Scotland, he was a sponsor of James Stewart's visit to the Zambezi in 1862—3.

(DNB.)

1195 12 Mar. 1862. Gave Stewart a hearty welcome, as there is room here for all missionaries. I invited him to accompany us up to Lake Nyassa, after the steamer is erected here. "Pioneer" cannot carry her sister ship and all our supplies too. Stewart seems well adapted for the job. The language must be reduced to paper, which will take many years. 15 Mar. Greatly saddened by the deaths of Mackenzie and Burrup.

CAPE TOWN MAIL, Editor of.

0258.7 [Sep.—Oct.? 1851] *Boer wrongs in treatment of natives.

CARDOSO, Candido José da Costa (ca. 1800 — 1890).
A trader and landowner of Tete, who may have visited Lake Nyassa in 1846, Cardoso (usually referred to as Candido) was Acting Chief Captain (Capitão Mor) of Tete 1851 — 61, and Chief Captain thereafter. Knight of the Order of Christ, 1863. During his long and varied career, Cardoso served Tete and the Province of Moçambique in many capacities. (Listowel, TOL.)

Letters to him of 16 May 1860 and 25 May 1860 are published in Portuguese in Wallis, ZEDL.

1024 16 May 1860. Advising him of the names of 10 Africans who are now to be considered as separated from Livingstone's expedition, and hence subject to the laws of the district, and of an additional three who remain attached to the expedition for service on the "Ma-Robert."

1025 25 May 1860. Advising him that six more Africans had left the expedition and are returning to Tete, some of which carry weapons which are not licenced. He lists the contents of the baggage they carry, and requests that Cardoso take inventory of the items, and deliver them safely to William Rowe, on board the "Ma-Robert."

CATO, George C.
The first mayor of Durban, Natal.

1359 3 Jul. 1863. If my son Robert comes your way, will you kindly direct him into any situation where he can earn an honest living. Give him a word on avoiding evil company, drink, etc. Our expedition was recalled due to Portuguese slaving, and we leave here in January next. If Robert reaches Durban, he may not be able to reach Quilimane before we depart.

CECIL, Richard (1799 — 1863).
Congregational minister, who served at Ongar (where Livingstone studied) 1838—47.

(Congr. Yearbook 1864, p. 200.)

0025   13 May 1841.   Charge that Philip a spiritual despot is false.   Any financial errors are from desire to advance the cause.   His church is divided and Philip treated shamefully.   Relations with Mr and Mrs Ross.   Wish for Inglis as companion.   First impressions of country.   Personal messages.

0057   11 Jul. 1842.   *On the number of patients and his determination to treat only serious cases in future;   and on the excess of clergy in Algoa Bay and his determination to move north despite Philip.

0080   15 Jul. 1843.   *On a new remedy for liver complaints and his visit to the Bokhatla.

CHAPMAN, William Cox (? — 1897).
Commander of the sloop 'Ariel' which towed Livingstone in the 'Lady Nyasa' from Quilimane to Mozambique in Feb. 1864.   Promoted Captain 1866, Rear Admiral 1882, and Vice Admiral 1888.   (Navy List.)

1585   25 Jan. 1865.   Welcome home.   Will send a copy of the new book as thanks for his kindness.

1594   6 Feb. 1865.   *Asks if Sunley has given up his consulship.

CLARE, Leigh.
Of Clare & Company, cotton merchants, Manchester??

0749   6 Mar. 1858.   Thank you for the seed.   We sail on Monday at 11 or 12.

CLARENDON, 4th Earl of (1800 — 1870).
George William Frederick Villiers, succeeded to the peerage in 1838.   After a diplomatic career he entered politics as a Liberal.   His principal office was as Foreign Secretary Feb. 1853 — Feb. 1858, Nov. 1865 — Jun. 1866, and Dec. 1868 — Jun. 1870, so that he was responsible for the planning and early stages of the Zambesi Expedition and also at vital moments of the final expedition.   He died in Jun. 1870, but Livingstone did not learn of this till Nov. 1871.   Livingstone gave his name to Mount Clarendon east of the Shire.   (DNB.)

0405   19 Mar. 1856.   Country suitable for trade by river.   Victoria Falls have been obstacle.   Healthy ridges.   Effect of slave trade.   Coal, gold, iron ore.   Plants.   **Agriculture.**   Native government.   British anti-slavery efforts successful.

0429   26 Aug. 1856.   People at the center of the cabinet are peaceful and generous;   tsetse killed our cattle, whick caused a lack of nourishment among us;   when 8 or 9 miles from Tette, Governor Sicard sent food and people to conduct us to the town;   also hospitable were Pereira and Ferrão of Senna, Nuñes of Quilimane, Neves of Cassange; the sketch of Nyanja by Rebman agrees with that of Sr Candido: with little doubt of its existence, we can proceed to that region via the Zambesi and the Shire.

0476   19 Mar. 1857.   Outlining a scheme Livingstone would undertake if he returned to Africa, which would include: making the Zambezi a path for commerce, which would contribute to the decline of the slave trade;   encouraging Africans to cultivate cotton;   form a chain of commercial stations along the river;   but this to be done with a modest beginning, requiring a small number of tools and implements, etc.

0514   2 May 1857.   Upon returning to Africa, he would promote legitimate commerce, emphasizing the cultivation of cotton.   Suggests Clarendon adopt a line of policy which would not offend the Portuguese.   Requests a salary as Clarendon deems suitable.

0632   1 Dec. 1857.   Outlining his plans for the Zambesi Expedition: establish stations on the higher portion of the region to introduce legitimate commerce and bring about an end to the slave trade.   Survey the river, examine Kebrabasa rapids, induce Africans to cultivate cotton and other produce, and open the river to ships of all nations: these steps will benefit all concerned.

0656   7 Jan. 1858.   Further ideas on the expedition: requests 6 European assistants for various duties;   plan to include depositing heavier luggage in Tete while rapids are examined, river surveyed, and local chiefs given cotton seeds and encouragement;   move upriver to healthy highlands and erect a headquarters beyond the confluence of the Kafue, where experiments will be made growing European crops on high ground and tropical crops on lower ground;   exploration conducted and scientific experiments carried out;   local Africans given religious instruction;   send dispatches from Tete at end of one year, and assemble there for further instructions at the end to two years.

1162   [Nov. — Dec. 1861?]   *Discusses the slave trade, describing the horrors he had witnessed. Details of his proposals for ending the trade, advocating the creation of an English colony near Lake Nyasa.   Determination not to abandon the cause.

1327   24 Feb. 1863.   *On the depopulation in the lower Shire valley since Paul Marianno II (Matakenya) was released from Portuguese custody.

1888   22 Mar. 1866.   Present thanks to naval officers.   Sultan showed every attention.   Hired dhow which 'Penguin' towed here.   24 Mar.   Rovuma too low to ascend and banks impassable;   therefore landing at Mikidani.

1892   18 May 1866.   No passage for camels through mangrove, so landed at Mikidani. Description of Pemba harbour.   Went south west to Rovuma.   Country, flora, people, geology.   Will be based at Ngomano.   Experiment with buffaloes and camels unsatisfactory.

1896-7 11 Jun. 1866.   British policy on slave trade in East Africa needs reconsideration. Weakness of the Sultan who owes his position to English power.   Limited concession of slave trade has been enlarged to allow northern Arabs to deal freely in Zanzibar. Sultan should be pressed to adhere strictly to treaty.   Arab domestic slavery is mild and will not change of itself.   Status of Zanzibar as slave market is due to its being an island; no inland substitute possible. 20 Aug.   Slave caravans. Depopulation. Guilt shared by chiefs, Arabs, and Sultan, who must be pressed vigorously.   English warship should be stationed at Zanzibar.   Benefits of ending of slave trade in West Africa.

1908   1 Feb. 1867.   Arabs who will take letter ready to leave.   Had to go south of Lake Nyasa to avoid Mazitu.   Chief Mataka.   Flight of Johanna men.   People around Nyasa. Crossing Chambeze.   Devastation and hunger.

1923   10 Dec. 1867.   Published in Waller, **LJDL** I, pp. 254–68.

1932   Jul. 1868. Nile sources probably between 10° and 12° S. The uplands; the Chambeze-Luapula-Lualaba.   Lake Moero.   Flooding.   His observations, checked by Maclear, better than theorising.   P.S.   Report of underground houses.

1974   1 Nov. 1871.   The watershed, its springs and rivers. Lake Bangweolo. Knows 600 miles of the watershed, but last 100 are most interesting: fountains of the Nile. Mistakes of Speke and Baker.   Ancient knowledge.   Course of the Lualaba.   Height of Lake Tanganyika. Manyuema cannibals; their markets, crops, and beliefs.

1975   1 Nov. 1871.   Thanks for search expedition.   Musa's story should not have been believed. Low-class Moslems quite untrustworthy; in East Africa they spread only syphilis. 15 Nov. Musa's false claim for pay.

CLOWES, George (1814–1886).
Partner in Wm. Clowes & Son, Printers, London who printed Livingstone's **Analysis of the Language of the Bechuanas**.

0478   22 Mar. 1857.   Thank you for handsome present you kindly sent my young folks, who are delighted with the pictures.   They are a better aid to "Sunday observance" than could be afforded by acts of Parliament.

COELHO DO AMARAL, José Rodrigues.
Major, army engineer, governor of Benguela from 1851, acting governor general of Angola from 1854.   (Schapera, **LAJ** I, p. 182 n.3.)

0406   25 Mar. 1856.   Account of reception by Sekeletu of letter and gifts from Loanda. The Victoria Falls.   Possibility of trade.   P.S.   Reached Quilimane 20 May and sent letter to governor 25 Jun.

COGHLAN, Sir William Marcus (1803 – 1885).
Major General, R.A., Coghlan was Great Britain's Political Agent at Aden, 1854–1863. Knighted 1864.   (Boase, **MEB**.)

1249   18 Jul. 1862.   You may recall that I landed with you at the end of 1856. When Rae appeared at Playfair's door in a doleful plight and ragged appearance the guards ordered him away, but you put in a good word for him.   I write to let you know that your kindness was appreciated.   Low on provisions, we must now proceed to Johanna. 19,000 slaves pass through Zanzibar annually. We get on well with the Portuguese, but their slaving is ingrained.

COLE, Miss.

1851   7 Dec. 1865.   *Shocked to learn of her sister's death. Can sympathise because of his similar loss.

CONEYS, Matilda.
Resident of Howth, Co. Dublin.

1483   6 Sep. 1864.   *Delayed replying for a month because he finds it hard to address one he never saw and because he had no photograph of himself.

CONYNGHAM, George Lenox (? — 1866).
Served in the Foreign Office as Supernumerary Clerk 1812—17, Clerk 1817—34, Senior Clerk 1834—41, and Chief Clerk 1841—66.   (F.O. List.)

0771   25 Mar. 1858.   Have sailed 200 miles per day since leaving Liverpool.   Into Sierra Leone today; "Pearl" does her duty and her captain is a good man.   Hope to reach Zambesi by 1 May.   Any expenses charged to me will be paid by Mr. Coutts.   It is not late enough to send home a life certificate.

0805   26 Jun. 1858.   About to sail upriver from "Pearl"; have been up all night writing. You must give me another little ship.   Tell Mr. Coutts to draw my salary.

0841   5 Oct. 1858.   Quarrel between Bedingfeld and Duncan.   We have taken the first coal ever from this country.   The Makololo were glad to see me.

1496   30 Sep. 1864.   Please send me the blue books in which my dispatches are printed.   I do not wish it known generally where I am.   Shells of the lake and the fishes were quite new. I hope you recovered your shells.

COOKE, Robert (? — 1891).
Cousin and partner of John Murray, Livingstone's publisher.

0566   10 Aug. [1857].   Returns corrected title page.   Wishes to see vignette of tsetse. Took Arrowsmith to church.

1642   20 Mar. 1865.   Owen's and Oswell's corrections.   Wishes information on stone age people.

1682   22 Mar. 1865.   Astonished at length of book, which he had been trying to enlarge. Only conclusion and appendix could readily be cut.   Will see him about Tuesday and discuss this and attribute drawings.

COWAN, Mrs.
A resident of Edinburgh, her husband may have been a Corporation official.

0584   14 Sep. 1857.   I wrote Sir Wm. Johnston fixing Monday 21st for the meeting in Edinburgh, but at what hour am I expected to arrive? If I leave Glasgow at 9 or 10 will I be in time?   Perhaps Mr. Cowan will be back by then.

CRAWFORD, Richard Borough (? — 1866).
Captain, R.N. (1856), commander of frigate "Sidon" stationed at the Cape of Good Hope, 1859—1862, retired 1862. The "Sidon" visited Livingstone at the mouth of the Zambezi in Feb., 1861. **(Navy List.)**

1075 9 Feb. 1861. Thank you for aiding the "Pioneer". We now proceed to Rovuma Bay,
a and request that you tow us.

CUMMING, Dr.

1477 1 Sep. 1864. *On his dread of his forthcoming speech at Bath and his having left a book presented by the medical men of Oban at his house.

DARLING, Sir Charles Henry (1809 — 1870).
Colonial administrator, who served as Lieutenant Governor of Cape Colony 1851—4, being in sole charge during the absences of Sir George Cathcart. **(DNB.)**

0290 29 Sep. 1852. Published in Schapera, **DLSAP**, pp. 55—9.

DARLINGTON, John.
A resident of Bradford, Yorkshire.

0623 21 Nov. 1857. *The map used at Birmingham was sufficient for the hall there, and as it is now at Bradford you may wish to look at it. If too small, get a larger one drawn from the one at the end of my book; not the detailed one in the pocket, as I bring one of that with me.

DAUBENY, Charles Giles Bridle (1795 — 1867).
Professor of Chemistry and Rural Economy at Oxford, and Professor of Botany there after 1834. **(DNB.)**

0538 17 Jun. 1857. With much pleasure do I accept Honorary Degree at Oxford and will dine with the Provost of University College as invited on the 23rd.

0615 3 Nov. 1857. Plans for a meeting at which L. is to lecture, and words on the forthcoming meeting of the R.G.S.

DENMAN, Hon. George (1819 — 1896).
Son of 1st Baron Denman. Barrister, M.P. for Tiverton 1859—65 and 1866—72, Judge of the High Court of Justice 1881—92. **(DNB.)**

1129 †[26 Sep. 1861?]. First encounter with the Ajawa. Bishop will now be at peace, if the Portuguese leave him alone. Sicard removed from Tette and made Governor of Iboe. Thus he is almost compelled to become a slave trader. Cruz married the daughter of the

Governor of Quilimane.   Do whatever you can to make Portuguese abandon their policy of exclusiveness.   Blakesley missed my weak point: not the Zambesi, which a Mississippi steamer could ply the whole of ordinary years, but the Portuguese settlements are the weak point.

DENMAN, Hon. Joseph (1810 — 1875).
Son of 1st Baron Denman.   Captain, R.N., Commander of the royal yacht "Victoria and Albert" 1854—62.   **(Navy List.)**

0697   11 Feb. 1858.   *On the trip up the Shire, the suspicions of the people, and their intention to return.

0872   19 Feb. 1859.   Examined rapid above Tette and found it a great curiosity.   We will need a strong steamer to go up.   We turned up the Shire, which we believe was never explored before.   The valley is 20 miles wide and bounded by lofty mountains.   Many hundred elephants.   Stopped by cataracts, but were told that a five days' journey overland brings us back to the river, at which point Arabs from Zanzibar come down in canoes.   We return in a month or so.

DENNY, Henry (1803 — 1871).
Entomologist and curator of the museum of the Leeds Literary and Philosophical Society.
                                        (DNB.)

0218   7 Dec. 1849.   On the parasitical insects of the larger African quadrupeds.

DICKSON, Henry (1818—1840).
A native of Edinburgh, he was a fellow student of Livingstone at Ongar.   He was appointed to Samoa, but died at Sydney **en route** on 4 Feb. 1840.   **(LMS Reg. no.410.)**

0008   8 May 1840.   Published in Chamberlin, **SLFL** no. 1 (omitting sentences on tracts to be sent to Dickson, expectation of letter from him, enquiries as to his health, news of Cecil and other friends, and personal exhortation).

DOUGLAS, John.
Possibly a photographer in Kendal.

0742   2 Mar. 1858.   Thank you for the photograph of me: I have seen no better.   We take photograph apparatus, which my brother manipulates.   He is now at Birkenhead;   if you gave him hints, I'm sure he'd be grateful.

DREW, Andrew (1792 — 1878).
Captain, R.N. (1843), Agent Victualler at the Cape of Good Hope, 1850—63, promoted to Admiral, 1875.   **(Boase, MEB.)**

0833   27 Sep. 1858.   Thank you for kindness shown me when I was with you, and to my wife after I left.   We took 1½ tons of coal near Tette, Which Rae says is better than the American coal he got in New York.   We have had many problems with the channels in this river, and our vessel should be named the "Asthmatic." It draws 8½ ft. when loaded and canoes pass us when going upstream.   The pinnace when loaded draws more than the launch.

0966   4 Nov. 1859.   *On the journey up the Shire to Lake Nyassa, whose length is unknown; its feeders; terraces along the Shire.   Intoxication and marriage rites of people. Mail service to Simonstown.   Does not know Marr's whereabouts.

1092   11 Mar. 1861.   We start today up the River Rovuma.   The mouth is wide, with no bar. Highlands begin 8 or 9 miles up.   People speak nearly same dialect as at Senna. We have the Bishop and Rowley aboard: fine characters.

DRUMMOND, George (1808 – 1893).

A native of Cumnock, he studied at Glasgow and Ongar, and was appointed to Samoa in 1839, remaining there till 1872.   **(LMS Reg. no. 407.)**

0010   25 Jun. 1840.   Published in Chamberlin, **SLFL** no. 2 (omitting passages on the death of Dickson and homecoming of his widow, Mrs Drummond's health, boxes to be sent out, T.L. Prentice, doubt as to whether he should marry, news of Cecil and other friends, reason for having written to Dickson; p. 9 1.20 **about Old Cumnock**).

0022   10, 18 Mar. 1841.   Published in Chamberlin, **SLFL** no. 6 (omitting passages on his visit to Rio, T.L. Prentice who has joined the Plymouth Brethern, Inglis and other friends, and a consumptive statue of a saint in Rio).

0071   20 Jun. 1843.   Published in Chamberlin, **SLFL** no. 13 (omitting passages of good **wishes**, on his success in learning the language, his tours to the north, Moffat's tendency to exaggerate, and news of friends; p. 40 1.30 **I have not**).

0112   21 Nov. 1844.   Published in Chamberlin, **SLFL** no. 20 (omitting passages on Chisholm's and Moore's families, bad character of the Bakhatla, Ross's exaggerated claims, success of the French mission, churches being regarded as political communities, circumlocutory nature of Sichuana, mutual friends, and the lack of suitable native teachers; p. 74 1.23 **viz. plastic**).

DRUMMOND, Henry.

A lace manufacturer in Hamilton, where he knew the Livingstone family, and later (ca. 1844–50) in Glasgow.

0030   4 Aug. 1841. Published in Chamberlin, **SLFL** no. 8 (omitting a few unimportant sentences and personal comment at the end).

0084   29 Jul. 1843.   Published in Chamberlin, **SLFL** no. 16 (omitting a paragraph on Williams and further details about Boers; p. 59 1.22 **sail cloth**; p. 61 1.25 **of the enamel**).

0185   19 Jun. 1848.   Published in Chamberlin, **SLFL** no. 30 (omitting the reason for not sending money order).

0190   Nov. 1848.   Apologies for delay in payment.   Box has arrived.   Further order for clothing, etc.   20 Dec. Letter will be taken tomorrow by a minister of the Dutch Reformed Church.

DUPRAT, Alfredo (1816 – 1881).
Portuguese consul and representative on the anti-slavery commission at Cape Town. Subsequently consul-general in London.   Created viscount 1870.   (Gr Enc Port.)

0333   9 Apr. 1854.   Journey from Sebituane's to Cassange, the country and people. Proposals to improve commerce.   15 Aug. Detained by illness. Kindness of all.

0378   12 Sep. 1855.   Suggests that seeds of a wax-producing plant be sent from Cape Town to be planted around Loanda and that seeds of Angolan coffee be sent to the Botanical Gardens in Cape Town.

0401   4 Mar. 1856.   Has reached farthest inland Portuguese station, received with the usual generosity.   Send news of discoveries to King of Portugal.   Do not reveal at the Cape that he wishes to promote a treaty between Sekeletu and Portugal.   Wax would be a boon to Angola.   Hopes to go with family to a point near Sekeletu.

0407   26 Mar. 1856.   Proposes an exchange of seeds between Tette and Cape Town.

DYKE, Hamilton Moore (1817 – post 1880).
The son of a London jeweller who emigrated to South Africa in 1822, he joined the French mission in Basutoland in 1840 and served it for many years.   His sister married Eugène Casalis of the same mission.   (Smith, MOB.)

0066   24 Feb. 1843.   Acknowledges his letter.   Progress of mission.   Perhaps Bechuanas not so degenerate as Moffat alleges;   idea of future life implied in fable of chameleon and black lizard;   translation of 'soul'.   Dried-up river beds; his finding of fossils.

0167   20 May 1847.   Does not have the books requested.   Congratulates him on his intended marriage, a state which can give much happiness especially to those who do not expect their partner to be perfect.   Amusement at clerical foibles.   Difficulties with Boers who oppress natives.   Reached the Limpopo;   country rich in minerals.   Strange organisation of French missionaries.   Personal greetings.

0183   7 Apr. 1848.   Sechele's writing to Mosheshe gives opportunity to write.   Building house. Sechele and he would like horses from Mosheshe.   Congratulations on marriage and ordination.   Progress encouraging.   Sechele desirous of improvement, but wives obstacle. Send gooseberry cuttings.

0262   1 Dec. 1851.   Regrets lack of personal details in Dyke's letter.   Tells him of his family, from whom he is soon to part as he is going to a feverish region and one ought not to risk the lives of one's children.   Doubts theory that much is to be expected from converting the young.   Seeks statistics.   Hunger and Boers make his people disinclined to learn, and he will move north.   Tsetse affects only domestic animals.   The Sesheke;   fruits;   the people and their languages.

EARDLEY, Sir Culling Eardley (1805 – 1863).
Religious liberal and philanthropist, Eardley served as M.P. for Pontefract 1830–1, and was longtime Treasurer of the London Missionary Society.   (DNB.)

1313 23 Jan. 1863.   After visiting Mackenzie's grave, I no longer think he was wrong in fighting. He defended his orphan children when there was no human arm to invoke· The country is now devastated;   the Tette people, the Ajawa and Marianno are behind it. Legalized slave hunting prevents the benefits of H.M. Squadron being felt inland.

EASTLAKE, Lady Elizabeth, née Rigby (1809–1893).
Authoress, married Charles Eastlake (1849).   (DNB.)

0520 18 May 1857.   *Accepting a dinner invitation.

0530 30 May 1857.   Sorry that I forgot your invitation last week, as I was busy leaving London.

EBURY, 1st Baron (1801 – 1893).
Robert Grosvenor, created Baron Ebury 1857.   A religious reformer within the Church of England, he presided over the revision of the Book of Common Prayer in 1874.
                                                          (DNB.)

0661 14 Jan. 1858.   Thank you for bringing the Homeopathic system to my notice.   L. discusses his medical training and his medical experience in Africa.

ELWIN, Whitwell (1816–1900).
Prose writer, Rector of Booton 1849–1900;   connected with the **Quarterly Review** 1843–1900, which he edited from 1853–1860.   He also edited various poetical works.
                                                          (DNB.)

0667 19 Jan. 1858. Please work into the abridgement your statement that the unusual amount of attention given to discoveries in Africa is the operation of the Spirit of God. Murray wants me to give you an outline of our expedition.   I have not mentioned this to any but the Duke of Argyll as I fear Portuguese jealousy.

0691 8 Feb. 1858.   He goes to Africa for more than mere exploration, taking a botanist, a geologist, and an artist, hoping to point out more than ever the salubrity of the healthy high region where Europeans may live and introduce civilization and Christianity.   Sometimes he thinks of a British colony.   His brother accompanies him to keep up Christian instruction.

0767 22 Mar. 1858. On the honeybees above Tette, perhaps notes for publication. Suggestions to be included in an abridgement of **MT**, including the type of mortar used by the ancient Egyptians, Owen's difference of opinion with L. about the lion, and illustrations of Oswell's.

FAIRBROTHER, William (1817 – 1882).
Missionary in Shanghai 1844–6, later Pastor of London Road Church, Derby, and an official of the London Missionary Society.   (LMS Reg. no. 469.)

0243   14 Jan. 1851.   Fairbrother's failure to write a real letter.   Mary's paralysis cured, but his uvula needs excision.   Boers menacing station.   Character of latter and their Scottish clergy.   Natives fighting them but will inevitably be defeated and retreat to fever-stricken areas.   Hopes of opening beyond Lake Ngami.   Progress of translation of Bible.   Would like copy of Krapf's dictionary.

FERGUSON, Fergus.
Deacon of Independent Church in Hamilton attended by Livingstone.

0083   28 Jul. 1843.   Apologies for not writing before.   Has been travelling to improve his knowledge of the language.   Prospect of establishing mission at Mabotsa.   Further progress in Africa doubtful because of malaria and tsetse.   Way to the interior must be by the lake which no white man has seen or could live near because of fever.   Divine aid needed for conversion.   Differences in language make conveying truth to native difficult.   Regrets being implicated in disagreeable circumstances by Moir, who is in error.

FESTING, John Wogom (1837 – 1902).
An Anglican clergyman who ended his career as Bishop of St Albans 1890–1902.   He was closely concerned with the Universities' Mission to Central Africa, as its Assistant Secretary 1863–82, Treasurer 1882–90, and President 1892–1902.   (DNB.)

1739   8 Jun. 1865.   Detained by mother's illness, but prepared to allow Committee to settle matter of payment for freight from Mozambique.   Has written to Rutherfoord in Cape Town to refund anything paid to him, but it was rather received by Captain Davis.

FIGANIÈRE E MORÃO, Jorge César de (1813 – 1887).
An official in the Portuguese Ministry for Foreign Affairs from 1844, and Director of that department from 1881.   (Gr Enc Port. XI, p. 280.)

0486   25 Mar. 1857.   Convey to your Government my gratitude for sending orders to Mosambique to maintain my men there at province expense until my return.   The announcement of this was greeted with great applause at the last meeting of the R.G.S.   The benevolence of your Government deserves the respect and admiration of all who are interested in Africa.   Please extend my greetings also to Viscount de Sá da Bandeira.

FITCH, Mrs.
Wife of Frederick.   For letters addressed to her jointly, see under Fitch, Frederick.

1220   29 Apr. 1862.   Grief over the death of Mary Livingstone;   requests Mrs. F. to aid his children.

FITCH, Frederick.
Associated with Fitch & Son, Provision Merchants and Importers, 66 Bishopsgate, London, Fitch regularly supplied the Zambezi Expedition with hams, cheeses, etc. In addition to handling the financial affairs of Charles Livingstone while he was on the expedition, Fitch and his wife were among the many who saw to the affairs of David and Mary Livingstone's children.

0462   27 Jan. 1857.   Thanking F. for his generous offer to aid L.'s work, which Mary will partially accept, and declining his invitation to spend the night as L. is too busy with his book.

0554   10 Jul. 1857.   Thanking F. for his kind note and whatever accompanied it, and indicating that he will visit F. when the book is completed.

0611   28 Oct. 1857.   L. accepts an invitation to visit F., and proposes Tuesday next.

0687   5 Feb. 1858.   Concerning the purchase of guns for the upcoming expedition.

0693   9 Feb. 1858.   Requesting F. order 4 cases of guns for the expedition.

0698   11 Feb. 1858.   Advising F. to press on with the purchase of guns.

0714   15 Feb. 1858.   Advising F. to purchase 4 instead of 5 cases of guns.

0725   18 Feb. 1858.   Advising F. on the correct procedure to deal with the paperwork relevant to the purchase of the guns, and requesting that they be forwarded to John Laird's Iron Works, Birkenhead.

0801   22 Jun. 1858.   Concerning the progress of the expedition to date. Mary L. left in Cape Town, whence she will proceed to Kuruman. Observations on the Zambezi Delta and River, and the good health and spirits of the party.

0954   28 Oct. 1859.   Telling of the exploration of the River Shire up to the Lake Nyasa, and elaborating L.'s prospects in a direction he never contemplated. Mentions his observation of the slave trading in the region. Derogatory words about the "Ma-Robert", and further comments about the men in his party.

1067   19 Jan. 1861.   Expecting the arrival of a new steamer daily. Sad news of the Linyanti Mission. Replacement of Sicard at Tete. Thanks for kindness to Mrs. L. Description of the Victoria Falls.

1148   25 Nov. 1861.   On the establishment of the OCDD (UMCA) mission to Central Africa, and the sad fate of the Linyanti Mission; the first skirmish with the Yao (Ajawa); the exploration of Lake Nyassa; guns turned out excellent.

1170   31 Jan. 1862.   Copy, letter of L. to Tidman, 24 Nov. 1861; if Tidman does not reply, please give me any information you can on the Makololo mission.

1191   1 Mar. 1862.   Thank you for cheeses and hams. New steamer and Mrs. L. arrived with aid of Capt. Wilson, HMS "Gorgon".

1224   1 May 1862.   On £15 loaned by F. to Mrs. L. Please look after boxes of clothing I send to my children. Please check prices of granite and iron tombstones.

1405 12 Dec. 1863. Thank you for papers you forwarded. We await rising of river to proceed to the sea. Late King of Portugal deceived by his ministers. New bishop will probably leave the country. Rowley blames L. for the mission's problems.
17 Dec. Bishop leaving. Tidman wrote exculpating Price entirely. Report of L.'s death is false.

1454 30 Jul. 1864. Sorry I have not seen you, but have had business and now leave for Scotland.

1689 26 Apr. 1865. In order to arrange for my last visit, please inform me when you will both be home.

1774 25 Jul. 1865. Advice to F. concerning a request he wishes to put to Miss Burdett-Coutts.

FITZGERALD, Sir William Robert Seymour Vesey (1818 – 1885).
A barrister and Conservative politician, he served as Governor of Bombay 1867–72.
(DNB.)

2003 13 Mar. 1872. Previous letters destroyed by slave traders; this goes by Stanley. The watershed and river system. Manyuema country. Difficulties of travel in forest. Still has to discover fountains and examine ancient excavations. Delays caused by slaves.

FLEETWOOD, Henry.
A bootmaker in Epsom, Surrey.

0657 7 Jan. 1858. Enclosed find £1 11/- for the boots. Linen arrived safely. As I did not know your initial, I put any letter down on the P.O. order, and you must endorse it accordingly. Mrs. L. will come to London on Saturday or Monday next.

FLETCHER, T. Sam.

0721 17 Feb. 1858. Please transmit packages from J.A. Turner of Manchester to John Laird's Ironworks, Birkenhead, for the Zambesi Expedition.

FOREIGN OFFICE.
Livingstone addressed his dispatches and letters to ministers and officials of the Foreign Office personally, and they will be found here under the headings CLARENDON, Earl of, CONYNGHAM, George L., HAMMOND, Edmund, LAYARD, Sir Austin H., MALMES-BURY, Earl of, RUSSELL, Lord John, SHELBURNE, Earl of, and STANLEY, Lord.

FOSTER, Peter Le Neve (1809 – 1879).
A regular contributor to many scientific and technological journals, he spent 13 years as secretary to the mechanical science section of the British Association, and was Secretary of the Royal Society of Arts, 1853–79. **(DNB.)**

0984   12 Jan. 1860.   Describing in detail the deterioration of the "patent steel plates" which were first used on the "Ma-Robert", and the several attempts by the expedition members to rectify the various problems resulting.

1552   8 Dec. 1864.   Requesting if certain statistics he recalls from a lecture about elephants given by Prof. Owen in Dec. 1856 or Jan. 1857 are correct.

1617   23 Feb. 1865.   Apologies for not thanking you earlier for the copy of the lecture you sent me.   Will you kindly forward the enclosed enquiry about ivory on the world market to Mr. Simmonds?

FRÉDOUX, Jean (1823 – 1866).
French missionary at Motito 1845—66.   In 1850 he married Ann Moffat, Mary Livingstone's younger sister.

0321   28 Sep. 1853.   Published in Schapera, **DLFL** no. 98.

0408   26 Mar. 1856 (also to Mrs. Frédoux).   Journey from Sekeletu's.   Description of the Victoria Falls and the lower Zambesi.   Kindness of Portuguese.

FREEMAN, Joseph John (1794 – 1851).
Missionary in Madagascar 1827—36, joint Foreign Secretary of the London Missionary Society 1841—6, and Home Secretary 1846—51.   (**LMS Reg.** no. 264.)

Livingstone's letters to him of 23 Sep. 1841 (0035), 22 Dec. 1841 (0045), 3 and 7 Jul. 1842 (0056), 18 Jul. 1842 (0061), 14 Nov. 1849 (0216), 8 Jan. 1850 (0219), and 24 Aug. 1850 (0230) are published in Schapera, **LMC.**

FRERE, George (1810 – 1878).
Clerk in the slave trade department of the Foreign Office from 1826;   commissioner to the Portuguese-British Commission for the Suppression of the Slave Trade (Cape Town) 1842—62;   and judge, United States-British Commission for the Suppression of the Slave Trade (Cape Town) 1862—7.   (Boase, **MEB,** Suppl.)

1144   13 Nov. 1861.   Describing the skirmish with the Ajawa in July 1861, and also of the recent exploration of the west side of Lake Nyassa.   Nothing but contradictory reports about the Rovuma.   Slaving here is successful under the French flag.

1289   19 Nov. 1862.   Am writing my opinion of Sa da Bandiera's map.   We went up Rovuma 114 miles as the crow flies, 156 in all, and twice touched the slave route from the lake to Kilwa.   We will tow the mission stores over the bar, but in future please send them to Mosambique.   I shall attend to Mrs. Burrup's request for her husband's belongings most carefully.

1294   2 Dec. 1862.   Details about Sa da Bandiera's map;   thank you for translating his paper. I enclose my paper: if you and Maclear think best, publish it.   Further observations on Portuguese slaving and claims to the interior.

1318   14 Feb. 1863.   On the depopulation of the valley by slavers from the north and north-west of Quilimane: panic seized the people around Zomba and they fled into the valley. Wilson's book on West Africa reveals the benefits of Palmerston's policy;   do whatever you can to give it the same chance here as it had on that coast, and do it quickly.

1414   22 Dec. 1863.   On the interdependence of the slave and ivory trade.   Mariano is dead; his people sell off his captives.   Hundreds go past Mt. Morambala every week while the mission remains in the clouds on top.   Sicard abusive to Kirk and made him pay for a licence to live in Quilimane.

1884   7 Mar. 1866.   Thanks to you and Layard for dealing with the mission's scandal: that I brought the people out in closed batches.   Saw from 70 to 300 slaves at the market at various times;   chief purchasers were northern Arabs and Persians.   Majority here are Mang'anja.   Sarcasm on Britain's slowness to end the trade of slaves in Zanzibar.

FRERE, Sir Henry Bartle Edward (1815 – 1884).
Entered the Bombay Civil Service in 1834, and concluded his service there as Governor 1862–7.   Livingstone first met him in 1864.   In 1872 he went to Zanzibar to negotiate the suppression of the slave trade.   Livingstone planned to give his name to one of the 'Fountains' of the Nile.   (DNB.)

1444   14 Jun. 1864.   Sends letter from Sultan of Zanzibar, with apologies for delay.

1447   23 Jun. 1864.   Prospects for trade between Bombay and Africa seem to be hindered by ignorance of coast north of Zanzibar.   Suggests going there in October next.   Large supplies of blackwood on Rovuma might be inducement to Indian merchants.   Leaving tomorrow.

1909   1 Feb. 1867.   Despatch to Clarendon does not coincide with views of Pelly, whose reasoning on the continuance of the Zambesi slave trade is untenable.   Arabs wait half a day for letters.   Long walk to this point.   Johanna men were thieves and it is good to be rid of them.   The people, country, forests, etc.   Death of Sultan who was kind and helpful.

1922   3 Dec. 1867.   Journey from Lobemba to Cazembe.   Now halted by excess of water in the country.

1933   Jul. 1868.   Description of the watershed, lakes, and rivers.   Friendliness of Arabs.   Delay at Cazembe from floods.   Paper for this and letter to Clarendon borrowed from Arab. Anxiety about Tom's education and preparation for Indian Civil Service.   His misunder-standing of Palmerston's offer of assistance.   Doubtful if doing good in accordance with Providence or serving insane geographers.   Excavations with animal drawings.

1943   Oct. 1869.   Northward course of the Lualaba.   Accuracy of Ptolemy's sources.   Must find confluence of Lualaba and Tanganyika and go round all the springs.   Speke wrong. The Manyuema people and country.   May 1870.   No evidence of cannibalism.   Rank vegetation.   No possibility of Nile source being further south.   Pupils from Price's school would have been better taught on a man-of-war.   Has received a few newspapers but no letters, which are probably detained at Unyanyembe.

1953   27 Nov. 1870.   Written on leaf of cheque book.   To the west two rivers, both called Lualaba, unite into a lake.   Mound with four fountains;   those on the north join into same lake and presumably form the Nile; those on the south are the Zambesi and Kafue. The watershed in general. Previous travellers. Longing to retire.

1987.1 20 Dec. 1871. Losses due to Kirk's use of slaves. Stanley's success. Delays caused by slavers. English settlement from West Africa desirable. Arabs spoil all tribes. 13 Mar. 1872. Came here on 2 Feb. Stanley leaves tomorrow. Eager to finish the sources.

2012 1 Jul. 1872. Sending map and observations to the coast. Short trip south about all the sources will finish his work. After the fountains will visit underground excavations. Banians have hindered him greatly; his complaints about them not intended as an attack on Kirk. Attempt to obtain longitudes. Glad to hear of Government grant to his daughters.

2026 [Jan. 1873?] Had to go south to avoid war. Geology of southern Tanganyika. Changes in chieftainships. Cloudy weather. Lake Bangweolo and its rivulets. Realisation that Chambezi is not the Zambesi. People not warlike till affected by Arab slavers. Food.

"FROLIC", HMS.
A sloop on the Cape of Good Hope station, which conveyed Livingstone from Quilimane to Mauritius in 1856. Her commander at this time was L.W. Peyton (q.v.).

0433 26 Sep. 1856. [To the gunroom officers.] Thanks for kind treatment.

FROST, Mr.
A servant at Newstead Abbey.

1686 25 Apr. 1865. Gives autograph and photograph with thanks for attention.

GABRIEL, Edmund (1821 — 1862).
British arbitrator from 1845 on the British and Portuguese Commission at Loanda for the suppression of the slave trade; in 1856 he was made Acting Commissioner and in 1859 Commissioner. Livingstone stayed at his house in 1854 and struck up a warm friendship.
(FO List 1864, p. 165.)

0338 1 Oct. 1854. Pleasant memories of Loanda. Plants. How to make metallic paint for painting birds. Good to study works of nature. Possibilities of developing trade. Cotton. Proceding to Cazengo. Donkey good. Servants excellent. Longitude of Golungo Alto.

0339 13 Oct. 1854. Trouble with mosquitos. Observations. Coffee apparently indigenous. Activities of Arsenio. Help to Costa in map-making. Churches decayed. Country suitable for railway and industry. Gabriel should visit it. Birds. Fowls adapted for hot climate. Fruit trees. 17 Oct. Clouds prevented lunar observations. Wild grapes. Bustards. Rope making. Sends coffee seeds. 21 Oct. Has received letters; regrets Gabriel's illness. Rope making. Cigars.

0340 21 Oct. 1854. Graça's estate at Monte Allegre. Kindness of planters. Extension of coffee plantations. Crops. Will write description of Angola, possibly for Government rather than Geographical Society. Correspondence after Cassenge will be difficult. Ancient iron works. Wild vines. Tsetse-like insects.

0341   24 Oct. 1854. Attack of fever cured by quinine. Seeds. To visit Piriz, a trader at Pungo Adongo. Project for museum at Loanda. How does one calculate a percentage?

0342   25 Oct. [1854]. Regrets accident to 'Philomel'. Thinking of purchasing a property for use as a hospital.

0344   28 Oct. 1854. Horse and men sick. Canto also ill. Child slavery. A deserted convent at Bango; immorality of its former priests. Plants. Route for Gabriel to visit interior; he could investigate reported petroleum and get many birds. Mysteries of bird migration. Dr. Welweitsch as a botanist. Papyrus plant. Supply statistics of rainfall and death. Slave trading. [End missing.]

0345   1 Nov. 1854. Ready to leave. Canto convalescent. Opportunities for cotton growing. Difficulty about hospital would be future administration. Plants.

0346   5 Nov. 1854. Canto seriously ill. Thanks for letter and Arsenio's literary curiosity. Difficulty with decimal arithmetic. Rope making. Tree rings and the baobab. [End missing.]

0348   9 Nov. 1854. Plants. Canto recovering. Sends letters for American brothers. Idea of hospital given up. Wished to benefit Angolese whose desire to learn to read contrasts with the Bakwains. Care of Providence. Maclear's scientific accuracy.

0349   12 Nov. 1854. Will leave tomorrow. Canto recovered. Does not intend to publish scandal about priests. Museum would be useful. Fig trees. Loadstone. P.S. Prevented from leaving by illness of horse.

0350   15 Nov. 1854. Horse's illness. One of the men has jaundice. Horse not made ill by grass. Will send map on tracing paper for transfer to cartridge paper.

0351   17 Nov. 1854. Plants. Horse seems mortally afflicted. Anxious to leave. Observations.

0352   21 Nov. 1854. Gabriel's health requires change of residence. Horse will neither live nor die. Jaundiced man better, another becoming insane through lack of activity. Canto recovered: his good character. Welweitsch less admirable. Seeds and mineral specimens. Geology. Idea of future life. Arrest of slave trader. Curious insect. Insect physiology. Clouds prevented observation of eclipse. Will take two extra men from a group like freemasons. Canto thinking of leaving here. Glad to get pocket-book back. Portuguese objection to quinine is prejudice. Horse prostrate. P.S. Plants.

0353   7 Dec. 1854. Change of residence always good in cases of fever. Never suffers from depression but occasionally from longing to see family. Advised to trick 'freemasons' into going all the way with him, but would rather do without them. Bite of a tampano. Experiment with distilling insects. Activities of Arsenio. Teaching of Jesuits better than heathen state. Centuries of degradation must have had effect on Africans, and several generations will be necessary before they reach European standards; compare Israelites after enslavement in Egypt. London Missionary Society agents have to respect governments. Spontaneous improvement in Angola possible. Leaving immediately for Pungo Adongo. Sends view of Ambaca and seeds.

0354   20 Dec. 1854.   Attack of fever.   Staying with Piris.   Latitudes.   Will visit Coanza. Canto here and unwell.   Conglomerate pillars.   Piris has cattle and vines.

0356   26 Dec. 1854.   Thanks for letters and papers.   Joy over safety of Bedingfeld outweighs loss of letters in 'Forerunner'.   Has re-written Murchison;   will write an account of Angolan geography.   Report to Clarendon difficult to compose.   Will be here at least till 1 Jan.   Will not remain long at Cassenge.   Man with insanity may be made to march. Visit to Coanza;   difference of climate.   Boy attacked by alligator.   Baobab.   Electric fish.   Birds already collected should be sent off.   Regards to Hoskins.   Thanks for paper and pens.   Is another bill on Tidman required?   Copy for Murchison not yet finished.

0357   31 Dec. 1854.   Sends letter for Murchison.   Boiling points of water and temperatures. Bulbs.   Canto ill with dysentery, but still conscientious about judicial duties.   Ascertain boiling point of water at Loanda.   Still trying to write to Clarendon.   Madman does not give much trouble.

0359   5 Jan. 1855.   Objects and letters entrusted to Pires, also geological specimens.   Did not see iron.   Hills probably result of denudation rather than volcanic activity.   Plants sent. His ox.   Notes from newspapers.   Falls at Lombe.   Affair of the slaves.   Use of a sketch map in Germany.   Costa's errors and pretensions.   Pires kind;   his farming.   18 Jan. Observations.   Money getting short.   Difficulty with servants.   Other travellers.   Will remain with Sekeletu for some months.   Vines, coffee, and other plants.   Will await mail before moving to Quango.   Good new blood in Navy to succeed indifferent Admirals. Does not think he was cheated over ivory at Cassenge.   Met black Catholic missionary from Loanda.   20 Jan.   Neves saw shells in rocks which he has overlooked.   Letter to Clarendon may be sent or burned.   Sends letter to Tidman with draft for his wife, and ideal section for Murchison.   23 Jan.   No letters for him in mail.   Working on map.   May settle in England on account of his family.

0362   30 Jan. 1855.   Sending seeds.   Intermittent fever.   Discussing future route with his men. Baptised a dying child of Neves;   shudders at theology which puts infants in hell.   Rocks. Future communication.

0363   4 Feb. 1855.   Mail brought no letter.   Will wait for next one before setting off.   Map completed;   many features omitted for want of space and positions unascertained for want of time;   observations go to Maclear for checking.   Letters sent.   Wishes to visit Matiamvo, but men wish to return to their families.   Madman recovered.   Learning Portuguese.   Regrets report to Clarendon was not better done.

0365   12 Feb. 1855.   Letter received.   Busy re-writing and map-making.   Copy of map might go to Clarendon and to Paris Geographical Society.   Corrections to positions.   Grieved by news from Sebastopool.   Sir George Cathcart.   Letters sent.   Birds.   Bills on Tidman. 13 Feb.   Going as far as Cobango.   Letters for Tidman and Maclear.

0368   14 Feb. 1855.   Sends map and letter for Murchison.   Has asked his wife to write care of of Gabriel.   All but certain they will go to Matiamvo.   Letters sent.   Definition of aliens. 15 Feb.   Neves wishes information about Casai to correct his pamphlet.   India rubber. Will continue writing even without hope of reply.   Birds.   Neves will be able to forward newspapers.

0369   2 Mar. 1855.   Left Cassange 16 Feb.   Delayed by sickness.   Troubles of Cypriano de Abreu.   Neves' agent dilatory but expected tomorrow.   Observations.   Letters sent. Kindness of Neves.   If he writes a book it will be overshadowed by interest in Russia. Hopes for another letter.   Working on dictionary of Ambonda language, which is of same structure as Caffre and Bechuana. Use of cotton cloth as money. Africans essentially like us. They are polytheists like the ancient Greeks. A trial for witchcraft. Gabriel's long burden at Loanda will ultimately be of benefit. Visit to Matiamvo would waste even more time; men anxious to go home; and he might not allow them to procede. River and mountain names repeated again and again. Why do climbing plants ascend trees as they do? What influences the colour of birds? Certain that rivers Quango and Casai form the Zaire. Slaves traded for ivory. 18 Mar. Slow progress because of rain and fever. Reception by Sansaue. Payment for passage. Tell Bishop of horse's death. Errors in locating rivers. Sends notes for Maclear, Murchison, and wife. Now passing out of correspondence. 19 Apr. Has had 22 days of rheumatic fever. Rock layers at Pungo Andongo. Vision of the creation. Insect experiment. 18 May. Much time lost by fever. Position. Not going to Matiamvo's. Letters sent. Almost blind.

0376 12 Aug. 1855. Goods finished but now in Barotse country. Men delighted to be home. Difficulties at Casai crossing. Hunting hippopotamus. Cormorants. Politics of Makololo. Letters etc. sent. Oswell and others have been at Chobe enquiring for him. Waiting for canoes. Moffat visited Mosilikatze, who has sent presents for him which Makololo would not receive and placed on an island. Donkeys excellent. Regards.

0380 12 Sep. 1855. Reached Barotse country in July, then came down river. Receipt of letters. Maclear happy with observations. Quarrel with Boers in South Africa. Vegetable wax from the Cape could be exported to Angola. Will go down river to Quilimane rather than discover Lake Nyassa because a sea route is his object. Forays by Makololo.

0393 7 Feb. 1856. Difficulties of communication. The eastern and western ridges. Victoria Falls. Elephant hunting. Venereal disease among Africans. Hopes of water route to healthy regions. Devastation of Zumbo. Slave trade. Absence of fever due partly to diet. Birds. Garden on island at Falls. 3 Mar. Rough journey to Tette. Exploitation of discoveries.

0409 [2 Mar. – 3 Apr. 1856.] [Beginning lost.] Unlikelihood of overland route being used. Lint plants. Sicard anxious to promote country. Ornithological books. Will write to Steele. Pieties.

0411 4 Apr. 1856. Sends letters to Governor, Schut, Canto, Pires; believes Neves has left Angola. Illness in kidneys. Waiting for more healthy period before going to Quilimane. In England the London Missionary Society will expect him to make speeches and raise funds. Use of brandy after fever. Wishes to establish mission among Makololo and get good name with heathen. Have written Steele. Pieties.

0421 27 Jun. 1856. Disappointed at receiving no letters from Loanda. Loss of five men from the 'Dart'. Then delighted to receive letter of 15 Jun. 1855. Letters sent. Geographical Society medal and degree from Glasgow. London Missionary Society in debt and may wish to transfer him to China, but will not now leave Africa. Waiting for vessel from the Cape. Kindness of Portuguese. Makololo remain at Tette. Poor state of country. English regarded with favour by natives. Captain Bobsein of Hamburg here.

0847 7 Oct. 1858. Bedingfeld's quarreling, slanders, and resignation; navigation better without him. Reception by men at Tette. Unsatisfactory launch. Coal from Tette. London Missionary Society annoyed at him. Kebra-basa said to be rocky and dangerous. Unfavourable to Germans. No fever. News of family.

0906. 4 Jun. 1859. Sends draft of his dispatch on the discovery of Lake Shirwa. African from

124

Loanda did not get beyond Tette. Returning to Nyinyesi. Need for British colony.

1007   25 Mar. 1860.   Treatment of fever.   Rae goes home to get steamer for Lake Nyassa. Settlement would help to eradicate slavery.   Hopes for free navigation.   Portuguese few and immoral. Slanders of Captain Gordon.   Steamer full of patches and holes.

1091   8 Mar. 1861.   Has heard Gabriel has gone to England.   Met Silva Porto in Linyanti in 1853 or 1854, who said he was prevented from going east;   his journal published in **Boletim** does not mention his reaching Mozambique;   his inability to go east, inter alia, induced him to go west.   Macqueen has published in PRGS a fraudulent journal which claims he reached Mozambique. Tell Murchison what really occurred.   Sorry to hear of Brand's death.

GARDNER, Alan Henry (? — 1878).
Captain, R.N. (1856), in command of H.M. Corvette "Orestes" at the Cape of Good Hope, 1861—5;   retired 1872, Rear Admiral 1874.   During his time off East Africa, Gardner rendered many essential services to the Zambezi Expedition.   **(Navy List.)**

1269   3 Sep. 1862.   Outlining the proposed movements of the expedition during the next 9 months, including a visit to the Rovuma, to Johanna in December and the Kongone by Christmas, and not back to the sea until late 1863 or early 1864.

1276   15 Oct. 1862.   Describing what the party saw on the Rovuma after Gardner left them and returned to his ship, including the topography and the encounter with the MaKonde. Also mentions crossing the slave route between the lake and the sea.

1433   7 Mar. 1864.   Telling of the Africans liberated from slavery in July, 1861 by his party in conjunction with the mission, many of whom now go to the Cape.   Requesting a passage to the Cape for the boys.

1769   15 Jul. 1865.   *After visiting Bombay he will ascend the Rovuma again, and then go inland around the lake.   If the Portuguese were angry over L's speech at Bath, they will be lunatics after reading his recent book.

GARFORTH, Edmund St. John (? — 1921).
Lieutenant in command of the gun-vessel Penguin' which conveyed Livingstone from Zanzibar to the Rovuma in Mar. 1866. Promoted Commander 1867, Captain 1876, and Rear Admiral 1891.   **(Navy List.)**

1887   16 Mar. 1866.   Delay and inactivity in Zanzibar are causing sickness in men and beasts and threatening expedition.   Therefore asks for immediate conveyance to Rovuma Bay.

1889   22 Mar. 1866.   Thanks for service rendered in allowing expedition to leave Zanzibar.

GEDGE, Johnson.

0638   11 Dec. 1857.   *In reply to a note sent me by your nephew, whom I met in Cambridge, I must say that my appearance there was the last I will make in England, and I decline your invitation.   I never lectured for pay and if you hear of any others wishing to so employ me, please tell them it is out of the question.

GLYNN, **Sir** Richard George (1831 — 1918).
Captain in the Royal Dragoons 1852–9.   Travelled in Central Africa, visiting the Victoria Falls in 1863.   Succeeded to the baronetcy in 1863.   (**Who Was Who** 1916–1928.)

1517   25 Oct. 1864.   Asks about progress of fruit trees he planted at the Victoria Falls, and thanks G. for cleaning initials he cut there.

GONNE, Charles.
Served in the Bombay Civil Service 1853–85.   He was Secretary to the Government of Bombay 1864–79, Chief Secretary 1879–85.   (**IO List.**)

1876   6 Feb. 1866.   Handing over of 'Thule'.   Help given by Sultan.   7 Feb.   Sultan's personal thanks.

GOODMAN, J.E.

0727   19 Feb. 1858.   *The account has been presented to Captain Washington, and will be paid whenever all other expedition accounts are paid.   Thank you for kind favours;   if I see opportunities for opening trade I shall let you know.

GORDON, William Edward Alphonso (? — 1907).
Captain, R.N. (1860), Admiral (1887).   Gordon commanded H.M. Sloop "Hermes" at the Cape of Good Hope, 1856–60, and escorted the "Pearl" carrying the Zambezi Expedition from Simon's Town to the Zambezi delta in Apr.–Jun. 1858.
(**Navy List.**)

0797   9 Jun. 1858.   As lower portion of the river is in turmoil, I request your assistance in aiding the "Pearl" reach Tette.   Forming a depot below that place is unwise.   May we have the use of a boat's crew?   As Capt. Lyster suggested we may borrow the pinnace if necessary, may we do so?

0962   3 Nov. 1859.   Published in Wallis, **ZEDL.**

GOULTY, John Nelson (1788 — 1870).
Congregational minister, served the Union Street Chapel, Brighton, 1824–61.   He was a friend of Robert Moffat.   (**Congr.** Yearbook, 1871, p. 314).

0452   9 Jan. 1857.   Declines an invitation to visit Brighton.

GRANVILLE, 2nd Earl (Granville George Leveson-Gower) (1815 — 1891).
Liberal politician; held office **inter alia** as Foreign Secretary 1851—2, 1870—4, and
1880—5. **(DNB.)**

1977 14 Nov. 1871. Wickedness of Governor of Unyanyembe who destroyed all his letters and
plundered his goods. Banians should be made to make restitution. Falsity of Shereef
and his men. Disgust at Ujijian bloodshed. The Bagenya; attack on their market.
Painful and dangerous return to Ujiji with traders.

1987 18 Dec. 1871. Now knows 600 miles of the watershed, but has still to see the four
fountains, of which he has heard on all sides; may be those mentioned to Herodotus.
Relation of fountains to rivers. Ignorance at Zanzibar about Government policy of not
employing slaves has caused much loss. Arrival of Stanley. Pleasure cruize on Lake
Tanganyika. American success in getting letters through. Geographical work will be
finished in one year. P.S. Asks for smallpox vaccine.

1996 20 Feb. 1872. Share of Banian English subjects in the slave trade, especially among the
Manyuema. Losses of goods sent from Zanzibar. Proposes to encourage emigration of
African Christians from West to East Africa. If Sultan of Zanzibar were relieved of
subsidy to Muscat, he would concede English settlements. Supplies recovered from
slaves and received from Stanley. Proposes to go round Lake Tanganyika, along Lake
Bangweolo, to the four fountains, to Katanga, and back. Former doubts that Lualaba
might be the Congo; still diffident. Discomforts of exploration. Journal goes with
Stanley.

2013 1 Jul. 1872. Losses caused by use of slaves. Formal complaint about this not a personal
attack on Kirk. He intended to stop more slaves coming, not an English expedition.
War going on. White man called Cherura who became chief of Basango six generations
ago; his descendents still pale; Darwin's theory. Repeats proposed route; expects to
be back in Ujiji in eight months. Could not retire immediately with honour. If he had
known of the Search Expedition, would have used it to explore Lake Victoria; native
accounts of that area. Longitude of Lualaba makes it less likely to be the Congo.
Various reports of fountains. Observations sent to Maclear. Anxiety about journal.
Thanks to all involved in Search Expedition.

GRAY, Mrs. (? — 1871).
Wife of Robert, née Myddleton.

1373 14 Jul. 1863. Thanking her for the mosquito curtain, the handsomest ever seen in this
country. Greatest folly of his life was travelling all over Africa without ever thinking
that the pest could be escaped from. Starts for the lake tomorrow.

GRAY, John Edward (1800 — 1875).
A naturalist connected with the British Museum 1824—75, Gray was a member of many
learned societies and the author of hundreds of scientific papers and catalogues. **(DNB.)**

0553 9 Jul. 185[7]. *Concerning a drawing of the tsetse fly for his book.

0563 31 Jul. [1857]. Instruct Mr. Ford to draw the tsetse on a small block of wood or on
paper which can be transferred to wood. Let it be life size in a natural position, with
two views. When completed send it to Cooke.

GRAY, Robert (1809 — 1872).
Bishop of Cape Town (1847—72) and Metropolitan of Africa, Gray was a committed supporter of the success of the Universities' Mission to Central Africa.   (DNB.)

0945   20 Oct. 1859.   Describing the Shire valley as an excellent spot for the foundation of a mission and the establishment of a trading station.

1006   21 Mar. 1860.   Heard Miss Coutts gave £2500 for an institution to educate the sons of native chiefs.   Zulu family reaches the Zambesi as "Landeens", to whom the Portuguese pay tribute.   While some individual Portuguese are kind, their settlements are small penal settlements.   I am trying to secure free navigation of the Zambesi for all nations.

1011   26 Mar. 1860.   Your letter informing me of the formation of the OCDD mission arrived since I last wrote;   now I can see divine Providence led us into an area we never contemplated exploring.   It is cotton country, but slaving is rife.   Fever treatment as follows.   Mission will need its own steamer.   Rae goes home to supervise a new one for us.   Dislike of Portuguese.   Local role of R.C. church.   Anglican mission should be first and foremost in East Africa.   No response from C.M.S.   Customs of the people around Shirwa.   Plans must be kept from Portuguese.   Plans to go to Makololo country, returning via Mosilikatse and Manica.

1016   8 Apr. 1860.   Have no wish to exclude mission from the Makololo country, but thought you would prefer "more inviting field" up the Shire.   Makololo are better prepared than others, and Shire language as yet unreduced;   yet missionary pluck here will overcome these disadvantages.

1049   † 28 Nov. 1860.   Seeking a route inland around Portuguese, which plan delays the work of the missionaries.   Sadness over the fate of the Linyanti mission.   Am pleased you recommended steamer and Manganja country to the mission.   Keep this letter secret as the Portuguese pick up all scraps.   Happy to hear the institution for chief's sons goes well.

1196   15 Mar. 1862.   Describing the deaths of Bishop Mackenzie, Henry Burrup, and speculating at length on the future of the mission.

1204   18 Mar. 1862.   Death of Mackenzie.   Wilson and gig arrived on the evening of the 14th with the tragic news.   Blair was dispatched with supplies for the mission next day.   Details of events leading to Mackenzie's death.   L. not clear on Bishop's decision to fight.   Mission requires a steamer.

1238   20 Jun. 1862.   I give mail from the mission to J.M. Nuñes who takes it to Quilimane.   Am sorry mission fled down to Chibisa's.   All but certain that 4 Tette slaves handled muskets against us in fight with Ajawa last July.   More fever and dysentery than ever before.   Negligence of engineer delayed our progress.

1302   23 Dec. 1862.   Hope you returned with no regrets.   Procter came down to get provisions for the mission.   Waller purchased 10 guns.   Rowley's assertions.

1367   8 Jul. 1863.   Welcomed the new bishop a few days ago.   He seems very cautious and thoroughly practical.   He does not like Mbame's as the 200 miles distance from the Shire would increase costs.   Morambala often has a table cloth as does Table Mountain.   Mission had to pay 4 pence per pound as dues.   Glad you have returned to your diocese.

1428   27 Feb. 1864.   Tozer left.   Alington and Waller on board with the orphans.   Wrote Tozer a long letter begging him to reconsider.   Waller is here;   other members of the mission are with "Orestes" and "Pioneer", whom we expect daily.

1438   30 Mar. 1864.   Waller prepares way in Cape Town for orphans, who arrive later.   Tozer said they did not want to leave country, and wanted them to go back to Chibisa's.   He also feared Portuguese would object to their leaving the country.   Boys may have had repugnance to leaving the country with him.   Some went to Chibisa's, and the rest stayed on Morambala.

GREY, Charles (1804 — 1870).
Brevet-Colonel, RA 1846, General, 1865.   Private Secretary to Prince Albert, 1849—61, and to Victoria, 1861—70.   (DNB.)

0630   30 Nov. 1857.   I return the letter of the Prince Consort sent two days ago for the King of Portugal as I regret my visit to Lisbon is delayed.

GREY, Hon. Sir Frederick William (1805 — 1878).
Captain, R.N. 1828, Rear Admiral, 1855;   from 1857 to 1860 he was Commander-in-Chief of the Cape Naval Station;   Lord of the Admiralty, 1861—66.   (Boase, MEB.)

0830   21 Sep. 1858.   Progress of the expedition thus far;   the events which brought about Bedingfeld's resignation;   problems navigating the river;   took coal from the ground near Tette;   engine consumes a ton of hardwood daily.

0848   13 Oct. 1858.   Send mail to Mosambique to avoid placing R.N. men in peril on the bar off Quilimane.   Slaves exported from delta region as part of French scheme.   Leave today for Senna, and on to Tette.

0859   25 Dec. 1858.   Description of Kebrabasa and its implications for the expedition.   A steamer sent to the delta in January of 1860 can surmount the rapids, with hawsers if necessary.

0866   15 Feb. 1859.   Results of the recent trip up the Kebrabasa rapids by Baines and C. Livingstone indicate that navigation may be possible.   Recent trip up the Shire revealed a new country;   Kirk delighted with the botany.   Can salt meat be sent to Kongone next May 24?

0924   31 Jul. 1859.   Thank you for prompt assistance of Saumarez.   If one of your cruisers should call in mid-Nov., we would welcome salt provisions.   Baines and Thornton are to be sent home.

0955   28 Oct. 1859.   Reached Lake Nyassa but could not explore it.   Details of the lake and the Shire River.   Good area for cotton;   slaving carried on;   an English mission and trading station is required.   A common road could easily be made past the cataracts.

0978   10 Dec. 1859.   Plans to explore the Rovuma;   it must have cataracts, but it may be our way around the Portuguese.   Kirk would not invalidate Thornton though he wished it. Details of Baines' behaviour.   Plans to go to Sesheke with the Makololo.   Rae to go home.

1005   21 Mar. 1860.   Published in Wallis, ZEDL I, pp. 157—8.

GREY, Sir George (1812 – 1898).
Distinguished colonial administrator. Governor of South Australia 1841–6, of New Zealand 1846–54, of the Cape Colony 1855–9, and of New Zealand 1861–7. Prime Minister of New Zealand 1877–9. (DNB.)

0783.3 21 Apr. 1858. I forward 2 letters for your Excellency. "Pearl" leaves Table Bay tomorrow to coal in Simon's Bay. I shall call upon you before she departs.

0792.5 10 May 1858. On a group of African vocabularies sent Grey via Moffat: larger volume is Sichuana = Serotse = English; several dialects are tabulated for comparison near end. Angolese words are in calico covers; the words are termed Bunda or Ambunda — also there are Lunda and Tete words. Ask Mr. Moffat to go over the Analysis and add or expunge as necessary.

0835 28 Sep. 1858. Engineer and Thornton think well of the coal of Tette. Makololo companions pleased to see me, and everyone was amazed by the steamer. War goes on here. The river is at its lowest, and we have another obstacle to surmount at Kebrabasa. We shall examine it as soon as we get up: now we are transporting gear. Lignum vitae, ebony and teak abound. Vessel draws more than intended, and the engine is a "wretched piece of gingerbread". I formerly thought river could be navigated only 6 or 9 months, but now I see a vessel of 2 feet draft might run year round. People blamed me for hurrying through the mangrove of the delta, but they would have blamed me more had I lost nearly the whole expedition. We take quinine daily.

0854 18 Dec. 1858. We have seen Kebrabasa, and it is not at all like the Portuguese described it. The river is confined by mountains to a bed at one point 50 or 60 yards wide. At flood this groove fills and water flows over the adjacent bed. To do so, it must rise perpendicularly 80 to 100 feet. This vessel cannot steam the river, but one of good power could do so easily. We use the Government House in Tette. Next week we go up the Shire.

0873 19 Feb. 1859. Baines and C. Livingstone fully confirm what I advanced as to the effect of a flood on Kebrabasa. We went up the Shire, and found it navigable for 100 miles. Morambala is 4000 feet high; oranges, lemons and pineapples grow there. Elephants abound at one part of the valley. People very suspicious of us. They grow two good kinds of cotton. As Arabs from Zanzibar sail down the river to the cataracts, we did not leave our vessel to go overland. A 2½ knot current probably kept the Portuguese below Morambala, and not duckweed, as they previously reported. I think more highly of the country, to produce what England needs, now more than ever.

0904 1 Jun. 1859. Have lately discovered Lake Shirwa, separated only by 5 or 6 miles from Nyanja. Has no outlet, hence the waters are bitter but drinkable. One portion is only 30 miles from a point on the Ruo reached by the launch. Mountains all around the lake. The country is well peopled, and they grow and weave cotton. The only trade is in slaves. There are no Maravi at or near Shirwa; they are west of the river, so this cannot be Lake Maravi. Those who claim that two black men with Portuguese names crossed the continent must explain why they did not cross Lake Shirwa.

0920 30 Jul. 1859. We send letters and buaze seeds by "Persian", please help them to their destination. Buaze will do well in Natal. Kirk and I send home a report on African fever. We have also completed a report on the navigation of the Zambesi. We are about to try Nyinyesi from the Shire. Why don't the Cape merchants push their merchandise farther up the coast?

0936.8 15 Oct. 1859.　Above 33 miles of cataracts the Shire is navigable into Lake Nyassa. Could not explore the lake as we left Laird's punt in a sinking state.　Discovered a cotton field of unknown extent.　Shire valley consists of three terraces.　A benefit of this expedition will be the curing of fever.　Purchased malachite from slavers at the lake. Propose an English station south of the lake, which will cut off the slave route to the east. A road past the cataracts will enable us to put a boat on the lake.

0945.1 20 Oct. 1859.　Have to dismiss Thornton for want of knowledge of the world and of field geology — could not get him to work though he would read geology all day.　Baines goes also:　left him at Tette to avoid exposing him to fever downriver, but he associated with certain "ticket of leave men" and made away with expedition provisions and stole private property of other members.　Were we within jurisdiction of the courts, I would deliver Baines over for justice.

1008　25 Mar. 1860.　Please help exert pressure upon the Portuguese to open the Zambesi to free trade.　Rae goes home to supervise the building of a steamer.　Portuguese restrain us while profiting from slave trade.　English settlers in the highlands would develop cotton and end the slave trade.

1013　6 Apr. 1860.　Since my last letter I have learned of your return to Cape Town, and of the formation of a mission by the Universities.　Portuguese erect a customs house at Kongone.　Details on the sending of slaves from Mozambique to Bourbon.　Hopes mission will locate in highland lake region.

1017　[10 Apr. 1860].　Published in Wallis, **ZEDL**.

1100　4 Apr. 1861.　Visited the Rovuma in February, but forced back by falling water.　From the little that we saw, it may be the entrance into eastern Africa.　Description of the river and its peoples follow.　Half-caste Arabs appear to lord it over the local population. Natives encourage the hope that the river flows from the lake.　Suggests a mission site near Mt. Zomba.　Slaves in Kilwa sell for $22 per head.

1145　15 Nov. 1861.　Published in Foskett (ed.), **ZmDc**.

1329.1 Feb. 1863.　Are engaged in transporting a steamer past the cataracts, and hope to stop the 20,000 slaves sent to the coast annually.　Tette people followed in our tracks, attacked the people, and famine and death followed.　Slaving system goes on with connivance of the officials.　Success of cruizers, missions and trade on the west coast should be realized here.　Death of Mackenzie a great misfortune.　Six Scotch mechanics may join us soon.　Went 156 miles up Rovuma in Sep. and Oct. last:　country well-wooded and coal abounds, but so does tsetse.　Glad to hear from Maclear that you are succeeding in your labours.

GRIMSTONE, Edward.
An artist or lithographer of London.

0492　2 Apr. [1857].　The other lithographs are caricatures rather than portraits of the undersigned.

GUEDES CARVALHO E MENESES, Vasco (1822 — 1904).
Portuguese general, who served as Governor General of Mozambique from 1856 to 1858.
(**Gr Enc Port.** xii.850.)

0420   20 Jun. 1856.   After crossing continent had intended to visit Governor, but must wait at Quilimane for ship to the Cape.   Intends to return to the Makololo.   Please forward letters to merchants of Loanda, telling them that Sekeletu received their gifts.   Earlier letter may not have arrived.

GURNEY, Hudson (1775 — 1864).
A wealthy antiquary from Norfolk and a Member of Parliament, Gurney was (like Livingstone's close friends, the Braithwaites) a member of the Society of Friends.
(DNB.)

0633.8 6 Dec. 1857.   Thanks for gift of £50.   Will try to make Zambesi an open highway to the healthy interior, where he will distribute cotton seeds.   If successful this will diminish value of slave labour in America.

0972.6 16 Nov. 1859.   Lake Nyassa.   Cotton.   Chance to interrupt slave trade.   Asking Government for steamer.   His brother will take charge of trading post.   Cheated by Macgregor Laird;   £2000 will secure a good vessel from Tod and Macgregor.

GUTHRIE, Thomas (1803 — 1873).
Minister of the Church of Scotland and the Free Church of Scotland;   famous as the advocate of ragged schools and temperance.   His interest in Kirk (see below) stems from the fact that he and Kirk's father were successive ministers of Arbirlot and both joined the Free Church in 1843.   **(DNB.)**

1767   13 Jul. 1865.   Charles Livingstone and Meller have received consulships, but the more deserving Kirk has received from Russell, after prompting via Lord Dalhousie, a minor appointment.   A written promise is necessary, as Russell broke a spoken one about his own salary.   Will Guthrie urge Lord Dalhousie to write again.

HAIDINGER, Wilhelm Karl Ritter von (1795 — 1871).
A geologist, he was President of the Vienna Geographical Society.   **(NDB.)**

0874   [21 Feb. 1859].   We are presently exploring the lower part of the river, which, due to the number of its arms reaching the sea, is not so well known.   The Shire below the falls abounds in elephant, hippopotami, and people who are cultivators.   We were held in great suspicion.   The ladies wear ivory or tin lip-rings (drawing included).   The Shire is navigable for 100 miles, and many crops (listed) will thrive here.

HALDANE, Mrs.

0539   17 Jun. 1857.   As I must be in Oxford on the 24th, will you kindly change the date of your invitation from the 24th to the 25th?

HAMILTON, James (1814 — 1867).
Minister of Regent Square Presbyterian Church, London 1841—67;   editor of **Evangelical**

Christendom 1864–7.   Livingstone attended his church and stayed at his house in 1865, and contributed a paper to his periodical (Papers and Reports no. 27).   He died on 24 Nov. 1867, but Livingstone did not learn of this until Nov. 1871.   **(DNB.)**

1697   4 May 1865.   Forward note to Brodie.   Robert Arthington of Leeds wishes to support agent in Loanda to introduce bible.   Advised him to be cautious and apply to Silva through Brodie.

1784   30 Jul. 1865.   Thanks for parcel.   Webb made better by travel talk.   Will go to Sedgwick on Wednesday, pack up and see Hamilton's friends on Friday, and return on Saturday. Hopes Mr. Binney can come.

1843   28 Nov. 1865.   Paper delivered at Malta.   Leaving for Zanzibar in a few days on Sultan's ship.   He has given a firman and transported buffaloes.   Governor an excellent man. Has seen Irish Presbyterian brethern.

1945   8 Apr. 1870.   Ivory traders among the Manyuema.   The country.   Boiled water prevents dysentery.   A variety of potato.   Example of commencing a mission in Central Africa needed because of Tozer's dawdling in Zanzibar.   Exploration the first step.   Nile sources are on the watershed, as placed by Ptolemy.   Speke, unlike himself, pursued a preconceived conclusion.   Once he discovers where the Lualuba joins the other arm of drainage, he will retire.   Cannot bear to give up.   Dutch lady explorer.   Manyuema not certainly cannibals.   Their food and customs.

HAMMOND, Edmund (1802 – 1890).
Hammond served in the Foreign Office from 1824–1873;   after serving as Chief of the Oriental Department, he became Permanent Undersecretary of Foreign Affairs (1854–1872).   Created Baron Hammond in 1873.   **(DNB.)**

0694   9 Feb. 1858.   Accepting Portugal's claim restricting free trade on the **Zambesi** implies their power over independent tribes beyond their control.   Please revise my commission to include Sekeletu and tribes beyond Portuguese control.

0699   11 Feb. 1858.   Portuguese position on the **Zambesi** resembles ours in China, except that they can hardly hold the forts they possess.   They possess neither bank, only isolated spots here and there, and nothing beyond 30° West.   Long. (sic).

0717   16 Feb. 1858.   I have received a copy of the Portuguese decree changing the name of the region to Zambesia, and note their estimate of their control coincides with mine.   I am thankful for the portaria which indicates their liberality, but as there is neither fort nor custom house I anticipated no duties.

0718   16 Feb. 1858.   May regulations requiring life certificates be received prior to salaries being paid be relaxed in the case of the Zambesi Expedition, as the opportunity to send the certificates to London may not occur until after salaries are due?

0729   20 Feb. 1858.   Requesting a final meeting with Clarendon.

0743   2 Mar. 1858.   Acknowledging the receipt of 10 letters from Clarendon to African chiefs, plus the instructions for the Zambesi Expedition.

0750   6 Mar. 1858. Acknowledging the receipt of his commission as H.M. Consul to Quillimane, exequator of the King of Portugal, and documents relating to marriages and deaths in his district. Weather only prevents our sailing.

0772   25 Mar. 1858. Enclosed are dispatches 4 and 5 for HMSSFO. Weather favourable thus far.

HANBURY, C.S.
A brewer of Spitalfield, London?

0716   [19 Jan.–15 Feb. 1858]. I have no doubt we shall find the ale superb wherever opened. We find it difficult to get a proper ship – a steam launch is building and will draw 18 inches. We are not yet certain which vessel will carry us out; perhaps one for the Ceylon Government.

HANNAN, James.
Associated with Henry Monteith & Co, turkey red dyers, Glasgow and Bailie of that city. He was one of Livingstone's three trustees.

1077   15 Feb. 1861. Re the enclosure to Mr. King: North American Africans should not come to this part of Africa. Even Kroomen catch fever here. The Bishop's party a fine set of fellows, and he is the "A–1" of the party.

HARDESTY, Charles.
Engineer of the "Pioneer" from its departure from England in September 1860 until he was dismissed by Livingstone for neglecting his charge, in July 1862. Part of this period he spent with the UMCA mission, at Magomero. As he was recommended for the "Pioneer" by John Penn & Sons, he was probably in their employ in 1860.

1214   10 Apr. 1862. Considering all of the hardship caused to this expedition, as well as to the officers and men of H.M.S. "Gorgon" as a result of your neglecting the engines last February, I must relieve you of this responsibility. Sand was allowed to remain in the condenser until the cyclinder was worn; the packing of the trunnions was not renewed for 20 months; and valves were burned by working the engine at high pressure.

HARE, Alexander.
Proprietor of a boys' school in London.

0480   23 Mar. 1857. Please keep Robert Livingstone at his literary lessons as he complains of headache when long detained at arithmetic. Give his mind plenty work.

0526   23 May 1857. I leave for the country on Tuesday next. Thank you for your kindness while Robert was under your tuition.

HAY, Charles Murray (1802 – 1864).
Commissioned in the Coldstream Guards in 1821, Hay became Lieut.-Colonel 1832,

Colonel 1846, and Major-General 1854.   As commander of the garrison in Mauritius 1855—7, he was host to Livingstone during the latter's only visit to that island.   He later became Colonel of the 91st Foot with the rank of Lieut.-General.   (Boase, **MEB.**)

1046   26 Nov. 1860.   Grateful for recuperation at his house.   Journey to Victoria Falls.   Glad at formation of Oxford and Cambridge Mission, which might be accompanied by a small colony.   Sekeletu's health.   Regrets deaths of L.M.S. party;   will now publish his cure.

1307.2 †[15 Mar.—31Dec. 1862].   *Deaths of Mackenzie and Burrup.

HAYWARD, Robert Newton (? — 1861).
A naval surgeon from 1836, he served on HMS Malabar in the Mediterranean 1841—4 and on HMS Locust in the same area 1844—6.   Livingstone presumably met him while studying medicine in London, as he became a Fellow of the Royal College of Surgeons in 1842.   (**Navy List; Medical Register.**)

0042   10 Dec. 1841.   *On his first journey to the interior, the character of the Bechuanas, etc.

0082   17 Jul. 1843.   Arrival in Bechuanaland and settlement at Kuruman.   Has learnt language and made three long journeys, on which he has penetrated farther than any other European and has almost reached a great freshwater lake.   Mosilikatze's cattle-raids. African customs at Kuruman and concerning iron-smelting.   Comments on the Boers.

0124   28 May 1845.   Effect of lion wound.   Reason for being near lion.   Natives suspect the motives of missionaries and are unwilling to change their ways.   Bamangwato have killed 23 Mosilikatze's people and revenge is expected.   Asks for news of friends.

HILL, Sir Stephen John (1809 — 1891).
Captain, RA 1842, Governor and Commander-in-Chief, Gold Coast 1851— 4;   Governor, Sierra Leone 1854—9, 1860—2;   Governor-in-Chief, Leeward and Caribee Is. 1863—9. He also saw service in Newfoundland from 1869 until his retirement in 1876.   (**DNB.**)

0925   1 Aug. 1859.   *On the failure of the "Ma-Robert" and the exploration of the Shire valley which resulted in the visit to Lake Shirwa.   An expedition toward Lake Nyassa is being planned.

HOOKER, Sir Joseph Dalton (1817 — 1911).
M.D. (Glasgow, 1839) and botanist, Hooker was assistant to his father (see below) at the Royal Botanical Gardens, Kew 1855—65, and Director there 1865—85.   (**DNB.**)

0556   11 Jul. 1857.   L. describes the names of many African plants, and requests Hooker provide their names.   They include the water-bearing melon of the Kalahari, two types of manioc, a palm, fruits, etc.

0560   28 Jul. 1857.   Requests identification of a plant which floats on the Zambesi and is called Alfacinya (lettuce) by the Portuguese;   of another plant which floats on the river;   and thanks Hooker for his and Mr. Westwood's notes.

0608   26 Oct. 1857.   Concerning the probability of an expedition to ascend the Zambezi. If it comes to pass, L. requests Hooker's aid in selecting the necessary personnel.   He doesn't want a German.

0641   16 Dec. 1857.   L. plans to dine with Clarendon tomorrow, thus he cannot meet Hooker and Nichol.   Ask if he would go for a year or so — L. writes to Edinburgh to learn of his antecedents.

0652   28 Dec. 1857.   Dr. Nichol has offered himself for naval service and will be guided by Sir John Liddel.   It is out of the question my expedition going begging to him   (Liddel). I have recommendations from Christison, Balfour, and Geo. Wilson for a Dr. John Kirk. From what is said of him I mean to see him.   I did not know Nichol's attitude until Sat.; up to that time I was bent on having him.

1154   9 Dec. 1861.   Telling of the trip he made 235 miles up the western shore of Lake Nyasa in Sept.–Oct.   Five boxes addressed to Kew were last seen in Mosambique, some of which had "Dr. Kirk" on the corner.   Robert ran away from his tutor but is now at St. Andrew's.

1466   9 Aug. 1864.   I sent crania of 2 hippopotami to James Young via your care: will you forward them soon?   I intend to visit you and your father soon.

1506   12 Oct. 1864.   Kirk is satisfied with Prof. Oliver's attainments and suitability for the work proposed.   He would do it for expedition pay.   Can you advise me on how to put the matter to Russell?

1512   19 Oct. 1864.   I wrote Kirk in Edinburgh re the arrangement, but learn he has gone to Kew.   Ask if he approves, so that I may submit the plan to H.M. Govt.

HOOKER, Sir William Jackson (1785 – 1865).
Professor of Botany at the University of Glasgow, 1820–41, Hooker directed the Royal Botanical Gardens at Kew, 1841–65.   The preceding was his son.   (DNB.)

0466   5 Feb. 1857.   I finally have my seeds and will prepare them soon.   By what means should I convey them?   Also fibrous tissues, leaves, unripe pods, and roots I would like you to examine.

0467   8 Feb. [1857].   *I shall have seeds ready for your servant.   Also the bark of a tree and a specimen of a plant, and Angolese coffee seeds.

0519   16 May 1857.   Ill due to overwork.   Attended L.M.S. anniversary on Thurs. and hurt my throat trying to speechify, hence I may come next Fri. or Sat.;   do not wish to meet Lady Hooker in this state.

1389   10 Aug. 1863.   Our letter of withdrawal remarked that only scanty information was received on the natural resources of the region.   I replied positively and mentioned how well Kirk did.   Testimony on behalf of Kirk follows.   With flood L. goes downriver and on to India.

1498   1 Oct. 1864.   I must apply for government assistance to enable Kirk to work on his plants.   What should I ask and how should I put it?

HOPE, William.
A businessman of Liverpool?

0669   21 Jan. 1858.   We do not leave Saturday next but hope to do so soon thereafter.   Thanks to all who contributed to the money testimonial: please place it in my account with Coutts & Co.   While we may meet with difficulties now beyond our comprehension, of the ultimate success of the endeavour I have no doubt.

HOSKINS, Sir Anthony Hiley (1828 — 1901).
Lieutenant, R.N. (1849).   Served on HMS "Castor" in East Africa and exploring the Zambezi delta, in conjunction with Captain Hyde Parker and HMS "Pantaloon", in the early 1850 s;   then with HMS "Philomel" in West Africa, where he met Livingstone at São Paulo de Luanda in 1854.   Captain, R.N. 1863;   Admiral, 1891;   retired 1893.   Served in later years as Commander-in-Chief in the Mediterranean, and as senior naval Lord of the Admiralty.   **(Navy List.)**

0449   5 Jan. 1857.   Discusses mutual naval acquaintances.   Thought of him while crossing continent as he read his gift of "Kosmos."   Requests he put on paper an outline of the depth of water at the mouth of the Zambezi.

HOULTON, Joseph.
Surgeon in London.

0016   28 Nov. 1840.   Declines invitation because of difficulties due to embarkation.   Ship expected from Dartmouth that night and will sail on Monday.

HOWARD, Sir Henry Francis (1809 — 1898).
A career diplomat, Howard was British Envoy in Lisbon, 1855—59.   For a number of incidental reasons, his efforts to arrange for Livingstone to visit Lisbon in 1857—8 failed.
                                            (Boase, MEB.)

0642   16 Dec. 1857.   *Referring to a meeting with Palmerston, Livingstone suggests that his trip to Lisbon may be cancelled, and that Clarendon will attempt to arrange matters with the Portuguese Government.

JAGO, Charles T. (? — 1891).
Commander of H.M. Sloop "Rapid" of the Cape Naval Station, 1862—65;   Captain, R.N. 1866;   Vice-Admiral 1889.   **(Navy List.)**

1363   4 Jul. 1863.   Informed by Gardner that you expect to meet expedition in August at Kongone, but we cannot get the "Pioneer" there by then.   Please convey Kirk, C. Livingstone and their party to the Cape.   Expenses incurred.

JOHNSTON, Thomas Brumby (? — 1897).
Partner in W. and A.K. Johnston, the Edinburgh printing firm, best known for its geographical work.

0596   3 Oct. 1857.   My address for the next 5 days will be (in Kendal).   The portraits may have gone to Glasgow but ought to have been here before now.   Give my address to Oliver & Boyd's.

0604   21 Oct. 1857.   The photographs were safe at Kendal, but I was not able to acknowledge them until now.   Mrs. L.'s is very good, and the only one of her that I have.   I left a small heart-shaped hairbrush at either Sir William's or Mr. Bullens (Cullen's?), which belonged to my uncle in the French War.

KEPPEL, Sir Henry (1809 — 1904).
Captain, R.N. 1837, Keppel saw extended service in Asian waters before becoming Commander-in-Chief of the Cape Naval Station in July, 1860.   Due to differences with Governor Grey, Keppel left this post in April, 1861.   In 1877 he was named Admiral of the Fleet.   **(DNB.)**

1090   †7 Mar. 1861.   Pleased to learn that you are well disposed toward this expedition. Description of Rovuma Bay.   Waited 10 days for coals, and the river is falling.   Hope to establish overland carriage from Rovuma to Lake Nyassa.   To get mission away from the Portuguese and to avoid the unhealthy months in the river we postponed the landing of mission in Africa.

1110   20 Apr. 1861.   Requesting provisions, and passage from the Cape to the Zambesi for Mary L.   Plans to take the new mission up the Shire River.   Requests also passage from Johanna to the Cape for D.J. May, and promotion for Able Seaman John Hutchins.

1114   1 May 1861.   Tells of his plans to continue up the Shire to explore Lake Nyasa, and requests 35 T of coal be shipped for his use by 15 December.

1125   21 May 1861.   Sends two packets of letters and a dispatch for Russell.   Sails today for the mouth of the Shire: expects to reach Murchison's Cataracts in three days.   Have had fever but now all are well.

KERR, Robert.
An official of the Blantyre Works Literary and Scientific Institute.

0445   19 Dec. 1856.   Declines an invitation to a soirée in his honour.

0447   27 Dec. 1856.   Changes his mind about the soirée because of the women in his family.

KINNAIRD, 9th Lord (1807 — 1878).
George William Fox Kinnaird, succeeded to the title 1826.   Agricultural reformer and philanthropist, concerned with the conditions of labourers.   **(DNB.)**

0877   2 Mar. 1859.   Resignation of our naval officer;   have escaped from fever.   My brother caught fever when trying photography while at Kebrabasa and overexposed himself. Africa is the country for both cotton and sugar.   Kirk saw indigo growing wild in the streets of Tette.

1149   25 Nov. 1861.   We collected 300 lbs. of excellent clean cotton from a six mile stretch of the river, out of season.   We must lead the way, establish markets, and gain confidence of the natives.   This region can produce a great deal of cotton, and thus I support the idea of a colony.   The Free Church sends out a Stewart to form a mission.   Details of the Bishop's fighting, and of Livingstone's recent exploration of Lake Nyasa.   Expect the Government will pay for the steamer after it is on the Lake.

1215   25 Apr. 1862.   Death of Mackenzie and unhealthiness of Magomero.   8 May.   Death of Mary Livingstone.   Details concerning the new steamer, and the neglect of the "Pioneer"'s engines, which caused party to delay in the delta region.

1955   Nov. 1870.   The watershed.   The Chambeze-Luapula-Lualaba.   Difficulties with men. When new men arrive, a few months will suffice to finish.   The fountains and lakes. Show this to Duke of Argyll, as he has no more paper to write him.   Speke's error.

1990   17 Jan. 1872.   Obtained paper at Ujiji.   No one realised the extent of his task.   Watershed 700 miles long with innumerable springs;   all covered on foot.   Kirk's failure.   When Stanley's supplies arrive, will go west to the fountains.   13 Mar.   Supplies received.   Will start when Stanley's men come.

KING, William (1812 – 1895).
A minister of Buxton, Ontario, who directed a settlement for escaped slaves at the northern end of the "underground railroad".

1078   15 Feb. 1861.   I do not encourage your idea of sending coloured people from Canada to Africa to cultivate cotton and sugar, as they would feel superior to local Africans and would be as susceptible to fever as Europeans.

KIRK, Christian (1803 – 1865).
Wife of John, minister of Arbirlot, and mother of Sir John.   (Scott, **FES** V, p. 422.)

1409   17 Dec. 1863.   Published in Foskett, **ZmDc.**

KIRK, **Sir** John (1832 – 1922).
Born in Barry and educated in medicine at the University of Edinburgh, Kirk in 1858 was named Medical Officer and Economic Botanist to Livingstone's Zambezi Expedition.   His service in this capacity was exemplary, and in 1865 he was appointed Surgeon to the British Consulate in Zanzibar.   Here he subsequently occupied a number of posts, and as H.M. Consul his skilful diplomacy increased British influence with successive Sultans, resulting in the demise of the East African slave trade, and the entrance of **Z**anzibar and Tanganyika securely into the British sphere of influence.   (**DNB.**)

Letters to him of 4 Jan. 1858 (0655), 14 Jan. 1858 (0662), 21 Jan. 1858 (0668), 22 Jan. 1858 (0672), 26 Jan. 1858 (0673), 28 Jan. 1858 (0679), 17 Feb. 1858 (0722), 22 Feb. 1858 (0731), 28 Feb. 1858 (0738), 18 Mar. 1858 (0765), 15 Apr. 1858 (0788), 21 Jul. 1858 (0811), 25 Aug. 1858 (0819), 17 Oct. 1859 (0944), 29 Oct. 1859 (0958), 3 Nov. 1859 (0963), 6 Nov. 1859 (0968), [28 Apr. 1863] (1343), 2 Jun. 1863 (1354), 5 Jul.

1863 (1365), 8 Aug. 1863 (1387), 9 Dec. 1863 (1402), 28 Jul. 1864 (1451), 1 Sep. 1864 (1478), 17 Oct. 1864 (1511), 21 Oct. 1864 (1513), 7 Nov. 1864 (1527), 24 Nov. 1864 (1541), 25 Nov. 1864 (1543), 27 Nov. 1864 (1544), 30 Nov. 1864 [sic] (1547), 1 Dec. 1864 (1550), 8 Dec. 1864 (1553), 12 Dec. 1864 (1556), 19 Dec. 1864 (1560), 11 Feb. 1865 (1605), 13 Feb. 1865 (1607), 14 Feb. 1865 (1609), 24 Feb. 1865 (1618), 28 Feb. 1865 (1623), 5 Mar. 186[5] (1632), 21 Mar. 1865 (1644), 24 Mar. 1865 (1650), 27 and 28 Mar. 1865 (1655), 28 Mar. 1865 (1656), 3 Apr. 1865 [sic] (1663), 5 Apr. 1865 (1668), 14 Apr. 1865 (1676), 13 May 1865 (1711), 8 Jun. 1865 (1740), 24 Jun. 1865 (1755), 30 Jul. 1865 (1783), 20 Sep. 1865 (1820), 15 Nov. 1865 (1837), 2 Dec. 1865 (1846), 13 Dec. 1865 (1853), 1 and 7 Jan. 1866 (1865), 12 Sep. 1867 (1919), 30 May 1869 (1938), Nov. 1870 [sic] (1956), 25 Mar. 1871 (1968), 14 May 1871 (1970), 26 Jun. 1871 (1971), and 20 (28?) Feb. 1872 (1998) are published in Foskett, **ZmDc**.

1179   17 Feb. 1862. Progress slow; have Vienna or Bandeira cut wood if you can arrange it. We may not reach Ruo before the officers must leave; if Wilson wishes you to go beyond Ruo and up to the Bishop's, do so. Rae must remain to help us unload.

1531   [14 Nov. 1864?]. The Webbs will be at 51 Upper Brook St. We expect to be in town by three, where I post this.

1562   [24–25 Dec. 1864]. A carriage was sent to the station 2 or 3 times, but Waller did not turn up. Guide enclosed. Thanks for Zoological paper. Follow instructions and a carriage will await you.

1706   11 May 1865. Concerning a drawing of a plant for **NEZT**. See you tonight at Sir George Lambert's. Had decided not to address L.M.S. today but Burton's nasty statements about missionaries stirred me to give testimony.

1864   [1 Jan. 1866?]. [Beginning missing.] If Waller should get an appointment on the West Coast he would always oppose slavery, etc. He wished me to write this to him, but it would sound better from you.

1918   †[28 Jul. 1866 – 23 Feb. 1867]. [Beginning missing.] Bad behaviour of sepoys. Will give them only enough cloth for rations to the coast.

1921   Oct. 1867. I expect to write from Ujiji in a month or two; the party that takes this is heading west. Syed bin Ali has been very kind. I have been with this party upwards of four months. Without medicine box, my health is bad when not travelling. (Livingstone goes on to describe the man who ran off with his medicine chest, whom he expects Kirk to meet.)

1928   8 Jul. 1868. *Has found what he believes to be the sources of the Nile between 10 and 12° S. Lat.; not one from a lake but upwards of 20 of them.

1961   5 Feb. 1871. Kirk's men arrived yesterday. Livingstone tells of the sickness he suffered in Bambarre, his stores at Ujiji, and the sources of the Nile, along with further information on his most recent travels and his financial state.

1965   †[11 Feb. 1871]. P.S. 2nd. Nine scoundrels said they were instructed to take him back to the coast, but really wanted more pay. Leaves tomorrow. Arab released from Cazembe received deserters. Mohamed Bugarib a good Moslem. Ostentatious prayers à la Bedingfeld. Send on thanks to Captain Richards. Goes down Lualaba in canoes to junction, then south to the watershed, back same way to Ujiji and Zanzibar. No doubt about size of watershed and vast bulk of water flowing north.

1967   13 Feb. 1871.   Difficulties with Banian slaves;   comparison with Baines.   Obstruction by Shereef.   Illnesses in successive rainy seasons.   Kindness of Bogharib.   Lack of medicine and goods.   Kirk alone could have withstood such hardships, but his work is more important.

1973   30 Oct. 1871.   Shereef's misdeeds.   Use of slaves a great mistake.   16 Nov.   £500 of Government goods also delayed by slaves.

1976   1 Nov. 1871.   On the difficulties Livingstone had with his men, some of whom he lists as being slaves to others also on his list.   Further details about Shereef.   Livingstone needed a pistol to keep his men moving.   His lack of supplies.   Contains an incomplete receipt for an unnamed captain of an unnamed ship for the loan of a pocket chronometer.

1980   17 Nov. 1871.   Overcharges in Ludha's bill.

2000   [Feb. 1872?]   *On the treatment of African fever.

2011   Jun. 1872.   *Livingstone never intended to attack Kirk personally.

KITCHINGMAN, James (1791 — 1848).
Missionary in South Africa 1816—48.   (LMS Reg. no. 167.)

0033   [4 Aug. 1841?].   Finally arrived, aided by people provided by him who were excellent in many ways.   Waggons.   Rested pleasantly in Griquatown.

LABOUCHERE, Henry (1790 — 1869).
MP for Michael Borough (1826—30) and Taunton (1830—59), Labouchere filled several political appointments, including Secretary of State for the Colonies (1855—9).
                                   (DNB.)

0493   2 Apr. 1857.   On the Sand River Convention: we hold to it rigidly while the Boers ignore the article against slavery.   Please lay these facts before the Cape Governor. Pretorius attacked Sechele and took 200 children into slavery.   Cathcart refused my offer to identify the children, whom I knew personally.   They are for domestic slavery: field hands are procured from Cashan and the Magaliesburg.   People all believe the English have given the country and its people to the Boers.   Although I lost £300 in my house at Kolobeng, about which they bragged to the Portuguese, I present no complaint on that score.   By adhering to this treaty we aid a policy which the Government makes great sacrifices to put down elsewhere.

0674   26 Jan. 1858.   *Livingstone's opinion on some reports of the Governor of Natal which Labouchere sent for his consideration.   Further attacks upon slavery and the Government, which in his view supports it.

0734   [27 Jan.—22 Feb. 1858].   *Making a point he neglected in his previous letter, concerning slavery in southern Africa.

LAIRD, John (1805 — 1874).
A shipbuilder, one of the first to turn his attention to building vessels from iron.   After retiring from business (1861), he represented Birkenhead in the Commons, 1861—74.
                                   (DNB.)

0799   21 Jun. 1858.   The launch was easy to assemble and has done admirable service ever since.   The Gov't should send out more of these to pursue slavers up creeks, but they should be broader and shorter.   Four feet wider plus more power would make her perfect.   Our bolts show symptoms of decay, and the plates should be made $^1/_8$ of an inch thick so they do not bend underfoot.

LAVRADIO, 2º Conde do (Francisco de Almeida Portugal) (1797 – 1870).
Career diplomat and constitutionalist, Lavradio had several European postings before serving as Portuguese Minister to Great Britain from 1851 to 1869.
(GrEncPort XIV, pp. 763–4.)

0503   17 Apr. 1857.   Published in Wallis, ZEDL I, pp. xxiv–xxv.

LAYARD, Sir Austin Henry (1817 – 1894).
Excavator of Nineveh and other Assyrian sites (1845–51), Layard was Under-secretary for Foreign Affairs, Feb.–May 1853, and Jul. 1861–Jul. 1866.   MP for Aylesbury 1852–7 and Southwark after 1860, Layard also served as British Minister in Madrid 1869–77 and in Constantinople 1877–80.   (DNB.)

1233   2 Jun 1862.   Describing the ill behaviour of the crewmen of H.M.S. "Gorgon", to insure that H.M. Government learns of the malfeasance from Livingstone rather than from the Portuguese.

1258   5 Aug. 1862.   Concerning the map of Sá da Bandeira, and its inaccuracies, plagiarisms, and the early Portuguese explorers of Africa.

1259   5 Aug. 1862.   Reply to yours of 17 Sep. 1861, requesting my opinion of Sá da Bandeira's map, enclosed.   No Portuguese map was published prior to that by Bowditch, our countryman, who worked in the Portuguese archives.   Bandeira's "New Portuguese map" is based upon Bowditch's errors and my tracings.

1518   25 Oct. 1864.   Requests order to Royal Geographical Society to deliver Baines's drawings to him, as promised by Admiral Washington.

1523   2 Nov. 1864.   Wishes drawings only on loan for use in his book.

1612   †17 Feb. 1865.   *On his salary.

1699   5 May 1865.   Baines's drawings have been returned to the Royal Geographcial Society.

1701   8 May 1865.   Requests recommendation to Admiralty or Board of Trade for loan of 3 barometers, 3 chronometers, and 4 thermometers for his next expedition.

1823   28 Sep. 1865.   Preparing to start in November.   Some Africans and Indians selected. Taking buffaloes to see if they withstand tsetse.   Governor helpful.   Will make arrangements with Sultan when he comes.   Has met John Wilson.

LAYARD, Edgar Leopold (1824 – 1900).
A brother of Sir A.H. Layard and a distinguished ornithologist, he was appointed by Sir

George Grey director of the South African Museum, Cape Town, a post he held from 1855 to 1872.   (**DSAfrB** I, p. 467.)

1014   7 Apr. 1860.   In reply to your enquiry about snails, I must confess there is great scarcity of them here.   Dr. Kirk has made a botanical collection and Mr. C. Livingstone one of birds, but this had been hampered by the damp in our steamer.   If the steamer reaches Tette we leave her there, as she is completely done.

LIVINGSTON(E), Neil (1788 — 10 Feb. 1856).
Tea-vendor in Blantyre and father of David.   On his spelling of the family name see Appendix 2.   Livingstone did not learn of his death till Nov. 1856.

Livingstone addressed letters to him alone on [6 Aug. 1843?] (0086) and 17 Jan. 1846 (0144);   to him and his wife on 19 May 1841 (0027), 13 Jul. 1842 (0058), [1 Sep. 1842?] (0063), 26 Sep. 1842 (0065), 21 Mar. 1843 (0067), 16 Dec. 1843 (0097), 27 Apr. 1844 (0099), 1 Oct. 1845 (0136), 15 Mar. 1847 (0161), 5 Jul. 1848 (0186), 25 Sep. 1849 (0211), and 26 Sep. 1852 (0289);   to him, his wife, and their two daughters on 29 Sep. 1841 (0036), 28 Jul. 1850 (0228), 4 Dec. 1850 (0240), 9 Feb. 1851 (0245), Oct. and 14 Nov. 1851 (0259), 30 Sep. 1853 (0324), 14 Feb. 1855 (0367), 18 Mar. and 28 Aug. 1856 (0404), and 1 Jun. 1856 (0419).   All except the following are published in Schapera, **DLFL**.

0063   [1 Sep. 1842?]   Leaves for interior next week.   Journey will be dangerous because of war.   Mahura's attack on Sebegwe.   Atrocities.   Must tell Sebegwe that Christians had no part in it.

0367   14 Feb. 1855.   Contrast between fertility of country and idolatry of population.   Need for admission of bibles.   Letters lost in wreck of 'Forerunner'.

LIVINGSTON(E), Agnes (1), née Hunter (1782 — 18 Jun. 1865).
Wife of Neil and mother of David.

For letters addressed jointly to her see under Livingston(e), Neil.   Those addressed to her alone of [21 Mar. 1843?] (0068), 14 May 1845 (0122), 4 May 1847 (0166), 19 Dec. 1852 (0307), and 11 Dec. 1856 (0439) are published in Schapera, **DLFL**.

0006   [1838–9.]   In view of her declining health and strength, exhorts her despite the trials of poverty to take heed of her soul.
0844   6 Oct. 1858.   Hasty letter sent by man-of-war.   Repairs to MaRobert.   Charles at Tette, recovered from slight illness.   Oswell at Kuruman.

0959   31 Oct. 1859.   No replies received to previous letters.   Those who accuse him of seeking glory from discovery know nothing.   Seeks to do good to men and glorify God.   Charles suffering a little from fever, but he has escaped: cure now found.   Large region opened which Church Missionary Society may occupy.   Hopes for cutting into slave trade.   Love to Tom.

1151   29 Nov. 1861.   Universities' Mission, despite its Puseyite nature, better than heathenism.   Near Lake Nyassa there is no trade except in slaves.   Northern shores littered with corpses.   Free Church proposal should not be discouraged by fate of London Mission to Makololo, who could have been saved if they had written to him. Slaves freed and given to Bishop Mackenzie. Lack of letters received. Expects to meet Mary soon.

1221   29 Apr. 1862. Death of Mary. Reasons for delay in the lowlands. Details of her illness and burial. Regrets that slander induced him to allow her to come before he was in the highlands.

1263   30 Aug. 1862. Published in Wallis, ZEDL II, pp. 215–216 (the PS of 21 Oct. is no. 1282).

LIVINGSTON(E), John (1) (1811 – 1899).
David's brother. He emigrated to Canada, where after some years he settled as a farmer at Listowel, Ontario. He married Sarah Mackenzie of Glasgow, and they had a large family.

0316   20 Sep. 1853. Travels from Kuruman; new route to avoid tsetse; moved fast to avoid Boers. Newly returned from Barotse country. Portuguese merchant wished to take him westward, but he could not endure the sight of chain-gangs and went north.

0726   18 Feb. 1858. James Young willing to appoint him agent for paraffin in Canada, which will bring him sufficient income.

1750   20 Jun 1865. Mother's death.

1941   [Sep. 1869?] Has received absurd instructions from Royal Geographical Society, who having voted $1/5$ or $1/6$ of expenses wish all his survey notes. Amused at Government offer of small salary should he settle somewhere.

1979   16 Nov. 1871. From his letter he learned of the transatlantic cable. Details of his recent travels.

2022   Dec. 1872. Complaints against Kirk. Geographcial comments. Regrets that his son abandoned the relief expedition; both his sons had been improvident with money. Seeking source of the Nile is merely a means to the end of stopping the slave trade.

LIVINGSTON(E), Janet (1818 – 1895).
David's sister. She provided the information on his early life given by Blaikie, **PLDL**; the notes she sent him are NLS, MS10767.

For letters addressed to her jointly with her parents see under Livingston(e), Neil. Those addressed to her of 21 Aug. 1843 (0087), 21 May 1844 (0101), 7 Nov. 1847 and 3 Jan. 1848 (0178), 31 Jan. 1849 (0197), and 20 Apr. 1849 (0202), and those addressed to her and her sister of 30 Mar. 1841 (0024), 8 Dec. 1841 (0040), and 28 Apr. 1851 (0250) are published in Schapera, **DLFL**.

0003   3 Oct. 1838. Encloses poem by John Barff 'The Christian's Hope' as token of affection and expectation of meeting after death.

0004   5 May 1839. Writes while watching at night over a sick fellow-student. Has just been told that he is to sail for South Africa in the coming summer, despite his desire for more education. Diligence necessary for holiness. She should persevere in her efforts to do good.

1163 1 Jan. 1862. Her letter received. High Church missionaries have come to a good school to cure their pretensions. Death of Helmores grievous. Cotton planted among Makololo thrives. Efforts to avoid Portuguese customs lead to attempt to reach Lake Nyassa by the Rovuma. Europeans will be able to live by the Lake, whose huge population is afflicted by slave trade. Regrets that she did not tell him of her financial difficulties.

1225 5 May 1862. Death of Mary. Absence of Anna Mary and Robert's unsettled state troubled her. Helpful spiritual advice by James Stewart. Look after children. When provisions arrive will proceed to Lake Nyassa.

2025 [Dec. 1872–Jan. 1873]. *On the reasons for his son Oswell's return to England.

LIVINGSTON(E), Charles (1821 – 1873).
Brother of David. Educated at Oberlin College, Ohio 1840–7, and Union Theological Seminary, New York 1847–9. Pastor in New York, Vermont, and Massachussetts 1849–57. David's assistant on the Zambezi expedition. Consul in the Bights of Benin and Biafra, West Africa 1864–73. Collaborated in the writing of **MT** and **NEZT**. (**DNB**.)

Letters to him of 16 Mar. 1847 (0162), 16 May 1849 (0204), 6 Feb., 18 Mar., and 7 Jun. 1853 (0311), and 8 Nov. 1854 (0347) are published in Schapera, **DLFL**; one of 10 May 1858 (0793) in Wallis, **ZEDL** II, pp. 431–432.

0207 19 Aug. 1849. At Zouga on way back from Lake. Lack of water. The Bakalahari and Bushmen. Eland. Their course. The lake and its people. Tradition of Solomon and harlots among Bechuanas. Inability to cross Zouga to visit Sebituane. 10 Oct. Trees. Wild life. Possibility of highway for missionary enterprise to the north. Waiting for oxen. Rivers. Mary and Thomas ill. Charles's engagement obstacle to being accepted by the London Missionary Society: therefore should go with American Board. 18 Oct. Home, all well.

0246 25 Mar. 1851. Dessication will make him leave Bakwains, but Boers and desert all around, and fever further north. Moffats' allegation about the death of his child and jealousy at his discovery of the lake. Perplexed as to how best to help the Bakwains. News of family. 26 Apr. Letters received.

0257 8 Oct. 1851. Visit to Sekhomi. Salt pans. Bushmen. Tsetse. Greeting by and death of Sebituane. The Sesheke. Various tribes. Need for Christian merchants to come up Zambesi and stop slave trade. Healthy season. Slave trade. Universal knowledge of God, sin, and futurity. No hills on which we may live safely, so family must leave, perhaps to live in Scotland. Thanks for offer of books etc. Directors wish him to make dictionary of Setchuana, but now has to deal with the only slightly related Zambesi language. Mary insists on calling new son Charles.

0270 12 Apr. 1852. Books not yet received. Met Newton, American Presbyterian missionary in the Punjab. Oswell bought clothes to make them more civilised. Operation to uvula. Sends curios, seeds, etc. Articles on Caffre War. P.S. Family sailed on 23 Apr.

0281 29 May 1852. About to leave for interior. In sorrowful widowhood. Sends daguerreotype. Missionaries in the interior are a sorry set. Shall be two years away.

0286 10 Sep. 1852. American provisions cheaper than South African, because everything goes to the army. Wishes to find healthy locality on the Zambesi and a way to the sea.

Also writing Sichuana dictionary and work on natural history. Look after children if he does not return. Evil nature of his brother-in-law. Afraid children will be spoiled in England. Congratulations on marriage. In a terrible fit about youngest child's name. Boers mean to attack Bakwains. Cruelty of English Army to Caffres and Hottentots. Sends speech of Sandillah to be printed.

0319   21 Sep. 1853. Takes up letter of 6 Feb. not yet sent. Delayed by fever, floods, and woods. European medicine better than native. Kind reception by young chief. Magnificence of Zambesi. Disgust at heathenism. Portuguese slave merchants. Unsuccessful conspiracy of Mpepe. Arabs from Zanzibar. The Makalaka.

0332   8 Apr. 1854. Excessive rain. The country. Delayed by demands of tribes, who are made unreasonable by slave trade. Need for road. Freeing of Balonda. Idolatry. Eating habits. 17 Jun. Reception by Gabriel.

0391   20 Dec. 1855. Feeding on hippopotamus. Description of Mosioatunya. Nursery made on nearby island. Travels in Angola. River Loembua which divides its waters between Atlantic and Indian Oceans. Geology of Central Africa. Lack of clothing among people. Ridges healthy. Prospects for missions and commerce. Will reach coast in a few months and be first European to cross continent, following many Arabs and two native Portuguese. Oswell not a captain, nor is the map his, but drawn by natives and polished by them. P.S. Reached farthest inland Portuguese settlement. Geology. Missionary opportunities.

0575   †28 Aug. 1857. As there is time before publication, will consult Murray who intended Falls at beginning of book. Send explanation of difference in amount of rain north and south of Equator, required for Monday's speech. 1400 admission tickets bought at Dublin. Bechuana reed-dance may be put in where Makololo dance is described. His movements.

LIVINGSTON(E), Agnes (2) (1823 – 1895).
David's sister.

For letters addressed to her jointly with her parents see under Livingston(e), Neil; for those addressed to her jointly with her sister see under Livingston(e), Janet. Those addressed to her of 4 Apr. 1842 (0050), 11 Nov. 1845 (0139), 5 Feb. 1850 (0222), and 29 Dec. 1851 (0263) are published in Schapera, **DLFL**.

1058   30 Nov. 1860. Her letter of 26 Jul. 1859 received. Has been to Makololo: glad to see old friends, but saddened by Helmores' death, especially when the cure was available in his waggon at Linyanti and the method mentioned in **Missionary Travels**. Sekeletu's skin disease not real leprosy. When goods transported up country, Makololo will move to highlands. Old ship a swindle. Regards to relations and friends.

LIVINGSTON(E), Mary, née Moffat (1821 – 1862).
Eldest daughter of Robert Moffat; married Livingstone 9 Jan. 1845; accompanied him on his early journeys, but sent to England 23 Apr. 1852; returned with him in 1858, but could not go beyond Cape Town; rejoined him 30 Jan. 1862, and died 27 Apr. 1862.

Letters addressed to her of 1 Aug. 1844 (0107), 12 Sep. 1844 (0109), [Oct. 1844] (0111), 5 May 1852 (0275), 20 Sep. 1852 (0287), 14 and 16 Jan. 1853 (0310), 25 Oct. 1854 (0343), [20 Mar. 1855] (0371), 14 Sep. 1855 (0386), and 27 Nov. and 6 Dec. 1856 (0438) are published in Schapera, **DLFL**.

0104.8 15 Jul. 1844. Wishes to become better acquainted with her.

0280 28 May 1852. *News of himself and the situation in Africa.

0313 6 Jun. 1853. Travel on the Chobe. Reception by Makololo. Will not speechify in England but may write a book.

0576 [28 Aug. 1857.] Good journey to Dublin which is full of foreigners for the meetings. Robert and Tom must be diligent.

0577 [29 Aug. 1857.] Invitations received. Papers by Scott Russell and Barth, whom he questioned about latitude.

0578 29 Aug. 1857. Wishes he could have taken her to Dublin. Interest in the cause from Lord Radstock and the Archbishop's daughters. Dinner and soirée on Monday, meets Trotter on Tuesday.

1097 14 Mar. 1861. On the Rovuma. Hopes to have her with him in a year. Rowley left his wife for five years.

LIVINGSTON(E), Robert Moffat (1846 – 1864).
Eldest son of David, named after R. Moffat 1 (q.v.). Went to England with his mother in 1852; returned to South Africa in 1863 to meet his father, but failing to do so went to the United States, where he was killed in the Civil War.

Letters to him and his sister and brother(s) of [Sep. 1852?] (0292), Nov. 1852 (0303), [10–14 Feb. 1853] (0312), and 2 Oct. [1853] (0325) are published in Schapera, **DLFL**.

0278 18 May 1852. Recalls parting in Cape Town. He is no longer his father; Jesus now is.

0773 25 Mar. 1858. Weather favourable. Oswell sick in Bay of Biscay. Southern Cross and Pole Star both visible. He should seek guidance of God. Write regularly. Landing for coal. Perhaps French should be added to Latin and Greek.

0790 7 May 1858. Mary sick all the way from Sierra Leone, and she and Oswell had to be left with Moffats at Cape Town; they will travel overland from Kuruman to the Zambesi when she is better. Now off Natal and lonely. Oswell has become a sailor and will now become a waggon driver. Prepare for the battle of life. Regards. Write frequently.

0900 31 May 1859. Too busy recently to write. Doing good service to the cause of Christ. Discovery of Lake Shirwa must be used to end slave trade. Personal advice.

1001.1 [28 Feb. 1860?]. Specimens of natural history sent with Rae. Exhortation. Seeds.

1130 26 Sep. 1861. Now 120 miles up Lake Nyassa; mountainous country; perhaps 30–40 miles wide and over 210 feet deep; stormy. About 140 slaves freed and given to Bishop;

attacked with poisoned arrows before slavers driven off. Strive to overcome fickleness (as Robert Moffat jr. never did) with God's help.

1322 20 Feb. 1863. Difficulties in getting 'Lady Nyasa' through elephant marsh and later because of lack of water. Dreadful results of slave hunting and famine. Contrast with good results of Palmerston's policy on the west coast. Universities' Mission has run into difficulties. Expects Jehan and five tradesmen. Family greetings.

LIVINGSTON(E), Agnes (3) (1847 – 1912).
Eldest daughter of David, named after A. Livingston(e) 1 (q.v.). Went to England with mother in 1852; her father's companion in 1864–5; married Alexander Low Bruce in 1875.

For letters addressed to her jointly with her brothers see under Livingston(e), Robert M. Livingstone commonly addressed her as 'Nannie'.

0277 18 May 1852. Published in Schapera, DLFL.

0301 26 Nov. 1852. Exhortation to goodness.

0585 14 Sep. 1857. Visit to church in Manchester where Moffats worshipped; their great contribution to Africa. Exhortation. Family news.

0592 27 Sep. 1857. Cannot remember what he said about her great-grandfather, but if she reads it again she will understand. Resting at Rossie Priory from speaking engagements. Family news.

0680 28 Jan. 1858. Regrets her eye trouble, but all is will of God. Starts if possible on 15 Feb. Has to purchase calico. On Monday unable to reach Geographical Society meeting because of crowd viewing illuminations for Princess Royal's wedding.

0751 6 Mar. 1858. 'Pearl' out of dock and sails on Monday. Mary packing. Exhortations and greetings.

0762 10 Mar. 1858. Just leaving. Weather stormy. Greetings.

0768 22 Mar. 1858. Will call at Sierra Leone in three days for coal. Very hot. Oswell was seasick. Flying fish. Pole Star now well down. Exhortation.

0789 7 May 1858. Now off Natal. Mary and Oswell left at Cape Town, to go on to Kuruman. Charles preaches on board.

0836 28 Sep. 1858. Charles at Tette. Mary and Oswell on way to Kuruman. Going to Tette immediately. Joy of Makololo. Exhortation and greetings.

0905 1 Jun. 1859. Have been to mouth of Zambesi, but no ship appearing buried a bottle with a letter. Has received no news from England. Kirk and he went up Shire to Lake Shirwa. Description of the Highlands. Country could be cultivated so as to make slave trading unprofitable. Exhortation and greetings.

0946 20 Oct. 1859. Hoping for letters. Discovery of Lake Nyassa. Meeting with slave party. Exhortation.

1000   28 Feb. 1860.   Letter and curios sent by Rae. No news from Mary.

1050   28 Nov. 1860.   Travel by canoe. Hippopotami. Cotton grown above Kafue. Greetings.

1079   20 Feb. 1861.   Thanks for letters. Cannot come home till work is completed. Will send for Mary when suitable place is found. Lake country beautiful. Has seen Bishop Mackenzie.

1120   20 May 1861.   So much to do that he cannot contemplate returning for years, if ever. Exhortation. Going up Shire to carry a boat past cataracts to Lake Nyassa, to stop slave trade. Bishop and party to be taken to the Highlands first. No serious fever. Weather. Greetings.

1131   12 Oct. 1861.   Could not reach end of Lake Nyassa because of lack of food and the mountains which tired the land party. War and slave trade have ruined country. Bishop has good opportunity with freed children. Size of lake. Slavery on the east shore. Immensity of task.

1216   28 Apr. 1862. Death of Mary.

1247   12 Jul. 1862. Sends gifts from José Nuñes, pieces of dinornis's egg from Madagascar, and curios. Cross erected at Mary's grave. Going to Johanna. Exhortation. Water falling fast. Greetings.

1265   1 Sep. 1862.   Published in Wallis, ZEDL II, pp. 216–217.

1270   [26 Aug.–4 Sep. 1862].   [Beginning missing.] Walked over mountains from Johanna through dense vegetation.

1273   10 Oct. 1862.   Published in Wallis, ZEDL II, pp. 220–221 (omits PS of 21 Oct. on arrival in Johanna).

1300   18 Dec. 1862.   Published in Wallis, ZEDL II, pp. 224–228 (minor omissions).

1328   24 Feb. 1863.   Her letters have improved. Held up by low rise of river. Country depopulated by slave hunting and famine. Bodies in the river. Palmerston's policy produced excellent results in West Africa. Exhortation. Family news.

1350   18 May 1863.   Cool weather may improve his health. Distressed at desolation. Waller sends insects. Greetings. Charles and Kirk go home.

1368   8 Jul. 1863. Now better. Hopes of progress baffled. Deceived by Portuguese statesmen. Robert in Natal, but there is no communication thence; has advised him to get a situation there. Family news and greetings.

1390   10 Aug. 1863.   Will come home after taking 'Pioneer' to the sea and 'Lady Nyasa' to India. Jealousy and slaving of Portuguese have thwarted hopes. Good laws in Lisbon mean nothing here. Tozer lacks courage and his followers fear difficulties. Robert [repeats previous letter.]

1401   7 Dec. 1863. Letters received. Loss of boat in cataracts. Mountains and hostile natives prevented reaching north of Lake on foot. Mountain journey; rivers and lakes. Chief source of Zanzibar slaves. Robert now at Cape Town. Going to India. Greetings.

1415   24 Dec. 1863. Has heard from Mrs Buchanan about her going to a finishing school in London — agrees; about her attending communion in Church of England — has no objection, it is up to her conscience; about not sleeping with an older woman — agrees it is not desirable. Avoid in yourself evils seen in others.

1425   25 Feb. 1864. Published in Wallis, **ZEDL II**, pp. 382—385.

1443   29 Apr. 1864. Prevented from sailing. Storms. Kindness of Seward. 30 Apr. Sailing today.

1448   [30 Apr.—23 Jun. 1864?] P.S. Performance by Indian jugglers. Family news.

1452   29 Jul. 1864. Dining with Palmerstons. Presents. If she had mentioned Robert's regiment, he would have applied to American Minister.

1471   27 Aug. 1864. Has seen Buchanans. She should come to Glasgow from Limefield on Monday. Tom need not come.

1636   11 Mar. 1865. No news of Robert. Social occasions. Write what books Moffat wants.

1638   [13 Mar. 1865?] Russell continues office to tribes north of Portuguese claims; tell only Mrs. Webb. Hopes to leave on Wednesday. Wishes he were fishing.

1808   19 Aug. 1865. Reached Marseilles at noon. Tiresome travellers. Visits in Paris. Greetings.

1811   22 Aug. 1865. Fine sailing. Kindness of officers. Fellow passengers.

1813   26 Aug. 1865. Will reach Alexandria in the afternoon and go straight by train to Suez. Cholera in Marseilles made Maltese refuse to come near them. Weather good. Greetings.

1815   3 Sep. 1865. Sweltered through Red Sea. Death of a passenger. Conditions in the engine and stoke rooms. Fish in the Red Sea. Ships seen. Will call at Aden to see Col. Merryweather. Fellow passengers. Saw Suez end of Lessep's canal: different views of its prospects.

1816   [22 Aug.—10 Sep. 1865.] [Fragment.] American passenger. What former slaves will do.

1818   11 Sep. 1865. Arrival in Bombay. Bereavement of fellow passengers. 20 Sep. Visit to Nassick school; eight pupils have volunteered. Some Marines also to go. Visit to Poona; country and climate. Theatrical entertainment. Ceremonial. Government favour to Hindus, some of whom are very rich. Not likely to go before November. 28 Sep. Avoid French novels. To deliver two lectures.

1828   12 Oct. 1865. Reception of Sultan of Zanzibar. Lectures at Poona and Bombay. To visit Taylor at Surat. Staying with Wilson.

1829   26 Oct. 1865. Letters received. Advice on health. Speech followed by subscriptions, which should be used for trade. Buffaloes shipped to Zanzibar. Assistance of Governor and Sultan. Cotton trade. Comfortable living. Letters received from Moffat and Frédoux. Land very valuable. Will remember request for seeds. 28 Oct. Sends report of speech.

1835   9 Nov. 1865. Waiting for ship. Will give money to Bombay merchants to start trade with Africa. Visit to tombs.

1836   14 [Oct. or Nov. 1865]. Letters received. Advice on health.

1840   17 Nov. 1865. Anxious to be off. Companions ready. Visit to Gujerat.

1841   24 Nov. 1865. Has to wait another month; would be infra dig to go on an Arab dhow. Intends to visit Nagpur. Climate of India. 27 Nov. Is to go by 'Thule'. Murchison wishes him to go straight to Lake Tanganyika but prefers to go via Rovuma and Lake Bemba, avoiding Burton's territory.

1847   2 Dec. 1865. Letter from Tom. Has written Hamiltons. Financial contribution. Governor's opinion of him. Greetings.

1852   7 Dec. 1865. Sudden death of a fellow passenger. Visit to Temples at Kanara; lecture by Wilson. Advice on studies. Handwriting could be better. Glove boxes from Surat and other presents. Change in India. Enquire again about Robert's death. 13 Dec. 'Thule' will not sail till Governor returns on 15th.

1854   20 Dec. 1865. Cannot leave till Governor returns. Favourable review in **Athenaeum**. Paper in **Evangelical Christendom**. Contribution from Mr. Justice Anstey; his sternness against speculators. 'Thule' is a fine boat. Contemplated purchase of opera cloak.

1856   26 Dec. 1865. Christmas customs. Best cashmere sent to Paris and London. Evening with Hindu family. Death of Lord Edward Seymour. Will sail on 1 Jan. Commissioned to make formal presentation of 'Thule' to Sultan. Sale of **Narrative**.

1860   [Dec. 1865.] [Beginning missing.] Visit to caves of Elephanta. Sad end of Rae. Learn by failings of others. Murchison wishes him to go Lake Tanganyika at once, but he is anxious to do more than discover. Advice and greetings.

1861   [11 Sep.–31 Dec. 1865.] [Beginning missing.] Traders prepare way for missionaries, who are not all over wise, e.g. Price. Helmore's mission not followed up. Great heat. Exhortation.

1871   22 Jan. 1866. Vessel rolls dreadfully. Rescue of men swept overboard. Shark bit vane of Patent Log. Personal news and advice. His sisters' house. Contact R.L. Tracey in Bombay about money invested. 29 Jan. Nine buffaloes dead. Visit to Sultan. Contemptuous conduct of Van der Decken. 6 Feb. Handing over 'Thule'. 'Penguin' comes in three weeks to take him to the Rovuma.

1878   8 Feb. 1866. Good that Kirk is coming to Zanzibar. Unhealthy locality. Description of slave market. Friendliness of Sultan; most of his income from slaves.

1881   17 Feb. 1866. Will be some weeks here. Doubtful if camels will come: Arabs afraid because of Von der Decken's murder. End of Ramadan.

1885   7 Mar. 1866. Previous letters by Seychelles mistakenly not prepaid. Waiting for 'Penguin'. Has got only one camel. Description of Zanzibar. Sending goods on to Lake Tanganyika. Greetings.

1890   22 Mar. 1866. Refused offer of Sultan's yacht and came down on 'Penguin', with animals in hired dhow. Write to Murchison. Foresees no impediment to finding watershed. Had to get rifles and ammunition from 'Wasp'. Life at Zanzibar. 24 Mar. Animals could not be landed at Rovuma, so going north to Mikindany.

1893   18 May 1866. Letters to be taken by Arab. Jungle. Lack of food. Buffaloes. Greetings.

1914   2 Feb. 1867. Now at watershed. Journey lengthened by need to avoid danger. Lack of animals and food. Reception by Chitapangwa. Loss of medicine very serious. Tell Oswell news because black slavers will not wait for more letters to be written. Personal advice.

1927   4 Jul. 1868. Stopped on way to Ujiji by inundation. Has borrowed paper from party going to coast to write her and Clarendon. Sources of Nile discovered near Lake Bangweolo. Still to follow down river. Tom's career. Teeth broken. Write to friends. Services of Maclear and Mann; criticism of Arrowsmith and Royal Geographical Society. Fever without medicine.

1940   Sep. 1869. Success and failure in treatment of fever. Detained by fear of Mazitu, hunger, war, and illness. Letters etc. inexplicably held up at Ujiji. Baker's intentions. Speke's error. His own scientific spirit. Ptolemy and his sources. Speke's false assertions. Sympathy for Miss Tiné. Letters sent. Greetings.

1959   †Nov. 1870. Lake Lincoln and the fountains. Speke's error. Reluctant to use Murchison's name again. The family name. Foot ulcers. Disease safura. Advice. Geographical details.

1962   5 Feb. 1871. Ten men have arrived from Kirk. Will leave on 12th to finish in four or five months. Determined to do his duty. Has grown old. Letters received. Cholera. Letters destroyed by governor who was annoyed at not being paid by Burton. Criticism of Royal Geographical Society and Arrowsmith. Personal advice.

1969   Mar. 1871. Writes in hope of meeting traders from the west coast at Lake Lincoln. Has been given baby gorilla. Way of life in Manyuema villages. Kirk's efforts against slavery. Attacks by gorillas. Death of Lady Murchison. Nature of after-life. Mrs Young failed to realise she was at the climax of life. No letters from Young or Murchison, unless waiting at Ujiji. Men sent by Kirk are Moslems, i.e. unmitigated liars; they refuse to send on his goods from Ujiji, but rather than waste six months in going back, he presses on to finish exploration. Moslems worst followers he has ever had.

1982   18 Nov. 1871. After going down Webb's Lualaba forced to return to Ujiji by Kirk's slaves. Destitute at Ujiji because of Shereef's activities, and in despair, but relieved by Stanley. His generosity. Letters brought by him showed Kirk's failure. Kirk's envy. Did not wish to use his few goods in making good Burton's account of Tanganyika.

1985   16 Dec. 1871. Keep all letters private or others will profit by them. Regrets Hamilton's death. Kirk's failure. Stanley's help. Kirk envious but would not take task himself without salary. Journal must be kept sealed. Hopes to get a little money for family.

2001   Feb. 1872. Letters received. Only waiting for men to be sent by Stanley. Length of time taken by Kirk's communications. Loss of goods by his neglect. Thanks for presents. Kirk wants him back to finish sources himself, a task he refused in 1865 unless there was a good salary. Presents from Stanley, who will deliver journal and chronometers. Messages to friends and family.

2004   13 Mar.   Send particulars of Robert's death by Stanley who will arrange transfer to Gettysberg.

2010   2 Jun. 1872.   Waiting for men to be sent by Stanley. No one will travel during Arab war. Pity financial loss at Bombay was made public. Advice on how to answer impertinent questions. Privacy. Has written New York Herald to earn some money. Kirk's failure to help due to desire to find source himself. 1 Jul. Oswell writes that he is coming. Loss of time and money because of slaves. Will not leave without completing work, for which eight months will do. Will go round south end of Tanganyika, along southern shore of Lake Bangweolo, west to ancient fountains, then to Katanga copper mines, north-east to excavations, back to Katanga, north-west to Lake Lincoln, then to Ujiji. Entrusted journal, chronometers, and curiosities to Stanley. Government award. Her marriage.

2016   15 Aug. 1872.   *Good that will be done by ending the slave trade; it is for this that he has been detained.

2018   23 Aug. 1872.   Has long letter ready but no reliable means of sending it during war. Letters received by Stanley's men. Tomorrow starts to complete work and come home. [End missing.]

LIVINGSTON(E), Thomas Steele (1849 – 1876).
Second son of David, named after T.M. Steele (q.v.). Went to England with his mother in 1852; always delicate, he finally lived in Egypt for the benefit of his health, but without result.

For letters addressed to him jointly with his brother(s) and sister see under Livingston(e), Robert M.

0302   26 Nov. 1852. Published in Schapera, **DLFL** no. 91.

0626   22 Nov. 1857. *Exhortation.

0684   2 Feb. 1858. Will soon go from this country, leaving him in God's care. Hopes he will learn quickly and well.

0763   10 Mar. 1858. Off again. Exhortation.

0791   7 May 1858. Mary and Oswell sick and had to be left at Cape Town. J.S. Moffat may be going to Mosilikatze. Hopes he is receiving knowledge of Jesus and getting on with school lessons.

1001   28 Feb. 1860. Natural history specimen being taken for him by Rae. Will soon be going to Makololo. Delay in lower Zambesi has led to discovery of Lake Nyassa. Much deceived by supplier of ship: unlike him be honest and sincere. Mailbag lost overboard and later recovered; may contain letter to him, but probably unreadable.

1051   28 Nov. 1860. When with Makololo saw two former wives of Sebituane who had fed him with honey and milk; association of ideas. Sekeletu suffering from skin disease, falsely believed to be caused by witchcraft. Makololo perishing from fever; awaits arrival of Mary so as to move to highlands. Contrast of climates. Now returning to sea to meet ship.

1132   12 Oct. 1861.   Blessing of living in a Christian country.   Here people flee before invaders, leaving their food supplies and consequently starving.   Ajawa invasion (urged on by Portuguese) will destroy many hundreds.   Mission with steamer required — good that Free Church of Scotland proposes to send one.   Seeking good healthy location (indicated by lack of mosquitos).   Universities' Mission well settled.   Attack by Ajawa.

1167   7 Jan. 1862.   Sends various curios.   Expects Mary soon.   Has passed through unhealthy marsh land, full of mosquitos.   If land were cultivated, it would be healthier and could support more people.   Ample space of Africa contrasts with crowded cities of Europe.

1217   28 Apr. 1862.   Death of Mary.

1274   10 Oct. 1862.   Published in Wallis, **ZEDL II**, pp. 217–220 (with minor inaccuracies; the PS of 21 Oct., letter 1282, which probably belongs to this letter, is ib. p. 216).

1391   10 Aug. 1863.   Disappointed to have received no letters from children.   Ask advice about career, as Robert never did.   New bishop likely to turn tail.   Work destroyed by Portuguese slave hunters: their method of operation.

1417   26 Dec. 1863.   Concerned about his illness.   Arab slavers on the Lake.   Recall of expedition shows that British Government has abandoned attempt to get free passage from Portuguese.   If Rovuma had not been so shallow, they could have been circumvented, and this may yet happen.   Abandonment of Universities' Mission even worse.   Marched west and were within ten days of another lake, but had to return.

1848   2 Dec. 1865.   Encouragement to study.   An English university would be preferable to a German.   Anxious to be off on the 'Thule'.   Details of his companions.   Changes in India.   Experiment with buffalo and tsetse.   Regards.

1877   †6 Feb. [1866].   Nine buffalo died from poisonous plant.   Death of Von der Decken and his contemptuous treatment of Africans.

1902   28 Aug. 1866.   Slave traders avoid him, so getting letters out is difficult.   Sepoys have failed.   Detailed description of country and people.   Advice on career.   1 Feb. 1867.   Journey to Benaba.   Death of poodle by drowning.   Desertion of Johanna men.

1939   24 Sep. 1869.   Living in Manyuema country: people reputed to be cannibals, but this is doubtful.   American Civil War has much advanced the cause of freedom;   reaction to riot in Jamaica shows how far behind England is.   His task to examine the watershed of South Central Africa and so discover the sources of the Nile and the Congo.   Ptolemy more correct than Speke, who was corrupted by Burton.   Advice on marriage, based on his own experience.   Advice on teeth;   most of his have come out.   [Later addition.] Cannibalism likely.   Delays because of rain, bad servants, and foot ulcers.   Probable explanation of rivers.

2023   Dec. 1872.   *Content if allowed to contribute to ending of slave trade.

LIVINGSTON(E), William Oswell (1851 – 1892).
Third son of David, named after W.C. Oswell (q.v.) and generally called 'Oswell' or 'Zouga' (the latter from his birthplace).   Went to England with his mother in 1852. Joined the Search Expedition in 1872, but did not reach his father.

For letters addressed to him jointly with his brother(s) and sister see under Livingston(e), Robert M.

0453   9 Jan. 1857.   Exhortation.

1133   14 Oct. 1861.   Hopes he may become missionary.   Numerous population, trading only in slaves and fighting each other.   Size of lake.   Meeting with Mazitu.

1218   28 Apr. 1862.   Death of Mary, who had collected curiosities for them and was pleased at the idea of his becoming a missionary.

1262   21 Aug. 1862.   Thanks for letter and present.   Now sailing to Johanna.   Current too strong to sail against it.   Education vital.   Glad he wishes to be a missionary.   Letters should not be shown to people who might publish.

1272   10 Oct. 1862.   *Expecting letters.   Alligator eggs.   Country and people.

1284.2 †[26 Oct. 1862.]   [Beginning lost.]   Voyage to Mohilla.   Reception by Abdullah and the Queen.   Bats.   Now sailing to Johanna.

1329.3 25 Feb. 1863.   Blacksmith William Macleod will take home hippopotamus tusk for Agnes, reason for its being round.   Now hauling ship through Elephant Marsh.   Tom has not written.   Trials of missionaries by death.   Numerous crocodiles.   Exhortation.

1418   26 Dec. 1863.   Waiting for rise in river to get to sea, then to India and home.   Loss of boat on Cataracts.   Encounter with elephants.   Country depopulated by slave wars.

LIVINGSTONE, Anna Mary (1858 — 1939).
Youngest daughter of David.   Married Frank Wilson in 1881.

1416   26 Dec. 1863.   Greetings.

1855   24 Dec. 1865.   Tea with Hindu family.

1870   22 Jan. 1866.   She will not remember crossing the Equator, when she still had a loving mother.   She should read 'Rose Douglas', autobiography of a minister's daughter near Lanark.   Slow journey to Zanzibar, seeing nothing but flying fish.   A shark left his tooth in the patent log.   Regards.

LIVINGSTON(E), Harriette C. Ingraham, (1825? — 1900).
Of South Attleboro, Massachusetts, was graduated from Oberlin College in 1847, and taught school for a time thereafter.   In 1852 she was married to Charles Livingstone.

1737   6 Jun. 1865.   Harper's and the NEZT.   I fear we shall hear of Robert no more.   Wish Charles were not on the West Coast.   Jefferson Davis;   the misleading of British newspapers.   America's task dealing with the liberated African.   Off to London, Paris and Africa.

LIVINGSTON(E), John (2) or Neil.
Sons of John (1).

1384   25 Jul. 1863.   Praises his handwriting; surrounded by people who never had the means of learning.   Taking boat past Shire cataracts to explore north end of Lake Nyassa.   The boat left previously had been burned in the burning of the high grass which takes place yearly.   This grass prevents the capture of game, as animals hear one before one sees them.

LIVINGSTONE, Neil 2.
Apparently a cousin of David's; a smith in Airdrie.

0472   27 Feb. 1857.   His sadness at not arriving home before his father's death, the more so as there were many things they could have discussed together.

LIVINGSTONE'S TRUSTEES.
James Young, Andrew Buchanan & James Hannan (q.v.).

1296   15 Dec. 1862.   Please apply £5589 5/9d plus any interest on £2100 and other trust monies received from John Murray to James Young for Tod and Macgregor for the Screw Steamer Lady Nyassa.   Apply £354 7/6d of the £210 and other trust monies received from John Murray to Captain Davies of the "Hetty Ellen" for additional freight from Mozambique to Kongone as agreed by Mr. Rae.

LOADER, John.
Thame, Oxfordshire.

1797   †11 Aug. 1865.   Has no information about a situation; try in Liverpool.   Is not taking an expedition of Europeans.

LOGAN, William (1813 — 1879).
A philanthropist who attended Anderson's College with Livingstone.

1323   20 Feb. 1863.   Thanks for your letter containing information about my children, especially the one I have never seen.   Slavers followed Kirk's path to this river; people panicked and fled across the river, resulting in death and devastation in this valley where Wilson thought a hundred tons of cotton could be collected.   The leading slavers here are Marianno, Belshore, Mello and Jose St. Anna; their captives are part of the French scheme.   Wilson's book and Palmerston's policy on the West Coast are similar.

1765   6 Jul. 1865.   *Praising a book written by Janet Hamilton.

LONDON, Lord Mayor of.

0551.8 8 Jul. [1857].   Thanks to subscribers to and organisers of London Livingstone Testimonial Fund.

LOUDON, James (? — 1902).
Physician in Hamilton.

0448   [30 Dec. 1856??]   Please call and treat hoarseness;   also wishes an aperient.

1763   [30 May — 4 Jul. 1865?]   Happy to accept invitation for any hour tomorrow afternoon. Anna Mary will play with his child.

LOWE, Mrs.

0752   6 Mar. 1858.   Thank you for the kind present you have generously sent me.

LUCAS, Charles Shaw de Neufville (? — 1887).
Officer in the Royal (Bombay) Artillery;   Captain 1863, Lieut. Colonel 1873, Colonel 1878, Major General 1883.   **(Ind. Army List.)**

1833   30 Oct. 1865.   Captain Mahomet is a drunkard but indispensable to the Sultan;   so must submit and hope that the beasts and men arrive safely despite him.

1827   †6 Oct. 1865.   Would like to see men selected and will call on Monday or Tuesday. Needs twelve, including good hunters and buffalo-managers.

MACGREGOR, Miss.

0581.9 9 Sep. 1857.   [Beginning unknown.]   Will fulfil duty.   God's kindness unbounded.

0593   27 Sep. 1857.   See the enormous cost of a sugar mill, which is too much for a private party to pay.   Show it to Miss Whately, and say I must pay for it out of the proceeds of the tusks at Quilimane.   Sekeletu will value it the higher he pays for it.

MACKENZIE, Miss.

0597   3 Oct. 1857.   I must vary topics due to continual newspaper coverage.   I have not submerged missionary work, but I do not consider a missionary as a dumpy man with a bible under his arm.   I have laboured at bricks and mortar, the carpenter's bench, at preaching, and medical practice.   I serve Christ when shooting buffalo for my men, taking an astronomical observation, or writing a letter to one of my children.   Am I to hide my light under a bushel merely because some consider my work not "missionary"?   Thus I do not take money from the Society.

MACKENZIE, Charles Frederick (1825 — 1862).
Archdeacon to John W. Colenso in Natal, 1854—9, serving first a parish in Durban and then a frontier post on the Umhlali River to the north. In November 1859 he was chosen to lead the Oxford, Cambridge, Dublin and Durham Mission to Central Africa (later the Universities' Mission to Central Africa), and was consecrated Bishop of Central Africa in Cape Town on 1 Jan. 1861. On 31 Jan. 1862 he died of fever at the confluence of the Ruo and Shire rivers. **(DNB.)**

1136   9 Nov. 1861. Livingstone returned, and waits only for Meller to go down to the sea. He could not give Procter a passage to the sea as I wished. He said in our second affair with the Achawa we were quite right to identify ourselves with the interests of our people. Sympathizes with us in our difficulties; act with a determined, vigorous will. Infers from the hydrographer's instructions that H.M. Government is favourable to assisting us if his own service is not hindered. Also he does so out of his own good will to the mission.

MACLEAR, **Sir** Thomas (1794 — 1879).
After studying medicine, he became interested in mathematics and astronomy, and was appointed astronomer of the Royal Observatory at Cape Town in 1833, a post he held till 1870. Knighted 1860. Livingstone met him in 1852 and thereafter depended on him to check and reduce his observations. He named Cape Maclear after him. **(DNB.)**

0276   7 May 1852. Requires map for a day or two. Wet weather prevents departure.

0279   24 May 1852. Sends map as means of reference for future communications. Leaves on Thursday. Domestic life of a toucan.

0306   13 Dec. 1852. Detained four months by Boers, but starts tomorrow. Their unprovoked attack on Bakwains and blockage of road north. Determined to find a way out to either coast.

0323   29 Sep. 1853. Sends observations; methods and errors. Plans for westward journey. Read enclosed letter to Steele and add note on longitude if desired. Sketch map. Meeting with slave merchant.

0331   7 Apr. 1854. Heavy rains. Threats by Africans. Fertile country. Sends observations.

0336   8 Jun. 1854. Sends observations. 15 Aug. Arrival in Loanda. Friendship of Gabriel.

0361   29 Jan. 1855. Sends observations. Splendid country, whose development is hindered by slave trade. Many literate through work of Jesuits.

0370   2 Mar. 1855. *His route from Cassange to Quango. Rainy season both ways. British trade up Casai and Zaire would be profitable.

0373   18 May 1855. Sends observations, but no map as he is nearly blind from a blow on the eye.

0381   12 Sep. 1855. Arrived two days ago. Cannot send observations because of dysentery. Letters and observations lost in 'Forerunner'. Hopes he received earlier observations. Weak from incessant rains and fever.

0383   13 Sep. 1855.   Sends observations and map.   Detailed account of the geography. Reports of Lake Tanganyika.

0394   15 Feb. 1856.   Journey from Linyanti to Tette.   Victoria Falls.   The people.   Physical geography of Central Africa.   Healthy ridges, deadly hollow.

0396   [22 Feb.–1 Mar. 1856.]   Observations and notes on them.   Desire to return.   Will write to the Royal Geographical Society about the country.

0397   2 Mar. 1856.   Notes on observations.   Geology.   A silicified forest.

0410   3 Apr. 1856.   Sends tracing, including rivers from information received at Tette.   Longitudes may be incorrect;   will not give them to anyone till checked.   Map should be in black for facts, in red for hearsay.   A person in Angola who was given his observations and claimed them for himself.   Observations for Tette.

0417   27 May 1856.   Observations.   Loss of Dart's boat.   Appreciates Maclear's drawing his observations to the attention of Government.   Better communications needed in the Zambesi.

0425   14 Aug. 1856.   Confusion of Jupiter and Mars in observations.   Existence of Lake Marawi;   accuracy of native reports.   Geology.

0426   17 Aug. 1856.   Fears work in Africa may end due to London Missionary Society.   They may send him to China but he would rather resign.   May investigate fever or spread gospel.

0456   21 Jan. 1857.   Tomorrow I begin to write my book.   Hope to be in Tete in April next year.   Work on the map delayed as we await your calculations on the bundle of observations sent from Mauritius.   Thank you for the kind things you said at the Cape Town meeting.   Here they laud me, but they ought to thank the Boers who set me free to discover the new country.

0470   16 Feb. 1857.   Thank you for your testimonial on my behalf.   I am up over my head into the book.   I may not be connected with the London Mission much longer.   Clarendon has decided on nothing yet.   Your calculations are not yet arrived.

0499   11 Apr. 1857.   *Very busy writing.   Comments on errors in his observations.   Draws no more money from the London Missionary Society.

0517   13 May 1857.   The fund people placed £1100 in my account with Coutts & Co.   Am nearly off with the Society, although I will be not a whit less of a missionary, and will not accept a Government appointment if it trammels my operations.   The book goes on — I may get £2000 for it, which will be for the youngsters.   Comments on Barth's 5 vol. book.   His brother has come to join him.

0617   10 Nov. 1857.   Ashamed at not writing, but have had good intentions.   Book sold out yesterday: many thanks to you for making it what it is.   Only my brother aided, as amanuensis — others added bits and pieces.   Various Chambers of Commerce interested in an expedition, but between ourselves we must obtain sanction of Portuguese first, and I go to Portugal on the 27th to try to obtain it.   Yellow fever prevented my going already.

0686   3 Feb. 1858.   We sail in the "Pearl", bought by Ceylon Government and chartered by

Foreign Office, on the 15th or thereafter. "Pearl" weighs 300 tons and has 10 h.p. If Cape people like, they can give the money to me at a meeting where I explain my journeys. I don't expect your praise in the map as I was too busy to watch Arrowsmith. I bring all my observations to you.

0807   26 Jun. 1858. The river at Mazaro changed since I was here. Skead will tell you of the delta. Lack of appreciation for armchair geographers at home. Have applied to the Government for a suitable vessel.

0813   31 Jul. 1858. *On Bedingfeld: he goes home after having quarreled with the Engineer, then with Capt. Duncan, and after the fourth row I told him I would have no more of it.

0824   10 Sep. 1858. Kirk and I navigate the "Ma-Robert" very well. Bedingfeld's follies. Details of the trip from Shupanga to Tette. Conditions of the river. "Ma-Robert" is a good vessel with a bad engine.

0845   6 Oct. 1858. Astronomical observations taken in September in Tette, in June and July at Expedition Island, Shupanga, Senna and in August at Expedition Island. Have applied for the "Ban." "Old Traveller" chronometer ran down on 30 Jun. Two of them fell off the seat of a railway carriage en route to Liverpool.

0857   19 Dec. 1858. Visited Kebrabasa in this frightfully feeble steamer. Had I come that way in 1856 I should never have reached Tette. We found smallpox in Tette. I was wrong in saying that natives do not know how to make sugar.

0861   13 Jan. [1859]. Returning from a trip up the Shire River. Clouds and rain prevented taking latitude. People suspicious. Description of the valley. Astronomical observations for November 1858 and February 1859. Further thoughts on Kebrabasa. Financial dealings between Livingstone, Wm. Thompson, and the London Missionary Society.

0887   12 May 1859. Since the Shire does not flow from Lake Shirwa, this must not be Candido's lake. If you write Sabine, let him know I take my brother back to Shirwa to take magnetic observations. Mt. Zomba is 6000 feet and inhabited. Further description of the region. We returned to the boat via the Shirwa valley, and visited the Ruo on the way down.

0922   31 Jul. 1859. Geologist's salary has been stopped. Baines and Thornton were left at Tette as they could not rough it. Have had to suspend Baines. Thoughts on the English colonization of the highlands.

0936   14 Oct. 1859. Traced this river right into Nyinyesi, or as we heard it called Nyassa. We went to Zomba by our old route, then descended into the Shire valley. The "Ma-Robert" is at Chibisa's in need of much repair. We don't believe Candido: he told Kirk he never said to me that he had been to Nyassa, then reasserted it to me.

0964   3 Nov. 1859. On missionaries in Africa and in general; colonization and the people who should take part; appeal of the old monastery system without the celibacy.

0999   22 Feb., 12 Mar. 1860. *Are now going down to the sea. Behaviour of the Portuguese is frightful. Conduct of Baines and Thornton.

1022   7 May 1860. *Pleased with the prospects of the Universities' mission. While the Makololo are better people than the Manganja, the latter are more crucially located for the extinction of the slave trade.

1028   17 Aug. 1860.   Description of trip up the north bank of the river, then westward across the highlands.   Underestimated dimensions of the Falls last time.   Sad losses sustained by the Linyanti mission.   Sekeletu's strange disease.   Extent of the coal field.   Further description of the middle Zambesi.   25 Dec.   We measured the Falls as follows.   Also further information on the middle Zambezi.   Pinnace used for firewood at Lupata; "Ma-Robert" sank here.   We visit Rovuma to avoid Portuguese.   Take notes on weather from the notebooks and forward it to Washington.   Mission news is welcome, but the mission will need its own boat.

1071   1 Feb. 1861   Came here to meet a ship.   I see one now, but it is too large to be ours.   The only good we do here is test fever remedy.   A sketch of the land from the Shire to Nyassa is enclosed.

1095   12 Mar. 1861.   *Description of first six miles of the Rovuma.   Mackenzie is A−1, and the missionaries with him seem very well adapted for their undertaking.

1111   20 Apr. 1861.   *Description of the Rovuma.   Ebony here 3 times larger than on the Zambesi.   Reasons for D.J. May's leaving.

1119   17 May 1861.   *Kirk, the Bishop, C. Livingstone, Scudamore and I all had a turn at navigating from Johanna.   Took us 1½ days to reach Mazaro from the ocean.

1142   † 12 Nov. 1861.   Warped "Pioneer" 20 miles up Shire, and went into the highlands with the Bishop.   At a spot 12 miles south of Zomba we had to defend ourselves against natives.   Then we went upriver to the lake, naming Cape Maclear, and explored west shore of Nyassa.

1192   1 Mar. 1862.   Keppel brings "Old Traveller" chronometer for cleaning and repair.   We have a skin disease, which began with Kirk and came around to us all.   No one saw Sekeletu except Kirk and myself;   he alone of our party understands Sichuana.

1209   28 Mar. 1862.   Published in Wallis, **ZEDL** II, pp. 365−368.

1226   5 May 1862.   Death of Mary Livingstone.   Rae and a few hands assembled the "Lady Nyassa."

1239   21 Jun. 1862.   Published in Wallis, **ZEDL** II, pp. 368−370.

1277   15, 27 Oct. 1862.   Published in Wallis, **ZEDL** II, pp. 374−377.

1287   17 Nov. 1862.   *On the winds and currents between Johanna and Quilimane.   Am taking supplies up to the mission.   Anticipate hearing of mission progress.

1291   20 Nov. 1862.   Rowley says the Bishop attacked the Ajawa on my advice, but the Bishop's journal says otherwise.   Anyway, I was at Lake Nyassa at the time.   Rowley wrote a letter on it to the Cape Town papers.   We took slaves from the Portuguese, not the Ajawa.

1303   23 Dec. 1862.   *Will proceed up the Shire after repairs have been effected.   Rowley's assertions.   Portuguese restrictions on both the Zambesi Expedition and the mission.

1364   4 Jul. 1863.   Recall of the Zambesi Expedition.   The mission will remove to Morambala.   Defence of the Makololo behavior in the Shire valley.

1369   8 Jul. 1863.   Recall of the expedition.   Proposed exploration of Lake Nyassa.   Rampant slaving impedes mission progress.   Son Robert in Natal.

1396   5 Nov. 1863.   Thoughts on Robert.   Trustees refused to pay additional freight bill charged by "Hetty Ellen";   Young paid it from his own pocket.   Detailed version of his recent exploration of the region west of the lake.

1412   19 Dec. 1863.   On Tozer's abandoning the country.   30 Dec.   Son Robert and his lost opportunity for a career as a seaman, perhaps with the P & O company.   18 Feb. 1864. Came down to Morambala, and picked up Waller, Alington, and some 40 Africans.

1426   26 Feb. 1864.   On the mission, and the ocean voyage from Kongone to Moçambique.

1437   22 Mar. 1864.   Mission orphans are 30 boys, 8 women, 3 infants and 3 girls.   Copy of letter sent to Tozer on 19 December 1863.   Further opinions on the Portuguese and the exporting of slaves.

1449   5 Jul. 1864.   Published in Wallis, **ZEDL** II, pp. 385—387.

1524   3 Nov. 1864.   Working at another book.   Speech at Bath.   Financial dealings with Universities' Mission.

1629   3 Mar. 1865.   Send observations book.   Still writing.   No news of Robert since his capture.

1725   27 May 1865.   Book delayed by disagreement with Arrowsmith;   will now be published in November.   Scientific appendices would make it too long.   Rowley supports him against Portuguese criticisms re Mackenzie.   Meller going to Madagascar.   Criticisms of Burton, Winwood Reade, McDouall Stuart.   Baron von Heuglin and Miss Tinné.   Would be mistake to hang Jefferson Davis.   Hopes to take Johanna men on next expedition.

1832   28 Oct. 1865.   Arrowsmith's grumbling.   Watches and chronometers.   Bombay merchants.   No exchange of prisoners between North and South in USA;   fears Robert will never return.   Sorry to hear of Basuto war.   Dissenters in Natal and Scotland.

1874   30 Jan. 1866.   True account of Von der Decken's contemptuous behaviour which led to his death.   Cowardliness of Von Schuft.

1883   2 Mar. 1866.   Expects a ship every day.   Zanzibar pleasant only to the eye.   Project for steamers to the Cape not carried out.

1915   2 Feb. 1867.   Had to go south of Lake Nyasa because of Johanna men's fear of Mazitu. The country.   Hopes to reach Lake Tanganyika in May.

1917   4 Feb. 1867.   Sent from Bombay comparison of chronometers on Zambesi Expedition, kept by Charles Livingstone.   Some observations on this journey.

1929   8 Jul. 1868.   Sends copy of letter to Clarendon.   Dispute with Baines.   Sends observations [present].

1942   Sep. 1869.   No hope of sending letters for months.   Sources of the Nile on the watershed. Miss Tinné a genuine explorer.   Has still to see where the two arms unite, back to Ujiji for supplies, then south round the sources to underground houses and copper mines. Does not know state of his affairs.

1957   Nov. 1870.   Writes on cheque book.   The fountains: native reports.   At mercy of slaves.   Rivers and forest.   Ivory trading.   Chronometers dead.   No medicine.

1981   17 Nov. 1871.   At Ujiji in 1869 concluded that Tanganyika is a lacustrine river.   Loss of goods.   Manyuema country.   Ivory and slave trading.   Difficulties of travel.   Loss of more goods.   Meeting with Stanley.   Cannot find outlet in Tanganyika.   Attempt to make chronometers work.   Reported fountains.   Manyuema cannibals.   The gorilla. Mohamedans worse than Christians.

2009   [Mar. 1872?].   *Must re-discover ancient fountains when men sent by Stanley arrive. Abundant supplies thanks to Bennett's generosity.   Agent failed him by using slaves.

2017   [18 Aug. 1872?].   *Stanley was his Good Samaritan;   local people considered the search for the Nile source a sham until he arrived.

2024   [1872?].   Sends rough map of explorations.

2027   [Jan. 1873?].   Retracing steps to take up exploration.   Has good men supplied by Stanley.   Heat beside Lake Tanganyika.   Disagreements with guides.   Confusion of Chambeze and Zambesi corrected by Cazembe.

MACLEHOSE, James (1811 – 1885).
Apprenticed to a bookseller in London 1833—8, where he met Livingstone.   Thereafter he ran a highly successful business as bookseller and publisher in Glasgow.
(Boase, **MEB.**)

0015   21 Nov. 1840.   Send copy of Williams' narrative as gift to Dr. Andrew Buchanan.   Supply rest of Penny Cyclopedia in cloth and of Pictorial Palestine unbound.   Will write at length from Africa.

0041   8 Dec. 1841.   Former arrogance of Bechuanas has been reduced by defeat of Matebele by Boers.   Distant tribes whose culture is primitive, more ready to listen to Gospel. Hope lies in continuous teaching of the young, and for this native agents required, as Griquatown mission has done.   Much disease in interior.   Much game, but excessive heat and little water;   Bakalihari succeed in living in desert.   Gifts of clothing tend to cause jealousy of recipients.   Church has treated Philip abominably.   Spectacles for old women would be useful.   Do not consult Moffat about native agents: his regrettable quarrel with Griquatown missionaries makes him unfavourable to this.

0055   28 May 1842.   Need to open friendly relations before successful preaching.   The Bamangwato, Bakaa, Makalaka.   Many lions.   Need to spread Gospel to the north, which would cut off supply of slaves.   Churches in Scotland could assist more by supporting native agents.   Visited by Sebegwe's men.   Progress in learning language;   Moffat's efforts have smoothed the way.   Sekomi wishes to change but still proud.   18 Jun. Parcels of books received.   Regrets some letters have not arrived.   Poverty in youth was not unpleasant though other things were.

0072   20 Jun. 1843.   Gifts of clothing cause trouble even when it is usable;   better to receive monetary value, but reluctance to offend induces silence.   Killing of Sebegwe's people by Mahura;   restoration of relations with him.   Iron works of Bakhatta.   Visit to Bakalihari. Desert food.   Parable shows idea of future state to exist among Bechuana.   Encounter with tiger.   Reluctance of Bakaa to give food.   Breaking of finger on rock and rebreaking when attempting to shoot lion.

0147   26 Feb. 1846.   Death of William Philip.   Parcels of reviews etc. received.   Send note-paper.   Prospects better than at Mabotsa.

0454   †20 Jan. [1857].   *Thanks for advice about Macmillan's offers which he rejects. Kinsley's imagination not suited to factual narrative.

0507   24 Apr. 1857.   Whish demands payment of account for which receipt is at Linyanti: do any friends recall matter?   Book will not be finished till middle of May.

McLEOD, Norman (1812 — 1872).
Minister of the Church of Scotland, and one of the founders of the Evangelical Alliance. Editor of **Good Words** 1860–72.   (**DNB.**)

1903   28 Aug. 1866.   *On the weary trudge from the coast, the harbour of Pemba and adjacent country, and various tribes met with.

MACMILLAN, Alexander (1818 — 1896).
Publisher, Cambridge and London.

0658   8 Jan. 1858.   Thank you for the gift of books, which are so long unacknowledged.

MACNAB, Samuel.
Ship and insurance broker, Glasgow.

0736   24 Feb. 1858.   My stay in Glasgow is regulated by the leaving of the "Pearl" for Liverpool and I wish you would inform me when that takes place.   Washington said it would be launched tomorrow, and I have ordered the men of the expedition to be in Liverpool on Saturday.

MACQUEEN, James (1778 — 1870).
Macqueen became interested in African geography while manager of a sugar plantation in Grenada.   After a period as editor of the **Glasgow Courier,** he moved to London and wrote much on African geography, and politics and economics generally.   Livingstone thought him a mere "armchair geographer".   (**DNB.**)

0508   24 Apr. [1857].   *On native nicknames.

McROBERT, — — — .
Apparently a brother of John.

0064   1 Sep. 1842.   Country at war.   Need for divine aid.   Best news is from a village 50 miles away which desires to see a missionary.

McROBERT, Catherine, née Copland.
Wife of John.

0037   2 Dec. 1841.   Just returned from a journey of 700 miles.   Sad condition of people. Met ivory traders who had been further into the interior.   Difficulty in convincing people that his teaching consisted of more than new customs.   Driver gave two-thirds of his pay to Edwards to assist in his work.

0075   24 Jun. 1843.   Thanks for contributions.   Native teacher to be theirs, and they must pray for him and make suggestions regarding him.   He is a deacon and as well informed as any Bechuana.   Most useful articles for friends to send would be nails, knives, beads, etc.   Clothes not needed for indiscriminate distribution, though presents for the teacher would be acceptable.   Influence of witchcraft.

0088   1 Sep. 1843.   Settling at Mabotsa.   Native goodwill worldly in nature.   Bechuanas no use for building.   Usefulness of native teacher.   Mountains remind him of Scotland. Name of village.   Formation of Committee.

0102   5 Jun. 1844.   Usefulness of Mabalwe.   Remnants of animal worship.   Depravity of people sub-natural.   Conversions in Lattakoo district have worked wonders.   Conversion has greater effect than cure of disease.   Injury from lion.   Objections to clothing do not apply to that brought by Moffat, which he gives as reward for labour.

0145   18 Jan. 1846.   Desire for outside news.   Sekhomi's ambush of Matebele.   Contrast with Mosheu's actions.   Sechele intelligent.   Tools for teachers required.

0159   9 Jan. 1847.   His native teachers.   Only one conversion, but definite progress has been made.   Sabbath observance.   Has to prevent believers using force to convince others. They are not unreasoning, as many believe.

0170   9 Jul. 1847.   Long silence makes him feel forgotten.   Mabalwe or David works well. Boers claim all Mosilikatze's country.   State of the people.

McROBERT, John (1793/4 — 1876).
Congregational minister at Ellon 1823—34, missioner at Falkirk 1834—6 and Grangemouth 1836—8, minister at Cambuslang 1838—46, and at Denholm 1846—76. Although both he and Livingstone were associated with George Street Chapel, Glasgow, their relationship seems to have been through Mrs. McRobert's school in Cambuslang. (Information from Rev. Dr. H. Escott, archivist-historian of the Congregational Union of Scotland, and Mr. M. Robson, Curator of Wilton Lodge Museum, Hawick.)

0079   14 Jul. 1843.   Community of feeling between them.   Low state of Bechuanas, their belief in witchcraft and joy in murder.   Their music has only two notes and their language is simple;   theological discussion difficult.   Procedure in preaching in a village.   Equal number of young and old converted.   A degenerate Boer.   Hope for revival of church under new missionaries.

0108   4 Sep. 1844.   Glad to hear of conversions in Scotland, but he has none to report.   Difficulties of preaching. Does not accept limited atonement.   His poverty in sheep and cattle. Goodness of Mabalwe.   Attitude of women and children to missionaries.   Greatness of his task.

0192   24 Dec. 1848.   His reason for not replying earlier is that ink was spilt over his unfinished letter.   Dates this Kolobeng because his location does not exist on maps.   Teacher settled with Mokhatla.   Opposition of Boers.   Training of native teachers to be begun. Slow progress with conversion.   Sympathy over unjust criticism.   Sechele continues faithful. 26 Jan. 1849. Whish's enclosure in Drummond's box has been plundered of the surgical instruments.

MACSKIMMING, – – –
Son of William MacSkimming, Livingstone's teacher at Blantyre.

0521   18 May 1857.   I cannot yet come to visit my old teacher, your father, but expect to be in Glasgow later in the year.

McWILLIAM, James Ormiston (1808 – 1862).
Medical Officer during Trotter's expedition up the Niger River in 1841, McWilliam's skills were severely tried by the onset of "African fever" among the expedition's members. He later wrote several articles on this topic, and on the health of seamen in general. (DNB).

1054   28 Nov. 1860.   Livingstone compares the effect of fever and his treatment of it thus far among the members of the Zambezi Expedition with the findings McWilliam exposed in his Medical History of the Great Niger Expedition.   Livingstone's main conclusion is that while quinine is not an effective preventative of the fever, it is valuable in bringing about the cure when used in conjunction with other medicines according to Livingstone's recipe. While current medical opinion may deem this recipe as "quackery", Livingstone assures all that it works.   Table of the difference between wet and dry bulb temperatures for 24 September 1860 (Victoria Falls) concludes this report.

1085   [5 Mar. 1861?].   Revising the proportion of the medicines given in his fever treatment recipe of 28 Nov. 1860.

MAJID IBN SAID (ca. 1835 – 1870).
Son of Said ibn Sultan, the first Omani ruler of Zanzibar, and himself Sultan 1856–70. He was unable to assert his authority on the mainland against slave-traders.
(Oliver et al., HEA, I, pp. 231–7).

1937   20 Apr. 1869.   Kindness of his subjects.   Loss of goods.   Asks his aid in recovery and protection of fresh stock.   Wishes to hire porters.   Expected route.

MALMESBURY, 3rd Earl of (1807 – 1889).
James Howard Harris, succeeded to the title in 1841.   A Conservative, he was Secretary of State for Foreign Affairs Feb.–Dec. 1852 and Feb. 1858–Jun. 1859.   (DNB.)

Livingstone's copies of his letters to him of 22 Mar. 1858 (0769), 23 Mar. 1858 (0770), 22 Jun. 1858 (0802), 31 Jul. 1858 (0814), 16 Aug. 1858 (0817), 10 Sep. 1858 (0825),

17 Dec. 1858 (0853), 14 Feb. 1859 (0865; partially), 4 Mar. 1859 (0879), 12 May 1859 (0888), 31 May 1859 (0901), and 26 Jul. 1859 (0917) are published in Wallis, **ZEDL**. Incl. 2 of 26 Jul. 1859 (0918) is described in Section 3, Papers and Reports no. 16.

0787   1 May 1858.   Arrived at Cape Town/Simon's Bay.   Have drawn £50 from expedition funds, bill to be forwarded to the Paymaster of the Navy.   Captain Duncan draws £130 from the same source, not for the expedition but for the "Pearl".   We sail today at 2½ o'clock.   H.M. "Hermes" sailed yesterday morning, and will present my credentials at Kilimane, then will see "Pearl" safely over the bar and on her way.   Moffat visited Mosilikatze, and says my men still at Tette. He awaits missionaries who will go to Mosilikatze's country.

0823   9 Sep. 1858.   *Progress thus far.   He and Kirk navigate the "Ma-Robert" all right. Information of coals, slaves, cotton & indigo.

0832   25 Sep. 1858.   Kirk, Livingstone, Thornton, Baines & Rae all well and performing duties. Bedingfeld's salary stopped 31 July 1858, pending the sanction of Her Majesty's Secretary of State for Foreign Affairs.   This date marks the end of the ½ year for which he had already been paid.   This is Life Certificate No. 1.

0842   5 Oct. 1858.   I enclose a tracing of Thornton's chart.   Will send C. Livingstone's observations by the next opportunity.

0865   14 Feb. 1859.   Baines and C. Livingstone were left to explore the Kebrabasa rapids while we went up the Shire.   Went up the Revubue River to examine the coal seam. (Remainder in **ZEDL**.)

MANBY, Charles (1804 — 1884).
A civil engineer who assisted in the building of the first iron steamboat, Manby served as Secretary of the Institution of Civil Engineers, 1839–1856.   (**DNB**.)

0500   14 Apr. 1857.   I am searching for a kind of copper boat made in America, like Burton took to East Africa.   The kind which can be taken apart and packed in pieces is the kind, and if equipped with wheels to aid in bypassing rapids, so much the better.   I would call to see your specimens if I had time.   Please send me the information you have.

MANN, William (1817 — 1873).
Astronomer, assistant to Maclear at the Royal Observatory, Cape Town 1839–70.
    (**DNB**.)

Livingstone's letters to Maclear of 2 Feb. 1867 (1915), 4 Feb. 1867 (1917), Sep. 1869 (1942), 17 Nov. 1871 (1981), [18 Aug. 1872?] (2017), [1872?] (2024), and [Jan. 1873?] (2027) are also addressed to Mann.

MARJORIBANKS, Edward (1776 — 1868).
London banker, senior partner in Coutts & Co.

0728 19 Feb. 1858.   I accept your offer of service while I am gone.   I spoke to Conyngham, but now put a stop to power of attorney papers.   He says it is necessary to have someone in the F.O. take charge of letters, etc.   Draw £150 annually from Consul's salary for J.S. Moffat through his agent at the Cape.   I do not intend to draw much, and my children's affairs are in the hands of Young, Buchanan and Hannan.   If the loose money amounts to £700 or £800, put £500 at interest.

0926 6 Aug. 1859.   *Discoveries and hopes for colonization.   Delayed due to faulty engine palmed off on us by a philanthropist.   I never appreciated the value of your business as highly as I do now.   Soon Africa will be considered far different than the sandy desert portrayed by mapmakers.

1427 27 Feb. 1864.   Portuguese slavers ruined 6 years of my life, and I am on my way home. While the mission remained there, there was hope, but now we learn that their withdrawal was planned all along.   Had we known it sooner, we could have been saved a great deal of trouble with the orphans.   If I were younger I would take up the mission single-handed.

MARSH, L.

2020.8 21 Nov. 1872.   Thanks for election to Medical Club.   Cut off by activities of Banian slaves.   Relieved by Stanley.

MAY, Daniel John.
Having served in the Royal Navy along the West Coast of Africa, May (as Master) took command of the "Pioneer" from its departure from Plymouth on 9 Sep. 1860 until he was dismissed by Livingstone at Johanna on 20 Apr. 1861.   His next post was as Assistant Surveyor at the Naval Station in Cape Town.

1099 25 Mar. [1861].   According to the Instructions of H.M. Govt. to this expedition, charge of this expedition devolves on Bedingfeld, Kirk and C. Livingstone in that order, in the event of my failure.   A careful reading of the order for your appointment to command the "Pioneer" gives me no reason to believe that the Foreign Office wishes to amend those instructions.

1112 20 Apr. 1861.   As it is undesirable to use valuable services as yours which may well be required elsewhere, to survey what may elsewhere be claimed as Portuguese possessions, I thank you for bringing out the "Pioneer", and wish you well in your future career.

MBURUMA   (? — 1860).
Title of the chief of the Ambo people, who occupied the region north of the Zambezi and west of the confluence of the Luangwa.   This particular chief was treacherously murdered by a band led by José Anselmo de Santos Anna.

For the letter addressed to Mburuma, see under Sekeletu.

MEDICAL TIMES AND GAZETTE, Editor of.

1313.8 26 Jan. [1863].   Missionaries did not die because of climate (healthy in the Highlands) but through lack of hygiene and food.   Elephant Marsh is no worse than cesspools around London.   Health must be looked after everywhere.   27 Jan.   Death of Scudamore.

MELLER, Charles James (1836 — 1869).
Surgeon of the "Pioneer", Meller served in the Zambezi region from Feb. 1861 to Apr. 1862, and Oct. 1862 to Jul. 1863.   He was Vice-Consul in Madagascar from Apr. 1865 to Apr. 1866, and was associated with botanical gardens in Mauritius and Queensland before his untimely death in Sidney.   His health was permanently undermined during his tenure with the Zambezi Expedition.

1381   20 Jul. 1863.   If you wish, you may hasten down to Kongone where the "Rapid" is to touch in August, and leave your luggage behind to go down with "Pioneer".   I could give you some pieces of cloth to pay your way.

1507   12 Oct. 1864.   Can you lend sketches showing scenery or native customs?   Waller lost money and his game licence sleeping in a railway hotel.   Don't make the pictures desperately ugly.

1659   [1 Nov. 1864—31 Mar. 1865].   Concerning an enclosed note from DL to CM: Meller should go to Russell and get a note from him too.   DL was only introduced to Sir George once.

METHUEN, Henry Hoare (1818/19 — 1883).
Curate in various parishes 1849—70.   (Crockford.)

0224   [1 Nov. 1849—28 Feb. 1850??].   [Beginning missing.]   The Bakaa.   Regards.

MILES, Thomas.

0725.5 6 Mar. 1858.   Apply to Washington for payment.   Would be advantageous to have the beads manufactured in England rather than imported from Venice.

MILLS, Arthur (1816 — 1898).
Member of Parliament (for Taunton 1852—3, 1857—65, and Exeter 1873—80) and writer on colonial affairs.   (Boase, MEB, Suppl.)

1622.3 25 Feb. 1865.   *On the relative mortality of cruisers on the China and Africa   stations.

1710   12 May 1865.   *Criticism of Burton's view of missionaries.

1720   23 May 1865.   *Received copy of answers but cannot rewrite corrections in Mill's copy. Give it to the clerk;   will leave this one for him at Murray's.

1779   28 Jul. 1865.   *Has had no time to call.   Thank Mrs. Mills for present.   Regrets that he was not re-elected.

MILNE, Thomas.
A resident of Halifax.

0537   13 Jun. 1857.   Thanks to you and friends for token of esteem which I received yesterday. I will visit Halifax on my trip south.   Coutts & Co. will apply to Smith, Payne & Smith for the sum (£100).

0606   24 Oct. 1857.   *Requesting the Chamber of Commerce present their solution concerning the development of the resources of Africa next week, as the British Association will interview Clarendon on the subject of granting a vessel for surveying the Zambesi.

0956   28 Oct. 1859.   No word from England since we left.   Failure of the naval officer; discovery of Lake Nyassa;   33 miles of cataracts to be surmounted.   Hopes the C.M.S. will consider a mission here.   Area a major cotton field.   Met slave traders with ivory. Steamer faulty.   Have been successful with fever remedies.

MOFFAT, Emily, née Unwin(1831 — 1902).
Daughter of a successful merchant in Brighton, she married Livingstone's brother-in-law early in 1858, less than a month before the Zambezi Expedition left Birkenhead.   Her journal kept while en route to and during her years in the MaTibele country is a rare blend of pathos, wit, charm, and compassion in the face of continual physical and psychological distress.   (Wallis, **TMaM**.)

Letters to her and her husband of 2 Oct. 1858 (0839) and 14 Jan. 1861 (1065) are published in edited form in Wallis, **TMaM**.

MOFFAT, John Smith (1835 — 1918).
Fourth son of Robert Moffat, he made a contract with Livingstone to spread the gospel into the Zambezi region.   Late in 1859 he and his wife, with other missionaries, took up residence among the MaTibele, in what today is Rhodesia.   In later years (after leaving the mission at Nyati in 1865), he served in administrative posts in the Transvaal, Basutoland, Bechuanaland, and Matabeleland.   (Moffat, **JSM**.)

For letters addressed to him jointly with his wife see under Moffat, Emily.   Letters to him of 14 Jan. 1858 (0663), 14 Jan. 1858 (0664), 6 Feb. 1858 (0689), 13 Feb. 1858 (0710), 20 Feb. 1858 (0730), 2 Mar. 1858 (0744), 16 Apr. and 1 May 1858 (0780), 15 Oct. 1859 (0937), 20 Apr. and 7 May 1860 (1021), 21 Aug. 1860 (1029), 29 Nov. 1860 (1056), 24 Dec. 1861 (1159), 23 Feb. 1862 (1188), [3 Apr. 1862] (1212), 29 May 1862 (1232), 25 Nov. 1862 (1293), 12 and 17 Dec. 1863 (1406), and 24 Sep. 1864 (1490) are published in edited form in Wallis, **TMaM**;   that of 8 Jul. 1863 (1370) is published in Wallis, **ZEDL**.

0550   4 Jul. 1857.   *Replies to questions asked of DL by JSM, on Kater's compass, Arrowsmith's map, a rifle, glycerine, etc.

1491 [24 Sep. 1864]. I used all my means to promote truth and righteousness, and believe money well spent. Went to Speke's funeral: his death threw gloom over the whole meeting of the British Association. Love to Emily and the children.

1637 [20 Feb.—11 Mar. 1865?]. Tidman told me nothing. I approve your joining the L.M.S., but am nettled at being kept in the dark as I always deal above board. Evidently we did not look on our connection in the same light: although you found other means of support, you continued to draw from Rutherfoord for two years. If I am wrong in assuming that L.M.S. salary began in April last, it is because of the underhanded way in which the transference was made. Hope you advise your money agent to give back whatever, if any, is overdrawn.

MOFFAT, Mary, née Gow, then Smith (1795 — 1871).
Wife of Robert.

0387 26 Sep. 1855. Published in Schapera, **DLFL**.

MOFFAT, Mary, eldest daughter of Robert: see Livingston(e), Mary.

MOFFAT, Robert (1) (1795 — 1883).
Missionary of the L.M.S. in South Africa 1816—70, chiefly at Kuruman; he also estab-lished the MaTibele mission. He translated the Bible into SeTswana, the first complete translation into a Bantu language. He influenced Livingstone to go to Africa, and became his father-in-law in 1845. Livingstone's first son was named after him.

(**DNB**; Northcott, **RM**.)

After 1845 Livingstone addressed him both as "Father" and as "Mr. Moffat". The letters to him have suffered greatly by being cut into fragments which Moffat gave to autograph collectors (cf. his letter in RHLO, MS.Afr. s.16.1, f.280). These can be very difficult to date accurately and to relate to other fragments.

The following letters are published in Schapera, **DLFL**: 15 Feb. 1844 (0098), [1 Apr. 1845] (0117), 12 May 1845 (0121), 6 and 18 Jun. 1845 (0125), [18 Jul. 1845] (0126), 13 Aug. 1845 (0127), 5 Sep. 1845 (0130), 22 Sep. 1845 (0132), [1 Nov. 1845?] (0138), 11 Feb. 1846 (0146), 11 Mar. 1846 (0148), 1 and 31 Jul. 1846 (0152), 8 Sep. 1846 (0153), 5 Oct. 1846 (0155), 27 Oct. 1846 (0157), Jul. 1847 (0171), 29 Sep. 1847 (0177), [Nov. 1847?] (0179), [Mar?] and 23 Mar. [1848] (0182), [11 Aug. 1848] (0187), 2 Sep. 1848 (0188), Nov. 1848 (0191), 18 Jan. 1849 (0196), 31 Jan. 1849 (0198), 23 Mar. 1849 (0199), 11 Apr. 1849 (0201), [4 May?] 1849 (0203), 26 May 1849 (0205), [17 Sep.?] 1849 (0209), [Nov?] 1849 (0217), [Jan.] and 4 Feb. 1850 (0221), 4 Mar. 1850 (0226), 8, 18, 31 Jul. and 1 Aug. 1850 (0227), 24 Aug. 1850 (0231), 18 and 27 Sep. 1850 (0236), 2 and [7] Oct. 1850 (0237), 17 Oct. 1850 (0238), 27 Oct. 1850 (0239), 14 Apr. 1851 (0247), 26 Apr. 1851 (0249), 29 Sep. 1851 (0254), 29 Nov. 1851 (0261), 22 Jan. 1852 (0264), Jan. 1852 (0265), 2 Apr. 1852 (0268), 26 Apr. 1852 (0271), 28 Dec. 1852 (0308), 16 Sep. 1853 (0314), 1, 9, and 10 Nov. 1853 (0329), 19 May and 9 Aug. 1854 (0335), 12 Sep. 1855 (0382, [2 Mar. 1856??] (0398), 5 Apr. and 12 Aug. 1856 (0413), and 17 Aug. 1856 (0427).

0115   10 Mar. 1845.   *On his gratitude for innumerable acts of kindness, and on a party of Bokhatla who are going to Kuruman.

0128   [13 Aug. 1845.]   *On his welding ability.   [?end of no. 0127.]

0131   5 Sep. 1845.   [End of no. 0130.]   Thanks for securing Hume's bill and sending equipment.   Door and frames made.   Still using celestial map.

0133   [Jun.—Oct. 1845?]   Murray and Oswell about to start;   their generosity. House-building. A grass fire.   [End missing.]

0134   [Jun.—Oct. 1845??]   *On Prata in Selinka, the destruction of cattle and goods of English travellers, powder for the Bakwains, fighting with Boers, Sechele, and Mrs. Moffat.

0135   [Aug. 1843—Oct. 1845??]   *On the coffee and tea drinking of Mosielele and the progress of the disease.

0154   [Feb.—Sep. 1846??]   [Beginning missing.]   Translation of Isaiah.   Relations with Lemue and Edwards.   Use sheep left at Mahatlema's.   Mary desires tin dishes.   Apologies to Taote for failure to salute him.   [End missing.]

0172   [Jul. 1847?]   [Beginning missing.]   Sichuana words.   Health of Monuaketze.   Conversation with Flaganyane.   Lemue's silence no defence.   Ross and Helmore going to Cape. [End missing.]   [? part of 0171.]

0175   [Jul.—Aug. 1847?]   [Beginning missing.]   Life with Sechele.   Attempts of Boers to make natives sign treaties.   Will start building a temporary residence on Tuesday.   Mary and children well;   will remain here till house is ready.   Greetings.

0194   [1848?]   [Beginning missing.]   On Malakane, former chief of the Bokhatla.   Send wood. Leaves for Sechele when Ann leaves for Kuruman.   Mary strong enough for journey. Pressing on with roof.   Keeping astronomical books a little longer.

0195   [1848.]   [Beginning missing.]   Increase in his goods.   Edwards.   J.R. Bennett would be grateful for skin.

0212   [1?] Oct. 1849.   Revised latitude of Bataoana.   Oswell and Murray will give other details. Account of the Bakolia, Botletli, Bakurutse, Batoana.   The Zouga and its rise.   Lung disease.   Still 150 miles from Kolobeng.   Lake Ngami further north than was thought. Bakoba language.   12 Oct. Arrived two days ago.   Family well despite prevalence of disease.   Oswell at Lopepe.   Murray pushed on with spare oxen.

0245.6 20 Mar. 1851.   Moyle's account of Robinson's death.   Sentuke and the Griquas.   Bakwains must move because of want of water, but he will not follow them but go north. News and letters.

0391.9 [22 Jan. 1856.]   [No information.]

0794   10 May 1858.   If this goes back by 'Hermes' and catches him at Cape Town, have prayers printed in Sichuana.   Points of vocabulary.   John Moffat would be free in Makololo country but under a tyrant in Matibele.   Has written Sir George Grey about vocabularies. 25 Jun.   Mouths of Zambesi.   'Pearl' has left.

1027   10 Aug. 1860.   *On the Helmores' death and the efficacy of his remedy for fever.

1069   †28 Jan. 1861.   PS. Delay in arrival of new steamer gives leisure to write.   Send new kaross to Lady Eardley.   Trade between Senna and Mosilikatze.   Mutual fear of Makololo and Matebele: reported fight below Victoria Falls seems not to have happened.   Pity John did not go by Baldwin's spoor direct to the Falls.   What made Helmore delay?   New steamer should be good.   Mary in England.   Universities' Mission prospering.

1086   6 Mar. 1861.   Correction to fever-powder recipe.   Rovuma promises well.   Dialect similar to that of Senna.   Bishop's party looks good.

1126   26 Aug. 1861.   Universities' Mission settled in healthy highlands.   Now going to Lake Nyasa to try to find communication with the Rovuma and Makololo country.   [Part missing.]   Freeing of slaves.   Murders by Ajawa.   [End missing.]

1127   23 Sep. [1861.]   Battle with Ajawa.   High Church ideas will soon be modified, but party happily constituted. 23 Sep.   Now 115 miles up Lake Nyasa.   Storm.   Dense population.

1150   †25 Nov. 1861.   Arab dhow on Lake Nyasa.   Skeletons on shore.   No satisfactory information about Rovuma, so new steamer will be carried up to the lake.   Bishop driving away Ajawa which will arouse criticism.   Helmores highly esteemed, but Price lost his head.   Tidman and Helmore did not write him.   London Missionary Society angry at his having left them.   Expects Mary soon.   'Trial at Tette.'

1177   8 Feb. 1862.   Arrival of 'Gorgon' and meeting with Mary.   New steamer aboard 'Pioneer'.   Different treatment by Makololo.   Regrets not acknowledging letters.

1178   [8 Feb. 1862?]   Survival of one volume of journal and other goods at Linyanti.   Sending a missionary who could not get on with heathen shows little wisdom.   Helmore did get on well.   Bishop thinks life easy after conveyance and cure for fever given him.   Sends seeds.

1219   28 Apr. 1862.   Death of Mary, with details of her illness.   Delay in low-lying areas caused by 'Lady Nyasa' being sent out in pieces.

1237   17 Jun. 1862.   Sends seeds.   Much fever in the delta.   Engineer who caused delay almost died.   Mary was fitter to live than he.   Need for provisions.   Possible to pass through delta in three days.   [End missing.]

1284   25 Oct. 1862.   Published in Wallis, ZEDL II, pp. 221–224.

1308.5 6 Jan. 1863.   Read enclosed letter to Mackenzie on mission to Makololo.   Sends photograph of Mary's grave, for which a stone is ordered.   Procter's linguistic work.   Blacks from Cape have turned out badly.   Slaving and famine.   Rowley's foolish article.   Navigation on Zambesi all important.   Scottish artisans to join him.   Seeds and beasts of burden.

1351   18 May 1863.   Sick with dysentery and depressed at desolation.   Seeds.

1372   †[5–11 Jul. 1863.]   [Beginning missing.]   State of the Universities' Mission.   Mackenzie would have been a model missionary bishop if he had had a wife to look after him.   Behaviour of Makololo.   [End missing.]

1392   10 Aug. 1863.   Lack of cooperation from Lisbon made retiral inevitable.   Had 'Lady Nyasa' been placed of the lake, the ivory trade would have been intercepted, which would have made slaving unprofitable. New restrictions on entering country. Should have begun at the Rovuma. Only hope is the Universities' Mission, which is ready to flee. [End missing.]

1403   10 Dec. 1863. Waiting to get to sea and home. To keep in health and pass time went to Lake Nyasa to determine if a large river flows in at north and if Zanzibar slaves come thence. Loss of boat at cataracts and hostile tribe prevented him getting to end of lake, but seems to be no river. Fever symptoms. Missionaries died from idleness. Mackenzie a good missionary but the rest a disappointment. Tozer sits on a mountain. Tell Sekeletu only one Makololo willing to return. Criticism of Rowley. Portuguese refusal to open up country. [End missing.] 17 Dec. Report of massacre untrue.

1702   8 May 1865. Busy with preparations since book finished. Hopes to see Helen. Agnes going to Paris. Tom has seen physician. No news of Robert. Should come home and get new teeth. Declined to speak at London Missionary Society meeting. Royal Academy dinner.

1905   [3–10 Nov. 1866.] *On his travels and problems with bearers since leaving Rovuma Bay. 1 Feb. 1867. Hunger and rain. Now on watershed. Medicine lost.

1926   7 Mar. 1868. Delayed by deep rivers. Insama and his people and dialect. Disagreement with Tozer. Prince Albert's support of Portugal. [End missing?]

2020   Sep. 1872. *On his presentiment that he would not finish this journey and belief that death will not be a great change.

MOFFAT, Robert (2) (1827 – 1862).
Son of Robert (1). After attending college in Glasgow, he became a surveyor in the Orange River Sovereignty 1848–9, when he laid out Harrismith, surveyor to a copper mining company in Little Namaqualand 1854–5, and finally a trader at Kuruman.

Letters to him of 13 Aug., Sep., and 30 Sep. 1847 (0174) and 28 Apr. 1851 (0251) are published in Schapera, DLFL.

0119   28 Apr. 1845. Acknowledges letter from London. Attack by lion. Home recently completed. Watch sent home by Birt to be taken to Young. Also writing to Arundel.

MONK, William (1826? – 1884).
Curate of St. Andrew's-the-Less, Cambridge, 1855–58; Wimpole, 1859–61; Bassingbourne, 1861–62; Wixoe, 1862–64; Rector of Wymmington, 1864–84. Editor of Livingstone's Cambridge lectures.   (DNB.)

0654   1 Jan. 1858. The requirements for a missionary include: robust health, "good flow of animal spirits", mental discipline, study of physical sciences (instead of dead languages), medical education helps, plus good sense, education and temper. Thanks to the donors of the books. My visit to Cambridge one of the most pleasant episodes of my life.

0878   3 Mar. 1859. I have not forgotten the men of the Missionary Union, but have been employed differently than I expected with no time to write. I have guided our steamer over 1,600 miles. Fever here is seldom or never fatal. Went up the Shire to see the cataracts. Makololo here are anxious to go home.

1164   2 Jan. 1862.   On the O.C.D.D. mission and its disputes with slavers and the Ajawa, and the problems in the Shire valley. Destruction of village after village produced no union of the Mang'anja against the Ajawa. After leaving the missionaries 15 miles south of Mt. Zomba, we took a boat past the cataracts and explored Lake Nyassa. Forced to return by want of food. A great field for missionary endeavour: room for more than will ever come. Burrup, Dickenson and Clarke came up the river in local canoes.

MOORE, Joseph (1816 — 1897).
Missionary in Tahiti 1842–5, Pastor of Congleton Congregational Church 1848–88. One of the closest of Livingstone's student friends, whom he visited in 1858.
                                         (**LMSReg.** no. 451.)

0173   9 Aug. 1847.   Continuing friendship. Despite criticism he should not again subject his body to a tropical climate. Need for foolishness to appreciate wisdom. Best for a missionary to begin single and then marry. Better prospects at Kolobeng than for Edwards and Inglis. Mrs. Ross no loss even to her children. Translation and printing proceed at Kuruman. Has just shot a wolf.

0299   23 Nov. 1852.   Apologies for not sending curios to Moore's son. Misses his family. Moore should emigrate to Australia. His ancestral poverty continues. Oswell's kindness. Boers have killed 60 Bakwains and plundered his house; losses about £300. Bakwains killed 30 Boers; he is blamed for this unprecedented act and is in danger. Determined to open path to the sea on east or west. Natives kind in worldly matters but hate the Gospel. Caffre war being lost by England; ought to convince everyone that Caffres are men. Personal greeting. Intends to start next week.

0403   16 Mar. 1856.   First opportunity to write friends. Rough march to Tette. Central Africa a trough with healthy ridges on each side. Has survived fever well. Portuguese kind. Bad effect of Christianity on heathen. Miscarriage of letters. Ignores criticism of his motives. Curios for Moore's son.

0675   26 Jan. 1858.   *Concerning a lecture he is to give, with no newspaper reporters, please.

1052   28 Nov. 1860.   Moore should have written. Progress despite obstacles, including a fundamentalist evangelical. Delighted at prospect of Church of England mission. Criticism is a good antidote to excessive praise. Hopes to do more good free from the London Missionary Society. Had Helmore read his book carefully he need not have died. Sketch of his travels.

1242   2 Jul. 1862.   Death of Mary. Can cure fever in the lowlands but cannot get rid of it. Any Christian welcomed by him; Church Missionary Society did not reply to his invitation. No communication received from Helmore; Tidman mistaken and Fairbrother's criticism strange. Character of Universities' Mission staff. Bishop's attack on slavers likely to involve him. Good if Moore went to Madagascar. Steamer ready for Lake Nyassa. Neglect of Pioneer's engines. Macgregor Laird dead, leaving behind all he made by cheating.

1421   14 Jan. 1864.   Portuguese refuse to make the Zambesi free, and follow up his discoveries by slave hunting. Shoals in Rovuma removed all prospect of success. Universities' Mission a disappointment; the new Bishop flees. James Stewart misled by missionaries.

Unfounded charges against the Makololo. When river rises, will go to hand over Pioneer to Navy, take Lady Nyassa to Bombay for sale, then free for home. Robert in Natal, misled by Trustees, who apart from James Young are obstinate. Trip with Pioneer's steward. Circumstances in Madagascar.

1460   5 Aug. 1864. Thanks for welcome. Good wishes to Moore's son. Robert in the Federal Army and no comfort. Returning to London to write and cannot stop at Congleton.

MORRIS, J.H.

1475   30 Aug. 1864. Limited time at home compels him to decline all such invitations.

MOYSEY, Miss.
A cousin of Edmund Gabriel who resided in Plymouth.

0543   27 Jun. 1857. Thank you for the loan of Gabriel's letters, which I return, along with a daguerreotype of him which you may copy but please return to him.

0546   Jun 1857. *Of his journal.

0624   21 Nov. 1857. Would like to send a book to Gabriel; I have a box of his which crossed Africa which he may look upon as a curiosity; how can I send it to you?

MURCHISON, Lady (? — 1869).
Charlotte, née Hugonin, wife of Sir Roderick I. An evidently charming woman, remarkable for her positive influence on her husband.   (DNB.)

0587   14 Sep. 1857. Please convey the following to Sir Roderick, as I know not when he will return. At Dublin Gen. Sabine asked if I objected to the Government sending a steamer up the Zambesi. My only reservation is that the Portuguese may object. At Manchester the Chamber of Commerce asked the same thing — all without my hinting or asking. From here I go to Glasgow and Edinburgh, and on to Portugal. Mrs. L. is well: the little girl goes to the coast for her weak eyes.

1222   29 Apr. 1862. On the death of Mary L. She went home with her father in 1839 and was educated in England. We married in 1844. Further details on her missionary experiences, her teaching, her travels, etc.

MURCHISON, Sir Roderick Impey (1792 — 1871).
One of the most famous geologists of his day, best known for his description of Silurian strata. He was President of the Royal Geographical Society for a total of 20 years between 1843 and his death and held office in the British Association. He also had very considerable social influence. Livingstone first wrote to him on geographical and geological matters; in 1856 they met and became close friends. He was to a considerable extent responsible for the Zambezi expedition and for the attempt to settle the question of the sources of the Nile. He became ill in Nov. 1870 and died 22 Oct. 1871;

Livingstone did not learn of this till Jul. 1872. Livingstone dedicated **MT** to him and gave his name to the Murchison Falls on the Shire. **(DNB.)**

0337   20 Aug. 1854.   Encloses sketch of route from Sekeletu's to Loanda. The rivers; reason for their frequency and depth.

0355   24 Dec. 1854.   Steele having gone to war, will now send geographical reports to Murchison. Sekeletu's assistance. Very detailed account of journey to Loanda. Trade in Angola. Naval officers should enquire about him in Mozambique at end of 1855. Courtesy of Portuguese.

0358   31 Dec. 1854. Sends copy [i.e. letter 0355] of letter lost in 'Forerunner'. Will send map from Cassenge. Believing map to be in Murchison's hands, has been rather free with positions. Gives position of various places, with comments.

0366   13 Feb. 1855.   General account of Angola, its crops, people, trade. Sends map.

0372   17 May 1855.   Sends corrections to map. Rivers all ooze out of bogs. Casai obstructed by cataracts.

0377   [Aug. 1855.]   [Beginning missing.]   Altitudes in Angola. Form of the southern part of Africa; ridges, plains, and rivers. Arab reports of Lake Tanganyika. Basically two north-south ridges with hollow between. Geological explanation. Desiccation of west-flowing rivers. Fossil site. Trading by Makololo. Trade in ivory may supplant that in slaves. [End missing.]

0390   16 Oct. 1855.   Portuguese routes to Matiamvo. Has been able to record rivers with precision. Rates of travel. Lack of goods prevented visit to Matiamvo, who will not allow passage on the Zambesi. Disagreement with Kawawa. Lotembwa flows in opposite directions. Commerce and Christianity both needed in Africa. Excuse poor paper; papyrus plant plentiful and might be used. 3 Mar. 1856. Reached Tette. This letter goes at once, others will follow.

0392   25 Jan. 1856.   Kindness of Sekeletu. Decision to avoid rapids. Detailed description of Victoria Falls. Creation of garden. Zambesi formerly a lake. Geology. Freedom from fever: better travelling conditions and diet. Ridges healthy. Denuded hills to east of ridge. List of boiling points of water at various places.

0402   4 Mar. 1856.   Influence of altitude on character, exemplified by hill tribes he has just passed through and the Bechuana. Misuse of term 'Caffre'. But race also important: Bushmen compared with Bakalahari, Bakoba with Sekote. Basic identity of southern African tribes. Bushmen's dialect. Character of Sichuana. New antelopes. Numerous animals. Generosity of people. Africans not susceptible to some European diseases. Has party of 110, with ivory to purchase goods for Sekeletu. There is apparently water carriage to the Falls. Portuguese and Arab attempts to cross the continent. End of geographical feat is beginning of missionary enterprise.

0414   23 May 1856.   Climate induces exhaustion after short marches. Account of the lower Zambesi. Missed seeing Kebrabasa rapids. Use of steamer would be possible. Delta at Quilimane gives no idea of the river; its position foolish and unhealthy; better harbours available. Coal, iron, gold. Agriculture. Native medicines. Gum plants, trees. Prospects for trade. Present low state of country due to slave trade and war. Bad reputation of Europeans among natives can be overcome by just dealing. So-called empires not too powerful. Lupata. Jesuits at Gorongozo. 26 Aug. Taken to Mauritius by 'Frolic'. Medicine and letters at Quilimane restored him. Companions wait at Tette. Wished to take headman to England, but excitement was too much for his brain and he drowned himself. Similar occurrence above Tette.

0423 5 Aug. 1856. Published in Wallis, **ZEDL** I, pp.xviii—xxi.

0440 12 Dec. 1856. Has a collection of African rocks. Geology of Africa from Victoria Falls to the sea.

0446 22 Dec. 1856. Leaves for Scotland tomorrow. Some London Missionary Society directors grumbled at spending money on his family and made Mary feel uncomfortable. Willing to consider roving commission. Difficulty of getting agents makes it best for trade to be started on a small scale and expanded if successful.

0450 6 Jan. 1857. L.'s cold makes him cancel his appointment to see M.; rock and coal specimens have arrived but L. has not seen them.

0458 23 Jan. 1857. Maclear says we may expect calculations in 2 to 3 weeks; L. will write statement for Clarendon tomorrow; first chapter of L.'s book is too frivolous and must be rewritten; de Lavradio asks two questions concerning the navigation of the Zambesi by steamer.

0460 26 Jan. 1857. L.'s hopes, plans and dreams for the future of Africa and his role in it. This is the statement referred to in the letter of 23 Jan.

0483 25 Mar. [1857]. L. cannot dine with M. as hoped; to Duke of Argyll's on Thursday; flax worth £50 to £60 per ton.

0490 [Feb.—Mar. 1857]. Concerning L.'s progress in his book; if the introduction is not good, L. will write another one.

0491 [Feb.—Mar. 1857]. L. has written a new beginning as M. suggested, and is now "on the way to Lake Ngami."

0501 15 Apr. 1857. Better to delay L.'s application for a governmental appointment until nearer his departure, or the Mission House will use it to damage L.'s character. Plan of M. and Clarendon to make L. Consul to the Makololo and other Central African tribes is admirable.

0594 27 Sep. 1857. On L.'s travels in the north of Britain, where he is "dead tired" with public spouting.

0600 6 Oct. 1857. More on L.'s current travels; he plans to meet with the Chambers of Commerce in Leeds, Halifax, Liverpool, and Birmingham to draw their attention to the resources of Africa.

0715 15 Feb. 1858. Concerning Cooley's letter to the "Athenaeum", and L.'s desire to have Baines' salary increased.

0732 22 Feb. 1858. Further comments on Cooley's letter.

0774 30 Mar. 1858. 5 days in Sierra Leone coaling; accomodation and prices; Mrs. L. to be left at the Cape of Good Hope; marine insurance will not permit a stop in St. Paul de Loanda.

0867   15 Feb. 1859.   The Kebrabasa Rapids;   first exploration of the Shire River;   ideas for a colony in Africa;   Thornton's laziness.

0886   9 May 1859.   First exploration of Shire highlands and Lake Shirwa;   including a small map of Shirwa, the Shire, and the lower end of Lake Nyassa.

0915   22, 30 Jul. 1859.   Thornton dismissed, and Baines may have to be dismissed also; derogatory comments about Macgregor Laird.

0929   8 Aug. 1859.   Further comments on Laird, Thornton and Baines;   his ideas for an English colony;   news of a German group en route to Mozambique to join Portuguese.

0932   10 Oct. 1859.   On the reaching of Lake Nyassa, the land between the Shire and Lake Shirwa (the Shire highlands) and trading opportunities in the valley.

0969   6 Nov. 1859.   Ideas for English colony;   L. greatly prefers the exploratory function of the expedition to the scientific functions.

0979   10 Dec. 1859.   Further comments on Thornton and Baines;   repairs carried out on the "Ma-Robert."

0991   7 Feb. 1860.   On the dismissal of Thornton and the possiblity of his reinstatement; Rae goes home to supervise the building of another craft.

1003   10 Mar. 1860. Waiting for a ship to take Rae home;   further repairs on the "Ma-Robert," and comments on the fever.

1036   10 Sep. 1860.   On the trip up the Zambesi to Sesheke;   L.'s revised opinion of the Victoria Falls;   and the fate of the Linyanti Mission.

1047   26 Nov. 1860.   Detailed statistical description of the Victoria Falls, and the locations of coal seams between Sesheke and Tette.

1072   1 Feb. 1861.   More on the Victoria Falls, and on papers L. and C. Livingstone enclose for M.

1080   20 Feb. 1861.   Derogatory comments about Macqueen;   on meeting Silva Porto at Linyanti and Naliele in 1853.

1101   9 Apr. 1861.   *Fall of water on Rovuma has prevented full exploration. Returning to Shire to make road past cataracts, to settle Universities' Mission, and to decide if Rovuma comes out of Lake Nyasa, which seems unlikely.

1113   20 Apr. 1861.   The Rovuma visit and a comparison of its waters with those of the Shire.

1128   23 Sep., 26 Oct., 11, 25 Nov. 1861.   On Lake Nyassa and its people;   the skirmish with the Ajawa;   L. learns of Mackenzie's two skirmishes with the Ajawa;   a representative of the Free Church of Scotland (J. Stewart) is coming out to confer with L. on the prospects of a mission.

1197   15 Mar. 1862.   Deaths of Mackenzie and Burrup;   anticipation that blame will be laid at L.'s door.

1223   29 Apr. 1862. Death of Mary Livingstone.

1243   7 Jul. 1862.   Kirk's conversation about the legality of slavery within Portuguese dominions, held with A.T. de Almeida, Governor of Tette.

1251   25 Jul. 1862.   L.'s opinion of Thornton, whom he treated as a son for M.'s sake; possibility of Thornton's return to the expedition in some capacity.

1266   2 Sep. 1862.   On the relationship between the Portuguese and the Zambesi Expedition; L.'s thoughts on the future success of the UMCA.

1275   10 Oct. 1862.   Description of L.'s second exploration of the Rovuma River.

1295   14 Dec. 1862.   Scotch artisans from the Cape Colony propose to make a settlement in Central Africa; Expedition returns to the Shire Valley; cost, etc. of the "Lady Nyassa"; L. deserves a higher salary.

1337   25 Apr. 1863.   Death of Thornton; Kirk and C. Livingstone to go home; Portuguese responsible for the depopulation of the Shire Valley; L. will probably sail the "Lady Nyassa" to India.

1399   4 Dec. 1863, 10 Feb. 1864.   Description of L.'s recent exploration of the country west of the Shire River and southwest of Lake Nyassa.

1431   Feb. 1864.   Slaves freed by L. and the mission will be taken to Cape Town; derogatory words about Tozer.

1446   18 Jun., 17 Jul. 1864.   Description of L.'s trip across the Arabian Sea from Zanzibar to Bombay, in the "Lady Nyassa."

1455   2 Aug. 1864.   Meeting with family. Agnes has received letter from Robert, who says he was drugged and found himself in the Federal Army.

1464   8 Aug. 1864.   Plans to visit Duke of Argyll, Mull, James Young. Has advised Robert to turn over new leaf.

1468   16 Aug. 1864.   Prof. Syme and Kirk recommend surgery for haemorrhoids. Off to Argyll tomorrow. Saw Playfair at Lochearnhead. Decline to join Lyons McLeod's project; he wants Livingstone's name.

1472   27 Aug. 1864.   Does not wish operation to be in newspapers. Delightful trip to Highlands; grandfather's farm on Ulva; crop failure in 1848 reduced population from 600 to 100.

1482   5 Sep. 1864.   Pressure from Webb to stay at Newstead. Charming visit to Inverary.

1505   9 Oct. 1864.   Thanks for getting consulship for Charles. Working on book, using Charles's journal. Murray thinks Charles's name on title page will help American sales; 30000 of **MT** sold there. Government gives £1200 for Kirk's publication on botany and natural history.

1516   23 Oct. 1864.   Has Palmerston thought of buying out Portuguese in East Africa; would be cheaper than keeping six warships there. Robert in hospital at Peterburg.

1530   12 Nov. 1864.   Webb's, Kirk's and Thomas's hunting successes.

1532   15 Nov. 1864.   Inaccuracies in Baines's book; people abused in it.

1533   17 Nov. 1864.   Recommends Meller as Inspector.   Kirk will find a position and devote spare time to natural history of the expedition.   Webb says if Livingstone asks nothing from Russell he will receive nothing; has not thought of anything to ask.

1534   18 Nov. 1864.   Encloses letter from American Geographical Society.   Where can he get Murchison's views on age of Africa.   Thornton received salary from paymaster of the navy.   He paid debt of £47 left by him, which does not look like being repaid.

1546   28 Nov. 1864.   Path north of Portuguese needed.   Can consular salary continue?   Book far from completed.   Palmerston and Russell need time to consider proposals.

1570   6 Jan. 1865.   Never intended settling in England.   Likes proposed expedition.   Must also talk to people about slave trade and Christianity.   Expects to sell 'Lady Nyasa' for half cost price; will use this and £800 from Cape people on expedition.

1577   16 Jan. 1865.   If possible will take 'Lady Nyasa' up the Rovuma.   Other possibilities are naval ship to Zanzibar or via Mauritius and Johanna.

1606   11 Feb. 1865.   Recommends Kirk for opening in Mozambique.

1633   5 Mar. 1865.   Will be in London on Friday or Saturday.   Stopping of Government salary.

1652   25 Mar. 1865.   Sections of the book.   Webb's health.

1666   4 Apr. 1865.   Carthaginian elephants.   Meller's commission; Kirk's superior merits.

1687   25 Apr. 1865.   Planned movements.   Webb's artist; better than originals.

1692   1 May 1865.   Possibility of free passage on P & O ship to Bombay.

1744   15 Jun. 1865.   Arrived in Oxford yesterday.   Goes on to Cambridge.

1747   19 Jun. 1865.   Has to go to Scotland because of mother's death.   Will return soon to London and then to Africa.

1752   21 Jun. 1865.   Funeral on Friday.   Preparations.   Will not again take untried companions.   Kirk would be invaluable but has no salary.   [End missing?]

1760   30 Jun. 1865.   Detained longer than expected.   Portuguese effusion easily answered. Rowley also blames mission troubles on Portuguese.   Perhaps answer in an appendix.

1770   21 Jul. 1865.   He wishes a salary, but Clarendon talks to Russell about a pension.   The Webbs' child.   Webb's coal.

1791   7 Aug. 1865.   Detailed vindication of his conduct vis-à-vis Baines.

1792   [7 Aug. 1865.]   [Beginning missing.]   Preparations for going to Bombay.   Russell's resentment means no salary.   On return may give services to the Viceroy of Egypt.

1809   19 Aug. 1865.   Bedingfeld's airs because of his higher salary.   Meeting with French geographer. Agnes in Paris.

1824   28 Sep. 1865.   Preparations for Africa.   Animals to be taken.

1830   26 Oct. 1865.   Preparations go well.   Lecture.   Commercial support from merchants. Governor is a great friend.

1842   27 Nov. 1865.   Rejects Murchison's advice to go direct to Lake Tanganyika.   Contribution of £645 in Bombay.   Selling 'Lady Nyasa' for £2300 against cost price of £6000.

1858   28 Dec. 1865.   Starts on 1 Jan.   Death of Lord Edward Seymour.

1873   29 Jan. 1866.   Death of Von der Decken;   brought it on himself.   Does not see why he should be subjected to degradation of having rejected claims which most people would endorse.

1894   18 [May] 1866.   Only time to write Agnes and him.   The Makonde quite civil this time. Mutumora or Ndonde is a very good fellow.

1916   2 Feb. 1867.   Flight of Johanna men.   Chief Mataka.   People near Lake Nyasa.   Hunger. Probably on watershed between Chambeze and Loapula.   Loss of medicines.   No news from coast.   Took rifles and ammunition from 'Wasp'.

1924   10 Dec. 1867.   Lobemba to Cazembe.   The marriage of a woman who fled.   Meller received £800 from scientific work in Madagascar, more than he gets now.   Criticism of Galton and Arrowsmith.   Back's paper on hydrography, sent with requests for rainfall figures.

1930   8 Jul. 1868.   Letter to Clarendon will explain his doings.   Sources of Nile are between 10° and 12° S.   Twenty-three sources converge into three lines of drainage, which have still to be followed.   Severe criticism of Galton and Royal Geographical Society council. Baines confessed and was allowed to stay, then forged storebook.   Glad Murchison prevented his being operated on by Syme.   Does not know if Kirk is in Zanzibar.   Hopes to be at Ujiji in two months, where he has goods and letters.   P.S.   Summary of sources.

1946   Apr.—Jul. 1870.   Ivory and slave trading among the Manyuema.   Difficult travel in rains. The forest.   Finally went into winter quarters.   Conviction that Ptolemy correct about Nile sources.   The watershed.   Ptolemy's Mountains of the Moon.

2005   13 Mar. 1872.   Concern at Murchison's illness.   Letters received.   Want of goods; Banians and governor of Unyanyembe responsible;   Kirk's failure and Webb's success in sending supplies.   Tanganyika of no importance to Nile;   interesting valley is to the west, with five lakes and three rivers;   correlation of these is his prize.   Watershed slopes gradually to the north.   Lady Murchison's death.   Hopes of ending slave trade.   P.S. Attentions to Stanley will gratify.   Agnes to keep box and journal.

MURRAY, Andrew (1794 — 1866).
A native of Aberdeenshire, he was one of many Scots who served the Dutch Reformed Church in South Africa, being minister at Graaf-Reinet 1822—66.   Livingstone passed through that town in 1841 on his way to Kuruman.   (DSAfrB, i.573).

0169   10 Jun. 1847.   Acknowledges letter.   Encourages Murray's son to be a missionary, but not in Cape Colony.   Other family news, including Charles Livingstone's studies.   Recent journey through fine country north of Mogale's Berg, but tribes live in hopeless ignorance.   Metal craft of the Bagalaka.   Dutch emigrants in that area live in ignorance and are very hostile to missionaries: can Murray help by sending tracts and writing them? Emigrants' attack on the Bagalaka, and their false belief that he is a Government spy. Progress of Bakwains. Chief learning to read and desirous of civilisation. Various trades to which a missionary must apply himself. Personal greetings. P.S. Boers' reluctance to go to Delagoa Bay explicable by danger of fever.

MURRAY, John (1808 — 1892).
Son of the founder of John Murray, Publisher, and third of that name, Murray was Livingstone's publisher and adviser. (DNB.)

0465   4 Feb. 1857. Routledge called with the pamphlet but I refused to look at it. He mentioned giving something handsome to the Testimonial Fund, but I replied "Satisfy Mr. Murray and you satisfy me." Drawing by Ryder of L. Ngami very good.

0474   5 Mar. [1857]. An antelope should be added to one of the pictures. Mrs. L. reacted routinely at Lake Ngami. Send for Harris and Smith tomorrow.

0479   22 Mar. [1857]. Enclosed you will find an example of Routledgism on a grand scale. J.P. Jewett of Boston wants this book: ten per cent in the retail price of all sold. Dr. Smith's book splendidly bound; an excellent present. Wish I had had it when in Africa.

0482   24 Mar. [1857]. Thank you for money and invitation; fear I cannot come to dinner due to another engagement. I send sections XVIII—XXIII.

0484   25 Mar. [1857??]. Requesting two woodcuts, one of oxen with twisted horns, brought to Egypt by Africans. Supposing that a request he received may be complied with without detriment to any future translation.

0488   27 Mar. [1857]. Trying to dictate my journal failed, as I cannot do it without seeing the first part of the sentence before me. Have paid Mr. Logadon (?) 7/6.

0489   30 Mar. 1857. Adams dedicates his book to the L.M.S.; Murchison thinks we should run an ad in the Times disowning it. We must change the picture of the tree with the falls.

0495   6 Apr. [1857]. Observations on the method of passing sections of the book on to others for inspection, correcting of spelling, etc. Have shortened section on the Caffre War. Duchess of Sutherland has a likeness of a bushwoman with a bundle of ostrich egg shells: we may use it if we wish.

0496   7 Apr. 1857. Do you know a respectable house agent? We must get away from the calls; people we live with do not behave well although we pay them highly.

0498   10 Apr. [1857]. I send £30 to Charles in Mattapoisett, the first use I have made of the fund we talked about. He has lost his health and wishes to go out to Africa. His church pays him only $800 per annum; another church owes him a portion of his salary from former years.

0510   28 Apr. 1857. Let Vardon have a peep at the Falls. Let him see any of the animals you have — he is a good judge.

0512   29 Apr. 1857.   My brother will be in London tomorrow evening.   Mr Binney has made many corrections, advising a few changes to convince religious people who otherwise would think the book merely an intellectual affair, and that I was not a religious missionary.   He has also smoothed sentences which would have irritated MacLehose of Glasgow.   I am to get a view of Loanda and a baobab from Capt. Need.

0515   8 May 1857.   Concerning the legal position of H.G. Adams;   L. was never asked permission to have his letters published by "Banner," Snow or L.M.S.   Mr. Prout sent my letters to the Banner.   It is mortifying to come from Africa to be so handled.

0522   [4, 11, or 18 May 1857].   I send sections XXXIII–XXXV, and more as soon as my brother has read them.   Mr. Binney is still ill.   Details of L.'s appointment schedule.

0524   22 May [1857].   Mr. Cowles' plate of lion encounter is abominable;   please suppress it. Everyone who knows what a lion is will die laughing.   Can the fellows be provided with loin cloths — all wear them but the Batoka.   This is worse than talking about urine.   A view of a marimba from the side is drawn herein.

0529   26 May 1857.   Will Kane's style be any help to me?   I also need Roget's Thesaurus and Maunder's Treasury of Words.   Here it is quiet and I shall get on well.   Your reviser suggests things to your mind and to that of my brother which I do not intend.   I am anxious about saying what I mean in my way.

0531   30 May [1857].   I forgot about Lady Eastlake's invitation, due to flitting.   I think I can promise 3 or 4 pieces of new matter weekly.   Engagement with Baptist Noel on Thursday next will be the last.   Will you lend me Maunder's Treasures of Natural History? I left mine in Africa.   3 pieces will go to the printer next Monday.

0532   30 May 1857.   Sorry you think the reviser is in any way qualified.   (A list of his errors follows;   L. berates this person characteristically).

0533   31 May 1857.   More criticism (negative) of the copy reader: Elwin, Owen, Murchison and Binney liked what L. wrote.   L. rejects in toto every change made in red ink.   Read Kane's book today.   Maybe I can get someone with a sympathy for African travel; Galton or Dr. Archer perhaps.   Further words of determination against the reviewer.

0535   3 Jun. 1857.   Dr. Norton Shaw will be better than Mr. Galton in looking over sheets.   I need drawings of fashion of dressing hair in Loanda.   Will send 2 pieces of the MS tomorrow.

0540   17 Jun. [1857].   Concerning drawings to be used in the book.   Next door neighbors recopying the manuscript.   Andrew Buchanan of Glasgow might like a hand at revision. Dr. Daubeny says they propose a D.C.L. for me at Oxford — that will look good on the title page.   The close resemblance of faces of Egyptian mummy cases and Sekeletu's mother is very striking.   Adams sends 3 copies of his letter — they threatened the editor of the Record with the law for what he said about it.

0542   20 Jun. 1857.   Ask Sir G. Wilkenson about the crooked stick or leg which is commonplace throughout central Africa as an object of worship.   Natives speak of their god having one leg or a crooked one.   I have the impression that Thoth was supposed to be lame.

0544   27 Jun. 1857.   Called on an old Mauritius family in Oxford Square, and met a first cousin of yours at New College.   I shall bring Kane the first time I come.   Arrowsmith always delays.

0551   6 Jul. 1857.   Concerning the wayward £30 note he sent to his brother in April.   Manuscript coming tomorrow to 1 Robert Street, Adelphi.   I bring Mrs. L. to Sir Harry Holland.   I shall bring Kane.

0557   11 Jul. 1857.   Working on proofs which I shall send soon.   Arrowsmith is famed for being late and blaming everybody but himself for it.   I enclose a musical instrument.

0558   14 Jul. 1857.   Can you give copy to Mr. Taylor?   Give him the medal too.   A lady here who draws well — she did the headdresses — will aid in illustrations.   I sent "Kane" with 3 pieces of manuscript yesterday.

0561   [1 Mar. — 30 Jul. 1857].   I enclose in one of these a drawing of a marimba.   I am going to see Windsor today.   3 more will finish manuscript;   1 is nearly finished.

0562   [1 Mar. — 30 Jul. 1857].   The corrections are proper;   I leave out the part concerning urine.   I know nothing which gives so good an idea of the lack of water than the bushmen softening their skins in the manner described.   I will carefully examine parts marked "meaning obscure".

0564   4 Aug. 1857.   Wants to dedicate it to Murchison, but as Maclear also helped greatly, is there a precedent for dual dedication?   Gray will get Ford to do tsetse.   Visited Sir H. Holland.

0572   24 Aug. 1857.   Admiral Smyth's son-in-law undertakes editorship of my appendix on observations calculated by Maclear.   Go to Dublin on Thursday.   Mr. Rae of Common Wealth Newspaper wants an early copy for review.   If you send one to the editor in Edinburgh pray correct an error on p. 96.   Capt. Need and Dr. Smith give drawings.

0574   [24 May — 27 Aug. 1857].   Can artist put rings on legs of Shinte up to the knees — gait of gentlemen of Balonda is regulated by real or supposed weight of them.   Sketch of the mirimba is mine;   I detain it for a lady friend who draws well now in childbed.   Mr. Grimstone wishes the drawing of L. Ngami.

0595   27 Sep. 1857.   Send the dedication to the printer — add his titles as they appear in Murchison's last address before R.G.S.   I would like him to see the proof.   Am now with your namesake Murray of Lintrose.

0601.7 [12–13 Oct. 1857].   A vitriolic denunciation of H.G. Adams and his colleagues, whom D.L. calls "ticket of leave" men, and whom he compares unfavourably with Africans.

0602   13 Oct. 1857.   I enclose Preface, plus a word on the Pirates.   If you wish soften it though they do not deserve it.   Edward Baines of Leeds Mercury wants a copy for early review.   Braithwaite wants a number of copies.   One to Captain Need.   I meet Chamber of Commerce here today and Birmingham tomorrow, and will return to London on Sat. or Mon. next.

0620   12 Nov. 1857.   Have received two notes each £1050 to be paid eight and ten months from this date, with thanks.   Dinner this evening with Captain Washington.   Friends call out against portrait by Philips: Vardon says it will do for any one between Captain Cook and Guy Fawkes!

0621   18 Nov. 1857.   Meeting here came off well yesterday — men attentive and attendance good.   I finish public spouting at Bradford on Sat. or Mon.   The copy I sent to Mr. Crawfurd has mollified him.   Went to Mayall & Pollybanks on Tues — if you need a new plate that may do it.

0643   17 Dec. 1857.   *Concerning Ballantyne, editor of the New Statesman.

0651   25 Dec. 1857.   A man in Manchester could only find my book by offering 2/6 to any boy who would find it.   New ones have not yet reached Glasgow.

0692   8 Feb. 1858.   Can you print the Analysis for private circulation?   Am going up to Wandsworth.   Do you have my observations book?

0708   12 Feb. 1858.   I have lighted on the Analysis — get someone to check for errors in English and I will do the same to native words before we sail.   One observation book has not turned up yet.   If you have it, send it to Maclear.

0719   16 Feb. 1858.   On an abridgement of Missionary Travels: I have fullest confidence in Mr. Elwin's sympathy and ability to do so, and the two of you can do as you please at your convenience.

0753   6 Mar. 1858.   We sail on Monday next, forenoon.   Forward letters via Lenox Conyngham of the Foreign Office.   Am very much knocked up and will be glad to get away. Shall write Mr. Elwin soon about the ants.   Have not yet seen the Analysis complete.

0843   5 Oct. 1858.   Two Dutch clergymen spread a story that a black pot was a cannon, with the result that I was denied gunpowder at the Cape.   Now they attack a footnote in which I mention their methods of getting land for their Church.   One, a Scotchman (Dr. Robertson) has written me.   Coal here is like the Welsh: burned 1½ T in coming down from Tette.

0960   1 Nov. 1859.   No word from England yet.   Have gone up river to Lake Nyassa, 250 miles on foot.   Faults of the Ma-Robert.   Description of Shire highlands and upper Shire valley. I send a photograph on bad paper which shows the similarity between ancient Egyptian and modern African pestles and mortars.

1456   2 Aug. 1864.   When renting a cottage remember my daughter will be housekeeper and needs a music master nearby, and my son has lost his health.   Scotch friends think I should tell of mission split and slave trade: difficult without giving offence.   Meller's brother is a house agent and may help.

1492   24 Sep. 1864.   Detained to visit Lord Taunton.   Then will go to Newstead to begin in earnest.   Charles's journal is at hand.

1497   30 Sep. 1864.   Lip-ring drawings might be done by Capt. Henry Need who lent us a portfolio of drawings done on the West coast.   Have written to Foreign Office for blue books.

1508   12 Oct. 1864.   Charles's visit to Boston.   Webb is copying and Need sketching.

1514   21 Oct. 1864.   Chapman may have published information from my journal stolen at Linyanti and taken to Mosilikatze's country.   Kirk will not agree to Hooker's proposition to write up the flora and zoa of the expedition;   Government will give £1200.

1520   30 Oct. 1864.   Dr. Waghorn implies that when he was with Tozer he was "in connection with Dr. L.'s expedition."   Should this be denied?   All from Bishop down like to say so.

1525   5 Nov. 1864.   Baines's paintings were paid for and are public property;   they go back to the Foreign Office when I am done with them.   Need is a confirmed invalid;   he has composed two which will do.

1528   7 Nov. 1864.   Mrs. Goodlake takes up two notebooks of astronomical observations to Arrowsmith.   Agrees with Archbishop Whately that iron-making by savages indicates divine aid.

1539   23 Nov. 1864.   Has two spirited sketches from Capt. Need.

1545   27 Nov. 1864.   Sends drawings of lip-ring women.   Need admits his figures are ugly, artist need not make them hideous.   Baines's drawing of Mazoro.

1548   30 Nov. 1864.   Kirk will call with photograph of Shupanga.

1558   15 Dec. 1864.   Mr. and Mrs. Charles Livingstone will call to discuss American profits from book.   Harpers seem to think they have a right.   American lawyer's advice.

1567   3 Jan. 1865.   Sends pages by Waller and picture of man weaving and smoking.   Brother and his wife have sailed for different parts;   she has a paper which makes the matter explicit.

1578   17 Jan. 1865.   Sends more pages.

1580   20 Jan. 1865.   Sends more pages.   Now revising journeys to Lake Nyassa and Bombay. Was informed by Mr. Young of £144-17-0.   Baobab should be more like photograph.

1583   24 Jan. 1865.   *On proofs and wood blocks.

1588   26 Jan. 1865.   Woodcuts for the book.

1608   13 Feb. 1865.   Waller draws method of putting poison on arrows.   An alkaloid like strichnine which Kirk took by accident, lowering his pulse and curing a cold.   Charles's birds and insects being prepared in the British Museum;   he is safe as far as Sierra Leone.

1615   18 Feb. 1865.   Illustrations for the book.

1616   20 Feb. 1865.   Give Waller introduction to the artist.   Waller's paper for Macmillan. Send first 40 or 80 pages to Mrs. Livingstone.

1619   24 Feb. 1865.   Encloses letter from Mrs. Livingstone.   Paper by a Mr. Stewart in **Good Words.**

1625   [Oct. 1864 — Feb. 1865.]   Portuguese response to Bath speech.   Difference between their claims and their control of Mozambique.

1630   3 Mar. 1865.   The book.   Baines's inability to draw human figures.

1631   4 Mar. 1865.   The book.   Murray's reader.   Perhaps attacks on Portuguese too savage.

1640   18 Mar. 1865.   Revises and slips.   Insert complimentary reference to Skead.   Can I borrow part of Denman [sic] and Clapperton on Mahometan proselytism?

1645   21 Mar. 1865.   Sends pages.   First revise goes to Clowes.

1647   23 Mar. 1865.   Books by Moffat and others.   Received Denman today.   Sends corrected pages.   Letter received tells of breakup of Makololo.

1653   25 Mar. 1865.   Sends appendix so that what is Archbishop's and what is his may be distinguished.   Owen to see about elephants.   Small alterations.

1657   31 Mar. 1865.   Mission should be a separate chapter.   Wishes to commend Mackenzie, but what to say about Tozer?   The frontispiece.   Will thank Layard for getting paintings from Royal Geographical Society.   Webbs are in London.

1661   1 Apr. 1865.   Revises and illustrations.   Denman and Clapperton returned.

1727   31 May 1865.   Oswell will attend to preface.   Agnes's finances.   Prof. Buchanan lost his only son.

1730   1 Jun. 1865.   Send sentence by Oswell for dedication.   Murchison revealed that Young gave the £1000.   Wrote to Mrs. C. Livingstone that publication was stopped till November.

1735   3 Jun. 1865.   Complimentary copies.

1741   9 Jun. 1865.   Cost of tuition in France.   Will call on Dr. Daubeny.   Remove dedication to Murchison even though he liked it.   Requires Rovuma notebook lent for woodcut. Has Bartle Frere resigned?

1746   17 Jun. 1865.   Sends last corrected sheet.   Gave a lecture at Daubeny's.

1748   19 Jun. 1865.   Mother dead.   Will return soon.   Forward letters.

1761   30 Jun. 1865.   Murchison thinks I should reply to Portuguese letters translated in the **Standard**.   May we add a leaf in the appendix for this?

1801   13 Aug. 1865.   Payments to be made for Agnes.   On any matter Murray's and Oswell's opinion will suffice;   Young's is always valuable.

1825   28 Sep. 1865.   Give copies of book to Lady Frere, Mr. Maine, and Rev. Dr. Wilson of Bombay.   Has eight Africans from a school and some marines.   Taking buffaloes to experiment with tsetse.   Gave two lectures.

NAISMITH, John.
Tanner in Hamilton, and deacon of the Independent Church there.

0038   2 Dec. 1841.   Have just returned from a 700 mile trip into the interior;   state of people is wretched in the extreme;   some had seen only one white man before;   description of his reception;   importance of churches at home aiding these people;   tribes inland are free from European contamination;   people at home should collect money to support a native teacher;   I will do anything to cooperate;   write c/o Philip in Cape Town.

NAPIER, James (1820 — 1884).
Fellow-student in Glasgow of Livingstone and James Young.   He remained associated with the latter's industrial activities, and wrote widely on scientific and antiquarian matters.   (**DNB.**)

1648   23 Mar. 1865. Wishes a drawing of a woman grinding corn on a stone, and includes a sketch to show what is required. [Cf. title-page of David and Charles Livingstone, **NEZT**.]

NAPIER, Robert (1791 – 1876).
A distinguished marine engineer and shipbuilder in Glasgow, from 1853 in partnership with his sons James R. and John.   (DNB.)

0640   15 Dec. 1857. Asks for estimate for steam launch as specified to be built by middle of January. Napier's interest in Christian civilisation his excuse for asking him.

1756   24 Jun. 1865. Cannot attend launch but hopes to be on trial trip of new ironclad. His mother's death.

NOEL, Mrs.

1465   8 Aug. [1864]. Declines offer of hospitality; anxious to get back to open up country north of the Portuguese slavers. Will do a little work, be near his daughter as much as possible, and avoid public engagements except Bath.

NUÑES, Gualdino José.
Military Commandant of Quilimane, Colonel Nuñes occasionally handled Livingstone's financial transactions. Until May 1857, he was Acting Governor of the district. He was the uncle of J.M. Nuñes.

1286   12 Nov. 1862. *We came into this river today to cut wood. Too bad José went to Senna to get married on a day we must cut wood. Hope you are in good health.

1324   21 Feb. 1863. *Lower Shire valley depopulated by Tette people, famine, and Marianno. We cannot buy food, and are 30 miles below Chibisa's waiting for the water to rise. We must go again in the "Pioneer" for provisions, so I may see you again.

NUÑES, José Militão.
Appointed British Vice-Consul by Livingstone, Nuñes served in this capacity at Quilimane from early 1858 to early 1864. From this position he handled many of the Zambezi Expedition's financial dealings, especially those between Livingstone and the Portuguese in Quilimane and Moçambique. Most of Livingstone's letters to Nuñes referred to in this catalogue are copies (see note 0428).

0428   20 Aug. 1856. Reached "Frolic" safely, then went to St. Augustine's Bay, where they remained a week watering, trading and hunting. Sekwebu's death. Remains in Mauritius until the arrival of the Commodore.

0437   1 Nov. 1856. Left Mauritius on 22nd and am now close to Ceylon. Intend to spend a week in Lisbon; sorry I do not have the address of your family in Lisbon as I would call upon them. An expedition is sent from Zanzibar to visit the lake visited by Sr. Candido.

0469   14 Feb. 1857.   Busy writing book, but intend to return for my men in June.   Request your uncle keep them there until I return;   tell them I need them to carry goods to Sekeletu.   Your uncle's watch is in the hands of Dent the Watchmaker.   I have ordered the watch pins for Sr. Candido.   Failure of ship's engine near Tunis prevented his visiting Lisbon.

0809   10 Jul. 1858.   Send the goods I left with you for sale to Wm. Thompson at the Cape, at my expense.   Out of my own money I purchased things for Sekeletu (a double-barreled rifle, etc.), for the ivory.   Send me the money or a full account and I will give him full explanation.

0818   17 Aug. 1858.   Thank you and Mr. Hines for the offer, but I expect the ship has sailed. I increased Bedingfeld's pay from £150 to £600.   I send you a harmonica as you are musical.

0849   13 Oct. 1858.   We shall probably go up Shire, then from Senna to Gorongozo.   Will remain some months in Tete to examine the adjacent country.   If he has Portuguese authorization, he would be willing to attempt to convince the rebels at Morambala to lay down their arms.

0860   27 Dec. 1858.   You managed the affair with Thompson nicely.   Livingstone has heard conflicting news about his expedition from sources outside Africa.   Three seams of coal have been found.   No fever except among Kroomen.   The gold spectacles have been ordered from London.

0862   15 Jan. 1859.   We are waiting for a steamer of greater power — this is between you and me.   A steamer of 60 or 100 h.p. would stem the current of Kebrabasa with ease.   Had the "Pearl" come now, she could have sailed up to Tette with ease, and the river is not one-half full yet.

0871   18 Feb. 1859.   Send letters for a man-of-war;   took 8 days from Senna to Tette, would have been 5 but we stopped to cut wood;   a strong steamer necessary to surmount Kebrabasa;   go down to Kongone to meet a man-of-war on the Queen's birthday.

0881   9 Mar. 1859.   Enclose letters to be forwarded;   go down to Kongone on 4th May; leave in two days for Shire.

0896   28 May 1859.   Thank you for sending our letters and the calico;   have been down to Kongone but met no ship;   others have had fever but Kirk and I have been relatively free of it;   on second trip up Shire we discovered a large lake;   longing much for letters from Europe. 30 May.   Shall send our dispatches in 8 days.

0907   11 Jun. 1859.   Went up Shire to buy rice and now proceed to Tette;   thanks for calico; pay yourself out of the money in your hands.

0919   27 Jul. 1859.   Again en route to Luabo to meet man-of-war;   missed mail on way down; take care of our letters whether loose or in packets;   Kirk, C. Livingstone and Rae are in company and we hope to meet ship on the 30th;   thanks for the coffee;   pay yourself.

0928   8 Aug. 1859.   Met 'Persian' which brought no mail;   are now en route up Shire;   please forward letters enclosed;   all in good health;   sent Kroomen away;   regards.

0943   17 Oct. 1859 is published in facsimile in Moir, **ALATR**.

0980   24 Dec. 1859.   Send two bales American calico as soon as convenient;   shall send 4 tusks which you will please sell for us at your convenience;   will be away in Makololo country 8 or 9 months;   if donkeys cannot be procured from Zanzibar within 2½ months do not order them;   war in Italy dreadful;   had to send artist away.

0983   9 Jan. 1860.   Pity bale of calico not sent sooner, next time buy regardless of price and send immediately;   delivered 4 tusks to Sr. Vianna;   regret loss of our mail bag on the bar.

0996   16 Feb. 1860.   Loss of mail bag brings us down river again;   Rae goes home;   astonished to learn that mail bag was found, as we searched 20 days for it;   reward the man who found it;   request to hire four of your Uncle's negroes to accompany us to Sekeletu's; had my first illness on the way to Tette.

1009   25 Mar. 1860.   Met no man-of-war at Kongone so Rae leaves via Mazaro;   treat Rae half as well as you did me and I will be grateful;   add any expenses to my account.

1018   10 Apr. 1860.   Thanks for taking care of my affairs.   I take three bales from Sr. Ferrao and wish you to place them to my account;   enclose another packet of letters;   if the donkeys are more than £12 or £15 do not order them;   will appreciate receiving any American papers before we leave Tette next month.

1023   14 May 1860.   Send another packet of letters;   am off to Sekeletu's country;   in event of my death pay yourself and return remainder to my successor;   our trip will take us till November next;   have found two donkeys in Tette.

1063   1 Jan. 1861.   Marched over 600 miles on foot, 1400 in all;   steamer sank above Senna; Thornton may be reinstated;   grieved to learn of Azevedo's death;   go to bar again hoping to meet a vessel.

1074   7 Feb. 1861. Send parcel for Thornton;   please send my account with you to Sr. Ferrao's at Senna;   in which ship did Rae put the specimens?

1115   1 May 1861.   Sympathy in the loss of your father;   good wishes for your brothers in Portugal;   industrious in this country are rich while lazy are all poor;   found a river to the north with no bar;   went to Johanna and take the Bishop and his mission upriver; Thornton offered no thanks for the loan of the theodolite;   Soares a thorough gentleman; MacLeod behaved ill toward him.

1121   20 May 1861.   Missed you at Mazaro;   hope to be down again by December next; received the box from America + a cask + two boxes of ale, also the theodolite;   heard from Rae in London;   have been waiting at Shamo for items Kirk went to fetch at Senna; have been unable to get gold spectacles ordered for Col. Nunes long ago, but will try again;   thank Soares for selling the tusks.

1168   22 Jan. 1862.   Again en route to sea, this time too late to meet ship;   delayed in Shire and Zambesi;   send account to Sr. Vianna's and I will settle it on my return, also 2 bales American calico;   40 bags of rice, and some ale if it comes via Quilimane.

1174   5 Feb. 1862.   Brig carrying new steamer arrived;   Captain of Brig wishes to take cargo of wood back, it may be a good venture for you or your uncle;   hope to start upriver in 2 or 3 days;   will return from Shire in a fortnight or three weeks to get things we store with "Mosquito";   wife here but no children;   also 4 other women;   man at Shupanga does not know that his landlord is our friend; Wilson wants to take a tree of Shupanga home to see if it is good for shipbuilding; thank you for the rice; send other supplies in three weeks or a month.

1183 21 Feb. 1862. Letter and good wishes received from Mr. Vianna, to whom he has paid balances. Vessel heavily laden and in need of wood. Freight for brig. Sale of liquor by "Mosquito".

1193 6 Mar. 1862. Problems going upriver, must unload ship and assemble steamer at Shupanga; as provisions are low, send rice; English sailors behaved ill when drunk; request men for help whom we will pay.

1207 25 Mar. 1862. Sad news of deaths of Mackenzie and Burrup; will you handle any supplies which may be sent missionaries, for which they will pay you; Soares may test authenticity of Makololo by asking the name of their headman when they left Sekeletu's; await arrival of 'Gorgon', which was driven to sea in a storm.

1314 27 Jan. 1863. Send a packet of letters; famine exists up here; canoe laden with gunpowder + spirits for Mariano was seized at Shire mouth, it was going upriver in the name of the missionaries; have written senior naval officer for common stores; do what you can to have them sent up; pay what you think necessary.

1325 21 Feb. 1863. Missionaries are sending some ex-slaves back to the Cape. Lower Shire depopulated. Must go again in "Pioneer" for provisions. P.S. MacLeod going to better climate; he is a good man.

1424 12 Feb. 1864. Must part without paying you a visit; delayed waiting for river to rise; the goods I requested you sell I must instead sell at Zanzibar; I leave with Sr. Soares a machilla cloth for your good wife as a marriage present; please send your and your uncle's accounts to Mozambique that I may settle them before I leave.

1441 12 Apr. 1864. Pleased to receive the accounts, which were higher than I expected; give me more information about the guns and I will investigate; Meller and Waller both agreed to pay Clementino for the chains; go to Johanna the day after tomorrow; Soares abundantly kind; compliments to your wife and her mother, sorry we were unable to visit you; Waller should be near the Cape by now. We may not sail until the 15th as it is blowing.

OLDFIELD, Radulphus Bryce (? — 1877).
As Commander of the "Lyra" (12 Nov. 1857 — 17 Aug. 1861) and the "Ariel" (17 Aug. 1861 — 22 Apr. 1862), Oldfield rendered assistance to the Zambezi Expedition on several occasions. He was by far the most successful prize-getter among the East African Squadron commanders during this period, although occasionally his enthusiasm overshadowed his discretion.   (Navy List.).

1252 26 Jul. 1862. As Lt. Burlton has never served in the expedition under my command, I have nothing to say about his passage to the Cape or elsewhere.

OSWELL, William Cotton (1818 — 1893).
After service in Madras Oswell came to South Africa in 1845 to shoot game and met Livingstone, with whom he travelled in 1849 and 1851. Livingstone's third son was named after him. He remained a close friend and gave much assistance in the writing of NEZT.   (DNB; Oswell, WCO.)

0165   22 Mar. 1847.   In Kuruman on visit.   Varden said Oswell had gone to India.   Has been 12 days due east of Chonuane, where they found the Limpopo came round.   Magnetic hills extend a long way to the east.   Visited three tribes in bend of Limpopo;   country more densely populated to the east.   Waggon from Oswell arrived before them.   Have decided to move to Kolobeng.

0184   10 Apr. 1848.   Knowledge and speculation about the course of the Limpopo.   Will wait for Oswell before going lakewards.   Sechele may go with them;   his character.   Their new location and its fruitfulness;   routes to it.   Cumming's hunting.   Dealings with Ashton and Hume.   State of his horse and cattle.   Boer expedition to Mosilikatze.   Routes to the lake.   Requests periodicals.

0213   11 Oct. 1849.   Wife and children recovering.   Details of journey from Boatlanama.   Oxen diseased because of drought but rain expected.   Discussion of whose oxen Oswell should use, and location of Oswell's.   Lack of sporting success of one Delman.   Meal from Hume has come.   Death of Bakwains in epidemic.

0260   [15 Nov. 1851.]   Inattention due to reading newspapers has caused them to take the wrong road: sketch of relative positions and proposed route.   Recent publications on South African geography.   Abuse of Sir Harry Smith.   Colonists have lost Caffre War.   Activity of Boers.   No game.   Hopes to see him at Boatlanama, but he is not to wait.

0274   27 Apr. 1852.   Difficulty of securing passages for family, but they finally sailed on 2 Apr.   Uvula excised.   Publication of account of their journey.   Maps sent from Zouga apparently lost.   Delay in getting permission to take gunpowder: if necessary will go without rather than smuggle.   Tuckey on Zaire dialects.   Plans of other travellers.

0288   20 Sep. 1852.   Delays in journey have prevented his falling into the hands of the Boers, who attacked Sechele.   Bakwains resisted, killing several, but had to retire for want of water.   Town burned and all cattle seized.   Sechele attempting to cut off parties of Boers.   His loss of books and medicine.   Fate of their map.   News of traders.   Will go north when it is safe.

0317   20 Sep. 1853.   Disturbances between Sekhomi's and Kuruman prevented communication.   Slow progress because of fever and vegetation.   A vineyard.   Floods. Sekeletu's 18°17'19" S., 23°47' E. (former longitude apparently wrong, but map need not be altered).   Attacks of fever.   Downfall of Mpepe.   Beauty of the Zambesi.   Provisional positions.   Various animals.   A slave trader from Mozambique, and Arabs from Zanzibar.   Portuguese maps not to be believed.   Possibility of commerce from Loanda. News of other travellers.   Leaving for Loanda when rains commence.

0412   4 Apr. 1856.   Could not write from Loanda.   No game in Londa.   Bogs and forest prevent travel by waggon;   has therefore returned to try the east.   Tsetse destroyed oxen and has had to walk.   Plenty of game on Kafue.   Natives are muscular farmers who have been fighting for two years with Portuguese.   Trade stagnant, though abundance of minerals and grain.   River magnificent, though spoiled by unhealthy delta.   Few letters received.

0745   2 Mar. 1858.   *Leaving for Kendal, then to Liverpool, and will sail in the 'Pearl' on Saturday or Monday.

0883   2 Apr. 1859.   Dismissal of Bedingfeld;   the harm he has done.   MaRobert an awful botch.   Shire a fine river but blocked by cataracts.   Elephant and other game cannot be hunted because of long grass.   14 May.   Mount Zomba, Lake Shirwa, River Ruo.   No news of Burton.   Killing of elephant.   Portuguese never went up Shire.

0970　7 Nov. 1859.　Shire traced to Lake Nyassa.　Sinking condition of MaRobert prevented full exploration.　An English missionary and mercantile settlement would stamp out slave trade.　Three terraces.　Climate of the Highlands.　Prospects for cotton.　Portuguese effete.　Evil conduct of Baines.

1060　†[Aug.–Nov. 1860.]　The Victoria Falls;　went down fissure (diagram);　water glides over.　Depth of the gorge below the falls must be enormous to admit of its being quiet so soon.

1503　8 Oct. 1864.　Belated congratulations on Oswell's marriage.　He is writing another book. Locations of family.　Praise of Webbs.　Invites Oswell to visit Newstead.

1515　21 Oct. 1864.　Invitation to visit Newstead.　Rawlinson and Murchison will be guests next week.　Disturbances after death of Sekeletu.　Situation of Robert.

1572　8 Jan. 1865.　Mrs. Oswell should also come, despite being an invalid.

1574　11 Jan. 1865.　Proof of first chapter　sent to him via Owen.　Much correction required. Regrets he cannot come to Newstead.

1576　12 Jan. 1865.　*Suggested improvements to the book.

1582　21 Jan. 1865.　Sends more proofs and invites suggestions.

1586　25 Jan. 1865.　Sends more proofs.　Death of an ox.　News of Steele.

1590　[Jan. 1865?]　Urges him and his wife to come to Newstead for the good of her health.

1592　3 Feb. 1865.　Revised proofs.　Oswell's brother suggests saying something good about 'Pearl' and 'MaRobert'.

1597　8 Feb. 1865.　Plain and readable text is all that can be expected.　Proofs.　Waller does not like his telling of advice to Mackenzie not to fight, but admits it is true;　has to be said because of what Rowley published.

1598　[8 Feb. 1865?]　*[Beginning missing.]　Explain the failure of the arts in the East to advance further.　Insert footnote about Rowley and the failure of the Mission.　Owen thinks we ought to bring out the Portuguese.　Compile contents note for Ch. XXX.

1602　9 Feb. 1865.　More proofs and illustrations.

1611　15 Feb. 1865.　Suggested alterations.　18 Feb.　Forgot to post this.　Sends page proofs. Printer to blame for unintelligible passages.　Difficulty of getting good illustrations of blacks.　Thanks for photograph.　He himself is old and gray.　Tozer not in high repute. Waller has written a good paper for Macmillan.　Name of a children's game.　Sat. a.m. More proofs, now almost perfect.

1620　24 [Feb. 1865?]　Murray has got a literary friend to make corrections.　Story in American paper about his marriage in Constantinople.

1627　1 Mar. [1865.]　[Beginning missing.]　Sends revised proofs.　Intended to leave for London but Webb would not hear of it.　[End missing.]

1635   9 Mar. 1865. Sends revised proofs. Goes to London to comment on a paper at the Royal Geographical Society. Webb is High Sheriff of Nottinghamshire. Murray hopes book will be out by Easter.

1643   20 Mar. 1865. *On the book; servants have misplaced a letter with changes.

1646   21 Mar. 1865. Captain Fraser's slaving venture. Long letter lost. Pressure of lip ring on teeth. Omissions by printer.

1649   23 Mar. 1865. Webbs unwell and he should postpone visit. Publisher's corrections. Tom's health; he and Oswell harmed by being sent to badly drained school near Glasgow. No word of Robert. His comments on America and Portugal have caused trouble. Thinks of going to London to sort out trouble with printer.

1662   1 Apr. 1865. *Has made new contents list only to find old one.

1664   3, 6 Apr. [1865]. *On the format and contents of the book.

1667   4 Apr. 1865. Who can tell us who tamed Carthaginian elephants? Dispure with Murchison about inferiority of those who did not tame them.

1672   7 Apr. 1865. *On the book.

1673   8 Apr. 1865. Murray's corrector may be a lady. Pages sent.

1674   10 Apr. 1865. Sends more manuscript. Uncertain whether to mention not selling 'Lady Nyasa'. Fever pills mentioned incidentally though treatment of fever is one great result of expedition. [End missing.]

1677   14 Apr. 1865. Corrections. Tom might become a tea planter in India; uncertain what to do with Agnes.

1678   15 Apr. 1865. Does not understand hiatus. Has full confidence in Oswell's judgement and none in Cooke's. Has restored one page just because Cooke deleted it.

1679   16 Apr. 1865. Sends end of manuscript. Mackenzie deserves to have some good said of him. If too artistic would not be natural.

1680   17 [Apr. 1865?] Must say something to butter Americans, who may take Cuba. Puzzled by charge about old English slavery.

1681   21 Apr. 1865. Man is an animal without feathers. Send part about old bachelors marrying young wives to Owen. Does not like Milton's criticisms.

1683   22 Apr. 1865. Various passages in the book.

1685   24 Apr. 1865. On the book. [End missing.]

1688   25 Apr. 1865. Going to London to see what causes delay. On various passages. Has found appropriate quotation sent by Mrs. Oswell, which has been omitted by his stupidity.

1688.9 [25—28 Apr. 1865.] Difficulty about length concerned only the price. Nothing need be cut.

1690   28 Apr. 1865.   Correction can only go in errata list which will not be read.   Sends corrected appendix.

1691   [Apr. 1865.]   Last sheets received and sent on.

1693   1 May 1865.   On the logistics of sending chapters to Oswell, Cooke, Murray, Owen, etc.

1694   [1 May 1865.]   At Academy dinner and the Crystal Palace.

1698   4 May 1865.   [Fragment.]   Oswell's corrections.

1700   5 May 1865.   Has apologised to Murray for Oswell not coming to dinner.   A deletion by Milton which he will restore.   Advantages of mixing races.

1703   8 May 1865.   On the book.   Murchison will advertise it in his Anniversary address: what are the chief points?

1704   10 May 1865.   On the book.

1707   11 May 1865.   [Fragment.]   On the book.

1712   [15 May 1865.]   Webb has a son.   Sends last sheets.   Thought of dedicating book to Webb, but Murchison would like it.

1714   18 May 1865.   Has said goodbye to Moffat's daughter.   Has been examined by House of Commons Committee on West Africa.

1718   22 May 1865.   Dedication to Palmerston.   Add acknowledgements to Russell, Owen and yourself in preface.   Going to Hamilton.

1722   25 May 1865.   Publication delayed till November.   Arrowsmith's claims.   Shaftesbury's question in the Lords will call attention to the book even if he is away.   A traveller's unorthodox method of courting.   P.S. Noting Burton's assertion about conversion in Africa.   Nonsense talked by Lord Stanley.

1729   [Feb. — May 1865.]   Believes progress of nations is part of the scheme of Creation.   But to eke out Oswell's theory, India and China have stopped and retrograded largely because they have been conquered by Mohammedans and Mongols.

1738   6 Jun. 1865.   Corrected preface and dedication sent to printer.   His mother declining.   Children's education.   Conflicting advice of Sir Bartle Frere and Col. Rigby about taking Indians.

1742   9 Jun. 1865.   Thanks for information about Indians.   Children's successes;   perhaps they should try for the Indian Civil Service.   Last sheet sent.   [End missing.]

1758   27 Jun. 1865.   Thanks for sympathy on mother's death, of which details are given.   Hopes to die as collectedly and does not expect to live long.   Translation of Lacerda's fulminations;   reaction on publication of book will be worse.

1773   24 Jul. 1865.   Details of movements.   Abuse by Portuguese.

1775   25 Jul. 1865.   Agnes and he will come tomorrow.

1790   7 Aug. 1865.   Sends proof of answer to Lacerda and copy of King of Portugal's speech. Starting in a week for Paris.

1795   10 Aug. 1865.   Parting from Webbs.   Dinner with Queen Emma.

1810   19 Aug. 1865.   Agnes with Rev. M. Calliatte, father of her instructor and brother-in-law of Mrs. Lemue.   Told her to write Oswell if she needed guidance.

1826   29 Sep. 1865.   Preparations going well.   Governor helpful.   Taking buffaloes to see if they withstand tsetse.   Sultan of Zanzibar to visit Bombay.   Playfair ill; wishes Kirk could be Resident.   Will sell 'Lady Nyasa'.   Anger of Portuguese an advance.   [End missing.]

1866   1 Jan. 1866.   Pleased with reviews.   Difficulties of Von der Decken.   Other travellers. Starting on 3rd in 'Thule'.   Free post at Rovuma would be good, but unlikely.   Reaction of Tozer's friends to book.   Baker's marriage and ignorance.   No news of Robert. Baines's description of the Victoria Falls not better than theirs.

1931   8 Jul. 1868.   The river system.   Annoyance caused by members of the Royal Geographical Society.   Errors of Arrowsmith and Galton.   Hopes Oswell is playing with his children, something he neglected at Kolobeng.

1944   Oct. 1869.   Writes with no prospect of sending it.   Wandering round lakes.   Moderns only rediscover what Ptolemy knew.   Mounts Kenya and Kilimanjaro have no connection with the Nile.   Taming of elephants.   Speke's discoveries.

1952   24 Nov. 1870.   Letters and goods plundered.   Attack on Arrowsmith.   Speke jumped to conclusions.

1988   6 Jan. 1872.   The four fountains and their rivers.   Trouble and losses caused by Kirk's repeated use of slaves.   Hopes for his son Oswell.   Criticism of Baker.   Structure of the watershed.

OWEN, Sir Richard (1804 — 1892).
Anatomist and naturalist;   as conservator of the Hunterian Museum (1827—56) and professor of comparative anatomy and physiology (1836—56), he taught Livingstone in 1840.   He was superintendent of the British Museum (Natural History) 1856—83. Knighted 1884.   (DNB.)

0023   29 Mar. 1841.   Boxes for anatomical preparations are with the Governor.   Will make every effort to collect specimens consistent with his main purpose, evangelisation.   Delays in journey.

0775   30 Mar. 1858.   Col. Hill will send him some mud-fish.   Some natural historians do not acknowledge specimens.   Mary is pregnant and will go to Kuruman.   Kirk has found a new mud-fish which will be sent from the Cape.

0898   [May] 1859.   Discovery of Lake Shirwa.   Elephant has been secured for him.   A small black ant.   A larva-depositing fly.   30 May.   No ship has come.   Returning to Tette and the lakes.   Infrequent communications.   Mary at Kuruman;   will meet possibly at end of year.

1062   29 Dec. 1860.   Peculiar lung formation of antelopes.   Darwin's theory not supported by his experience in Africa, where there is no great struggle for existence nor evidence of natural selection.   Division of antelopes by habitat.   Other animals seen and eaten. Delighted at prospect of Universities' Mission.

1535   18 Nov. 1864. His book. Asks opinion on Charles Livingstone's theory that only female mosquitos have poisonous proboscis.   Kirk's lack of situation, and thus no botanical publication from the Expedition.

1538   22 Nov. 1864.   Sends note on mythical beast in Africa.   Persistence of such ideas in the native mind.

1599   †8 Feb. 1865.   First revise of early chapters has gone back to printer and when they return he will trouble Owen again.   Sends Charles Livingstone's address.

OXFORD AND CAMBRIDGE MISSION, Honorary Secretaries.

1057   29 Nov. 1860, 14 and 22 Jan. 1861.   Draft published in Wallis, **ZEDL** II, pp. 351—362.

PAGET, Sir James (1814 — 1899).
Surgeon at St. Bartholomew's Hospital, London, and Professor of Anatomy. Surgeon to Queen Victoria.   Vice-Chancellor of London University.   Created a baronet 1871.
                                                                            (DNB.)

0705   11 Feb. 1858.   *On the rarity of defects of speech and hearing in Africa.

PAKINGTON, Sir John Somerset (1799 — 1880).
Conservative politician, **inter alia** minister for war and colonies 1852.   Created Baron Hampton 1874.   **(DNB.)**

0304   12 Dec. 1852. Published in Schapera, **DLSAP** pp. 59—62.

PALMERSTON, 3rd Viscount (1784 — 1865).
Henry John Temple, succeeded to the title (an Irish peerage which did not debar him from the House of Commons) in 1802.   Foreign Secretary 1830—41, 1846—51; Prime Minister 1859—65.   Livingstone had almost unlimited admiration for him, and was in complete agreement with his anti-slavery policies.   **(DNB.)**

0889   13 May 1859.   Description of the Shire valley, highlands, and of the discovery of Lake Shirwa.   Portuguese cooperation in French slaving program.

0947   20 Oct. 1859.   Exploration of upper Shire valley, reaching Lake Nyassa.   Above 33 miles of rapids one finds a cotton field of unknown extent.   As the lake is of unknown length, and extends parallel to the east coast, slave traders must cross certain fords on the way to Mosambique, etc. Chief of these fords is the one between Lake Nyassa and Shirwa, where the Shire River leaves Lake Nyassa.   Here we met a large party, who slipped away into the night upon learning we were English.

1066   15 Jan. 1861.   On his second visit to the Victoria Falls, which after careful measurement I call the most wonderful in the world.   They are twice the depth of Niagara and over a mile wide.   Cotton much more widespread than I anticipated formerly.   Coal field from Tete almost to the Falls will probably be important in the future of the Cape Colony.   Pleased to hear of a Universities' mission.   Hope to find a route around the Portuguese.   We believe we now have a remedy for fever.

1143   12 Nov. 1861.   Detailed description of his recent exploration of Lake Nyassa.   Shores highly populated.   Arab dhows seen carrying slaves across the lake.   People civil away from the slave route, and welcomed trade.   Left the Oxford and Cambridge mission in the highlands east of the river, among the Mang'anja.   Slaves were freed from four different parties and the people turned over to the mission.   An attack by poisoned arrows forced us to defend ourselves.   That the Portuguese can follow in our footsteps, enslave people and keep all other nations from lawful trade in our discoveries is depressing.

1279   16 Oct. 1862.   We were delayed in the lower part of the river and had to go to Johanna for a new crew.   Then we went up Rovuma to seek an outlet north of the Portuguese.   Attacked by "river pirates" sixty miles up the river.   Description of the land around the river.   Crossed twice the slave route to Kilwa.   This river has the disadvantage of the tsetse, but a steamer drawing 18 inches could ply it when loaded 7 or 8 months of the year.

1312   14 Jan. 1863.   Districts around Portuguese settlements depopulated by slave trade.   French scheme now being supplied from north of Quilimane and Shire valley.   Local persons owning slaves and arms capture people at will, and are not brought to account until he can be mulcted, after which he is set free.   Our cruizers on the west coast helped lead to the founding of over 20 missions, but here on the east paltry peddling and slaving go on.   Cannot something be done to prevent Portuguese from keeping the land from Delagoa Bay to Cape Delgado as a private slave preserve?   Free navigation of the Zambesi seems essential.   The lower Shire valley is rapidly becoming a wilderness.   It is galling that no Portuguese dare enter a district before we do.

PARIS, Société de géographie.

0322   28 Sep. 1853.   Award of their medal an unexpected reward for his attempts to improve the condition of Africa.   Now trying to find healthy locality for mission.   Difficult journey through bush and floods.   Reception by Sekeletu. Assassination attempt.   The Leeambye or Sesheke.   Borotse country.   Portuguese maps based on inadequate information.   Minor corrections to his and Oswell's map.   Degradation of natives.

0395.5 [Feb?] 1856.   The physical geography of Central Africa.   Rivers and peoples of Angola and the Zambesi valley.   Makololo expedition to the north-east.   Geological speculations.   2 Mar.   Reached Tete.

PARKER, John Henry (1816 — 1858).
A fellow-student of Livingstone at Ongar, missionary in Calcutta 1843—58.
(LMSReg. no. 460.)

0100   11 May 1844.   Method of communication.   Christian view of polygamy.   Now in a delightful country, but morally in darkness.   Praise of Moffat.   Trouble from lions.   No news of Lattakoo district.   Personal comments.

PATERSON, Thomas Macdougall Brisbane (1844 – 1921).
Minister of Hamilton West (United) Free Church 1875–1920, and apparently at the date of this letter in charge of its Young Men's Association.   (Lamb, **FUF**, p. 189.)

1473   27 Aug. 1864.   Limited time at home compels him to decline all such invitations.

PEDRO V (1837 – 1861).
King of Portugal 1853–61.   (**GrEncPort. xx.   788.**)

0395   24 Feb. 1856.   Thanks to subjects who assisted in Angola.   It is less prosperous than English colonies;   introduction of wheat would help.   Lack of cooperation among more intelligent Portuguese.   Large number can read, but great want of books.   Absence of Portuguese women.

PENNELL, John.
First Class Stoker, R.N., Pennell served aboard the "Pioneer" from Mar. 1861 to Mar. 1864.   He accompanied Livingstone from Zanzibar to Bombay (and on to London) in mid-1864, and survived at least until 1913.

1434   7 Mar. 1864.   A very high testimony of Pennell's service to the Zambezi Expedition.

PETO, Sir Samuel Morton (1809 – 1889).
Builder/contractor in the railroad industry, of the firms Grissell & Peto (1830–46) and Peto and Betts (1846–66), also a Baptist philanthropist, he represented Norwich (1847–54), Finsbury (1859–65), and Bristol (1865–8) in the Commons.   (**DNB.**)

0800   21 Jun. 1858.   *Have been exploring the delta, and now make for Tette.   I apply by this mail for the vessel described by you.   When visiting Mazaro, people were glad to see we were English rather than Portuguese.

0828   17 Sep. 1858.   *Bedingfeld could not have brought the "Bann" out as he suffers from seasickness.   Faults of the "Ma-Robert".   Coal in the region, and with coal and iron we can begin to open up Africa.   Rocks above Tete I may have to turn quarryman and blast away.

PEYTON, Mrs.
Wife of Lumley W.

0457   22 Jan. 1857.   Sympathy for her in her long absence from her husband.   Her likeness and those of her daughters hang in the cabin of the "Frolic."   Tells of the kindness of her husband to him;   brings a package from him to her.   I am writing a book.

PEYTON, Lumley Woodyear.
Lieutenant on HMS 'Frolic' 1854–6 and its Acting Commander 1856–7;   this was the ship which conveyed Livingstone from Quilimane to Mauritius.   Commander 1868.
(**Navy List.**)

0432   26 Sep. 1856.   Thanks for kind treatment received when on board.

PHILIP, – – (? – 1847).
Wife of John.

0034   5 Aug. 1841.   Published in Chamberlin, **SLFL** no. 9 (with the omission noted;   p. 27 1.19
Uitenhage).

PHILIP, John (1775 – 1851).
Superintendent of the London Missionary Society in South Africa 1820–50.
                                                    (**DNB**;   **LMSReg.** no. 194.)

0105   21 Jul. 1844.   Bill to David Hume for £20.

0106   29 Jul. 1844.   Bill to Rev. W. Ashton for £12 for native teacher's salary.

0142   †[1845??]   *Describes mauling by lion and missionary work.

PHILLIPS, John (1800 – 1874).
An eminent geologist;   Keeper of York Museum 1825–40;   Professor of Geology, Trinity
College, Dublin 1844–53;   Keeper of the Ashmolean Museum 1854–70.   He was also
Assistant Secretary of the British Association 1832–59.   (**DNB**.)

1728   [Sep. 1864–May 1865??]   *[Beginning missing.]   On the pottery fragments found on the
Zambesi, his old African friend Webb, and his interest in the British Association.

PLAYFAIR, Lyon (1818 – 1898).
A classmate of Livingstone's at Anderson's College, Playfair was on the faculty of the
Royal School of Mines in the 1840's before occupying the Chair of Chemistry in the
University of Edinburgh, 1858–69.   He represented the universities of Edinburgh and St.
Andrew's 1868–85, and South Leeds 1885–92.   Created Baron Playfair in 1892.
                                                    (**DNB**.)

0957   28 Oct. 1859.   Visit to Lake Nyassa opens up a cotton field superior to the American.
The valley is divided into three distinct terraces of differing climate.   33 miles of cataracts
can be surmounted by a road.   We feel we can cure fever.   The slave traders pass between
Lake Nyassa and Shirwa;   met some slavers there but they could not speak Arabic.   We
would have explored the lake, but returned as we left our steamer in a sinking state.

1155   10 Dec. 1861.   Thank you for your kindness in our son's escape from Glasgow.   We carried
a boat past the cataracts and explored the lake, but the gales prevented our crossing, and
the lack of food prevented our going around.   Something in sun's rays besides heat
affects our bodies, and we must wear thick clothing to sit in its rays.   Can you make
nothing from mica?   It is very beautiful, and I ask this question every time I see mica
schist.

PLAYFAIR, Sir Robert Lambert (1828 — 1899).
Brother of Lyon Playfair, he rose to the rank of Lieut.-Colonel in the Madras army, serving mostly on the political side. Consul at Zanzibar 1863—7, and for Algeria 1867—96. Knighted 1886. **(DNB.)**

Livingstone's letters of 30 May 1869 (1938) and Nov. 1870 [sic] (1956), addressed either to Playfair or to Kirk, are published in Foskett, **ZmDc.**

PORTER, William (1805 — 1880).
Attorney General of the Cape Colony, 1839—65, who on the sole basis of Baines' testimony against Livingstone believed Livingstone to have been unfair and perhaps unjust in dismissing Baines. **(DNB.)**

0785   30 Apr. 1858.   Advising Porter on how to dispose of the 800 guineas which were presented him by the city of Cape Town, in case of Livingstone's death on the Zambezi.

PRENTICE, Manning.
Younger brother of T.L. Prentice; considered becoming an artisan missionary.

0052   8 Apr. 1842.   Building of dam at Bubi's village. Character of natives, who ought to be stimulated to industry rather than become recipients of gifts of clothing etc. Trades spread civilisation better than missionaries. Wonders whether to build house for Prentice and his brother. Advice on what to bring, especially beads the universal currency. Language not difficult **pace** Moffat. Better to be ordained before coming.

PRENTICE, Thomas.
From Stowmarket, Suffolk. Father of T.L. and Manning.

0053   8 Apr. 1842.   Advice on his sons' future. If they come to South Africa they must not stop in Cape Colony (too many missionaries) or Caffreland (missionaries and a scattered population) or near Kuruman (enough missionaries for a slight population), but move to the interior, where one missionary with native teachers can cover a large area. Climate also better than at Kuruman. In three day will set out to prevent bloodshed. 8 May. Letter to Thomas explains why westward journey was prevented.

PRENTICE, Thomas Lomas.
Friend of Livingstone while he was a student; he also wished to be a missionary (Livingstone later claimed this was a device to win Catherine Ridley, who was attracted to the missionary life; letter to his son Thomas 24 Sep. 1869), but became instead a corn merchant.

0009   †7 Jun. 1840.   Thanks for financial help, though his position is not desperate. It has enabled him to assist one more deserving.

0019   27 Jan. 1841.   Published in Chamberlin, **SLFL** no. 3 (omitting details of seasickness suffered by Mr. and Mrs. Ross, pieties, intention of distributing tracts, and regards to Miss R. and family).

0021   5, 17 Mar. 1841.   Published in Chamberlin, **SLFL** no. 5 (omitting passages on his reason for sending details of voyage, the Ridley family, drunken sailors in Rio, Manning's study of medicine, pieties, and regards to family).

0029   3 Aug. 1841.   Published in Chamberlin, **SLFL** no. 7 (omitting sentences on racialism in the anti-Philip party, Manning's training, and regards to Mr. Fison).

0039   2 Dec. 1841.   Climate salubrious but summer trying for females.   Chiefs hostile to Christianity. Griqua Town missions surround Kuruman, forcing them to the north. Small population.   Iron smelting, the surrounding country.   Need for native teachers.   His travels. Hopes for letters. Regards to friends and family. 15 Dec. An excellent native teacher found.

0093   9 Oct. 1843.   Published in Chamberlin, **SLFL** no. 17 (omitting sentences on his feelings when no letters received, pieties, arrival of new missionaries, and the death of a native from fever).

PRICE, W.S.
In charge of the school for freed slaves at Nasik, near Bombay, from which Livingstone received some of his followers for the final expedition.

1821   27 Sep. 1865.   Details of what he requires of his men. He will return them to Zanzibar if no suitable residence is found.

1834   7 Nov. 1865.   *On the type of knapsack required and what will be carried in them, and on the importance of teaching agriculture to his pupils.

1845   Nov. 1865.   *On the boys to be sent and their outfit.

1857   27 Dec. 1865.   *Thule ready. Provisions must be husbanded. Bombay not a good place to idle in.

PROCTER, Lovell James (1833 — 1910).
An Anglican clergyman who served with the UMCA 1861—63, Procter after leaving the Zambezi was associated with several churches in Yorkshire, St. Giles, Reading (1869—76), and St. Columba's, Salem, New Brunswick (Canada, 1886—8). His last post was as Rector of Radwell, near Baldock, Hertfordshire.   (**Crockford**; Bennet & Ylvisaker, **CAJLJP**.)

1198   15 Mar. 1862.   Sorrow at learning of Mackenzie's death. Canoes will bring mission provisions up to you at once. New mission members had no supplies on board, so we shared with them. We will buy one of the two mission mules. About to start for the sea.

1253   30 Jul. 1862.   Forwarding your mail which arrived via "Ariel." I wrote Governor about Belshore. Oldfield is sorry you do not live in houses like Sunley; I mentioned you fled your original position and are now uncertain of permanent habitation. Bishop of Cape Town has gone home to get a new chief pastor for you. All are well here; some of the seamen are gone.

1315   27 Jan. 1863.   Distressed at the death of Scudamore. Advised Johnson to go on to you.

We are delayed a few days, but shall be up soon. All well except Pearce. Commandant at mouth of Shire seized a canoe of arms, ammunition, wine & spirit, for Mariano, going up in the name of the missionaries.

1330   26 Mar. 1863.   Are past Mankokwe's and moving toward you; hope to be nearer in a few days.   Kirk says Clark is recovering.   The decision of leaving the highlands for the lowlands should be rectified before more deaths occur.   Once we have landed above you, I intend on going down-river.   Mankokwe fears the Makololo more for their revenge upon him for attacking them than for any harm they have done his people.

1356   5 Jun. 1863.   Thankful to be well and hope you are too.   Rowley is awful; I waded through his book.   Wilhelm Meister was a fool.   I never read such dreary stuff.   Etc. on German drivel.

PYE Brothers.
Owners of a London textile business.

0923   31 Jul. 1859.   Through the Foreign Office I send buaze to see if it can be converted into cloth, or other materials proper for a thorough trial of its properties.   The seed contains oil valuable for painting, and the plant grows on soil unfit for other cultivation.   It may well be introduced in Natal or India, or any of our colonies.

PYNE, Benjamin T.
A resident of Ongar, with whom Livingstone became friendly when a student.

0017   8 Dec. 1840.   Settled on board ship.   Passengers seem friendly;   majority Scotch but none the better for that.   Gratitude for divine guidance and Pyne's kindness.   Mrs. Ross improves on acquaintance.

0026   13 May 1841.   Philips most obliging.   Thanks for box of useful articles.   Baby clothes given to Mrs. W. Philip who is an old friend.   Trip to Hankey;   affecting welcome to Williams.   Please transmit £20 to parents and tell Moore to bring thermometer and quadrant.

0046   22 Dec. 1841.   Kindness of Mr. and Mrs. Edwards.   Journey to unvisited tribes.   Great heat.   Game.   Character of people, their idea of prayer and superstitions.   Degraded state of women.

0049   11 Mar. 1842.   Settling native teacher with Bubi.   Largeness of country;   more animals than people.   Population so scattered that to station European missionaries here would be impossible without a route to the west coast.   School began today.   Bubi most sensible of Bechuana chiefs.   Travel by ox-waggon;   his driver and leader.   Reluctance of Bechuanas to eat fish.   Character of Bechuanas.   Tea popular.   Kindness of Lemue.   17 May.   Visit to Sekomi.

0077   25 Jun. 1843.   Attack by Mahura on Sebegwe's people.   Visit to Sebegwe.   Effect of comet on Africans.   Bakwains have all changed locations.   Visit to Bakalahari and Bakaa.   Broke his finger.   Sent message to Mosilikatse.

0103   6 Jun. 1844.   Mauling by lion.   Bechuanas have no thought of heaven.   Traces of animal worship.   Of seeds sent only sunflower has grown.   Chinese oats and Egyptian corn grow well.

0114   28 Jan. 1845.   Will write for Williams' Welsh magazine.   Now married.   Respect for deceased Miss Marshall.   Distress of Joseph Moore.   Moving to Mabotsa, but it is too small for two, and will soon move on.   Criticism of Inglis.   Visit of English hunters. Chance to send parcels at expense of East India Company Botanical Gardens at Calcutta. P.S. Sends specimen for [autograph] album.

0143   1 Jan. 1846.   No external news for months.   Mends guns for all tribes on condition that they are not used against people.   Visit of group of Zulus.   Meeting with Sir William Cumming.   Gardening activities.   Wild life.   Send thermometer and dresses.

0150   28 May 1846.   Gardening at Kolobeng because of drought at Chonuane.   Robert growing. He will never see the Pynes in this life.   Mary very busy.   Indian visitors.   Kindness of Oswell, with whom he has arranged to travel.   Adventure of Ann Moffat.   Inglis settled at Mabotsa.   Attack by Sechele on Bubi's people.

0158   Dec. 1846.   Banks of Botletle so swollen they must wait.   Forced from ESE course to NW by range of mountains.   People know we wish them to live in peace.   Supplies will be gone before they reach home.   Natives call the Limpopo the mother of all rivers.   The chief of the Bagalaka.   Times now worse because of Boers than when Mosilikatze was here.   Robert ill but now restored.

0168   31 May 1847.   Has been repairing waggon wheels, damaged by journey of thousands of miles.   Waiting for birth of child.   An ungrateful Griqua.   Box not yet received. Necessity of always carrying a gun.   Sends trinkets.   Pleasant visit from Oswell.   Visit previous year by him and Murray resulted in latter praising him greatly to the London Missionary Society.   Robert grows finely.   Advice on avoiding colds.   Personal news. P.S. Birth of Agnes.

0214   15 Oct. 1849.   Has reached River Zouga and Lake Ngami.   Birth of Thomas.

0225   4 Mar. 1850.   Box most acceptable but seeds spoiled.   Garden useless from want of water.   Visit with Freeman to a cave and to Bubi's old village.   Freeman attempted in vain to take daguerreotype of Livingstone.   He has unfortunately accepted Philip's view about colonial stations.   Nichols and fellow travellers do not realise what they are attempting.   About to set off for the north.   Personal news.   2 Aug.   Forgot to post letter which has been to the lake and back.

0233   27 Aug. 1850.   *On the plundering of waggons by Boers, the goodness of great people, drought, and the likelihood of doing the Bakwains good by leaving them for some years.

0241   4 Dec. 1850.   Published in Chamberlin, **SLFL** no. 35 (p. 142 1.20 future ages be extensively useful).

0252   30 Apr. 1851.   En route to lake.   Country drying up.   Mrs. Pyne to send clothing.

0269   2 Apr. 1852.   Preparations for journey of family to England.   Oswell's help.   Needs information on cost of living and schooling in England.   Would like Mrs. Pyne to take Agnes if she still keeps a school.   Children will forget him.

0294 15 Oct. 1852. Mary could not visit them because of his mother's illness. Receipt of box. Elephants. Boers attacked Bakwains and plundered his house, and now threaten his life.

0443 15 Dec. 1856. After meetings and seeing mother will quietly return to Africa. Has received no letter since 1852. Will stay near London to write.

PYNE, Elizabeth.
Wife of Benjamin T. Livingstone's fourth child (born Aug. 1850, died six weeks later) was named after her.

0074 22 Jun. 1843. Annoyed at T.L. Prentice. News from Drummond. Moffat's 50 tons of luggage, much of which is useless. Williams has gone back to England. His correspondence with Mrs. Sewell. Dissatisfaction with Ross. Will soon begin mission among the Bakhatla. Ruins of Mosilikatze's town.

0091 5 Oct. 1843. Death of friends. Has bought land from the Bakhatla. Description of the site. Visit of hunters from India. Steele promises to open channel for sending money to Charles Livingstone. Final station not settled.

QUEKETT, John Thomas (1815 — 1861).
Professor of Histology, Royal College of Surgeons, 1851—61; Conservator of the Hunterian Museum, 1856—61. Author of several publications on various forms of histology and anatomy. **(DNB.)**

0701 11 Feb. 1858. *Thanking him for a list of items most in demand by the museum. Discusses busy schedule which prevents a visit before his departure.

RAE, George (? 1831 — 1865).
Said to have been born in Blantyre, Scotland, Rae served as a ship's engineer on the North Atlantic run. After working in the yards of Tod & Macgregor, Glasgow, he was appointed Engineer to the Zambezi Expedition in February 1858. Rae served in this capacity until 30 April 1864. He went into business in Zanzibar, but died prematurely in Glasgow a year later.

0779 15 Apr. 1858. Published in Wallis, **ZEDL** II, pp. 418—419.

1311 10 Jan. 1863. Chastizing Rae for stating he will not enter the "Pioneer" except when on duty; reminding him of his original agreement to serve the expedition; telling him that two establishments in one expedition cannot be permitted.

RANDALL, Mr.
A resident of Southampton.

0997 20 Feb. 1860. I did not write you earlier as I remembered everything about you but your name. We have not yet reached Makololo country, due to a bad vessel and a bad naval officer. Instead we reached the cotton country of the Shire and Lake Nyassa. Our mode of treating fever has rendered it not more formidable than the common cold. Greetings to Adkins and Nicholson.

RATCLIFFE, Mrs.
Of Castle Hill, Reading, Berkshire, mother of David Livingstone Ratcliffe.

0683   1 Feb. 1858.   Thanks for your present I received some time ago.   I pray that your wishes for your son may be realized.

RATCLIFFE, David Livingstone.
A child named after the explorer.

0681   28 Jan. 1858.   Advice on growing up as a good Christian.

RAWLINSON, Sir Henry Creswicke (1810 — 1895).
Served with the East India Company in the Middle East, where he deciphered Assyrian cuneiform.   Member of Parliament 1858, 1865—8.   President of the Royal Geographical Society 1871—2, 1874—5.   Created a baronet 1891.   **(DNB.)**

2028   [Jan. ?] 1873.   Thanks for Search Expedition; if they had come on he would have directed them to Victoria Nyanza.   Effect of rains.   Marshes near Lake Bangweolo. Lake Tanganyika.   Letters intercepted.

2029   [Jan. 1873?]   Thanks for Search Expedition.   Plunder of his goods and letters.   Lake Tanganyika.   Errors of longitude excusable.   Geology.   Villainy of Shereef and Ludha. Stoppage of his salary.

RAWSON, Sir Rawson William (1812 — 1899).
Colonial administrator, served as Colonial Secretary of the Cape of Good Hope 1854—64.
        (Who Was Who 1897—1916.)

0374   18 May 1855.   *On his journey, with geographical positions, the large rivers, and an attack of fever.

REIS, Joaquim Moreira.
Bishop of Angola, 1849—56;   Acting Governor, 1854;   later Commissario Geral da Bula da Santa Crusada.   **(GrEncPort. xvii. 873.)**

0379   12 Sep. 1855.   Please report the following to the Governor-General: arrived Libonta at the end of July, then descended the Zambesi slowly, being happily received by the people all the way; arrived at Sekeletu's village at the end of August; parcels received from my father-in-law were stored on an island near the falls; Sekeletu pleased with the gifts you sent; he sends his cordial thanks; today people discussed the possibility of moving north toward Libonta, and Sekeletu and most of the people are in favor, but some old members hesitate to leave the line of defense provided by the Chobe; people good to me; keep trade prospects open; ben Habib carries this tomorrow; I will write the Governor-General from Quilimane.

RICHARDS, Sir George Henry (1819 — 1876).
Captain R.N. (1854), succeeded John Washington as Hydrographer of the Admiralty 1863–74; Rear Admiral (1870).　　　　　(Boase, **MEB**.)

1422　10 Feb. 1864. Saddened by the death of Admiral Washington. Describing trip down the Shire, and telling of plans to go to Bombay.

1440　11 Apr. 1864. Enclosing Account of the expedition for 1863. With Shire depopulated by slave trade we had to procure food from Tette, Senna, Quilimane and Kongone, requiring three times the calico anticipated. Had to use Col. Nunes as an agent. Meller went from Quilimane to Kongone, where he suffered much sickness, then back to Quilimane and on to Mozambique. Further particulars about the 1863 budget.

1595　6 Feb. 1865. Detailed refutation of George Thornton's claim for his brother's expenses: Thornton had no authority to charge instruments, food, or servants to the Expedition, especially after he left to work for Von der Decken. His journals and collections should be requested. P.S. If principle admitted for Thornton, he can claim £5957 for 'Lady Nyasa', and smaller sums for other purposes. Other members would have similar claims.

1992　8 Feb. 1872. Letter will be taken by Stanley. Thanks for support of Young's expedition. Complaints about Kirk and Ludha. The sources, watershed, and fountains. The savage Manyuema slave trade. Sends back two pocket chronometers and two watches, all dead.

RICHARDSON, Sir John (1787 — 1865).
Surgeon on Franklin's Arctic expeditions and in charge of the search expedition for him. Knighted 1846.　　　　　(**DNB**.)

1628　2 Mar. 1865. Will refer to Arctic trees putting forth leaves while roots are frozen without mentioning his name. Weather atrocious.

RIDLEY, Catherine.
Daughter of Charles Ridley of Felstead; friend of Livingstone when he was at Ongar; later married T.L. Prentice.

0020　26 Feb. [1841]. Published in Chamberlin, **SLFL** no. 4.

RIGBY, Christopher Palmer (1820 — 1885).
Political Agent in Zanzibar, 1858–61.　　　　　(Russell, **RZST**.)

1081　25 Feb. 1861. We seek an opening around the Portuguese. In 1855 Ben Habib ben Salem Lafifi took 95 Makololo on an expedition to Loanda: they are unheard of after leaving there. Do you know of him? Can horses be produced for the Zambezi? Kirk and I send fever powder to Speke.

1169   23 Jan. 1862.   The party of Makololo about whom I wrote last year are en route back to their country, evidently as a result of your action.   When we visited the Lake we saw an Arab dhow carrying slaves across.   Heard that the Governor-General went to Zanzibar recently to settle the boundary on the Rovuma.   The Portuguese have built a fort at the mouth of the Shire and a Customs House at the mouth of the Kongone.   Is the Rovuma within the territory of Zanzibar or not?

1554   8 Dec. 1864.   At Nyassa we heard of no white man ever having been there.   Oldfield compared dates, found that we were there first, and remembers that Roscher was told that a party of whites reached the southern end first.   I lost Oldfield's letter and I wish you could supply the dates.   I hope to publish your letter as a footnote as the Germans claim it a German discovery.

ROBERTS, Samuel (1800 — 1885).
Pastor of Llanbrynmair 1834—57;   writer on social, political, and religious questions.
(DNB.)

0120   29 Apr. 1845.   Sends for young Welsh friends an account of an adventure [as in letter to Cambuslang Girls' School, 21 June, 1843], which if published should be anonymous.

ROBERTSON, William (1805—1879).
Born in Aberdeenshire, he was a minister of the Dutch Reformed Church in Swellendam, Cape Colony, 1832—72.   (DSAfrB I, p. 672.)

0831   22 Sep. 1858.   Regret any pain caused to any in Dutch Reformed Church by my footnote to which you refer, concerning the methods by which the church gained land following the battle at Boomplaats.   The behavior of the DRC clergymen toward the Government and other missionaries.   I regret you did not communicate with me when I was in Cape Town.

ROBINSON, Mrs.
A resident of Port Louis, Mauritius, visited by Livingstone in 1856.

0435   18 Oct. 1856.   Sends four roots of a kind of snowdrop for Miss Blanche's garden;   do not water or manure.   If they succeed give one to the Botanic Gardens.   Scold man who cheated us yesterday and made parting visit so short.

1283   24 Oct. 1862.   Sorry to hear of your sad bereavement like that I recently suffered.   Glad one of your daughters married my friend Keppill.   Kindest salutations to my friend Miss Blanche. We went up the Rovuma 114 miles in a straight line, came to cataracts, and now return to the Zambesi.   Mention my objects to Bishop Pryan.   I am getting old, so my young friends at Bagatelle may not know me.

ROUGH, George.
A glove manufacturer in and Lord Provost of Dundee, Scotland.

0502   15 Apr. 1857.   *Regret having caused you pain;   I laboured under anxiety about my men in Tette, to whom I am anxious to return.   However, since the Portuguese Government supports them at public expense, I am now at ease.   As my letters have been abused already, I do not answer a list of questions, but if you or anyone else wishes particular information, I will bear it in mind in the narrative.

0625   21 Nov. 1857.   Thanks to you and people of Dundee for additional £13 4/- which I received lately, which added to the £120 16/- received earlier equals £134.   I am proud of my connections with Scotland.

ROWLEY, Henry (? — ?1907).
A deacon connected to the Universities' Mission to Central Africa, 1860—64, Rowley went on to become Secretary to the Society for the Propagation of the Gospel, from 1865 to 1900.

1199   15 Mar. 1862.   The deaths of Mackenzie and Burrup a blow to the mission, which must now stick together more than ever.   We cannot serve you with the steamer, and can get no provisions unless we go to Johanna.   On the way down we were detained 6 weeks in a large marsh.   Reached the sea in late Jan.

1600   8 Feb. 1865.   Thank you for your letter which I think valuable as the Portuguese quote you as asserting that the disasters of the mission came from taking my advice instead of from slaving.   I did not want to appear in opposition to the mission.

RUSSELL, Rev. James, D.D.
Apparently a Catholic clergyman, possibly an Irishman and a Jesuit.

1304.9 29 Dec. 1862.   Seeks information on Jesuit translations into language of Senna and Tette, because help in mastering language will increase his influence.

1572.5 8 Jan. 1865.   Encloses proof sheet with regard to Catholic translations.   Portuguese worthless.

RUSSELL, Lord John, 1st Earl Russell (1792 — 1878).
Third son of 6th Duke of Bedford, created Earl Russell 30 Jul. 1861.   Member of Parliament from 1813 and for long leader of the Whigs.   Paymaster General 1830—4, Home Secretary 1835—9, Colonial Secretary 1839—41, Prime Minister 1846—52, Foreign Secretary 1852—3, Colonial Secretary 1855, Foreign Secretary 1859—65, Prime Minister 1865—6.   (DNB.)

Livingstone's copies of his letters to him of 15 Oct. 1859 (0938), Incl. 1—3, 7 Dec. (0939—41), 20 Nov. 1859 (0973), Incl. 1, 6 Dec. (0974), 9 Dec. 1859 (0975), Incl. 2, 12 Dec. (0977), 7 Feb. 1860 (0992), Incl. 2, 20 Feb. (0993), 10 Apr. 1860 (1019), Incl. 1, 10 Apr. (1020), 6 Sep. 1860 (1031), Incl. 1—3, 6 and 9 Sep. (1032—4), 24 Nov. 1860

210

(1040), Incl. 1–2, [24 Nov.] and 29 Dec. (1041–2), and 10 Nov. 1861 (1137; PS [17 Dec.] not published, see below), Incl. 1–3, 15 Nov. and [Nov.] (1138–40; Incl. 2 only partially published, see below) are published in Wallis, **ZEDL**; those of 2 Sep. 1862 (1267) and 16 and 21 Oct. 1862 (1280) are published in Shepperson, **DLatR**.

0976   Incl. 1, 9 Dec. 1859.   Ran down Shire to beach vessel and repair leaky bottom.   Rae made a new funnel.   She may float for a month or two, but we cannot bring her down-river again.   Hope to leave in a fortnight for Tette, and then on to the Makololo country. Admiral Grey assisted us in every way.

1043   Incl. 3, 29 Dec. 1860.   No marriages in Consular District thus far;   I will notify you if and when any take place.

1044   Incl. 4, 28 Dec. 1860.   Kirk, Livingstone, Rowe and Hutchins are well and performing their duties as of this date.

1076   9 Feb. 1861.   "Pioneer" arrived safely, in good condition and well stocked.   The Oxford and Cambridge Mission also arrived, and all are optimistic of their success.   Kirk's botanical report enclosed.   Dr. Roscher.   Cotton-growing potential of the Shire Valley.   The Rovuma.

1083   4, 10 Mar. 1861.   Description of Rovuma Bay, and intentions of going upriver.   European crew must be retained as Makololo cannot run the "Pioneer".

1093   11, 13 Mar. 1861.   Departure from Rovuma Bay delayed as we awaited arrival of coals from Johanna.   Prospects of the Rovuma as an alternative to the Shire.   Results of exploration after two days' journey upriver.

1104   16 Apr. 1861.   Had to return when the Rovuma fell;   "Pioneer" arrived two months too late.   It may yet be navigable.   It may be an outlet of Lake Tanganyika, but the people in the area say it comes from Lake Nyassa.   We will take the missionaries to a place near Mt. Zomba, then take a boat to Lake Nyassa.   Some men took ill at the river's mouth.   Landed at Mohilla for supplies, then went to Johanna.   Mr. May goes home.

1105   Incl. 1, [20 Apr. 1861].   His reasons for dismissing Daniel J. May: May would not consider himself subordinate to Kirk, and Livingstone had no orders from London that he should be so elevated.

1106   Incl. 2, [20 Apr. 1861].   Concerning Thornton's salary: Livingstone was unable to get in touch with him in Mosambique, and will return to the question when he again hears from Thornton.

1107   Incl. 3, [20 Apr. 1861].   With overland postal communications established with the Seychelles, may dispatches for Livingstone be sent to H.M. Commissioner Captain Wade for transmission to Mosambique or Johanna as Consul Sunley may direct.

1122   20 May 1861.   Reached Zambesi eight days from Johanna, waited a day for a smooth bar and entered the river on 1 May.   After cutting wood we went to Mazaro: 80 miles in sixteen hours.   I write to order new bushes for our paddle shaft, broken on the Rovuma. Also require copper tubing to prevent engine filling with sand.   Drawings and details have been sent to John Washington.

1123   Incl. 1, 20 May 1861.   Recommending Thornton's salary be restored without deduction whenever he applies for it.

1137 [17 Dec. 1861] (PS to 10 Nov.). Inclosure 3 an attempt to answer by anticipation a circular I expect to receive regarding cotton supply. A newspaper brought by one of the missionaries mentioned you intend to request this information from H.M. Consuls. I also enclose a paper for the R.G.S. and a list of dispatches received in 1861. We have lost our carpenter by fever; details sent to Captain Washington.

1139 Incl. 2, [Nov.] 1861. Price of two mules and two Scotch carts for carrying the steamer past the cataracts has probably been requested by Sir George Grey from the Foreign Office.

1160 25 Dec. 1861. Acknowledge receipt during this year of No. 1—5, plus a copy of May's appointment and the "Pioneer's" orders by the Hydrographer, a dispatch from Wodehouse, and a circular not requiring to be specified.

1185 22 Feb. 1862. Slaving on the Shire sends captives up the Zambesi, where they are sold for ivory. A fort erected at the Shire mouth said to be temporary. The sultan of Zanzibar met with the Governor of Mosambique; the latter wanted to include both banks of the mouth of the Rovuma within Portuguese claims, but Rigby kept our option open. 19,000 slaves pass through Zanzibar annually. H.M.S. "Gorgon" arrived with the brig in tow.

1186 Incl. 1, [22 Feb. 1862]. The party of Makololo who visited Loanda in 1855 were detained in Kilwa for 6 years by an Arab. They crossed the Lake en route to the Makololo country in Aug. or Sep. last. This was probably brought about though Rigby's energetic action.

1187 Incl. 2, [22 Feb. 1862]. Have I authority to prevent the mission from attacking the Ajawa again? Can I issue a formal protest or order the bishop not to engage in hostilities again? With regard to the Rovuma-Cape Delgado boundary dispute: is it part of my duty to take possession of our discoveries on Lake Nyassa in the name of Her Majesty?

1200 15 Mar. 1862. On the death of Bishop Mackenzie and Henry DeWint Burrup.

1235 5 Jun. 1862. I am living on this day and write to enable Coutts & Co. to draw from the Treasury the salary now due me.

1240 27 Jun. 1862. In a recent conversation with Dr. Kirk, the Governor of Tette upheld the principle of slaving operations within the country being legal, and that slaves and slave traders will defend selves and property. This is contrary to Portugal's anti-slavery legislation of 1854, 56 and 58. These, coupled with Sa da Bandeira's assertions concerning Portuguese explorations published in **Almanac** for 1862, and the willingness of the Governor at Mosambique to make a demonstration against slavery beyond his boundaries indicate that the Portuguese intend to extend their boundaries to include the Shire valley.

1241 1 Jul. 1862. Due to the "culpable negligence" of Charles Hardesty we have been detained 5 months in the delta. Fever and dysentery resulted, but the only death was that of Mary Livingstone. The Portuguese learned from us and moved their troops upriver. Mr. Rae never saw the engines in such a wretched state. I allowed Hardesty to retire. The detention added considerably to our expenses. The particulars have been forwarded to Captain Washington.

1281 21 Oct. 1862. I am alive on this day and write to enable Coutts & Co. to collect my salary from H.M. Government.

1297   15 Dec. 1862.   Acknowledge receipt this year of Dispatches No. 1 & 2 of 1861 & No. 1 of the present year, and the circular Dec. 16, 1861.

1305   29 Dec. 1862.   Have communicated to Mr. Thornton that in joining this mission again his salary without any deduction will be given him.   He has been working at different parts of the Zambesi under my direction with improved health and energy, and will likely give a good account of the geology of this region.

1306   29 Dec. 1862.   Slavery continues to thrive between Shire and Tette.   The Makololo freed a few parties but refrained on seeing white men present out of a reluctance to shed white man's blood.   At Quilimane they now fetch 1 fathom of calico each rather than 8. Six Scotch traders in Cape Colony wish to join me;   I have approved their coming by sea as soon as possible.   We may employ them a short time in transport and erecting a station above the cataracts.   We require free navigation only between Mazaro and the Shire, as the Portuguese do not use the delta.   When in Quilimane we encountered the "Joven Carlotta" laden probably with slaves.

1307   Incl. 4, [29 Dec. 1862].   Slave hunting on east bank of Shire began in 1856 by Marianno for his brother-in-law Cruz.   Marianno spent only 3 years in prison although condemned for over 40 murders, and was back in Quilimane last year.   Since then he has been ravaging the area around Mt. Clarendon with 1000 armed slaves: the fugitives crowded into the Shire valley.   It is not known where his captives go.   Col. de Portgual, Governor of Inhambane I met in Angola in 1854 was publicly disgraced for misconduct, returned to this region from Bombay via H.M.S. "Orestes," again carries on slave exporting from Inhambane.   The west coast is so different from this one: there we have 8 settlements, trade flourishes, dialects are reduced, peace and blessings follow;   but none of this is here.   Please send extracts of this to Palmerston and Clarendon.

1316   28 Jan. 1863.   We are now towing the steamer, and met with no obstructions until within forty miles of the cataracts.   Review of the slaving in the Shire valley in the wake of his opening it in 1859.

1339   28 Apr. 1863.   Drought, famine and slave trade has in one year produced unbelievable devastation in the Shire valley.   In former droughts, people cultivated in the marshes and survived; now this is not possible due to the slaving.   Hence our food supplies must come from the south, and Dr. Kirk and C. Livingstone go home in failing health.   Details on the death of Richard Thornton.   Health and spirits of the expedition are low.

1340   Incl. 1, 28 Apr. 1863.   Kirk and C. Livingstone return home, after having served the expedition well.   Kirk I confidently recommend to H.M. Government in any capacity they wish to employ him.   The collections they made go with them: the British Museum gets the first refusal, also Hooker and Owen and Murchison, to keep specimens from going into private collections.

1341   Incl. 2, 28 Apr. 1863.   On the death of Richard Thornton.   His effects and papers have been sealed, and his two Zanzibari servants are due wages since March, 1862.   I send the two men to Mr. Rick in Zanzibar, requesting he fulfill their terms and be reimbursed by English Consul, who will draw the amount against Thornton's salary, from the Foreign Office.

1347   1 May 1863.   My dispatches have indicated that unless the slave trade can be suppressed, the objects of this mission cannot be realized.   If the Portuguese restrict the mouths of the rivers, our utmost efforts will produce no permanent effect.   The steamer cost twice what I expected;   had she reached the lake, I would have asked ½ the expenditure returned.   Should I send her to India for sale there?

1378   17 Jul. 1863.   *Current and future state of the Universities' mission. Livingstone's dissatisfaction with the way the orders recalling the expedition were treated: contents were known in Mosambique, and those who delivered the dispatch to him announced its contents in a rude manner before they had even landed.

1382   20 Jul. 1863.   Orders for withdrawal received, relieving us from the suspense into which the depopulation of the valley had thrown us. I regret having given credit to the Portuguese desire to end the slave trade. The river fell before the dispatch arrived. Kirk takes home proof of the economic and vegetable productions of the country: the complaint by H.M. Government that scanty information was received was premature. On the west coast, the squadron's success was derived in part from the zeal and benevolence of the missionaries; hence I saw the success of the Universities' mission as vital. Comparison of the two coasts. H.M. Government should not give up on this region, as it is "scarcely probable that another leader would meet with half the hindrances which have baffled me." Before leaving I intend to go north to account for the perennial flow of the Shire.

1383   Incl. 1, 20 Jul. 1863.   I have attempted to give the Universities' mission the benefit of my opinion and experience, but Tozer only wanted me to agree with his preconceived views. He likes Morambala, as stores can be got easily and retreat is easy if necessary, but there are no people there to be taught. I told him that by sowing wheat in May and irrigating it, the mission could become independent of the Cape for flour. Tozer thinks I advised Mackenzie to make war on the Ajawa, in spite of Mackenzie's own journal. Mackenzie and Burrup died from walking in the stream when dressed — it would not have killed them in England. The rest died in the unhealthy lowlands, and not in the healthy highlands.

1407   12 Dec. 1863.   On the trip to the region west of Lake Nyassa, we found evidence of the trade route extending westwards from Kotakota. Here I hoped the missionaries would work; here alone can the trade be stopped. The Shupanga men were sick, due to the high altitude and the change of air. The Luapula is reported to flow westward, forming lakes Mofue and Moero, and after being joined by the Lualaba turns around the town of Cazembe and enters Lake Tanganyika. An outlet may exist on the S.W. of that lake, allowing water to reach the Kasai northwest of where I crossed it. Instead of going on to Bemba, the Steward and I turned back. Many crops are found in the country. 24 Feb. 1864. The river rose on 19 Jan., but we were further delayed by a rudder accident. Met H.M.S. "Ariel" and "Orestes" at Kongone on 13 Feb., and proceeded in their company to Mosambique.

1408   Incl. 1, 12 Dec. 1863.   I have learned with regret that Tozer will leave the Zambesi as early next year as possible. I hope this will not be a step toward Madagascar, where all the work has been done by missionaries from another society, and where the addition of Anglican priests can only add discord among the French Catholic religious orders. 24 Feb. 1863. Upon reaching Morambala I found that Tozer had left the country and gone to Quilimane. I took on board 2 missionaries and 35 orphans. Gardner says Tozer had plans to wind up the affairs of the mission and retire, when he first arrived here.

1413   19 Dec. 1863.   Acknowledge receipt during the past year of Dispatch No. 2 of 1862, and No. 1 of Feb. last, plus the "Merchant Seaman's Act," the "Patent Law Amendment Act," etc., and 3 circulars.

1716   19 May 1865.   Please pay the £500 authorized by you for me to Coutts & Co.

1721   23 May 1865.   In reference to your dispatch No. 2 of 28 March last: I understand from

Clarendon and Murchison that the concluding clauses do not reflect your current views, so I return it for your reconsideration.

1844   28 Nov. 1865.   Arrived here 11 Sep.; as steamer is too small to sail back, I go by "Thule". Have 12 sepoy volunteers and a native officer plus 8 liberated Africans, and 14 buffalo. Governor Frere has helped me in every way possible.   Gentlemen of Bombay gave me £645, which I deposited with a mercantile firm until I find a place for an establishment. Instructions from you and the R.G.S. will receive my earliest attention.

RUTHERFOORD, Howson Edward.
Merchant in Cape Town and director there of the London Missionary Society.   (Schapera, **DLSAP**, p. 147, n. 4.)

0285   8 Sep. [1852].   *Difficulties with Boers, who attacked natives and sacked his house.

SABINE, Sir Edward (1788 — 1883).
2nd Lt. R.A. (1803), became interested in astronomy and terrestrial magnetism and was instrumental in conducting the first systematic magnetic survey ever made in Great Britain (mid-1830's), which he repeated in 1858—61.   President of the Royal Society, 1861—71.   Promoted to General R.A. in 1870, he retired from the Army in 1877.   A prolific writer on scientific matters.   **(DNB.)**

0612   30 Oct. 1857.   Liverpool Chamber of Commerce has not yet decided whether to send a deputation or a messenger.   It will be proper for me to accompany the deputation to expound upon matters as required.   I shall be happy to hear from you as soon as you know when an interview will be granted.

SALT, Sir Titus (1803 — 1876).
Manufacturer who made his fortune by developing a method of using alpaca hair, then built manufacturing town of Saltaire, near Bradford.   He represented Bradford in Commons, 1859—61;   created a baronet in 1869.   **(DNB.)**

0611.5 29 Oct. 1857.   Visit to Portugal delayed by epidemic, will therefore come to Bradford on 10 Nov. and will stay with either Salt or the Mayor.

0618   10 Nov. 1857.   *Regretting he is unable to visit Bradford.

SAUMAREZ, Philip (? — 1889).
Lt. of H.M. Sloop "Persian," at the Cape Naval Station, 1859—60, which visited the Zambezi Expedition at Kongone in July—August 1859;   Captain R.N. (1866), Rear Admiral (1883).   **(Navy List.)**

0921   30 Jul. 1859.   May we have sheet iron to repair our sinking vessel, and also white and red lead paint for our whalers?   Also we require oil, salt provisions, shoes, blankets, stockings, blue check shirts, serge and blue cloth (enough for a jacket of two), and a piece of sheet lead.   Can you take 10 Kroomen and use them on board so their contract is not broken? We have 46 Makololo and expect to work on land for 6 months. Walker must go due to illness; we give double full pay for two seaman volunteers.

SCHUT, Alberto.
A leading merchant of Loanda; financial member of the committee administering the local almshouse, 1853—56.   (Schapera, **LAJ I**, p. 156, n.)

0383   12 Sep. 1855.   We arrived two days ago, and presented to the people the presents of yours, the Bishop of Angola, and the Governor General.   A meeting was convened to consider moving residence toward a city which is 240 miles closer to Loanda.   This and other communications will be delivered tomorrow to an Arab of Zanzibar, who is said to have relations with Sr. Pires and Carvalho Bastos.   The presents were delivered just as you packed them.   I explained to the people your desire to trade in ivory and wax, and of your ability in the business due to your proximity to the sea; the custom and benefit of free trade, and your good will, which will benefit Sekeletu and all his people.   Sekeletu sends his sincere gratitude.   Another expedition to Loanda is preparing.   My old companions are eager to return, in spite of the fact that their earnings were all exhausted on the journey home.   It is hoped that trade will lead to amicable relations and the disappearance of wretched jealousies and isolation between the different people here.   Sentiments of brotherhood, good will and reciprocal dependency are the result of introducing Christianity, commerce and civilization.   My sincere compliments to you and all those who assisted toward the success of my visit to Angola, and toward the establishing of friendly and commercial relations between distant peoples and the civilized inhabitants of Angola.

SEDGWICK, Adam (1785 — 1873).
Professor of Geology at Cambridge after 1818, he was later a fellow of the Geological Society, of the Royal Society, and was President of the British Association in 1833, and of its geological section in 1837, 1845, 1853 and 1860.   (**DNB.**)

0690   6 Feb. 1858.   I appreciate your support in my expedition.   List of the positions (not names) of his men follow, with the hopes that it may lead to the establishment of an English Colony in the healthy highlands of Africa.

0758   †8 Mar. 1858.   *There was so little probability of my adding to it during my present enterprise that I sent it to the press and had 25 copies printed.

0895   27 May 1859.   Discovery of Lake Shirwa and exploration of Shire valley.   Highlands are promising for Europeans and the development of cotton.   French emigration scheme.

1319   16 Feb. 1863.   Review of the last four years: Tette people followed in his footsteps, introducing slavery.   Marianno depopulates region around Mt. Morambala.   Slave trade, and the situation on the west coast of Africa.   Commerce, Christianity and civilization. Sorrow over the Universities' mission.

1397   5 Nov. 1863.   Recommending the university Boat Club contribute a vessel to the UMCA. Wheat may be grown in the Shire valley.   Visited Lake Nyassa recently: Zulus are depopulating the land to the west.   24 Dec.   Regret Tozer's decision.   No Europeans died of disease where I placed them.

1654   26 Mar. 1865.   Thanks for letter.   Totally involved in book;   extra labour in working his and his brother's journals together.   Hopes it may help stop Portuguese activities. Tozer has dissipated opportunities created by Mackenzie.   After finishing book and visiting Scotland will return to find a way north of Portuguese.   No stone age in Africa.

1745   †15 Jun. 1865.   If possible will call to say goodbye.

1777   27 Jul. 1865.   *Hopes to get to Cambridge to see him.

1780   28 Jul. 1865.   *Came from Newstead on Tuesday and on return on Thursday will begin to pack in earnest.

1901   24 Aug. 1866.   Avoided by Arab slave traders.   Country rises quickly;   well watered; geology. Mataka.   Depopulation.   Missionary opportunity lost by Tozer.   Dean of Ely's offer of help with children's education.   1 Feb. 1867.   Now on watershed.   No news since leaving coast.   Having a belated Christmas feast tomorrow.

SEKELETU (?1834 — 1864).
Son of Sebituane and chief of the Kololo, 1853—64.   Treated for a skin disease by Livingstone in 1860.   His people disintegrated as a political unit after his death.

The letter is also addressed to Mburuma, and was subsequently copied for several other African chiefs.

0741   [Feb. 1858].   Thanking Mburuma, Sekeletu and others for helping Livingstone during his travels, and indicating that H.M. Government would welcome establishing trading links with them all.

SEWARD, Mrs.
Wife of George E.

1443.1   [23—30 Apr. 1864.]   He is rating chronometers on the roof.   Sorry her husband is ill.

SEWARD, George Edwin (? — 1909).
Graduated in medicine at Edinburgh in 1855;   appointed Assistant Surgeon in the Bombay establishment 1855, Surgeon 1867.   From 1863 to 1867 he served as Agency Surgeon, Acting Political Agent, and Acting Consul in Zanzibar, where Livingstone met him in Apr. 1864.   Retired in 1884.   (Ind. Army List; Medical Register.)

1443.7   1 Jun. 1864.   Apologies for bad manners.   Difficulty in starting engine.   Biliousness of crew.   Other medical details.   Steamer uses more coal than was stated;   glad he did not sell her under false pretences.   12 Jun.   Details of voyage.   23 Jun.   Bartle Frere's invitation.   Instead of selling ship will go home for counsel. Sultan's letter delivered.

1891   5 Apr. 1866.   Beast of burden now ready for use.   Sending back boat and contents. Description of the harbour.   Difficulties in getting carriers and guides.   Buffalo wounded a donkey.   Do not publish this but send it to Agnes.

1912   1 Feb. 1867.   Party of Bagamoyo slaves take this.   Problems with sepoys and other groups of porters. Hunger. Supplies required, which should be sent to Ujiji; keep them light as heavy things cannot be carried.

1920 25 Sep. 1867. Hears goods have reached Ujiji. Detained by war for 3½ months. Kind treatment by party of Arabs. Desertion of Nassick boy. Buffaloes all died on way to Ujiji.

1925 14 Dec. 1867. Letters sent. Needs shoes, tracing paper, pencils, etc. Going to Ujiji in two days. Moero one of a chain of lakes connected by a river.

1938.8 Nov. 1871. *Previous letters plundered. Box of guns and medicine detained at Unyanyembe. Supplies lost because of Kirk's failure. Stanley rescued him from despair. Will finish Nile sources before retiring. P.S. Disappointment in Kirk. Stanley will enquire in India where to send this letter.

SEWELL, Margaret.
A widow who kept a boarding-house in London, where Livingstone lodged when a student.

0011 3 Aug. 1840. Shares joy at Charles's success. Reason for not writing earlier. Sleeping on deck on the voyage did no harm. Family's thanks for her kindness.

0012 8 Aug. 1840. Health restored. She should go to the country. Liston's prejudicial remark about an Edinburgh surgeon. Maclehose's hop very impressive. Parcel with specimen dress for sister sent. Greetings. Brother enjoying Oberlin.

0013 25 Aug. [1840]. Time is short. Leaves tomorrow and will be in London on Friday or Saturday.

0051 7 Apr. 1842. Apologies for light-hearted letters. At present with Bubu, whose people are much more obliging than Bechuanas to the south. Intends to travel practising medicine and leaving native teachers behind. Irrigation of garden. Intends to travel west to warn Sebegwe of danger from Mahura. Celibacy comfortable and does not arouse suspicion. Bechuanas all married because women work and are stronger than men; more northern tribes are physically superior. Northern vegetation also better than that at Kuruman. If Mrs. Moffat criticises missionaries' wives she is not to be believed. Some mission stations in Cape Colony excellent, but many places there do not require missionary. Most Bechuanas remain selfish even after conversion. Awaits letters. Regards to mutual friends. Folly of Ross. A wife might be useful, but no possible candidate in South Africa; her previous criticism of his obstinacy here is based on ignorance of his history.

0060 14 Jul. 1842. Regrets she has not received letters. If possible recommend Edwards to Tidman. Recollects with pleasure his early toils. Hears that Gospel is being well received in Rio de Janeiro.

0069 †17 Jun. 1843. Journey to Bakhatla. Meeting with Sebegwe, whose initial hostility was overcome. Drinks native beer which is not intoxicating. Want of good men prevented him from visiting a reputed lake.

0176 20 Sep. 1847. Travel has improved his strength but made Mary thin. Chief at Kolobeng insists on building house. Gossip about missionaries.

0210   21 Sep. 1849.   Has reached Lake Ngami.   People on the Zouga.   Plans to return.   Still 200 miles from home.

0223   20 Feb. 1850.   Visit of Freeman, who wishes to reduce London Missionary Society spending in South Africa from £9000 to £4000;   unfortunately he agrees with Philip on keeping up Colonial stations.

0235   9 Sep. 1850.   Thanks for periodicals.   Frédoux driven back from Bampala by Boers. Fever and tsetse prevented their going to Sebituane.   Robert Moffat now a surveyor. Salaries of London Missionary Society agents less than those of any other society.

0248   19 Apr. 1851.   Thanks for parcels and periodicals.   Criticism of Inglis.   War everywhere. Details about James Wilson.

0297   22 Nov. 1852.   Misses children.   Boers' attack on Kolobeng.   They blame him for the Bakwains' fighting ability.   Natives' defeat is punishment for their rejection of the Gospel.   Progress of the Caffre War;   criticism of Cathcart and Calderwood.   Thanks for periodicals.

SHAFTESBURY, 7th Earl of (1801 – 1885).
Antony Ashley Cooper, succeeded to the title in 1851.   Famous philanthropist, with an interest in a multitude of benevolences.   A member of various religious societies, including the Church Missionary Society.   (DNB.)

0653   [Nov.–Dec. 1857?].   I send you a copy of my book in hopes that Africa and England can be linked more closely than before.   The discoveries discussed therein indicate that raw material may be got by labour, which may lead to the freeing of the African from heathenism.   May your mind be directed to Africa.

SHAW, H. Norton (? – 1868).
Born in St. Croix, Danish West Indies.   Qualified as a surgeon in Copenhagen;   M.D. (London).   Travelled widely as a surgeon for a shipping line.   Assistant Secretary of the Royal Geographical Society 1849–54, Acting Secretary 1854–63.   British Consul at St. Croix. (Information from Mrs. C. Kelly, Archivist to the Royal Geographcial Society.)

0244   [Aug. 1850 – Jan. 1851].   *Did not receive guides from Sebituane and could not proceed without them because of tsetse.   Intends to visit him with Oswell in May. Native reports of rivers north of Lake Ngami.

0455   20 Jan. 1857.   I forward letter of Lt. Hoskins, commander of the "Pluto," whom I met in Loanda and who gave me a copy of Humboldt's "Cosmos."   Capt. Parker examined the river up to Mazaro;   I did not see this section due to my lack of nautical experience.

0464   [2 Feb. 1857].   I return paper with corrections.   Morning Times places the mistake upon my shoulders;   after this save me from my friends.

0471   20 Feb. [1857].   Mrs. L. requires a surgeon: can you introduce her to one of your friends?   Thanks for the journals;   the observations have not come yet.   If you copy them, won't Cooley get them out in Germany before I do?   Saw your friend Prince Albert yesterday.

0473   3 Mar. 1857.   At your suggestion, I'd like to draw £50 from the testimonial fund.   I could draw from L.M.S., but it would be for 1857 and I have no intention of so doing.

0481   [23 Mar. 1857?].   The government of Portugal has sent orders to Mozambique to support Dr. Livingstone's late companions at province expense until he returns.

0485   25 Mar. [1857].   L.M.S. put £200 at my disposal.   I had only £100 out of 4 years salary; Mrs. L. drew it, having only £45 after paying for the children.   I have no intention of drawing more money from the L.M.S.

0487   26 Mar. [1857].   Will try to see you tomorrow.   Get me a copper boat like Burton's. Clarendon is agreeable.

0505   21 Apr. 1857. Glad you are better. I wrote Lord Mayor, wishing fund be paid to Coutts' bank.   Saw Capt. Denman today;   we agree it best to appear not to quarrel with the Society.

0536   5 Jun. 1857.   Discusses his astronomical observations, Maclear's reductions of them, and Arrowsmith's use of the reductions.   Progress of **MT**:   L. is working on new material and not proofs. Agnes's eye problem.

0545   27 Jun. 1857.   Requests the letter in which he describes the Falls of the Zambesi. Arrowsmith puts the blame for his own delaying on L. Give my daguerreotype to Brand to return to Gabriel.

0547   1 Jul. 1857.   I return letter on Falls with thanks.   Please send daguerreotype of me which Gabriel sent from Loanda to Brand.   Moffat's son made the map, and he will be much pleased with your notice of him.   Miss Moysey is Gabriel's cousin.

0552   8 Jul. 1857.   Heard from Lord Mayor yesterday and wrote acknowledgements to Hon. Secretaries and his Lordship.   Am writing new matter;   approaching Tete.   I am not well, have giddiness and headaches.

0555   10 Jul. [1857].   Agnes's eyes worse;   have treated them accordingly.   Tells of his plans for the next day and Sunday.

0580   4 Sep. 1857.   On L.'s movements to Manchester and from Dublin, and the possible publication of a table of longitude and latitude.   L. wishes his map sent to Manchester. Toynbee is pleased with his astronomical observations;   you remember Murchison said R.G.S. would publish them.   Have you heard anything of a steamer for the Zambesi?

0581.2 5 Sep. 1857.   Please send to Manchester the map I used in Dublin.

0582   9 Sep. 1857.   Please send map to Manchester. I put "corresponding member" on the title page believing that will make me one afterwards.   I leave **Analysis** at Murray's.

0583   12 Sep. 1857. I mention you and Sir Roderick in the Preface. (Details on **MT** follow).

0614   2 Nov. [1857].   Further details on **MT**, especially about Shaw's corrections on the size of Livingstone's ammunition.   L.'s plans for Thursday, and Monday 9th.

0700   11 Feb. 1858.   I went once to Society's house and you were busy.   I met Sir R. and walked to the end of the street with him, and on to the F.O.

1082   1 Mar. 1861.   We await "Lyra" which brings us coal.   The journal of Silva Porto is a literary fraud;   he told me he tried but failed after reaching the Kafue.   If in England, Gabriel will corroborate the story.

1172   [13 Nov. 1861 – 31 Jan. 1862].   A list of 26 latitudes, mostly taken during the exploration of Lake Nyasa in 1861.   Lake is 15 to 40 miles wide and 200 miles long, as a minimum.

SHELBURNE, Lord (1816 – 1866).
Henry Thomas Petty Fitzmaurice, succeeded as 4th Marquis of Lansdowne in 1863. Member of Parliament 1847–56;   Under-Secretary for Foreign Affairs 1856–8.
(DNB.)

0647   21 Dec. 1857.   If Lt. Bedingfeld, who knows African rivers, is chosen, he might be put on the Admiral's ship at the Cape for a full year, and have his time counted as service.   The additional expense to the country would be only ½ pay.

0930   9 Aug. 1859.   Having spent so much time as Skipper I was unable to write you previously. Vessel badly constructed.   Description of the Shire valley and highlands.   Portuguese never came up here.   A colony of Germans coming out here will probably work at coal we have begun.   A small English colony will do immense good.   We owe our health more to good food than to quinine.   Must sleep wet as we cannot keep our cabin dry.

SICARD, Tito Augusto de Araújo (? – 1864).
Major, Military Commandant of Tete up to 1859, when he became Governor of Ibo. From 1862 until his death he was Commandant of Mazaro and the Shire.   He was very hospitable to Livingstone in 1856, and again in 1858–59, but in the following years relations between the two were strained.

Letters to him of 23 Jun. 1859 (0908), 23 Jun. 1859 (0909), and 26 Jun. 1859 (0911) are published in Wallis, **ZEDL**.

SILVA, Custódio José da.
Governor of Quilimane during the entire period of the Zambezi Expedition, which position carried with it more autonomy and hence more power than did the other regional governorships within the Provincia da Moçambique.   Da Silva was rescued by Livingstone and a Portuguese sergeant when wounded under fire at Mazaro on Jun. 22 1858, after which his wounds were treated by John Kirk.

0784   26 Apr. 1858.   Presenting his credentials as H.M. Consul to Quilimane, and requesting aid from authorities in Sena and Tete.

1116   1 May 1861.   I have communicated your offer of service to Bishop Mackenzie, who expresses his thanks.   So many lives were lost on the bar of the Zambesi, including lately an officer of H.M.S. "Lyra," that I have examined a river to the north.   Having spent unhealthy months of Feb., Mar., and April in Johanna, we now take the bishop as close to Lake Nyassa as possible.

1248   14 Jul. 1862.   Apologizing for the unruly behaviour of the crew of H.M.S. "Gorgon," and expressing Captain Wilson's apologies and determination to punish the guilty men. Thanking him for hospitality toward Lt. Burlton. Mentions an attack on Chibisa by Belshore.

1308   5 Jan. 1863.   Your letter implied that my expedition and the mission under the late Bishop Mackenzie were one and the same, but the mission now under Procter is neither an exploring nor a scientific expedition. Mackenzie brought papers from Duprat containing I suppose "all necessary explanations." Their luggage and provisions were never intended nor used for commercial purposes. In future address them separately. The crew of the "Pioneer" are Royal Navy men, and use provisions as do those in Portugal's navy. They buy food in this country using calico bought from the Portuguese in this country. I regret that the Governor-General has been led to believe that we have abused our privileges. The misunderstanding arose because I used our steamer to transport their goods, the same as I would have done for the Governor-General if necessary. Our arms and ammunition were introduced into the country in 1858 and until recently stored in the fort at Tette.

SKEAD, Francis (1823 — 1891).
A career sailor, Skead was the Royal Navy's Surveyor at the Cape of Good Hope from 1856 to 1863. He accompanied the Zambezi Expedition from Cape Town in 1858, surveying with them the West Luabo and the Zambezi delta. His discovery of the Kongone River/Canal at this time was vital to Livingstone's interests. Skead resurveyed the delta of the great river in 1861, and after his retirement worked many years as Port Captain at Algoa Bay, South Africa.

0776   3 Apr. 1858.   Request the loan of a sextant for use by this expedition, in addition to the one already being used.

1087   6 [Mar.] 1861.   I was pleased when Washington said you were coming, not even thinking you'ld be here for anything less than half a year. I thought you would at least survey Nyassa. The Rovuma promises well: a large deep bay, no bar, and Mr. May found no bottom with seventeen fathoms across the mouth. Country well wooded. People speak nearly the same language as at Tete. Best wishes.

1993   8 Feb. 1872.   On his explorations during the past 6 years, and of his search for the sources of the Nile River. A long time since he heard from Skead. The Arabs and Banians are not reliable mail carriers: this one is taken to the coast by an American gentleman.

SMITH, Sir Andrew (1797 — 1872).
Staff Surgeon, R.A. 1837. From 1821 to 1837 Smith was stationed in the Cape Colony and Natal, where he conducted serious ethnic studies on the Khoi-San and the Zulu people. From 1837 to 1858 when in Britain he rose regularly through the ranks of the Army Medical Department, becoming its Superintendent. Knighted 1858. (DNB.)

0902   31 May 1859.   In saying that the Balonda have square huts I misled you. (Discussion of African huts follows.) Have just visited a country similar to Londa. Local fever is so mild that Kirk and I failed to recognize it at first. Method of treating it. Our artist fails miserably with the natives, but I will have photographs to aid your work of ethnology.

SMITH, R.M.

1521   31 Oct. [1864].   Busy writing and cannot visit him to discuss proposals for his son, who is with him and will do well.   If he is still of the same mind, he should write.

1542   24 Nov. 1864.   Too busy to accept invitation to dinner.   P.S.   Thanks for writing to Dr. Sherman on Robert's behalf.   He was kidnapped into army, his reluctance being shown by his refraining from taking life.

1546.2 28 Nov. 1864.   *Robert has been kidnapped and has changed his name.   Efforts to secure him a passage to England.   News of his other son.

SMYTH, Annarella.
Wife of Admiral William H. Smyth, née Warington.

0676   26 Jan. 1858.   On an instrument L. wanted to buy.   I know Taylor well, also the circumstances which caused him to write the Admiral.   A Mrs. Bevan, wife of a London banker, wanted to give us something, and he mentioned the instrument;   that was two months ago.   I shall see Taylor in 2 days and get the instrument [a chronometer?] myself.   Where in London may I find one?

SMYTH, William Henry (1788 — 1865).
Captain, R.N. (1824), retired as Rear Admiral in 1853.   (DNB.)

0665   18 Jan. 1858.   Had hoped to accept invitation you extended to instruct me on determining longitude, but as I have been so busy will you kindly tell me about the instrument's probable cost and size?   If my funds can meet it, I will get one as soon as possible. Hope to get away next month but the vessel is not ready yet.

SNOW, John.
Publisher and bookseller in London.

0309   12 Jan. 1853.   Last box of books suffered damage because of bad packing.   Orders books on theology, medicine, natural history, etc.

SOUTHAMPTON, Above Bar Sunday School.

0110   17 Sep. 1844.   Thanks for £15 for native teacher;   difficult to find a suitable recipient at once.   All have duties with regard to mission.   Youth is a happy time only with Christian commitment.   Yesterday began Sunday School in Mabotsa.

SPENCER, Thomas (1796 — 1853).
Curate of Hinton Charterhouse 1826—47;   social reformer.   (DNB.)

0298   22 Nov. 1852. Has totally abstained from alcohol for over 20 years. Does not intend to experiment if his duties would be better performed if he used it. English drinking customs and drinks destroy natives' souls and bodies.

STANLEY, Lord (1826 — 1893).
Edward Henry Stanley, succeeded as 15th Earl of Derby in 1869. Conservative politician, **inter alia** Foreign Secretary Jun. 1866 — Dec. 1868 (Livingstone did not know of the change of Government till Nov. 1871).   **(DNB.)**

1935   26 Mar. 1869. Supplementary to despatch of Jul. 1868, gives information on Lake Bangweolo, its islands and size. The nature of the watershed: primary sources are natural sponges, which form into large streams or secondary sources. Great humidity is due to direction of prevailing winds and altitude. No zone of continuous rainfall. Information on fountains which seem to be sources of the Nile and Zambesi. Dispute between Muabo and traders prevented him examining ancient buildings. Future plans. Speke's errors.

1950   15 Nov. 1870. Journey north-west along watershed. Meeting with Ujijian ivory and slave traders. The Lualaba. Beautiful country, but difficult to travel through. Vegetation. Forest. Lust for ivory. Rested during rains. Manyuema afraid to travel. Balagga country. Foot ulcers. Difficulty in getting men. Hostility of Governor of Unyanyembe. Exaggerated stories about Manyema.

1951   15 Nov. 1870. [As previous letter to 1.4 foot ulcers.] The Lualaba. Lake Lincoln. The fountains; native reports. Ptolemy's account of the sources good, but his Mountains of the Moon mysterious.

STANLEY, Sir Henry Morton (1841 — 1904).
Journalist and explorer. As roving correspondent of the **New York Herald** he was sent by J.G. Bennett 2 to find Livingstone, and met him at Ujiji in Nov. 1871; he remained with him till 14 Mar. 1872, and on his return to Zanzibar organised supplies. He later travelled extensively in Central Africa.   **(DNB; Hall, Stanley.)**

2007   14 Mar. 1872. Slaves employed by Kirk have caused so much loss that if Stanley meets another party he is to send them back.

2008   15 Mar. 1872. Telegraph from London about Murchison's health. Will return when satisfied about sources. Has copied observations from Kabuire to Cazembe to Lake Banguelu. Forwards Arab letters. 16 Mar. Has written to Murray to help in sending journal to Agnes.

2030   [Jan. 1873?] Gratitude for sending supplies and men, which and who are mostly excellent. That Chambezi is not Zambesi was indicated by Cazembe, whose empire was much exaggerated by Portuguese. Other exaggerations. Election of Baurungu chiefs. False reports of his former visit to Lake Banguelu.

STEARNS, William French (1834 — 1874).
A merchant from Massachusetts, partner of Stearns, Hobart and Co. in Bombay 1857—68. Livingstone met him on board ship in 1865 and lived in his house for much of his stay in Bombay.

1875   2 Feb. 1866.   Nine buffaloes dead because of some plant;   send more.   Has to wait three weeks for 'Penguin'.   Von der Decken killed because he treated natives with contempt;   River Juba closed by his conduct.   Ammunition lost.

1879   15 Feb. 1866.   Apply to Tracey for payment for buffaloes.   Arrangements for getting them to the Rovuma.   Brava people may not bring camels because of Von der Decken's death.   Kirk coming here.   Living at Sultan's expense.

1882   19 Feb. 1866.   Repeats message of previous letters, sent by Seychelles, in case this, by Sultan's ship, arrives first.   Two Nassick boys have gone home with free passage.

1958   Nov. 1870.   No paper, so uses leaf of cheque book.   Expected in 1866 to examine watershed in two years and then begin a mission, which is much needed as Tozer dawdles in Zanzibar.   The watershed, its springs, rivers, and lakes.   No one cared where rivers ran.   Hindered by wars, illness, and unsuitable men.   Lake Lincoln and the four fountains, probably those mentioned to Herodotus.   Manyuema country;   exaggerated stories about them.   Give extracts of this to New York Geographical Society.   P.S. Speke's error.   Sympathy for Dutch lady explorer.   Buffaloes ill-treated and died.   Has had no letters for years and does not know how his affairs stand.

2006   13 Mar. 1872.   This, with previous letter enclosed, goes with Stanley;   now has greater knowledge.   Plunder of goods by slaves.   Financial loss in crash of Agra Bank.   Destruction of letters.   Now equipped for final journey by Americans.

STEBBING, J.R.
Polytechnic Institution, Southampton.

1480   1 Sep. 1864.   Declines invitation because of limited time in England.

STEELE, Sir Thomas Montague (1820 — 1890).
An officer in the Coldstream Guards and aide-de-camp to the Governor of Madras, he met Livingstone on a hunting trip in South Africa in 1843, and remained a close friend. Livingstone's second son was named after him.   He later served in the Crimea, became a general, and was commander-in-chief in Ireland.   Knighted 1871.   **(DNB.)**

0088.1 3 Sep. 1843.   Despite reluctance to beg, asks for meat;   Rulph is useless and he cannot spare time from building to hunt.   Politics of the Bakhatla: influence of Wanketze. Will communicate only in writing.   Monotwane feared by Bakhatla.

0090.3 [Sep. 1843].   Thanks for skins.   Sechele now half a day east of here.   Hunting party of Boers wishes to meet him.   Steele's route.   Have begun to build.   P.S.   Sechele's messengers go in his direction.

0113.1 7 Dec. 1844.   A hunting party, including Methuen and Bain, whose exploration was limited.   Sebegoe dead.   Progress at Mabotsa, but he will go farther north.   Road to the east dependent on goodwill of Portuguese and Boers.   Tubers and fruit.   Lake and river to north-east.

0143.8 14 Jan. 1846. Please write.   Now with Sechele and married.   Oswell's visit.   A large tree. Elephant shooting by Cumming.   Activity of Boers.   Visit of Matibele who have often defeated Mosilikatze.   Lake still the great unknown.   Building house.   Exhortation.

0152.8 25 Aug. 1846.   Thanks for sextant.   Now able to explore the Lake.   Visit to Boers and Bechuanas to the east.   Animals killed by natives.   Boers' method of civilising.   Game. Hunting parties.   Would like vegetable seeds.   Bain's debts.

0169.4 21 Jun. 1847.   Thanks for letter.   Intended to give Steele's name to his child but it turned out to be a daughter.   Anxious about need to educate his own children.   His varied occupations.   Hopes of Sechele.   Patience required.   The Bechuanas to the east are more advanced.   Caffre war brings no renown;   failure of Boer detachment to achieve anything.

0182.9 5 Apr. 1848.   Delight in their correspondence.   Move to Kolobeng.   Now building. Kindness of Sechele, who promises to accompany him to the Lake, but does not wish to leave Mrs. L. and will now wait for Oswell.   Hopes Steele will come too.   Reports of tribes beyond the Lake.   Little of geological interest.   Cumming is a trader and elephant-hunter, not an explorer.   Oswell's gift of his waggon.   Would like old periodicals.

0191.9 20 Dec. 1848.   Projected expedition to the Lake will require great determination. Griqua party forced back by thirst.   One route lacks water, another is impassable by waggon and blocked by Sekome.   Sechele and he plan to go by waggon and ox.   Dreams of opening up passage to the sea.   Meeting with Pretorius.   Failure of crop.

0215   Sep.—Oct. 1849.   [Beginning missing.]   People and animals of the desert.   Method of obtaining water.   The Zouga and its annual rise.   People quite distinct from the Bechuanas. Trees. Lake Ngami. Prospects of water-route to the north. Need for boat, which Oswell will supply.   Explanation of sketch map.   [End missing.]

0235.1 9 Sep. 1850.   Why has he not written?   Second visit to the Lake.   Turned back because of tsetse.   Fever attacked English party who were ungrateful for help.   Thomas also ill. Meeting with Oswell.   Said to be another lake where Sebitoane lives;   his dealings with Mosilikatze.   Less water this year.   Height of Ngami.   Mission now shut in to the east by Boers.   Maclear gives method of getting longitudes, but a good watch is needed.   No progress in mission.

0239.9 3 Dec. 1850.   Sympathizes with his accident, though hunting a fox is scarcely hunting at all.   Geographical Society has awarded him 25 guineas;   would like a good watch instead, to cooperate with Maclear in observing occultations.

0243.1 14 Jan. 1851.   25 guineas probably in hands of Tidman and Challis.   Trouble with Boers. Moffat busy with translation.   Hamilton very weak.

0255.9 1 Oct. 1851.   Journey of Oswell and himself to Sebitoane on the Chobe.   His career and death.   The magnificent Sesheke, its size and tributaries.   Flat marshlands and tsetse obstruct settlement.   Hills exposed to Mosilikatse.   Cannot therefore begin missionary work at once as he expected, which was why he took his family.   Spread of slaving might be prevented by trade via the Zambesi, on which only Mosioatunya is obstacle to navigation.   Map sent to London Missionary Society.

0266.9 30 Mar. 1852.   Cannot write well to an abstraction like the Geographical Society, but only to a known individual.   Ridicule of Galton's expedition.   His and Oswell's trip very good.   Oswell's progress to the sea stopped by tsetse and swamps.   Death of Sebitoane and fever prevented him settling.   Having family was an advantage.   Thanks for trouble over watch.   Unjust criticism of Sir Harry Smith.   Oswell takes presents. Disappointed with Cummings' book;   he is much inferior to Oswell.   P.S.   Wishes to call new antelope after Captain Vardon.

0274.1 28 Apr. 1852.   Wrote long letter by Oswell.   Sent map via London Missionary Society but fears they have not forwarded it.   Will return to Sebitoane's country, find a healthy residence and a way to either coast.   Doubtful if he will get gunpowder.   How Caffres get ammunition.

0288.1 20 Sep. 1852.   Congratulations of promotion and letter-writing;   remarks on Rio de Janeiro correspond to his own recollections.   Delays have prevented his falling into hands of Boers, whom he will now avoid.   Looting of his house and battle with Bakwains. Misses books and medicines most.   Bakwains will follow example of Caffres.   Boer influence at the Cape.

0318 20 Sep. 1853.   Journey north by new path through wooded country and flooded plain. Crossed river by pontoon.   Assisted by Makololo with canoes.   Reception by Sekeletu. Expedition up the Leeambye;   description of river and country.   The succession to Sebituane.   Slave merchants.   Going alone to the west.   Corrections to former observations of latitude.   Game.

0319.9 24 Sep. 1853.   Requires advice.   Amelioration of condition of Africans is his sole aim. Failure to discover healthy locality for mission may mean stopping of support from London Missionary Society.   Travelling agents better suited to a suppression of slave trade by introduction of commerce.   Healthy region may yet be found.   Lakes and rivers.   Would Government support him?   Would work without salary but for family. Cannot retire from interior.

0360.7 24 Jan. 1855.   Journey to the west coast.   Now going back to the Zambesi and then to Quilimane.   Country fertile but unhealthy.   Waiting for mail to get accounts of the war. Press criticism of army has no popular support.

0408.1 26 Mar. 1856.   Despaired of Steele's being alive.   The falls on the Zambesi, which must have proved a total barrier to European trade.   Tedious walk through jungle.   Abundance of game.   Fertile soil.   Coal, iron, gold.   But slave trade has caused decay.   English cruizers **have** helped.   Salubrious ridges, to the eastern of which he will return.   Kindness of Portuguese.

STEPHENS, Henry Eusely (? — 1913).
Captain, R.N. (1883), Acting Lt., H.M.S. "Frolic," 1856—7, on which ship Livingstone sailed from Quilimane to Mauritius following his trans-Africa journey, early in 1857.
(Navy List.)

0639 11 Dec. 1857.   Thank you for your invitation, but I must go to Portugal on the 17th. Aye, the bar at Quilimane was one to be remembered, and I think contributed to Sekwebu's insanity.   I wear a cap with a gold band ever since being with you.

STEWART, James (1831 — 1905).
Sent to the Zambezi by the Free Church of Scotland for the purpose of conducting reconnaissance for a future mission, Stewart was close to Livingstone and the Zambezi Expedition from 1 Feb. 62 to 1 Apr. 63.   In 1867 he went to join the Lovedale mission in the eastern Cape Province.   He became Principal of Lovedale in 1870, and remained connected with this mission for the remainder of his life.   Stewart took a two-year leave of absence in 1876—8 to aid in the founding of the Livingstonia mission, on Lake Nyassa.
(DNB.)

Letters to him of 1 Apr. 1862 (1210), 30 Jul. 1862 (1254), 24 Dec. 1862 (1304), 7 Jan. 1863 (1309), 17 Aug. 1864 (1469), 7 Oct. 1864 (1501), 22 Dec. 1864 (1561), 24 and 25 Mar. 1865 (1651), 31 Mar. 1865 (1658), and 13 Apr. 1865 (1675) are published in Wallis, **ZJJS**.

1320   19 Feb. 1863.   Sorry to hear of Stewart's illness.   Hopes the change of residence will aid his recovery.   Country completely disorganized;   death is everywhere.   Let me know how Free Churchmen deal with the important question.

STOCKPORT, Ragged School for Boys.

0459   23 Jan. 1857.   Assure the boys that their expression of approbation of my labours in Africa, their honest, spontaneous deed, has delighted me.   I ought to be back to my men in April.

STRONG, Sidney (? — ?1863).
A secretary of the Universities' Mission at the time of his death.

1208   25 Mar. 1862.   Deaths of Mackenzie and Burrup, with details of the circumstances which led to them.   Took all mission females on board, plus Blair, leaving Hawkins at Kongone to guard the supplies.   Hawkins left in the "Gorgon" suffering from ulcers in mouth and limbs.   Procter cannot control mission;   they need guidance.

STURGE, Joseph (1793 — 1859).
Philanthropist who espoused the anti-slavery cause, joined the Anti-Corn Law League, was a member of the Society of Friends and President of the Peace Society.   (**DNB.**)

0852   11 Dec. 1858.   Published in Chamberlin, **SLFL**, no. 66.

SUNLEY, William (? — 1886).
Took up residence on Anjouan (Johanna) in 1848, eventually becoming a prosperous sugar plantation owner.   From 1851 to 1865 he served as H.M. Consul in the Comoro Islands.

1102   [10 Apr. 1861??]   Steamed over to Johanna today.   If you can spare us coal, we shall come to your side of the island and then depart for the Zambesi.

1108   17 Apr. 1861.   Thank you for intending to get 2 mules and 2 Scotch carts for us from Mauritius.   I am obliged by the way you have done all in your power to help us.

1146   18 Nov. 1861.   On Livingstone's exploration of Lake Nyassa, and his expedition to the Rovuma.   Details of skirmish in which 84 slaves were freed last July.   Ajawa raid Manganja to supply slaves to Portuguese.

1157   [18 Nov. — 22 Dec. 1861].   Can you engage 12 or 14 other Johanna men at same rate of pay?   Talks of selling "Pioneer."   Saw at Nyassa a small green collecting box which may have been Roscher's.   The owner was said to be buying slaves.   I fear my coming to

Johanna has imposed a burden upon you: Burrup says Mrs. L. is coming there. We go down to the sea as the water rises.

1290   19 Nov. 1862.   Left you on Wed. and were within 30 miles of the Zambesi on Mon. I am in Col. Nuñes' house, and he is pleased with your invitation. Four of our English crew had to be brought down to the ship, victims of grog. Unsuccessful attempt to deliver letters to Prince Mahomet.

1432   4 Mar. 1864.   Describing the trip from the Zambesi to Mosambique, with H.M.S. "Orestes" and "Ariel". Waller takes the orphans to the Cape. The Johannamen. We probably go to Bombay to sell "Lady Nyassa." Portuguese and their slaving activities.

1442   25 Apr. 1864.   Describing the trip from Mosambique to Zanzibar; unable to stop at Johanna due to the current. I send £18 for Johanna men yet unpaid. The loss of Rae is a disadvantage to me, but I hope he will be all you wish.

1486   13 Sep. 1864.   I regret we were unable to speak of future before I left the Zambesi. Sorry you did not advise Captain Frazier to try his sugar plantation on the mainland: now he will have the same difficulties with slave owners which have always hampered you. Are you still interested in expanding to the continent? I have kept my steamer to see if I can get a good spot up one of the rivers. The consular uniform is on the way home and I may need it.

1724.5   26 May 1865.   Hire 20—25 porters at £1 per month; funds are short. Musa must have connived at other porters' stealing. Prefers going to Johanna to Zanzibar. News of Thornton, Meller, Kirk. Will start at end of June or in July.

1732   2 Jun. 1865.   I have written you by way of India, Sir Thomas Maclear, and now Meller. Will you assist me by getting 20—25 carriers for my next trip? I propose £1 for common men per month, and more as you direct for headman and cook.

1886   14 Mar. 1866.   As your letter did not arrive until I was leaving Bombay, I hired sepoys and Africans, but would have preferred the whole to be Johannamen. Am glad to receive the men you sent. Musa was not a bad one, and I am glad to see him again. Old Seedy also. Dr. Kirk comes out to Zanzibar soon. My brother is now at Fernando Po. My son perished at Richmond; was captured by the Confederates.

TAVARES DE ALMEIDA, António.
Named Governor of Tete and Sena in March 1859, he took up residence in Tete in mid-1860, and held this office until after the Zambezi Expedition was recalled.

1245   10 Jul. 1862.   Calling his attention to Belshore's attacks on Chibisa and asking he prevent this form of securing slaves. Thank you for polite attention to Kirk and C. Livingstone during their recent visit to Tete.

1301   22 Dec. 1862.   Thanking him for his prompt action against Belshore, which from letter of 30 Aug. seems to have been spontaneous.

TAVARES DE ALMEIDA, João.
Governor General of Moçambique, 1856?—1864. His seizure of the "Charles et Georges" early in his administration, in an effort to discourage the export of Africans from Moçambique by the French, produced a temporary strain in Luso-French and Luso-British relations.

1246   12 Jul. 1862.   Concerning the paper recently published in the **Almanac** by Sá da Bandeira, which accused L. of claiming Portuguese discoveries for himself.   Examining Candido's case for having visited Lake Nyasa.   Bowditch and the work he did in Lisbon's archives.   Bandeira's patriotism exceeds his geographical knowledge.

TAYLOR, Wilbraham.
A resident of Hadley Hurst, Barnet, Taylor served for a time as Secretary of the Church Protestant Defence Society.

0629   28 Nov. 1857.   Yesterday I was packed and ready to go to Lisbon, but plans were changed when the Portuguese minister informed me that no business is being transacted there due to an epidemic.   I expect to be there in a fortnight.   I may go to Cambridge as they want me there.

0746   2 Mar. 1858.   Get Tidman to put it in writing: he said the same to me, but Thompson would react more to it in writing than verbally.

0822   Aug., 28 Sep. 1858.   [Beginning missing.]   Men totally different since he assumed command.   Portuguese war with the rebels.   Nature of the river;   rescued the Governor of Quilimane, a medical heretic, and poured quinine into him;   surely in light of the resources of Africa it was designed as something more than a slave market.

0948   20 Oct. 1859.   Describes the Shire valley, about which he has written to Mr. Venn. The failures of the "Ma-Robert," Laird, and Bedingfeld.   Visited Lake Nyassa, and longed for a glass of bitter ale upon our return.   The chronometers.

1798   [12 Aug. 1865?].   I cannot come and must say goodbye: am off to Paris on Monday next.   Steamer sails from Marseilles on the 20th.

THOMPSON, William (1811 — 1889).
Missionary in South India 1836—48;   agent of the London Missionary Society in Cape Town 1850—88.   (**LMSReg.** No. 341.)

Letters to him of 27 Aug. 1850 (0234), 9 Jun. 1852 (0282), [20?] Jul. 1852 (0283), 6 and 20 Sep. 1852 (0284), 30 Sep. 1852 (0291), 12 Oct. 1852 (0293), 24 Nov. 1852 (0300), 17 Sep. 1853 (0315), 11 and 17 Oct. 1853 (0328), 14 May and 14 Aug. 1854 (0334), 13 Sep. 1855 (0385), 27 Sep. 1855 (0388), 2 Mar. 1856 (0399), [Nov. 1855— Jun. 1856] and 2 Jul. 1856 (0422), 8 and 12 Aug. 1856 (0424), 17 and 28 Sep. 1856 (0431), and 31 Oct. and 3 Nov. 1856 (0436) are published in Schapera, **LMC.**

0786   30 Apr. 1858.   Account presented is for appeal for LMS funds and expenses of it ought to be borne by LMS.

0840   4 Oct. 1858.   Published in Chamberlin, **SLFL**, no. 65 (omitting postscripts on expenses and the arrival of new missionaries).

0864   5 Feb. 1859.   Goods and money from Quilimane have been transmitted, in payment of LMS's debt to Thompson for his appeal.   The misunderstanding between them on financial matters.

2021   Nov. 1872.   Published in Chamberlin, **SLFL**, no. 68.

THORNTON, George.
Brother of Richard, who assumed control of Richard's papers, effects, and financial affairs following Richard's death.

1334   22 Apr. 1863.   Advising him of his brother's death, and assuring him that Richard was well cared for by Dr. Meller, assisted by Dr. Kirk.   All of his papers have been sealed and will be sent to you by the first opportunity.   Sale of his effects will not cover wages he owes Ali & Mabruck.   He also had debts in Quilimane: those he incurred in Tette on behalf of the mission will be paid.

1348   1 May 1863.   Kirk goes home, and will take charge of the articles to be sent.   Rae had an arrangement with your brother for the Enfield rifle;   the two-barrelled shotgun he wanted to give to Sr. Clemintino to repay a debt.   An unspecified amount is also due José Nuñes.   Passage home for his two servants must come from his salary.

1429   27 Feb. 1864.   Further details concerning the sale of the possessions of Richard.   Rae has erected a 12 foot tall cross over the grave.

1453   29 Jul. 1864.   Young brought all of your brother's boxes, and I have requested he contact you.   Tozer declined to pay the balance of the bill Richard incurred at Tette, and I have paid it all.   Tomorrow I go to Scotland;   if you know anything of the sum owed me, send it to Murray the publisher.

1579   19 Jan. 1865.   Criticizing George for not replying to his earlier letter, Livingstone explains further the financial intricacies resulting from Richard's death, and declines to have anything further to do with the matter.

THORNTON, Richard (1838 – 1863).
After graduating from the Royal School of Mines, Thornton was appointed Geologist to the Zambezi Expedition.   Having been dismissed by Livingstone for laziness, he joined Klaus von der Decken in exploring and climbing Mt. Kilimanjaro in 1861–62.   Returning to the Zambezi, Thornton worked in conjunction with Livingstone's expedition, and died on the Shire as a result of malaria contracted while he was rendering service to the UMCA.

Letters to him of 16 Apr. 1858 (0781), 25 Jun. 1859 (0910), 6 Feb. 1860 (0990), and 1 Jan. 1861 (1064) are published in Wallis, **ZEDL**;   those of 25 Aug. 1858 (0820), 25 Jun. 1859 (0910), and 1 Jan. 1861 (1064) in Tabler, **ZPRT**.

0850   [29 Nov. 1858].   Hippo shot 7 miles above you;   we go on to the high hill today, and return to men left here to cut up the meat either tonight or tomorrow morning.   I send a piece of meat.   Come or remain where you are as you think best.   If you remain, send someone to cut, dry, and carry down the meat.

0876   24 Feb. 1859.   *It was expected that as a mining geologist you would take an early opportunity of performing that duty . . .

0995   8 Feb. 1860.   Kirk will supply any medicines you may need.

1255 30 Jul. 1862.   Ran aground twice coming down;   it may be better to spend Aug.—Nov. in boat exploration of the Rovuma.   Exchanged crew men with "Ariel."   The Baron grumbled to Oldfield's men about your publishing a paper;   better let your friends know where you stand on this.   If you go to Gorongozo, look for the inscriptions;   in Manica, ascertain exact gold-bearing stratum.

1321 19 Feb. 1863.   On no account enter a dangerous locality alone, as the black men will protect you only as long as there is no danger.   When we get up we shall require your help with the steamer.   Thank you for trying to get wood for us.   If you go to the cataracts, seek a level place for a road.

TIDMAN, Arthur (1792 — 1868).
Congregational minister at Salisbury 1814–18, at Frome 1818–28, and at Barbican Chapel, London 1828–51.   He was also and latterly exclusively Foreign Secretary of the London Missionary Society 1839–68, and Livingstone's principal correspondent in the Society both while he was a missionary and later.   (**Congr. Yearbook** 1869, p. 281.)

Letters to him of 24 Jun. 1843 (0076), 30 Oct. 1843 (0095), 9 Jun. 1844 (0104), 2 Dec. 1844 (0113), 23 Mar. 1845 (0116), 17 Oct. 1845 (0137), 10 and 12 Apr. 1846 (0149), 17 Mar. 1847 (0163), [30 Dec. 1847] (0180), 1 Nov. 1848 (0189), 26 May 1849 (0206), 3 Sep. and 14 Oct. 1849 (0208), 24 Aug. 1850 (0232), 30 Apr. 1851 (0253), 1 Oct. 1851 (0256), 17 Oct. 1851 (0258), 17 Mar. 1852 (0266), 26 Apr. 1852 (0272), 26 Apr. 1852 (0273), 2 and 12 Nov. 1852 (0296), 12 Dec. 1852 (0305), 24 Sep. 1853 (0320), 8 Nov. 1853 (0330), 14 Jan. 1855 (0360), 10 Feb. 1855 (0364), 12 Oct. 1855 (0389), 2 Mar. 1856 (0400), 23 May 1856 (0415), 23 May 1856 (0416), and 26 Aug. 1856 (0430) are published in Schapera, **LMC**, together with his replies.

0007 [Apr. 1840.]   Applies for the fee for study at St. Bartholomew's Hospital of clinical medicine, midwifery, gynaecology, paediatrics, physics, botany, etc.

0461 26 Jan. 1857.   His throat complaint, which renders public speaking painful, has apparently been forgotten.   Found that this was still so in Mauritius, when he appealed for a sailor's home.

0475 †13 Mar. 1857.   *On the Grahamstown horde who blame the Caffre Wars on missionaries.

0497 7 Apr. 1857.   Prout informed him there was £200 in his account, and he is therefore supposed to have money.   But as Directors will not aid him in his plans, he will not draw this money, and asks for silence about these resources.

0513 [20 Jan. — 30 Apr. 1857.]   Must withdraw from pecuniary dependence on any Society. Aged mother and two sisters need help.   After the letter referred to, learned of father's death and loss of income for family, and resolved to act independently of the Society.

0586 14 Sep. 1857.   *Declines an invitation to attend a meeting.

0605 21 Oct. 1857.   *Moravian Missionary Society asked by Pretorius to send missionary to Sechele.   Hopes men have been found for new Zambesi mission.

0733 22 Feb. 1858.   Hopes that new Zambesi mission will start soon.

0754 6 Mar. 1858.   Sails on Monday.   Glad that young missionaries are to leave in May; will assist them at the Victoria Falls;   they might proceed by the hill Ngwa.   He is not responsible for J.S. Moffat leaving the Society.

1038   10 Nov. 1860.   Published in Chamberlin, **SLFL**, no. 67 (omitting a paragraph on the plans of the Makololo).

1039   Incl. 1, 26 Nov. 1860.   Published **ibid.**

1147   24 Nov. 1861.   Corrects slight error in fever prescription sent previously.   Asks if mission to Makololo is to be continued.   If he is told he will give all possible assistance.

1189   25 Feb. 1862.   Astonished at misrepresentation.   Sekeletu ill and not universally popular, but all parties spoke well of Helmores.   But Price was not respected.   Still hopes for a successful mission.   P.S.   His treatment by Makololo not the result of presents.   Helmore lacked horses.

1499   1 Oct. 1864.   Regrets not having seen him.   Would like news about Moffat.

1723   25 May 1865.   Surprised at uneasiness caused by Burton's unwarranted aspersions on missionaries; he is a moral idiot and his conduct is disgusting.   Perhaps Moffat should come home to show what a missionary really is, and get his revised New Testament printed.

1733   2 Jun. 1865.   Meller going as consul to Madagascar where he will be favourable towards missionaries.

TIMES, Editor of.
These letters are addressed impersonally.   The editor at this period was John Thadeus Delane (1817 – 79; **DNB.**)

0444   18 Dec. 1856.   *Will give information on cotton growing; short silence does not imply insensibility to the honour done him.

0446.4 24 Dec. 1856.   Introduction of cotton growing to Africa need not lead to slavery on the American pattern.   Detailed description of society, products, etc. in Bechuanaland and Angola to prove this.   Need for expert examination of ports at mouth of Zambesi.   Small attempts to introduce trade better than grandiose.

0463.2 28 Jan. [1857].   Disowning a proposed publication of his discoveries by Routledge and Co.

0633.1 [24 Nov. – 1 Dec. 1857].   Despite reports and his own earlier scepticism, the British squadron on the west coast has significantly reduced the slave trade.

1088   [5 Feb.], 6 Mar. 1861.   On the capability of the Shire region to produce cotton.

1098   [15 Mar. 1861?]   "Pioneer" began ascent of the Rovuma on 11 Mar.   At mouth it is 19 fathoms deep and 1 mile wide with no bar.   Shoals need skilful navigation.   Natives know of no cataracts and believe river to flow from Lake Nyassa.   Mackenzie and Rowley on board.   Party will split; one group goes overland to Nyassa; "Pioneer" returns to Johanna.

1103   [11 Apr. 1861.]   Reporting the discoveries made by the expedition on the Rovuma, and the conclusions Livingstone drew therefrom.   Observations on the slave trade with reference to Johanna.

1201   [17 Mar. 1862.]   Reporting the death of Bishop Mackenzie.

TORRESÃO, José Leocádio Botelho.
Lieutenant, 2nd Battalion Light Infantry stationed at Tete during the period of the
Zambesi Expedition, Torresão was Acting Commander of the garrison for a period in
1862.   In 1863 he was appointed Chief Captain of Zumbo, which position he took up in
mid-1864.   (Almeida, **IdDDL**.)

1419   31 Dec. 1863.   The Landeens to the north have given me no trouble.   Congratulations on
your appointment to Zumbo, and also for the birth of your son.   The meteorological
instruments belong to H.M. Govt., and I am not at liberty to sell them.   As yet I have
received no instructions from Mr. Thornton's heirs regarding the sale of his rifles (of
which detailed descriptions follow).   As Sr. Clementino has returned, I hope he has the
gundpowder.   Mr. Rae and I send greeting to your family.

TOYNBEE, Henry.
After 33 years experience at sea, Toynbee worked for the Meteorological Office, and
published various works on meteorology.

0559   25 Jul. 1857.   Thanks for your work on lunars, and for the offer that comes with it.
As the sextant was damaged en route to Mauritius, I cannot do as you suggest.

0570   20 Aug. 1857.   Requesting he edit L.'s notes on some of his astronomical observations,
for inclusion in the **JRGS**.   I believe Arrowsmith wants some of them suppressed.

0571   22 Aug. 1857.   I leave Maclear's work as I have it, your work, and my observation book
at 3, Royal Exchange Buildings.   How many pages will it require?   When I know, I will
tell Murray.   I am grateful that you take up this work.

0573   [22—27 Aug. 1857].   Murray is willing to print 25 copies;   you are in for the editorship.
I would like the Admiral's opinion.   I go to Dublin on Thursday morning.   My book
delayed until November.

0581   4 Sep. 1857.   Spoke at a large meeting Monday;   as your notes and observations went to
Hadley Green I could not attend to your invitation.   I wrote Shaw, telling him I accept
your plan to give table of Longitude and Latitude at the end of the book, and refer to
more remarks of yours in **JRGS**.   Murray has no objection to printing 150 copies to
whoever may want them.   12,000 is too many for such an esoteric item;   **JRGS** seems
the better vehicle.

TOZER, William George (1829/30 — 1899).
Bishop, UMCA 1862—3;   Bishop of Zanzibar 1863—73;   Bishop of Jamaica 1879—80;
Bishop of Honduras, 1880—81.   Livingstone never forgave him for moving the UMCA
from the Shire highlands and Morambala to Zanzibar in 1862—3.   (**Crockford**.)

1374   [14 Jul. 1863?].   By the lawful introduction of commerce and the gospel, your mission
may bring about the final extinction of the slave trade.   Coastal squadron does its part in
spite of calumnies heaped upon it.   God grant the Church of England use the opportunity
placed before it.

1410   18 Dec. 1863.   With great regret I learn that you plan to abandon this country, and I earnestly beg you to reconsider. This is the first time Protestant missionaries have bolted, without reducing the language, and having only tried from the top of an uninhabited mountain. You will be blamed, and will regret it till your dying day. You will be perfectly safe among the Ajawa; not a single European died of disease in those hills. Reconsider and do not abandon these downtrodden people.

TROTTER, Henry Dundas (1802 — 1859).
Captain R.N. 1835. In command of the Niger Expedition in 1841. Commodore at the Cape of Good Hope 1856—7. Rear Admiral 1857.   **(DNB.)**

0434   9 Oct. 1856.   Gives up hope of meeting him in Mauritius. Letter from London Missionary Society unfavourable: assumes directors mean to send him elsewhere. This means his resignation and continuing in a private capacity. Potentialities of Central Africa in resources and people. Thanks for passage to Mauritius. Kindness of Portuguese.

TURNER, Mrs.
Wife of James A.

0755   6 Mar. 1858.   Thanks for your kind present and good wishes. I am not sure we shall be as successful as we expect, but I shall try to do my duty. Remember me to Mr. Turner. "Pearl" is in the river and sails Monday forenoon.

TURNER, James Aspinall (1797 — 1869).
A cotton manufacturer in Manchester, Turner had a great interest in the Zambezi Expedition, for obvious commercial reasons. He represented Manchester in Parliament 1857—65.   (Boase, **MEB.**)

0569   19 Aug. 1857. I propose going to Manchester on the 5th, and will devote the 7th and the 8th to meeting the gentlemen. Should another time be more convenient, I can meet them upon my return from Scotland.

0797.3 10 Jun. 1858.   After prosperous voyage, now exploring mouths of Zambesi. Cotton found at Kongone. Other seeds. Rebellion against Portuguese. 21 Jun. "Pearl" sent back as river falling.

0882   9 Mar. 1859.   Hope to send you a package by the end of May. It is not necessary to give seeds to natives as they have their own. Cucumber and melon seeds make excellent table oil. Africa north of 15° S. is incomparably the best adapted for cotton in the world. Have set up the sugar mill and the small engine. On the Free Emigration Scheme: colonization will bring the slave trade to an end.

0899   30 May 1859.   Discovery of Lake Shirwa: such cotton country we saw nowhere except Angola. I send a box of cotton we collected. Trade is ready to be developed, but Portuguese only carry on a paltry trade in ivory. We have had mild fever.

1589   26 Jan. 1865.   Have not been in Manchester so I could not call on you. Please send by sea the value (£22) of the cotton, to Bombay to help pay some black men who accompanied me from Africa. Make it common grey calico 16 yards each.

TWEEDIE, William King (1803 — 1863).
Convenor of Foreign Missions Committee, Free Church of Scotland.

(Scott, **FES I**, p. 121.)

1134   2 Nov. 1861.   Recommending the region around Lake Nyasa as an ideal place for a mission: telling of the observations made during the exploration of the west side of the lake.   Mission would lack Government protection;   and must have its own steamer. Portuguese carry on slaving activities in the region.   18 November the Bishop attacked Ajawa on two occasions.   1 Mar. 1862.   Have shown this to Mr. Stewart who is now with us.   He should encounter no serious obstacles.

VAVASSEUR, James.
Husband of Helen Moffat, Livingstone's sister-in-law.

0634   7 Dec. 1857.   *Due to a previous engagement I cannot speak to the Fishmonger Company. Prevented by an epidemic from going to Portugal.   Cannot get to Epsom.

VENN, Henry (1796 — 1873).
Secretary of the Church Missionary Society, 1841—73.   Anxious to check the slave trade in West Africa, he advocated developing the trade in the natural products of the country.   **(DNB.)**

0890   15 May 1859.   Describing the country around Lake Shirwa, and suggesting that the C.M.S. send a mission to the region.   The country is high and cool, well-watered, and the lake is said to be separated from Lake Nyassa by only a narrow strip of land.   The people in the highlands grow cotton.

0942   15 Oct. 1859.   Tells of his recent visit to Lake Nyassa, near which the presence of an "English Establishment" would do much to end the slave trade of Zanzibar through legitimate commerce.   Cotton grows both above and below the Murchison Cataracts, and the east side of the valley is divided into three terraces affording slightly different conditions of climate.   Met with more intoxication in 40 days in the highlands than in the previous 16 years.

VIGORS, P.

1234   2 Jun. 1862.   Your letter arrived by "Ariel."   Missionaries fled to the lowlands, but Waller is in favour of returning.   Their prestige is gone.   After Mr. Rae assembled the "Lady Nyassa" in a fortnight, we took him down to the sea for fresh air.

WALKER, Sir Baldwin Wake (1802 — 1876).
Lieutenant, R.N. (1820);   accepted command in the Turkish Navy, 1840—5;   Surveyor of the Navy 1848—60;   Commander-in-Chief at the Cape Station, 1861—4;   created Baronet, 1856;   Admiral, 1870.   **(DNB.)**

1180   17 Feb. 1862.   Thanks for the services of Wilson of the "Gorgon."   On the first encounter with the Ajawa, the visit up the Lake of Nyassa, on the Portuguese vigilance towards the expedition, and the need to get around them to allow English merchants into the country.

Proposes going up the Rovuma with naval assistance. Wondering of the second encounter with the Ajawa, at which English sailors were present, and of the legal implications, if any. Requesting provisions.

1205   19 Mar. 1862.   Meller goes to the Cape for reasons of health; please aid him and extend to him benefits of a naval hospital. Please send by merchant ship 10 draught oxen, 2 cows and a Hottentot driver, plus 20—30 feet of bulk's head, some angle iron and iron plates.

1377   15 Jul. 1863.   Meller entitled to a passage home; Kirk and C.L. left on 19 May. Portuguese slave hunters depopulated Shire valley. Wrote to Russell on need to end slavery; reply was recall. Portuguese hypocrisy. Await river rising: will explore Nyassa. Lack of provisions. Good wishes.

1394   18 Aug. 1863.   In leaving Young in charge of "Pioneer" I gave him a statement of good conduct. If I do not return to testify on his behalf, may he be promoted.

1430   27 Feb. 1864.   Not killed as Portuguese report but alive and in Mosambique. River rose on 19 January. Had given up discovery of Lake Bemba to get back in time to meet flood; it is in another drainage system, perhaps the Congo. Slaving dhow plys Lake Nyassa. Towed to Mosambique by "Orestes" and "Ariel." "Orestes" takes boxes of Thornton and those for Kew. Have borrowed two chronometers.

WALLER, Horace (1833 — 1896).
Lay Superintendent, Universities' Mission to Central Africa, 1860—4; Curate, St. John's, Chatham 1867—70; Vicar of Leytonstone, 1870—4; Rector of Twywell, 1874—95. In addition to editing Livingstone's **Last Journals,** Waller wrote several articles on slavery and the slave trade in Africa.   (**DNB.**)

1244   7 Jul. 1862.   Leave for Johanna in a day or two. Rae needs a sea voyage due to dysentery. "Penguin" went past Quilimane without leaving provisions, so we must go to get them. Chibisa was active in aiding Tette slavers cross the Shire to invade Manganja country, and he may be aiding those now active in Ajawa country. I told the Makololo that if they live quietly, I'll taken them home as soon as I can.

1256   30 Jul. 1862.   Met Oldfield and "Ariel" on the 24th: got no Johanna men and as "Ariel" goes to Cape we must go to Johanna. From August to November we will probably explore the Rovuma. Dispute between Hawkins and Stewart in Natal. Oldfield disappointed that by this time you have no houses as good as Sunley's, but he does not realize the difficulties.

1331   26 Mar. 1863.   Expect to be up soon; we are now searching for wood. Compelled yesterday to separate vessels to get through a shoal spot. Mankokwe complains of the Makololo. Will waste no time in returning downriver after reaching you, and would do so now except no one here understands yoking oxen.

1332   20 Apr. 1863.   Sorry I spoke to you as I should not have; take my apology as it is meant and such will not be necessary again.

1333   21 Apr. 1863.   Thornton expired at 10 a.m. We rigged a place for him on the "Pioneer" in hopes that the change would benefit him. Meller was with him constantly and did all that man could do. Magrath, Pearce and Wilson plus one Johanna man also sick, Charles

was down but is better today.   Have cut a few miles into the vegetation and found a
gradual slope up to the plateau.

1336   24 Apr. 1863.   Kirk and I agree £5 will cover the boat.   Look into Thornton's boxes for
manuscripts etc. which his friends will value, and put them in a box which I can take.
Oxen difficult to manage yesterday due to long idleness.   I mean to send to Senna for
more.   The deaths of so many cast a deep gloom over the future, and I should [not]
wonder in the least to be recalled.   As famine and drought never fully exterminate, I
blame the condition of this valley on the Portuguese.

1342   28 Apr. 1863.   Meller goes down to see Procter: I hope you are relieved.   Nine of our
party are leaving.   The boats will bring up anything Nuñes may have purchased.   Kirk
will hire ten Shupanga men to allow those with us to return.   Somewhat lightened, I can
now concentrate on the slave trade.   Observations on some individuals in the Zambezi
region, and thoughts on the anniversary of Mary's death.

1345   30 Apr. 1863.   The five Ajawa would never have got the canoe up with three Shupanga
and Quilimane men.   I gave each a fathom: they wanted "Merikano!"   The boat is yours
after Ali and Mabruk are taken down.   In the course of the next month we may draw our
supplies from the Lake region.   The green boat will bring up any rice, salt beef and pork
left for us.

1346.5 [Mar. — Apr. 1863].   Sends insects to Agnes, who is about 15.   She and his third son
are his best correspondents and increasingly dear to him.

1349   1 May 1863.   Whoever sends up food will man the "Galzo."   If the Governor does not
receive something in the Cape papers from his Government more stiff than from me, I am
mistaken.   He would like Rowley to state that he on the spot is in no position to judge
the merits, but I will bear all like a Briton.

1352   23 May 1863.   Thanks for invitation to visit, but am disinclined to move or to speak.
Recovering from illness, I am disinclined to take to a canoe.   I send down a canoe with
25 lbs of pork and 25 lbs of beef.   Rain yesterday: pity the voyagers.

1353   30 May 1863.   I return your books with thanks.   One is not at hand, the others were
damaged by cockroaches.   I retain Keble a little longer.   Sorry you did not succeed as
well as you wished — I guess your terrific puns made Procter ill.

1355   2 Jun. 1863.   I send the brass wire you requested by the Senna men who brought the
cattle.   We have four bulls to break in.   Weather completely changed, and our health is
improving.

1357   10 Jun. 1863.   On the activities of individual Africans: Enda Moshule's women are
returning after conveying their lord and his leprosy up here for relief;   a woman went to
get grain from the old gardens and returned with an arrowhead through diaphragm and
lungs up to near the heart.   Seseho did well in not hunting, as I told them to spend more
time in agriculture.   King very low due to haemorrhage: can you lend us two bottles of
Port and ammoniate of iron?

1358   14 Jun. 1863.   I send the seven rings which came from Clementino to Thornton with
Wikatani this morning.   Sorry I let some of your books out of my sight: we may have a
book thief on board.   I will be glad if you lose some of mine.   King improving and no
one else either sick or skulking.

1360   3 Jul. 1863.   I send down beef for you and companions.   Meller says the new bishop is
vegetarian: glad you have a new head, and an energetic one.   All feel better for our trip.

Took seven days from the boat to this seeking level paths — a pleasure, not a chore. Sorry Procter's ill health continues. Our boat was burned by a grass fire. I was aware no good could be done by this expedition while the Portuguese slaved in our tracks, but Russell does not mention this in his withdrawal instructions. We cannot go down until the flood: hope Tozer is content with a paper welcome. I will hand Thornton's rifles, gear and bills to the mission, to be sent to his brother.

1366   5 Jul. 1863. Morambala seems as healthy looking as up here. Bishop — whom we liked very well indeed — ought to visit Mbame's and Morambala before deciding. Clementino will be glad of bills on Bombay for his money from Thornton. We go north of the lake if we can.

1371   [10 Jul. 1863?] Return your axe by Chibisa. I enclose a letter to Thornton's brother: you should know its contents. Are getting ready as fast as we can. Hope to leave Tuesday, and to see you and Mr. Alington tomorrow. I gave Chibisa 2 fathoms of moleskin.

1375   14 Jul. 1863. We start for Nyassa tomorrow: thanks for the quinine and the notebook. We forgot to send the bullets to Mr. Alington. I return the report with hearty thanks for the kind things you say about me, and wish they were better deserved.

1379   17 Jul. 1863. Transport difficulties: can you send Ajawa to carry the boat? About 40 strong fellows would do, and I will pay them well (lists items they will receive). Ferrão will supply the orphans with food for one year at my expense. As Mesquita is a spy, don't let him know our plans. Between Makololo and Ajawa it is 6 to one and ½ dozen to the other, except in addition to Makololo vices, the latter are low thieves. Anyone who maintains the goodness of either has not learned the first lesson in native character. Would Bishop lend Thornton's boat to the "Pioneer"? If so, we could send it up with mail. He may not be cordial with me.

1386   6 Aug. 1863. Ajawa went off laughing, saying they were sick. This is breach of contract and should be punished. Tozer, using Mesquita as interpreter, humbly asked Tito's permission to settle on Morambala! His good sense will get over this stuff, but you old hands should stick around to prevent such follies. Wilson sends salt provisions and greetings. Poor Ramsay is dead.

1388   8 Aug. 1863. Lost our boat Monday in the rapids. The Makololo could not negotiate them, and unknown to me 5 Shupanga men tried and lost it. Remaining Ajawa behave capitally. Divide the wages of the seven who left after 6 days among the rest.

1393   15 Aug. 1863. Sorry to hear discouraging news of the mission. I thought Tozer would honour his predecessor's work. I shall take the boys and girls to Johanna and keep them there until I hear from the Metropolitan. I cannot view Makololo in the same light as do you and the Ajawa women. I know their wickedness, but much not theirs is laid at their door. Even one of the twelve was a devil. They were not left to shift for themselves, but voluntarily broke from us. Reid, Wilson and the steward all past cure. Young says that when there is work to do, all go on the sick list. My good wishes follow Meller to Madagascar. I may yet work alone in Africa.

1398   28 Nov. 1863. Tozer wishes to segregate the sexes — I think the precaution a wise one. They shall either be supplied by Ferrão or go to Johanna. Came here 31 October tired of walking 660 miles. We wait for high water. Ajawa and Makololo drove Mankokwe to an island and burned his village, or so say the people. Lost a Johannaman yesterday to a crocodile.

1411   18 Dec. 1863.   Had a slight sunstroke while coming home.   Blair writes that Tozer is glad to hear that I am taking steps to make Waller independent of the mission: I didn't think objection could be taken to a member of the mission becoming a vehicle of Christian benevolence to poor people.   He will probably go to Madagascar where others have done work, as in Honolulu.   Not murdered by Mazitu.

1459   4 Aug. 1864.   Col. Sabine's box goes to him.   Boys better where they are.   Tell Miss Mackenzie and Mr. Halcome he will call.   Imitates Waller's fast style.

1462   6 Aug. 1864.   Send enclosed to Meller about getting a cottage near London.   Has given plain opinion of Tozer's conduct;   Central Africa is abandoned but they will get nice comforts at Zanzibar.

1479   1 Sep. 1864.   Explain to Thornton about his outlay for the mission.   Anxious about speech.   Hears Colenso is invited to Bath.

1484   6 Sep. 1864.   To stay with Dr. Watson at Bath.   Labouring at speech.   Will write book thereafter.   Has written twice to Miss Mackenzie.   Splendid visit to Ulva.   Compliments to Chinwala.   Successful fishing.

1488   [19 Sep. 1864.]   Draw large head with lip-ring to show at the Theatre tonight.   Will not mention Tozer.

1493   24 Sep. 1864.   Send two copies of photographs so that he can present one to Miss Watson. Speke's funeral;   inaccurate reporting of Grant's behaviour.

1500   1 Oct. 1864.   Returns photographs;   banter about Waller being robbed of them.   Money and George Thornton.

1509   13 Oct. 1864.   His accounts with the mission.   Shooting.

1522   31 Oct. 1864.   Returns Lightfoot's letter.   Daoma done for so near the coast.   Sekeletu dead.   Sorry at reaction to financial statement and horrified that Davies has deceived them.   Miss Watson's gratitude for photographs.   Compliments to Stewart.   May send him proofs.   Where are sketches?

1529   8 Nov. 1864.   Send sketches of loom and furnace.   Agnes wishes insects set up. Message to Stewart.

1536   18 Nov. 1864.   Oldfield says that a black boy brought home by some of us is in a reformatory: enquire.   Ask for Archbishop Whately's tract on revelation;   or his daughter's address.   Draw bellows, loom, spinning apparatus, foundry.

1540   23 Nov. 1864.   Details of Manganja language and names.   Has written about the mission and its failure.   Capt. Gardner will deny his statement but he is prepared to swear to it. Thanks for beetles.

1555   8 Dec. 1864.   Speeches.   Thanks for drawings.   Thank Meller for what he sent.   Tozer writing book.

1557   14 Dec. 1864.   Send lip-ring with drawing of head.   Will not attack Tozer as he deserves in order not to exaggerate his importance.   Lecture at Mansfield.   Opportunities of publishing in magazines.   Secretary wishes to discuss accounts.

1559   18 Dec. 1864.   Wrote this morning.   Repeats invitation.   Speeches.

1563   28 Dec. 1864.   How to get to Newstead.

1564   [Dec. 1864.]   Come when you can.

1565   [26 Sep. — 31 Dec. 1864.]   [Beginning missing.]   Ask Young name of gunner.   Mixture of names is to secure profits for his brother's family.

1566   [26 Sep. — 31 Dec. 1864.]   [Beginning missing.]   Send on enclosed, adding that he sent character of Young to Admiralty and Admiral Walker; but case is hopeless.   Letter from Rowley.   Murray's artist will welcome help.   Mrs. Burrup will be spoken about by Rev. Bentinck.   Gedge owes £20 and does not reply.   Unless Young eats his accusation, will not trouble about him.

1568   4 Jan. 1865.   Sorry for cause of his absence.   Meeting at Mansfield.   Mrs. Webb recovering.

1573   8 Jan. 1865.   Hopes his father is better, as Mrs. Webb is.   An article in Blackwood's. Burton a nasty fellow.   Kirk's movements.   Meeting ill reported.

1575   12 Jan. 1865.   Write soon.   Sermon by Rowley.

1584   24 Jan. 1865.   Glad his father is better.   Asks for translations.   Rowley.   Waller's writing.

1587   25 Jan. 1865.   May be Baines's book which Longman has got reviewed favourably. Waller's writing will do more good.   Egyptians and Assyrians were Africans.   Mrs. Webb stronger.   Will send proof for correction.

1593   3 Feb. 1865.   Thanks for proof.   His account of the mission.   Contributions to next expedition.   Wishes his son were home to go.   Lacerda's response to his Bath lecture; wait till they see the book!   Exposure of Almeida to Russell.

1596   7 Feb. 1865.   Sent further proof yesterday.   Wishes to be as brief as possible.   His son if alive now educated in roughing it.   Capt. Wilson home.   Mrs. Webb as well as ever.

1601   8 Feb. 186[5].   Thanks for emendations.   Instructions for corrections to illustrations. Criticism of Baines's ability.   Going to London on Saturday.

1603   9 Feb. 1865.   Thanks for loan of Clark's letter.   Reasons for not writing a simple personal narrative.   Cannot be silent about Rowley.   [End missing.]

1610   14 [Feb. 1865?]   Rowley's retraction.   Sends more proofs.

1613   17 [Feb. 1865?]   If he cannot hit Rowley, he will hit Waller!   Wants name of Terere who killed Chibisa.   Portuguese angry at what he said about Sá da Bandeira.   Evidence for slaving at Tette.   Brother well.   If Devil doesn't catch these fellows, he is not worth his sulphur.

1621   24 Feb. 1865.   On Manganja phrases.   Thanks for seeing artist.   Recommendation for Young's promotion.   Sá da Bandeira's errors.

1624   [Feb. 1865??]   Type of retraction required from Rowley.   Thanks for arrows.   London coffee house has files of South African papers.   Tom going to London for medical advice.

1634   8 Mar. 1865.   Omitted wood cuts yesterday.   Faces should be less prognathous and fish basket corrected.

1669   6 Apr. 1865.   Praise of article.   Sorry to hear of father's illness.   Webbs in London about his knee.   Bishop of Lincoln's promise about Mrs. Burrup;   could speak to Bishop of Oxford if he saw him.   Writings.   Call on Cooke for drawings.

1684   23 Apr. 1865.   Sympathises in loss of father.   Goes to London briefly next week.   MS complete.   Call on Cooke for drawings.

1695   2 May 1865.   Has he Tozer's letter about repudiation, in case his accuracy is questioned. Will he come to help settle with Universities' Mission Committee.   [End missing.]

1708   11 May 1865.   Make drawing for outside of book: slave and slaver would be best. Went to London Missionary Society, not to speak, but was stirred by Burton's criticism of missionaries to bear testimony.   P.S.   Sorry he was out when Waller called;   when he may be found.

1731   1 Jun. 1865.   Miss Coutts's invitation.   Call on MacDougall about clothing.   Has not had time to make list of medicines.   Sending to Sunley.

1736   5 Jun. 1865.   Does not know Abel Smith, but might work at him through a Mr. Chapman who is related.   Mother very low.   Find out about Miss Coutts's agent, named Sinclair. £2000 will soon go.

1743   9 Jun. 1865.   Flying visit to Oxford next week;   possibly also to Cambridge to see Sedgwick.   May see Waller or visit Miss Coutts.   Waller should speak to Venn of Church Missionary Society.   Get Chapman's address.   Never spoke to Kirk about Borneo;   it was Sewell.

1753   21 Jun. 1865.   Mother dead.   Will be in London next week.   Waller should not have paid George Thornton.   Kindness in Oxford.   Sends autograph.

1754   22 Jun. 1865.   Thanks for sympathy.   Details of death.   Thornton's affairs.

1759   27 Jun. 1865.   Thornton's affairs.

1762   [Jun. 1865?]   [Beginning missing.]   Thornton's affairs.   Portuguese fulminations. [End missing.]

1768   13 Jul. 1865.   Came to town yesterday.   Had note of condolence from Miss Coutts.

1771-2   21 Jul. 1865.   Set Agnes to answer Waller's letter.   Saw Miss Coutts and is invited to eat; will introduce Waller's mission.   Wrote to Rajah but no reply.   Does not know when he will get away.   Should like to tell committee his ideas of Tozer's staying in Zanzibar. P.S.   Sends letter of Sir J. Brooke.   Grant's wedding and good fortune.

1778   27 Jul. 1865.   Settlement with Universities' Mission.   Collect medicine chest from Apothecaries' Hall.   Tea with Miss Coutts tomorrow.   Other commissions and meetings.

1785   [26 Sep. 1864 – 30 Jul. 1865.]   Waller right to say what he thought.   Intended to state missionaries' opposition to slave trade at a later point.   He did oppose Mackenzie. Rowley's letter in the **Times** was not contradicted.   Spelling of Manganja word.   Wishes drawings of arrow and arrowhead.

1786 [26 Sep. 1864 — 30 Jul. 1865.] [Beginning missing.] Mission's opposition to slaving was the first step to success; wheat available and Portuguese ashamed. Abandonment therefore regrettable and to be ascribed to Tozer's ignorance of missionary enterprise, evidenced in his statements to naval officers. Personnel were inadequate apart from Mackenzie and Scudamore. Prospects were encouraging. [End missing.]

1787 [26 Sep. 1864 — 30 Jul. 1865.] [Beginning missing.] His hopes for the Universities' Mission and distress at its decline into a chaplaincy. Privation was real; Thornton risked his life to supply wants; native grain cannot be kept and unfit for European stomachs.

1793 8 Aug. 1865. Instead of finishing packing went to zoological with Kirk and Webb. Going to lunch with Queen Emma at Miss Coutts's. Come and help tomorrow.

1796 10 Aug. 1865. *Going to Maidstone to say goodbye to Duchess of Sutherland. Hopes he has put mosquito fenders in the boxes.

1803 [26 Sep. 1864 — 13 Aug. 1865.] [Beginning missing.] Manganja words.

1804 [26 Sep. 1864 — 13 Aug. 1865.] Suggested corrections.

1805 [26 Sep. 1864 — 13 Aug. 1865.] [Beginning missing.] Rutherfoord's doubts about use of money.

1807 [1 Jan. — 13 Aug. 1865.] [Beginning missing.] Sends a ticket which may be shown at the meeting of the British Association.

1814 26 Aug. 1865. Satisfied with Agnes's settlement. Smooth voyage. Maltese panic about cholera. Railway from Alexandria to Suez.

1822 27 Sep. 1865. Africans from Nassick school selected. Also to get sepoys. Taking buffaloes which may withstand tsetse; good beasts of burden and give milk. Governor helpful. To give two lectures. Juma and Wikatani to be baptised. Chuma goes with him to Government House. The call on the Church to take up Honolulu. Does not leave till November.

1831 26 Oct. 1865. Prospects fair. Subscription by merchants. Will select spot, do what Royal Geographical Society desires, and come back to establishment in the Highlands. Sultan has given passage to buffaloes; experiment worth making. Doubts about Nassick boys. Chuma very sharp. Endemic cholera. Tozer's activities. Tell Arrowsmith to return observations.

1838 15 Nov. 1865. Shocked by Rae's end. Church's attitude to marriage. Company which has taken up Zanzibar will not be tools in the hands of a slaver. Sunley does not reply to letters about getting Johanna men; he deserves some credit for paying wages. Has been to Ahmedabad.

1849 2 Dec. 1865. Explains Wikatani's letter. Wilson will baptise him and Chuma; most eminent missionary in Western India. They go with him as soon as 'Thule' is ready. Tozer's new leaf. Has not agreed to Murchison's plan. Prosperous merchants.

1850 4 Dec. 1865. Enclosed notes show what Wilson thinks of boys; he is Scottish Free Church and more particular about qualifications than High Church folk. Nassick Africans all baptised, confirmed, etc.

1867 [1 Jan. 1866?] [Beginning missing.] Send this to Kirk. Names of animals.

1868 1 Jan. 1866. Thanks for letter. Leaves tomorrow. Has written Kirk in his favour. Oswell's fight with Tozer; their relations.

1880 [16 Feb.] 1866. Encloses note given him at Bombay. Rae's brother died. Declined invitation by Bishop. Sultan kind. This is last day of Ramadan. Waiting for 'Penguin.'

1904 3 Nov. 1866. Writes on chance of meeting slave trader. These generally flee from him. Lack of food. Sepoys killed buffaloes and have been sent back. Description of the country. Delight at seeing Lake Nyasa again; but Arab dhows are there instead of mission steamer. Fear of Mazitu caused Johanna men to flee. Boyish activities of Wikatani and Chuma. Mission in Zanzibar mainly a chaplaincy to the consulate. 1 Feb. 1867. On watershed.

1963 5 Feb. 1871. *Terribly knocked up, but sticks to work despite everything.

1984 Nov. 1871. Lack of letters. Size of watershed. Loss of goods; infamous to employ slaves. Missionary bishop should not be sent to Madagascar to steal converts. Faulkner is a moral idiot like Baines. Fraudulent boots. Wekotani's feet all right when he left. Regards to his wife. Relieved by Stanley. Cannot find outlet to Lake Tanganyika. Kirk does not write and baffles him by giving goods to slaves.

1994 19 Feb. 1872. Boots and clothing received. March to Unyanyembe. Gratitude to Young. Wekotani, his feet and activities. Banians are worst slaves; Kirk could not have known this or he would not have engaged Ludha.

2002 8 Mar. 1872. Praise of Stanley. Delay in Kirk's sending of letters and goods. Now supplied by Stanley. Introduce him to Murchison etc. He will inform about geography.

2019 2 Sep. 1872. Various phenomena observed in 1869 led him to believe Lake Tanganyika had an outlet. Destruction of letters. Arab lies about outlet. Use of his work by Royal Geographcial Society; their instructions. Kirk's failure. Men sent by Stanley. Grateful for boots. Hopes Waller will become missionary bishop. He will require lodgings in London. Stanley's achievements. Kirk would not take this expedition without salary. He could have settled with Mataka and had £500 p.a., but respected Murchison's wishes. The White Nile slave trade. Tozer. Cheap living in Zanzibar. Kirk's eagerness to force him back inexplicable. Rae's end a warning. [Unfinished?]

WARD, Thomas.
As Steward, Ward was one of only two men who served on the "Pioneer" during the entire period it was placed at Livingstone's disposal. In addition to working with the UMCA at Magomero from 14 Sep. to 11 Nov. 1861, Ward accompanied Livingstone on his expeditions south and west of Lake Nyasa in Jul. — Nov. 1863.

1435 7 Mar. 1864. *Testimony on behalf of Ward's service and very good conduct during his 3½ years' service on board the "Pioneer."

WASHINGTON, John (1800 — 1863).
Hydrographer to the Admiralty and Head of the Harbour Department from 1855 till his death, Washington functioned as chief supply officer for Livingstone's Zambezi Expedition. From his office in London he handled Livingstone's requests for provisions,

material, personnel, etc.   Having been a Captain since 1842, he was promoted to Rear Admiral on 12 Apr. 1862.   (DNB.)

Letters to him of 1 Feb. 1861 (1073), 5 Mar. 1861 (1084), 11 Mar. 1861 (1094), 18 Apr. 1861 (1109), 1 May 1861 (1117), 20 May 1861 (1124), 6 Dec. 1861 (1152), 20 Dec. 1861 (1156), 6 Jan. 1862 (1165), 31 Jan. 1862 (1171), 21 Feb. 1862 (1184), 7 Mar. 1862 (1194), 17 Mar. 1862 (1203), 24 Mar. 1862 (1206), 1 Apr. 1862 (1211), 3 Apr. 1862 (1213), 5 May 1862 (1227), 15 May 1862 (1229), 21 May 1862 (1230), 6 Jun. 1862 (1236), 22 Jul. 1862 (1250), 15 Aug. 1862 (1261), 2 Sep. 1862 (1268), 4 Sep. 1862 (1271), 15 Oct. 1862 (1278), 1 Nov. 1862 (1285), 15 Dec. 1862 (1298), 23 Feb. 1863 (1326), and 29 Apr. 1863 (1344) are published in Clendennen, **DLJW.**

0619   11 Nov. 1857.   Arrowsmith sends map.   L. hopes to accept W.'s invitation for tomorrow. Outline of L.'s notes on African languages.

0636   9 Dec. 1857.   Answers to seven questions, all of which concern the navigation of a steam vessel on the Zambezi River.

0645   18 Dec. 1857.   Forwarding a letter from G. Rennie & Sons, Marine Engineers.

0648   22 Dec. 1857.   HP of Laird's vessel too small;   Rennie's have 10 HP each.

0659   9 Jan. 1858.   L.'s plan for the Zambezi Expedition, including the names of 5 persons to accompany him.   Requests a boat of three compartments which may be taken apart.

0709   12 Feb. 1858.   Explains an accusation that a chronometer was allowed to run down, and complains about Mr. Welsh, who made the accusation.   Hopes that Welsh will not handle the Expedition's magnetical observations.

0711   13 Feb. 1858.   Comments on the purchasing of provisions for the Expedition.

0723   17 Feb. 1858.   Murchison advises against lowering Thornton's pay;   L. hopes the matter may be comfortably arranged with Baines.   Portuguese name the river valley "Zambezia," and allow us to pass duty-free although they have no custom house at the mouth.

0739   28 Feb. 1858.   Steamer launched today and proceeds to Liverpool Tuesday.   Supposes Bedingfeld and Baines there already;   we join them Wednesday.   Steamer looks well to a landsman.

0757   8,9 Mar. 1858.   Received enclosures for Sierra Leone and the Cape.   Only weather prevents departure.   Thank you for your labour on our behalf.

0759   9 Mar. 1858.   Kirk requests expenses from London.   Weather bad.

0760   9 Mar. 1858.   Kirk's account enclosed.   Weather bad.   My last accounts for present sent yesterday.

0764   10 Mar. 1858.   We are off with fair prospects;   shall do our duty with God's blessing. Thanks for all your polite attentions.

0783   19 Apr. 1858.   Hope to reach Cape tomorrow.   Companions in good health and spirits; not so Mrs. L., whom we leave in Cape Town.   Have written our instructions for companions.   Original plan slightly revised.   As Duncan had no money for provisions, L. covered his bills.   28 Apr.   Moffats here;   Skead and "Hermes" go with us.   Maclear well.   Sail on 30th.

0826   13 Sep. 1858.   Your placing Bedingfeld on proper footing with Duncan at Liverpool very wise.   Reasons for dismissing Bedingfeld.   Nature of river thus far; Kebrabasa reputed to be rocks jutting out of the stream.   My men at Tete pleased to see me.   Launch ought to be called "Asthmatic."

0838   28 Sep. 1858.   Men agreed Bedingfeld must go.   No fever, just colds.   Sicard very helpful.   Coal in abundance, other products being studied.   If rocks in river are small, I may blast them.   Portuguese war ended.

0846   6 Oct. 1858.   Cook's idea of Luabo differs from ours; his report enclosed.   Survey required.   Repaired Launch and took on two new men.   Hope to see inscriptions on Gorongozo.   On expenditures and supplies.   Next time I shall tell you of Kebrabasa.

0855   18 Dec. 1858.   Describes Kebrabasa, which a 'good, strong steamer' will pass through.   Scarcity of food prevents side explorations.   Three seams of coal found.   Harmony prevails.   New vessels and supplies needed.   Keep our affairs out of the hands of Mr. Laird.

0870   16 Feb. 1859.   Further information on Kebrabasa; report on lower Shire.   Makololo requested to go home, then had second thoughts.   Comments on the Portuguese.   We have had slight touches of fever.   Favourable report about Rowe.   Remain here a month.

0892   25 May 1859.   Came here for provisions, found none.   Lake Shirwa, its land and people.   Natives say Shirwa separated from Nyinyesi by 5 or 6 miles level land.   Cotton cultivated widely.   Fever among us in spite of quinine.   Landeens prevented C. Livingstone from exploring gold region to the southwest of Tete.   Thornton too young, Baines 'a little heady sometimes.'   Hope to ship out Kroomen and use Makololo.

0933   10 Oct. 1859.   Traced river to Nyinyesi, or Nyassa.   Are delighted with the country; finest cotton & sugar country in world.   From Kongone to this is all English discovery.   Require a steamer capable of being unscrewed and carried 30 miles.

0949   20 Oct. 1859.   Baines dishonest: I put it down at first to fever.   Send him and Thornton away.   I never anticipated the opening of the Shire into Nyassa.   Cotton will thrive here.   Greatest boon the expedition has given is the cure of fever.   30 Nov. "Lynx" in sight.   Thornton has gone up to Zumbo with a Portuguese trader.

0967   5 Nov. 1859.   Copy, Macgregor Laird's letter to Admiralty, 16 Jan. 1858.   This in reply to Mr. Laird's letter of 4 Jan. 1859.   Details of the failures of the "Ma-Robert."   Copy, report on that vessel dated 1 Aug. 1859 and signed by Kirk and the two Livingstones.

0971   10 Nov. 1859.   First mail from England arrived 8 days ago.   Magnetical observations made at Chibisa's.   Vessel requires constant pumping; steel plates become thin due to scaling.   Highlands adapted for European colonization.   Must take Makololo home early in 1860.

0972   13 Nov. 1859.   "Statement respecting a turning lathe furnished by Mr. John Laird to the Zambesi Expedition."   The cylinder is a low pressure one applied to high pressure purposes.   Vessel altogether an ill-planned affair.

0988   4 Feb. 1860.   Mr. Rae goes home, on duty.   Small vessel required to eradicate slave trade over a large district.   It will also render us independent of Portuguese.   Have submitted to Russell a plan to put her on Nyassa.   Sketch map and description of Kongone Bar.   Copy, L. to W.E.A. Gordon, P.S. 3 Nov. 1859, about Bedingfeld.   Further discrepancies in the reputed performance of the "Ma-Robert."

0998   20 Feb. 1860.   On Baines and Thornton, and the "Ma-Robert."   Requests W. aid in getting free navigation of the Zambesi for vessels of all nations.   On Bedingfeld, health and dietary problems, and expenses.

1010   25 Mar. 1860.   Waited 23 days at Kongone, then left for Mazaro.   Doubtful if 'Ma-Robert' ever reaches Tete.   What do you think of our prospects from a business point of view?   Portuguese jealous.   Have requested Russell secure freedom of trade on this river. If not, we ought to try Rovuma.

1037   12 Sep. 1860.   Tells of trip up Zambezi to Sesheke, including visit to Batoka country and Victoria Falls.   Sekeletu ill with skin disease.   Sad fate of Linyanti mission.   Makololo perishing due to fever.

1048   26 Nov. 1860.   Tells of trip down Zambezi to Tete, including second visit to the falls. Sketch of the fissure and measurements.   Could not visit Mosilikatze as we had to hurry to be at Kongone this month.   Description of Kebrabasa.

1053   28 Nov. 1860.   General description of country south of the Zambezi;   Portuguese claim to sovereignty is flimsy.   Thanks for supplies and other aids.   Rowe plastered and kept vessel afloat.   20 Dec.   Ship sunk one day above Senna.   "A Note on Fever for Dr. MacWilliam transmitted by favour of Captain Washington."

1335   23 Apr. 1863.   On the death of Thornton, the recent trip up the Shire, the departure of Kirk and C. Livingstone, the state of the Universities' Mission to Central Africa, the slave trade in the region, and the Expedition's provisions.   27 Apr.   L. will not accompany Kirk and C.L. downriver as planned.   Ale you often sent drunk by some fellow at the Cape. Kirk a good man.   28 Apr.   Meller wishes to go also, but fails to consider the seven months he spent at the Cape. I consider his time up in July.   Four seamen will accompany Kirk home.   Collection of plants, birds and insects will go to British Museum.   Our quinine nearly done; please send more.   Details about C.L.'s salary.   12 May.   Weakened by a fortnight's dysentery;   first real illness I have had.

1376   14 Jul. 1863.   *Financial transactions concerning the time Kirk and his party spent at Quilimane en route to England.

1400   4, 22 Dec. 1863.   Details of his trip up the west bank of the Shire, along the west coast of Lake Nyasa, and then inland, with Thomas Ward.   Expenses of 1863, which was the most expensive year for the expedition.   His attempt to undermine the slave trade caused the Portuguese to oppose him with all of their power, and he hopes that future operations in the interior under a more able leader will not be lost sight of by the government.

1424.9   [1 Jan. — 9 Feb.] 1864.   UMCA a sore disappointment;   Tozer plans to leave the country. Waller disagreed with Tozer's plan to abandon the Africans freed by Mackenzie, and resigned his connection with the mission.   In Quilimane, the Portuguese taxed heavily Kirk and his party when passing through.   The Rovuma may be navigable 8 or 9 months of the year for a vessel of light draught.   24 Feb.   Bishop [Tozer] has gone;   Livingstone takes the 40 boys and children he abandoned and sends them to the Cape.

WATKINS, G.
A minister.

0548   2 Jul. 1857.   I must decline the invitation to the meeting as I must get my narrative to press as speedily as possible.

WATT, David Gilkinson (1817 — 1897).
A native of Irvine, student at Glasgow and Spring Hill College.   Missionary in Benares
1840—5; pastor of various independent churches in England.   (LMSReg. no. 436.)

0028   7 Jul. 1841.   Impression of Rio.   Now half way to Kuruman.   Enjoys travelling.
Disputes among the missionaries.   Philip has been much maligned: he has favoured
natives against colonials.   All missionaries wish to be first to see the reported lake; Ross
has blabbed that Moffat has been given money for an expedition, and if French missionaries hear of it they will set out first; if he can learn the language he may forestall them.
Criticism of Ross's education.   Married missionaries as open to scandal as unmarried.
Should he spend some years in Abyssinia?   Method of communication.   Learned navigation from the Captain.   Want of sound spiritual companionship.   4 Aug.   Arrived at
Kuruman.

0054   14 Apr. 1842.   Despite lack of instructions from Directors has left Kuruman for Bakwain
country.   People have dug canal for irrigation.   Description of country.   Population
scattered.   Too many missionaries at Kuruman and in Cape Colony generally.   18 Jun.
Visit to Bamangwato, Bakaa, and Makalaka.

0070   18 Jun. 1843.   Journey to Sebegwe.   Bubi has fled, Sechele now kind.   Companions
would not go beyond Bakwains, which prevented him seeing lake.   Friendship with
Bakalihari.   Prof. Owen has one box, a second awaits instructions, a third is entrusted to
Williams of Hankey, an excellent Welshman returning home, who intends to establish a
Welsh missionary magazine.   Appointed member of district committee: will vote against
its existence and then ignore it.   Comments on mutual friends.

0089   27 Sep. 1843.   Watt is wrong to condemn Finney unheard.   Progress of Charles at
Oberlin.   Has written Directors about population.   Wishes Watt happiness in marriage:
here is no one suitable for him, even if he had time to think about it.   Visit with Edwards
to Bakhatla.   New mission to be at Mabotsa, where a hut has been erected.   Steele and
Pringle accompanied them.   Moffat not yet returned.   He and Edwards could not wait
for Committee's sanction.   Moffat's book contains map of the lake, which must be a leap
in the dark.   Will try not to quarrel with anyone.   Mrs. McRobert has collected money
for native teacher.   If Moffat asks he will go with him to the lake to observe fever more
closely.   Has corresponded with Prof. Buchanan of Glasgow about medicinal plants.

0118   2 Apr. 1845.   Quarrel with Edwards over credit for journeys.   Does not seek fame.
Moffat withstood similar envy;   regrets having believed anything to his disadvantage.
Mary is a good wife.   Watt should go to China, with an unromantic wife.   Has built house.
Committee has agreed that he should move further on when Edwards returns from the
Cape.

0123   23 May 1845.   Watt's pessimism about India due to his illness.   With regard to marriage
he should ask again.   Institution to train native teachers very desirable, but cannot succeed
without support of older missionaries who are all opposed.   Quarrel with Edwards about
credit for establishing mission.

0129   15 Aug. 1845. Seeks news of his doings.   Atonement controversy.   Quarrel with Edwards
now before committee.   Next week fresh start with Sechele.   Education scheme failed
because support of elders had not been secured.

0151   8 Jun. 1846.   Seeks news of Watt; mission field needs men like him, where life is hard.
In company with an Indian hunter proposes to visit a large tribe to the east, where it is
proposed to settle two native teachers.   Both hope and fear about chief, who is literate,

intelligent, and with many good characteristics. Edwards, having got Mabotsa to himself, claims to have made no accusations.

0160 17 Jan. 1847. Rejoices in Watt's recovery, but advises against return to India. Has been among populous tribes to east of Chonuane, where the bad influence of the Boers is spreading. Far too many missionaries in Cape Colony. Rebuked by Directors for not prompting other missionaries to set up training institution: to tell truth would be to accuse colleagues; best to keep apart from them. Inglis has gone to Cape for supplies, a quite unnecessary procedure. Geological specimens stolen on railway. Seeds have been sent to Calcutta. Tsetse will stop waggons or horses going further north; but beyond that are Arabs.

0181 13 Feb. [1848.] On journey to recover from incessant manual labour and teaching. Sechele cannot put his wives away. Sympathy on death of Watt's wife. News of Charles Livingstone. Progress of mission and translation. Missionaries driven out by Caffre War. Doubts whether continual supply of Europeans is correct policy. Institution now unlikely. Criticises collection of money for Hankey tunnel.

0214.7 26 Oct. 1849. Requires more letters. Would like help from home, but not from begging. If he had been as close as Watt, he would have visited Jerusalem. Watt would do better in England than Scotland and should remarry. Boers make his removal from Mokhatla necessary. Seeks way to the north. Description of the Zouga and its people. Prevented from advancing up the Tamunakle. Lake discovered by missionary enterprise. Recent articles written. His correspondents. Low salaries lead to difficulties for those who really carry out missionary duties.

0220 13 Jan. 1850. Freeman's visit friendly but unlikely to be beneficial, as he accepts Philip's view that the Cape missions must be maintained to uplift the blacks there, overlooking the fact that LMS concern for blacks is regarded by other denominations as excuse for ignoring them. Affectations of Dutch Reformed Church clergy. Available money should be used to advance frontier. Ross's actions argument against Presbyterians being used by LMS. Elliot — Philip controversy. Has compiled a grammar of Sichuana, not relating it to Latin and Greek but on its own terms: what would be cost of printing a few copies? Correspondence with Fairbrother. Examine **Banner** to see if letters have been published. Send copy of Tattam's **Lexicon Aegyptiaco-Latinum**.

0229 18 Aug. 1850. Ministers at home should not require more mental effort than missionaries. The most ignorant and unprincipled missionaries require a bishop, ones less so a committee or presbytery, the best can be independent. No Christian affection between missionaries. Inglis's criticisms of Sechele have had a bad effect. Regrets attack by students on Dr. Wardlaw. Second visit to Lake Ngami. Prevalence of fever. Must be better climate to the north, and there is the only hope for the mission. Will return for a year while family stays at Kolobeng. Thinly populated country. Resolutions passed at Leeds illiberal, confusing freedom and coercion. Practice more important than theology.

0242 10 Jan. 1851. Exhortation to write. Pious character of Tyndale as described by Christopher Anderson. Folly of Hughes's irrigation scheme from River Vaal: discourage subscriptions. Draft paper on missions in South Africa. Contribution from Geographical Society. Terrible state of Ross's church. What are results of Freeman's visit? Boers troublesome. News of Robert Moffat jr. Moffat's translation proceeds. Method of communication.

0255 29 Sep. 1851. Glad to have received letter. Asked to compile dictionary and grammar may form preface to this; but Moffat may do it instead, if his son helps him. Watt should consider going to New South Wales. Hottentot rebellion. Colonists hate missionaries.   Journey with Oswell to Sekhomi;   north across Zouga and through desert; guide wandered;   reached Chobe;   character of Sebetwane.

0267   Mar. 1852.   Has sent paper for **British Quarterly**;   delete passages about whites.   Cape Colony is no longer a mission field: prepared to accept odium for stating this.   Has not yet had time to write down his grammar.   Presently busy with sending back family.   Oswell exceptionally kind.   Treatment of uvula not yet successful.   Sympathizes with Caffres.   State of missionaries involved in the war.

0295   Oct. 1852.   Banter on Watt's family.   Another paper for **British Quarterly** sent.   Thompson largely agrees with him on missions.   Caffre War.   Fighting with Boers.   Will go north whenever danger is past.   Speech of Sandile in United Presbyterian Missionary Record and sent to America for publication.

0327   3 Oct. 1853.   *On his articles which cannot pay their way;   he has two (on the Boers and slavery and on missionary work) which he will not publish.

0402.9 15 Mar. 1856.   Reason for not writing.   Rough journey down the Zambesi.   Geology and rivers of South Central Africa.

WAY, Mrs.

0541   19 Jun. 1857.   Cannot accept your invitation as I must go to Oxford at that time.   We came here to finish my narrative in quiet, and as a general rule accept no invitations until it is completed.   The visit to Oxford is an exception.

WEBB, John F.
A merchant from Salem, Mass., who spent some time in Zanzibar, and was American Vice-Consul, Acting Consul and Consul there between Jul. 1871 and Mar. 1873.

2014   2 Jul. 1872.   *Hopes Stanley reaches coast safely;   his health;   his bravery in passing through war country.

WEBB, William Frederick (1829 — 1899).
A big-game hunter whom Livingstone and Oswell met in 1850.   Livingstone stayed at his house, Newstead Abbey in Nottinghamshire, in 1864—5 while writing **NEZT**.   Livingstone gave his name to "Webb's Lualaba" river.   (Fraser, L&N.)

1670   6 Apr. 1865.   Glad that no operation is required on Webb's knee.   John Livingstone will provide wild rice seed in the autumn.   Fishing excellent.   Has commission but no salary.   Has written to Lord Dalhousie about Kirk.

1726   27 May 1865.   *High opinion of **Tom Brown's Schooldays** and Dr. Arnold, whose good influence is shown in W.C. Oswell.   Errors of Burton school in claiming that Christianity makes people worse.

1799   12 Aug. 1865.   *Oswell offers to help Agnes in any way;   their mutual but undisplayed affection.

WELLINGTON, 2nd Duke of (1807 — 1884).
Arthur Richard Wellesley, succeeded to the title in 1852.   Soldier and politician.
(Boase, **MEB**.)

1012   [Mar. 1860?]   Thank you for the supply of filters.   I entrusted my naval officer with the duty of selection, but fear he took all he could get.   We have traced this river up to Lake Nyassa.   (Description of the three terraces in the Shire highlands follows.)

WHEWELL, William (1794 — 1866).
Master of Trinity College, Cambridge, 1841—66;   Vice-Chancellor, 1843—56.   (**DNB**.)

0950   20 Oct. 1859.   Traced this river up to Lake Nyassa, where we met a slaving party.   The solution to the slave trade is the introduction of legitimate commerce and the gospel.   Our needs for raw materials can be supplied without utilizing slave labour.   Our Christian poor will shine here as lights in the darkness.

WHISH, Charles.
Millinery manufacturer in Glasgow, and friend of the Livingston family.

0156   9 Oct. 1846.   Published in Chamberlin, **SLFL** no. 25 (omitting the list as specified, and a few other sentences).

WHITAKER, J.N.

1404   10 Dec. 1863.   *The thermometer I used was made by Newman, Bond Street, London.   The scale was made of boxwood and had a hinge two or three inches above the bulb.

WHITBOY, Klaso.

0031   4 Aug. 1841.   Testimonial to his abilities as a waggon driver.

WHITE, — — —
Captain of the P. & O. steamer 'Massilia' on which Livingstone travelled from Suez to Bombay in 1865.

1819   11 Sep. 1865.   Thanks for polite attention on the voyage.

1978   15 Nov. 1871.   Thanks for present which he hears is at Zanzibar.   His error in giving steward on the 'Massilia' sixpence instead of half a sovereign.   Goods squandered by carriers.   Waiting for other men from the coast.   Lower class Christians are gentlemen, while similar Moslems are blackguards.

WHITE, Henry.

0598   3 Oct. 1857.   Thank you to the children of your school for the gift of £1, which I shall probably use to purchase books.

WILBERFORCE, Samuel (1805 — 1873).
Bishop of Oxford 1845—69, and of Winchester 1869—73, Wilberforce was a prolific writer on church and religious matters, with several books, pamphlets and articles to his credit.
(DNB.)

0627   23 Nov. 1857.   On the 26th I hope to be bound for Southampton en route to Lisbon. This visit has already been delayed by yellow fever. I hope to see you on my return, and regret not doing so now, to acquaint you with the revival of the slave trade. The idea of free emigration among people who believe that slaves are taken away to be fattened and eaten is preposterous.

0803   22 Jun. 1858.   Upon entering the West Luabo, we had the "Ma-Robert" in steaming order in three days. Up the river we found very good cotton, superior due to the presence of the sea air. Commandant of Tette feared to pass between Mazaro and Senna for the past 6 months. If we had a paddle boat 4—5 feet draught we could survey the delta region and communicate regularly between Tette and the Cape. The "Ma-Robert" can carry nothing but her fuel. Washington favours a shallow steamer for us, and we welcome your support also.

1015   7 Apr. 1860.   Formation of Universities' Mission welcome news. Outline of prospects in the Shire highlands. Rae home to supervise the construction of a boat. I rejoice that Miss Coutts supports institution for the sons of African chiefs.

1317   12 Feb. 1863.   Desolation of the Shire valley caused by spread of slaving from region northwest of Quilimane, practiced by Marianno, Belchoir, and Mello. The same chaos exists south of the Zambesi, where slaves are exported through Inhambane. This contrasts with the achievements of the missions in West Africa. I see our prospects being swept away; only the hope of stopping the trade between Lake Nyassa and Kilwa keeps me going. Although I originally thought the mission wrong in fighting, I now suspect that even Dr. Pusey would have defended his orphans.

1420   31 Dec. 1863.   Disappointment at Tozer's leaving: the missionaries here recommended returning to the highlands, but he had already made up his mind in favour of Morambala. Review of the accomplishments of the mission: far more left undone than done. Have lately returned from a visit to the west of the lake: it is well-watered and well-peopled, and it was there I anticipated the extension of your mission.

1457   2 Aug. 1864.   Will visit W. after spending some days with elderly mother and children. Wishes to discuss abandoned mission.

1461   5 Aug. [1864].   Cannot agree with Tozer on abandonment of mission. Atmosphere in Zanzibar strongly opposed to missionary influence. French Catholic mission there looks to the mainland. Zanzibar trade is with mainland north of Cape Delgado, from which foreigners are excluded. Privation in Highlands inevitable but would have decreased. Already mission had influence and members and had shamed Portuguese. In Zanzibar they will have comfort but no influence. Must be reestablished on the mainland by men specially educated who will give a lifetime to it.

1526   5 Nov. 1864.   Mackenzie was let down by his associates who were pious but (except Scudamore) unsuited to be missionaries. He was too gentle to order them to work, and they wrote journals while he built. Their sedentary life might have killed all in the lowlands. Does not wish to be an accuser, but only specially educated men should be sent in future.

1641   18 Mar. 1865.   Wishes to quote Colenso on bigamy but needs verification of what Mackenzie told him. Is there anyone from the Church in Natal in England?

WILLANS, J.S.
The recipient is said to be an officer of the Royal Engineers;   in that case he must be Thomas Joseph Willans, 1841—86, Lieutenant 1861, Captain 1873, Major 1881, who served in Abyssinia and Assam.   (**Army List.**)

1839   16 Nov. 1865.   *[No information.]

WILLIAMS, Francis.

1494   24 Sep. 1864.   *Not likely to obtain desired situation in an African expedition.

WILLIAMSON, Mrs.

1487   18 Sep. 1864.   Cannot accept invitation.   Greetings.

1537   18 Nov. 1864.   Thanks for present to his followers in Africa, where his work may do a little good.   At a geographical meeting and with the Bishop of Oxford.   Though he likes Colenso, he would not wish his name used in his defence.

WILSON, George (1818 — 1859).
Professor of Technology, Edinburgh, 1855—9, Wilson was a chemist who made Livingstone's acquaintance at University College in London, in 1838—9.   He conducted research into many areas, including colour-blindness and the life of Henry Cavendish.   (**DNB.**)

0649   22 Dec. 1857.   Concerning one Nichol, whom L. was considering as economic botanist of the Zambezi Expedition.   He must be acquainted with medical plants, dye-stuffs, fibrous substances, and act medically too.   Dr. Hooker is highly pleased with him, and if you and Prof. Balfour are satisfied I will have him.   What should his salary be?   Is he a religious man?   This is the main thing, then economic botany.   I go to Hamilton tomorrow evening.

WILSON, J.H.
Trader in South Africa.   (Schapera, **DLSAP**, pp. 117—18.)

0326   2 Oct. 1853.   Published in Schapera, **DLSAP**, pp. 119—23.

WILSON, John (1804 — 1875).
Missionary in Bombay 1829—75;   Vice-Chancellor of the University of Bombay 1857—75. Distinguished orientalist.   Livingstone met him in 1864.   (**DNB.**)

1991   24 Jan. 1872.   Obstructed by slavers.   Destruction of their trade more important than source of the Nile.   Kirk has unintentionally caused loss of £1000 and much time and effort by entrusting goods to slaves.   Success of Stanley.   Disappointment with Nassick boys.   13 Mar.   Letter goes with Stanley, not to be published.   Not finished till he sees the fountains of Herodotus, if they exist.

WILSON, John Crawford (1834 — 1885).
Son of the Chief Justice of Mauritius, Wilson became a Commander on 30 Jan. 1861, and assumed command of H.M.S. "Gorgon" two months later. After aiding the "Hetty Ellen" and Mary Livingstone reach the Zambezi in late Jan. 1862, Wilson accompanied John Kirk up the Shire (where they first received word of the deaths of Charles Mackenzie and Henry Burrup) and on to Magomero. Promoted to Rear-Admiral in 1881, Wilson was Second-in-Command of the Channel Fleet at the time of his death. (Boase, **MEB**.)

1173 1 Feb. 1862. Livingstone requests the aid of the Captain and men of H.M.S. "Gorgon" in getting the "Lady Nyassa" assembled and transported to the cataracts of the Shire. He also describes the slaving activities of the Governor of Tete.

WILSON, William.

0588 14 Sep. 1857. It would be nice to visit the pleasant haunts to which you invite me, but I must decline to lionize for Africa. If Mr. Cecil is with you, present my kind regards.

WILTON, J.H.
Theatrical agent?

0702 11 Feb. 1858. Thanking him for his book, which he hopes to read on the way to Africa. Not aware we were such near neighbours. Good wishes.

WODEHOUSE, Sir Philip Edmond (1811 — 1887).
Entered the Ceylon Civil Service in 1828, and held several posts there before serving as Superintendent of British Honduras, 1851—54; Governor of British Guiana, 1854—61; Governor, Cape Colony 1861—70; and Governor of Bombay from 1872 until his retirement, in 1877. (**DNB**.)

1361 3 Jul. 1863. The expedition cannot leave the country until the river floods next December. In the meantime I will see if a large river enters the northern end of Lake Nyassa, which would account for the perpetual flow of the Shire. This will entail no delay as the "Pioneer" is stuck here. Upon realizing that no good would come while the Portuguese controlled the rivers I sent Kirk, Livingstone, and 4 seamen away. Now we have only 8 sailors, and a native crew to take back to Johanna.

WOODMAN, William Bathurst (1804 — 1882).
Congregational minister at Cadnam 1834—7, Paignton 1837—44, Newport 1844—9; retired to Stonehouse, Glos. Interested in missions. (**Congr.Yearbook** 1883, p.319.)

0703 11 Feb. 1858. I will be pleased to take the gift to Sekeletu.

0740 28 Feb. 1858. I return the post order which you kindly sent for Sekeletu and Shinte, as it is payable in London's GPO and I leave for Liverpool in order to sail on Wednesday next. Thank you for your kindly feelings.

WRIGHT, Margery (1798 — 1886).
Wife of Peter.

0090   29 Sep. 1843.   She should get another medical certificate at Cape Town.   Apologises for hasty letter.

0096   5 Nov. [1843].   Has written to McMurdo of Royal Ophthalmic Hospital in London, who will assist her.

WRIGHT, Peter (? — 1843).
Missionary in South Africa, mostly at Griquatown (where Livingstone stayed with him in 1841), 1821—43.   (**LMSReg.**,no. 221).

0032   4 Aug. 1841.   Settled at Kuruman.   Sends medical books.   Do not bleed females of 14—22 years.   Send pack ox.   Suggests joint subscription to a review.

0047   Jan. 1842.   Desires Wright and Edwards to be reconciled without his mediation.   Various peregrinations.   Medical essays.

0048   7 Feb. 1842.   *On Mahura's attack on Sebegwe, assisted by Boers, and Philip's tour.

0062   11 Aug. 1842.   Hopes to assure Sebegwe of friendship.   His hopes of sending native teachers to the interior dashed by the war.   Philip's visit has had bad effect on the natives.

YOUNG, Edward Daniel (1831 — 1896)
Gunner of H.M.S. "Gorgon."   Young joined the Zambezi Expedition in February, 1862 and served Livingstone in several capacities for more than two years.   In 1867 he led a Livingstone Search Expedition up the Shire, which proved that the explorer was not dead as reported;   and in 1875 he led up the Shire the expedition which founded the Livingstonia mission.   When he retired from the Coast Guard in 1891 he was given rank as honorary Lieutenant, by which title he is usually remembered today.   (Boase,**MEB.**)

1260   8 Aug. 1862.   "Pioneer" to remain here at anchor until I return or Kirk returns from Rovuma.   Carpenter is to erect bulkheads between cabin and engines, and between engines and front of ship.   Also have sides caulked, scraped and painted as far as possible: defer repairs to bottom until our return.   Engineer has given orders to the stokers; please see that King winds the chronometers.

1380   17 [Jul. 1863].   Have written Waller to send 40 Ajawa to carry the boat.   Your deep gully was close at hand when you turned yesterday.   Have been hauling waggon all morning;   oxen not behaving like gentlemen.   I have mentioned to Waller the payment I promise to give, and he will give you a list of the same if they do not wait for my return.

1436   7 Mar. 1864.   Testimony on behalf of Young's good service to the Zambezi expedition since 1 February 1862.

1439   2 Apr. 1864.   Authorizing Young and Waller to receive cases of beer sent by Admiral Washington via Cape Town for the use of the Zambezi Expedition.

1474   29 Aug. 1864.   When I return to London in a few days I will be happy to go with you to the Admiralty on your account.   The Paymaster of the "Seringapatam" neglected sending papers as soon as might have been done.   I gave certificates to all hands — yourself included — before leaving Moçambique.

YOUNG, James (1811 — 1883).
A Scottish industrialist who made a fortune distilling paraffin from shale, Young first met Livingstone when the latter was attending Anderson's College.   He became one of Livingstone's three Trustees, charged with administering his finances with reference to his family during the Zambezi Expedition, and he also supported Livingstone generously from his own pocket after 1857.   (**DNB.**)

0504   17 Apr. 1857.   Cannot stay with you in Glasgow as I have a prior commitment with Andrew Buchanan.   Yesterday I met your daughters playing music at Mrs. Lindsay's — they should play Scotch tunes instead of Italian.   I suspect their Mama will think me heretical in this.

0631   Nov. 1857.   *Extract published in Blaikie, **PLDL**, p. 218, n. 1.

0666   18 Jan. 1858.   I think it best not to buy "Dechmont," but thank you anyway.   Give up the tunnel idea and try to bore through "Dechmont."

0795   10 May 1858. *Extract published in Blaikie, **PLDL**, pp. 247—8.

0804   23 Jun. 1858.   Good weather since leaving Liverpool.   We entered the Zambesi through a natural canal 5 miles long.   The "Pearl" was too deep for exploring.   Next week we go to Tete.   My brother found cotton in the delta.

0827   14 Sep. 1858.   I formerly believed the river could be navigated only six or eight months in one year;   now I believe a 30 inch steamer could navigate it ten months or the whole year.   We dug out 1½ tons of coal near Lupata, and the country is rich in coal seams.   I offered to mediate in the war between the rebels and the Portuguese, but the Governor-General would not hear of it.

0851   8 Dec. 1858.   Inquire if the Bann will be sent out;   if not, I must have my own, and would use £2000 of my money in your charge for it.   This area can produce raw materials. Let Washington know I will have a Government vessel or my own.

0868   15 Feb. 1859.   *I wrote you in dispatches which left this on 20th Dec. last and told you about a steamer.   If the Government does not feel inclined to do its duty . . .

0885   8 May 1859.   *While waiting for another ship, if one is to be sent, we might try to reach Nyinyesi.

0916   22 Jul. 1859.   *I am trusting you for another ship.   If the Government fails, £2000 is at your service.

0927   6 Aug. 1859.   *You will recollect I authorized you to use £2000 if the Government refused the Bann or another vessel . . .

0935   12 Oct. 1859.   I want a steamer capable of carrying 100 tons, which can be screwed together and transported in pieces not weighing more than 400 or 500 pounds, around 30 miles of cataracts.   If the Government does not give, I will have it myself.   Our path is open and the way plain before us.

0982   [1859]. Trading prospects in the Zambezi region. Now struggling upriver. Rae navigated yesterday — he never had any idea how tedious it was.

0987   28 Jan. 1860. Our mail was lost at sea. Rae goes home to supervise the building of a new ship. Intend to take the Makololo home. Send me a book by Bishop Selwyn, which contains all the words in the Bible.

0994   [7 Feb. 1860??]. Chapman's partner, Samuel Edwards, stole a volume of my journal, or at least the Makololo say they gave it to him. Send me a copy of Chapman's book: I'm curious to see if he used it. Ask Rae about Bedingfeld's performance on the battlefield at Mazaro. Have you tried getting rid of the smell of your oil by putting a single drop of terpentine on it?

1002   29 Feb. 1860. *As soon as you know that the Government will not give another boat for Lake Nyassa you must order one from Tod. Rae knows what we want.

1026   22 Jul. [1860]. Have made our way around the Kebrabasa and are en route to the Makololo country. The river is quite smooth to about 25 miles above the Kafue. Coal field more extensive than I thought. Pleased to hear of Universities' mission to the interior. 11 Aug. We saw the falls 20 miles off and I could not resist the pleasure of showing them to my companions. Charles says they throw Niagara into the shade.

1061   4 Dec. 1860. Measurements of the Victoria Falls. Came downstream by canoe; Kirk's upset and he lost his notes. We are en route to the sea in hopes of getting a new steamer. Although well patched, the "Ma-Robert" springs new leaks lately daily. Our pinnace is also very bad, so we take both and stick to that which floats longest. 20 Dec. One day above Senna "Ma-Robert" stuck on a bank and filled, so we had to leave her and go ashore.

1070   [Jan. 1861]. Extract published in Blaikie, **PLDL**, pp. 279—280.

1118   14 May 1861. Send a new blue frock coat. Discussion of steamers. Rae not to be trusted. John's suit regarding paraffin sale in Canada.

1135   7 Nov. 1861. Description of Lake Nyassa, and of the ferocity of its sudden storms. Brief discussion of the first hostile encounter with the Ajawa, which took place in July.

1175   [2—7 Feb. 1862]. Arrival of "Hetty Ellen." Robert's flight from a threatened caning at school convinces Livingstone that his son is much like his father (i.e. David), and that he needs a free rein in order to find himself.

1176   [7 Feb. 1862?]. Rae tells of Robert's activities in Edinburgh, and realizing his dereliction as a parent, David wishes Robert with him.

1182   19 Feb. 1862. "Gorgon" with brig in tow arrived on 31 January. Give mother an extra £50, but suggest to my sisters that if they can, they ought to work.

1228   5 May 1862. On the death of Mary Livingstone, and the wanderings of their son Robert.

1231   28 May 1862. Came down on 11th as Rae has dysentery and fever. He was treated by Stewart. "Lady Nyassa" almost ready. Sorry my actions caused you a great deal of trouble. Financial matters concerning his family. Dissatisfaction with the Universities' mission.

1299   15 Dec. 1862. Financial affairs involving the Trustees, Livingstone's family, and his salary. Thoughts on Mary's death; requests Young send a gravestone to mark her resting place.

1346   30 Apr. 1863.   At work on the road around the rapids.   Slave hunting followed the expedition to this region.   Death of Thornton and two missionaries.   Kirk and Livingstone go home.

1362   3 Jul. 1863.   Extract published in Blaikie, **PLDL**, p. 313.

1395   [Jul. — Aug. 1863?].   Surprised Hannan and Buchanan oppose Young against Livingstone's wishes.   Realizes his great financial debt he owes Young, and intends to pay every farthing.   Robert at Cape Town and Natal.   Deprecating intrusion of High Church missionaries and their behavior in Hawaii.

1423   [10 Feb. 1864?].   Water rose on 19 Jan.   Started down but lost rudder.   Hope stupid tale of my murder has not reached the children.   Sorry to hear of Washington's death.   Robert shipped to N.Y. on a brig as a common sailor.   Hope to get enough from the sale of the "Lady Nyassa" to pay off everything.   Have 40 of the Bishop's liberated captives on board.

1458   2 Aug. 1864.   Will meet on Thursday.   Children arrived today.   Wishes to spend two days with them.

1495   26 Sep. 1864.   Agnes delighted with present of watch.   Webbs all he expected and more.   Going to London to get journals.

1549   30 Nov. 1864.   Possibility of his return as consul or otherwise.   Murchison wants him to settle the Nile watershed question, but a purely geographical task has no interest.   Wishes to do good by opening up a path north of the Portuguese.

1569   4 Jan. 1865.   Banter on Young's silence.   If sons turn out fools, it is inherited.   [End missing.]

1571   7 Jan. 1965.   Will go as soon as possible, but not solely as a geographer.

1581   20 Jan. 1865.   *Will have to sell 'Lady Nyasa' as monsoon will be blowing before he gets out.   Will go to Seychelles, then to Rovuma, then on foot.   Will be a missionary, doing geography by the way.

1660   [Mar. 1865?]   [Beginning missing.]   Inscription on naughty lady's tombstone.   Asks for sketch of millstone.   Thanks for paper.   Murray will print 10000 copies to begin with.

1705   †10 May 1865.   [Beginning missing.]   Concerning Messr. Aston, Brown, Hannan and Braithwaite.

1713   [8 or 15 May 1865].   Intends to go to Scotland on 23rd or 24th.   If Young is in London, they should travel together.   Saw Dr. Stenhouse at Royal Society.   [End missing.]

1751   20 Jun. 1865.   His mother's death.   Anna Mary not alarmed.

1757   24 Jun. 1865.   Funeral yesterday.   Will Youngs join him on trial run of Turkish ironclad to which he is invited by Napier.   Struck by comment of Dr. Thomas Brown on neglect of his body.

1766   [1 Aug. 1864. — 6 Jul. 1865?].   Wishes a few pounds of paraffin candles.

1776   [25 Jul. 1865].   [Beginning missing.]   At Grant's wedding.   Charles has had fever at Fernando Po.

1788   [26 Sep. 1864 — 30 Jul. 1865].   Adjutant of Robert's regiment sure he was not left dead or wounded.   Agnes at two balls.   Tom still ill;   he should go to India as a tea-planter.

1794   8 Aug. 1865.   Cannot stay longer.   Must get to Bombay to sell 'Lady Nyasa.'   Goes to Paris on Monday.   Expects no salary from Russell, who resents his giving anti-slavery credit to Palmerston.

1800   12 Aug. 1865.   Farewell and thanks.   Means of forwarding letters.

1812   22 Aug. 1865.   At Malta in an hour.   Russell says he can have £500 if settled with some chief;   but then he could not do what Royal Geographical Society wishes, and he could not lie, as Burton would.

1869   [2 Jan. 1866?]   Death of Von der Decken.   Lady Franklin here.   Leaves tomorrow. Beke and his wife going to Abyssinia to try to free prisoners.

1872   26 Jan. 1866.   *Rolling voyage.   Failure of Edinburgh instrument maker to include Scripture slides.   Prospect of Kirk being in Zanzibar.

1906   10 Nov. 1866.   Send £400 from his account at Coutts to Zanzibar for wages etc.   Had to go south in case men would desert, which they did in any case.   Jan. 1867.   Delayed by rain.   Thanks for trip to Loch Fyne.   Loss of medicine.   Dean of Ely promised help with children's education.

1934   [Jul. 1868?]   [Beginning missing.]   The Portuguese.   Observations.   Baines.   Desire to be home to guide Tom.

1986   16 Dec. 1871.   Regrets Bombay affair but should be able to give him something as he has Government salary.

2015   [15 Mar. — Jul. 1872?]   Statistical denunciation of Kirk.

2031   [Jan. 1873?]   *Glad that Young is able to retire: he cannot, as he must still work against slavery.   Presentiment that he would not live to complete this journey now weakened;   it did not interfere with his performance of his duty.

COMMANDER, H.M. SHIP.

0816   13 Aug. 1858.   On this island, the Zambesi Expedition erected an iron house, and removed the luggage upriver in five trips.   At the lignum vitae log, Skead observed for Latitude & Longitude;   at the tree marked with the broad arrow, C. Livingstone took observations for magnetical dip, deflection, vibration and declination.   Quit island this day to go to Shupanga and Tette;   hope that three trips may place all of expedition in Tette.   Some goods may have to be left in Senna and Shupanga.   All well since our arrival.   Baines suffers a little due to slight stroke of sun.   Expect to be at Kongone on Christmas day.

0893   25 May 1859.   Have visited various mouths of the Zambesi since the 18th, but having met no ship with provisions we depart from the Luabo tomorrow.   Discovered Lake Shirwa.   Natives say it is separated from a larger lake, Nyinyesi, by only 5 or 6 miles. Shirwa does not seem to be the Lake Maravi of maps as no Maravi are near.   We go to Tette and return to the Lake region in July.   Expect the vessel to be in Kongone on 30 July.   We have had fever but not in its severest form.

0903   31 May 1859.   Expected ship at Kongone on 24 May but found none.   A note left in a bottle in the harbour entrance sets an appointment for 30 July.   It contains our account of the discovery of a lake.   We have had fever in its mild form.

CAPTAIN, MAN OF WAR.

1329   25 Feb. 1863.   Due to famine and depopulation in the lower Shire valley it is difficult to find provisions for the crew of the "Pioneer."   The black men from the Cape who were with the UMCA are being returned.   As the expedition cannot get to Johanna, may provisions be sent to Kongone, Quilimane or Mosambique.   Blacksmith of the "Pioneer" to be invalided.

CAPTAIN, H.M. SHIP.

0400.5   3 Mar. [1856].   Please take letters to Maclear.   Reached Tette yesterday, tired but well. Portuguese very kind.

1338   28 Apr. 1863.   Due to depopulation of the valley, we must rely entirely upon stores we left in Johanna last November.   With reference to the following list please send provisions to Quilimane.   These will last till January, when we expect a ship from the Cape at Kongone.   Pearce and Wilson invalided, both good men; Magrath will do well but Saunders and Newell are indifferent characters.   Kirk and C. Livingstone are entitled to a passage home via the Cape: please help them and their baggage.   Thornton hired two men, who return to Zanzibar: wages due Kirk for them from Consul who will charge FO.

L — — — — — —, — — — .

0140   15 Nov. 1845.   Busy building house.   Unlike at Mabotsa, has started teaching at once. Sechele's progress and example.   Visitors from other tribes.   Long account of the 'science' of proleptics.

UNKNOWN RECIPIENTS.

0085   Jul. 1843.   Exhortation.   The people, their degraded state.   Native medicine.   Baptisms. Murders.   Hopes to start new mission.   Regards to Mrs. C.

0164   22 Mar. 1847.   [To 'Young Friends'.]   Delay in receipt of their letter.   They are fortunate compared with African children.   Death of Ashton's son.   Basis of true happiness. [End missing.]

0375   [Jul. 1855.]   *Men prepared for another trip, though they have made little profit.

0442   13 Dec. 1856.   His correspondent's influential literary position would make his negotiation an honour, but has already agreed with Murray.

0451   6 Jan. [1857].   Must decline your invitation as my time in England is short and my English faulty with disuse, and from a conviction that my usefulness does not lie in public exhibitions.

0463   27 Jan. [1857].   I have not the smallest desire to receive any civic honours, but will visit you for the honour after my last visit to my mother in Hamilton.   No demonstrations.

0516   8 May 1857.   I cannot come to Scotland when I expected, but will let you know when I can.   Publisher etc. detains me.

0527   [20 Jan. – 23 May 1857].   Went to R.G.S. to get a ticket for you, then to Admiralty and forgot it.   I send a card which will admit you at once.   The papers are on the Congo, the mouth of the Zambesi, and a journey to Persia.

0528   [20 Jan. – 23 May 1857].   *I have specimens of a human parasite generally unknown, and also tsetse, in my luggage.   You will hear from me when I get to them.   Am very busy with my book.

0565   6 Aug. 1857.   The only authorized version of **MT** is that published by Murray.   The collection of letters produced by the **British Banner** was unauthorized, but he took no legal action, not wishing to injure the society with which it was connected.

0567   13 Aug. 1857.   Supporting the petition of Mrs. Maclune, widow of a man of the H.M.S. "Dart" who lost his life off the bar at Quilimane while attempting to aid Livingstone.

0568   16 Aug. 1857.   Concerning an article in the **Natal Mercury**, on the subject of Moffat, Pretorius, and Sechele: Livingstone doubts Sechele would ask the Boers for a missionary, although he is notorious for wanting one.   Has no objections to the Moravian Society taking up the site if we are unable to do so.   Lists 8 other tribes who need a missionary more than does Sechele.   C.M.S. may go to Sechele, but I dare say you would object to this.   I shall be in London tomorrow.

0579   29 Aug. 1857.   *Sir Duncan and Lady Macgregor all you said.   Their son, hero of the Kent East Indiaman, is a worthy son of such parents.   He gave an amusing paper on ship's propulsion.   Wish I could say a word or two for Christ which would come in naturally and be useful.

0589   21 [Sep. 1857].   Your note came a minute ago when leaving for Edinburgh.   On Thurs. we are in Dundee;   Sat. Kendal en route to Liverpool and Leeds if mother's illness does not worsen.   I may be off without seeing you.   Lionizing very disagreeable.   Mrs. L. follows me tomorrow;   part with the Canadian brother today.

0590   [14–21 Sep. 1857?].   I send a note for Mr. Buck: he felt very much hurt at not getting an appointment and asked for a testimonial that he had volunteered.   I don't feel inclined to do so and if he calls, please give him his trash.   Never thought much of a man dismissed from the Navy.   Am off to address the University and am in a funk.

0599   3 Oct. 1857.   *I am not sure if the R.G.S. will provide the instrument you mention, but will know when I return from Portugal and will let you know.   Seems just the thing for my purpose.

0607   24 Oct. 1857.   Return Moffat's letter: glad Sechele and the Kuruman mission are cooperating in spite of the Boers.   Pleased he supports a mission to Mosilikatze;   someone should take Mosilikatze a new waggon.

0609   26 Oct. 1857.   Cannot lecture in Birmingham due to events beyond my control.

0613   30 Oct. 1857.   Invite any friends you like to be present Tuesday evening.   Large public meetings are distasteful, but not this type.

0633   1 Dec. 1857.   At Kendal you invited me to speak to the young men at Cambridge on African missions.   Having received an invitation from Rev'd Monk and Prof. Whewell, I let you know I avail myself of the opportunity.   I told Monk I had a previous invitation from you.   Murray gave me your note acknowledging the copy.

0635   7 Dec. 1857.   The Lisbon Co. did not receive the sanction of the Portuguese government, and was said to have been concocted by a man "cracked," but seemed a feasible idea. If they give free passage to all nations, it will benefit themselves.   The work of Sr. Botelho gives a glowing account of the resources of East Africa.

0644   17 Dec. 1857.   Thank you for the gift of knives.   Up over my head preparing to return to Africa.   I will convey your gift to my friends the Makololo.   Thanks for the pretty hymn book.   Mrs. L. is in Scotland.   Regards to your nieces and their governess; salutations to your husband and yourself.

0650   22 Dec. 1857.   Thank you for your reply to my enquiries.   In order to lose no time, the FO ordered a steam launch from Macgregor Laird.   Though he will probably do the thing well, I would have preferred it had it come from my fellow townsman.

0670   21 Jan. 1858.   *There is no room for you in the expedition.   Our plan is a tentative one, and we take as few Europeans as possible.

0671   21 Jan. 1858.   *Acknowledges receipt of 10/- for work in Africa.

0696   10 Feb. 1858.   Washington expected to have orders for half year's advance ready today, so you may have them by calling on him.   I forgot the tent yesterday: please ask the Captain about it.

0704   11 Feb. 1858.   *Will attend to Gurney's suggestion as far as possible.   Will manage Ackworth on our way to Scotland.

0706   11 Feb. 1858.   Coningham my agent;   send letters through him.   Breakfast at Trotter's tomorrow.   Arrangement with my brother-in-law is **entre nous**.   L.M.S. agent at the Cape sends a bill for £258 against me.

0724   17 Feb. 1858.   I gave John a copy and he signed both, so you may keep the one you have. Last night at Miss Coutts' we were with the Bishops of Oxford, Cape Town and Exeter — don't know what gauge I employ to find out if I have become Puseyite in consequence.

0756   6 Mar. 1858.   *Thanks for the present of seeds, which are now in the charge of Dr. Kirk, and for the £5.

0806   26 Jun. 1858.   We attempted a branch described by Lt. Hoskins as the southernmost navigable, and found it so for 60—70 miles.   Skead sounded the Luabo bar.   Following Gordon's advice, we entered the Kongone and soon were in the mainstream.   No fever yet: Bedingfeld works hard but keeps well.   We shall leave our heavy baggage at Senna.

0869   15 Feb. 1859.   A cataract, which we wish to name after Sir Roderick, prevented our going to Nyanja, from which the Shire flows.   Ascended Morambala.   A ragged school came down to Hadley Green;   some had never seen green fields.   It must come to national colonization.   Left orders for Baines and C. Livingstone to explore Kebrabasa. Cucumbers are coming in now;   the best cotton country is undoubtedly north of this.

0934   10 Oct. 1859.   Met a slaving party from Cazembe's country, and bought malachite from them.   They appeared to be from the Angoxia River.   When they knew we were English, they slipped off in the night.   Not more than 1/5 of the available land here has been put under the hoe.   A colony of our own English honest poor would be a great advantage to England and Africa.

0951   Shire 20 Oct. 1859.   Shire is cotton country, also grows indigo.   Nile and Shire similar. Slaving party with tusks and slaves.   I never encouraged any scheme when at home, but this seems like a fair opening.   Reached Lake Nyassa.   A road can be built around the cataracts.   Three terraces of Shire valley have different climates.   We ought not to pay dues, as Shire, Luabo and Kongone are all English discoveries.

0961   1 Nov. 1859.   The Shire, Lake Nyassa, the Highlands, cotton growing.   Commerce and mission would do good.

0981   [1 Sep. — 31 Dec. 1859?].   Every day I feel more certain that an English colony will end the slave trade.   This land is for cotton and sugar, yet the Portuguese export labourers. We return to the lakes in July.   Portuguese stand in the way.   They think a company will be formed and they as masters of the land will become rich without taking the cigars out of their mouths.   If you can bring forth the idea of a colony being formed, you will do a good service.   I mean a Christian colony to end this trade of men.

0986   26 Jan. 1860.   Published in Wallis, ZJJS, pp. 205—208.

1035   8 Sep. 1860.   Went to Linyanti to get medicines and papers he left there earlier.   Disappearance of Makololo who went to Angola with Ben Habib ben Salem Lafifi in 1855. Marched 600 miles;   learned of loss of Linyanti mission when near the falls.   Fever remedy in MT.   Coal field extends further than Zumbo and the Kafue.   28 Nov.   This was to have been sent by an elephant hunter who departed before we saw him again. Description of the Victoria Falls, and of the trip back to Tette.

1055   28 Nov. 1860.   With reference to your account of the decease of Joseph Sturge: he wrote me a letter on the subject of peace, which I read and then lost.   It remained on my mind, so I wrote him stating difficulties which stand in the way of peace.   You appear to have answered them fairly.   I pray never to be forced to fight with black or white, but believe that in some cases war is necessary and just.   In Africa we have the worst evils of war;   but I think lawful commerce will forestall the advances of the bad.   Some of the Friends should appear among us as the harbingers of peace.   Lately I marched 600 miles carrying only a stick, but I carried a revolver after a rhinoceros charged and stopped short when within 3 yards of me.

1153   7 Dec. 1861.   Carried a boat past the cataracts and explored Lake Nyassa.   Went along the western shore: it is from 20 to 50 or 60 miles broad, and over 200 miles long. Very deep.   Excessively stormy, and we did not find out about the Rovuma.   Depopulated near the north end, pirates live on detached rocks and skeletons lying everywhere. Two Arabs we met on the lake reported another lake, Moelo.   They came from a place called Katanga, which seems S.S.W. of Cazembe, and had come to buy cloth.

1158   24 Dec. 1861.   Was delayed going down to meet Mrs. L. and those with her.   On the mission, the lands of the Shire, and the slave trade.   The mission needs a steamer of three feet draft.

1288   17 [Nov.] 1862.   Came to this river to cut wood, and met a boat from the "Rapid" with your letter.   We cannot take mission provisions on board.   Col. Nuñes will send his launch for the mission provisions.   Waller was here and took what provisions and grog he could.   Please give what little information I have to the bishop.   Salutations to your lady.

1310   8 Jan. 1863.   *Requesting translations of the Bible in the languages of Senna and Tette. Now engaged in carrying a steamer past the cataracts.   Slaving continues.   Death of Mary L.

1467   15 Aug. 1864.   Cannot accept invitation to lecture.

1470   17 Aug. 1864.   *No hope of good from Portuguese;   need for English commerce and missions.

1481   1 Sep. 1864.   Absence in the Highlands prevented answer sooner.   Insects collected were forwarded to British Museum;   details of parasites.

1489   [18 – 23 Sep. 1864].   [No information.]

1502   7 Oct. 1864.   Ship on which he and Smith came from Malta was the 'Ripon', due in Southampton about end of July.   He of Smith & Burry & Co. is the man;   too late to communicate with him, as he must be off by the end of the year.

1504   8 Oct. 1864.   Declines invitation.

1622   24 Feb. 1865.   Way smooth for another attempt to end slave trade because the Royal Geographical Society, the Foreign Office, and an anonymous friend are giving money. If only Robert were available to go.   Russell's promised commission.   Sends letter of John Moffat.   Tidman showed him letters only from Robert Moffat.

1626   [25 Jan. – 23 Feb. 1865?]   [Beginning missing.]   Tozer would not keep the women among his crew, but could do no good without them. Mrs. Webb going on well.   Hayward asked what Palmerston could do: wishes free access to the Zambesi and Shire.

1665   3 Apr. 1865.   *Sends proof of wood cuts.

1717   [25 Apr.—19 May 1865?]   *On the lack of religious conviction among the Portuguese.

1734   2 Jun. 1865.   Hopes to be in London in a fortnight and will call.

1781   28 Jul. 1865.   Delighted to come to Norwich on Wednesday and should like to stay overnight.   Comes up from Newstead on Tuesday and will begin to pack on Thursday.

1782   28 Jul. 1865.   By a note of 26 Jul. signed G.E. I am said to be under a delusion because I did not know that an objectionable letter had been cancelled.   Never asked for pension. Objectionable letter was returned.   Salary is all required.   PS   Russell said I would get salary when I settled, which is hard.

1817   [27 Aug.—10 Sep. 1865].   [Beginning missing.]   *Description of voyage.

1859   31 Dec. 1865.   *On obtaining boatman.

1862   [11 Sep.—31 Dec.] 1865.   *Religious advice to a girl.

1863   [Nov.—Dec. 1865?]   *Returns proof;   considers lecture very well reported.

1895   4 Jun. 1866.   Unsatisfactory conduct of sepoys.

1898   18 Jun. 1866.   Notes on conversation with person in Bombay.

1899 20 Aug. 1866. [To 'Friends in Scotland'.] *On the weary journey from the coast; the peoples of the Rovuma; Dr. Roscher.

1907 10 Nov. 1866. Impossible to send letter to the coast. Slave traders avoid him. Desertion of Johanna men. Could not go around north end of Lake. Manganja were hospitable. Has zig-zagged to avoid depredations of Mazitu.

1910 1 Feb. 1867. [To 'Friends in Scotland'.] *On the journey across the Chambeze to the watershed; desertion of Johanna men.

1913 2 Feb. 1867. [To 'Friends in Scotland'.] *Long journey north to the watershed; Luapula before him; Nassick boys; visit to Chitapangwa.

1964 7 Feb. 1871. Short of paper. Impertinent letter from Under-secretary Murray. Better treatment given to Meller and Thornton. Dispatch lost.

1966 12 Feb. 1871. Previous explorations of the Nile and their defects.

2032 [1873?] Reports that on the — — — he reached the fountains, which rise at the base of a mound — — — feet high, at a distance of — — — from each other.

SECTION 3

BOOKS, ARTICLES, JOURNALS, DIARIES, NOTEBOOKS.

BOOKS

1)   **Missionary Travels and Researches in South Africa,** London: John Murray, 1857.

An early draft of Chapter 1, dated 30 May 1856, is in NARS, LI 1/1/1, pp. 479–94, (16 pp.).   A draft, frequently fuller than the published work, of which sections I–XXXIX are autograph, most of the rest is in Charles Livingstone's hand with corrections and additions by David, and the last few folios are in another hand, survives incompletely as follows: sect. I–XXXV (= pp. 1–356) JMPL (formerly SNMDL;   photocopy NLS, MSS. 10712–13); XXXVI–XXXIX, XLI, XLIII–XLIV, XLVII–XLVIII, and unnumbered section (= pp. 356–88, 406–63, 503–62, 659–77) NLS, MS. 10702;   stray leaves NLS, MS. 10702 (3 ff., = pp. 92–3, 477–9), BLL, Add. MS. 36297, f. 22 (1 f., = p. 363;   microfilm NLS, MS. 10780 (3)), BLJ 6507 (2 ff., = pp. 366–7, 454–6), and Myers Cat. 386 (1956) no. 188 (1f., = p. 383).   Draft introductions are in NARS, LI 1/1/1, pp. 621–4 (4 pp.).   Two sheets of galley proofs with autograph corrections, numbered 433–4 and corresponding to p. 626 1.31 – p. 631 1.19 of the published work, are in NMLZ on display.

On variants of the first edition see Frank R. Bradlow in Lloyd, **Liv,** pp. 6–19, **Quart. Bull. S. Afr. Libr.** xxviii, 1973, pp. 29–30, and **Mendelssohn Revision Project Bulletin** xxii, 1976, p. 6.   At first there was no index: this was printed separately (copy in RHLO), and included in later copies.

The author received 250 copies.   Without carrying out a thorough search we have noted the following presentation and inscribed copies (arranged by date of inscription):

1.   'To Mrs Dick in kind remembrance of her departed husband Dr Thomas Dick whose memory is revered by David Livingstone.   50 Albemarle St. London 26th Oct 1857.' JPLAM.
Dick, the scientific writer (**DNB.**), died 29 Jul. 1857.

2.   'To Revd Dr Keith with kindest salutations from David Livingstone London 26th Octr 1857.' BLJ 6506.
Peter Hay Keith, minister of Hamilton (Scott, **FES** III, p. 261).

3.   'To Dr Loudon with kindest salutations from his friend David Livingstone   London 26 Oct 1857.'   SNMDL.
James Loudon, physician in Hamilton.

4.   'To Professor R. Owen with the kindest salutations of his affectionate and obliged friend David Livingstone London 26th Oct 1857.'   Location uncertain.
Sir Richard Owen (**DNB.**).

5.   'To Rev. Dr Williams with the kindest salutations of David Livingstone, London 26 Octr. 1857.'   Sawyers Cat. SA/45 (1965) no. 41.
Possibly Rowland Williams (**DNB.**).

6.   'Lady Emma Campbell with respectful salutations from David Livingstone London 29th Octr 1857.'   NCLE.
Daughter of the 7th Duke of Argyll (Paul, **SP** I, p. 389).

7.   'Sir George Grey with respectful salutations from David Livingstone.   London, 29th Oct. 1857.'   SALCT Grey Coll.
Apparently Grey, colonial governor (**DNB.**);   cf. no. 25 below.

8.   'Rev David Russell with kind regards from David Livingstone, London, 29th Oct 1857.'
Sotheby's Cat. 11 Apr. 1967, lot 418.

9.   'Titus Salt Esq. with kindest regards from David Livingstone, London, 29th Oct. 1857.'
Sawyers Cat. SA/83 (1974) no. 51.
Sir Titus Salt (**DNB.**).

10.   'E. Pye Smith Esqr with kind regards and thanks from Mrs and David Livingstone, London, 29th Octr 1857.'   SNMDL.

11.   'Mrs Vavasseur with the kindest salutations of her affectionate brother David Livingstone London 29 Oct 1857.'   Privately owned.
Helen Vavasseur, née Moffat, Mary Livingstone's younger sister.

12.   'Colonel Sykes with the kindest salutations of David Livingstone   London   30th Octr 1857.'   USPGL.
William Henry Sykes of the East India Company.

13.   'Sir Roderick I. Murchison with the kindest regards of his affectionate friend David Livingstone.   London 2d Novr 1857.'   Privately owned.
Murchison, geologist and president of the Royal Geographical Society (**DNB.**).

14.   'Chas. Ratcliffe Esq.   With the kindest salutations of David Livingstone London 2d Novr 1857.'   SALCT.

15.   'To Agnes Livingstone with the prayer that God may protect her through life and admit her at last into his Heavenly Kingdom.   David Livingstone.   London 9th Novr 1857.'   SNMDL.
His eldest daughter.

16.   'David Livingstone London, 14th Nov., 1857.'   Sawyers Cat. SA/48 (1965) no. 50.

17.   'His Excellency the Count di Lavradio with the respectful salutations of his obliged & grateful David Livingstone London 20 Novr 1857.'   BSGL.
Francisco de Almeida Portugal, Conde do Lavradio, Portuguese Minister in London (**GrEncPort.**).

18.   'To Mr William Macskimming with the kindest remembrance of his grateful pupil David Livingstone London 20th Novr 1857.'   SNMDL.
Macskimming was Livingstone's teacher in Blantyre.

19.   'Walter Maclellan Esq with kindest regards David Livingstone   London   12th Dec 1857.'   SNMDL.
Maclellan was a partner in P. and W. Maclellan, ironmongers in Glasgow.

20.   'John Thom [?] Esq, with the kind regards of David Livingstone   24th Dec. 1857.'
K Books Cat. 239 (1977), no. 277.
The name of the recipient may be Thom or Thorn;   his identity is unknown.

21.   'Revd Dr Goold with the kindest salutations of David Livingstone.   Glasgow, 26th Decr 1857.'   SNMDL.
William Henry Goold, Professor of the Reformed Presbyterian Church and later Secretary of the National Bible Society of Scotland (Ewing, **Annals** I, p. 170).

22. 'Sir Thomas Dyke Acland with the kindest salutations of his friend David Livingstone London 18th January 1858.' Sawyers Cat. SA/42 (1964) no. 60.
Acland, politician and philanthropist (**DNB.**).

23. 'Mr John Darragh with the kind regards of David Livingstone London 22nd Feby 1858.' NMLZ.

24. 'Mr J. Buchanan Mirrlees with the kindest regards of David Livingstone London 22nd Feby 1858.' BLJ 3345.

25. 'To Sir George Grey, KCB from David Livingstone. Cape Town, 26 April 1858.' Privately owned.
Grey, colonial governor (**DNB.**); cf. no. 7 above.

26. 'Mary Moffat Livingstone 1862. Mama bought this at the Cape and intended that I should write her [sic] on it. I now do it on the second day after her departure and send it home to one of the children who may not have a copy. David Livingstone Shupanga 29th April 1862.' 'Mary Moffat Livingstone, to whom this book belonged, died at Shupanga on the evening of 27th April 1862.' NMLZ on display.

27. [To Heinrich Barth.] 'This work is offered as a token of kind regard, and high appreciation of his services in opening Africa; by his friend and fellow labourer.' [David Livingstone.] Location unknown (quoted by A.H.M. Kirk-Greene, **Barth's Travels in Nigeria** (London, 1962), p. 33).

See also Section 1, no. 0653.

A related item is the inscription 'David Livingstone. Unyanyembe July 1872' on a copy of **A Popular Account of Missionary Travels and Researches in South Africa**, London: John Murray, 1868. SNMDL.

2)   **Analysis of the Language of the Bechuanas**, privately printed, 1858. MS not located.

An early draft is in the first half of notebook 3 below. A condensed account of the printed version is given in Monk, **DLCL**, 2nd edition, 1860, pp. 250–69.

Only 25 copies were printed, intended primarily for the use of members of the Zambesi Expedition. The location of eleven is known:

1. NLS, RB.m.68. Presented to J. Bevan Braithwaite.

2. WCLUWJ. 'Professor Daubeny, with the kindest regards of the author. Only 25 copies printed. Please show it to anyone interested in these matters. We sail tomorrow. 8th March, 1858.' Damaged by fire 1931 (full text of inscription known from Sotheby's Cat. 3 Dec. 1913, lot 299, item 2).
Charles Giles Bridle Daubeny, chemist and botanist (**DNB.**).

3. NMLZ. 'Rev'd Robert Moffat to be sent to John Moffat, Brighton. 25 copies only — printed with wide margin for corrections & additions. D. Livingstone.'

4. SNMDL, Misc MS Material. 'Rev. Dr. Somerville with the kindest regards of David

Livingstone.   8 March 1858.   Mr Waddell may feel an interest in this — 25 copies alone are printed.'

Andrew Somerville was Foreign Mission Secretary of the United Presbyterian Church, and Hope M. Waddell missionary of that Church at Calabar, Nigeria.

5.   SNMDL, Relic Case E.   Presented to Richard Thornton.

6.   MDNHLL, P587.   'Captain Washington RN Private.'

7.   DMLDSA.

8.   · LCUSWDC, PL. 8651. L5.   (In catalogue, but book could not be located, 1976.)

9.   LPCT.

10.   NARS.   Inscribed 'Robert Livingstone' in pencil in an unknown hand.

11.   NYPL, P184792.   (Microfilmed and original destroyed.)

One was sold at Sotheby's,   10 Nov. 1936, lot 510.   For another possible copy see Section 1, no. 0758.

3)   [with Charles Livingstone] **Narrative of an Expedition to the Zambesi and its Tributaries,** London: John Murray, 1865.

Livingstone wrote this book by substantially revising, adding to, and subtracting from a narrative written by Charles Livingstone in the first half of 1864;   this narrative (the 'journals' of Charles referred to in David's correspondence), in Charles's hand and much corrected by David, is in OCLOO, 091.916 L763 (vol. 1, 304 pp.;   vol. 2, lost;   vol. 3, 313 pp.;   vol. 4, 155 pp.; 176 x 110 mm.).   David's resultant MS is in JMPL, storeroom (not seen).   MS of the footnote to p. 600 with a related note is in JMPL.   A corrected proof of the dedication is in NMLZ, G 17/6. A corrected proof of the preface is privately owned.

Livingstone had left England before this book was published in Nov. 1865, and so there can be no inscribed copies.   Presentation copies were however sent out;   one to David Hutcheson is privately owned.

4)   **The Last Journals of David Livingstone,** edited by Horace Waller, 2 vols., London: John Murray, 1874.

For the MSS used by Waller see the sections Journals and Field Diaries below.   The proofs with Waller's alterations and corrections are RHLO, MS. Afr. s. 16. 6—8.

PAPERS AND REPORTS

This section includes essays, papers published or apparently intended for publication, and drafts of these, together with some summaries of letters etc. published by others. It could have been much expanded, if sections of notebooks, enclosures to letters, and the like, had been included; but its size has been deliberately restricted.

1. 'The Divinity of the Holy Spirit, and his operation on the human heart', essay submitted to the London Missionary Society, [1837?]. 4 pp. 228 x 184. ULSOASL (photocopy NLS, MS. 10778, f. 19).

2. 'The Peace Makers of the Interior of South Africa', written early 1849. MS not located. Published in **British Banner**, 4 Jul. and 14 Nov. 1849 (Schapera, **DLSAP**, pp. 6—20).

3. Notes on missionaries and the Government of Cape Colony, [1850?]. 2 pp. 246 x 203. NARS, LI 1/1/1, pp. 2343—4.

4. Notes on the affairs of Cape Colony, [1850?]. 4 pp. 249 x 165. NARS, LI 1/1/1, pp. 2345—8.

5. Review of John Philip, **Letter to the Directors of the London Missionary Society, on the Present State of their Institutions in the Colony of the Cape of Good Hope**, Cape Town, 1848, written Nov. 1850 — Jan. 1851. MS not located; what appears to be a draft is NARS, LI 1/1/1, pp. 2305—29 (32 pp., 6 blank; 200 x 129). Published in **British Quarterly Review**, xiv, Aug. 1851, pp. 106—13 (Schapera, **DLSAP**, pp. 99—109).

6. [with William Cotton Oswell] Report to the Royal Geographical Society on his explorations beyond Lake Ngami in 1851, written early 1852. 24 pp. ca. 200 x 125. NARS, LI 1/1/1, pp. 55—77. MS copy (17 pp. folio) RGSL, DL 1/2/4 (photocopy NLS, MS. 10779, no. 13a). Published with omissions in **JRGSL**, xxii, 1852, pp. 163—73, and with an additional preface on missionaries and trade (of which the MS has not been located) in **South African Commercial Advertiser**, 7 Apr. 1852 (also separately, Cape Town: Pike and Riches, n.d.), under the title 'Notes of a Tour of the River Sesheke in the Region North of Lake Ngami' and in **Cape of Good Hope Almanac**, 1853, pp. 275—83, under the title 'The Great Lake' (the preface only in Schapera, **DLSAP**, pp. 114—16).

7. On the Eighth Frontier War and the Xhosa chief Sandile, [1852—3?]. 78 pp. NARS, LI 1/1/1, pp. 6—50.

8. 'The Story of the Black Pot alias The Story of Selling the Gun', written mid 1852. 16 pp. 180 x 111. ULSOASL (photocopy NLS, MS. 10778, f. 475). Published in **Cape Town Mail**, 26 Apr. 1853 (Schapera, **DLSAP**, pp. 28—35).

9. 'The Transvaal Boers', written early 1853. MS not located. Published in **Catholic Presbyterian**, ii, 1879, pp. 412—23, and Blaikie, **PLDL** ed. 2 (1881), pp. 490—511 (Schapera, **DLSAP**, pp. 70—95).

10. Paper on slavery among the Boers left with William Thompson in 1853. MS not located. Published by Thompson in a letter (signed 'Scrutator') in the **Cape Town Mail**, 4 Jun. 1853, p. 2.

11. On Angola, written in August 1854. 38 pp. (wants 4 pp. at the beginning). 272 x 210. GMAG (photocopy NLS, MS. 10777, no. 17). A Portuguese translation appeared under the title 'Apontamentos' in **BOdGGdPdA**, 1854, undated Supplement (photocopy in

ULSOASL, Afr.:   Odds & Ends 22);   this is retranslated into English by Douglas Wheeler in **RLJ**, xxxii, 1962, pp. 23—45.

12.   On Portuguese possessions in Eastern Africa, 17 Mar. 1855.   28 pp.   310 x 203.   NARS, LI 1/1/1, pp. 114—41.

13.   'Winds in Africa', [1856?].   4 pp.   307 x 202.   NARS, LI 1/1/1, pp. 2330—3.

14.   'Easy Chair Geography vs. Field Geography', 25 Nov. 1856.   22 pp.   226 x 184.   RGSL, DL 2/12 (microfilm NLS, MS. 10780, no. 5).   MS aut copy (19 pp.   227 x 185) NARS, LI 1/1/1, pp. 552—70.   This paper, critical of the opinions of W.D. Cooley expressed in the **Athenaeum**, was sent to the editor of that journal but apparently not published.

15.   Report of activities, 13 Aug. 1858.   4 pp.   322 x 203.   SNMDL (photocopy NLS, MS. 10779, no. 3).

16.   [with John Kirk]   'Remarks on the African Fever in the Lower Zambesi', sent to Sir James Clark, Jul. 1859.   Enclosure 2 in dispatch to Earl of Malmesbury 26 Jul. 1859 (see Section 1, no. 0917); draft NARS, LI 1/1/1, pp. 2338—41 (4pp.   310 x 195).   Published in Monk, **DLCL**, (2nd edition, 1860), pp. 370—5 and in Wallis, **ZEDL** II,   pp. 309—14 (from MS aut copy in journal 5.).

17.   'Latest Accounts from Dr Livingstone, F.R.G.S., of the Central African Expedition', a summary of several letters and reports read to the Royal Geographical Society 28 Nov. 1859, and published with the ensuing discussion in **PRGSL** iv, 1860, pp. 19—29.

18.   'A Note on Fever for Dr McWilliam transmitted by favour of Capt. Washington', 28 Nov. 1860.   4 pp.   322 x 203.   MDNHLL, MS. 120 (photocopy NLS, MS. 10777, no. 23, f. 159).   Published in **The Lancet**, 24 Aug. 1861, pp. 184—6 and Gelfand, **LtD**, pp. 297—303.

19.   'Latest Intelligence from Dr Livingstone and his Party in Central Africa', communicated to the Royal Geographical Society by Sir R.I. Murchison and Sir G. Back, 22 Apr. 1861, and published in **PRGSL** v, 1861, pp. 128—31.

20.   'Paper prepared for the Royal Geographical Society by Dr Livingstone', Jan. 1862, dealing with his activities in the second half of 1861.   12 pp.   323 x 200.   RGSL, DL 3/13/3 (microfilm NLS, MS. 10780, no. 5).   Published in **JRGSL** xxxiii, 1863, pp. 258—65.

21.   (a). Translation of an article by the Marquês Latino Coelho a Sá da Bandiera on Portuguese discoveries in **BOdGGdPdM**, no. 43, 26 Oct. 1861, pp. 177—8, made in August 1862.   8pp.   folio.   PROL, FO 63/894 II, ff. 93—6 (microfilm NLS, MS. 10780, no. 4 reel 2).
(b). 'Explanatory Note of a Map published by the Viscount de Sa da Bandiera & sent to the different European Governments as a 'New Portuguese Map' ', written 1 Dec. 1862.   6 pp.   325 x 205.   NMLZ on display (photocopy RHLO, MS. Afr.s.18 and NLS, MS. 10779, no. 20).

22.   'Exploration of the Niassa Lake', communicated to the Royal Geographical Society 24 Nov. 1862, and published in **PRGSL** vii, 1863, pp. 18—20.

23.   On the Portuguese in Africa [probably sent to George Frere], 6 Jan. 1863.   3 pp.   8vo.   NARS, LI 2/1/1.

24. On Portuguese discoveries, [1863?]. 5 pp. folio. NARS, LI 2/1/1. [Possibly a draft of no. 21(b).]

25. Comments on the 16 'Makololo' who remained in the Shire, [1863]. Published from field diary 11 by Wallis, ZEDL II, pp. 242–3.

26. 'Letters from the Zambesi to Sir R.I. Murchison, and (the late) Admiral Washington', communicated to the Royal Geographical Society 13 Jun. 1864, and published in PRGSL viii, 1864, pp. 256–8.

27. On slavery in Africa, [1864?]. 36 pp. 176–9 x 113–14. NARS, LI 1/1/1, pp. 1975–2009.

28. 'Missions in Africa and Elsewhere', written mid 1865. MS not located. Published in Evangelical Christendom, N.S. vi, 2 Oct. 1865, pp. 469–73.

29. 'Conjecture', on the ancient authorities for the source of the Nile, with consideration of the possiblity of his view being mistaken and of his exploring the Congo, [Jan. 1873?]. 7 pp. irregular folio. PROL, FO 2 49A, pp. 6–12, with a draft (same size) pp. 13–19 (microfilm NLS, MS. 10780, no. 4). Extract published by Waller, LJDL II, pp. 65–6.

30. Paper on atmospheric strata, the watershed of the Nile, the economy of the watershed, rains, floods, and inference therefrom, Feb. 1873. 14 pp. irregular folio. PROL, FO 2 49A, pp. 20–33, with a draft (4 pp. irregular folio) pp. 34–7 and a copy (9 pp. irregular folio) pp. 38–46 (microfilm NLS, MS. 10780, no. 4).

JOURNALS, FIELD DIARIES, AND NOTEBOOKS

A distinction has been made for convenience between journals (fairly large volumes, covering a considerable period, in a reasonably finished form), field diaries (smaller volumes, mostly restricted to a few months, often no more than rough notes), and notebooks (containing miscellaneous material; notebooks containing mostly astronomical observations and accounts have also been listed separately): but the distinction is not and cannot be hard and fast, and anyone interested in this type of manuscript would be well advised to read all three sections. As a general rule all of the field diaries and notebooks contain at least a few pages of astronomical observations, financial transactions, sketches, etc.; while those devoted mainly to observations and accounts also contain daily entries which are not found elsewhere.

JOURNALS

1. 10 May 1848 – 16 Oct. 1849. Fragments of journal destroyed at Kolobeng in Sep. 1852, later copied into journal 2, pp. 316 sqq. Schapera, **LPJ**, pp. 297–307.

2. 24 Apr. 1851 – 8 Jun. 1853. 355 pp. 179 x 112. Calf binding. NARS, LI 1/4/1. Schapera, **LPJ**, pp. 1–153, 297–310.

3. 9 Jun. – 10 Nov. 1853. 358 pp. 179 x 112. Three-quarter vellum binding. NARS, LI 1/4/2. Schapera, **LPJ**, pp. 153–296, 311–19.

4. 11 Nov. 1853 – 26 May 1856. 849 pp. 233 x 200. Brown calf binding (much rubbed), with brass lock. Wilson collection (microfilm NLS, MS. 10775, no. 1). Schapera, **LAJ** (omissions specified on p. xx).

5. 12 Mar. – 25 Jun. 1858. 355 pp. (many blank). 222 x 186. Half leather binding. NARS, LI 1/4/3. Wallis, **ZEDL** I, pp. 1–29, II, pp. 272–305. 308–14, 411–35 (A1). The published version omits a copy of a letter from the Marquês Sá da Bandiera and J.V.D. Oliviero to Livingstone (6 pp.), copies of letters from Livingstone to the Governor of Quilimane [Custodio José da Silva], 26 Apr. 1858 (2½ pp.), to William Thompson, 5 Feb. 1859 (4 pp. + margins of 5 pp.), and to William Robertson, 23 Sep. 1858 (6 pp.); and a copy of the agreement to serve signed by the four officers of the 'Pioneer', 30 Aug. 1860 (2 pp.).

6. 2 Aug. 1858 – 9 Jan. 1859. 42 + 317 pp. 178 x 112. Rough calf binding, with brass lock. Wilson collection (microfilm NLS, MS. 10775, no. 2). Wallis, **ZEDL** I, pp. 29–80, II, pp. 306–8 (A2). The published version omits astronomical observations for 6, 7, 12, 20, 21 Aug., 9, 10, 12, 16 Sep.; poem or passage in an African language (1 p.); pencil map of the Shire valley (1 p.); notes of the boiling point of water, 29 and 30 Dec. (2 pp.); list of 17 Makololo who received muskets, n.d. (1 p.); astronomical observations for 9, 10, 11 Jan. (4 pp.); pencil sketch of a Shire cataract; and index (3 pp.).

7. 21 Feb. – 12 Dec. 1859. 380 pp. 222 x 186. Half leather binding. NARS, LI 1/4/4. Wallis, **ZEDL** I, pp. 80–134, 137–9, II, pp. 263–71, 315–40 (A3). The published version alters inexplicably the table published on p. 80, and omits a translation of the Pater Noster, Ave Maria, Santa Maria, and Creed, 27 Feb., and the payment of 18 Makololo in calico, 27 Jun. The entry for 11 Dec. (**ZEDL** I, p. 139) is not in this journal, but in no. 8 below.

8. 1 Dec. 1859 – 11 Jun. 1860, 3 – 30 Dec. 1860, 31 Dec. 1860 – 30 Jan. 1861, 1 – 2 Feb. 1861, 16 – 23 Mar. 1861. 365 pp. 190 x 118. Red leather binding, with brass lock. Lett's Diary No. 8 for 1858. Wilson collection (microfilm NLS, MS. 10775, no. 3).

Wallis, **ZEDL** I, pp. 135—7, 139—80, II, pp. 340—410 (A4). The published version omits the freeing by H.M.S. 'Lynx' of a woman whom Livingstone saw near Lake Nyasa (1 p.); summary of speech by Prof. R. Owen at the British Association, Leeds, copied from **The Times** of 24 Sep. 1858 (3 pp.); a list of Africans who 'Received guns on 8th Feb. 1860', and another of 'Those who went to Nyassa, received guns too'; a comment from Bishop Thirlwell's **History of Greece**, copied from the **Saturday Review** of 15 Jan. 1859, p. 62; and comments on a missionary meeting held in Leeds in April 1860 (4 pp.).

9.   9 Nov. 1861 — 1 May 1863. 246 pp. 310 x 200. Half calf binding. SNMDL (photo-copy NLS, MS. 10715). Copies of an unpublished annotated transcript by Dr V.L. Bosazza are available in various institutions (including NLS, MS. Acc. 6373). In addition to daily entries for most of the period, this journal contains copies of many dispatches and letters, some in Portuguese, some written as late as 24 Feb. 1864, all of which are included in the appropriate sections of this catalogue. There are also financial notes on the Zambesi expedition and its personnel.

10.   26 Mar. 1864 — 23 Jan. 1866. 404 pp. 190 x 118. Red leather binding, with brass lock. Lett's Diary No. 8 for 1863. Wilson collection (microfilm NLS, MS. 10775, no. 4). Extracts are published by Seaver, **DLLL**, pp. 440—449. This journal contains daily entries for 26 Mar. 1864 — 13 Jun. 1865, 7 — 13 Aug. 1865, and 15 Dec. 1865 — 23 Jan. 1866; copies of letters which are included in the appropriate sections; and notes of financial transactions, occasional thoughts, etc.

11.   28 Jan. 1866 — 5 Mar. 1872. 763 pp. (numbered 1—769; 621—6 have been torn out). 315 x 195. Brown leather binding, with brass lock. Lett's Perpetual Diary. SNMDL (microfilm NLS, MS. 10734). Waller, **LJDL**; an omitted passage (11 Feb. 1866, on the death of Baron von der Decken) in J. Simmons, **JRAS** xl, 1941, pp. 335—46; other passages omitted in **LJDL** are mainly copies of dispatches and letters (28 Nov. 1865 to 28 Feb. 1872), personal items, and scientific tables; the removed pages were critical of Prince Albert. Livingstone made entries in this volume during periods when he was detained in one place, chiefly from field diaries 14 — 26. It was left at Ujiji from Jul. 1869 to Oct. 1871 (see field diary 34), and was completed while he was with Stanley, who took it back to England. There are hardly any entries for 23 Jul. 1870 — 1 Jan. 1871.

FIELD DIARIES

1.   6 Oct. 1856 — Mar. 1857. 90 pp. 135 x 68. Purple leather binding with clasp. Patent Metallic Memorandum Book. Wilson collection (microfilm and photocopy NLS, MS. 10775, no. 5). The diary covers his voyage from Mauritius to London, ending 10 Dec. 1856; thereafter the notebook contains appointments with and addresses of persons in Great Britain and a few pages of notes on natural history. The pocket contains a printed sheet of a mock 'Senatus Decretum' dated 25 Feb. 1858, and a letter in Portuguese from Tito Sicard to Livingstone, 18 May [1856].

2.   4 Apr. — 13 May 1859. 108 pp. 133 x 85. Black leather binding. Wilson collection (microfilm and photocopy NLS, MS. 10775, no. 6). This diary contains daily notes of his first visit to the highlands east of the Shire, when with John Kirk he first saw Lake Shirwa (Chilwa); watercolour sketches of the landscape; pencil sketches of the people and their way of life; a table of air and water temperatures from 20 Mar. to 17 Apr.; astronomical observations; and linguistic notes.

3.   23 Aug. — 8 Oct. 1859.   48 pp.   153 x 80.   Brown paper cover, marked I. Wilson collection (microfilm and photocopy NLS, MS. 10775, no. 7).   Wallis, **ZEDL** II, pp. 245–9 (C1).   The published version omits a note on the economic potential of the region of Lake Nyasa and the Upper Shire (6 pp., between the entries for 3 and 4 Oct.).

4.   29 Apr. — 17 May 1860.   24 pp.   153 x 85.   Brown paper cover, marked II. Wilson collection (microfilm and photocopy NLS, MS. 10775, no. 8).   Wallis, **ZEDL** II, p. 249 (C2).   The published version gives entries for 16 and 17 May only. The diary also contains a 'List of names of Makololo who received muskets on 29th April 1860' (4 pp.); 'Names of children of Makololo who have been born of slave women at Tette' (3 pp.); 'Masakasa's party who went to sea last time' (1 p.);   lists of goods and persons, possibly with reference to his trip from Tette to Sesheke from May to Sep. 1860;   a list of Makololo who 'Returned to Tette or fled';   and chronometer readings, etc (4 pp.).

5.   18 May — 3 Jun. 1860.   32 pp.   152 x 92.   Brown paper cover, marked III.   NMLZ on display.   Wallis, **ZEDL** II, pp. 250–2 (C3).   In addition to the daily entries as published, this diary contains a few pencil and watercolour sketches.

6.   3 — 27 Jun. 1860.   32 pp.   153 x 82.   Brown paper cover, marked IV.   Wilson collection (microfilm and photocopy NLS, MS. 10775, no. 9).   Wallis, **ZEDL** II, pp. 252–5 (C4).   The published version omits the entries for 3 — 11 Jun.   (13½ pp.;   not the same as the corresponding entries in journal no. 8 above);   topographical bearings throughout;   and entry for 27 Jun. and astronomical observations for 19 Jun. (2 pp.).

7.   28 Jul. — 24 Aug. 1860.   116 pp.   132 x 72.   Original cloth cover covered with brown paper, marked V.   Wilson collection (microfilm and photocopy NLS, MS. 10775, no. 10).   Wallis, **ZEDL** II, pp. 256–62 (C5).   Entitled 'Taba Cheu & Sesheke'.   The published version omits notes of 11 — 13 Aug. (2 pp.), observations (many pp.), and two small maps.

8.   27 Sep. — 22 Nov. 1860.   140 pp.   145 x 87.   Brown paper cover, marked VI.   NMLZ on display (photocopy NLS, MS. 10759).   This includes his attempts to measure the Victoria Falls, and notes of his trip from Sesheke to Tette, with tables of temperatures, etc.

9.   3 Jul. — 26 Oct. 1861.   179 pp.   154 x 88.   Purple leather binding, with clasp, originally labelled XIII.   T.J. and J. Smith's Metallic Book.   Loose sheets in pocket: 30 Oct. — 7 Nov. 1861;   8 pp.;   182 x 108.   Wilson collection (microfilm and photocopy NLS, MS. 10775, no. 11).   Wallis, **ZEDL** I, pp. 180–211 (B1), II, pp. 213–14 (D).   The published version omits various notes, sketches, distances, African vocabulary, and maps   (38 pp.).   The pocket also contains needles and blue feathers.

10.   23 Aug. 1862 — 19 Mar. 1863.   148 pp.   140 x 80.   Black leather binding, with clasp. Harwood's Patent Metallic Memorandum Book No. 6.   NLS, MS. 2249.   Shepperson, **DLatR**.   The published version overlooks the fact that the last 17 pp. are written from the end towards the front.

11.   19 Mar. — 12 Jul. 1863.   142 pp. (some blank).   148 x 85.   Red leather binding, with clasp.   Henry Penny's Metallic Memorandum Book No. 43.   Wilson collection (microfilm and photocopy NLS, MS. 10775, no. 12).   Wallis, **ZEDL** II, pp. 228–44 (B2).   The published version omits notes on similar tools and smelting processes observed in different parts of Africa,   freshwater tropical fish, birds, eggs, elephant population, and flies, quotations from religious writers, and vocabulary (40 pp.).

12.   15 Jul. — 22 Sep. 1863.   138 pp.   146 x 85.   Blue leather binding, with clasp.   Henry

Penny's Metallic Memorandum Book No. 43. Wilson collection (microfilm and photo-copy NLS, MS. 10775, no. 13). Daily record of his trip from Murchison Cataracts to Muazi's village with Thomas Ward, plus notes (36 pp.) on his men and their trials, financial transactions, sketches and diagrams, natural history, etc.

13. 22 Sep. 1863 — 25 Mar. 1864. 140 pp. ca. 195 x 90. Soft leather binding, with case. E.M. Privately owned (microfilm NLS, MS. 10771). Covers the final days of the Zambesi expedition, including the return trip with Thomas Ward from Chinanga's village, roughly 100 miles west of Kotakota Bay on Lake Malawi to the foot of Murchison's Cataracts. For a more detailed description with facsimile of two pages, see Maggs Cat. 889 (1963) no. 371.

14 — 30. These form a continuous numbered series, and are the main source for journal 11.

14. 4 Aug. 1865 — 31 Mar. 1866. 106 pp. 151 x 90. Green cloth binding, marked I. SNMDL (photocopy NLS, MS. 10719). Notes on the journey from France to the Rovuma, via Suez, Bombay, and Zanzibar, including expenses and preparations for his final expedition into the interior of Africa.

15. 4 Apr. — 14 May 1866. 106 pp. 151 x 90. Green cloth binding, marked II. SNMDL (photocopy NLS, MS. 10720). Daily entries and sketches.

16. 14 May — 30 Jun. 1866. 106 pp. 151 x 90. Green cloth binding, marked III. SNMDL (photocopy NLS, MS. 10721). Daily entries and sketches.

17. 1 Jul. — 5 Sep. 1866. 106 pp. 151 x 90. Green cloth binding, marked IV. SNMDL (photocopy NLS, MS. 10722). Daily entries and sketches.

18. 5 Sep. — 23 Oct. 1866. 106 pp. 151 x 90. Green cloth binding, marked V. SNMDL (photocopy NLS, MS. 10723). Daily entries and sketches.

19. 24 Oct. — 23 Dec. 1866. 106 pp. 151 x 90. Green cloth binding, marked VI. SNMDL (photocopy NLS, MS. 10724). Daily entries and sketches.

20. 26 Dec. 1866 — 1 Mar. 1867. 136 pp. 136 x 81. Green leather binding, marked VII. SNMDL (photocopy NLS, MS. 10725). Daily entries and sketches.

21. 4 Mar. — 19 May 1867. 138 pp. 136 x 81. Brown cloth binding, marked VIII. Privately owned (photocopy NLS, MS. 10776, no. 1). Daily entries and sketches, with miscellaneous notes.

22. 20 May — 7 Sep. 1867. 138 pp. 136 x 81. Brown cloth binding, marked IX. Privately owned (photocopy NLS, MS. 10776, no. 2). Daily entries and sketches, with a voca-bulary and geographical and other notes; the entry for 11 Jul. contains the Arabic alphabet.

23. 9 Sep. 1867 — 2 Jan. 1868. 138 pp. 136 x 81. Brown leather binding, marked X. SNMDL (photocopy NLS, MS. 10726). Daily entries and sketches.

24. 1 Jan. — 12 Jun. 1868. 138 pp. 136 x 81. Black cloth binding, marked XI. Privately owned (photocopy NLS, MS. 10776, no. 3). Daily entries and sketches, with notes of rainfall, etc.

25. (a) 14 Apr. — 10 Nov. 1868. 136 pp. (some loose and some probably missing).

140 x 88.   Brown leather binding, marked XII.   NMLZ on display (microfilm NLS, MS. 10780, no. 2a). Daily entries and sketches, with astronomical observations and vocabulary. The entry for 3 Aug. reads 'Copied thus far for Sir T. Maclear, 15 March 1872'.

(b) 24 — 28 Dec. 1868. 2 pp. 134 x 81.   Leaf torn from diary, probably XII (given to Edith Kerr, 31 Jul. 1886, by Anna Mary Wilson, née Livingstone).   WIHMLL, 67551 (photocopy NLS, MS. 10779, no. 15, f. 89).   Brief notes of a bleak Christmas.

26.   28 Jun. 1869 — 25 Feb. 1871. 138 pp. 136 x 81.   Black cloth binding, marked XIII. Privately owned (photocopy NLS, MS. 10776, no. 4).   Daily entries and sketches, with notes on rainfall, geography, etc.

27.   14 Nov. 1871 — 14 Sep. 1872. 137 pp. 139 x 80.   Brown leather binding, marked XIV. SNMDL (photocopy NLS, MS. 10727).   Daily entries and sketches.

28.   7 Jul. — 1 Dec. 1872. 150 pp. 155 x 85.   Black leather binding, marked XV. SNMDL (photocopy NLS, MS. 10728).   Daily entries and sketches;   fuller than 27 where it overlaps, and used by Waller, **LJDL**.

29.   1 Dec. 1872 — 6 Apr. 1873. 179 pp. 153 x 86.   Black leather binding, marked XVI. SNMDL (photocopy NLS, MS. 10729).   Daily entries and sketches.

30.   9 — 27 Apr. 1873.   30 + many blank pp.   153 x 86.   Purple leather binding, marked XVII.   SNMDL (photocopy NLS, MS. 10729A).   Facsimile of entries for 20 — 27 Apr. in Waller, **LJDL** II, between pp. 298—9 and Listowel, **TOL**, p. 227.   Daily entries. On the third last page, possibly in the hand of Jacob Wainwright, is the note '11 o'clock night 28th April', with a list of coins, watches, measuring instruments, etc.

31 — 33.   These form a series and were given to Livingstone by Stanley.   Waller, **LJDL** apparently used 31 and 32, but not 33.

31.   16 Apr. — 1 Jun 1872. 90 pp. (7 blank). 221 x 171.   Mottled paper cover, marked I. SNMDL (photocopy NLS, MS. 10731).   Daily entries, plus references to Baker, St Paul, the Nile, and Dr Buckland's insanity.

32.   1 Jun. — 12 Jul. 1872.   80 pp. (some missing?). 221 x 171.   Mottled paper cover, marked II. SNMDL (photocopy NLS, MS. 10732).   Daily entries, plus geological notes.

33.   22 Jul. — 7 Oct. 1871, and (on an envelope enclosed) 28 Sep. — 7 Oct. 1871 (apparently copied Apr. 1872). 86 pp. (21 blank). 222 x 177. Mottled paper cover, marked III. SNMDL (photocopy NLS, MS. 10733).   Daily entries, plus items copied from diary 26 (XIII), astronomical observations (made in Feb. — Mar. 1871), and vocabularies of Suaheli, Batusi, Buganda, and Manyuema.

34 — 39.   Notes made on various pieces of paper when his notebooks were full.

34.   10 Mar. 1870.   'Retrospect to be inserted in the Journal if I get back to where it is left in Ujiji.' 8 pp. 135 x 188. NLS, MS. 10703, ff. 40—3.   Thoughts on his mission to the Bakwains (1845—51).

35.   Aug. 1870?.   Notes for journal written in the margins of a printed book.   70 pp. 25—30 x 130—150. SNMDL (photocopy NLS, MS. 10763).

36.   25 Aug., 4 Oct., 8 Oct. 1870.   Notes for journal written over a letter to Livingstone. 4 pp.   269 x 208.   NARS, LI 1/1/1, pp. 2277—80.   Includes a description of the

Manyuema country, thoughts on Speke and the sources of the Nile, Arabs he met at this time, and his realisation that the Chambesi is not an eastern branch of the Zambesi.

37. 18 Aug. 1870 — 10 Aug. 1871. Diary and other notes written on scraps of paper, printed books, and newspapers (some made into a notebook now dismembered and incomplete), paginated with Roman numerals. 156 pp. Various sizes. Facsimile of one page in Waller, **LJDL** II, facing p. 114.

I — IV	18 — 24 Aug. 1870	4 pp.	BLL, Add. MS. 50184, f. 169 (microfilm NLS, MS. 10780, no. 3).
X — XIII	10 Oct. 1870	4 pp.	NLS, MS. 10703, ff. 1—2.
XIV	13 Oct. 1870	1 p.	JMPL (formerly SNMDL; photocopy NLS, MS. 10717).
XVII — XX	20 Oct. — 1 Nov. 1870	4 pp.	JMPL (formerly SNMDL; photocopy NLS, MS. 10717).
XXI — LXI (LV repeated)	2 — 13 Nov. 1870 with a copy of letter to Lord Stanley 15 Nov. 1870.	42 pp.	NLS, MS. 10703, ff. 3 —23.
LXII — LXIX	22 Nov. — 10 Dec. 1870	8 pp.	SNMDL (photocopy NLS, MS. 10718).
LXX — LXXV	10 — 30 Dec. 1870	6 pp.	NLS, MS. 10703, ff. 24—6.
LXXVI	16 Jan. 1871	1 p.	JMPL (formerly SNMDL; photocopy NLS, MS. 10717).
LXXVII — CI	24 Jan. — 22 Mar. 1871	26 pp.	NLS, MS. 10703, ff. 27—35.
CII — CLXIII (CXXXII, CXXXIII repeated)	23 Mar. — 10 Aug. 1871	64 pp.	JMPL (formerly SNMDL; photocopy NLS, MS. 10717).

38. 11 Aug. — 9 Sep. 1871. Diary written on an envelope. 8 pp. 190 x 136. NLS, MS. 10703, ff. 36—9. Also includes temperatures, rainfall, observations, etc. for Mar. — Nov. 1871.

39. 23 Oct. — 3 Nov. 1871. Diary written on an envelope. 2 pp. 166 x 154. RHLO, MS. Afr. s. 16.1, f. 172 (microfilm NLS, MS. 10780, no. 8). Recording his arrival at Ujiji, just prior to the appearance of Stanley.

NOTEBOOKS

1. 10, 24, 28 Jul. 1849. Notes of the boiling point of water on these dates, copied from a notebook found in his waggon at Linyanti in 1860 into Observations notebook no. 3 below, (1) p. 40.

2. 1850—4. 275 pp. 123 x 70. Black cloth binding, with clasp. Good's Railway Share Application Book. Privately owned (photocopy NLS, MS. 10776, no. 5). This is in two parts, one added at a later date. (1) 18 Mar. 1850 — 24 Apr. 1851. Notes on Makololo, travel, vocabulary, etc., elementary sketches, and diary for 18 Mar. — 27 Jun. 1850. 83 pp. (many removed). (2) On blue paper inserted at the end, and written from back to front. 7 Nov. 1853 — 20 May 1854. Daily entries, calculations, maps, linguistic notes, sketches, and alphabetical Portuguese vocabulary. 192 pp. (37 blank).

3. 1852. 106 pp. 243 x 203. Red half leather binding. SNMDL (photocopy NLS, MS. 10711). The first half contains an early version of the **Analysis of the Language of the Bechuanas,** completed in Aug. 1852. The second half contains 'Notes on Wild Animals'; the names of the Bakwain children (56 girls and 68 boys) taken by the Boers in Sep. 1852; comments on the local Africans; his conversation with a Rain Doctor; and an essay 'Missionary Sacrifices'.

4. 1852—3. 203 pp. 130 x 82—85. Black cloth binding, with clasp. Approved Patent Metallic Book. Privately owned (photocopy NLS, MS. 10776, no. 6). This is in two parts, one added at a later date. (1) 8 Jun. 1852 — 23 Mar. 1853. Daily entries, with notes on the trial of Andries Botha, May 1852, on Ephesians 4.26, on language, on birds (full and systematic), on the Bakwain mission, etc. 139 pp. (2) On blue paper inserted between pp. 1 and 2 of the original book. Jun. — Jul. 1853. Linguistic and geographical notes, etc. 64 pp. (2 blank).

5. 20 Sep. 1854 — 19 Aug. 1856. 311 pp. Various sizes. Brown binding. NMLZ on display (photocopy NLS, MS. 10757). Livingstone began this notebook in Loanda and filled it just after he left Sesheke en route for Quilimane. Sections 1 and 3 were kept on loose paper and added later. (1) 20 Nov. 1855 — 2 Feb. 1856. pp. 1—79. 100 x 63 (pp. 1—31) and 123 x 80 (pp. 32—79). Daily entries, with notes on wild life, his African companions, and geology, sketch maps, astronomical observations, and a few book titles apparently for future reading. (2) 20 Sep. 1854 — 16 Nov. 1855. pp. 80—224. 125 x 74. Daily entries, with addresses of several Portuguese residents of Angola, boiling points of water, astronomical observations, maps, and his first estimate of the extent of the Victoria Falls. (3) 1 Feb. — 19 Aug. 1856. pp. 225—311. 116 x 69. Daily entries, with maps, astronomical observations, sketches, a list of chiefs below Mozinkua's place, African vocabulary, and notes on Portuguese history in Africa.

6. [1854—5?] 52 pp. (many blank). 250 x 203. NMLZ on display. (1) Comparative vocabulary of Bakholea, Bashubea, Balogorzi, Baponda, Barotse, Matibele, Batoka, Banyenko, Bechuana, and English. 28 pp. (2) MaShona — English dictionary. 13 pp.

7. [1855?] 272 pp. 241 x 198. Quarter vellum binding. SALCT, Grey Coll. 38b (microfilm NLS, MS. 10780, no. 1, reel 1 (1) + 2 (9, 10)). Contents: ff. 1—8 a dialect of SeTswana, probably Bashubea, with notes by Robert Moffat; ff. 9—108 and 124—132 dictionary of SeTswana; ff. 109—23 comparative vocabulary of Bayeiye, Bashubea, Balojarzi, Bamaponda, Barotse, Batoka, Banyenko, Bechuana, and English [Livingstone's headings]; ff. 133—4 scriptural passages in SeTswana written by Robert Moffat for Livingstone to memorise; ff. 135—6 miscellaneous notes and word lists.

8. 18 Oct. 1855 — 26 Jul. 1856. 96 + 136 pp. (several blank). 247 x 187. Two notebooks, red and white cloth bindings, joined by string. SALCT, Grey Coll. 38b (microfilm NLS, MS. 10780, no. 1, reel 1 (6)). (1) pp. 1—65 Barotse [SeLozi] vocabulary; pp. 67—93 vocabulary of language of Tette and the lower Zambesi; pp. 94—5 Malagasy words collected at St Augustine's Bay, Madagascar, 26 Jul. 1856; pp. 17, 22, 23, and 96 are blank. (2) pp. 1—29 SeLonda vocabulary; pp. 30—3 sketch maps of Angola; pp. 35—65 further vocabulary, probably SeLonda; pp. 66—8 descriptions of BaLunda marriage and funeral ceremonies; pp. 71—132 further vocabulary lists; p. 132 'Ambonda words' and equivalents of English numbers one to ten; pp. 52—3 are duplicated and p. 64 is blank.

9. [1856—60.] 44 pp. 226 x 187. NARS, LI 1/5/1. Vocabulary of an African language, perhaps that spoken at Tette.

10. [1857—8.] 101 pp. 130 x 70. Black binding. NMLZ on display (photocopy NLS, MS. 10758). Addresses and appointments; notes on geology, mammals, and birds;

account with the London Missionary Society; and a draft of a speech given in or near Glasgow, probably in Sep. 1857.

11. [1858–64.] ca 350 pp. 220 x 185. NARS, LI 1/5/4. 'Cisena Vocabulary.'

12. 16 Jan. – Jun. 1858. 106 pp. 124 x 74. Green cloth binding. NARS, LI 1/7/1. Contains the addresses of many of Livingstone's acquaintances in 1858; lists of items prepared for shipment to Cape Town and the Kafue, etc.; and notes made in the early days of the Zambesi expedition; also notes for a letter to Admiral Sir Frederick Grey, 23 Jun. 1858, which may never have been sent.

13. 4 – 25 Sep. 1859. 60 pp. 150 x 78. No cover. NMLZ on display. This notebook was with Livingstone when he first saw Lake Malawi, and in addition to daily notes contains many sketches of indigenous peoples.

14. 27 Jun. – 31 Oct. 1860. 32 pp. 138 x 95. No cover. NMLZ on display (photocopy NLS, MS. 10760). Livingstone's watercolour sketchbook made during his second visit to the Victoria Falls. Several sketches are published in **Illustrated London News,** vol. 210 (1947), pp. 360–361.

15. Mar. 1866 – Mar. 1870. 114 pp. 192 x 121. Lett's Analytical Index. Green cloth binding. SNMDL (photocopy NLS, MS. 10762). Contains notes on his African bearers; African fables; essays on atonement, Darwin and natural selection, the history of exploration in Africa and America, the origins of the American Civil War, Michelangelo and Raphael, etc.; financial notes; a Suaheli vocabulary; observations of nature; a map of the Zambesi delta in 1856; and daily entries for 2 Jul., 29 Sep. 1869, 28 Feb., 13 Mar. 1870.

16. 1867–9. 122 pp. 140 x 88. Lett's Sons Metallic Book. Brown binding. NMLZ on display. An apparently disorganised notebook containing daily entries, statistics of rainfall, boiling point of water, barometer readings, etc. for various dates during these three years.

17. 1868–72. 88 pp. Brown leather binding. SNMDL (photocopy NLS, MS. 10730). This is in two parts, the second on separate paper and added at a later date. (1) Jul. – Oct. 1868. 40 pp. 180 x 115. A collection of thoughts and essays on various topics, including antiquity, African history and the Nile sources, with a map; a 'Note on the Climate'; 'A Mission'; thoughts on the watershed and a description of the country through which he travelled; list of Masai words; Kavirondo words; a 'Note' of 5 Oct.; Lunda words; and some astronomical observations. (2) See below Observations 8.

18. n.d. 12 pp. 323 x 204. NARS, LI 1/5/3. This undated African language dictionary is written in an unidentified hand, with only two words and meanings on p. 3 in Livingstone's hand.

ASTRONOMICAL OBSERVATIONS

1. 26 Jan. — 13 Jun. 1853. MS copies by Sir Thomas Maclear (16 pp., folio) ULSOASL; RGSL, DL 2/4/3. Maclear's explanatory notes (26 pp., large folio) are RGSL, DL 2/4/2, published **JRGSL** xxiv, 1854, pp. 302—6.

2. 1853—8. 125 pp. Various sizes. Some MS copies. NARS, LI 1/3/1. Included is 'Comparisons of Chronometers of [Zambesi] Expedition for Mr Maclear'. Observations for Dec. 1854 — Jun. 1855 were published in **JRGSL** xxv, 1855, p. 219; a table of results for 1 Jan. 1854 — 11 Jan. 1855, sent by Maclear, in ib. xxvi, 1856, pp. 82—4 (a MS copy of observations for these dates is in ULSOASL); and an extract of a letter of Maclear, 3 Nov. 1856, on Livingstone's observations and Maclear's reductions of them, in **PRGSL** i, 1857, pp. 268—9.

3. 7 Apr. 1859 — 8 Nov. 1860. 117 pp. 325 x 202—204. Four notebooks (and a letter), paper cover, bound together with string. SALCT, MSS. SA. Sect. A (microfilm NLS, MS. 10780, no. 1, reel 1 (7) — (11)).
   (1) 15 Dec. 1859 — ca. 28 Aug. 1860. 42 pp. Most of these observations were taken between 16 May and 28 Aug. 1860, between Tette and Linyanti, to revise the sightings of 1855—6. There are also comments on the malfunctioning of his chronometer and other instruments, and some entries taken from the notebook left in his waggon at Linyanti from 1855 to 1860. The final two pages contain explanations and instructions to Maclear (to whom he sent this notebook), dated 8 Nov. 1860.
   (2) Letter to Maclear of 1 Feb. 1861 (see letters section).
   (3) 27 Sep. — 13 Oct. 1859. 20 pp. Observations taken between late Jul. and Oct. from Dakanamoio Island to Lake Nyasa to Mount Dzomba, and entered here between the dates given. Pp. 17—20 contain notes of instruction and news for Maclear, written between 11 and 20 Nov. 1859.
   (4) Observations reduced by and in the hand of Maclear. 24 pp.
   (5) 7 Apr. — 31 Jul. 1859. 31 pp. Observations taken during the trip to Lake Shirwa, the return to the Shire and on to the sea, and the ascent of the Zambesi to Tette. On pp. 23—31 are personal messages to Maclear of 17 May, 12 May, and [5 Jul.?].

4. 24 Aug. — 11 Nov. 1861. 94 pp. (ca. 12 blank). 181 x 110. Red leather binding. SNMDL (photocopy NLS, MS. 10761). Entitled by Livingstone 'Observations on River Shire & Lake Nyassa or Nyinyesi, 1861', this notebook was received by Maclear from Captain John Wilson of H.M.S. **Gorgon** on 26 Apr. 1862. Completely devoted to astronomical observations, with the exception of a small map of islands near the south end of the lake (p. 61) and the names of two Arabs met at Kaombe on 17 Oct. (p. 78).

5. 7 Oct. 1863 — 14 Jun. 1864. 157 + many blank pp. 176 x 115. Brown leather binding. SNMDL (photocopy NLS, MS. 10716). Completely devoted to astronomical observations with the exception of one page of African vocabulary and a drawing of part of a Mawawa (?) plant.

6. 27 Mar. 1866 — 22 Dec. 1868. ca. 400 pp. 186 x 117. Lett's Diary No. 8 for 1858. ERSHH (microfilm NLS, MS. 10766). The pages for 26 — 29 Dec. 1858 were removed and used for a letter to Robert Moffat of 7 Mar. 1868 (see letters section).

7. 17 Apr. — 19 Oct. 1868, 14 Mar. 1872. 24 pp. 344 x 215. NARS, LI 2/5/3.

8. 8 Jun. — 13 Dec. 1869, 1871—2. 48 pp. (11 blank). 158 x 100. SNMDL (inserted into Notebook 17 above) (photocopy NLS, MS. 10730).

9. 15 Oct. 1872 — 10 Apr. 1873. 51 + many blank pp. 204 x 104. Brown cardboard cover. RGSL, DL 4/19 (microfilm NLS, MS. 10780, no. 4).

ACCOUNTS

1. 26 Mar. 1858 — 14 Apr. 1864. 68 pp. (several blank). 187 x 117. SNMDL (photo-copy NLS, MS. 10714). 'Zambesi Expedition Account Book.' Contains miscellaneous financial transactions, including occasional entries of monies paid or loaned to his African, European, and 'Johanna' companions; sums paid for provisions; sums received from the periodic visits of Royal Navy vessels, and two pages of comments on slavery carried on by the Dutch at the Cape from Van Riebeck to 1792, including a comment on church history during that period.

2. 1861. 4 pp. 320 x 200. NARS, LI 1/1/1, pp. 1337—9.

3. 1862. 4 pp. (1 blank). 320 x 200. NARS, LI 1/1/1, pp. 1479—81.

4. Jan. — May 1862. 4 pp. (1 blank). 318 x 197. NARS, LI 1/1/1, pp. 1434—5.

5. May — Dec. 1862. 4 pp. 258 x 202. NARS, LI 1/1/1, pp. 1590—2.

6. 1863. 4 pp. (1 blank). 325 x 200. NARS, LI 1/1/1, pp. 1860—1.

SECTION 4

MISCELLANEOUS

In the following section are listed various items in Livingstone's hand which according to their nature do not merit a place in any of the three preceding sections. Indeed, they are so diverse that it was only with difficulty that each was placed in one of the four subsections of this section, and in some cases general rules have been stretched to accommodate them. It may be argued that some of these items have no historical value whatsoever, but we choose to leave this to the user: each may determine the importance (or lack of it) of each entry according to his or her needs. Descriptions of portraits, photographs, published reports of speeches and lectures and similar items are not included here, nor are signatures which have been cut from letters and documents by autograph hunters, which lack textual material above, or on the verso of the signature.

The symbols and abbreviations used are uniform with those used in the preceding sections; hence explanations will be found elsewhere. All items in double quotation marks (" . . . ") are from the document and in Livingstone's hand; single quotation marks (' . . . ') have occasionally been added by the editors in a variety of circumstances. Punctuation has been regularized in Livingstone's quotations. Finally, as the scope and contents of this section were not delineated until just prior to going to press, it proved impossible to provide the same type of information for each item listed.

A. Sketches, Envelopes and Odd Scraps.

The number arbitrarily assigned to each entry is followed by a word or phrase describing the item, after which date, size and location are given whenever possible. Notes of interest are occasionally included.

1.	Sketch,	"Ideal section of the fizzure," pencil, [1855–57]. 157 252. JMPL. Perhaps the Victoria Falls.
2.	Sketch,	Victoria Falls, watercolour, [1860]. 125 156. RGSL, DL 3/5, Mf. copy NLS, MS. 10780, no. 5. A similar sketch is found in Debenham, **TWtI**, opposite p. 112.
3.	Sketch,	"Achowa" woman, pencil, [1861–63]. ca. 254 204. Privately owned. Includes a note suggesting that Agnes may like to have a similar lip-ring fitted.
4.	Sketch,	Shupanga House and Mary's grave, brown ink, [1862–63]. 212 312. JMPL. Contains descriptive comments and "D. Livingstone."
5.	Sketch,	Sanjika [a fish] of Lake Nyassa, black and blue pencil, [1868–70]. 273 192. JMPL. Livingstone's notes on both sides are summarized as follows: found potato growing in the Shire highlands when exploring with Kirk; lotus grows in shallow water; primeval forest is found between each district; Manyuema country and Ujiji; descriptions of several types of African wildlife. A reference to what may be a similar sketch is found in **ZEDL** I, p. 192, n. 1.
6.	Illustration,	"Bechuana reed dance by moonlight," [1857?]. 147 223. JMPL. Artist unidentified; title only in Livingstone's hand.

7.   Envelope,   "J. Bevan Braithwaite, 65 Mornington Road, Regents Park, London," postmarked (hereafter pm) 8M8 AP 30 57; 61 102. NLS, MS. Dep. 237. '4) Original given to L.P. Davies [S.P. Dawes?] 1220 10 [word illegible] April 29, 1857. About salary from L.M.S.' in an unidentified hand. Contains a penny red stamp.

8.   Envelope,   "Bevan Braithwaite Esq, 3, New Square, Lincoln's Inn," pm London 1 FE 17 58; 68 123. NLS, MS. Dep. 237. '5) Nov. 27, 1857 about Mr. Anderson's book and a lion attacking a giraffe supposed to be a false story.' in an unidentified hand. Contains two penny red stamps.

9.   Envelope,   Richard Thornton, Esqre, Livingstone's Expedition, Cape of Good Hope, pm Bradford, JY 3 1858, Devonport, JY 5 58, Cape Town AU 13 1858; 67 120. NARS, LI 2/1/1. Via Royal Mail Steamer 'Dane' from Plymouth. "Found at Linyanti, DL."

10. Envelope,   "John Blanche, Gracechurch St. London," pm 27 Sep. 1859. ULSOASL, Africa, Odds, Box 11, folder 5.

11. Envelope,   "Miss Anna Braithwaite," franked "Dr. L." pm London 24 Aug. 1860; Kendal 24 Aug. 1860; 80 138. NLS, MS. Dep. 237. '9) March 6 1858. To Father about private matters' in unidentified hand [the recipient's?]. Admiralty stamp.

12. Envelope,   "Miss Burdett Coutts, 1 Stratton St., Piccadilly, London," franked "Dr. L." pm LN Bombay AP 29, 61; 95 215. Privately owned. India unpaid.

13. Envelope,   Richard Thornton, Esq., [1858–63], 89 218. NMLZ, G17/1H1. "This was wetted on the Bar, opened by Captain Oldfield and dried — It was seen by him alone. We put it up thus. D. Livingstone."

14. Envelope,   "H.W. Esq., Mission," [Horace Waller], [1861–63]. RHLO, Waller MSS. Afr. s. 16, I, f. 213.

15. Envelope,   "Bevan Braithwaite Esq., 3 New Square, Lincoln's Inn, London," franked "Dr. L." pm Mansfield, C FE 23 65; 78 140. NLS, MS. Dep. 237. '29) John S. Moffat Care of H.M. Arderne, Fairbridge & Arderne, Cape Town. Livingstone, England, Feb. 2, 1865. Slave trade, copy of letter from Dr. to J.S. Moffat on his becoming a missionary under the L.M.S. in Africa,' in an unidentified hand. Contains four penny red stamps; pm London MA Fe 24 65 on verso.

16. Envelope,   "Miss Currie, Almada Street, Hamilton," franked "Dr. L." pm Hamilton, JU 20 65. SNMDL, on display. Contained a 1/4/1 8vo page announcing the death of Livingstone's mother.

17. Envelope,   "Mr. John Loader, Thame, Oxfordshire," pm London WC AU 12 65, B Thame AU 12 65; 78 132. WIHMLL, MS. A 167. Contains one penny red stamp.

18. Envelope,   "Rev. Horace Waller, Sydenham Road, Croydon, London," "Via Marseilles." pm Alex 27 [Aug. 65], Marseilles 2 Jan 66, AX JA 4 66; RHLO, Waller MSS. Afr. s. 16, I, f. 211.

19. Envelope, "Rev. Horace Waller, Clover, near Chatham," [Jul. 64—Aug. 65]. RHLO, Waller MSS. Afr. s. 16, I, f. 212.

20. Envelope, David Livingstone from Thomas Maclear, "dated 9 Oct. 1866, Received Aug. 13, 1872." RHLO, Waller MSS. Afr. s. 16, I, f. 214.

21. Envelope, "Bevan Braithwaite, Esq., 3, New Buildings, Lincoln's Inn, London," franked "Dr. L." [Nov. 1870]. 70 115. NLS, MS. Dep. 237. Made from a cheque from Livingstone's Bombay Chequebook.

22. Envelope, "The Duke of Argyle," 62 102. WIHMLL, MS. 64757. 'From Dr. Livingstone' written in unidentified hand.

23. Envelope, "Bevan Braithwaite, Esq., 3, New Square, Lincoln's Inn," 80 137. NLS, MS. Dep. 237. '£3 7 6 2) Ap. 4. 1857 + letters from L.M.S., Church Protestant Defence and John Smith Moffat' in unidentified hand.

24. Envelope, "Miss Burdett Coutts, Stratton Street, Piccadilly, London," franked "Dr. Livingstone," 95 215. Privately owned.

25. Envelope, "Miss Burdett Coutts, Stratton Street, Piccadilly, London," franked "Dr. L," 96 218. Privately owned.

26. Envelope, "The Reverend E. Glover, Cape of Good Hope, HMS 'Rapid', D.L. " Privately owned.

27. Envelope, "Sir William Hooker, Kew Gardens," 67 107. RBGK, African Letters, 1844—58, vol. LIX, f. 190.

28. Envelope fr, "W.W. Cazabet, 6, Grosvenor St., Grosvenor Sq., W." BLO, Clarendon dep. C. 80, f. 528.

29. Envelope fr, "T.B. Johnston, Esq., 4, St. Andrew Square, Edinburgh." NLS, MS. 10707, f. 39.

30. Visiting card, 'Mrs. John Smith Moffat,' signed by Livingstone on verso. Sotheby's Cat., 25 Jul 1970, lot 348.

31. Visiting card, 'Rev. John Smith Moffat,' signed by Livingstone and his wife on verso. Sotheby's Cat., 17 Dec 1974, lot 307.

32. Visiting card, 'Mrs. John Smith Moffat,' signed by David and Mary Livingstone, John Smith and Emily Unwin Moffat on verso. Sotheby's Cat., 17 Dec. 1974, lot 307.

33. Label, on an African cup. NMLZ, on display. "Champagne cup for J. Young, Esq. Sent home because there is no champagne."

34. Postscript, to a letter from Mary to Thomas S. Livingstone, 16 March 1862. 209 267. SNMDL, Ph copy NLS, MS. 10707, f. 66. At the top of page 1, Livingstone wrote: "Look at Oswell's + Agnes' pictures by Dr. Meller and send letter + picture to Robert + picture to Oswell."

35. Notes, pencil, on "Bad Weather," "Fever," "Alarm at night lions roaring," "Fever again, very weak." Sotheby's Cat., 25 Feb 1946, lot 200.

36.   Benediction card, Wedding, John Smith Moffat to Emily Unwin, Union Street Chapel, Brighton, 15 Feb 1858. 72 113. NLS, MS. 10707, f. 44. Printed on one side, with Livingstone's note to Agnes on the other: "My Dear Agnes, I enclose the wedding cards of your uncle John. We were at the wedding today 15 Feb/58 I saw & spoke to the Queen on Saturday. She said her good wishes would follow me".

B.   Autographs and Autographed Books.

Books authored by Livingstone are not included here, but in Section 3 above.

1.   Autograph,   "Morimo o loa rata Lehatsi yalo, ka o loa naea moroa ona go le shuela. John III − 16. Sitchuana or language of Bechuanas. Written for Miss Poyser at Professor Owen's, 3d May 1857, David Livingstone." 182 116. WIHMLL, MS. 56360.

2.   Autograph,   biblical quotation, Hadley Green, Barnet, 18 June 1857. Three lines in an African language with English equivalent beneath, 1 p. 8vo. John Wilson Cat. No. 20 (1975), item 60. This autograph may also be described in less detail in Sotheby's Cat., 15 Apr 1975, lot 540.

3.   Autograph,   "Ena eo o tlañ go 'na ga 'nkitla ki mo leleka ka gope. (Lehu ku ya Jesu). Him that cometh unto me, I will in no wise cast out. (The word of Jesus). Then if we are not saved, the fault will be our own for ever and ever.   David Livingstone.
Jesu dulcis memoria, Dans corde vera gaudia,
Sed super mel et omnia, Ejus dulcis praesentia.
                    St. Bernard
Hadley Green, 1st July 1857" lge. fol. CLRUGSA, Ph copy NLS, MS. 10777, no. 19.

4.   Autograph,   "Ena eo o tlañ go 'na ga 'nkitla ki mo leleka ka gope. Him that cometh unto me, I will in no wise cast out. Drumcondra Castle, 31st August 1857, David Livingstone." 1/4/1, 181 116, WIHMLL, MS. 63319.

5.   Autograph,   two autographs, biblical quotations in English with African equivalents, both signed and dated Hamilton, 14 Sep. 1857. Sotheby's Cat., 17 Jun 1957, lot 140.

6.   Autograph,   "Ena eo o tlañ go 'na ga 'nkitla ki mo leleka ka gope. Him that cometh unto me, I will in no wise cast out. 17 Sept. 1857, Glasgow, David Livingstone." 200 126, SNMDL.

7.   Autograph,   "Ena eo o tlañ go 'na ga 'nkitla ki mo leleka ka gope. Him that cometh unto me, I will in no wise cast out. 10 Oct. 1857, Leeds, David Livingstone." 1/4/1, 8vo, ULSOASL, Africa, Odds, Box 11, folder 4.

8.   Autograph,   'David Livingstone, the Son-in-Law of Rev. Robert Moffat, was born so long ago he has forgot all about it, and does not like to deal in hearsay! After hardy training in youth, he was enabled to endure some toil in the cause of his loving Saviour in South Africa, and hopes the privilege may still be awarded him of serving his good master there. David Livingstone, 13 October 1857, Liverpool.' 1 p., TS copy. ULSOASL, Africa, Odds, Box 10, folder 4.

9. Autograph, "David Livingstone." 14 Nov. 1857, London. Also signed by Mary and Charles Livingstone. 157 120, JPLAM. Partially destroyed.

10. Autograph, "Ga 'nkitla ki go tlogela ile esiñ ki go tloboga. I will never leave thee, nor forsake thee. A verse in the language of the Bechuanas, South Africa. David Livingstone. 19 Decr. 1857, London." SNMDL.

11. Autograph, "With the kindest regards of David Livingstone. 20 Feby 1858, London." 130 120, privately owned.

12. Autograph, "Ena eo o tlañ go ['na] ga 'nkitla ke mo leleka ka gope. Him that cometh unto me, I will in no wise cast ou[t]. this is the Language [of] the Bechuanas. 20th Feby 1858, David Livingstone." WCLUWJ, partially damaged by fire in 1931.

13. Autograph, "If Mrs. Wyon wished an autograph in the envelope I have just lighted on, here it is. If anything else I am off at 5½ P.M. for Scotland. David Livingstone. Kind regards to Mrs. W. 22 Feby 1858." WIHMLL, MS. 68010 B.

14. Autograph, "4th March 1858. David Livingstone." 1/4/1, 182 113. SNMDL.

15. Autograph, "Re timetse rotle yaka linku ra hapoga moñue le moñue tseleñ ea gague; mi Jehova o mo belesitse boleo you nona rotle. Isaiah 53 — v. 6. 6 Novr. 1864, Newstead Abbey." Rendell Cat. No. 44. [All we like sheep have gone astray; we have turned every one to his own way; and the Lord has laid on him the iniquity of us all].

16. Autograph, quotation from Scriptures in English and Arabic. Sotheby's Cat., 25 Jan 1949, lot 499.

17. Book, autographed. Forbes, William. **The Duty and Powers of Justices of the Peace, etc.** "David Livingstone, Manyuema Country." SNMDL.

18. Book, autographed. Gray, James. **An Introduction to Arithmetic,** 22nd edition, Edinburgh, 1825. "Blantyre Works, 12 June 1825, David Livingston." SNMDL, also autographed by Charles Livingston.

19. Book, autographed. McLeod, Norman (ed.). **Good Words,** 1862. "David Livingstone." NMLZ, on display.

20. Book, autographed. Sigourney, L.H. **Lays of the West.** "To Miss Catherine Ridley with the Best wishes + Christian regard of D.L. London, 25 June 1840." SNMDL; see also Sotheby's Cat., 25 Apr. 1934, lot 553.

21. Book, autographed. Taylor, Jeffreys. **The Young Islanders and What Came of their Adventures.** London: Simpkin, Marshall & Co., n.d. "David Livingstone." CSBL.

22. Book, autographed. Watts, Isaac. **The Psalms of David, In Metre. Hymns & Spiritual Songs, in 3 books.** London: A.K. Neuman & Co, 1840. "D. Livingston." NMLZ, on display.

23. Book, autographed. Webster, Noah. **Dictionary.** "David Livingstone, Unyanyembe, June 1872." SNMDL, on display.

24. Book, autographed. **The Holy Bible.** "The Bible of Dear Mary Moffat Livingstone. Robert May Have it. 28 April 1862, David Livingstone." Privately owned; Ph copy of inscription in SNMDL.

25. Book, autographed. **The Holy Bible.** "The Bible which went with me in all my wanderings in Africa. David Livingstone, Feby 1858." Privately owned.

26. Book, autographed. **The Holy Bible.** "For Agnes Livingstone on her tenth birthday, June 13th 1857, from her father David Livingstone. My dear Nanie, May our God and Father lift up the light of his countenance upon you and grant you his peace." SNMDL.

27. Book, autographed. **The New Testament.** "This book was presented by me to my son Oswell in 1858, but his dear Mama brought it out to Africa in 1862, and now after her departure to the Heavenly Home I send it back to Oswell. David Livingstone, 29 April 1862." SNMDL.

28. Book, autographed. **Le Nouveau Testament.** "Found in Mama's pocket after she died. 28 April 1862, David Livingstone." SNMDL.

29. Book, autographed. **Η ΚΑΙΝΗ ΔΙΑΘΗΚΗ [The New Testament].** "To Neil, Janet or David Livingstone, who ever learns to read it first. From their Uncle David, South Africa." NMLZ, on display.

C   Documents.

While all items referred to throughout this section, and indeed in this entire catalogue, are documents, the terms in the context of this subsection is used simply to denote all items which are neither letters nor letter fragments, and which do not fit into either of the two preceding subsections. Because of their disparate nature, and since the terms used to describe them are arbitrary at best, they are presented chronologically rather than by category.

1. Prescription, for William Mason [?]. 6 Feb 1840, 77 116. WIHMLL, MS. 25612.

2. Poems, of a religious nature, in Livingstone's hand, one written by a Mr. Reid of Bellany, a second apparently anonymous. Sep 1840, 184 116. NLS, MS. 10701, f. 7.

3. Receipt, "Received from Mrs. J. Phillip the sum of Eighteen Pounds fifteen shillings sterling, being the salary for one quarter from London Missionary Society, 8th April 1841, David Livingstone." SNMDL.

4. Certificate, of marriage, 9 Jan. 1845; copy, Duplicate original register, NARS, LI 2/1/1 (photocopy NLS, MS. 10779 (21)). Signed by David Livingston and Mary Moffat; witnessed by Robert Hamilton, William Ashton, Jean Lauga, and David Lemue; accuracy of copy attested by Robert Moffat.

5. Receipt, from "Claremont, Mauritius, 17th Septr. 1856," from William Thompson while at Quilimane: 500 Spanish dollars and 50 sovereigns, also clothing, beads, and writing materials. 229 186. ULSOASL, Africa, Wooden Box of L's letters. Published in **LMC**, p. 324.

6.	Hymn,	"We've no abiding city here," written in SeTswana [1856], Sotheby's Cat. 15 Nov. 1937, lot 195.
7.	List,	of seeds, to Sir William Hooker, 5 Feb 1857. Copy in KCLUND.
8.	List,	of seeds, including descriptions of the habitats of Masuka, Mashoma or Mokuchong, Koma, Maceas, Two Square Pods, Seeds of the Senna of Tete, Mokorongo, A Long Pod, marked flower seeds and fruit seeds. n.d. [rec. 10 Feb 1857], 317 195. 1/4/4. RBGK, African letters 1844—1858, vol. LIX, f. 190.
9.	Prescription,	n.d. [20 Jan — 23 May 1857], WIHMLL, MS. unnumbered, 182 117.
10.	Agreement,	an unsigned copy of the paper making Buchanan, Young, and Hannan Livingstone's Trustees. n.d. [1 Oct. — 19 Dec. 1857], NARS, LI 1/2/1.
11.	Indenture,	between Livingstone and his Trustees, (A. Buchanan, J. Young and J. Hannan), placing £5,100 and the profits from **MT** in trust for his children. 19 Dec 1857, NARS, LI 1/2/1.
12.	Note,	"Any friends may attend meetings," unknown recipient. 1857, 1 p. 8vo. Sotheby's Cat., 28 Jul. 1930, lot 111.
13.	Agreement,	between John Murray and the Librairie de L. Hachette Et Cie, Rue Pierre-Sarazin 14. 6 Jan 1858, "approved by David Livingstone." 250 174, 1/2/2, JMPL. Regarding a translation of **MT** into French.
14.	Note,	from T.M. Drysdale of Glasgow to Wm. Hodgson of London, requesting a picture or illustration from Livingstone to aid Drysdale in publicizing Africa. Livingstone refuses, not knowing Drysdale, and leaves the matter to Murray. 9 Feb 1858, 1/4/4, 235 207, JMPL.
15.	Indenture,	between Livingstone and John S. Moffat, defining the terms under which Livingstone would give Moffat financial support for the latter's founding a mission station south of the Zambezi. 13, 15 Feb 1858, NARS, on display.
16.	Agreement,	entered into and signed by 6 Europeans agreeing to follow Livingstone's leadership on the Zambezi Expedition. London, 22 Feb 1858, MDNHLL, MSS 120; duplicate in PROL, FO 97/322, f. 275; Livingstone's copy in NARS, LI 1/1/1, p. 765.
17.	List,	of African chiefs provided for Clarendon by Livingstone. "1. Mburuma, chief on the Zambesi; 2. Mpende, chief on the Zambesi; 3. Katolo-sa, chief on the Zambesi; 4. Shinte, chief of Balonda; 5. Cazembe, chief of Balonda." Verso reads: "1. 2. 3. to be addressed as **chiefs** and **our friend** and in reference to the Zambesi **Bonga**-chief." n.d. [Feb 1858], PROL, FO 63/842, f. 198.
18.	Receipt,	"Received from Mr. Skead one Sextant No. Da. 20 for use of the Zambesi Expedition. David Livingstone, Steamer 'Pearl,' 3d April 1858." Location of original unknown; ph copy in NLS, MS. 10777, no. 28.

19. Receipt,   from Sir George Grey, £105 on the account of the Zambesi Expedition, to be refunded at the Foreign Office from their funds. 28 Septr 1858 Kongone Harbour, MS copy, MDNHLL, MSS 120.

20. Postscript,   "Enclosure No. 1. Dr. Kirk's tracing of the river from Tette up through Kebra-basa — bearings magnetic compass." Tette, 18 Dec 1858, 696 924; MDNHLL, MSS. 120.

21. Account,   of Livingstone's royalties from **MT**, up to 30 June 1859. NARS, LI 1/1/1, pp. 1027—1028, MS aut copy.

22. Translations,   "Pater Noster in the Dialect of Senna," "Ave Maria," "Signal da Cruz," "Santa Maria," "Ave Maria," "Pater Noster." n.d. [1858—59], 2/8/6, 327 200, NARS, LI 1/5/2, Livingstone copied these from versions written down by Portuguese residents of the lower Zambezi. These aids to worship were taught to the indigenous people by Jesuits prior to their expulsion from the region in 1759.

23. Accounts,   for the Zambezi Expedition, 11 Mar, 21 Mar, and May 1861. NARS, LI 1/1/1, pp. 1337—39.

24. Life Certificate,   David + Charles Livingstone, Gedye, Meller, Hardisty, Gwillam, John Neal, Thomas Ward, John Pennell, Charles Neale, Richard Wilson, Wm. Rowe + John Hutchins are alive and performing their duties as of this day. 24 December 1861. MS aut, MDNHLL, MSS 120. These certificates were sent quarterly to the Admiralty to enable relatives or agents of the men to draw their salaries from H.M. Govt. One wonders why John Kirk is not included.

25. Receipt,   given by David Davies of the 'Hetty Ellen' to Livingstone, for £354 7s 6d for use of brig and crew from 8 Jan to 23 Feb 1862. Witnessed by John Kirk. 21 Mar 1862, Mouth of the Zambesi. MS aut copy, SNMDL.

26. Note,   to James Young, advising him to draw £354 7s 6d from available funds to pay David Davies of the 'Hetty Ellen.' 21 Mar 1862, Mouth of the Zambesi. MS aut copy, SNMDL.

27. Note,   "Found in Mama's box." Part of an almond plant plucked by Mary Livingstone at Wynburg, Cape Town. 1/4/1, 180 114, privately owned, n.d. [28—30 Apr 1862]. See Sotheby's Cat. 8 Nov 1960, lot 203, where it is listed as being to Agnes Livingstone 3 and dated April 1862.

28. Receipt,   concerning a financial transaction between Livingstone and John C. Plow, Acting Paymaster of H.M.S. 'Ariel.' Livingstone notes receiving £42 10s in gold, £19 in shillings, and £28 in florins, totalling £89 10s. Subtracting this from £100, Livingstone gets a balance of £10 — 10s. Verso in Plow's hand indicates that he gave Livingstone £100 in public money. 18 [?] July 1862, privately owned. At a later date a dispute arose between the two over this transaction.

29. Receipt,   for naval stores from Wm. Sunley, including beef, pork, sugar, suet, tobacco, soap, potatoes, peas, lime juice, oil, boots, and lime. "H. M. Exploring ship 'Pioneer,' 3rd Sep 1862." MS aut copy, PROL, FO 97/322, f. 258.

30.   Agreement,   signed by 10 Johanna men to work aboard the 'Pioneer' for a year. Witnessed by Wm. Sunley. In the left margin of the agreement, Livingstone wrote: "2 months pay each and a velvet jacket and strong calico trousers each — for the church or poor." 4 Sep 1862, 1p. fol. Privately owned; ph copy in NLS MS. 10777 (9).

31.   List,   stores taken by 'Pioneer,' including bread, spirits, chocolate, tea, pork, peas, beef, flour, suet, mustard, pepper, vinegar, lime juice, preserved meats, potatoes, tobacco, soap, candles (returned), raisins (condemned). "29th Octr 1862, Pomony." MS aut copy, PROL, FO 97/322, f. 259.

32.   List,   ' . . . of Articles belonging to the late Mr. Thornton, for transmission home.' n.d. [Apr–May 1863], 2pp. fol. Sotheby's Cat. 10 Nov 1936, lot 506.

33.   Note,   Livingstone writes that he began where no one had ever appeared except Cowan and Donovan, who were never again heard of; and if he were to begin again he would not sit down where others had led the way, such as in Madagascar or Honolulu. n.d. [1863–4?] BLJ.

34.   Note,   requesting that the address of Dr. Kirk be given to James Young at the Royal Hotel, recipient unidentified. n.d. [Jul 1864 – Aug 1865], 12 mo, 1p. Sotheby's Cats., 14 Jul 1970, lot 564, and 15 Apr 1975, lot 539.

35.   Note,   by a picture of a tombstone, taken from a trade catalogue: "Poor Mary's gravestone is like this without the railings + a cross on the top because the Portuguese respect that emblem. An English inscription on one side and a Portuguese one on the other to be sent in July." n.d. [1863–1865]. 115 155, SNMDL.

36.   List,   "Wages to be paid at Zanzibar," for 1st Jan 1869. Livingstone lists the wages he wanted paid to Simon, Amoda, Gardener, Mabruki, Abram, Chuma, Susi, and James, and his reasons for so doing. 2/4/4, 227 180, NARS LI 1/1/1, pp. 2256–59 (photocopy NLS MS. 10779 (21)).

37.   Notes,   on various specimens of wildlife; including birds, insects, shells + fishes; shells of Lake Nyassa and of the Sea of Galilee so similar as to indicate that a chain of lakes might have once existed from Palestine to South Africa: certain species collected by Kirk cause Livingstone to make deductions about Africa and Madagascar. 1/2/1, 316 205, n.d. [1866–69?], NARS LI 1/1/1, p. 2342. Paper watermarked 'Thomas James, 1864.'

38.   Cheque,   payable to John Kirk, H.M. Consul, for 4000 rupees. 5 Feb 1871, NLS MS. 10705, f. 3 (see illustration).

39.   Agreement,   with porters and others, Manyuema, 5 Feb 1871. MS not located. Printed in **The Times**, 27 Sep 1872, p. 3 c. 3.

40.   Receipt form,   for loan of a pocket chronometer from Captain, H.M. Ship. Never used. 1/2/1, 215 240, Unyanyembe, Feb 1872. Location of original not known; ph copies in SNMDL and NLS MS. 10708, f. 123.

41.   List,   " . . . of men + goods from Zanzibar to H.M. Stanley," requesting Whittier's **Poems,** a blank journal, nautical almanacks, padlocks, 50 freemen, hatchets, muskets, powder and horns, etc. 1/2/1, n.d. [Mar 1872?], MS aut, NLS MS. 10705, f. 4.

D. **Letters and Letter Fragments.**

The first two items are letters in Livingstone's hand which were excluded from Sections 1 and 2 above on the grounds that they are copies of letters written by others. The remaining items are included here because there was not enough concrete information to warrant their inclusion above.

1.	Letter,	"To Mrs. Hamilton," signed "David Livingston for Robert Hamilton." 16 Jan 1851, Kuruman. 1/4/4, 227 185, JLUCT, Misc. MSS. Liv. Ph. copy in NLS MS. 10779, no. 5. As Hamilton was very ill (he died not long thereafter), Livingston acted as his amanuensis.
2.	Letter,	To A. Januarie from J.W. Viljoen, Field Coronet to the Transvaal River Company, 11 Jun 1852, Grootwater. 1/4/4, 274 219, ULSOASL, Africa, Odds, Box 10, folder 2. In Afrikaans, the letter gives Januarie power to inspect all non-company wagons. Ph copy in NLS MS. 10780, no. 6. "The above is a true copy, errors included, of the original in the possession of the above-named A. Januarie, a Griqua. D.L." See Schapera, **DLSAP**, p. 52, n. 7.
3.	Fragment,	To [Robert Moffat 1?], n.d. [1845–52]. 1p. oblong 12 mo. Rendell Cat. No. 23, item 101. 'Mary much better this evening. Mose goes off tomorrow morning. I have enclosed the yellow paper. With kind love to Mrs. M. + all. D. + M. Livingstone.' Final 'e' dubious.
4.	Fragment,	To Robert Moffat 1, n.d. [1844–53]. 2pp. 4to. Sotheby's Cat., 23 March 1936, lot 170. Dealings with natives.
5.	Fragment,	Recipient unknown, n.d. [1853–55]. 'I am recovered from fever, and think I am getting rid of intermittent too. If spared, will impart knowledge of Christ to those who have never heard his name. Many large tribes in the direction we go. I hope to establish the gospel in this region, and to see commerce + Christianity stay the bitter fountain of African misery.' **NDLDSCA**,p. 34.
6.	Fragment,	Recipient unknown, Jun 1857. Sotheby's Cat., 20 Nov 1972, lot 410. Concerning an application for money.
7.	Fragment,	Recipient unknown, n.d. [1857?]. 1/2/2, 94 108, privately owned. "you. I told Mr. Milne that I would advise you to apply for the sum at once if he had no objection." Verso: "By attending to this matter at your convenience you will much oblige Yours Most truly, David Livingstone."
8.	Letter,	To Thomas Baines, 20 Feb 1858, 18 Hart St., London. Sought by J.P.R. Wallis in a letter to the editor of the **Observer**, 29 Aug 1937. '. . . asks Baines to call, if it does not interfere with Commander Bedingfeld's orders, to take charge of the plans of [the] house designed to be built on the Zambezi, and gives instructions concerning instruments.'
9.	Fragment,	Recipient unknown, said to have been written to his host in Manchester [Thomas Clegg??]. 23 Feb 1858 [dated in an unidentified hand]. 48 119. SNMDL, ph copy in NLS, MS. 10779 no. 3. ". . . kindly lent me for perusal was returned. It must . . ." Verso: "I am most truly yours, David Livingstone."

10. Fragment, Recipient as 9. above. n.d. [Apr 1857 – Feb 1858]. 78 112. SNMDL, ph copy in NLS, MS. 10779 no. 3. ". . . thankful if you kindly give my brother a bed during our stay. I had a previous . . ." Verso: "I am Dear Sir Yours +c, David Livingstone."

11. Two letters, To J.R. Liefchild, 1857 and 1858, 7pp. 8vo. Sotheby's Cat., 25 Jan 1949, lot 499. Declining an invitation to a party. 'I like the quiet sort of thing you invite me to better than a party, these I never . . . did like. A great want of taste I suppose, but so it has always been. I prefer the old friends; for thee I hope will continue friends still, when the tide of popularity ebbs or flows the other way.'

12. Fragment, To Samuel Wilberforce, n.d. [1859–60?]. 2pp. oblong 8vo, Sotheby's Cat., 19 Jul 1960, lot 392. Calling for the establishment of a colony of 'our own hardworking Christian people' in Africa, as the only means of ending the slave trade.

13. Letter, Recipient unknown, 15 Feb 1861, 'Pioneer at Sea.' 4pp. 8vo, Sotheby's Cat., 23 May 1922, lot 540. Relating to missionary work in Africa. This may well refer to letter 1077 in the chronological tables.

14. Fragment, Recipient unknown, n.d. [May–Dec 1862]. 1/2/2, 166 204. NLS, Acc. 6903. Following Mackenzie's death, missionaries moved down to Chibisa's. Inspiration for this came from Rowley. Makololo we sent home remained and attacked a Portuguese caravan + gave the slaves over to the mission. I shall start them again and pass Tette with them, but unless something is done to the Portuguese now that Ma Robert is gone, Lake Nyassa will employ all my energies. [Verso:] The Mombari insolent? Maybe, but I never saw a more cringing set. All who are under Portuguese seem spirit broken. I asked where they got their best slaves and the prices at Lobale and Benguela. I made enquiries about slaving by Makololo — a few secret cases had occurred at great distances from Linyanti, but even enemies of the Makololo know little of slaving by them. If I was deceived by Sekeletu, he must be a cleverer fellow than you will find him. The fear that I should come to rule them did not exist.

15. Letter, To Charles A. Alington, December 1863, Murchison's Cataracts. Sotheby's Cat., 25 Feb 1946, lot 200. 'Describing his struggles to reach Lake Bemba and the Upper Congo.'

16. Letter, Recipient unknown, 29 July 1864, Tavistock Hotel. 4pp. 8vo. Sotheby's Cat., 6 Jun 1950, lot 311. On financial matters and a forthcoming visit to Scotland.

17. Two letters, 'My Dear D.' 5 Nov 1857, 10 Soho Square; and 7 Feb 1865, Newstead Abbey. Both 8vo. Sotheby's Cat., 30 Oct 1973, lot 363. Offering more 'information about Lake V' although 'I am always afraid of being prosy.' No indication which quotation is from which letter.

18. Fragment, [Horace Waller?], n.d. [Feb 1865?], Newstead Abbey. 1/2/2, 79 113. RHLO, Waller MSS. Afr. s. 16, I, f. 210. Rowley implies that not the Governor of Tette but I am the cause of all the ills that befell the mission. Verso: Send back the proof soon. Tell Meller he was proposed for . . . .

19. Fragment, [William C. Oswell?], n.d. [10–14 Jun 1865]. 1/2/2, 75 115, SNMDL, ph copy NLS, MS. 10779 no. 3. "—duced. I am going in a day or two to Oxford to fulfill a promise of meeting some of the Dons there." Verso: " . . . before I can leave India. With kind words to Mrs. Oswell, I am affectionately, David Livingstone."

20. Fragment, [Horace Waller?], n.d. [Jul 1864–Aug 1865]. 1/2/1, 95 113. RHLO, Waller MSS. Afr. s. 16, I, f. 208. I told Mrs. W. about Mrs Burrup — she will write if she sees an opportunity of doing service — you need not mention this.

21. Fragment, [Horace Waller?], n.d. [Jul 1864–Aug 1865]. 1/2/2, 41 113. RHLO, Waller MSS. Afr. s. 16, I, f. 209. I fear I am as sorry as yourself — look at the enclosed. Verso: please return the note.

22. Fragment, Recipient unknown, n.d. [Mar 1872–Apr 1873]. Blaikie, **PLDL**, pp. 425–6. 'He laid all he had at my service, divided his clothes into two heaps, and pressed one heap upon me; then his medicine chest; then his goods and everything he had, and to coax my appetite, often cooked dainty dishes with his own hand.' Livingstone obviously writes of H.M. Stanley.

23. Letter, [Robert Moffat 1?], n.d. [1848–49]. 2pp. 4to. Sotheby's Cat., 15 Nov 1937, lot 195. 'Preparation for 1st interior journey.'

24. Letter, Recipient unidentified, n.d. 1p. 8vo. Sotheby's Cat., 24 Oct 1972, lot 425. Hoping God will prolong the recipient's life + usefulness and that he and Livingstone will have 'several more such happy meetings.'

25. Fragment, [Harriette C. Livingstone?], n.d. Mf copy, LCUSWDC, MSS. Div., AC 6907. "Agnes writes in love to you + all the children. David Livingstone."

26. Letter, To Dr. Percy, Albemarle St., n.d. 3pp. 8vo. Sotheby's Cat., 30 Jul 1937, lot 734. 'stupid neglect.'

APPENDIX 1

NOTES ON SECTION 1

The number of the note is identical with that of the letter to which it refers.

0002   Arundel wrote to Livingston on 17 Jan. 1838, asking 17 questions for prospective missionaries. This letter is an MS copy of Arundel's letter, with Livingston's replies inserted. As it was read to an L.M.S. Examination Committee on 23 Jul., Livingston obviously wrote his replies between those dates. The copy consists of 23 pp. in all, of which 11 are Livingston's replies.

0003   The second page of this letter is blank; pp. 3 and 4 consist of a poem to the tune of "Auld Lang Syne" in the hand of the lyricist John Barff.

0004   See also Seaver, **DLLL**, p. 36, ex.

0005   See also Campbell, **Liv**, pp. 61—63.

0006   This letter is dated by the Library holding it.

0007   This letter is dated by the Archive holding it.

0008   See also Gelfand, **LtD**, p. 24, ex.

0009   This letter was probably written to Thomas Prentice junior.

0014   The published version of this letter has it dated 13 and 15 Nov. 1840.

0018   At a later date, someone added an "e" to "Livingston" in the signature of this letter. At first Livingston wrote "1840", but struck over the "0" to make "1841."

0020   Livingston dated this letter in error as "26 Feby 1840." The published version dates it as 24 Feb. 1841, also in error.

0025   See also Seaver, **DLLL**, p. 44, ex.

0028   Livingston's place for 7 Jul. reads "Outspanned, alias anchored in loco innominato."

0044   See also Blaikie, **PLDL**, pp. 50—51, ex., where the letter is published as 18 Dec.; and Gelfand, **Ltd**, pp. 28—30, ex.

0047   Livingston's "Jany 1842" may easily be misread as "Jan 7 1842."

0049   Livingston gives his location as "Tropic of Capricorn, Long. $28^{\circ} 10'$ E."

0056   See also Chamberlin, **SLFL**, pp. 32—37.

0057   See also Sotheby's Cat. 22 Dec. 1915, lot 495; and Maggs' Cat. Autumn 1920, no. 2353.

0061   See also Chamberlin, **SLFL**, pp. 37—40.

0063   This "letter" is an extract taken from a letter of Neil Livingston to "My Dear Friend", dated 24 Dec. 1842.

0064   This and all other items in NLS, MS. 10773 are from a letter copy book compiled for William Garden Blaikie.

0066   Livingston wrote at least four letters to Dyke between 1843 and 1851, addressing them variously to M., M.T. (or H.T.), and T.M. Dyke.   Since Dyke was associated with the French mission in the Basuto country, it is possible that the "M." was for "Monsieur", or even "Mister."   It is the editors' opinion that all were meant for Hamilton Moore Dyke, although no explanation for the variations can be offered.

0068   This letter is dated by Professor Isaac Schapera in the publication referred to.

0073   See also **DD,** vol. 1, no. 7 (Oct. 1848), pp. 133–136.

0076   See also Chamberlin, **SLFL,** pp. 42–49.

0078   The first four pages of this letter are in the NLS;   the second four are in the SNMDL. The NLS copy referred to is of the second four pages.

0084   See also Schapera, **DLSAP,** preface, ex.

0086   This letter is dated by Professor Isaac Schapera in the publication referred to.

0087   Livingston gives his place as "In sight of the Hills of the Bakatla."

0107   Mary Moffat married Livingston on 9 Jan. 1845;   her husband's name is added to hers in parentheses before that date to distinguish her from her mother.   See also Blaikie, **PLDL,** pp. 71–72, ex.

0109   See also Blaikie, **PLDL,** pp. 71–72.

0110   Livingston wrote this to the Above Bar Sunday School in Southampton.

0111   Dated by Professor Isaac Schapera in the publication referred to;   place taken from the text of the letter.   See also Blaikie, **PLDL,** p. 72, ex.

0117   The date and place on this item are written in the hand of Robert Moffat 1.

0126   The date and place on this item are written in the hand of Robert Moffat 1.

0128   The date and place on this item are written in the hand of Robert Moffat 1;   other fragments from the letter of this date are still at large.

0131   Most of the letters in this collection were partially destroyed by fire in the University of Witwatersrand Library in 1931.

0133   Livingston dates this letter "Monday morning."

0134   Robert Moffat 1 dated this fragment "about 1846".   See also Myers' Cat. No. 6 (Spring 1967), no. 12.

0135   Robert Moffat 1 endorsed this item "This specimen of Dr. Livingstone's writing is about 1849."

0142   The printed copy referred to dates this letter "28 April 1843", which was a year before he was mauled by the lion and four months before he went to Mabotsa for the first time. See also Sotheby's Cat. 18 Feb. 1930, lot 427.

0146　See also Gelfand, **LtD**, p. 40, ex.

0154　Robert Moffat 1 endorsed this item "This was written before his first interior journey to Linyanti and the Barotse country to the west coast = just before the commencement of his travels."

0175　Robert Moffat 1 endorsed this item "Rec'd 11 Sept. 1847." This may well be the completion of letters 0171 and 0172.

0180　The date and place of this letter were removed from the manuscript and added later in an unidentified hand.

0187　Robert Moffat 1 endorsed this item "Livingston, 11 Augt. 1848."

0188　Postscripts were added to this letter on "Monday evening" and "Tuesday morning," probably 4 and 5 Sep. 1848.

0193　While the text of this item indicates that it may have been written as early as mid-1844, the editors, lacking any other copy of it, choose to honour the date under which it was printed.

0200　This copy was made stealthily in Kuruman shortly after the letter's arrival there, and was forwarded immediately to Cape Town and perhaps on to London. It is not a complete copy of the letter.

0207　Livingston's first postscript was written between the Zouga and Kolobeng, and the second after he had reached Kolobeng.

0208　See also Listowel, **TOL**, pp. 32—34, ex., and **JRGSL**, vol. 20 (1850), p. 138, where a small portion of this letter is rewritten.

0227　Livingston's places for the four dates given are respectively: Logagnen, Bamangwato, Kolobeng, and Kolobeng. See also Listowel, **TOL**, p. 42, ex.

0232　See also **JRGSL**, vol. 21 (1851), pp. 18—24.

0233　MS copy in the hand of C. Reeve.

0241　See also **The Times**, 22 Aug. 1938, p. 7, c.1.

0244　This "letter" is paraphrased in a footnote of one paragraph in length.

0246　Livingston's postscript was written two days north of Kolobeng.

0257　See also **Bull.Amer.Geog. and Stat.Soc.** vol. 1 (1852), pp. 48—59. The sections of this letter published in each periodical differ significantly.

0260　Livingston dates this letter "Saturday evening;" the place is taken from the text; the date is from Schapera, **LPJ**, p. 76, n. 2.

0265　Brelsford, W.V. **Handbook of the David Livingstone Memorial Museum.** Northern Rhodesia: Rhodes—Livingstone Institute, 1937, p. 137 dates this fragment as 7 January 1852. However Robert Moffat 1 endorsed it "This letter is dated Jany 1852." Schapera, **DLFL** II, p. 166, n. 10 implies that the MS is in RHLO, where one finds a Ph copy of the original in the NMLZ. A TS copy of this elusive fragment, in ULSOASL, Africa, Odds, Box 10, folder 2, dates it "Cape Town, April 1852."

0274   See also **JRGSL**, vol. 22 (1852), p. 173, ex.

0275   See also Blaikie, **PLDL**, pp. 131–132.

0277   See also Balikie, **PLDL**, p. 132.

0278   In 1859 this letter was found in a wastebasket in a former residence of James Young.

0283   This letter is dated by Professor Isaac Schapera in the publication referred to.

0287   See also Blaikie, **PLDL**, pp. 133–135;   and Seaver, **DLLL**, pp. 155–156.

0290   See also Campbell, **Liv**, pp. 145–148.

0292   This letter is dated by Professor Isaac Schapera in the publication referred to.

0293   The final two pages of this letter contain Livingston's text of a speech made by Sechele. It is not published in the work cited.

0298   See also Gelfand, **LtD**, p. 60.

0304   MS copy in the hand of Ira Smith.   See also **PP** Sess. 1852–53, v. LXVI [1646], pp. 125–126.

0309   See also Sotheby's Cat. 20 Dec. 1937, lot 216, and 6 Jun. 1950, lot 306.

0311   See also **The Atlantic Monthly**, v. 130, no. 2 (Aug. 1922), pp. 212–213.

0312   Dated by Schapera, **DLFL** II, p. 204, n. 1.

0313   Following the death of Mary Livingstone on 27 Apr. 1862, James Stewart burned a number of David's letters to her, which she had given him, behind Shupanga House. This is the only letter Stewart preserved, probably by accident. It is this letter to which David refers when writing to Stewart on 7 Oct. 1864; "You are welcome to the letter you mention" (Wallis, **ZJJS**, p. 232), in reply to Stewart's offer to return it.

0316   In an unidentified newspaper dated 3 Jun. 1854, this letter is addressed to "his brother in Canada West."

0322   This letter is published in French.

0325   This letter is addressed to "My Dear Robert, Agnes, and Thomas, and Oswell." See also Blaikie, **PLDL**, pp. 148–149;   and Christie's Cat. 6 Apr. 1977, lot 17 (which gives the length and size).

0326   Livingstone heads page 1 of this letter "A true copy.   D.L.   To be returned" and concludes page 4 "A true copy to Mr. Wilson at Lake Ngami."

0328   An extract from this letter is in Glasgow University Library, MS. Gen. 539/6 (published in **NDLDSCA**, pp. 31–32, Myers' Cat., no. 360, Winter 1949, no. 5, and **The College Courant**, vol. 25, no. 50, 1973, p. 5). A signature of doubtful authenticity is appended to the extract.

0339   Livingstone's place for the middle date is "Cazengo."

0343   See also Blaikie, **PLDL**, pp. 166–167.

0346   Livingstone heads this letter "No. 5", indicating that he may have considered some of the letters in this collection listed above as mere postscripts.   This inconsistency continues to be apparent throughout the remainder of this series of letters Livingstone wrote to Gabriel in 1854–1856.

0359   Livingstone wrote no places for 20 and 23 January, when he was in Cassange.   Portions of this letter dated 5 and 18 Jan 1855 are published in **OB**, vol. III, No. 27 (Dec 1922), pp. 191–196;   portions dated 20 and 23 Jan 1855 are in **OB**, vol. III, No. 28 (Jan 1923), pp.289–290;   see also Sotheby's Cat. 3 May 1971, lot 276.   The NLS copy, acquired under Export Licence regulations, is sealed until 11 May 1978;   there is a copy in SNMDL.

0361   Livingstone denotes his place as "Cassange, Angola, West Coast of Africa."

0371   See also Blaikie, **PLDL**, pp. 172–173.

0373   Copy in the hand of Thomas Maclear, who gave the original to Rawson Rawson.

0375   This publication contains extracts from other Livingstone letters which are not easily identified, but which may be included in this listing.

0379   Livingstone wrote from the "Capital of Sekeletu, Linyanti, on the River Chobe."

0380   On further publication and copies see note to letter 0359.

0384   Livingstone lists his place as "Linyanti, banks of the Chobe River."

0389   An incomplete draft of this letter is in NARS, LI 1/1/1, pp. 178–202.

0390   An incomplete draft (or drafts) of this letter is in NARS, LI 1/1/1, pp. 204–240.

0391   Livingstone denotes his position as "River of the Bashukulompo near its Confluence with the Zambesi, Lat. 15° 47'S. Long. 28° 50'E."

0392   Livingstone's place of writing reads "Hill Chanyuné, on the banks of the Zambesi."   A draft in NARS, LI 1/1/1, pp. 266–288 reads "Opposite Chanyuné on the Zambesi."

0393   This letter was given by Gabriel to John S. Coker, agent of a Salem, Massachusetts trading concern in Loanda.   It is published as two letters.

0394   A photocopy of an MS copy of this letter in ULSOASL, Africa, Odds, Box 21 says that Maclear gave this letter to Sir George Grey at Grey's request.

0395   It is likely that this is a draft of the original.

0396   Livingstone denotes his place as "Southwest of Zambesi before reaching Tete."

0397   Livingstone denotes his place as "Tette or Nyunkwe the farthest inland station at present occupied by the Portuguese in Eastern Africa."

0401   The publication cited is in Portuguese;   between pp. 6 and 7 this letter is reproduced in facsimile.

0402   What seems to be a draft of this letter is in NARS, LI 1/1/1, pp. 387–394.

0405   This letter is published in Portuguese in **BOdGGdPdM**, 20 Feb. 1858, No. 8, pp. 35—36; 6 Mar. 1858, No. 10, pp. 42—43; 13 Mar. 1858, No. 11, pp. 47—48; and 17 Apr. 1858, No. 16, pp. 67—68; and in the **BOdGGdPdA**, 18 Mar. 1857, No. 600, pp. 8—11; and 4 Apr. 1857, No. 601, pp. 9—11.

0409   On further publication and copies see note to letter 0359.

0411   The published version dates this letter as 5 Apr. On further publication and copies see note to letter 0359.

0414   Drafts of this letter are in NARS, LI 1/1/1, pp. 413—444.

0415   See also Blaikie, **PLDL**, pp. 483—487. According to Schapera, **op. cit.**, this letter was never sent to Tidman.

0416   See also Blaikie, **PLDL**, pp. 483—487.

0421   On further publication and copies see note to letter 0359.

0423   Livingstone's place reads "At Sea, on Board H.M. Brig Frolic."

0428   This and all subsequent MS copies of letters from Livingstone to José Nuñes held by the NARS were copied in Nuñes' presence at Quilimane on (or around) 21 Apr. 1880 by Jane Elizabeth Waterston, Principal of the Girls' School at Lovedale and later a physician in Cape Town.

0429   A copy of this letter was sent to the Marquis de Loule by Henry Howard on 12 Nov. 1856; where the original lies remains to be seen. Archival copy by Emilio Achilles Monteverde, Secretary of State for Foreign Affairs.

0433   See also Maggs' Cat. No. 954 (Summer 1973), no. 91; and Sotheby's Cat. 11 May 1970, lot 159.

0441   Blomfield Street was the address of the L.M.S. Mission House.

0444   This letter does not appear in **The Times** between 18 and 25 Dec. 1857.

0445   This letter is published as though to John Ness, in spite of the fact that Livingstone wrote "Robert Kerr, Esqu" above the greeting. It is also published in **The Glasgow Herald**, 17 Mar. 1913, p. 11.

0447   See note to letter 0445. All applies likewise to this letter, except that in the absence of the original it cannot be ascertained if Livingstone wrote Kerr's name on the letter or not. The newspaper referred to prints this letter as to Kerr.

0448   Livingstone dates this letter merely "Tuesday morning." There is a possibility that it was written in 1858, or even in 1864—5, but the date indicated seems most likely.

0451   This letter, which Livingstone dates erroneously as 6 Jan. 1856, was written to an unidentified Y.M.C.A. official.

0452   Only the signature of this letter is in Livingstone's hand.

0453   The published version includes a facsimile.

0455   The address was Livingstone's lodging between 20 Jan and 23 May 1857. He left it to get away from dishonest owners and also from incessant interruptions caused by well-wishers as well as the curious.

0459   Livingstone wrote this letter to the Director of a Ragged School for Boys in Stockport.

0460   Livingstone wrote this letter for the eyes of the Earl of Clarendon, using Murchison as an intermediary.   A corrected draft, dated 24 Jan., is in Christie's Cat. 6 Apr. 1977, lot 19.

0463   Livingstone wrote this letter to an Edinburgh city official.

0472   MS copy in the hand of Robert G. McCallum, Warden, SNMDL.

0473   Livingstone signs his name "David Zambesi."

0475   The catalogue referred to gives the recipient as "Rev. Dr. Fielman", which the editors suspect may be a misreading for "Tidman".

0484   This letter may have been written in 1865.

0486   Copy in the hand of Emilio Achilles Monteverde, Secretary of State for Foreign Affairs.

0491   This letter was written later than letter 0490.

0493   What appears to be an early draft of this letter may be found at the beginning of the draft of Livingstone, MT (see Section 3, Books).

0494   The NLS copy, acquired under Export Licence regulations, is sealed until 20 Jan 1982; a TS copy is in NLS, MS. Acc. 6509.

0505   Livingstone wrote the date as April 20, then struck over the "0" to indicate 21.

0509   On the NLS copy see note to letter 0494.

0511   NLS, MS. Dep. 237 actually contains a Ph copy of the MS copy, and not the original of the MS copy as the table implies.

0513   This letter is a fragment of a copy sent to the L.M.S. by James I. Macnair.

0514   An MS copy in an unidentified hand fills four pages in Journal no. 6.

0516   This letter is probably written to the same Edinburgh city official as is letter 0463.

0521   Livingstone wrote this letter to the son of his childhood teacher, William Macskimming.

0522   Livingstone dates this letter merely "Monday morning".

0534   There is no letter under this number.

0550   This letter consists of Livingstone's replies to seven questions asked by J.S. Moffat, which were forwarded to Moffat in a letter from his sister, Mary Livingstone.

0561   Livingstone's place reads "London, Monday morning."

0563   The place of writing is printed on the stationery, and not written in Livingstone's hand. The address was and is that of John Murray, Publishers.

0567   This may well be a draft of a letter written to some official in the Admiralty.

0577   The first two pages of this letter contain an invitation to Livingstone from Archbishop Whately of Dublin.

0590   The address from which this was written was the home of Andrew Buchanan.

0610   On the NLS copy see the note to letter 0494.

0615   See also Sotheby's Cat. 7 Dec. 1976, lot 409.

0620   This and all subsequent letters written from Highbury New Park were written from Hadleigh House.

0628   On the NLS copy see the note to letter 0494.

0630   This is apparently a draft of the letter.

0645   This letter is written on page 3 of a 1/4/2 letter to Livingstone from G. Rennie & Sons, Engineers.

0650   See also Sotheby's Cat. 2 July 1962, lot 235.

0652   The NB in the place stands for North Britain, the nineteenth-century postal designation of Scotland.

0653   This letter was included in a presentation copy of **MT**.

0654   The date and place given for this letter make one wonder if one or the other is printed in error.

0655   See also Coupland, **KotZ**, p. 95.

0665   This letter is written on printed stationery, from "9, Great George Street, Westminster, S.W." which Livingstone struck over.

0673   See also Coupland, **KotZ**, p. 98.

0679   See also Coupland, **KotZ**, p. 99.

0681   The recipient's middle name was Livingstone.

0682   In letter 0678 Livingstone states that he will write to the son of a lady he had met who lived at 34 Berkeley Square, London; this was the residence of Lord and Lady Colchester, whose only son was at this time a sixteen-year-old schoolboy. It cannot however be proved conclusively that this is the letter referred to.

0683   Livingstone wrote this to the mother of the recipient of letter 0681.

0690   See also Sotheby's Cat. 9 Jun 1936, lot 500.

0696   This letter was written to one of the members of the Zambezi Expedition.

0710   See also Edwards' Cat. 1012 (1977), no. 304.

0719   The place on this letter is printed, and not in Livingstone's hand; as the address is that of the recipient, Livingstone may have written it elsewhere.

0722   See also Coupland, **KotZ**, p. 99.

0731   See also Coupland, **KotZ**, pp. 99—100.

0734   See also the Pr copy of letter 0674.

0736   The address is that of James Young.

0737   There is no letter under this number.

0738   See also Coupland, **KotZ**, p. 100.

0741   This is a draft of a letter Livingstone wrote for the Earl of Clarendon, who was to give him an official copy to present to various chiefs in South Central Africa.

0758   This may be an inscribed copy of **ALB** rather than a letter.

0765   See also Coupland, **KotZ**, pp. 103—108; Wallis, **ZEDL II**, pp. 420—425; Foskett, **ZJJK II**, pp. 599—605; and Sotheby's Cat. 21 Mar 1966, lot 182.

0769   Livingstone heads this letter "No. 4."

0770   Livingstone heads this letter "No. 5."

0778   See also Coupland, **KotZ**, p. 108; and Sotheby's Cat. 21 Mar 1966, lot 183.

0780   See also Moffat, **JSM**, pp. 57—58, and Seaver, **DLLL**, p. 320, ex.

0784   MS copy in English in the hand of José Maria Pereira e Almeida, Secretary to the Governor of Quilimane. Livingstone's copy in his journal no. 5 was not published by Wallis in **ZEDL**.

0785   MS copy in the hand of Thomas Maclear.

0787   Livingstone heads this letter "No. 7."

0794   Livingstone gives his place for the latter date simply as "Zambesi."

0799   See also **The Times**, 14 Sep. 1858, p. 10 c. 5. Seaver, **DLLL**, p. 327, claims that this letter was not sent; this can hardly be correct.

0800   Length and size taken from Sotheby's Cat. 6 Jun 1950, lot 308.

0802   Livingstone heads this item "Des. No. 8." It left the Zambezi for London in HMS "Hermes" bound for Cape Town. A duplicate in Livingstone's hand left on the "Pearl" bound for Ceylon, and is in PROL, FO 63/843 I, ff. 118—127.

0806   Written to an unnamed correspondent in Cape Town, this letter was printed in an unidentified Cape Town newspaper. Alfredo Duprat sent the newsclipping to Sá da Bandeira on 13 Jul 1858. It may be that this is from the letter to Maclear of the same date.

0811 See also Coupland, **KotZ**, p. 119, and Sotheby's Cat. 21 Mar 1966, lot 184.

0812 A copy in the hand of Charles Livingstone is in **NARS**, LI 1/1/1, pp. 812–813.   Much longer than the version printed by Wallis (**op. cit.**), this copy also includes Livingstone's letter to Bedingfeld of 12 Aug 1858.

0814 Livingstone heads this letter "1st part of No. 10."   Rough drafts of it are in **NARS**, LI 1/1/1, pp. 822–869.

0815 See note on letter 0812.

0816 During his tenure as Commander of the Zambezi Expedition, Livingstone often buried notes in bottles to be picked up by the first Royal Navy ship in the area, and he also gave letters to Portuguese officials in Moçambique to be delivered to the first such ship to arrive.   Such letters were almost invariably addressed to "Commander, H.M. Ship" (or equivalent expression), as Livingstone naturally could not know which vessel of the East Africa Squadron would be the next on the scene.

0817 Livingstone heads this letter "2d part of No. 10."   Although the copy in Livingstone's journal is also dated 16 Aug., Wallis publishes it as 6 Aug.

0819 See also Sawyer's Cat. SA/54 (1967), no. 40.

0822 The beginning of this letter is missing.   There is a TS copy in the **SALCT**, S.A. MSS. Sect. A; the **NLS** copy cited in the text is of this.

0823 This is apparently a draft of the letter to Malmesbury of 10 Sep.

0828 Length and size taken from Sotheby's Cat. 6 Jun. 1950, lot 308.

0831 Two further drafts/copies are in **NARS**, LI 1/1/1, pp. 893–900.

0835 Monk publishes this letter dated incorrectly as May 1858.   It is also published in Portuguese in the **BOdGGdPdM**, 15 Oct. 1859, No. 12, pp. 166–167, where it has been translated from an undated copy of the **Cape Monitor**.

0837 There is no letter under this number.

0839 See also Seaver, **DLLL**, p. 330, ex.

0840 Also published in **The Times**, 30 Dec. 1858, p. 7 c. 1, and in the **BOdGGdPdM**, 15 Oct 1859, No. 12, p. 167, where it has been translated from an undated copy of the **Cape Monitor**.

0842 Livingstone heads this letter "Supplementary note."

0845 As is the case with most letters from Livingstone to Maclear during this period, this letter contains both astronomical data and information of passing interest from many dates earlier than that upon which the letter was written.   Such items are too numerous to be entered in the "date" column.

0847 The published version dates this letter as 5 Oct.   See also Sotheby's Cat. 3 May 1971, lot 277.   On copies see note to letter 0359.

0851 Most of the MS copies in this collection are in the hand of James Young, and are exceptionally brief.

0853   Livingstone heads this letter "No. 12."   See also **JRGSL**, vol. 31 (1861), pp. 256–262.

0854   See also **Cape Monthly Magazine**, vol. 6 (1859), pp. 114–118.

0858   An extract copy in an unknown hand is in BLO, MSS. Wilber. c. 19, ff. 1–4.

0861   Livingstone erroneously dates this letter "13 Jany 1858."

0864   Livingstone's copy in his journal no. 5 was not published by Wallis, **ZEDL**.

0865   Livingstone heads this letter "No. 13 or No. 1 of 1859."   It is also published in **JRGSL,** vol. 31 (1861), pp. 262–264.

0867   This letter is published by Seaver as 5 Feb.

0873   See also **Cape Monthly Magazine**, vol. 6 (1859), pp. 114–118, and McLeod, **TiEA** I, pp. 231–234.

0875   A German translation of this letter is published in **MJPGA** 1860, pp. 149–150.

0876   The catalogue refers to this as a "carbon copy," implying that it is a TS copy.

0878   MS copy is in the hand of William Monk.

0879   Livingstone heads this letter "Slave Trade No. 2."   See also **PP Sess. 1860, v. LXX [181]** Class B, p. 110, ex.

0884   An extract copy in an unknown hand is in BLO, MSS. Wilber. c. 19, ff. 5–7.

0887   Livingstone wrote this letter in his Observation Notebook no. 3, and sent the book to Maclear as a later date.

0888   Livingstone heads this letter "No. 2."

0894   There is no letter under this number.

0895   See also Sotheby's Cat. 9. Jun 1936, lot 501.   A MS copy in the hand of William Monk is in KPLSA.

0900   See also Christie's Cat. 6 Apr. 1977, lot 20 (which gives the length and size).   The NLS copy, acquired under Export Licence regulations, is sealed until 13 June, 1984.

0903   This letter was picked up by HMS "Persian," Philip Saumarez commanding, on 25 Jul. 1859.

0904   The publication dates this letter 1 Jul. 1859.

0906   Most of this letter is a rough copy of Livingstone's dispatch to Malmesbury of 12 May 1859.   See also Sotheby's Cat. 3 May 1971, lot 278.   On copies see note to letter 0359.

0908   Also published in the **BOdGGdPdM**, 27 Aug. 1859, No. 55, p. 138, in Portuguese.

0910   See also Wallis, **ZEDL** I, pp. 112–113.

0911   MS copy in the hand of José Maria Pereira e Almeida, Secretary to the Governor of Quilimane.

0912   An extract copy in an unknown hand is in BLO, MSS. Wilber., c. 19, ff. 7—8.

0913   See also Wallis, **TBKL**, pp. 170—171.

0914   See also **South African Advertiser and Mail**, 6 Feb. 1861.

0917   Livingstone heads this letter "No. 3." Malmesbury's tenure as Secretary of State for Foreign Affairs ended in June 1859, but of course Livingstone had no way of knowing this. Inclosure No. 1 to this dispatch was the essay by Livingstone and Kirk entitled "Remarks on the African Fever in the Lower Zambesi" (see Section 3, Papers and Reports no. 15).

0918   Inclosure No. 2 is entitled "Report on the Navigation of the Zambesi."

0920   Monk publishes this date in error as 1 Jun 59.

0925   The NLS copy, obtained under Export Licence regulations, is sealed until 27 July 1983.

0927   This letter is discussed in Blaikie, **PLDL**, p. 262.

0934   This may be an extract of letter 0932.

0935   MS copy in the hand of James Young.

0937   See also Seaver, **DLLL**, pp. 356—357, ex.

0938   Although the manuscript is addressed to Russell, the published version is addressed to Malmesbury. While it is possible that the three inclosures following (0939—0941) should be associated with Livingstone's dispatch to Russell of 20 Nov 59, their position in Livingstone's journal as well as their subject matter indicate that the order presented here is more likely. Inclosure No. 3 is undated in the published version, leaving the remote possibility that it goes with 20 Nov 59 and that an Incl. No. 2 to that date is lost.

0942   Livingstone lists his position as "River Shire, Lat. 15° 55′ S., Long. 35° 1′ 30″ E."

0943   Nuñes gave this letter to Moir in 1878.

0944   See also Coupland, **KotZ**, p. 158, and Sotheby's Cat. 21 Mar 1966, lot 185.

0948   There is a TS copy in the SALCT, S.A. MSS. Sect A (copy in NLS, MS. 10780 (1)). See also Edwards' Cat. 691 (1948), no. 355.

0961   A German translation of this item is published in **MJPGA** 1860, pp. 160—161.

0962   This is a postscript to an unidentified letter of an earlier date; a copy in Livingstone's hand, with further comments, is included in letter 0988.

0965   As this letter implies but does not specifically mention the fact that Livingstone visited Lake Nyasa, it may be that the printed version is merely an extract.

0966   See also Sotheby's Cat. 21 Jun. 1977, lot 540A.

0972   This item is entitled "Statement respecting a turning lathe furnished by Mr. John Laird to the Zambesi Expedition."

0973   Livingstone heads this letter "No. 5."

0974   This item is entitled "Suggestions for the extension of lawful commerce into the slave market of Eastern Africa."

0975   Livingstone recorded an abbreviated version of this dispatch in his journal, and it is this which Wallis published. Livingstone heads this letter "No. 6."

0986   Wallis publishes this letter as though written to James Stewart, which is impossible since Livingstone did not meet Stewart until over two years later. Furthermore the salutation and tone of the letter are more intimate than in any known letter of Livingstone to Stewart. Blaikie, **PLDL**, pp. 266—267 publishes it as written to an unnamed Secretary of the Commission for a Universities' Mission.

0992   Livingstone heads this letter "No. 7."

0993   In his journal (published by Wallis), Livingstone dated this inclosure 27 Feb 60. The location of Inclosure No. 1 is not known.

1002   MS copy in the hand of James Young.

1007   On copies see the note to letter 0359.

1008,   Grey sent copies of these letters to the Duke of Newcastle on 6 Oct 1860, and these are
1013   now in UNLNNE, NeC 11023 and 11024 (photocopies in NLS, MS. 10779 (17)). Other copies are in the PROL, FO 63/871, ff. 456—63 and 464—9 (mircofilm in NLS, MS. 10780 (4)).

1015   See also Seaver, **DLLL**, pp. 363—364.

1016   An MS copy is in USPGL, B4 ii, 56—57.

1019   Livingstone heads this letter "No. 8."

1024   This letter is addressed by Livingstone to "O Capitão Mor de villa de Tette," the Chief-Captain of the settlement of Tete, who at that time was Candido José da Costa Cardoso.

1025   See note 1024 above.

1026   Although the date of this letter in Young's copy book seems to read 18 Jul., both **The Glasgow Herald** and Blaikie (**PLDL**, pp. 272—273, ex.) publish it as 22 Jul.

1028   This letter is not copied into the journal referred to, but is folded and placed between the end papers. All other letters with this location are MS aut copies unless otherwise specified, and are entered into the journal proper.

1030   Livingstone gives his place as "The Town Sesheke, in the Makololo Country, South-Central Africa."

1031   See note 1030. Livingstone heads this letter "No. 9." Also published in **JRGSL**, vol. 31 (1861), pp. 290—293, ex.

1034   Although there is no copy of this inclosure in the PROL, and in spite of the fact that letter 1043 (see relevant note below) is kept where one would expect to find this letter (compare entries in the location column), it is the compiler's opinion that letter 1034 is entered here in its proper place, and that the original manuscript has been lost.

1035   **The Glasgow Herald** reprinted this letter from the **Cape Argus**, 18 Apr. 1860.

1040   Livingstone heads this dispatch "No. 10." See also **JRGSL**, vol. 31 (1861), pp. 294–296.

1043   Livingstone addressed this item to the "Register General, General Register Office, Somerset House." On page 2 of this inclosure Livingstone wrote "Inclosure 3, Dispatch No. 9." However the subject matter of the item concerns marriages performed in his consular district, which H.M. Consuls were required to report annually near the year's end. Along with the information presented in note 1034 above, it is the compiler's opinion that Livingstone erred when writing "No. 9" on this inclosure: he should have written "No. 10." If this speculation is not correct, it is difficult to explain the existence of letter 1034, which Wallis publishes correctly (although out of order as written by Livingstone), but which most unfortunately Livingstone did not date. Nevertheless it is worth considering that Livingstone learned of the circumstance he describes in 1034 upon arrival at Sesheke in Aug. 1860, and it seems likely that he would have written his protest shortly thereafter, rather than waiting until late Dec. (should anyone think 1034 is Inclosure 3 to Dispatch No. 10 of 24 Nov. 1860). A further possibility is that Livingstone destroyed 1034 after copying it in his journal, never sent it, and substituted 1043 in its place, which although disarmingly simple and logical enough seems unlikely.

1049   Although "Robert Gray, Bishop of Cape Town" is pencilled atop this letter in an unidentified hand, Livingstone's salutation "My Dear Friend" suggests it was written to Maclear. He invariably addressed Maclear (and after his first return to Great Britain, very few others) in this manner, while always greeting Gray as "My Dear Bishop," "My Lord Bishop," or on one occasion (8 Apr. 1860) "My Dear Sir." Livingstone in 1049 may possibly have varied his practice, but as he was very conscious of and consistent in such matters, it is unlikely.

1057   Wallis, **op. cit.** pp. 360–361, publishes a postscript of 14 Aug. 1861, which can only be 14 Jan. 1861. This postscript was cancelled by Livingstone in the final version. A second MS aut copy is in NARS, LI 1/1/1, pp. 1180–1193. The postscript of 22 Jan. is undated in Wallis, **op. cit.** pp. 361–362.

1061   A more complete copy of this letter was published in **The Glasgow Herald**, 20 Jun. 1861, p. 2, as though written on 4 Dec. 1861.

1064   See also Wallis, **ZEDL** I, p. 177, and Martelli, **LR**, p. 163.

1069   A postscript to an earlier unidentified letter, this may have been written to either Robert Gray or Robert Moffat 2.

1075   This copy is an incomplete draft of the letter.

1076   Livingstone heads this letter "No. 1." A draft of it is in NARS, LI 1/1/1, pp. 1232–1239.

1083   Livingstone heads this draft "No. 2." Another, shorter draft is in NARS, LI 1/1/1, pp. 1248–1250. It may be that Livingstone never sent this dispatch, as there is no copy in the PROL, and as he heads his next dispatch "No. 2."

1085 This may have been an inclosure to letter 1084.

1087 Livingstone erroneously dates this letter 6 Feb. 1861.

1093 Livingstone heads this letter "No. 2."

1099 In the published version this letter is dated 25 Mar. 1859.

1100 Livingstone wrote the postscript from the home of William Sunley, Pomoni Bay, Ile d'Anjouan (Johanna). A short extract is published in the **PP Sess.** 1862, v. LXI [50] Class A, p. 134. An MS copy is in USPGL, B4 ii, ff. 72—80 (photocopy in NLS, MS. 10779 (15)).

1103 When Livingstone gave his place as "Johanna," he was usually in that island's captial city of Musamoodi; when elsewhere on the island, he usually preceded "Johanna" with "Pomony Bay," "H.M. Consulate," "Sunley's Residence," etc.

1104 Livingstone heads this letter "No. 3." His draft is in NARS, LI 1/1/1, pp. 1263—1272.

1112 MS aut copies are in MDNHLL, MSS. 120, and NARS, LI 1/1/1, pp. 1273—1275.

1116 The copy, made by Francisco de Salles Machada on 19 Jun. 1861, is in English.

1122 Livingstone heads this dispatch "No. 4." His brief notes for it are in NARS, LI 1/1/1, p. 1307 (photocopy NLS, MS. 10779 (21)).

1127 The date given is that of a postscript. This may be the end of letter 1126.

1128 Facsimiles of the first and last pages appear in Pachai, **LMA**, opposite pp. 153 and 184, and in Listowel, **TOL**, pp. 200 and 170.

1130 See also Seaver, **DLLL**, p. 421.

1136 The MS copy is in Mackenzie's hand, in his journal entry for 12 Nov. 1861.

1137 Livingstone heads this dispatch "No. 5." It is published without the postscript in Wallis, **ZEDL** II, pp. 401—407.

1138 See also Wallis, **ZEDL** II, pp. 409—410.

1139 See also Wallis, **ZEDL** II, p. 409, where a paragraph is omitted and the text differs.

1140 See also Wallis, **ZEDL** II, pp. 407—409, where it is published as Inclosure No. 1.

1142 What may be NS copies of this letter are in RGSL, DL 3/11/2 and MDNHLL, MSS. 120.

1145 See also **South African Advertiser and Mail**, 21 May 1862, and **Cape Monthly Magazine**, vol. 11 (1862), pp. 269—271.

1157 Livingstone heads this letter "P.S." and it is probably a postscript to letter 1146.

1158 This letter may be to Samuel Wilberforce or Robert Gray.

1160 Livingstone heads this letter "No. 6."

1161 There is no letter under this number.

1164   The complete publication reference is: **John Bull**, vol. 42, no. 2172 (Saturday, 26 Jul. 1862), p. 474, c. 3, and p. 475, c. 1. Extracts of this letter appeared in various newspapers, such as **The Daily News**, 12 Aug. 1862; **The Glasgow Herald**, 7 Aug. 1862, p. 4, c.1 (reprinted from the **Liverpool Mercury**); **The Glasgow Herald**, 13 Aug. 1862, p. 4, c. 3; **The Times**, 20 Aug. 1862, p. 8, c. 7; and also in **The Athenaeum**, No. 1818 (30 Aug. 1862), p. 279. A German translation is published in **MJPGA** 1863, p. 109.

1175   The MS has been torn into several pieces and reassembled using staples.

1176   In a similar condition, this may be a postscript to letter 1175.

1178   This is probably the second half of letter 1177.

1180   An MS copy of this letter is in the PROL, FO 63/894 II, ff. 23—24.

1185   Livingstone heads this dispatch "No. 1." His draft is in NARS, LI 1/1/1, pp. 1361—1368.

1186   Livingstone's draft is in NARS, LI 1/1/1, p. 1372.

1187   A draft in an unidentified hand is in NARS, LI 1/1/1, pp. 1369—1371.

1189   Livingstone's copy is in Journal no. 9, pp. 236—240.

1195   The 12 Mar. portion of this letter is also published in Wells, **SoL**, pp. 84—85.

1196   This is a draft of letter 1204.

1199   See also Sotheby's Cat. 31 Oct. 1950, lot 174, and 9 Apr. 1974, lot 658.

1200   Livingstone heads this letter "Separate"; his copy is in the NARS, LI 1/1/1, pp. 1381—1384.

1201   The date and place on this MS were added in an unidentified hand, perhaps Braithwaite's.

1205   An MS copy of this letter is in the PROL, FO 63/894 II, ff. 35—37.

1212   The date and place were added to this MS in an unidentified hand.

1238   The published version dates this as 25 Jun 62.

1239   Also published in the **South African Advertiser and Mail**, 25 Aug. 1862; a shorter version is in the **JRGSL**, vol. 33 (1863), p. 273.

1240   Livingstone heads this dispatch "No. 2." His copy is in Journal no. 9, pp. 55—60.

1241   Livingstone heads this dispatch "No. 3." His copy is in Journal no. 9, pp. 198—199.

1245   A copy in English in an unidentified hand is in the AHUL, Moçambique Papeis, Pasta 19.

1248   The copy is in English, in an unidentified hand.

1258   Livingstone's copy is in Journal no. 9, pp. 78—87.

1259   Livingstone's copy is in Journal no. 9, pp. 87—89.

1262   The two sheets of this letter came to the NLS from different sources at different times. The publication given is of the first sheet only; for the second see Christie's Cat. 6 Apr. 1977, lot 22. A TS copy of the second sheet is in ULSOASL, Africa, Odds, Box 10, folder 4.

1264   There is no letter under this number.

1267   Livingstone heads this dispatch "No. 4." His copy is in Journal no. 9, p. 93.

1269   This may in fact by a draft of the letter.

1270   This may be a postscript to letter 1265.

1275   See also **The Times**, 13 Jan 1863, p. 5, c. 5, and **PRGSL**, vol. VII (1862–63), pp. 52–53.

1276   The published version is not of the actual letter, but of the recipient's summary of it in his logbook.

1277   The version Wallis published is dated 10 Oct 1862; extracts are in Blaikie, **PLDL**, p. 309, and Seaver, **DLLL**, pp. 421–422.

1280   Livingstone heads this letter "No. 5." A copy in Charles Livingstone's hand is in Journal no. 9, pp. 99–106.

1282   This is a postscript to a recent letter to one of his children, perhaps to letter 1274; the published version indicates that it was written to his mother (i.e. PS to letter 1263).

1286   Although in Portuguese, this may be a draft.

1288   Livingstone erroneously dates this letter "17 Oct. 1862."

1296   Livingstone's Trustees were Andrew Buchanan, James Hannan, and James Young. This is copy of two letters to them sent together.

1297   Livingstone heads this dispatch "No. 6." His copy is in Journal no. 9, p. 111.

1299   Middle pages from this letter may be missing.

1301   The copy is in the hand of Francisco de Salles Machada. Livingstone's copy is in Journal no. 9, p. 112.

1304   See also Wells, **SoL**, pp. 85–86.

1305   Livingstone's copy is in Journal no. 9, p. 111.

1306   Livingstone heads this dispatch "No. 7." His copy is in Journal no. 9, pp. 113–119.

1307   Livingstone's copy is in Journal no. 9, pp. 133–138. He heads this item "Separate of No. 7." Inclosures 1–3 are not by Livingstone, but were forwarded by him to the Foreign Office.

1308   MS copy in the hand of Francisco de Salles Machada. Livingstone's copy is in Journal no. 9, pp. 139–142.

1310   This letter is written to an unidentified Portuguese Bishop.

1313   See also Goodwin, **MoBM**, pp. 262—263, ex.

1316   Livingstone heads this dispatch "No. 1." His copy is in Journal no. 9, pp. 144—149.

1324   This letter is an extract of a letter from George Tozer to T. Harry Woodcock dated 15 May 1863. As the content is similar to that of letter 1325, it may be that Tozer erred in referring to Nuñes as "Col." and that letter 1324 is a phantom.

1329   Addressed to "Captain of Any Man of War Touching at Mozambique," this letter was delivered to Admiral Sir Baldwin W. Walker at Cape Town by Commander John Wilson of H.M.S. "Gorgon."

1334   See also Sotheby's Cat. 9 Jun 1936, lot 496.

1337   The NLS copy is in Murchison's hand.

1338   Livingstone addressed this letter "To Captain of H.M. Ship, Mozambique Channel."

1339   Livingstone heads this letter "No. 2." His copy is in Journal no. 9, pp. 189—192.

1340   Livingstone's copy is in Journal no. 9, pp. 186—187.

1341   Livingstone's copy is in Journal no. 9, pp. 187—188.

1342   According to Chadwick, **MG**, p. 185, no. 1, Livingstone erred in dating this letter, which should have read "21 April 1863."

1344   Foskett publishes this letter dated "1863?"

1347   Livingstone heads this letter "**Private** and **Confidential**." His copy is in Journal no. 9, pp. 193—196.

1348   This is a postscript to letter 1334.

1354   See also Sotheby's cat. 21 Mar. 1966, lot 186.

1365   See also Sotheby's cat. 21 Mar. 1966, lot 187, and 23 Jun. 1969, lot 161.

1378   As this letter is neither in the PROL nor copied in Livingstone's Journal, it may be that this is a draft that was not sent.

1380   The date and place of this letter read merely "Thursday, 17th 2 P.M." At this time Livingstone was a day off in his reckoning (17 April 1863 was a Friday); this letter is dated from information contained in letter 1379.

1382   Livingstone heads this letter "No. 3." His copy is in Journal no. 9, pp. 206—211.

1383   Livingstone's copy is in Journal no. 9, pp. 213—217.

1384   This letter is written to either John or Neil Livingstone, David's nephew in Canada.

1394   This item appears in a printed testimonial for E.D. Young addressed to the Lords of the Treasury, published in Sep—Oct 1891 by Agnes Livingstone (3) Bruce and others interested in Young's application for a pension.

1400   The published version consists of summaries of Livingstone's letters to Washington and Murchison of 4 Dec 1863 (1399 and 1400).

1402   See also Sotheby's Cat. 21 Mar 1966, lot 188.

1407   Livingstone heads this dispatch "No. 4." His copy is in Journal no. 9, pp. 219–230.

1408   Livingstone's copy is in Journal no. 9, pp. 231–233.

1410   This is a draft copy. Livingstone's copy is in Journal no. 10, pp. 1–3, written in an unidentified hand.

1415   Livingstone may have considered this a PS to letter 1401.

1419   This letter is written in Portuguese.

1423   Livingstone considered this a PS to an earlier (unidentified) letter.

1425   See also Blaikie, **PLDL**, pp. 326–327, where it is dated 24 Feb. 1864.

1433   This copy is entered in the journal in an unidentified hand.

1436   See note 1394; this letter is in the same item.

1444   Livingstone gives his place as "Lady of Nyassa, Bombay Harbour."

1445   At that time Bombay had two Deputy Commissioners of Customs: Forster Fitzgerald Arbuthnot and Gilbert Wray Elliot.

1448   This is a postscript to an earlier unidentified letter.

1450   This is on printed stationery, thus Livingstone may have written the letter from another location.

1470   See also Sotheby's Cat. 14 Feb. 1929, lot 844.

1473   Livingstone wrote on this letter: "To Hamilton Young Men's Association."

1475   See also Sotheby's Cat. 31 Oct. 1950, lot 240.

1495   The stationery is printed: "Newstead Abbey" is not in Livingstone's hand. Livingstone wrote so many letters on such stationery that no further notice will be taken in the notes unless it is evident that the letter in question was written at a place other than Newstead. There are several types of such stationery, including block captials in red, blue, and black, each of which may be embossed or otherwise; colorless embossed; and black longhand script, to name eight of the most common. The paper is almost universally ivory-coloured. In many cases the type of stationery may give a clue to the date the letter was written. As this chronological listing of Livingstone's letters indicates, more letters written by him from Newstead Abbey than from any other location have survived.

1521   The catalogue in which this item appears has it dated 31 Oct 1866.

1531   This letter is on printed stationery and is dated by Livingstone merely "Monday morning."

1532   This letter is on printed stationery.

1541   Livingstone corrected to this date after writing "24 Oct."

1547   This letter is published in error as 3 Nov. 1864.

1566   This may be a postscript to an earlier unidentified letter.

1579   Livingstone's copy is in Journal no. 10, p. 372.

1625   Livingstone heads this item "PS to Preface."

1636   On printed stationery, the complete place of which reads: "Paraffin Light Company, 19, Bucklersbury, London, E.C.", which was James Young's London office.   The paper is edged in black.

1638   This letter is written on paper edged in black.

1660   This letter is dated from the words "Newstead Abbey" written on it in pencil in an unidentified hand, and from a sentence in the text.   Nevertheless it could very well have been written in 1857.

1663   In the published version this letter is erroneously dated as 30 Apr. 1865.

1671   Although an unidentified hand wrote "Walker Brodie, 29 Park Road, Havestock Hill, London N.W." across the top of this letter, it is the compiler's opinion that Livingstone wrote it to Arthington, who in turn gave it to Brodie.

1691   Livingstone's place and date read merely "One o'clock Monday."

1694   The published version dates this letter erroneously as 14 Apr. 1865.

1696   Note to letter 1671 applies equally to this letter.

1705   This letter is written on printed stationery similar to that of letter 1636, but without the black edging.

1712   Livingstone's place and date read merely "Monday."

1713   Livingstone's place and date read merely "Monday morning."

1716   This letter is addressed to "The Secretary of State for Foreign Affairs."

1719   See also Sotheby's Cat. 17 May 1922, lot 507.

1726   Another extract of this letter may be published in Blaikie, **PLDL**, pp. 353–354.

1732   A shorter extract is published in Simpson, **DC**, p. 53.   See also Sotheby's Cat. 6 Jun 1950, lot 313.

1744   The place on this stationery, and on that of letters 1745–1748 is printed in red Old English type.

1749   The paper of this letter is edged in black, as a sign of Livingstone's mourning at the death of his mother.   Other letters so edged from this period are 1750–1754, 1756–1759, 1762, 1764, 1769, 1774, 1775, 1778, 1781, 1792, 1793, and 1801.   As the manuscripts of letters 1755, 1765, 1777, 1779, 1780, and 1782 have not been examined, it may be that some of them are also edged in black.   This is theoretically possible for any of the remaining letters written by Livingstone up through his departure from England in mid-August 1865.

1760   This and letter 1761 are written on printed stationery.

1762   This letter is bound into the volume back to front.

1767   This and letter 1768 are written on printed stationery.

1772   This letter is a postscript to letter 1771, and is written on pages 3—4 of a 1/4/2 letter from James Brooke ("of Sarawak") to Livingstone, dated 18 Jul 1865.

1777   See also Sotheby's Cat. 9 Jun 1936, lot 505.

1782   Livingstone's salutation reads simply "My Lord."

1786   The conjunction of the two fragments of this letter is due to the editors.

1789   See also Myers' Cat. No. 1 (Spring, 1958), no. 175, where the recipient is given as Angela Burdett-Coutts;   however this letter refers to an evening with Queen Emma, and it was at Lady Franklin's that Livingstone met her in the evening, having had lunch with her at Miss Burdett-Coutts'(Journal no. 10 for 8 Aug 1865, quoted by Blaikie, **PLDL**, p. 356).

1791   Seaver publishes this letter erroneously as dated 7 Aug 1863.

1792   Murchison destroyed the first four pages of this letter.

1797   An envelope addressed to Mr John Loader, Thame, Oxfordshire, apparently relates to this letter.

1798   The date is added to this letter in an unidentified hand.

1802   There is no letter under this number.

1805   This letter is bound into the volume back to front.

1806   There is no letter under this number.

1810   See also Fraser, **L&N**, p. 164, ex.

1813   The pages of this letter have been bound in the wrong order;   they should be read as follows: 113, 114, 112, and 111.

1814   Livingstone records his position as "Near Alexandria on board S.S. Massilia."

1816   This is apparently a postscript to one of letters 1811, 1813, or 1815.

1819   Livingstone wrote this letter from "G.M. Stewart's, Esq, Kambala Hill, Bombay."

1836   This is a postscript to an earlier unidentified letter.   Livingstone gives the date and place merely as "14th."

1844   Livingstone's copy is in Journal no. 11, pp. 9—13.

1850   This letter is written on the three blank pages of a 1/4/1 letter from John Wekotani to Horace Waller, dated "Bombay, 30 November 1865."

1857   Livingstone wrote from "Mr. Tracey's, Kambala Hill."

1860   This letter was probably written before 26 Dec.

1871   See also Starritt, **LtP**, p. 121, ex.   Livingstone gives his position as "Crossing the Line in Long. 49° E."

1875   This letter is reprinted from the **New York Herald,** 29 Aug 1872.

1879   See note to letter 1875.

1882   See note to letter 1875.

1887   See also Maggs' Cat. No. 798 (1950), no. 430.   This is the letter referred to by Genesta Hamilton, **Princes of Zinj** (Lond., 1957), p. 138 n., as having been found by soldiers of the Black Watch in 1955 in a shack in the Aberdare forest in Kenya (copy of letter from Rev. W.G.A. Wright, chaplain to the Black Watch, to Rev. Dr. James I. Macnair, 28 Feb 1955, in Glasgow University Archives).

1888   Livingstone heads this letter "No. 1."

1892   Livingstone heads this letter "No. 2."   See also **PRGSL**, vol. XI (1866–67), pp. 15–17.

1894   Livingstone erroneously dates this letter 18 Mar 1866; his place reads "Ingomano, Confluence of Rovuma & Loendi."

1896   Livingstone heads this dispatch "Political, Slave Trade No. 1."   His place reads "East Africa, Lat. 11° 18' South, Long. 37° 10' East."   His copy is in Journal no. 11, pp. 131–143.

1900   The two Copy Books in the RCSL were compiled for and/or by Sir John Gray.

1901   See also Sotheby's Cat. 9 Jun 1936, lot 504.

1902   Livingstone gives the position of Bemba as "10° 10' S. + 31° 50' E."   There is a TS copy of the postscript in RCSL, Copy Book I.

1903   See also Sotheby's Cat. 16 Feb. 1926, lot 472, and 6 Jun. 1950, lot 316.

1904   Waller published the date of this letter as "September, 1866."   Extracts from the postscript are published in **PP** Sess. 1871, v. XII [420], p. 87.

1905   Livingstone gives the position of the Chipeta country as "Lat. 14° 8' S., Long. 33° E."

1907   This letter may well be a printed copy of letter 1906.   See also **Christian News,** 25 Apr. 1868, p. 11.

1908   Livingstone heads this letter "No. 2, Geographical."   See also **PP** Sess. 1868–69, v. LVI [145] Class B, pp. 17–18.   He gives his position as "Lat. 10° 11' South, Long. 31° 50' East."

1911   There is no letter under this number.

1912   An MS copy of this letter is in RGSL, Archives, DL 4/4/5.   It is published in **PP** Sess. 1868–69, v. LVI [145] Class B, pp. 67–68, and **PRGSL**, vol. XII (1867–68), pp. 179–180.

1917   Livingstone gives his place as "Country called Lobemba, vil. Molemba."

1918   A German translation is published in **MJPGA**, 1870, pp. 185—186.

1923   Livingstone gives the position of Casembe's as "Lat. 9° 3—7'13"S., Long. 28° E." As he was low on paper at this time, this letter was never sent.

1925   See also **PRGSL**, vol. XIII (1868—69), pp. 8—9.

1928   See also **The Athenaeum**, No. 2194 (13 Nov 1869), p. 631, ex.

1930   See also **The Times**, 6 Nov. 1869, p. 5 c. 4.

1932   See also **PP** Sess. 1870, v. LXI [C—141] Class B, pp. 13—16. A German translation is published in **MJPGA**, 1870, pp. 186—189. Letter 1934 refers to a copy Livingstone sent to Thomas Maclear, requesting that Maclear return it as Livingstone was low on paper and this was his only copy. The location of the original is not known, though it is probably somewhere in the PROL.

1933   This item is entitled "Privately printed for the perusal of Dr. Livingstone's personal friends only." A long paragraph from this letter is published by Martineau, **LCBF** II, pp. 115—116, dated Jul 1867.

1938   See also **The Times**, 13 Dec 1869, p. 9 c. 6, and **The Bombay Gazette**, 20 Nov 1869. A German translation is published in **MJPGA** 1870, p. 189.

1939   Starritt, **LtP**, pp. 126—30 dates this letter Nov — Dec 1867.

1940   See also Starritt, **LtP**, pp. 131—132, ex.

1941   Starritt dates this letter Nov — Dec 1867.

1942   See also **Cape Monthly Magazine**, n.s. vol. 10 (1875), pp. 65—70, and Starritt, **LtP**, pp. 130—131, ex.

1943   See also **The Times**, 28 Apr. 1874, p. 7 c. 5.

1944   Livingstone's place reads "Manyuema Country, say 150 miles West of Ujiji."

1945   Livingstone writes this letter from "the country of the Manyuema who are reputed to be cannibals, and about 150 miles N.W. of Ujiji on Lake Tanganyika."

1946   Livingstone writes this letter from "Manyuema or Cannibal Country, say 180 miles W. of Ujiji."

1947   There is no letter under this number.

1948   There is no letter under this number.

1949   There is no letter under this number.

1950   Livingstone writes from "Bambarre = Manyuema country, say about 150'W. of Ujiji." His copy is in Journal no. 11, pp. 537—550. He heads this dispatch "No. 1." See also **The Times**, 6 Aug. 1872, p. 12, and **LFDL**, pp. 246—258.

1951   Livingstone writes from "Manyuema country, say 180 miles W. of Ujiji." This is basically another draft or copy of letter 1950, with the different place and different ending.

1952   Livingstone considered this letter a postscript to letter 1944.

1954   Livingstone writes from "Manyuema country, say 180 miles W. of Ujiji." See also **The Times**, 13 Aug. 1872, p. 9 c. 5.

1957   See also **Cape Monthly Magazine**, n.s. vol. 5 (1872), pp. 242–249. There is a TS copy, erroneously dated Sep 1870, in RCSL, Copy Book I.

1958   See also **New York Herald**, 27 Nov 1872.

1959   Livingstone's heading reads simply "PS."

1960   Livingstone considered this a postscript to letter 1954.

1961   Livingstone's copy is in Journal no. 11, p. 535.

1962   See also Blaikie, **PLDL**, p. 405, ex. There is a TS extract, erroneously dated Sep 1870, in RCSL, Copy Book I.

1964   The copy, in an unidentified hand, is written on India Office stationery.

1965   The heading on this letter reads "PS 2nd."

1966   See note to letter 1964.

1967   Livingstone heads this "3rd PS." It is written across a printed page reporting an **R.G.S.L.** meeting of 8 Nov 1869.

1968   Written on paper similar to that of letter 1967, this letter is also published in Coupland, **LLJ**, pp. 109–114. Livingstone wrote from "Webb's Lualaba or Lacustrine River across another great bend to the West of about 100°."

1969   Livingstone wrote from "Webb's Lualaba or Lacustrine River." See also Blaikie, **PLDL**, pp. 405–407, ex. There is a TS extract, erroneously dated Sep 1870, in RCSL, Copy Book I.

1970   This and letter 1971 are written on the same piece of paper. See also Coupland, **LLJ**, pp. 115–116.

1971   See note to letter 1970, and Coupland, **LLJ**, pp. 116–117.

1972   Printed by the Government of India, Foreign Department, No. 17 of 1872. See also **The Times**, 27 Sep 1872, p. 3 c. 3.

1973   See also **The Times**, 27 Sep 1872, p. 3 c. 3; **LFDL**, pp. 291–296; **PP Sess.** 1872, v. LXX [C–598], pp. 15–17; and the Government of India print referred to in note to letter 1972, which gives a third postscript dated 15 Nov. Livingstone's copy is in Journal no. 11 pp. 583–589.

1974   This dispatch is headed "No. 2, Geographical." See also **The Times**, 6 Aug 1872, p. 12; **PP Sess.** 1872, v. LXX [C–598], pp. 6–10. Livingstone's copy is in Journal no. 11, pp. 554–564, in the hand of Henry M. Stanley. An extract German translation is published in **MJPGA** 1872, p. 405.

1975   See also **The Times**, 6 Aug. 1872, p. 12; **PP Sess.** 1872, v. LXX [C–598], pp. 5–6. Livingstone's copy is in Journal no. 11, pp. 551–553, in the hand of Henry M. Stanley.

1977   See also **The Times**, 6 Aug. 1872, p. 12;   **PP** Sess. 1872, v. LXX [C–598], pp. 10–15. Livingstone's copy is in Journal no. 11, pp. 565–583.

1978   The NLS copy, obtained under Export Licence regulations, is sealed until 3 August 1979.

1980   The Government of India print cited in note to letter 1972 also has this item, including a postscript dated 16 Nov.

1981   See also Blaikie, **PLDL**, pp. 426–427, and **Cape Monthly Magazine**, n.s. vol. 5 (1872), pp. 242–249.   There is a TS extract, erroneously dated 18 Aug 1872, in RCSL, Copy Book II.

1983   See also Stanley, **HIFL** (1890), pp. 486–489;   **LFDL**, pp. 219–224;   **New York Herald**, 26 Jul 1872;   **The Times**, 27 Jul 1872, p. 5 c. 3;   **The Daily News**, 27 Jul 1872, p. 5 c. 3.

1985   The date and opening of this letter are on p. 5;   the preceding four pages were apparently written in the Manyuema country.

1987   See also **PP** Sess. 1872, v. LXX [C–598], pp. 17–19.

1989   Livingstone heads this letter "PS to a letter written long ago in Manyuema," referring to letters 1954 and 1961.   See also **The Times**, 13 Aug. 1872, p. 9 c. 5.

1990   Livingstone writes this letter from "Ten Days East of Tanganyika," and "Unyanyembe."

1991   Livingstone writes this letter from "About 12 days East of Tanganyika."

1992   Livingstone writes this letter from "Ngombe Nullah, near Speke's Kazeh."

1994   Livingstone heads this letter "PS" — probably to letter 1984.

1995   Livingstone writes this letter from "District of Unyanyembe about 2' South by Speke's Kazeh."   A bonded photocopy of this letter in the NLS will be opened on 25 Sep 1977; The NLS copy mentioned in the text is a TS.

1996   Livingstone heads this letter "No. 5," and writes it from "Unyanyembe = near the Kazeh of Speke."   See also **The Times**, 6 Aug. 1872, p. 12;   **PP** Sess. 1872, v. LXX [C–598] , pp. 19–24.   Livingstone's copy is in Journal no. 11, pp. 737–742 and 767–769;   three leaves of this copy are missing from the journal.   A portion of another copy of this dispatch is in the NARS, LI 1/1/1, pp. 2290–1, headed "Continuation of des. No. 5." A further fragment is in the BLL, Add. MS. 50184, ff. 180–181.

1997   There is no letter under this number.

1998   This letter is published by Foskett as 28 Feb, and the true date is debatable.   See also **The Times**, 27 Sep 1872, p. 3 c. 3;   Stanley, **HIFL** (1872), pp. 707–708;   and the Government of India print cited in note to letter 1972.   There is a TS extract in RCSL, Copy Book I.

1999   Also published in the **New York Herald**, 27 Jul 1872, and **The Times**, 27 Jul 1872, p. 12 c. 1.   See aslo Sotheby's Cat. 29 Jun 1939, lot 1488.

2000   There is no letter under this number.

2001   Livingstone wrote from "Unyanyembe, near Speke's Kazeh."

2002   Livingstone heads this letter "PS", perhaps to letters 1984 and 1994. It is written from "Unyanyembe, 2' south of Speke's Kazeh."

2003   Copy in the hand of G. Gildy(?).

2004   This is a postscript to letter 2001.

2005   Also published in Stanley, **HIFL** (1890), pp. xlviii—lii.

2006   Livingstone wrote from "Unyanyembe, i.e. Sixty Days Smart Marching from the East Coast, Africa." Published in the **New York Herald**, 21 Sep 1872.

2007   A facsimile of this was published in the "Supplement to the Graphic," 10 Aug. 1872, which may easily be mistaken for the original.

2008   Also published in Stanley, **HIFL** (1890), pp. 500—501. Livingstone addressed this letter "To Henry M. Stanley, Esquire, wherever he may be found."

2010   Livingstone wrote from "Unyanyembe—Kwihara near Kaze." This letter was published in **The Times**, 23 Oct 1872, p. 5 c. 5, and **The Glasgow Herald**, 22 Oct 1872, p. 4 c. 1.

2011   **The Times**, 19 Oct 1872, p. 9 c. 6 mentions this letter as being dated 1 Jul 1872.

2012   See also **LFDL**, pp. 318—320 and **PRGSL**, vol. XVI (1871—72), pp. 440—441.

2013   Livingstone heads this dispatch "No. 1, 1872." See also **LFDL**, pp. 321—328; **PRGSL**, vol. XVI (1871—72), pp. 437—440; and **The Times**, 22 Oct 1872, p. 10 c. 1.

2015   Livingstone heads this letter "PS", probably to a letter not known at this time.

2017   There is no letter under this number.

2022   See also Seaver, **DLLL**, p. 614, and Sotheby's Cat. 27 Feb 1962, lot 531. There is a TS copy of the extract in Blaikie in RCSL, Copy Book II, wrongly stated to be addressed to Thomas Livingstone.

2023   There is no letter under this number.

2025   Seaver indicates that this letter was written from the south side of Lake Bangweolo.

2026   See also **The Times**, 28 Apr 1874, p. 7 c. 5.

2027   This letter was never completed and was found in Livingstone's papers after his death. See also **Cape Monthly Magazine**, n.s. vol. 8 (1874), pp. 380—383.

2029   See also **The Times**, 28 Apr 1874, p. 7 c. 5, and Sotheby's Cat. 20 May 1969, lot 404. An MS copy of this letter is in the RGSL, DL 4/18/2. This letter is sufficiently different from letter 2028 to warrant inclusion here as a separate entity.

2030   See also Stanley, **HIFL** (1890), pp. lxx—lxxi.

2032   This undated item is addressed to "Your Lordship," and was received at the Foreign Office on 7 Apr 1874.

APPENDIX 2

OBSERVATIONS ON THE SPELLING OF LIVINGSTONE

Anyone who works with Livingstone's papers for any length of time soon notices that in many cases he signed his name "Livingston," thus omitting the final "e" which is included in the universally accepted method of spelling his name today. This was no slip of the mind or pen on Livingstone's part — such documents are far too numerous — but was in fact the way the family chose to spell the name during the first two-thirds of Livingstone's life. While it is generally agreed that Livingstone added the final "e" at his father's suggestion or insistence, it is not always agreed upon as to why Neil Livingstone wished to have the change made. As a beginning toward examining this problem in detail, let us turn to the information provided by some of the missionary-explorer's greatest biographers.

Blaikie, who wrote with the active support of Livingstone's siblings and children, notes simply: "David wrote it for many years in the abbreviated form, but about 1857, at his father's request, he restored the original spelling."[1] Almost fifty years later J.R. Campbell elaborates on Blaikie's implications: "The family name at this period [i.e. the period of Neil Livingstone's father] appears to have been spelt without the final e and continued to be so until about the middle of the 19th century, when for some reason the longer form was adopted, probably as being more in harmony with the usage of other Scottish Livingstones."[2] James Macnair advances a different reason: "A tradition which may well be correct says that Neil, the father, objected to 'Livingston' because local pronunciation turned the 'stone' into 'stun', and that David fell in with the old man's wish and changed the spelling. The change 'dates' all manuscripts, 1857 being the dividing line."[3] Simmons however disagrees with Blaikie and Macnair as far as the effective date of the change is concerned, and writes that David "abandoned Livingston" in 1855.[4] Two years later Seaver supported Simmons, noting that the change was made "about the year 1855."[5]

Tim Jeal goes into greater detail on this point than any of his predecessors, observing that Livingstone spelled his name without the "e" "until the latter part of 1855," and adding that Neil (and not his father as Campbell wrote) dropped the "e" "because he thought his name long enough without it." He goes on to comment: "For reasons best known to himself, he [Neil] resumed it in the mid-fifties. Shortly after using the final 'e' in spelling his name on the title deeds of a new cottage in Hamilton, he wrote to the children asking them to revert to the old spelling. David Livingstone did so from September 1855."[6] Listowel merely notes that he changed the spelling in 1857 at his father's request.[7]

From among the group of biographers briefly discussed above, Jeal seems closest to the apparent truth. His source of information is no less an authority than David's sister Janet, who in 1879 or 1880 prepared notes to assist Blaikie in preparing Livingstone's "official" biography. She wrote "My father's family all spelt their name with the e at the end but my Father thought the name long enough without the e and spelt his name Livingston, but when the title deeds for our cottage & garden came to be drawn out he resumed the e and wrote to his sons to do the same."[8]

1	Blaikie, **PLDL**, p. 2.
2	Campbell, **Liv**, p. 29.
3	Macnair, **LtL**, p. 372.
4	Simmons, **LaA**, p. 1, n. 1.
5	Seaver, **DLLL**, p. 15.
6	Jeal, **Liv**, "Note on Spelling," p. [xvi].
7	Listowel, **TOL**, ch. 1, n. 1, on p. [268].
8	NLS, MS. 10767, f. 17.

The cottage to which Janet refers still stands on Burnbank Road in Hamilton, and she indicates that it was built in 1852, when she and her sister Agnes went into the millinery business. Exactly when the deeds were drawn out remains to be discovered, but from letters written by members of the family it is possible to narrow down the date somewhat. On 18 November 1852, Mary Livingstone wrote a letter to the London Missionary Society from 46 Almada Street, Hamilton, where the family had lived since mid-1839 at the very latest; in this letter Mary's signature bears the final "e".[9] A letter from Neil Livingstone to the L.M.S. from the same address on 14 April 1852 did not include the "e", but his letter to Arthur Tidman from Ingraham Cottage, Burnbank Road, Hamilton of 25 June 1853 did incorporate the change.[10] It appears then that the change of spelling was adopted prior to December 1852, and that the move into the new residence was completed by the end of June 1853.

Having ascertained this information, it is relevant to discover when Neil Livingstone wrote his sons of the change and when they reacted to it. Unfortunately this is easier said than done. John and Charles were in North America at the time, and would presumably have received word in due time, but evidence of the exact date in either case has yet to surface. In the case of David evidence is scanty, but there is much on which one may speculate.

The greatest of the Livingstones left Kuruman in mid-December 1852, perhaps at the very time the family was changing residence in Hamilton. He was bound, eventually, for points north, west, and east: after reaching São Paulo de Loanda on the Angolan coast on 31 May 1854 and staying there till 20 September, he turned his steps back toward the vast interior and walked across the continent, arriving at Tete in Moçambique on 2 March 1856 and reaching the port of Quilimane on 20 May 1856. During this period of three years and five months, Livingstone received mail only once, at Linyanti in September 1855; and if he learned of the spelling change at that time, he seems to make no mention of it. There were letters awaiting Livingstone at Quilimane, but it is possible that he did not learn of the change until he reached Cairo (17 — 19 November 1856), where he heard of his father's death, which had taken place in Hamilton on 9 February 1856. Indeed it is remotely possible that Livingstone did not become aware of it until he reached Great Britain a month later.

Lacking concrete evidence as to when Livingstone learned of his father's wishes, we may turn to his letters to discover when the change became apparent. Again the issue is not to be cut and dried: for there was no month when he stopped spelling his name the one way and began the other way. In fact, by accident or design, Livingstone varied the spelling over the better part of a decade. The following table, in which the letter number is that used in Section 1, lists the letters known to this writer in which Livingstone adds the "e" to his name prior to 1 January 1857. The * indicates a note.

No.	Recipient	Date
0218	Henry Denny	7 Dec 49
0226	Robert Moffat 1	4 Mar 50
0228	His Parents	28 Jul 50
0266*	Arthur Tidman	17 Mar 52
0289	His Parents	26 Sep 52
0380*	Edmund Gabriel	12 Sep 55
0388	William Thompson	27 Sep 55
0389	Arthur Tidman	12 Oct 55
0390*	Roderick I. Murchison	16 Oct 55
0392	Roderick I. Murchison	25 Jan 56

9   ULSOASL, Africa, Wooden Box of Livingstone's Letters.

10   **ibid.** The name of the cottage is interesting: as Charles Livingstone married Harriette Ingraham in Massachusetts on 29 January 1852, it may have been named after her (however this is the only reference to "Ingraham Cottage" that the present writer has seen).

No.	Recipient	Date
0400	Arthur Tidman	2 Mar 56
0404	His Parents	18 Mar 56
0413	Robert Moffat 1	5 Apr 56
0414*	Roderick I. Murchison	23 May 56
0415	Arthur Tidman	23 May 56
0419	His Parents	1 Jun 56
0424*	William Thompson	8 Aug 56

Notes

0266   Livingstone does not use the "e" in the signature but in the body of the letter where he refers to "Mrs. Livingstone & family."

0380   Livingstone signs this letter twice: on page 12 he uses the "e" but in a postscript written in the margin of page 2 he does not.

0390   Livingstone signs this letter twice, using the "e" in the main part of the letter, but omitting it in the postscript of 3 March 1856.

0414   Livingstone uses the "e" in the draft of the letter, but omits it in the original sent to Murchison.

0424   Livingstone's signature follows the postscript of 12 August 1856.

As one studies the above table, it becomes apparent that it raises more questions than it removes. If Livingstone decided to make the change in September 1855, what prompted him to do so, and why was he not more consistent about it? And the fact that he did so prior to that time makes one wonder if Neil Livingstone raised the idea earlier, or if David experimented with it on his own. Five mis-spellings of his own name prior to September 1855 does seem somewhat overly coincidental. And orderly speculation becomes chaotic when one realises that on two occasions he spelled his name both ways in the same letter. If the family letters written to David had survived, they would have shed much light on these matters; but without them let us now list those letters written after 1 January 1857 in which Livingstone does not use the final "e".

No.	Recipient	Date
0463.2	**The Times**	28 Jan [57]
0464	H. Norton Shaw	2 Feb 57
0470	Thomas Maclear	16 Feb 57
0471	H. Norton Shaw	20 Feb 57

Obviously the great majority of his letters written after 1 January 1857 do contain the final "e" in the signature. This may be due to the fact that on this date he was at home in Hamilton with his mother and sisters, and it seems likely that at some time during his first visit home, this subject would have come up in conversation. Nevertheless Livingstone did not reach a final decision while in Hamilton, for he wrote to Norton Shaw on 3 March 1857: "Am going to the Archbishop's tonight and as I am not sure about the 'stone' & 'ston' I imitate him & sign myself David Zambesi."[11] Livingstone must have made up his mind not long thereafter, perhaps as a result of his ever increasing interaction with Government officials, for on 25 May 1857 Roderick Murchison proclaimed to a meeting of the Royal Geographical Society of London: "Since his return to England this traveller has changed the spelling of his name, adopting the form used by his father, and adding the e to Livingston."[12] In fact it appears that on only two occasions after expressing doubt to Shaw on 3 March 1857 did Livingstone sign his name to a letter without adding the eleventh letter: to John Murray on 11 July 1857 (letter no. 0557)

---

11   RGSL, Archives, DL 2/15/3.
12   **JRGSL** vol. 27 (1857), p. cxlviii.

and to an unknown correspondent on an unknown date (letter no. 0590, [14—21 Sep 57?]).[13] Perhaps these last two examples may be justly regarded as slips of the mind.

Thus it seems that few definite statements can be made with regard to Livingstone's use of the final "e". Signatures lacking it were probably written prior to 1849, perhaps before September 1855, and certainly before 31 December 1857, while those with it may have been written as early as 1849, or more likely September 1855, and most probably after 1 January 1858. Obviously anything was possible between September 1855 and March 1857. And if this brief study reveals anything, it indicates that Livingstone wrote his signature according to no easily discernible pattern, and at any time new documents may be found to necessitate revision of any of all of the above generalisations.

There remains yet one phenomenon which we must come to grips with before leaving this subject, and that is the censor. Always the plague of reality, the censor appears wherever mankind has its business, and hence the letters of David Livingstone are not to be excepted. To his letter of 27 January 1841 to John Arundel (letter 0018) someone obviously added the "e" to Livingstone's signature at a later date: perhaps in their blindness they feared people would thing Livingstone too ignorant to spell his own surname correctly. A similar but less serious example, and doubtless there are more, may be seen in connection with an obituary of Livingstone written by his father-in-law, Robert Moffat. The article[14] is accompanied by a reproduction of a portrait made of Livingstone by Mayall in 1857, under which is reproduced one of David Livingston's signatures, to which someone has added the final "e". Whether this was done to the original portrait or merely the published version referred to cannot be easily determined, but in any case this is another pitfall of which those who work with the papers of David Livingstone must be wary.

---

13   Perhaps this fact in itself indicates that this letter may have been written at an earlier date. It must be kept in mind that the information presented in Section 1 must not be considered complete. Certainly it is accurate as far as it goes, but for many reasons it cannot be conclusive. From many letters the signature has been removed by or for autograph collectors, and such mutilations are not noticed. Also the final "n" was frequently written at the edge of the paper, or the final letter may have been covered by adhesive which bound the letter in a volume. Often the smudge or blot following the "n" may be interpreted as an "e" by one reader and as an error by another. Finally in this question copies of whatever kind cannot be trusted implicitly.

14   Moffat, Rev. Dr. "David Livingstone." **The Sunday at Home**, no. 1061 (29 Aug. 1874), pp. 549—554; portrait on p. 553.

APPENDIX 3

LIVINGSTONE'S LETTERS IN THE PARLIAMENTARY PAPERS

The following is a list of Livingstone's letters which have been printed in the Parliamentary Papers of Great Britain, in so far as such are presently known to the compilers. It is hoped that omissions will be brought to the attention of the Project, for inclusion in future editions. The final reference in the list is not to a letter, but to Livingstone's testimony before the House of Commons Select Committee on Africa (Western Coast), given on 18 May 1865.

No.	Name	Date	Publication
0304	John S. Pakington	12 Dec 52	PP Sess. 1852–3, vol. LXVI[1646], pp. 125–6.
0331	Thomas Maclear	7 Apr 54	PP Sess. 1856, vol. LXII [174] A, pp. 86–7.
0333	Alfredo Duprat	9 Apr 54	PP Sess. 1856, vol. LXII [174] A, pp. 84–5.
0394	Thomas Maclear	15 Feb 56	PP Sess. 2 1857, vol. XLIV [212] A, pp. 32–5.
0405	The Earl of Clarendon	19 Mar 56	PP Sess. 2 1857, vol. XLIV [212] A, pp. 62–6.
0879	The Earl of Malmesbury	4 Mar 59	PP Sess. 1860, vol. LXX, [181] B, p. 110.
1100	George Grey	4 Apr 61	PP Sess. 1862, vol. LXI [50] A, p. 134.
1137	Lord John Russell	10 Nov 61	PP Sess. 1863, vol. LXXI [58] B, pp. 191–4.
1138	Inclosure No. 1	15 Nov 61	PP Sess. 1863, vol. LXXI [58] B, pp. 194–5.
1139	Inclosure No. 2	[Nov 61]	PP Sess. 1863, vol.LXXI [58] B, p. 195.
1140	Inclosure No. 3.	[Nov 61]	PP Sess. 1863, vol.LXXI [58] B, pp. 195–6.
1185	Lord John Russell	22 Feb 62	PP Sess. 1863, vol. LXXI [58] B, pp. 196–7.
1186	Inclosure No. 1	22 Feb 62	PP Sess. 1863, vol. LXXI [58] B, p. 197.
1240	Lord John Russell	27 Jun 62	PP Sess. 1863, vol. LXXI [58] B, pp. 197–8.
1306	Lord John Russell	29 Dec 62	PP Sess. 1864, vol. LXVI [60] B, pp. 118–20.
1307	Inclosure No. 4	[29 Dec 62]	PP Sess. 1864, vol. LXVI [60] B, pp. 121–2.
1316	Lord John Russell	28 Jan 63	PP Sess. 1864, vol. LXVI [60] B, pp. 123–4.
1887	Edmund St. J. Garforth	16 Mar 66	PP Sess. 1867, vol. LXXIII [65] A, p. 97.
1889	Edmund St. J. Garforth	22 Mar 66	PP Sess. 1867, vol. LXXIII [65] A, p. 97.
1892	The Earl of Clarendon	18 May 66	PP Sess. 1867, vol. LXXIII [66] B, pp. 39–40.
1896	The Earl of Clarendon	11 Jun 66	PP Sess. 1868–9, vol. LVI [145] B, pp. 13–17.
1904	Horace Waller	1 Feb 67	PP Sess. 1871, vol. XII [420], p. 87.
1908	The Earl of Clarendon	1 Feb 67	PP Sess. 1868–9, vol. LVI [145] B, pp. 17–18.
1912	G.E. Seward	1 Feb 67	PP Sess. 1868–9, vol. LVI [145] B, pp. 67–8.
1920	G.E. Seward	25 Sep 67	PP Sess. 1868–9, vol. LVI [145] B, pp. 80–1.
1925	G.E. Seward	14 Dec 67	PP Sess. 1868–9, vol. LVI [145] B, p. 81.
1932	The Earl of Clarendon	Jul 68	PP Sess. 1870, vol. LXI [C–141]B, pp. 13–16.
1938	J. Kirk or R. Playfair	30 May 69	PP Sess. 1870, vol. LXI [C–141] B, pp. 16–17.
1951	Lord Stanley	15 Nov 70	PP Sess. 1872, vol. LXX [C–598], pp. 1–5.
1973	John Kirk	30 Oct 71	PP Sess. 1872, vol. LXX [C–598], pp. 15–17.
1974	The Earl of Clarendon	1 Nov 71	PP Sess. 1872, vol. LXX [C–598], pp. 6–10.
1975	The Earl of Clarendon	1 Nov 71	PP Sess. 1872, vol. LXX [C–598], pp. 5–6.
1977	Lord Granville	14 Nov 71	PP Sess. 1872, vol. LXX [C–598], pp. 10–15.
1987	Lord Granville	18 Dec 71	PP Sess. 1872, vol. LXX [C–598], pp. 17–19.
1996	Lord Granville	20 Feb 72	PP Sess. 1872, vol. LXX [C–598], pp. 19–24.
	Testimony, HCSCA (WC)	18 May 65	PP Sess. 1865, vol. V [412], pp. 227–33.

APPENDIX 4

THE LETTERS H.M. STANLEY BROUGHT BACK FROM AFRICA

These letters as a group are of interest to the students of Livingstone and his papers for a number of reasons. This was the one time during Livingstone's final years when he knew there was a reasonable certainty that those to whom he wrote would eventually receive the letters — this is contrasted with 42 he wrote from the Manyuema country, of which only two reached the coast.[1] Perhaps some may wonder to which persons Livingstone would choose to write — or not to write — under such circumstances. This collection is of further interest as it provides an interesting study of the problems one encounters when dealing with any group of Livingstone's letters.

Stanley narrates that after he and Livingstone arrived back in Ujiji from their cruise on Lake Tanganyika on 13 December 1871, Livingstone began to write to his many friends and to copy his field diaries into his journal; he wrote first to James Gordon Bennett junior.[2] In the latter part of December he wrote to his children, to Sir Roderick Murchison, and to Lord Granville; he intended to write to the Earl of Clarendon, but Stanley told him of his death.[3] By (apparently) the end of February 1872 the letters were finished: Stanley brought back from Unyanyembe 29 letters, of which 20 were bound for Great Britain, six for Bombay, two for New York, and one for Zanzibar; those for New York were to James Gordon Bennett 1 and 2.[4] After he had been four days on the trail, on 17 March, Stanley received two additional letters — one for Thomas Maclear and one for himself.[5] In a postscript to the latter Livingstone says he has written a note to John Murray (which was presumably enclosed).[6] If we omit the letter to Stanley and also the one to Stanley of 14 March 1872, we are considering a total of 31 letters. On reaching Zanzibar Stanley, apparently on 7 May, delivered two letters, one to John Kirk and one to William Oswell Livingstone.[7] In London he delivered dispatches to Lord Granville on 31 July and the journal and letters to Thomas S. Livingstone on or before 2 August.[8]

Another contemporary source gives information about this particular group of letters. "Mr. Stanley brought letters from Dr. Livingstone to Lord Granville; to the President of the R.G.S., to Mr. Bates, Sir Bartle Frere, Miss Agnes Livingstone, to his eldest son now living (Thomas), Mr. Charles Livingstone; Miss Anna Maria Livingstone; Dr. Wilson (formerly of Bombay); Sir Seymour Fitzgerald, ex-governor of Bombay; Mr. Webb; Dr. Edwin Seward, of Bombay; Captain White, of the P. & O. Company; Horace Waller; and W.F. Hearnes, of Bombay; and John Murray; plus one or two others in England whom Mr. Stanley cannot recall."[9] The unidentified author goes on to say that Kirk and Oswell Livingstone received letters in Zanzibar, and that there were also two letters to the **New York Herald**.

By comparing these two sources, the following may be deduced. Obviously there are no questions about the two letters to New York and the one to Zanzibar. It seems likely that the six to Bombay were to Frere, Wilson, Fitzgerald, Stearns, Seward, and White. This assumes that if any of the first four had already left Bombay, Livingstone was not aware of it; and that Captain White could at least receive mail there, if he did not live there. This leaves the 21 (20 +

---

1   Livingstone to Kirk, 13 Feb. 1871, NLS, MS. 10701, f. 154. It should be considered that David may have been mistaken, as the lost letters may well have turned up after he wrote Kirk. This catalogue lists 29 letters written from Manyuema, no. 1939—1967.

2   Stanley, **HIFL** (1872), p. 563.

3   **Ibid.**, p. 564.

4   **Ibid.**, p. 615.

5   **Ibid.**, p. 628.

6   **Ibid.**, p. 629.

7   **Ibid.**, p. 662.

8   **Ibid.**, p. 718.

9   LFDL, p. 153. "Anna Maria" should read "Anna Mary", and "Hearnes" is W.F. Stearns.

Murray) letters to Great Britain, of which ten recipients have been identified in LFDL, and an eleventh (Murchison) referred to.   Stanley identifies another: William Oswell Livingstone, whose letter was delivered to him in Zanzibar, but which was certainly addressed to Great Britain.   Ignoring for a moment the letter to Maclear, this leaves nine letters to Great Britain, the recipients of which remain to be identified.

Having reached this point in our examination, let us now turn to the main sequence of Livingstone's letters in this catalogue.   While it cannot with certainty be determined from this source which letters were delivered by Stanley it seems a fair beginning to assume that they included letters numbered 1978 through 2006.[10]   These 29 letters are addressed to 19 different persons, and since Livingstone probably put all postscripts or additional letters to each individual in one envelope, it seems safe to assume that they represent 19 of the 29 letters (excluding Maclear's and Murray's) Stanley carried.   This would indicate that the identity of 10 recipients are as yet unknown, but as we shall see there is yet more mystery to be considered.

Of the 19 recipients listed in letters 1978–2006 of this catalogue, nine were not mentioned by the author of LFDL.   They are in order John Livingstone, Thomas Maclear (and William Mann), James Young, William C. Oswell, J. Bevan Braithwaite, Lord Kinnaird, George H. Richards, Francis Skead, and Roderick Murchison.   Although Murchison was no longer the President of the R.G.S.[11] it is likely that LFDL refers to this letter, leaving eight actual recipients to account for nine letters not identified in that work.   It appears that we are getting closer.

But instead of finding a simple answer, the plot thickens: of the ten recipients identified in LFDL, no letters are known to us for seven, viz. Bartle Frere, Dr. Seward, Frederick Webb, John Murray, Thomas, Anna Mary, and Charles Livingstone.   Thus it is necessary to examine very carefully the discrepancy between LFDL and the tables in this catalogue in an attempt to synthesise the two.

As Stanley mentions having carried six letters for Bombay, and since LFDL lists six persons connected with Bombay, it appears that letters were written to Frere and Seward.   And we can be certain that he would have sent a letter to W.F. Webb.   Webb was his host for seven months in 1864–5, while he was writing **NEZT**.   Furthermore Livingstone seems to have been particularly close to Mrs Webb.   In fact as she considered his letters so precious and personal, she may have destroyed them before her death.   The letter to Murray is apparently not to be included in the 29, and its location is also not known.   There is no reason to doubt that he wrote to Thomas and Anna Mary, since at this time he wrote his other two surviving children; with the exception of Agnes, to whom he wrote very frequently, Livingstone throughout his career tended to write to all of his children at the same time.

This brings us to the case of Charles Livingstone.   We have seen that a letter was received by his brother John (no. 1979), but apparently Charles's letter does not survive.   Indeed it seems likely that he never received it.   From Old Calabar he wrote his wife on 20 September 1872: "I saw from the papers that Stanley brought me a letter but it has not yet arrived here."[12] He expressed similar sentiments to Harriette in letters of 27 September, 17 October, and 26

---

10   At first sight 1972 would appear a better starting point.   But Stanley as quoted above rules out the letters to Clarendon, 1974–5;   and 1972–3 and 1976–7 do not mention Stanley's arrival.   So it seems likely that these were taken out of Ujiji by another courier shortly before Stanley arrived.   This is connected with the still unresolved question of what date Stanley reached Ujiji, what date he thought it was, and what date Livingstone thought it was.

11   Henry Rawlinson was President at this time.

12   NMLZ, G5/134.   It is interesting that Charles first heard about the letter from the newspapers.

December of that year, and also to David in a letter of 9 January 1873,[13] which is his last known reference to the subject.   Certainly Stanley makes no mention of a letter to West Africa, but David may have addressed the letter to Hamilton for forwarding, as he frequently did when Charles was living in North America.   From there his sisters may have forwarded it to Old Calabar, to Harriette on the European continent, or anticipating Charles's return from West Africa they may have retained it.   Although the existing form of John's letter is a newspaper copy, and hence subject to error, it seems a reasonable assumption that Livingstone would have written both his brothers at this time.   Whether or not he would have written his sisters at this time is a very open question.

There is one string yet to be tied before seeking conclusions, and that is the letter to Thomas Maclear which Stanley received four days after leaving Livingstone.   This is assuredly letter no. 2009, but how does one account for no. 1981, addressed to Maclear and Mann?   Stanley mentions no letter to Cape Town among his original 29, but perhaps the following explanation is relevant: Livingstone obviously wrote Maclear and Mann on 17 November, but he may have misplaced the letter among his papers until after Stanley had departed.   Upon finding it, he wrote either a postscript or another letter, put the two in one envelope, and sent them off down the path Stanley had taken.

Thus if in addition to the letters to the 19 recipients listed in the tables, one assumes that Stanley delivered letters for Frere, Seward, Webb, Thomas, Anna Mary, and Charles Livingstone , we have a total of 25.   But we know that one to Maclear was added later, so that there are five unknown recipients.   While it may be amusing to speculate as to who they were (Janet Livingstone, Robert 1 or J.S. Moffat??), such an exercise is rendered fruitless by the fact that something at this time moved Livingstone to write to Francis Skead, with whom he seems to have had no contact for almost a decade, and to whom he wrote only a few letters during his entire life.   The possibilities are endless, and the careful reader can no doubt raise a few of his or her own.   But until more letters are uncovered, we can only guess;   such are the vicissitudes of working with the papers of David Livingstone.

[After the above was written the letters to Seward and Frere came to light: see no. 1983.8 and 1987.1 in the Addenda.]

---

13   NMLZ, G5/135, 136, 139, and 141 respectively.

APPENDIX 5

LIVINGSTONE'S CONSULAR APPOINTMENTS

For the student of the career of Livingstone, and especially the student of the Zambezi Expedition, it is a relatively simple matter to become confused when questioning the nature of Livingstone's Consular commissions. It is hoped that the following essay will help to clarify the confusion.

Livingstone was first commissioned as H.M. Consul on 15 January 1858, to Quilimane, Sena and Tete, and directed, among other things, to reside in that district.[1] This appointment was of course a part of his preparation for the trip up the Zambezi River to the highlands near the Kafue River. However, upon reading the commission, Portuguese authorities in Lisbon refused to grant their exequatur for this appointment. Their reason was explained in a coded telegram from the British Minister to Portugal, Henry Howard, to the Foreign Office, dispatched at 6 p.m. on 7 February 1858: the Portuguese authorities would only recognize Livingstone as Consul to Quilimane, on the grounds that while Quilimane was open to foreign trade, Sena and Tete were not.[2] On the next day, H.M. Govt. presented Livingstone with a new consular commission, this time only to Quilimane.[3]

This interpretation meant that the Zambezi River was closed to non-Portuguese vessels, a state of affairs which Livingstone knew well would thwart his plans for establishing a long-term British settlement in Central Africa. On 9 February, he protested in a letter to Edmond Hammond, then Under Secretary of State for Foreign Affairs, requesting that his new commission be amended to accredit him to Sekeletu, chief of the Makololo, and to other independent tribes beyond Portuguese possessions and claims, in addition to Quilimane.[4] As Quilimane was not on the Zambezi, and was only connected with that great river for a part of the year via the Kwakwa River (or Mutu River/Canal), the commission of 8 February could indeed be interpreted to deny him all access to the Zambezi. Furthermore, acceptance of this second commission implied Portuguese control of the river, which although it was accepted de jure by most European nations, was in fact hardly de facto, since Portuguese settlements on the river were few and far between, and those on the right bank had to pay tribute annually to the Zulus of the region, known as the Landeens.[5]

Livingstone's protest caused the Foreign Office to raise a few questions of its own. When these had been carefully answered by the missionary-explorer, Livingstone received on 22 February 1858 his third consular commission within 5 weeks. This one named Livingstone as H.M. Consul to several tribes of interior Africa, as Livingstone desired, as well as to Quilimane.[6] The Portuguese must have found this acceptable, as Livingstone's commission underwent no further revision before its expiration in 1864.

Within a year, Livingstone had his fourth and presumably final appointment as a member

---

1   Original in the SNMDL; ph copy in the NLS, MS. 10753.

2.   PROL, FO 63/842, f. 124. Quilimane only became open to ships of all nations as late as 17 October 1853.

3   This document is privately owned.

4   PROL, FO 63/842, ff. 139–142.

5   An eyewitness account of tribute being levied on Shupanga, on 29 March 1862, is found in Wallis (ed.), ZJJS, pp. 37–39.

6   Location of original unknown. Note, FO to Livingstone, PROL, FO 63/842, f. 221/236.

of the Consular Service. He was in London from 11—14 March 1865 helping Layard draft his commission, which Livingstone describes as including the region of the chiefs inland of the Portuguese on the south, to the lands of Abyssinia and of the Pasha of Egypt on the north.[7] However, the commission he was issued on 28 March 1865 is described as having been to "the Territories of the African Kings and Chiefs in the Interior of Africa," and there is a slight possibility that a first commission in mid-March 1865 had also to be revised.[8] At any rate, the commission of 28 March enabled him to have some prestige during the wanderings Livingstone undertook during the final seven years of his life. Prestige was all he received for a time, as no salary was granted him by H.M. Govt. at the outset, and he held this final appointment until his death.

---

7   Letter, Livingstone to J.B. Braithwaite, 15 March 1865, NLS, MS, Dep. 237. Austin Henry Layard was now Under Secretary of State for Foreign Affairs.

8   Location of original unknown. Note, PROL, FO 2/49 B. Another note in this same volume, from Roderick Murchison to the Earl of Clarendon, dated 7 April 1870, notes: "Dr. Livingstone was gazetted as Consul to 'all the native states in the interior of Africa' on the 24th of March 1865." Perhaps the hiatus between gazetting and dating of the appointment was not unusual.

ADDENDA

The following letters came to our attention too late to be included in Section 1 and Appendix 1. Summaries of them have however been included in Section 2.

NO.	RECIPIENT	DATE	PLACE	LENGTH	SIZE	TYPE
0088.1	[Thomas Steele]	3 Sep 43	Mabotsa	1/ 4/ 4	250 202	MS aut
0090.3	[Thomas Steele]	[Sep 43]	Mabotsa	1/ 4/ 4	250 200	MS aut
0104.8	Mary Moffat (Livingston)	15 Jul 44	Kuruman	1/ 4/ 2	226 183	MS aut
0113.1	Thomas Steele	7 Dec 44	Mabotsa	1/ 4/ 4	322 203	MS aut
0143.8	Thomas Steele	14 Jan 46	Bakwain Country	1/ 4/ 4	320 200	MS aut
0152.8	Thomas Steele	25 Aug 46	Chonuane, Bakuena Country	1/ 4/ 4	320 198	MS aut
0169.4	Thomas Steele	21 Jun 47	Kuruman	1/ 4/ 3	400 249	MS aut
0182.9	Thomas Steele	5 Apr 48	Kolobeng, Bakwain Country	1/ 4/ 4	400 249	MS aut
0191.9	Thomas Steele	20 Dec 48	Mogale's berg	1/ 4/ 4	227 183	MS aut
0214.7	David G. Watt	26 Oct 49	Kolobeng	1/ 4/ 4	380 240	MS aut
0235.1	Thomas Steele	9 Sep 50	Kolobeng	1/ 4/ 4	400 250	MS aut
0239.9	Thomas Steele	3 Dec 50	Kuruman	1/ 4/ 4	251 202	MS aut
0243.1	Thomas Steele	14 Jan 51	Kuruman	1/ 4/ 3	228 183	MS aut
0245.6	Robert Moffat 1	20 Mar 51	Kolobeng	1/ 4/ 3	252 200	MS aut
0255.9	Thomas Steele	1 Oct 51	Banks of the Zouga	2/ 8/ 7	252 199	MS aut
0258.7	Editor of **Cape Town Mail**	[Sep—Oct ? 51]				NS copy
0266.9	Thomas Steele	30 Mar 52	Cape Town	1/ 4/ 4	400 250	MS aut
0274.1	Thomas Steele	28 Apr 52	Cape Town	1/ 4/ 4	275 219	MS aut
0288.1	[Thomas Steele]	20 Sep 52	Kuruman	1/ 4/ 4	400 254	MS aut
0319.9	[Thomas Steele]	24 Sep 53	Town of Sekeletu, Linyanti	1/ 4/ 4	275 220	MS aut
0360.7	Thomas Steele	24 Jan 55	Cassange, Angola, W. Africa	1/ 4/ 4	235 186	MS aut
0391.9	[Robert Moffat 1]	[22 Jan 56]	[Below Zumlo on the R. Zambesi]	1 p		Pr copy
0400.5	Captain, H.M. Ship	3 Mar [56]	Tette			NS copy
0402.9	David G. Watt	15 Mar 56	Tete or Nyungue	4 pp	fol	Pr copy
0408.1	Thomas Steele	26 Mar 56	Tete, on the Zambesi	2/ 8/ 8	334 214	MS aut
0446.4	Editor of **The Times**	24 Dec 56	Kendal			NS copy
0463.2	Editor of **The Times**	28 Jan [57]	57 Sloane Street			NS copy
0551.8	Lord Mayor of London	8 Jul [57]	London			NS copy
0581.2	H. Norton Shaw	5 Sep 57	Drumcondra	1/ 2/ 1		TS copy
0581.9	Miss Macgregor	9 Sep 57				Facs
0601.7	John Murray	[12—13 Oct 57]		3/ 6/ 3	411 258	MS aut
0611.5	Titus Salt	29 Oct 57	50 Albemarle St.	1/ 4/ 4	180 113	MS aut
0633.1	Editor of **The Times**	[24 Nov —1 Dec 57]				NS copy
0633.8	Hudson Gurney	6 Dec 57	50 Albemarle Street	1/ 4/ 4	250 188	MS aut
0752.5	Thomas Miles	3 Mar 58	Birkenhead	1/ 4/ 4	182 110	MS aut
0783.3	George Grey	21 Apr 58	"Pearl" Steamer	1/ 4/ 2	220 180	MS aut
0792.5	George Grey	10 May 58	Steamer "Pearl"	1/ 4/ 4	325 205	MS aut
0797.3	J. Aspinall Turner	10, 21 Jun 58	Screw Steamer Pearl			NS copy
0875.2	Wilhelm H.I. Bleek	22 Feb 59	Tette	1/ 4/ 4	250 200	MS aut
0875.3	Inclosure No. 1	5 Jun 59		1/ 4/ 4	330 195	MS aut
0936.8	George Grey	15 Oct 59	River Shire 15° 55′ Lat. S.	1/ 4/ 4	325 200	MS aut
0945.1	George Grey	20 Oct 59	Shire	1/ 4/ 4	215 185	MS aut
0972.6	Hudson Gurney	16 Nov 59	Kongone Harbour	1/ 4/ 4	165 102	MS aut
1001.1	Robert M. Livingstone	[28 Feb 60 ?]		1/ 4/ 4	210 184	MS aut
1284.2	William O. Livingstone	[26 Oct 62]		1/ 4/ 4	212 164	MS aut

NO.	N	LOCATION	NLS COPY	PUBLICATION
0088.1		Privately owned.	MS. 10777 (10aa)	
0090.3		Privately owned.	MS. 10777 (10aa)	
0104.8		NLS, Ms. Acc. 6900.		Christie's Cat. 6 Apr. 1977, lot 16.
0113.1		Privately owned.	MS. 10777 (10aa)	
0143.8		Privately owned.	MS. 10777 (10aa)	
0152.8		Privately owned.	MS. 10777 (10aa)	
0169.4		Privately owned.	MS. 10777 (10aa)	
0182.9		Privately owned.	MS. 10777 (10aa)	
0191.9		Privately owned.	MS. 10777 (10aa)	
0214.7		NLS, MS. Acc. 6940.		
0235.1		Privately owned.	MS. 10777 (10aa)	
0239.9		Privately owned.	MS. 10777 (10aa)	
0243.1		Privately owned.	MS. 10777 (10aa)	
0245.6		NLS, MS. Acc. 6901.		Christie's Cat. 6 Apr. 1977, lot 18.
0255.9		Privately owned.	MS. 10777 (10aa)	
0258.7	n			Cape Town Mail, 4 Nov. 1851.
0266.9		Privately owned.	MS. 10777 (10aa)	
0274.1		Privately owned.	MS. 10777 (10aa)	
0288.1		Privately owned.	MS. 10777 (10aa)	
0319.9		Privately owned.	MS. 10777 (10aa)	
0360.7		Privately owned.	MS. 10777 (10aa)	
0391.9	n			Sotheby's Cat., 4 Oct. 1977, lot 21.
0400.5	n			The Times, 28 Jul. 1856, p. 6 c. 5.
0402.9				Rendell Cat.
0408.1		Privately owned.	MS. 10777 (10aa)	
0446.4				The Times, 29 Dec. 1856, p. 4 c. 6.
0463.2				The Times, 31 Jan. 1857, p. 7 c. 6.
0551.8				The Times, 11 Jul. 1857, p. 5 c. 2.
0581.2	n	RGSL, Archives, DL 2/15/13.		
0581.9				Kumm, AMHaH, frontispiece (ex).
0601.7		JMPL.		
0611.5		NLS, MS. Acc. 7070.		Myers' Cat. No. 10 (1977), no. 5.
0633.1				The Times, 2 Dec. 1857, p. 6 c.2.
0633.8		Privately owned.	MS. 10777 (22b)	
0752.5		CNSMUN.	MS. 10777 (23a)	
0783.3		APLANZ, GL: L30.	MS. 10777 (10a)	
0792.5		APLANZ, GL: L30.	MS. 10777 (10a)	
0797.3				The Times, 2 Sep. 1858, p. 4 c. 6.
0875.2		APLANZ, GL: L30.	MS. 10777 (10a)	
0875.3		APLANZ, GL: L30.	MS. 10777 (10a)	
0936.8		APLANZ, GL: L30.	MS. 10777 (10a)	
0945.1		APLANZ, GL: L30.	MS. 10777 (10a)	
0972.6		Privately owned.	MS. 10777 (22b)	
1001.1	n	NLS, MS. Acc. 6903.		Christie's Cat. 6 Apr. 1977, lot 22.
1284.2		NLS, MS. Acc. 6903.		Christie's Cat. 6 Apr. 1977, lot 22.

NO.	RECIPIENT	DATE	PLACE	LENGTH	SIZE		TYPE
1304.9	James Russell	29 Dec 62	River Zambesi				Pr copy
1307.2	[Charles M. ?] Hay	[15 Mar — 31 Dec 62]		2 pp			Pr copy
1308.5	Robert Moffat 1	6 Jan 63	Shupanga	1/ 4/ 4	326	204	MS aut
1313.8	Editor of **MTG**	26, 27 Jan [63]	River Shire				NS copy
1329.1	William O. Livingstone	25 Feb 63	River Shire	2/ 8/ 8	210	134	MS aut
1329.2	George Grey	Feb 63	River Shire	1/ 4/ 4	325	205	MS aut
1346.5	[Horace Waller]	[Mar—Apr 63]		1/ 2/ 2	115	175	MS aut in
1424.9	[John Washington??]	[1 Jan—9 Feb], 24 Feb 64	[Moçambique?]	2 pp			Pr copy
1443.1	Mrs Seward	[23—30 Apr 64]	[Zanzibar]	1 p		4to	Pr copy
1443.7	G.E. Seward	1, 12, 23 Jun 64	At Sea	3/12/12	204	132	MS aut
1546.2	R.M. Smith	28 Nov 64	Newstead Abbey	4 pp		8vo	Pr copy
1572.5	James Russell	8 Jan 65	Newstead Abbey				Pr copy
1622.3	Arthur Mills	25 Feb 65	Newstead Abbey			8vo	Pr copy
1688.9	William C. Oswell	[25—28 Apr 65]	8 Dover Street	1/ 4/ 4	176	110	MS aut
1724.5	William Sunley	26 May 65	Burnbank Road, Hamilton	1/ 4/ 4	182	114	MS aut
1983.8	G.E. Seward	Nov 71	Ujiji	2 pp		fol	Pr copy
1987.1	H. Bartle E. Frere	20 Dec 71, 13 Mar 72	Ujiji				NS copy
2009.2	James Gordon Bennett 2	9 Apr 72	Unyanyembe, S.E. Africa				NS copy
2020.8	L. Marsh	21 Nov 72	South Central Africa				Pr copy

NOTES

0258.7   See also **Colonial Intelligencer**, vol. 3, no. 45 (Jan. 1852), p. 340.

0391.9   This is a 20—line fragment in an autograph album. The date and place are given in an annotation by Robert Moffat 1, from which it is inferred that he is the recipient. It may be part of the beginning of 0398.

0400.5   Livingstone addresses this letter to the Captain of any Royal Navy vessel at Quilimane.

0581.1   As it is unlikely that Livingstone was in Dublin on the date of this telegram, its sending must have been delayed for some reason. Certainly it was late at its destination: someone wrote "Too late" across the bottom.

1001.1   Place, date, and signature are cut from this letter.

1307.2   The General Hay who was the recipient of this letter was a relation of Bishop Mackenzie. We have not been able to establish which of the three possible General Hays (Charles Crawford, Charles Murray, Lord James) this was, but follow Seaver (**DLLL**, p. 404) in assuming it to be the one whom Livingstone met in Mauritius.

1313.8   The place of the P.S. is "Elephant Marsh." See also **The Times**, 7 Aug. 1863, p. 6 c.3.

No.	N	LOCATION	NLS COPY	PUBLICATION
1304.9				**Irish Monthly**, vol. 18 (1890), pp. 89–90.
1307.2	n			Goodwin, **MoBM**, pp. 425–426 (ex).
1308.5		NLS, MS. Acc. 6902.		Christie's Cat. 6 Apr. 1977, lot 21.
1313.8	n			MTG, 1863, vol. 2, pp. 127–128.
1329.1		NLS, MS. Acc. 6903.		Christie's Cat. 6 Apr. 1977, lot 22.
1329.2	n	APLANZ, GL: L30.	MS. 10777 (10a)	
1346.5		RHLO, Waller MSS. Afr. s. 16, I, f. 200.	MS. 10780 (8)	
1424.9	n			JRGSL, vol. 34 (1864), pp. 250–251.
1443.1				Sotheby's Cat. 6 Jul. 1977, lot 237.
1443.7	n	NLS, MS. Acc. 6982.		Sotheby's Cat. 6 Jul. 1977, lot 236.
1546.2				Sotheby's Cat., 4 Oct. 1977, lot 188.
1572.5				**Irish Monthly**, vol. 18 (1890), pp. 90–91.
1622.3				Sotheby's Cat. 12 Dec 1967, lot 483.
1688.9		USPGL, SPG Autographs XIV.	MS. 10779 (14)	
1724.5		NLS, MS. Acc. 6983.		Sotheby's Cat. 6 Jul. 1977, lot 241.
1983.8				Sotheby's Cat. 6 Jul. 1977, lot 239.
1987.1	n			**The Times**, 9 Aug. 1872, p. 10 c. 3 (ex).
2009.2	n			**The Times**, 10 Apr. 1874, p. 10 c. 1.
2020.8	n			Marsh, **EAtCR**, pp. 43–46.

1424.1 Printed as though to John Washington, this is a most puzzling letter. By the time that the postscript was written, Livingstone knew that Washington was dead. Furthermore included in the text, prior to the postscript, is the phrase "Before I left the Zambesi..." On 14 Feb. Livingstone left the river on board the "Lady Nyassa," which was being towed by HMS "Ariel," and as the voyage to Moçambique was unusually rough, one wonders if Livingstone was able to begin the letter while on board.

1443.7 Livingstone's location on 12 Jun. was "40 miles off Bombay"; the PS of 23 Jun. was written from India.

1987.1 The place of the PS is Unyanyembe.

2009.2 See also **Cape Monthly Magazine**, n.s. 9 (1874), pp. 57–63; French translation in **La Revue Scientifique de la France et de l'Etranger** (Revue des Cours Scientifiques, 2e Série), vol. 13 (1874), pp. 1005–1015.

2020.8 The publication referred to includes a partial facsimile. See also **The Times**, 11 Apr. 1874, p. 6 c. 3.

FURTHER ADDENDA

NEW LETTERS

No	RECIPIENT	DATE	PLACE	LENGTH	SIZE	TYPE
0016.2	— — Moore	30 Nov 40	London	3 pp	4to	Pr copy
0108.5	William C. Oswell	7 Sep 44				Pr copy
0112.9	John Philip	1 Dec 44	Kuruman	1 p	8vo	Pr copy
0394.1	— — Mathieu	16 Feb, 2 Mar 56	Above Tete or Nyunkue	11 pp	lge fol	MS aut
0508.2		24 Apr 57	57 Sloane Street	3 pp	8vo	Pr copy
0536.8	Edme F. Jomard	12 Jun 57	Hadley Green, Barnet	1/ 4/ 4	230 188	MS aut
0764.7	Livingstone's Trustees	16 Mar 58	At Sea	4 pp	4to	MS copy
0791.9	[Charles L. Braithwaite?]	10 May, 25 Jun 58	Screw Steamer Pearl	4 pp	fol	MS copy
0891.1	[Joseph B. Braithwaite?]	24 May 59		2 pp	4to	MS copy
0898.5	Editor of the "Times"	30 May 59	River Zambesi	3 pp	fol	MS copy
0936.8	[Editor of the "Times"?]	15 Oct 59	River Shire	5 pp	fol	MS copy
0955.1	Earl Grey	28 Oct 59	River Shire, E. Africa	1/ 4/ 4	321 205	MS aut
1022.7	James Young	12 May 60	Tette	1 p	4to	MS copy
1151.3	Editor of the "Times"	[Nov 61?]		28 pp	8vo	MS copy
1232.5	Baldwin W. Walker	30 May 62	Kongone	1/ 4/ 4	fol	MS aut
1252.2	Baldwin W. Walker	26 Jul 62	Kongone	1/ 4/ 4	fol	MS aut
1260.9	Baldwin W. Walker	15 Aug 62	HM Exploring Ship Pioneer	2/ 6/ 5	fol	MS aut
1284.5	Baldwin W. Walker	28 Oct 62	Johanna	1/ 4/ 4	fol	MS aut
1316.7	[Joseph B. Braithwaite?]	7 Feb 63	River Shire	7 pp	8vo	MS copy
1331.2	Baldwin W. Walker	[Mar?] 63		1/ 4/ 4	fol	MS aut
1344.9	Baldwin W. Walker	30 Apr 63	Murchison Cataract	1/ 4/ 4	fol	MS aut
1680.8	— — Brown	21 Apr 65	Newstead Abbey	2 pp	8vo	Pr copy
1738.5	William C. Oswell	7 Jun 65	Hamilton	1/ 4/ 3	176 109	MS aut
1843.8	W.S. Price	28 Nov 65	Malabar Hill	1/ 4/ 4	180 113	MS aut
1850.3	W.S. Price	5 Dec 65	Bombay	1/ 2/ 2	195 125	MS aut
1897.2	[Charles L. Braithwaite?]	12 Jun 66, 1 Feb 67	East Africa	3 pp	fol	MS copy
1945.5	John Livingstone 1	Apr 70	Manyuema	9 pp		Pr copy

No	N	LOCATION	NLS COPY	PUBLICATION
0016.2				Sotheby's Cat. 24 Jul. 1978, lot 197.
0108.5				JRGSL, vol. 20 (1851), p. 239 n.
0112.9				Sotheby's Cat. 20 Feb. 1978, lot 153.
0394.1	n	Institut de France, Bibl. MS. 2656[21], ff. 19—24	MS. 10779 (20a)	Bull., Paris Geog. Soc. s. 4, vol. 12 (1856), pp. 155—168.
0508.2				John Wilson, list 32 (1978), no. 56.
0536.8		Société de Géographie, Paris, Bibl.	MS. 10777 (25a)	
0764.7		NLS, MS. Acc. 7222.		
0791.9	n	NLS, MS. Acc. 7222.		
0891.1		NLS, MS. Acc. 7222.		
0898.5		NLS, MS. Acc. 7222.		
0936.8		NLS, MS. Acc. 7222.		
0955.1		Grey Papers, Dept. of Palaeography, Durham.	MS. 10777 (14a)	The Scotsman, 25 Jul. 1959, p. 5 c. 3 (ex).
1022.7		NLS, MS. Acc. 7222.		
1151.3	n	NLS, MS. Acc. 7222.		
1232.5	n	Privately owned.		Stanley Gibbons Cat., 7 Sep. 1978, lot 1.
1252.2	n	Privately owned.		Stanley Gibbons Cat., 7 Sep. 1978, lot 1.
1260.9	n	Privately owned.		Stanley Gibbons Cat., 7 Sep. 1978, lot 1.
1284.5	n	Privately owned.		Stanley Gibbons Cat., 7 Sep. 1978, lot 1.
1316.7		NLS, MS. Acc. 7222.		
1331.2	n	Privately owned.		Stanley Gibbons Cat., 7 Sep. 1978, lot 1.
1344.9	n	Privately owned.		Stanley Gibbons Cat., 7 Sep. 1978, lot 1.
1680.8				Sotheby's Cat. 6 Jun. 1978, lot 173.
1738.5		WCLUWJ.	MS. 10779 (10)	
1843.8		Privately owned.		
1850.3		Privately owned.		
1897.2	n	NLS, MS. Acc. 7222.		
1945.5	n		MS. 10779 (23)	Life and Explorations of David Livingstone (Cincinnati: US Book and Bible Co., 1879), pp. 473—481.

BRAITHWAITE, C.L.

0791.9 † 10 May 1858.   Good voyage to Delgoa Bay.   Meeting with Moffats and news of Makololo.   Good work being done in Sierra Leone.   [ca. 17 May.]   Arrival at Zambesi and launching of MaRobert.   25 Jun.   Mouths of the Zambesi.   No fever.

1897.2 † 12 Jun. 1866.   His correspondence.   Experiences in Egypt and India show good done by individuals.   Slave trade fostered by people themselves.   Knowledge of God among Makanda.   Failure of seopys.   Now at tract of country totally devastated.   1 Feb. 1867.   Probably now on watershed at 4500 feet.

BRAITHWAITE, J.B.

0891.1 † 24 May 1859.   *Has written to C.M.S.   Laird's meanness over lathe and forge.   Quinine no prophylactic.

1316.7 † 7 Feb. 1863.   *Difficulties in getting "Lady Nyassa" up river.   Effects of slave hunting.   Comparison of east and west coasts.   Natives better workers than white sailors but cannot stay long.   Scotch artisans coming.   Encouragement from Russell.

BROWN, – – –

1680.8 21 Apr. 1865.   *Repeats request to have locks on two tin boxes repaired.

GREY, Earl (1802 – 1894).
Henry George Grey, succeeded as 3rd Earl in 1845.   Previously an M.P., he then became Whig leader in the Lords.   Colonial Secretary 1846–52.   (**DNB.**)

0955.1 28 Oct. 1859.   The Shire valley and its suitability for cotton growing.   Three terraces, suitable for European occupation.   English colony desirable.   Steamer on the lake would stamp out slave trade.

JOMARD, Edme François (1777 – 1862).
French geographer and archeologist.   Keeper of maps in the Bibliothèque Royale.   President of the Société de Géographie de Paris.
(**La Grande Encyclopédie** [Paris, 1887], xxi. 184.)

0536.8 12 Jun. 1857.   Thanks him for gold medal and apologises for delay in naming someone to collect it, which will now be done by R.W. Pentland.

LIVINGSTONE, John 1.

1945.5 Apr. 1870.   Journey from Tanganyika; the Manyuema country and people.   Herodotus and Ptolemy had genuine information about Nile sources.   Errors of Speke and Baker.   Dutch lady explorer.   Difficulties in exploring watershed.   Cannibalism doubtful.   Portuguese visits to Cazembe were slaving expeditions.   The Lualaba and the four fountains.   His attendants useless but not typical Africans.   Loss of letters.

LIVINGSTONE'S TRUSTEES.

0764.7 16 Mar. 1858.   Suggestions on education of Robert, Thomas and Agnes.

MATHIEU, – – –
French admiral and President of the Paris Geographical Society.

See below, addenda to Section 2.

MOORE, – – –
A brother or sister of Joseph Moore (q.v.).

0016.2 30 Nov. 1840.   *Thanks for gift and recipe.   Moral and spiritual counsel.

OSWELL, W.C.

0108.5 7 Sep. 1844.   *On the course of the Limpopo.

1738.5 7 Jun. 1865.   Dedication and other details about the book.

PHILIP, J.

0112.9 1 Dec. 1844.   Bill to David Hume for £50.

PRICE, W.S.

1843.8 28 Nov. 1865.   To sail in "Thule".   Additions to boys' outfit may be obtained in Bombay.

1850.3 5 Dec. 1865.   "Thule" requires alterations which will take 5 or 6 days.   Will let him know in time for boys to spend a day in Bombay.   Is new volunteer able-bodied?

TIMES, Editor of

0898.5 30 May 1859.   Sends report of Lake Shirwa.   Expects to reach Lake Nyinyesi in a month.   Healthy country.   Portuguese claims.   Prevented from going to Makololo country by want of powerful steamer.

0936.8 15 Oct. 1859.   Fine country.   Testing of fever remedies.   Portuguese settlements are not colonies.   First visit to Lake Nyassa.

1151.3 [Nov. 1861?]   Activities of the Ajawa;   their attack on the mission party.   Detailed description of the Murchison Cataracts, the upper Shire, and Lake Nyassa.   Effects of slaving; involvement of Portuguese, supported by Prince Consort.   Regrets Mackenzie's fighting.

WALKER, Sir B.W.

1232.5 30 May 1862.   Need for Mackenzie's sister to control him.   "Pioneer" 's engines.   Fever attacks repeatedly in the delta.

1252.2 26 Jul. 1862.   Burlton not required and apparently came without authority.   May's ignorance of the language and insistence on precedence.   Plans for Rovuma.

1260.9 15 Aug. 1862.   No disrespect intended by not taking Burlton.   Discrepancies in money and cloth received.   30 Aug.   Going to Rovuma.   Will respect instructions about ships going up rivers.   PS   Sends E.D. Young's certificates.   Ale from Washington does not arrive.

1284.5 28 Oct. 1862.   The Rovuma.   Pirates.   Possibilities for trade.

1331.2 [Mar.?] 1863.   Sends W. Macleod for pay and treatment.   Slaving.   No provisions available.   Low water level.

1344.9 30 Apr. 1863.   Give Kirk and Charles Livingstone passage.   No provisions.   Sends away seamen.   Death of Thornton.

YOUNG, J.

1022.7 12 May 1860.   *Have steamer built for which he will pay.

Unidentified recipient.

0508.2 24 Apr. 1857.   *On a forthcoming meeting of the Geographical Society at which Sir John Davis is to speak on China.

NOTES

0394.1 The publication cited is a French translation.   The full place is "Above Tete or Nyunkue, on the River Zambesi, Africa";   that of the PS is presumably Tete.

0791.9 The place of the PS is "Zambesi".

1151.3 The MS copy is partly in the hand of J.S. Moffat.

1897.2 The full location is "East Africa Lat. 11° $18'$ S. Long. 37° $10'$ E.";   that of the PS is "Lat. 10° $10'$ S. Long. 31° $50'$ E. due of town of Bemba."

1945.5 The full location is "Manyuema or Cannibal Country, say 150 miles northwest of Ujiji."

1232.5, 1252.2, 1260.9, 1284.5, 1331.2, 1344.9.   Information on these letters additional to what appears in their catalogue was kindly supplied by the auctioneers.

0066   An extract from this letter is published in **African Studies,** vol. 6 (1947), p. 180, from an MS copy in Gubbin's Library, University of the Witwatersrand, which gives as the recipient the Rev. Ad. Mabille, of the French Basuto Mission.

0506   Facs in **The Continent,** 6 Mar. 1913, p. 317.

0591, 0601, 1463 See also Sawyer's Cat. 299 (1978), no. 61 (photocopies, acquired under Export Licensing Regulations and totally restricted until 3 Apr. 1985, are in NLS, MS. 10769).

0593   See also Sawyer's Cat. 299 (1978), no. 60.

0615   See also Maggs' Cat. 988 (spring, 1978), no. 109.

0938—0941, 0973—0974   When the order of these items was being settled and the note to letter 0938 written, Livingstone's endorsements were unfortunately overlooked.   These make it certain that 0939—0941 are Inclosures 1, 2, and 3 to letter 0973, and probable that 0974 is Inclosure 1 to letter 0938.   The latter had three inclosures: for 2 see below on 0965;   3 may have been the sketch-map which is still present (PROL FO 63/871, f. 248) or the magnetical observations referred to in the text of the letter.   Livingstone's order in his journal appears to be misleading.

0965   This is, despite the heading in the published version, not a letter of Livingstone and should be deleted.   It is a letter of Charles Livingstone to David which the latter sent as Inclosure 2 in his dispatch 0938.   The original letter (PROL FO 63/871, ff. 242—247) has lost 1 or 2 folios at the beginning;   the published version omits the greeting and the final paragraph.

1145   See also **Cape Monthly Magazine,** vol. 11 (1862), pp. 269—271.

1275   See also **The African Times,** 23 Feb. 1863.

1324   This is certainly a phantom.

1377, 1430   The originals were included in Stanley Gibbons Cat., 7 Sep. 1978, lot 1 (information kindly supplied by the auctioneer).

1542   Sold at Sotheby's, 24 Jul. 1978, lot 198, and now NLS, MS. Acc. 7237.   The summary in Section 2 is misleading: the son for whom Dr Sherman was writing was not Robert.

1625   This is not really a letter, but the MS of the postscript to the preface of **NEZT.**

1956   This letter was published erroneously as "November 2nd, 1870."

2005   8 pp. fol. Sotheby's Cat. 24 Jul. 1978, lot 184 (with facs of p. 1).

2008   The original (2/6/5, misc.) is privately owned.

2009.2 An incomplete preliminary draft (with some pages in several versions) is privately owned.

2022   A little more than in Blaikie l.c. is published in **Life and Explorations of David Livingstone** (Cincinnati: US Book and Bible Co., 1879), pp. 481—482 (copy in NLS, MS. 10779 (23)).

2031   An MS copy (1 p. fol.) with a few more sentences than in Blaikie l.c. is in NLS, MS. Acc. 7222.

NLS internal reference for the following letters should read MS. Acc. 7176 (instead of Dep. 237): 0506, 0748, 0792, 0834, 0897, 0952, 0985, 1068, 1088, 1089, 1098, 1141, 1201, 1202, 1292, 1385, 1639.

Photocopies of the following are in NLS, MS. 10779 (12a):   the letters to John Murray listed in Section 2 (except 0482, 0484, 0643, 1583 and 1588, which are not in JMPL), letters 1642 and 1789, the illustrations to **MT** noted below, the footnote to **NEZT** (Section 3, Books 3), and Section 4, A.1, A.4—6, and C. 13—14.

SECTION 2

s.v. Burdett-Coutts, Angela.   Delete 1789 here and insert the entry under the new heading FRANKLIN, Lady (Jane, née Griffin, 1792—1875), wife of Sir John Franklin and traveller in her own right (**DNB.**).   (See 1789 n.)

s.v. Paris — Société de Géographie.   In the second entry change the reference to 0394.1 and the date to 16 Feb. 1856.   The letter was in fact addressed personally to the President, Admiral Mathieu.   (See above, New Letters.)

s.v. Unknown Recipients, no. 1489:   Has none of the objects requested;   good wishes for Sunday School.

SECTION 3

Books 1   Also in JMPL are proofs of the illustrations facing pp. 291, 332, and 380, with MS captions by Livingstone.

Inscribed copy 9:   also in Sawyer's Cat. 299 (1978), no. 126.

Books 2   Add at end: (that a copy was sent to Adam Sedgwick is indicated by Monk, l.c.)

Books 3   For the postscript to the preface see above, addenda to letter 1625.

SECTION 4

A.4   Reproduced in **NEZT**, facing p. 31.

A.6   Reproduced in **MT**, facing p. 225.

B.21   Sawyer's Cat. 299 (1978), no. 127.

C.11   Another unsigned draft is in NLS, MS. Acc. 7222.

C.15.5   Note, on the copy of Sir Roderick Murchison's **Address at the Anniversary Meeting of the Royal Geographical Society**, 1852, presented by Murchison to Livingstone: 'This address was sent by the author to me through the Cape Colony and was delivered by the Revd Robert Moffat to some Matibele who laid it down on the south bank of the Leeambye just above the Victoria falls.   It was taken by the Makololo and placed on an island about 14th September 1854 and remain[e]d there till we returned from Loanda when I received it from the Makololo about the same date in 1855.   It was then brought home and delivered by me to Sir Roderick Murchison 19th February 1858 David Livingstone.' Sotheby's Cat. 24 Jul. 1978, lot 182.

C.41   Another MS aut is privately owned;   probably it is the real MS aut, while the one in the text is an MS aut copy.

APPENDIX 2

0394.1 is to be added to the list of signatures before 1 Jan 1857 which have the final "e".

APPENDIX 4

Add to note at end: It has also become known from some Braithwaite papers now in the NLS (MS. Acc. 7222) that the letter to J. Bevan Braithwaite (no. 1989) was delivered by Stanley on 1 Aug. 1872.

ILLUSTRATIONS

The illustrations of Livingstone's signatures and handwriting are actual size; in some cases this has meant that a complete page could not be reproduced.

1) *[signature in handwriting]*

2) *[handwriting: "Believe me your very Affectionate David Livingston"]*

3) *[signature: "David Livingstone"]*

4) *[signature: "affectionate David Livingstone"]*

Signatures

1)	28 May 1842	(letter no. 0055)
2)	4 April 1856	(letter no. 0412)
3)	13 May 1859	(letter no. 0889)
4)	Dec. 1870	(letter no. 1960)

Bakwain Country 28th May
1842

My Dear Friend

I have related to our very dear and mutual friend Mrs Sewell a few particulars relating to the Bechuanas in this part of the country and as she may perhaps be kind enough to give you anything that may be worth a second narration in these letters. I shall say nothing in this of what has already been told. I am most anxious to hear from you, and as I am now about to proceed to Kuruman shall be much disappointed if succeeding ones of your kind remembrance does not meet me there.

I left this about two months ago for the purpose of visiting and opening up a friendly intercourse with some tribes which lie still farther north. This seems the first step necessary in preparing the way for the spread of the gospel among this people. Believing that the motives of all men are just like those which actuate our own bosoms. The natives usually receive a first visit of strangers with suspicion. They suppose we come for some selfish purpose & are therefore on the alert lest they should be imposed on by our superior cunning, and so long as this state of mind exists it is in vain we attempt to preach the gospel. We have therefore to endeavour to overcome their suspicions and this we can do most effectually by an easy open frank association with them.

I shall give you a few particulars respecting three tribes of Bechuanas with which I have recently become acquainted and as they were never before visited a messenger of the gospel the reception and treatment I met with will I hope prove interesting to you. Their names are the Bamangwato, the Bakaa and Makalaka, and their country lies between Lat. 21° & 22°. and Long 29° or 30°. My route alongside the great sandy desert which flanks the whole of the Bechuana country to the West, presenting an impassable barrier to the traveller in that direction. It occasionally crossed portions of the sand which stretch out to the East in the form of waves and there were exceedingly distressing for the oxen. We however were within two days of the Bamangwato before they were entirely exhausted. I then instructed the people to endeavour to take back the oxen to a pool we had found the day before while I pursued my journey on foot —. The chief was evidently pleased that I had come unprompted into his vicinity without distrust for before I had been 10 minutes with him & seated in the midst of hundreds of his people watching every motion & look. We commenced cramming me with flesh of the rhinoceros and such other dainties as this royal party afforded. And as we became better acquainted he presented one with an elephants tusk frequently and emphatically exclaiming "you have come just like rain on us" and "you have brought your majesty a friend have held on to his lion looking at you". He has more people under him than any other chief I have seen in this country. He has numerous tributaries and his own town upwards of 600 houses

Early letter (no. 0055)

<u>Private</u>   "Senna 13th May 1859

My Lord

 We have just returned from
the discovery of a magnificent
inland Lake, and as you took a
kind interest in our Expedition
I feel anxious to tell you about
our success so far. We ascended
a branch of the Zambesi called the
Shire about a hundred miles from
its confluence in January last.
The people were very much
alarmed never having been
visited by whites before for the
Portuguese have always been
afraid of them as a very warlike

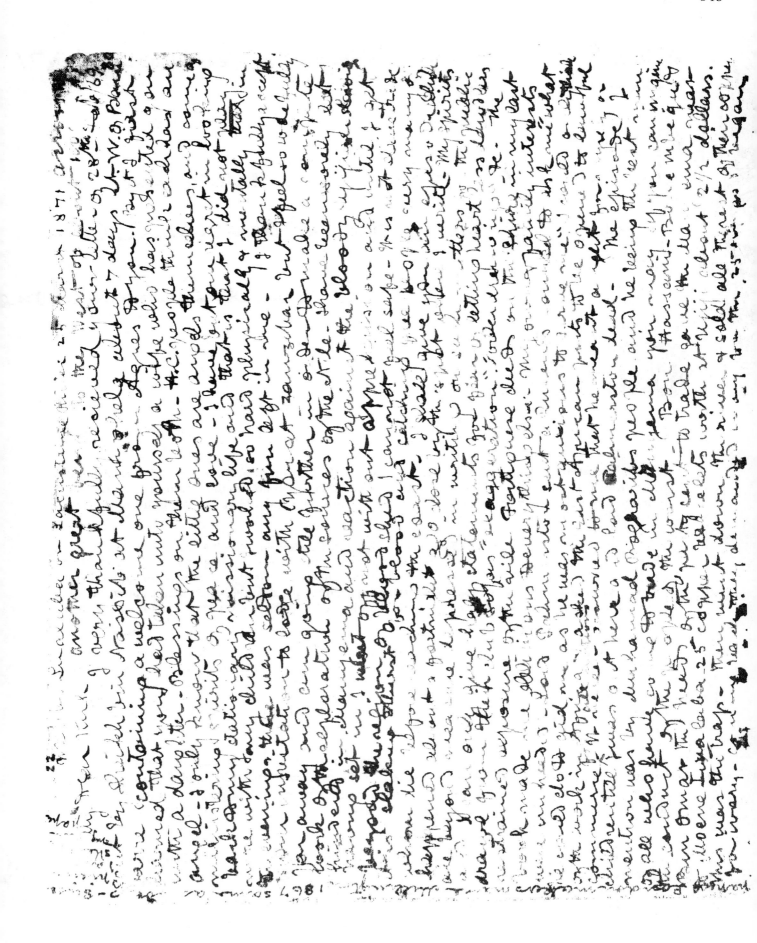

Late letter (no. 1968)

No. 5 Duplicate Bombay, 5 February 1871

Messrs. Ritchie, Stewart, & Co,

Please pay to Dr John Kirk HM consul Bearer the Sum of Rupees Four thousand — on Account of David Livingstone

Rs 4000 —

A CHEQUE OF LIVINGSTONE'S

The above is a reproduction of a cheque on Livingstone's account with Messrs. Ritchie, Stewart, & Co. of Bombay (NLS, MS. 10705, f.3). It is worth noting that Livingstone's account number was 186, which in this case he partially struck over and added "71" to indicate the date of writing.

When in the Manyuema country west of Lake Tanganyika (in what today is Zaire) late in 1870 Livingstone's supply of paper was running very low. In order to supplement his dwindling stocks, he wrote a number of letters on such blank cheques. As their size was considerable by modern standards (the above example has had at some time quite a bit of blank paper cut off both sides) and as Livingstone wrote in a tiny hand on both sides, such letters contain a great deal of information.

Three such letters are known to survive today. They are letters numbered 1952 (NMLZ), 1954 (NLS: one side reproduced on the next page), and 1959 (BLL). Two others are known to have been written on such cheques: the copyist of 1949 indicates he saw the original, and in the printed text of 1958 Livingstone himself says that he writes on a page from his cheque book. Further in NLS, MS. Dep. 237 is an envelope manufactured out of a cheque (Section 4, A 21; this came to the NLS from the same source as letter 1954 and probably went with it originally).

Prior to letter 1949 and after letter 1959 there are no clues that any letters were so written. Between these two numbers we know that letters 1950, 1951, and 1956 were not, as the originals survive on other paper (from the text of 1956 we know that it was written on the last piece of ordinary paper he had). This leaves letters 1953, 1955, and 1957, any or all of which might have been written on cheques.

It is quite possible that other letters, notes, lists, etc, were written by Livingstone on such paper (it was at this time that he was keeping his diary on pages of newspaper and other scraps), and should they eventually surface undated, the likelihood is that they were written between September and November 1870.

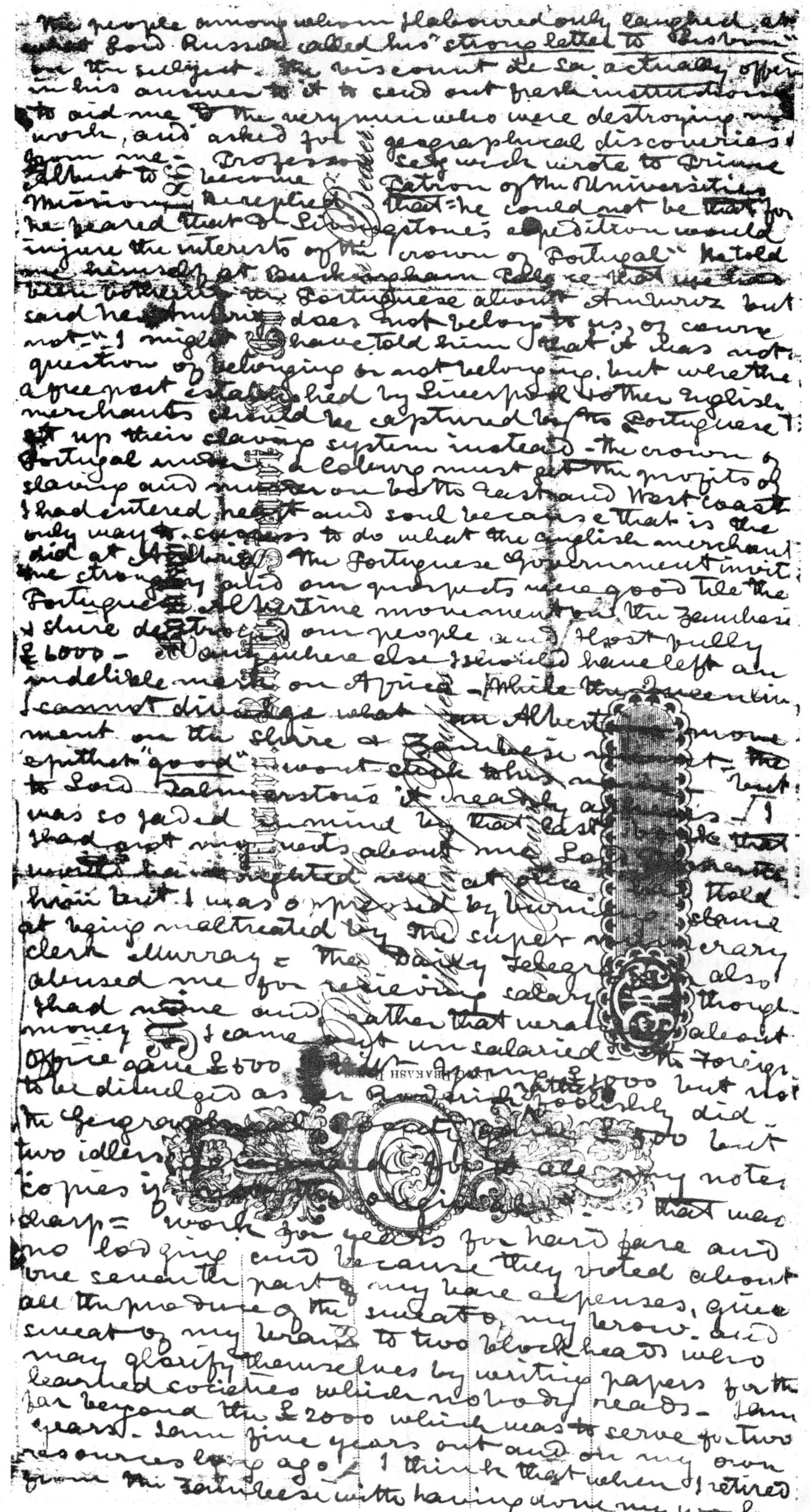

Cheque-form used for letter (no. 1954).

we got in we saw Cazembe seated in front of a huge hut & two umbrellas is held over him

On his right were about 30 people sitting behind him in the door way sat his principal wife & attendants — on his left some fifty men. Still farther off on both hands sat a hundred Mohamados and attendants were placed directly in front Cazembe & about 30 yards off — While behind & on our right & left we had groups with marimbas drums & other instruments of music — Each band came up playing & then took up stand near ourselves

Sept 1867
6ᵃ 20
6 = 68° 7 = 70° 8 = ? 9 = 9?
10 = 80° = 11 = 85°
12 = 89° — 1 = 89°
2 = 92° — 3 = 92
4 = 92° — 5 = 90°
6 = 83

Nasrajite a man of Mohamad

Kongolo pa whirlwind

Karungu — Itawa Dis Mteta a priest chief W Juma merkaw pass Manda Morumbi which is near to Tanganyika on his way to Rua — Philikongo west of Karungu —

Choma is W.S.W. of this — Logarawa goes into Moero & Moero comes from Cazembe's

Groundnuts or Mteza or Mbalala roasted in a frying pan — Then rubbed between the hands & take off the skin & pounded fine, then mixed with water & boiled make an excellent substitute for milk in the porridge — add s 4

ISBN 0 902220 22 5

Printed in Scotland for the National Library of Scotland.